King James Version

Standard Lesson Commentary
1999-2000

International Sunday School Lessons

Edited by

Douglas Redford and Jonathan Underwood

Published by

STANDARD PUBLISHING

Eugene H. Wigginton, *President*
Mark A. Taylor, *Publisher*
Richard C. McKinley, *Director of Curriculum Development*
Carla Crane, *Assistant Director of Curriculum Development*
Jonathan Underwood, *Senior Editor of Adult Curriculum*
Hela M. Campbell, *Office Editor*

Forty-seventh Annual Volume

©1999
The STANDARD PUBLISHING Company
division of STANDEX INTERNATIONAL Corporation
8121 Hamilton Avenue, Cincinnati, Ohio 45231
Printed in U. S. A.

In This Volume

Fall Quarter, 1999 (page 1)
From Slavery to Conquest

Writers

LESSON DEVELOPMENT: Orrin Root

VERBAL ILLUSTRATIONS: Charles R. Boatman

LEARNING BY DOING: Thomas Hutchison (1-4), Richard A. Lint (5-9), Steve Simpson (10-13)
LET'S TALK IT OVER: Kenton K. Smith

Winter Quarter, 1999-2000 (page 113)
Immanuel: God With Us

Writers

LESSON DEVELOPMENT: Johnny Pressley

VERBAL ILLUSTRATIONS: L. D. Campbell (1-4), David Roadcup (5-9), Richard W. Baynes (10-13)

LEARNING BY DOING: Ronald G. Davis (1-4), Rick Shonkwiler (5-9), Everett Brewer (10-13)
LET'S TALK IT OVER: Larry Jones (1-4), Tom Claibourne (5-9), Charles E. Cook (10-13)

Spring Quarter, 2000 (page 225)
Helping a Church Confront Crisis

Writers

LESSON DEVELOPMENT: Robert C. Shannon (1-4), John W. Wade (5-13)
VERBAL ILLUSTRATIONS: Charles R. Boatman

LEARNING BY DOING: Virginia Beddow (1-4), Richard A. Koffarnus (5-9), Ronald L. Oakes (10-13)
LET'S TALK IT OVER: Kenton K. Smith

Summer Quarter, 2000 (page 337)
New Life in Christ

Writers

LESSON DEVELOPMENT: Edwin V. Hayden (1-4), J. Michael Shannon (5-13)
VERBAL ILLUSTRATIONS: Robert C. Shannon

LEARNING BY DOING: Alan Weber

LET'S TALK IT OVER: Ronald G. Davis

Artists

TITLE PAGES: James E. Seward

Cover design by DesignTeam

Index of Printed Texts, 1999-2000

The printed texts for 1999-2000 are arranged here in the order in which they appear in the Bible. Opposite each reference is the number of the page on which it appears in this volume.

Cumulative Index

A cumulative index for the Scripture passages used in the STANDARD LESSON COMMENTARY
for the years September, 1998—August, 2000, is provided below.

The *Standard Lesson Commentary*:
Your Tool for Better Teaching

FOR ALMOST FIFTY YEARS, the *Standard Lesson Commentary* has provided a valuable resource for adult Sunday school teachers. Many churches, desiring lessons that focus on what the Bible says and how it applies to our times, have found that the *Commentary* helps them achieve these important goals.

The strength of the *Standard Lesson Commentary* has always been its **thorough treatment of the lesson Scripture.** Five of the eight pages in each lesson are devoted to this. Printed texts are taken from the International Sunday School Lessons. These are arranged in a six-year program that provides a comprehensive survey of the entire Bible. The lessons to be covered in a given year are highlighted at the beginning of every fall quarter. See page 2 of this *Commentary*, and you will note that the 1999-2000 lessons make up the second year of the current six-year program.

We want to call your attention to some of the special features that we introduced in the 1998-99 *Commentary*. Most of these are found within the eight introductory pages that appear at the beginning of every quarter. For example, each set of introductory material includes a page of Bible helps relevant to the upcoming quarter. On one side of the page an appropriate map for the quarter is shown, while on the other side you will find a time line, chart, or other feature that will call attention to something noteworthy about that quarter's lessons. (See pages 5 and 6, 117 and 118, 229 and 230, and 341 and 342 of this *Commentary*.) Note that these pages are perforated so that you can tear them out if you wish to save them. By the end of the six-year lesson plan, you will have assembled a rather comprehensive set of **maps and charts** for studying the Bible.

Another special feature in the introductory pages accompanies the winter, spring, and summer quarters. This is a two-page article called **"Teacher Tips."** These articles are written to provide you as a teacher with some practical suggestions as to how to communicate God's Word more effectively to your students. Illustrations of specific principles stated in these articles are taken from the upcoming quarter's lessons, making these "tips" of immediate value.

Within the introductory pages, we have kept what we hope are features that will continue to be an asset to your teaching. There is always a two-page essay previewing the lessons that will be studied during the new quarter. You will also find the **quarterly quiz** at the beginning of each quarter. As the instructions at the top of the quiz explain, there are a number of ways in which you can use this quiz in your teaching. You may photocopy the quiz if you like (or feel free to add any other questions that you wish).

A valuable supplementary item is also available to assist you in teaching the lessons in this *Commentary*. That is the packet of **visual teaching posters,** available each quarter from Standard Publishing or your local curriculum supplier. Keep in mind that the small visual pictured in each of the lessons (see, for example, page 13 of lesson 1 in the fall quarter) is only a reproduction of a large, full-color poster included in the *Adult Visuals* packet for the quarter. These colorful posters measure nineteen by twenty-five inches, making them ideal for classroom use. If you have not used this resource before, you may find it very helpful in highlighting an important Scripture verse, summarizing the theme of the lesson, mapping out the geographical setting, or charting the historical/chronological background.

Standard Publishing also now has an Internet web page. The address is **www.standardpub.com.** If you have access to the Internet, check us out! And if you have any questions or comments about any of our adult curriculum material (either in the annual *Commentary* or in the quarterly products), e-mail us at AdultCurriculum@standardpub.com.

Finally, we want to let you know about an addition to our curriculum that we introduced in the fall of 1998. This is a **large-print edition** of the material found in this *Commentary*. It is a quarterly teacher's manual called the *Bible Teacher and Leader* (Large Print). If you are interested in obtaining this large-print material for your adults—or any of the other teaching aids we have to offer—contact your local curriculum supplier or call a customer service representative at Standard Publishing, at 1 (800) 543-1353.

The changes described above are designed to help make the *Standard Lesson Commentary* the most helpful tool it can be in equipping you to teach the changeless truths of God's Word to your students. We hope that you will see that purpose accomplished as you prepare and teach these lessons.

How to Say It

Listed below are some of the names and other hard-to-pronounce words that you will encounter in the lessons covered in this book. (Because of space limitations, not every word that appears in the "How to Say It" boxes in each lesson has been included, but these will be the ones most often needed for general Bible study.) Notice that the page is perforated so that you can tear it out and keep it for later use in teaching or personal Bible study.

ACHAIA. Uh-*kay*-uh.
ACHAN. *Ay*-can.
ADAM. Uh-*dahm*.
AGABUS. *Ag*-uh-bus.
AHAZ. *Ay*-haz.
AHOLIAB. Uh-*ho*-lih-ab.
ALEXANDRIA. Al-ex-*an*-dree-uh.
ALPHEUS. Al-*fee*-us.
AMALEKITES. *Am*-uh-leh-kites or Uh-*mal*-ih-kites.
AMMINADAB. Uh-*min*-uh-dab.
AMORITES. *Am*-uh-rites.
ANAK. *Ay*-nack.
ANANIAS. An-uh-*nye*-us.
ANTIOCH. *An*-tee-ock.
ANTIPAS. *An*-tih-pus.
APOLLOS. Uh-*pahl*-us.
APPHIA. *Af*-ee-uh or *Ap*-fee-uh.
AQUILA. *Ack*-wih-luh.
ARABAH. *Air*-uh-buh.
ARAMAIC. Air-uh-*may*-ick.
ARCHIPPUS. Ar-*kip*-us.
ARIMATHEA. *Air*-uh-muh-*thee*-uh (strong accent on *thee*; *th* as in *thin*).
ARTEMIS. *Ar*-teh-miss.
ASSYRIA. Uh-*sear*-ee-uh.
ATHENS. *Ath*-unz.

BAAL-ZEBUB. *Bay*-ul-*zee*-bub (strong accent on *zee*).
BABYLON. *Bab*-uh-lun.
BABYLONIANS. Bab-uh-*low*-nee-unz.
BARAK. *Bair*-uk.
BARBARIAN. Bar-*bare*-ee-un.
BARNABAS. *Barn*-uh-bus.
BARTHOLOMEW. Bar-*thah*-luh-mew.
BATHSHEBA. Bath-*she*-buh.
BEELZEBUB. Bih-*el*-zih-bub.
BEELZEBUL. Bih-*el*-zih-bull.
BEERSHEBA. Beer-*she*-buh.
BETH-PEOR. Beth-*pea*-or.
BETHPHAGE. *Beth*-fuh-gee.
BETHSAIDA. Beth-*say*-uh-duh.
BEZALEEL. Bih-*zal*-ee-ull.
BOAZ. *Bo*-az.

CANAANITES. *Kay*-nuh-nites.
CAPERNAUM. Kuh-*per*-nay-um.
CENTURION. sen-*ture*-ee-un.

CEPHAS. *See*-fus.
CHLOE. *Klo*-ee.
COLOSSAE. Ko-*lahss*-ee.
COLOSSIANS. Kuh-*losh*-unz.
CONCUPISCENCE. con-*kew*-pih-sense.
CORINTH. *Kor*-inth.
CORINTHIANS. Kor-*in*-thee-unz.
CORNELIUS. Kor-*neel*-yus.
CRISPUS. *Kris*-pus.

DAMASCUS. Duh-*mass*-kus.
DEUTERONOMY. Due-ter-*ahn*-uh-me.
DIDYMUS. *Did*-uh-mus.

EBAL. *Ee*-bul.
ECCLESIASTES. Ik-*leez*-ee-*as*-teez (strong accent on *as*).
EDOM. *Ee*-dum.
ELATH. *Ee*-lath.
ELI (Aramaic). *Ee*-lye.
EPAPHRAS. *Ep*-uh-frass.
EPAPHRODITUS. Ee-*paf*-ro-*dye*-tus (strong accent on *dye*).
EPHESIANS. Ee-*fee*-zhunz.
EPHESUS. *Ef*-uh-sus.
ETHAM. *Ee*-thum.
EUNUCH. *you*-nick.
EUODIAS. You-*o*-dee-us.
EZEKIEL. Ee-*zeek*-yul or Ee-*zeek*-ee-ul.
EZION-GABER. *Ee*-zee-on-*gay*-ber (strong accent on *gay*).

GAIUS. *Gay*-us.
GALATIA. Guh-*lay*-shuh.
GALLIO. *Gal*-ee-o.
GERIZIM. *Gair*-ih-zim or Guh-*rye*-zim.
GETHSEMANE. Geth-*sem*-uh-nee.
GIDEON. *Gid*-ee-un.
GILGAL. *Gil*-gal.
GIRGASHITES. *Gur*-guh-shites.
GOLGOTHA. *Gahl*-guh-thuh.

HEROD. *Hair*-ud.
HERODIAN. Heh-*roe*-dee-un.
HEZRON. *Hezz*-ron.
HITTITES. *Hit*-ites.
HIVITES. *Hi*-vites.
HOREB. *Ho*-reb.

HORMAH. *Hor*-muh.
HOSANNA. Ho-*san*-uh.
HYMENEUS. High-meh-*nee*-us.

IMMANUEL. Ih-*man*-you-el.
ISAIAH. Eye-*zay*-uh.
ISCARIOT. Iss-*care*-ee-ut.

JAIRUS. *Jye*-rus or *Jay*-ih-rus.
JEBUSITES. *Jeb*-you-sites.
JEREMIAH. Jair-uh-*my*-uh.
JERICHO. *Jair*-ih-co.
JOSES. *Joe*-sez.

KADESH-BARNEA. *Kay*-desh-*bar*-nee-uh
        (strong accent on *bar*).
KIDRON. *Kid*-ron.
KORAH. *Ko*-rah.

LAMA (Aramaic). *lah*-muh.
LAODICEA. Lay-*odd*-uh-*see*-uh
        (strong accent on *see*).
LEBBEUS. Leh-*bee*-us.
LEVITES. *Lee*-vites.
LEVITICUS. Leh-*vit*-ih-kuss.
LYSTRA. *Liss*-truh.

MACEDONIA. Mass-eh-*doe*-nee-uh.
MAGDALENE. *Mag*-duh-leen or Mag-duh-*lee*-nee.
MEDITERRANEAN. *Med*-uh-tuh-*ray*-nee-un
        (strong accent on *ray*).
MELCHIZEDEK. Mel-*kizz*-eh-dek.
MESSIANIC. Mess-ee-*an*-ick.
MICAH. *My*-kuh.
MIDIANITES. *Mid*-ee-un-ites.
MIRIAM. *Meer*-ee-um.
MOAB. *Mo*-ab.
MOLECH. *Mo*-lek.
MOSAIC. Mo-*zay*-ik.
MYRRH. mur.

NAHSHON. *Nah*-shahn.
NAPHTALI. *Naf*-tuh-lye.
NATHANAEL. Nuh-*than*-yull.
NEBO. *Nee*-bo.
NEGEV. *Neg*-ev.
NICODEMUS. Nick-uh-*dee*-mus.
NINEVEH. *Nin*-uh-vuh.

OBED. *O*-bed.
ONESIMUS. O-*ness*-ih-muss.

PARAN. *Pair*-un.
PEREA. Peh-*ree*-uh.
PEREZ. *Pair*-ezz.
PERIZZITES. *Pair*-ih-zites.
PHARAOH. *Fair*-o or *Fay*-ro.

PHAREZ. *Fair*-ezz.
PHARISEES. *Fair*-ih-seez.
PHILEMON. Fih-*lee*-mun or Fye-*lee*-mun.
PHILIPPI. Fih-*lip*-pie or *Fil*-ih-pie.
PHILIPPIANS. Fih-*lip*-ee-unz.
PHILISTINES. Fuh-*liss*-teens or *Fill*-us-teens.
PHRYGIA. *Frij*-ee-uh.
PHYLACTERIES. fih-*lack*-ter-eez.
PONTIUS PILATE. *Pon*-shus or *Pon*-ti-us *Pie*-lut.
PRISCILLA. Prih-*sil*-uh.

RACHAB. *Ray*-kab.
RAHAB. *Ray*-hab.
RECONCILIATION. *rec*-un-sill-ee-*ay*-shun
        (strong accent on *ay*).

SABACHTHANI (Aramaic). suh-*back*-thuh-nee.
SADDUCEES. *Sad*-you-seez.
SALMON. *Sal*-mun.
SALOME. Suh-*lo*-me.
SANHEDRIN. San-*heed*-run or *San*-huh-drin.
SAPPHIRA. Suh-*fye*-ruh.
SCYTHIAN. *Sith*-ee-un.
SEIR. *See*-ir.
SEPULCHRE. *sep*-ul-kur.
SHECHEM. *Shek*-em or *Shee*-kem.
SHEOL. *She*-ol.
SICHEM. *Sigh*-kem.
SIHON. *Sigh*-hun.
SILAS. *Sigh*-luss.
SIMEON. *Sim*-ee-un.
SINAI. *Sigh*-nye or *Sigh*-nay-eye.
STEPHANAS. *Stef*-uh-nass.
SUCCOTH. *Soo*-kawth.
SYNAGOGUES. *sin*-uh-gogs.
SYNTYCHE. *Sin*-tih-key.
SYRIA. *Sear*-ee-uh.

TAMAR. *Tay*-mer.
THADDEUS. *Thad*-ee-us.
THESSALONIANS. *Thess*-uh-*lo*-nee-unz (strong
        accent on *lo*; *th* as in *thin*).
THESSALONICA. *Thess*-uh-lo-*nye*-kuh (strong
        accent on *nye*; *th* as in *thin*).
TROAS. *Tro*-az.
TYCHICUS. *Tick*-ih-cuss.

URIAH. Yu-*rye*-uh.

ZACCHEUS. Zack-*kee*-us.
ZARAH or ZERAH. *Zair*-uh.
ZARETAN. *Zair*-uh-tan.
ZEALOT. *Zel*-ut.
ZEBEDEE. *Zeb*-uh-dee.
ZEBULUN. *Zeb*-you-lun.
ZECHARIAH. Zek-uh-*rye*-uh.
ZELOTES. Zeh-*low*-teez.

Fall Quarter, 1999

From Slavery to Conquest

(Exodus, Leviticus, Numbers, Deuteronomy, Joshua)

Special Features

Lessons

Unit 1: Exodus and Covenant

Unit 2: Wandering in the Wilderness

Unit 3: Entering the Promised Land

About These Lessons

The lessons in this quarter trace the history of Israel from the exodus to the conquest of the promised land. They highlight God's deliverance of His people from bondage in Egypt, the establishment of His covenant with them, the initial failure of the people to enter the land, and their eventual success in doing so under Joshua.

Sep 5
Sep 12
Sep 19
Sep 26
Oct 3
Oct 10
Oct 17
Oct 24
Oct 31
Nov 7
Nov 14
Nov 21
Nov 28

Forward in Faith, Not in Fear

THE YEAR 2000! It's hard to believe that the lessons covered in this book will take us into the year that once seemed so far away. Now we wonder where the time went!

Our thoughts as we prepare to cross this milestone may be similar to those of the Israelites as they prepared to enter the promised land. The lessons for the Fall quarter of this year, entitled "From Slavery to Conquest," cover the period of Israel's history from the exodus to the possession of the promised land. We will be reminded of a time when fear triumphed over faith, when the people failed to enter Canaan because of unbelief.

The Winter quarter's lessons are all taken from the Gospel of Matthew. They focus on the impact of Immanuel ("God With Us"). His death and resurrection ushered in a new era, establishing a New Covenant and calling us to faith in Him.

Life under the New Covenant carries its own challenges. This is clear from the Spring and Summer lessons, drawn from some of the New Testament epistles: the Spring from 1 and 2 Corinthians and the Summer from Paul's prison epistles. We will see that the issues that faced both the first-century church and the soon-to-be twenty-first century church are not really much different. Our times and our challenges, like those of the Israelites and the early church, call for faith, not fear.

May these lessons help you answer that call.

International Sunday School Lesson Cycle
September, 1998—August, 2004

YEAR	FALL QUARTER (Sept., Oct., Nov.)	WINTER QUARTER (Dec., Jan., Feb.)	SPRING QUARTER (Mar., Apr., May)	SUMMER QUARTER (June, July, Aug.)
1998-1999	God Calls a People to Faithful Living (Old Testament Survey)	God Calls Anew in Jesus Christ (New Testament Survey)	That You May Believe (John)	Genesis: Beginnings (Genesis)
1999-2000	From Slavery to Conquest (Exodus, Leviticus, Numbers, Deuteronomy, Joshua)	Immanuel: God With Us (Matthew)	Helping a Church Confront Crisis (1 and 2 Corinthians)	New Life in Christ (Ephesians, Philippians, Colossians, Philemon)
2000-2001	The Emerging Nation (Judges, 1 and 2 Samuel, 1 Kings 1-11, 1 Chronicles, 2 Chronicles 1-9)	Good News of Jesus (Luke)	Continuing Jesus' Work (Acts)	Division and Decline (1 Kings 12-22, 2 Kings 1-17, 2 Chronicles 10-28, Isaiah 1-39, Amos, Hosea, Micah)
2001-2002	Jesus' Ministry (Parables, Miracles, Sermon on the Mount)	Light for All People (Isaiah 9:1-7; 11:1-9; 40-66; Ruth, Jonah, Nahum)	The Power of the Gospel (Romans, Galatians)	Worship and Wisdom for Living (Psalms, Proverbs)
2002-2003	Judgment and Exile (2 Kings 18-25, 2 Chronicles 29-36, Jeremiah, Lamentations, Ezekiel, Habakkuk, Zephaniah)	Portraits of Faith (Personalities in the New Testament)	Jesus: God's Power in Action (Mark)	God Restores a Remnant (Ezra, Nehemiah, Daniel, Joel, Obadiah, Haggai, Zechariah, Malachi)
2003-2004	Faith Faces the World (James, 1 and 2 Peter, 1, 2, 3 John, Jude)	A Child Is Given (Samuel, John the Baptist, Jesus) Lessons From Life (Esther, Job, Ecclesiastes, Song of Solomon)	Jesus Fulfills His Mission (Death, Burial, and Resurrection Texts) Living Expectantly (1, 2 Thessalonians, Revelation)	Hold Fast to the Faith (Hebrews) Guidelines for the Church's Ministry (1, 2 Timothy, Titus)

Lessons Learned on the Move

by Orrin Root

AN YOU IMAGINE an entire nation of people tramping for forty years through rugged country without even wearing out their shoes? It happened (read Deuteronomy 29:5). The account of that migration is as fascinating as Homer's mythic *Odyssey*, and centuries older. Most important, it is true. It is actual history—and it is the subject of our Sunday school lessons for September, October, and November.

Throughout the Bible, God frequently taught His servants many important lessons while they were "on the move." Hebrews 11:9, 10 says of Abraham, "By faith he sojourned in the land of promise, as in a strange country, dwelling in tabernacles with Isaac and Jacob, the heirs with him of the same promise: for he looked for a city which hath foundations, whose builder and maker is God."

Moses, who is a central figure in this quarter's lessons, fled from Egypt to Midian as a fugitive, then returned to Egypt when God called him to lead the Israelites out of bondage in that land. Moses' experiences in the desert prepared him for the long, hard years of wandering that the Israelites would have to endure.

David also learned much while "on the go" as a fugitive from the angry, jealous King Saul. A number of David's Psalms were written during this period of his life. They express his love for and trust in God, in spite of the disheartening circumstances he was facing. For example, read Psalm 57, noting what the heading says about the time when it was written.

In the thirteen lessons of this quarter, we shall trace the Israelites' forty-year journey in the wilderness. Obviously we can touch on only the highest of the high points and the lowest of the low. As we observe the Israelites, we shall see the depth of fear and the height of faith, the depth of man's need and the height of God's care. We shall see the wisdom of trusting God and obeying Him, and if we are wise we shall determine to trust and obey Him too.

What follows is a preview of the thirteen lessons for September, October, and November. They are divided into three one-month units.

Unit 1. September
Exodus and Covenant

Lesson 1: God Calls Moses. Most people recall the story of Moses, who was born a Hebrew slave but reared a prince of Egypt. For killing an Egyptian whom he saw mistreating one of the Hebrews, Moses became a fugitive from Egypt and lived as a shepherd in Midian for forty years. Then God sent him back to Egypt to lead the Hebrew slaves to freedom. At first Moses was reluctant to answer God's call; however, assured of God's presence and power, he undertook the task vigorously.

Lesson 2: Crossing the Red Sea. Ten plagues compelled the Pharaoh of Egypt to release the Hebrew slaves. Starting their journey to the land God promised them, they camped beside the Red Sea. Then Pharaoh changed his mind about his decision to release the Hebrews and sent his army after them. But the Lord continued to protect His people. He opened a way through the sea, and the Hebrews passed between walls of water. When the Egyptian soldiers forged ahead into the same path, the liquid walls collapsed and drowned them all.

Lesson 3: The Covenant. The Israelites camped by Mount Sinai, where the Lord demonstrated His presence through an impressive array of sights and sounds. There He gave His people the laws that would govern their life as a nation.

Lesson 4: The Tabernacle and Obedience. While they were encamped at Sinai for approximately a year, the Israelites built a beautiful tabernacle to serve as God's tent among the tents of His people. God promised to bless the people with prosperity and peace if they would obey His law.

Unit 2. October
Wandering in the Wilderness

Lesson 5: The Cloud and the Fire. In the wilderness, God showed the way for His people by going before them in a cloud by day and a fire by night. The cloud served as a signal to indicate when the people should break camp and resume their travels and when they should stop and rest.

Lesson 6: The People's Rebellion. This is perhaps the most tragic incident to be considered in this quarter's lessons. As the Israelites neared the promised land, Moses sent twelve men (one from each of the twelve tribes) to explore the land and to bring back a report. The spies gave an encouraging description of the fruit of the land (they even brought with them an impressive visual aid), but their report as a whole was not encouraging. They described the residents of the land as "giants" and themselves as mere "grasshoppers" in comparison.

Disheartened by the negative elements in the spies' report, the people refused to enter the land. Instead of trusting God to overcome whatever obstacles existed, they became intimidated by those obstacles. They determined to walk by sight, not by faith. As a result, faith was smothered by fear.

Lesson 7: The Desert Years. God ordered the frightened people to turn back to the desert and spend the rest of their lives there. At this they rebelled yet again, and tried to take control of the promised land. But God was not with them in their act of defiance, and they were soundly defeated. Some thirty-eight years would pass before they had another opportunity to enter the land of promise. How foolish it is not to do something when God says, "Do it!" and to do something when God says, "Don't do it!"

Lesson 8: The Great Commandment. While the two previous lessons focus on the Israelites' rebellion against God, this lesson calls attention to the importance of loving and obeying the Lord. It also stresses how vital it is to teach future generations to love and obey Him, and to use every available opportunity to do so.

Deuteronomy 6:7 describes a series of settings where the faithful teaching of God's Word is to take place: indoors ("when thou sittest in thine house"), outdoors ("when thou walkest by the way"), nighttime ("when thou liest down"), and morning ("when thou risest up"). All Christian parents should be engaged diligently in this kind of "homeschooling"!

Lesson 9: A Warning. Here God renewed His promise of a good and fruitful land for His people, but warned that they would be destroyed if they forgot His blessings and turned away from Him. How necessary is this reminder in our time!

Unit 3. November
Entering the Promised Land

Lesson 10: Joshua Succeeds Moses. Moses died at the border of the promised land, without ever entering it. He had provided, however, for a successor so that the task of bringing God's people into the land could be completed. Joshua, who had faithfully served as a kind of "apprentice" to Moses, was appointed to provide the necessary leadership.

Lesson 11: Israel Crosses the Jordan River. At the time of year when the Israelites approached the Jordan River, the river was overflowing its banks. However, in a miracle reminiscent of the parting of the Red Sea, God made the water stand up in a heap, leaving an empty riverbed for Israel to cross.

Lesson 12: God Destroys Jericho. Jericho was a well-fortified city, but at Israel's shout the wall "fell down flat" (Joshua 6:20). Charging in from every side, the Israelites took the city. All of its people and its contents were set apart to the Lord to be destroyed. Any items of value were placed in the treasury of the Lord. Only Rahab and her family were spared from the destruction because she had helped the Israelite spies when they entered Jericho.

Lesson 13: Israel Chooses to Serve the Lord. Israel conquered the rest of the promised land in about seven years of warfare, then settled down to peaceful and prosperous living. In a farewell address, aged Joshua challenged the people: "Choose you this day whom ye will serve" (Joshua 24:15). Together the people promised to sever any ties with idols and to serve the Lord who had given them the good land they possessed.

The challenge of this final lesson is an appropriate one with which to end the quarter. Will we choose to serve the Lord—this day and every day? Are we willing to declare unashamedly, "As for me and my house, we will serve the Lord"? Only by exhibiting such faith can we enter the "promised land" prepared for us—Heaven!

Answers to Quarterly Quiz
on page 8

Lesson 1—1. Jethro. 2. kept his flock. 3. I Am That I Am. **Lesson 2**—1. Philistines. 2. Joseph's. 3. a strong east wind. **Lesson 3**—1. eagles' wings. 2. priests, holy. 3. "that thy days may be long upon the land which the Lord thy God giveth thee." **Lesson 4**—1. the laver. 2. rain. **Lesson 5**—1. the glory of the Lord. 2. cloud, fire. **Lesson 6**—1. true. 2. grasshoppers. 3. Caleb. **Lesson 7**—1. Amorites. 2. Kadesh. 3. forty, nothing. **Lesson 8**—1. "Hear, O Israel: The Lord our God is one Lord: and thou shalt love the Lord thy God with all thine heart, and with all thy soul, and with all thy might." 2. "when thou sittest in thine house, and when thou walkest by the way, and when thou liest down, and when thou risest up." **Lesson 9**—1. iron. 2. bless the Lord. **Lesson 10**—1. Sihon and Og. 2. 120 years old. 3. 30 days. **Lesson 11**—1. the ark of the covenant. 2. Jericho. **Lesson 12**—1. seven, seven trumpets of rams' horns. 2. Rahab. **Lesson 13**—1. Shechem. 2. gods.

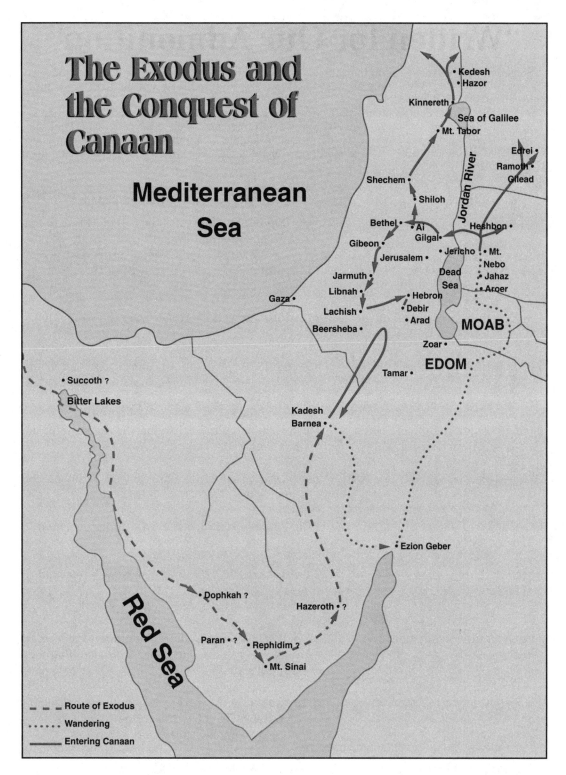

The Exodus and the Conquest of Canaan

Mediterranean Sea

Red Sea

Route of Exodus
Wandering
Entering Canaan

Kedesh
Hazor
Kinnereth
Sea of Galilee
Mt. Tabor
Edrei
Ramoth
Gilead
Shechem
Shiloh
Bethel
Ai
Gilgal
Gibeon
Jerusalem
Heshbon
Jericho
Mt. Nebo
Jahaz
Aroer
Jarmuth
Libnah
Hebron
Gaza
Lachish
Debir
Arad
Beersheba
MOAB
Zoar
Tamar
EDOM
Kadesh Barnea
Ezion Geber
Dophkah ?
Hazeroth ?
Paran ?
Rephidim ?
Mt. Sinai
Succoth ?
Bitter Lakes
Jordan River
Dead Sea

"Written for Our Admonition"

Sometimes Christians question the value of studying the Old Testament. "We belong to the 'New Covenant,'" they say. "Why study all this stuff about law and sacrifices and the like? We want to know about Jesus and grace!"

But the New Testament frequently cites the Old Testament. In fact—as the chart below shows—many of the lessons of our present quarter's study find reference in the New Testament. Paul said, "These things happened unto them for ensamples ["examples"]: and they are written for our admonition" (1 Corinthians 10:11). If we would know of Jesus and grace, the Old Testament is a good place to start!

Old Testament Event	New Testament References
God Calls Moses (Lesson 1)	**Acts 7:30-34.** Stephen cites the call of Moses in his defense before the Council.
The Passover (Lesson 2)	**1 Corinthians 5:7.** Jesus is "our passover." (See also 1 Peter 1:19.)
Crossing the Red Sea (Lesson 2)	**1 Corinthians 10:1, 2.** Israel "passed through the sea."
The Law Given Through Moses (Lesson 3)	**Mark 7:9, 10.** Jesus quotes one of the Ten Commandments as the "commandment of God" and as the words of Moses. (See also John 1:17; 7:19.)
Israel to be a "kingdom of priests," "a holy nation" (Lesson 3).	**1 Peter 2:9** paraphrases Exodus 19:5 in reference to Christians.
Building the Tabernacle (Lesson 4)	**Hebrews 9** describes the tabernacle as a "pattern" of heavenly things (v. 23).
Israel Led by Pillar of Cloud/Fire (Lesson 5)	**1 Corinthians 10:1, 2.** Israel was "under the cloud."
Rebellion in the Desert (Lessons 6, 7, 9)	**1 Corinthians 10:5-13** describes Israel's repeated rebellion. (See also John 3:14; Acts 7:39-43; Hebrews 3:15–4:6.)
The Great Commandment (Lesson 8)	**Mark 12:28-34.** Jesus cites Deuteronomy 6:4, 5 as the "greatest commandment." (See also Matthew 4:10; Luke 10:25-27.)
The Fall of Jericho (Lesson 12)	**Hebrews 11:30, 31** says it was faith that brought down the walls of Jericho, noting also the faith of Rahab in hiding the spies. (See also James 2:25.)

Meaningful Memories

by Lloyd Ludwick

"MOMMY, TELL ME AGAIN about when I was a little baby and. . . ." The end of the sentence may change, but our youngest daughter always asks about an event she is too young to remember. In such cases, Rachelle relies on her mother's recollections to make the memory meaningful.

Remembering has always been an important part of God's relationship with His people. In the Old Testament, God remembers both His promises (Genesis 9:15-17; Exodus 2:24; Leviticus 26:45) and His people (Genesis 8:1; 19:29; 30:22; 1 Samuel 1:11, 19; Nehemiah 13:14, 22), because He is holy, loving, and faithful. Israel, on the other hand, remembers because God instructs her to do so (Deuteronomy 5:15; Joshua 1:13). Israel's failure to remember God's commandments and His mighty acts on her behalf plagued her throughout her history, and eventually led to her downfall (Judges 8:34; Isaiah 57:11).

God knows how prone we are to forget that which is essential to our spiritual well-being. He has always encouraged His people to observe special spiritual landmarks.

Meaningful Models

The most meaningful memory that God commanded His people to keep was the Passover. The elements of that observance (items that could be seen and tasted) prompted the telling of the story of God's mighty work of deliverance (Exodus 12:26, 27). That act became the cornerstone of God's subsequent acts and commands (Exodus 20:2). It was meant to provide Israel with the motivation to live as God's holy people (Exodus 19:3-6). The failure to keep such observances as the Passover led Israel into spiritual decline.

It is no coincidence that Jesus instituted the Lord's Supper at His final Passover meal with His disciples. Three and a half years earlier John the Baptist had called Jesus the "Lamb of God" (John 1:29, 36). In the same way that God delivered the Israelites from slavery in Egypt by means of the blood of lambs, He performed a mighty act of deliverance at Calvary by means of His Son—the spotless Lamb (Hebrews 2:14, 15; Revelation 5:6-12).

The Lord's Supper provides us with a sacred opportunity to remember God's act of deliverance and to thank Him for what He has done for us and for all others who have accepted His grace and forgiveness. We are reminded of Jesus' sacrifice through Communion meditations, hymns, and through our reading of the Scriptures during Communion time. We remember His death and resurrection, and we recall our personal participation in these events through our baptism (Romans 6:3-11). It is a participation that continues as we "walk in newness of life" (v. 4) and give ourselves to the service of Jesus as "living sacrifices" (Romans 12:1).

Making Meaningful Memories

According to Numbers 15:37-41, God told the Israelites to place "fringes" or "tassels" (*New International Version*) on the edges of their garments. When the Israelites saw these tassels, they were to remember God's commands and renew their commitment to obey Him. Like Old Testament Israel, Christians also have many opportunities for meaningful memories of God's mighty acts. Such memories are important for our churches, our families, and our personal growth.

Christmas, for example, offers us many opportunities to establish meaningful memories and traditions, particularly within our families. We can begin by making sure that the season is filled with opportunities both to see and to hear the story of Jesus' birth. These "tassels" cause us to reflect on the importance of Jesus' incarnation, of the angels' words of salvation, and of the words spoken to Mary and Joseph. Such reflections should stir us to live so that others may see Christ living in us.

Special celebrations such as church anniversaries, wedding anniversaries, and birthdays present us with opportunities to trace the hand of God in our yesterdays. Through these occasions, we are challenged to continue making Him the center of our churches and our families. On a more personal level, an object such as a bookmark, a note written on a calendar, or a child's picture can serve as a "tassel" that provides a meaningful memory.

Meaningful memories are an essential part of our health and maturity as children of God. If such memories are not a regular part of your life and worship, why not begin to collect some today? Celebrate God's mighty works so that you can continue to be aware of His power and grace at work in your life.

Quarterly Quiz

The questions on this page may be used in several ways: as a pretest at the beginning of the quarter; as a review at the end of the quarter; or as a review after each lesson. The questions are based on the Scripture text of each lesson (King James Version). ***The answers are on page 4.***

Lesson 1

1. Give the name of Moses' father-in-law. *Exodus 3:1* JETHRO
2. What work did Moses do for his father-in-law? *Exodus 3:1* Sheep HCARDEE
3. What did God tell Moses that His name was? *Exodus 3:13, 14* I AM

Lesson 2

1. When the Israelites left Egypt, God did not lead them through the land of the Philistines. (Edomites, Syrians, or Philistines?) *Exodus 13:17*
2. Whose bones did Moses take when the Israelites left Egypt? *Exodus 13:19* Joseph
3. What did the Lord use to cause the sea to go back? *Exodus 14:21* STRONG EAST WIND

Lesson 3

1. God told the Israelites that He had borne them on _____ _____. *Exodus 19:4*
2. God called Israel to be a kingdom of _____ and a _____ nation. *Exodus 19:6*
3. God linked a specific blessing with obeying the command to honor father and mother. What was it? *Exodus 20:12* LONG LIFE

Lesson 4

1. Moses was told to put water into which of the tabernacle's accessories? *Exodus 40:7*
2. God said that if the people kept His commandments, He would give them _____ in due season. *Leviticus 26:4*

Lesson 5

1. What filled the tabernacle when it was completed? *Exodus 40:34, 35*
2. During their travels, God guided the Israelites by a CLOUD during the day and by FIRE at night. *Exodus 40:38*

Lesson 6

1. God told Moses to appoint one man from each tribe of Israel to search the land of Canaan. T/F *Numbers 13:2*
2. Compared with the "sons of Anak," ten of the Israelite spies saw themselves as GRASShoPPers *Numbers 13:33*
3. Whom did God say had "another spirit with him"? *Numbers 14:24*

Lesson 7

1. What group of people pursued the Israelites like bees when they first tried to take the hill country? *Deuteronomy 1:44*
2. In what place did the Israelites abide "many days"? *Deuteronomy 1:46*
3. The Lord told the Israelites that He had been with them for _____ years and that they had lacked _____. *Deuteronomy 2:7*

Lesson 8

1. Quote Deuteronomy 6:4, 5.
2. Name the four settings in which the Israelites were commanded to teach their children God's words. *Deuteronomy 6:7*

Lesson 9

1. The promised land was described as a land whose stones were _____. *Deuteronomy 8:9*
2. Which of the following were the people to do after they had eaten and were full? (return to their work, bless the Lord, or offer a sacrifice?) *Deuteronomy 8:10*

Lesson 10

1. What two kings of the Amorites did Israel destroy? *Deuteronomy 31:4*
2. How old was Moses when he died? *Deuteronomy 34:7*
3. How long did Israel weep for Moses after his death? *Deuteronomy 34:8*

Lesson 11

1. What did the priests carry as they entered the Jordan River? *Joshua 3:14* ARK OF COVENENT
2. The Israelites crossed the Jordan at a place near what city? *Joshua 3:16*

Lesson 12

1. How many priests were to circle Jericho? What were these priests to carry? *Joshua 6:4*
2. Only RAHAB and her family were spared when the city of Jericho was destroyed. *Joshua 6:17*

Lesson 13

1. To what city did Joshua gather all the tribes of Israel? *Joshua 24:1* JERICHOO
2. Joshua challenged the people to put away their IDOLS. *Joshua 24:14*

God Calls Moses

DEVOTIONAL READING: Exodus 6:2-8.

BACKGROUND SCRIPTURE: Exodus 3.

PRINTED TEXT: Exodus 3:1-14.

Exodus 3:1-14

1 Now Moses kept the flock of Jethro his father-in-law, the priest of Midian: and he led the flock to the back side of the desert, and came to the mountain of God, even to Horeb.

2 And the angel of the LORD appeared unto him in a flame of fire out of the midst of a bush: and he looked, and, behold, the bush burned with fire, and the bush was not consumed.

3 And Moses said, I will now turn aside, and see this great sight, why the bush is not burnt.

4 And when the LORD saw that he turned aside to see, God called unto him out of the midst of the bush, and said, Moses, Moses. And he said, Here am I.

5 And he said, Draw not nigh hither: put off thy shoes from off thy feet; for the place whereon thou standest is holy ground.

6 Moreover he said, I am the God of thy father, the God of Abraham, the God of Isaac, and the God of Jacob. And Moses hid his face; for he was afraid to look upon God.

7 And the LORD said, I have surely seen the affliction of my people which are in Egypt, and have heard their cry by reason of their taskmasters; for I know their sorrows;

8 And I am come down to deliver them out of the hand of the Egyptians, and to bring them up out of that land unto a good land and a large, unto a land flowing with milk and honey; unto the place of the Canaanites, and the Hittites, and the Amorites, and the Perizzites, and the Hivites, and the Jebusites.

9 Now therefore, behold, the cry of the children of Israel is come unto me: and I have also seen the oppression wherewith the Egyptians oppress them.

10 Come now therefore, and I will send thee unto Pharaoh, that thou mayest bring forth my people the children of Israel out of Egypt.

11 And Moses said unto God, Who am I, that I should go unto Pharaoh, and that I should bring forth the children of Israel out of Egypt?

12 And he said, Certainly I will be with thee; and this shall be a token unto thee, that I have sent thee: When thou hast brought forth the people out of Egypt, ye shall serve God upon this mountain.

13 And Moses said unto God, Behold, when I come unto the children of Israel, and shall say unto them, The God of your fathers hath sent me unto you; and they shall say to me, What is his name? what shall I say unto them?

14 And God said unto Moses, I AM THAT I AM: and he said, Thus shalt thou say unto the children of Israel, I AM hath sent me unto you.

GOLDEN TEXT: And God said unto Moses, I AM THAT I AM: and he said, Thus shalt thou say unto the children of Israel, I AM hath sent me unto you.—Exodus 3:14.

> ## From Slavery to Conquest
> ### Unit 1: Exodus and Covenant
> ### (Lessons 1-4)

Lesson Aims

After this lesson a student should be able to:

1. Tell the story of God's call to Moses.

2. Compare the call and task God gave Moses with the call and tasks God gives to Christians today.

3. State what he or she believes God has called him or her specifically to do, and suggest one step that can be taken in the coming week to obey that call.

Lesson Outline

INTRODUCTION
  A. God and Mankind
  B. Lesson Background
 I. GOD IN THE FIRE (Exodus 3:1-6)
  A. Shepherd in the Desert (v. 1)
  B. God and His Angel (vv. 2-4)
  C. Holy Ground and Holy God (vv. 5, 6)
    A Mountaintop Experience
 II. GOD'S MESSAGE (Exodus 3:7-12)
  A. A Cry and a Reply (vv. 7, 8)
  B. A Job for Moses (vv. 9, 10)
    Delayed Response
  C. Objection Overruled (vv. 11, 12)
III. GOD'S NAME (Exodus 3:13, 14)
  A. Need for a Name (v. 13)
  B. I AM (v. 14)
CONCLUSION
  A. Qualification
  B. Help
  C. The Lord's Approval
  D. Prayer
  E. Thought to Remember

Introduction

A. God and Mankind

Opposition to God always ends in failure or even disaster. We saw that in our lessons from Genesis last summer. Adam and Eve chose to go their own way, and they lost their home in Eden. Mankind after them opposed God till "every imagination of the thoughts of his heart was only evil continually" (Genesis 6:5), and only eight people survived the flood that followed.

When descendants of those eight grew godless, God chose Abraham (then called Abram) to be the father of a nation that God could call His own. The Lord took Abraham from idolatrous Ur and led him to the land that would belong one day to that nation—the land of Canaan.

Approximately two hundred years later, when there were some seventy people in Abraham's family, the family was welcomed as honored guests in Egypt. But when the family of seventy became a throng of millions, the king of Egypt grew wary of their numbers. Hoping to retard their growth, he made them slaves instead of guests. Yet God remained in control. He had told Abraham that his descendants would dwell in a "land that is not theirs" for four hundred years (Genesis 15:13). Now it was time for them to go back to the land that was theirs, which God had chosen for their home.

B. Lesson Background

Nearly every Sunday school student remembers the story of baby Moses. Pharaoh had decreed that any newborn Hebrew boy should be thrown into the river. Moses' mother, however, placed him in a basket and sent the basket floating down the river. Eventually Moses was found by Pharaoh's daughter, who immediately "had compassion on him" (Exodus 2:6). She brought him up as her own son and gave him the best education that Egypt had to offer (Acts 7:22). Romantic readers like to think he might have been the next king of Egypt if he had been more cautious. One day, however, Moses saw an Egyptian beating a Hebrew, and his anger flared. He killed the oppressor and buried his body in the sand. Moses, a man of great promise and potential, found himself a fugitive, fleeing for his life across the eastern desert.

In the land of Midian, Moses joined the household of a priest named Jethro. He stayed there for forty years, married a daughter of the priest, and started to rear a family. Our text takes up the story at that point.

I. God in the Fire
(Exodus 3:1-6)

Moses' father-in-law was a sheep owner as well as a priest. Moses' first contact with the family was at a watering place where Jethro's daughters brought their father's sheep (Exodus 2:15-17). Forty years later, Moses was taking care of the family sheep.

A. Shepherd in the Desert (v. 1)

1. Now Moses kept the flock of Jethro his father-in-law, the priest of Midian: and he led the flock to the back side of the desert, and came to the mountain of God, even to Horeb.

The land of *Midian* was a vast desert area. Pasture is scarce in such country; sheep had to keep moving to find enough to eat. Eventually Moses and his *flock* came *to Horeb*, also called Sinai. The phrase *the back side of the desert* suggests that Moses had traveled a long way from home at this point. Perhaps Horeb is called *the mountain of God* because God spoke to Moses and later gave the law there; or possibly the Midianites themselves had given the mountain that name for reasons unknown to us.

B. God and His Angel (vv. 2-4)

2. And the angel of the LORD appeared unto him in a flame of fire out of the midst of a bush: and he looked, and, behold, the bush burned with fire, and the bush was not consumed.

Students are puzzled because at many points in the Old Testament there seems to be no clear distinction between *the Lord* and His *angel*. Some scholars explain in various ways that the angel either provided the *fire* or was the fire, but God spoke from it. Others believe that the angel was God Himself "in one particular phase of His self-revelation." Verse 2 says plainly that *the angel of the Lord appeared . . . in a flame of fire out of the midst of a bush*; and verse 4 says that *God called . . . out of the midst of the bush*. We can accept the facts without understanding all about them.

What Moses saw is quite clear: *he looked, and, behold, the bush burned with fire*. That in itself was startling when there was neither a man nor a flash of lightning to start the fire. But it was still more startling to see that *the bush was not consumed*. Moses was close enough to see that the small leaves of the desert plant were not withered in the heat, and that the twigs and stems were not being reduced to smoke and ashes.

3. And Moses said, I will now turn aside, and see this great sight, why the bush is not burnt.

Moses had never seen such a *sight* before. He went closer to try to determine *why the bush* was *not burnt*.

4. And when the LORD saw that he turned aside to see, God called unto him out of the midst of the bush, and said, Moses, Moses. And he said, Here am I.

Seeing that the fire had Moses' full attention, God spoke his name clearly and repeated it. If Moses was startled before, now he must have been shocked, if not terrified. But he stood his ground and answered, *Here am I*. [See question #1, page 16.]

C. Holy Ground and Holy God (vv. 5, 6)

5. And he said, Draw not nigh hither: put off thy shoes from off thy feet; for the place whereon thou standest is holy ground.

Holy ground! If Moses was still moving toward the bush, surely this brought him to a sudden stop. If he was frightened before, now his trembling fingers must have found it hard to untie the thongs of his sandals.

6. Moreover he said, I am the God of thy father, the God of Abraham, the God of Isaac, and the God of Jacob. And Moses hid his face; for he was afraid to look upon God.

Now the Lord identified Himself plainly. He was the God of Heaven and earth who had called the descendants of *Abraham* to be His own. Upon hearing these words, Moses could no longer stare at that fascinating fire. He *hid his face; for he was afraid to look upon God*. Later God said to Moses, "Thou canst not see my face: for there shall no man see me, and live" (Exodus 33:20); but already Moses understood that the sight of Almighty God is not for human eyes.

A MOUNTAINTOP EXPERIENCE

At 29,028 feet, Mount Everest stands as the highest mountain in the world. Not until 1953 did its peak feel the pressure of human footsteps, when Sir Edmund Hillary and Tensing Norgay became the first climbers to see the spectacular view from the "top of the world." Thousands have sought glory in that experience, but through the end of 1996, only 846 people had reached the summit. Only one man, Reinhold Messner, has climbed the mountain alone.

Moses thought that he was alone on "the mountain of God." He had gone there, not in a quest for glory or a spectacular view, but in search of food for his sheep. Instead, what Moses found was a bush that burned with the presence of God and yet was not consumed. As a result, Moses' trip to the mountain was not the culmination of a lifelong quest, but the beginning of a life of service.

How to Say It

ABRAM. *Ay*-brum.
AMORITES. *Am*-uh-rites.
CANAAN. *Kay*-nun.
EGYPTIANS. Ee-*jip*-shunz.
HITTITES. *Hit*-ites.
HIVITES. *Hi*-vites.
HOREB. *Ho*-reb.
JEBUSITES. *Jeb*-yuh-sites.
JETHRO. *Jeth*-ro.
MIDIAN. *Mid*-ee-un.
MIDIANITES. *Mid*-ee-un-ites.
PERIZZITES. *Pair*-ih-zites.
PHARAOH. *Fair*-o or *Fay*-ro.

Whether our search for meaning in life is as mundane as obtaining our daily bread or as challenging as climbing a breathtaking mountain peak, we should not be surprised to be confronted by God.

He still speaks to those willing to be awed by His presence.   —C. R. B.

II. God's Message (Exodus 3:7-12)

Eyes tightly closed and hands covering his face, Moses was humbled, frightened, and trembling with reverent awe. Now he was ready to hear God's message to him. When we approach God's Word with an attitude like that, perhaps we shall understand it better, remember it better, and obey it better. Moses' eyes were closed, but his ears and his mind were opened wide as God continued to speak.

A. A Cry and a Reply (vv. 7, 8)

7. And the LORD said, I have surely seen the affliction of my people which are in Egypt, and have heard their cry by reason of their taskmasters; for I know their sorrows.

Moses was now eighty years old, and the *affliction* of his people had begun long before he was born. Both he and his suffering people must have wondered at times if God really knew or cared about their misery, or if He really *heard their cry*. But He did hear; He did know; He did care. That was cheering news to Moses, and it is cheering news to us when we cry in times of suffering. [See question #2, page 16.]

8. And I am come down to deliver them out of the hand of the Egyptians, and to bring them up out of that land unto a good land and a large, unto a land flowing with milk and honey; unto the place of the Canaanites, and the Hittites, and the Amorites, and the Perizzites, and the Hivites, and the Jebusites.

If news of God's knowledge of His people's misery was encouraging, how Moses' heart must have leaped at this additional news! God had *come down*. He was on the scene, ready for action. The end of bondage was at hand—the liberation of God's people. God Himself would *deliver them out of the hand of the Egyptians*. He would lead them to *a good land and a large*, a land with plenty of room and resources.

Perhaps Moses' enthusiasm waned a bit upon hearing the list of people already living in that land. It would take courage to invade a country so filled with hostile warriors. But *God* was taking His people there. If He could burn a bush without harming it, couldn't He bring His people unscathed through the fire of battle?

Today we see no bush burning with strange and miraculous fire; we hear God's message from the printed page instead of a living voice. Yet we know all Moses did, and more, about God's mighty power and His unfailing goodness. How can we shrink from any great undertaking when we are sure it is His will?

B. A Job for Moses (vv. 9, 10)

9. Now therefore, behold, the cry of the children of Israel is come unto me: and I have also seen the oppression wherewith the Egyptians oppress them.

The Lord repeated the assurance He had already given Moses.

10. Come now therefore, and I will send thee unto Pharaoh, that thou mayest bring forth my people the children of Israel out of Egypt.

On hearing these words, Moses' soaring heart must have dropped with a thud. That he should go to *Egypt* and rescue his enslaved *people* was not what he had been praying for. When a hard job needs to be done, aren't we all more eager to pray for God to do it than we are to dig into it ourselves? God does many mighty works with no help from us, from the creation of the world to the sunshine that warms us today; but there are also some mighty works that He will do through us or not at all! [See question #3, page 16.]

DELAYED RESPONSE

Anne-Merete Christensen was a Swedish teenager when she put a letter in a bottle and threw it into the Baltic Sea. After years with no response, she gave up hope of hearing from a pen pal.

However, thirty years later, eight-year-old Otto Fransson found the bottle bobbing near Sweden's eastern shore and retrieved it. He wrote a long-delayed response to Christensen, who by then was a forty-three-year-old married woman with two children of her own.

When God spoke to Moses on the mountain, He was responding to a cry that Israel had been voicing for some four centuries. Moses may well have wondered why it had taken so long for God to respond. But from God's vantage point, that time was well spent in preparing Moses to be His instrument of deliverance.

Who among us has not questioned why God's response to our prayers is so often delayed? Moses' experience teaches us that God always hears us; however, his response often comes through people who, according to His timetable, have finally been prepared to act on His behalf.

Is God preparing you to be an answer to someone's prayer today?   —C. R. B.

C. Objection Overruled (vv. 11, 12)

11. And Moses said unto God, Who am I, that I should go unto Pharaoh, and that I should bring forth the children of Israel out of Egypt?

Who am I? This was a reasonable question. Moses was a fugitive from *Egypt*. There was another *Pharaoh* now, though not the one from whom Moses had fled (Exodus 2:15); but would he be any kinder to a runaway killer? Would even the enslaved *children of Israel* pay any attention to a fugitive who had resurfaced after forty years in hiding?

12. And he said, Certainly I will be with thee; and this shall be a token unto thee, that I have sent thee: When thou hast brought forth the people out of Egypt, ye shall serve God upon this mountain.

I will be with thee. This was the encouraging promise that put a different face on the job to be done. What appeared too much for Moses was not too much for Moses and God. And how was Moses to know that God would be with him in fulfilling this assignment? When the job was done, Moses and his people would worship God on this very *mountain* where God was speaking. In the meantime Moses was to walk by faith. He was to trust and obey.

III. God's Name
(Exodus 3:13, 14)

After asking, "Who am I?" Moses next asked, "Who is God?" While it may seem odd to us today, this too was a reasonable question. The people of Israel had been in Egypt for approximately four hundred years. During the early stages of that time, they had been treated as honored guests, favored by the government, and allowed to live in Goshen, among the most fertile parts of all the land of Egypt.

Probably the knowledge of God became less rather than greater during those prosperous years in Egypt. Then came a change in the government and the beginning of what became many years of oppression and slavery. Perhaps the people thought of God and cried to Him for relief; but the cruel burden of bondage made it hard, if not impossible, to do much effective teaching. Imitating their parents, the children learned to cry

plaintively to God, but with little concept of who He was.

A. Need for a Name (v. 13)

13. And Moses said unto God, Behold, when I come unto the children of Israel, and shall say unto them, The God of your fathers hath sent me unto you; and they shall say to me, What is his name? what shall I say unto them?

If Moses would come announcing that the slaves' deliverance was near and claiming to speak on behalf of the *God* of their *fathers*, they would want to know more about that God. It did not seem to them that He had done much for them recently, so why should they expect His help now? *What is his name?* they would ask, hoping His name would give them some insight into His character, His nature, or His power.

B. I AM (v. 14)

14. And God said unto Moses, I AM THAT I AM: and he said, Thus shalt thou say unto the children of Israel, I AM hath sent me unto you.

The name *I AM*, spoken by *God*, declares that God is always living and always the same. Coupled with the words of verse 6, this name told the slaves in Egypt that the God calling them to freedom was the same God of majesty and power who had called Abraham from Ur and had brought him to Canaan with wealth and power and honor. That same God could break the shackles of their slavery and bring them to that same land with similar wealth and power and honor.

To all of us, these two verses carry several great thoughts: First, the God who sent Moses is the only God who really is, the only one who actually exists. Other so-called gods are figments of human imagination. They are without life and without power. [See question #4, page 16.]

Second, the God who sent Moses is eternal. Forever He is, and forever He is the same—past, present, and future. His people can depend on Him, not only for all the years of this life on

This visual reminds us of the nature of the God we serve, the great and eternal "I AM," who called to Moses from out of the burning bush.

Visual for lesson 1

earth, but also throughout the eternity beyond this life.

Third, in a special sense the God who sent Moses is the God of the Hebrews. He is the one who called, blessed, and helped Abraham, Isaac, and Jacob. He is the one who gave special promises about their descendants as well as about them. In a similar special sense He is the God of Christians, for they are "the Israel of God" (Galatians 6:16). By faith they are "children of Abraham," and thus "are blessed with faithful Abraham" (Galatians 3:6-9).

Conclusion

Moses doubted his ability to do the job, but he could not doubt that God was calling him to do it. Without a clear voice from a flame, how can I recognize God's call? When I see an opportunity, how do I know whether it is God's call to a great work or the devil's invitation to disaster? When I need a leader to follow, how do I know whom to choose?

A. Qualification

God calls people to do what He qualifies them to do. Several factors combine to qualify a person for a job.

1. *Training.* During the first forty years of his life, Moses became "learned in all the wisdom of the Egyptians, and was mighty in words and in deeds" (Acts 7:22). Who could be better qualified to confront the rulers of Egypt?

2. *Experience.* Many employers are looking for people with experience. During the second forty years of his life, Moses was a shepherd in Midian. He became well acquainted with the desert country and with the needs of livestock as well as people. Who could be better prepared to lead

---

Home Daily Bible Readings

Monday, Aug. 30—Birth and Youth of Moses (Exodus 2:1-10)

Tuesday, Aug. 31—Moses Flees to Midian (Exodus 2:11-15)

Wednesday, Sept. 1—Moses Settles in Midian (Exodus 2:16-25)

Thursday, Sept. 2—Moses at the Burning Bush (Exodus 3:1-10)

Friday, Sept. 3—Moses Called to Deliver Israel (Exodus 3:11-22)

Saturday, Sept. 4—Moses Empowered by God (Exodus 4:1-9)

Sunday, Sept. 5—Moses Responds to God's Call (Exodus 4:10-20)

---

his people and their flocks through such rugged terrain over the next forty years?

3. *Natural talent.* A singer needs a voice. A scholar needs high intelligence. A mechanic needs mechanical aptitude. An evangelist needs to be a "people person." A fine teacher may fail as a farmer, and a fine farmer may fail as a teacher. Moses had talent as well as training and experience. He was the man for the job!

Haven't we all seen a well-schooled preacher who couldn't preach well, or a good preacher who was not good at personal evangelism, or a fine evangelist who was too aggressive in visiting the sick? A big church may have a team of specialists; but a church with only one minister looks for a man of many talents, or one who is strong in the ability most needed in that church.

B. Help

The new president of a corporation noted, "The secret of success will be to surround myself with people smarter than I am." One who would lead must ask, "Is competent help available?" Anyone looking for a leader must ask, "Is he able to make use of competent help?" Moses needed a talker to help him, and his brother Aaron was just what he needed (Exodus 4:10-16).

A preacher who can't sing looks for a church that has a good song leader, and a church without such a leader may look for a minister skilled in music. A beginning preacher looks for a place with experienced elders, but a new church may need a minister with experience. A preacher unskilled in business looks for a church with a competent treasurer, but a church unskilled in business may look for a minister with knowledge and experience in the business world. [See question #5, page 16.]

C. The Lord's Approval

In choosing a career or a hobby, a task or a game, an employer or an employee, a leader or a follower, a Christian asks, "Will God be pleased with this choice?" If you see anyone or anything that would turn you away from the Lord, turn away from that person or thing. Make a choice that will make you a better Christian.

D. Prayer

How good and gracious You are, our Father, to give us so many abilities and to place before us so many opportunities! Give us wisdom to choose, we pray, and remind us always that "the fear of the Lord is the beginning of wisdom." In Jesus' name. Amen.

E. Thought to Remember

God knows best. Let Him lead.

Learning by Doing

This page contains an alternate lesson plan emphasizing learning activities.
Classes desiring such student involvement will find these suggestions helpful.

Learning Goals

After this lesson, each student will be able to:

1. Tell the story of God's call to Moses.

2. Compare the call and task God gave Moses with the call and tasks God gives to Christians today.

3. State what he or she believes God has called him or her specifically to do, and suggest one step that can be taken in the coming week to obey that call.

Into the Lesson

Bring with you the classified section from a local newspaper. Read several of the "Help Wanted" ads that are very different from each other. Next, ask class members to work in small groups to suggest various tasks God uses people to do today. Provide each group with "Post-it Notes," and ask the students to write their ideas on these notes and then post them on the board to be shared with the rest of the class.

Discuss the following questions. What are some specific situations where God might use a person to speak for Him? *(Sharing the gospel, serving in community organizations, etc.)* How can people with particular training, experience, or talent be used by God? *(Teaching ability for preaching and teaching Sunday school classes, musical ability for leading worship, business ability to help administer the church, etc.)*

Into the Word

Once Moses heard that he was the one God would use to deliver His people, he responded with objections and questions (Exodus 3:11; 4:1, 10). Write on the board the following three column headings: "Task Assigned," "Questions and Objections," and "God's Answers." Write, "Go to Egypt and deliver the Israelites (Exodus 3:10)" under "Task Assigned." Review Moses' responses to God by listing them under the next heading. (Who am I? Who is God? What is His name? They will not believe me. I am not qualified. Send someone else. See Exodus 3:11, 13; 4:1, 10, 13.) Under the final heading summarize the response of God to each of these questions or objections. (See Exodus 3:12, 14-22; 4:2-9, 11, 12, 14-17.) In the next section, you will work to identify specific tasks God has for your class members. At that time come back to this chart, and see what questions or objections people

might present to God today in light of those special assignments.

Into Life

God met Moses in the ordinary routine of his daily work, and challenged him to a specific task that God had prepared him to accomplish (Exodus 3:1-7). Ask class members, "If God appeared to you and said: 'I have a job for you to do,' what do you think that job might be?"

While God doesn't communicate with us that way today, He still guides us into tasks that are specifically suited for each of us. To help your class members identify specific tasks God may be directing them to accomplish, help them put together a resume to consider ways in which God has prepared them to serve Him.

Training: What skills and abilities have you developed through formal or informal classes, job training, seminars, personal study, etc.?

Experience: Have you gone through certain experiences that might equip you to minister more effectively to particular people or in particular situations?

Talents: Has God given you specific abilities that could be used to promote spiritual growth in the lives of others?

Passions or burdens: Do you have a burden for a particular person or a certain group of people? When you think of serving God, is there a particular area of ministry that really excites you?

Opportunities: Are you aware of a particular need that you believe you could meet? Are you in a situation at home, work, the church, or the community that gives you unique opportunities to serve God?

Have class members look over what they have written and then write job descriptions for the ministries they believe God has called them to perform. As a few volunteers name their tasks, write them on the board under the column marked "Task Assigned." Next, ask the entire class to suggest objections or questions that some might offer in resistance to accepting each task. Write these under the "Questions and Objections" heading. Then discuss what God's answer might be to those responses.

Close the class time in prayer, thanking God for His direction in our lives. Leave time for class members to commit themselves silently to the task God has for them.

Let's Talk It Over

The questions on this page are designed to encourage review of the lesson Scriptures and to promote discussion of the lesson by the class. The answers provided are only discussion starters. Let your class talk it over from there.

1. God got Moses' attention in dramatic fashion when He called Moses. How can we recognize God's call today? How do we know when God wants us to leave the familiar and ordinary—as He called Moses to do—and when He wants us to stay and do His work from *within* our present situation?

No one else on record ever received a call from a burning bush. God calls today in a variety of ways. Of course, the call to salvation is open to all, to "whosoever will" (Revelation 22:17). But He calls individuals to a variety of ministries through the gifts and skills that He gives to them, through a burden laid on a person's heart, or through unique opportunities that He opens before us. Encourage class members to share how they believe God has led them into the ministries in which they currently serve Him.

2. Surely Moses' heart often must have yearned for the deliverance of his people whom he had left in bondage when he fled Egypt forty years before. How reassuring it must have been to hear God say He had seen their affliction and heard their cry! How can we assure suffering people today that God sees and hears them?

Caution is in order here. Mere mouthing of platitudes offers no comfort at all, but may lead instead to cynicism on the part of the sufferer. A careful look at Scriptural examples of God's deliverance combined with an honest compassion and willingness to be God's vessel of comfort will be much more helpful.

Perhaps class members can cite examples of how God has demonstrated His care for them or how they have been used by God to minister to some other hurting person.

3. The lesson writer says, "When a hard job needs to be done, aren't we all more eager to pray for God to do it than we are to dig into it ourselves?" How can we avoid this mistake of trying to substitute prayer for an obedient response to God's call for service?

Prayer was never meant to be a substitute for obedience. Instead, it should be a way in which we express our obedience and seek God's guidance and strength for completing such obedience. We should make it a habit to say in our prayers, "Lord, what do You want me to do? Where do You want me to go? Reveal to me the tasks that You want me to accomplish."

4. This is an era of compromise and of tolerance gone awry. Many who regard themselves as Christians actually see Christianity as no more authentic than Islam, Buddhism, Hinduism, and other pagan religions. They would regard it as a serious breach of political correctness to speak of the Christian faith as the only way to salvation and eternal life. Yet by revealing Himself as I AM, God has demonstrated that He is the only God. How can we emphasize the exclusive nature of worshiping the true God in this age of pluralism?

Being a Christian used to be accepted as a positive trait in a person's life—even by non-Christians. Today, however, being a Christian is more and more a liability on the secular scene. To believe that Jesus—or anyone else, for that matter—is the only way of salvation (as per John 14:6; Acts 4:12; and others) is considered intolerant and bigoted. We take a stand on this issue the same way the apostles did, by being glad to suffer for the name of Jesus! (See Acts 5:41.) You may want to discuss ways of cultivating such determination among believers or of encouraging those who are suffering for taking such a stand.

5. Whatever our task in the church, we need not only divine help, but human help as well, to accomplish it. When Moses indicated that he needed help, God assigned Aaron to assist him. Jesus enlisted His apostles to help Him, and Paul characteristically had assistants with him during his missionary journeys. Why do you think some Christians are hesitant to ask for help in fulfilling their duties in the church?

Two very different reasons may be behind such reluctance. Some may be too proud to admit they need help, or too proud to share the credit for the completion of the task. Such pride gets in the way of doing God's will! Others may be too embarrassed to ask for help. They may believe that others will think they are lazy or weak, or that their tasks will be taken from them and given to others. These need encouragement and comfort. Even if they are weak, it is only with support and assistance that they will become stronger and more mature.

Crossing the Red Sea

DEVOTIONAL READING: Psalm 106:1-12.

BACKGROUND SCRIPTURE: Exodus 13:17—14:31.

PRINTED TEXT: Exodus 13:17-22; 14:21, 22, 26-31.

Exodus 13:17-22

17 And it came to pass, when Pharaoh had let the people go, that God led them not through the way of the land of the Philistines, although that was near; for God said, Lest peradventure the people repent when they see war, and they return to Egypt:

18 But God led the people about, through the way of the wilderness of the Red sea: and the children of Israel went up harnessed out of the land of Egypt.

19 And Moses took the bones of Joseph with him: for he had straitly sworn the children of Israel, saying, God will surely visit you; and ye shall carry up my bones away hence with you.

20 And they took their journey from Succoth, and encamped in Etham, in the edge of the wilderness.

21 And the LORD went before them by day in a pillar of a cloud, to lead them the way; and by night in a pillar of fire, to give them light; to go by day and night.

22 He took not away the pillar of the cloud by day, nor the pillar of fire by night, from before the people.

Exodus 14:21, 22, 26-31

21 And Moses stretched out his hand over the sea; and the LORD caused the sea to go back by a strong east wind all that night, and made the sea dry land, and the waters were divided.

22 And the children of Israel went into the midst of the sea upon the dry ground: and the waters were a wall unto them on their right hand, and on their left.

26 And the LORD said unto Moses, Stretch out thine hand over the sea, that the waters may come again upon the Egyptians, upon their chariots, and upon their horsemen.

27 And Moses stretched forth his hand over the sea, and the sea returned to his strength when the morning appeared; and the Egyptians fled against it; and the LORD overthrew the Egyptians in the midst of the sea.

28 And the waters returned, and covered the chariots, and the horsemen, and all the host of Pharaoh that came into the sea after them; there remained not so much as one of them.

29 But the children of Israel walked upon dry land in the midst of the sea; and the waters were a wall unto them on their right hand, and on their left.

30 Thus the LORD saved Israel that day out of the hand of the Egyptians; and Israel saw the Egyptians dead upon the seashore.

31 And Israel saw that great work which the LORD did upon the Egyptians: and the people feared the LORD, and believed the LORD, and his servant Moses.

GOLDEN TEXT: Fear ye not, stand still, and see the salvation of the LORD, which he will show to you today.—Exodus 14:13.

From Slavery to Conquest
Unit 1: Exodus and Covenant
(Lessons 1-4)

Lesson Aims

After this lesson a student should be able to:
1. Tell how God led Israel out of Egypt and through the Red Sea.
2. Tell how God has delivered him or her from a specific sin or difficult circumstance.
3. Praise God for His deliverance and seek to go forward in faith.

Lesson Outline

INTRODUCTION
 A. Teaching a King to Obey
 B. Lesson Background
 I. STARTING OUT (Exodus 13:17-22)
  A. The Long Way (vv. 17, 18)
  B. Keeping a Promise (v. 19)
  C. Guidance for the Journey (vv. 20-22)
   A Divine Pilot
 II. RESCUE (Exodus 14:21, 22, 26-28)
  A. Deliverance of Israel (vv. 21, 22)
  B. Destruction of Egypt (vv. 26-28)
 III. SAFE AT LAST (Exodus 14:29-31)
  A. The Saved (v. 29)
  B. The Savior (v. 30)
  C. The Result (v. 31)
   Splendid Isolation
CONCLUSION
 A. God's Purpose for Israel
 B. God's Purpose for the Church
 C. God's Purpose for You
 D. Prayer
 E. Thought to Remember

Introduction

A. Teaching a King to Obey

Last week's lesson focused on Moses, the Hebrew who became first a prince of Egypt, then a fugitive running for his life. After living forty years in Egypt, Moses became a shepherd in Midian for forty years. It seems he was content with that life, and not pleased when the Lord sent him back to Egypt to lead his people to freedom. But the Lord insisted, and Moses went (Exodus 3, 4).

The king of Egypt was not pleased either when Moses came asking him to release God's people so they could observe a religious festival in the desert. Instead of granting the slaves a holiday, he increased their work load. But the Lord had ways of disciplining a disobedient king and his cruel slave drivers: the ten plagues broke their stubborn wills. When the final plague brought death to the firstborn in every Egyptian family, king and people not only agreed to let God's people go, but begged them to go quickly and take whatever items of value they wanted. All of this is recorded in Exodus 5–12.

B. Lesson Background

Swiftly a huge caravan was assembled. It included about six hundred thousand men, besides women and children, and countless sheep and cattle (Exodus 12:37, 38). In the Israelites' haste to obtain all they could from the Egyptians (12:35, 36), they must have loaded wagons or oxcarts with lumber, leather, jewelry, and fabrics. We know this because they later used those items to build the tabernacle in the desert (35:4-9). We can imagine that there was more confusion than order in organizing the departure from Egypt, but soon the huge throng was ready to move forward (12:37).

I. Starting Out
(Exodus 13:17-22)

The last part of chapter 12 and the first part of chapter 13 are filled with instructions to be followed by God's people throughout the coming centuries. However, for today's lesson we bypass these commands and go on to the record of the actual exodus from Egypt.

A. The Long Way (vv. 17, 18)

17. And it came to pass, when Pharaoh had let the people go, that God led them not through the way of the land of the Philistines, although that was near; for God said, Lest peradventure the people repent when they see war, and they return to Egypt.

The people of Israel had lived in Goshen, located in the fertile delta of the Nile River. The direct route to the promised land would have taken them northeast along the Mediterranean seacoast. However, *the Philistines* lived along that route. They were a tough and hostile people. The Israelites knew nothing about waging war; they had been submissive slaves all their lives. Confronted by such a possibility, they might *repent* and *return to Egypt*.

The word *repent* is normally associated with turning from sin. Here it simply means "change." The Israelites, if faced with an early clash against battle-tested veterans, might change their minds and have second thoughts about leaving Egypt.

They might be tempted to go back, since they were not far from there at this point. So God led them to Canaan by a much longer route.

18. But God led the people about, through the way of the wilderness of the Red sea: and the children of Israel went up harnessed out of the land of Egypt.

Instead of leading His people northeast toward the promised land, God led them southeast toward the desert country near the Red Sea. Thus they bypassed the hostile Philistines. [See question #1, page 24.]

Harnessed is taken by some to mean "armed for battle," as the *New International Version* has it. The only other time the term is used in the Old Testament it is translated "armed" (Joshua 1:14), so it seems good to some to translate it here consistently with the other use.

Some, however, note that Israel was taking a long way around the Philistines in order to avoid battle, so they believe the term ought not to have a military connotation. Some of them think that the term simply means "equipped." In Joshua 1:14 the Israelites were "equipped" for battle, or "armed." In this case, however, they were "equipped" for travel, with wagons and provisions. Others think the word could be translated "organized" and could have reference to military preparedness, but not necessarily. Whatever the word means, these travelers were expecting a long trip and were prepared for it.

The exact location of where the Israelites crossed the Red Sea has been a matter of much discussion among Bible students. Much of the uncertainty lies in the Hebrew term rendered "Red Sea," which actually means "Sea of Reeds." In addition, this term is used in a variety of ways in the Old Testament. Sometimes it designates the western "arm" of the Red Sea, or the Gulf of Suez (Numbers 33:10, 11); elsewhere, the eastern "arm," or the Gulf of Aqaba, is being described (1 Kings 9:26). Some liberal Bible scholars, attempting to deny the miraculous nature of the crossing, have suggested this "Sea of Reeds" was merely a marshy area in which the Egyptian chariots got bogged down, allowing Israel to escape. This denies too much of what the Bible says, however, and certainly does not account for the great impression the event made on both the Israelites and the Canaanites (Joshua 2:9, 10).

Some Bible students believe that the crossing occurred at the northern end of the Gulf of Suez. Others point to Exodus 15:22, which says that when the Israelites crossed the sea, they entered the "wilderness of Shur." Most scholars locate this desert in the northern part of the Sinai Peninsula, so some suggest that the crossing occurred at an area known as the Bitter Lakes (see

the map on page 5), which may have been at that time an extension of the Gulf of Suez.

B. Keeping a Promise (v. 19)

19. And Moses took the bones of Joseph with him: for he had straitly sworn the children of Israel, saying, God will surely visit you; and ye shall carry up my bones away hence with you.

Joseph was a son of *Israel* (Jacob), who had gone to Egypt before his family had. He had become a ruler there and had welcomed his family when a famine drove them to Egypt. Jacob, the head of the family, had died in Egypt, but his body had been taken back to Canaan for burial (Genesis 50:12-14). Confident that God would someday lead all of His people back to the promised land, Joseph had made his fellow Israelites swear to take his remains there instead of burying them in Egypt (Genesis 50:24-26). That oath had been made long before Moses was born, but it had been handed down from generation to generation. Now Moses was in a position to honor it. Since Joseph's body had been embalmed, the remains were what we would call a mummy rather than merely Joseph's *bones*.

C. Guidance for the Journey (vv. 20-22)

20. And they took their journey from Succoth, and encamped in Etham, in the edge of the wilderness.

In many Bible atlases, as on the visual for today's lesson and the map on page 5, these place names are printed with question marks because no one knows exactly where they were; but it is clear that the travelers were going southeast toward the Red Sea, and that *Etham* was *in the edge of the wilderness*, or the desert.

21. And the LORD went before them by day in a pillar of a cloud, to lead them the way; and by night in a pillar of fire, to give them light; to go by day and night.

The travelers needed no road map or native guide. *The Lord* Himself led them with visible

This visual shows a suggested route of the exodus from Egypt. You may want to keep it on display for reference through most of the quarter.

Visual for lesson 2

signs to show the way. *A pillar of a cloud* moved ahead of them every day. By night *a pillar of fire* gave *light* as well as guidance. Thus they could travel by *day* or by *night*. When the pillar moved, they moved; when the pillar stopped, they stopped. [See question #2, page 24.]

22. He took not away the pillar of the cloud by day, nor the pillar of fire by night, from before the people.

A *pillar* was always there, *day* or *night*, when *the people* traveled and when they rested. It served, not only as a guide, but also as a constant reminder that God was there and was taking care of them.

A DIVINE PILOT

Bob Frayser was piloting his own plane eastward over Kansas at an altitude of fifty-five hundred feet. A leaking exhaust system allowed carbon monoxide fumes into the cabin, and Frayser lost consciousness. But he didn't die in a fiery crash! He had put his plane on autopilot; and when he passed out, the autopilot kept the plane on a level, straight course.

After some 250 miles, the plane finally ran out of fuel; however, the autopilot kept the plane level as it glided to a landing in a snowy field in Missouri. The plane skidded five hundred feet and stopped in a row of trees. Frayser awakened in a confused state and found his way to a farmhouse a quarter of a mile away. Speaking of his survival with only minor injuries, he said, "Most of the credit I give to the Lord."

The Israelites could see the pillars of cloud and fire that were directing them to their unknown destination. But the real power leading them was God Himself—a far surer guide than Frayser's autopilot. And unlike a malfunctioning airplane that caused Frayser to black out, God sustained and protected Israel during their journey from Egypt through the wilderness to the promised land. He fed, healed, and protected them as He led them to freedom.

Today, while God may use less spectacular means, He still protects and guides His children. In all our ways, let us acknowledge Him (Proverbs 3:6). —C. R. B.

II. Rescue
(Exodus 14:21, 22, 26-28)

From Etham the pillar led the travelers on to the shore of the sea (14:1, 2). Meanwhile, however, Pharaoh was having second thoughts about releasing the Hebrews. He had brought on the plagues, including the death of the firstborn, by refusing to let the Hebrews go. Then he had relented and let them go; so his people had lost

How to Say It
AQABA. *Ock*-uh-buh.
CANAAN. *Kay*-nun.
ETHAM. *Ee*-thum.
GOSHEN. *Go*-shun.
MIDIAN. *Mid*-ee-un.
SUCCOTH. *Soo*-kawth.
SUEZ. *Soo*-ez.

both their firstborn and their slaves. Many of those grieving over their losses would be blaming Pharaoh personally. Would some of them be thinking of replacing him? If they were, would the army be on their side? What could the king do to regain the respect and support of his people? He knew he could not bring back the dead children, but perhaps he could bring back the slaves. Quickly he marshaled his army—infantry and cavalry and chariots—and raced after the Hebrews. He caught up with them as they were camped by the sea (Exodus 14:5-9).

At first the Israelites panicked. They cried out to Moses, asking why he had led them into that barren wilderness to die. Moses assured them that the Lord would fight in their behalf and that "the Egyptians whom ye have seen today, ye shall see them again no more for ever" (v. 13).

Then the guiding cloud became the people's defense. Leaving its place in front of the Israelites, it moved behind them and blocked the pass between them and the Egyptians, keeping the pursuers at bay all night long (vv. 19, 20).

A. Deliverance of Israel (vv. 21, 22)

21. And Moses stretched out his hand over the sea; and the LORD caused the sea to go back by a strong east wind all that night, and made the sea dry land, and the waters were divided.

Moses did exactly what God told him to do (v. 16), and God did the rest. He made *a strong east wind* do what no wind could do without His express order. It pushed the water to the left and right, exposing the bed of the sea and swiftly turning it into *dry land* over which the people could cross.

22. And the children of Israel went into the midst of the sea upon the dry ground: and the waters were a wall unto them on their right hand, and on their left.

It seems the guiding cloud now returned to its usual place in front of the Israelites, and they followed it *into the midst of the sea*. It must have been quite frightening at first to walk between walls of water, but they bravely followed their guide and were safe. [See question #3, page 24.]

Once the pillar of cloud was removed and no longer blocked the way before them, the army of Egypt went into action, swift and terrible. Probably the chariots were in the lead, rolling like a wave of death after the fleeing people (v. 23); but then they met the Lord and disaster. Suddenly the chariots lost their wheels. The onslaught of death slowed as horses plunged and swayed, struggling to drag those chariots without wheels. Then panic caught the drivers. The Lord was fighting against them, they realized— the same Lord who had overwhelmed Egypt with those terrible plagues! Desperately they tried to swing the chariots around and race back over the way they had come, but they soon met the oncoming cavalry. Men, horses, and wheelless chariots mingled in wild confusion.

B. Destruction of Egypt (vv. 26-28)

26. And the LORD said unto Moses, Stretch out thine hand over the sea, that the waters may come again upon the Egyptians, upon their chariots, and upon their horsemen.

By this time, all the children of Israel had reached the other side of *the sea*. That dry passageway through the water had served its purpose; now it was time to close it. At Moses' outstretched *hand* the *waters* had been driven back (v. 21); now it summoned them to return.

27. And Moses stretched forth his hand over the sea, and the sea returned to his strength when the morning appeared; and the Egyptians fled against it; and the LORD overthrew the Egyptians in the midst of the sea.

Now the towering walls of water came crashing together. Weighed down with battle garb, the men could not swim in that tempestuous sea. Still hitched to the heavy chariots, the horses were helpless too.

Home Daily Bible Readings

Monday, Sept. 6—The Feast of Unleavened Bread (Exodus 13:3-10)
Tuesday, Sept. 7—Led by Pillars of Cloud and Fire (Exodus 13:17-22)
Wednesday, Sept. 8—Caught Between Pharaoh and the Sea (Exodus 14:1-9)
Thursday, Sept. 9—Going Forward at God's Command (Exodus 14:10-18)
Friday, Sept. 10—Israel Crosses the Red Sea (Exodus 14:19-25)
Saturday, Sept. 11—God Saves Israel From the Egyptians (Exodus 14:26-31)
Sunday, Sept. 12—Israel Sings of God's Victory (Exodus 15:1-13)

28. And the waters returned, and covered the chariots, and the horsemen, and all the host of Pharaoh that came into the sea after them; there remained not so much as one of them.

Thus Pharaoh's army was destroyed. *Not so much as one* man survived. Sooner or later, such is the fate of all those who persist in fighting against God.

III. Safe at Last (Exodus 14:29-31)

These verses provide a summary of what happened and its impact on those who witnessed it.

A. The Saved (v. 29)

29. But the children of Israel walked upon dry land in the midst of the sea; and the waters were a wall unto them on their right hand, and on their left.

The children of Israel had been in deadly peril from the pursuing army and the towering walls of water; but they *walked upon dry land*, safe from both dangers.

B. The Savior (v. 30)

30. Thus the LORD saved Israel that day out of the hand of the Egyptians; and Israel saw the Egyptians dead upon the seashore.

The *Egyptians* could have crushed the Israelites, and the sea could have drowned them; but *the Lord* overpowers the armies of nations and controls the movements of the waters of the earth. He made the waters a source of life for His people, and a source of death for their enemies.

C. The Result (v. 31)

31. And Israel saw that great work which the LORD did upon the Egyptians: and the people feared the LORD, and believed the LORD, and his servant Moses.

The people of *Israel* were alive and safe from the *Egyptians*, but this verse mentions other results no less important: they *feared the Lord*, and they *believed*, not only *the Lord*, but also *his servant Moses* whom He appointed and inspired.

We know of this miracle, and Scripture tells us of many others that Moses and his people never saw. Shouldn't we also fear the Lord, believe Him, and obey Him? [See question #4, page 24.]

SPLENDID ISOLATION

Juneau, the capital of Alaska, sits in splendid isolation in the southeastern corner of the state. The city backs up against the spectacular glacier-riven, eight-thousand-foot peaks of the Coast Range. On the opposite side is water— what is called the "inside passage" that stretches a thousand miles along the Pacific coast of North America.

Juneau is four and one-half hours by ship from the nearest Alaskan city that has a road system connecting it to the rest of the state. This isolation is both bane and blessing. It is also the subject of continuing debate as to whether the state capital should be moved to Anchorage and whether a road should be built to connect Juneau with the "outside."

The blessing of Juneau's isolation is that it has enabled the city to maintain a pristine beauty, undefiled by the hordes of motor vehicles that crowd most other state capitals. The bane is that the city is inaccessible except by plane or ship.

The Red Sea was first bane, then blessing, to Israel. As Pharaoh's army bore down on the Israelites (standing on the western shore), the sea appeared to be their barrier to salvation. But when they stood on the opposite shore watching the destruction of Egypt's army, the Red Sea became a blessing. Now Israel stood in splendid isolation, separated by those same waters from the world that had enslaved it.

In such circumstances as these, the difference in perspective depends on where one stands with God.   —C. R. B.

Conclusion

Why did the Lord take such care to keep the Israelites alive and make them a free people? He had a specific purpose for them. Why has He preserved the church through the centuries, in spite of attacks from without and frequent faithlessness within? He has a purpose for His church. Why has God called you, forgiven you, and made you His own? He has a purpose for you, too.

A. God's Purpose for Israel

God stated His purpose for Israel when He called Abraham to be the father of that nation: "In thee shall all families of the earth be blessed" (Genesis 12:3). In spite of their many faults and failures, God preserved Abraham's people until they brought into the world the Savior who offers all mankind the blessing of eternal life.

B. God's Purpose for the Church

Today we who follow the Savior are God's chosen people—chosen for the purpose of bringing to all families of the earth the blessing promised through Abraham and given through Christ. How are we doing? Is your church keeping the whole community aware of Christ's offer of life? Is it also supporting missionaries who hold forth the Word of life in distant lands?

C. God's Purpose for You

I like to think God has called me to prepare Sunday school lessons like this one. I know a young lady who is such a fine teacher that I think God has called her to that work; and she does her best teaching in Sunday school. I once knew an auto mechanic so skilled and so benevolent that I felt sure God had given him a special talent and calling. His chief joy was to take care of the cars that Bible college students drove to their week-end preaching appointments. He did that at reduced rates, and often for no payment at all.

Whatever God has equipped you to do for a living, are you also finding a way to take part in His great purpose of bringing the blessing of eternal life to all mankind?

Whom do you know who is not a Christian? Have you ever made an opportunity to tell him or her about the way of salvation and the joy of Christian living? Are you ready to begin the great adventure of such telling?

You don't know how? Then whom do you know who does know how? Maybe you can go with him a few times and see how he does it. Or maybe you can find some other Christians who don't know how. Maybe they would like to meet once a week for a month and get an expert to teach them how to start talking about the most important matters in the world. Between meetings you can practice what he tells you, and then come back for more coaching.

Involvement in this kind of personal evangelism program is not easy, but what joys it can bring! However, if you keep trying for a year and then are convinced that God did not design you for that service, increase your missionary offering and turn to some ministry better suited to your talent. You can still share your faith informally in personal settings even if evangelism is not your ministry strength.

If you start out with courage and vigor to do what God wants you to do, He will be with you all the way. Prayer will help; however, a time does come when God tells us to "go forward" (Exodus 14:15). [See question #5, page 24.]

D. Prayer

Our Father, our Leader, and our God, we are overwhelmed by the greatness of Your blessings. To be free from the bondage of sin, to be Your people, to be on the way to the promised land— these fill us with joy unspeakable and full of glory. Grateful for Your guiding presence, we pray for the strength and courage and good sense to follow where You lead. Amen.

E. Thought to Remember

Go forward!

Learning by Doing

This page contains an alternate lesson plan emphasizing learning activities.
Classes desiring such student involvement will find these suggestions helpful.

Learning Goals

After this lesson a student should be able to:

1. Tell how God led Israel out of Egypt and through the Red Sea.

2. Tell how God has delivered him or her from a specific sin or difficult circumstance.

3. Praise God for His deliverance and seek to go forward in faith.

Into the Lesson

Use a bold black marker to write the letters of the word PROBLEM on seven sheets of paper (one letter per sheet). On the backs of the sheets spell RED SEA (the back of the B is blank) with a bold red marker. Display the word PROBLEM at the front of the room before students arrive.

When it is time to begin, ask, "What are some very difficult (or even seemingly impossible) situations you have faced—times when you knew you would make it through only with God's help?" Prompt the discussion with questions like, "How did you react?" "Did you learn any new lessons about God through those experiences?" "Did you wonder why God allowed them to happen, or how He could possibly use the circumstances for any good purpose?"

Observe that in today's lesson we will examine a time when the Israelites faced a similar situation. Begin turning over the letters to reveal the words RED SEA as you tell the class, "Just as God delivered the Israelites through the Red Sea, He will deliver us through our problems and difficult circumstances, too."

Into the Word

Ask a volunteer to read Exodus 13:17-22. Ask the class to listen for the answers to the following questions as the text is read. After the reading, discuss the questions.

• Why did God lead the Israelites through the longer route, avoiding the Philistines? *(So they wouldn't face war and turn back; Exodus 13:17.)*

• What is the significance of carrying Joseph's bones with them on their journey? *(It was a visual memorial of God's faithfulness, the fulfillment of a promise made over 400 years earlier; Genesis 50:24-25.)*

Make the transition to the next portion of today's text by noting that God led the Israelites to an impassable route and brought the Egyptian army from behind to trap them completely. God

allowed the Israelites to face such difficult circumstances to bring glory to Himself and to make Himself known as the only true God (Exodus 14:1-4). He protected the Israelites from war with the Philistines but then brought the Egyptian army to them, putting them in an apparently inescapable position (Exodus 14:5-9).

Discuss what lessons this should teach us about difficult (or seemingly impossible) situations and about God's providence. *(God protects us from what we cannot handle [1 Corinthians 10:13], but He may also allow us to experience situations where He receives the glory by demonstrating His power [2 Corinthians 12:7-10; Ephesians 3:20, 21; 1 Peter 1:5].)*

Have a volunteer read Exodus 14:21, 22, 26-31. Then divide the class into small groups (four to six members in each). Ask the groups to work together to summarize how God delivered Israel from an impossible situation and what effect the rescue had on the Israelites. Ask each person in the group to tell how God has delivered him or her from a specific sin or difficult circumstance. Are there parallels between God's deliverance of the Israelites from Egypt and His deliverance of His people today from problems or difficult situations? If so, have the groups list as many as they can. Discuss what these experiences did for the faith of those who went through them.

Allow about ten minutes for the groups to discuss these issues; then call for reports. List on the chalkboard or a large poster the cumulative list of parallels between Israel's rescue and the rescue of God's people today.

Into Life

Perhaps there are "Red Seas" facing some of your students even now. Ask, "What is one battle you are facing in which you know you need God's help?" Allow volunteers to tell of their situations, but don't pressure anyone to participate. Those who do tell their stories will become models for others, even those unwilling to open up about their situations.

Ask, "What is one risky step of faith that you know you need to take to move forward?" Discuss what is "risky" about such a step, why it is necessary, and what results might be expected.

Close with prayer for courage as you and your students seek to "move forward" with God in faith.

Let's Talk It Over

The questions on this page are designed to encourage review of the lesson Scriptures and to promote discussion of the lesson by the class. The answers provided are only discussion starters. Let your class talk it over from there.

1. The Lord led the Israelites away from the warlike Philistines, but then He led them to the Red Sea, with the Egyptian army in hot pursuit. Why do you think He did not let them face the Philistines and deliver them with a miracle as He eventually delivered them from the Egyptians anyway? How do we know when to avoid a confrontation (as with the Philistines) and when to face the problem head on with the power of the Lord (as with crossing the Red Sea)?

The Israelites were not looking for a fight. The Egyptians were, so there was no way to avoid that confrontation. But to "invade" Philistine territory would have been seen as an act of aggression, to which the Philistine response would have been quite predictable. Perhaps the Israelite path is an illustration of Paul's exhortation in Romans 12:18: "If it be possible, as much as lieth in you, live peaceably with all men."

2. Suppose a member of your class said, "I wish I had a pillar of fire or a cloud to direct me! It seems so hard to determine what God's will is sometimes." How would you respond?

It is appealing to imagine how a pillar of cloud could lead us to the church God wants us to attend or lead us away from a place where we are in danger of being tempted. But such a cloud would have limited usefulness. The Bible gives us a comprehensive set of moral and spiritual principles to guide us in all decisions. Even the Israelites had to make decisions for themselves about most daily activities. The pillar of fire/cloud only gave them instructions about the direction to go and when to go or stay. The rest was up to them. From the record we have, they didn't do very well!

3. The Israelites' path to deliverance from the Egyptians took them between towering walls of water. That must have been an awesome—perhaps even frightening—experience. From what frightening situations has God delivered you or someone you know?

Some Christians can testify to God's help in delivering them from an addiction (e.g., to drugs, alcohol, or the like). It was without doubt a frightening, soul-shaking, painful trial to overcome their craving. But they can now glorify God by describing how He brought them through.

And this is only one form of addiction to which people are subject. Other Christians can speak of deliverance from enslaving fears, gambling, pornography, profanity, and other burdensome habits. Again, the deliverance was frightening because the habit was deeply ingrained and difficult to give up. Still another frightening deliverance may have been experienced by people who have overcome racial prejudice. God has helped them work their way through hate and rejection to the point of love and acceptance.

4. "Israel saw that great work which the Lord did upon the Egyptians: and the people feared the Lord, and believed the Lord, and his servant Moses" (Exodus 14:31). That's fine for the Israelites, but how about our unbelieving neighbors? How can we lead them to believe in the Lord, or in us as faithful witnesses to Him? We can't part the water in the neighborhood pool—can we?

Miracles in Scripture did have the purpose of producing faith, as we see here and in the New Testament. (See for example, John 2:11.) But we ought to remember that Pharaoh saw many great miracles, too; yet the experience did not lead him to faith. So even "parting the water in the neighborhood pool" would not guarantee a faith response by our neighbors. Far better is the witness of a faithful Christian demonstrating his or her faith and love. Then, as the opportunity presents itself, the believer can share what the Bible says about Jesus and lead the neighbor to Christ.

5. What do you think God's purpose is for you? Why do you think so? What are you doing about fulfilling that purpose?

Some of your students may never have considered this concept. God has a basic will for all of us—He wants us to be saved and to serve Him in some tangible way. But determining what specifically God has called each of us to do is harder to determine. Help your students explore the issues that concern them—is God calling them to make a difference there? What skills and talents has God given them, and where might those talents be useful? What special circumstances do some face—like a chronic illness, a temporary layoff, or parenting a handicapped child? How would God use them to testify of His power and grace?

The Covenant

DEVOTIONAL READING: Deuteronomy 4:32-40.

BACKGROUND SCRIPTURE: Exodus 19:1—20:26.

PRINTED TEXT: Exodus 19:3-6; 20:2-4, 7, 8, 12-17.

Exodus 19:3-6

3 And Moses went up unto God, and the LORD called unto him out of the mountain, saying, Thus shalt thou say to the house of Jacob, and tell the children of Israel;

4 Ye have seen what I did unto the Egyptians, and how I bare you on eagles' wings, and brought you unto myself.

5 Now therefore, if ye will obey my voice indeed, and keep my covenant, then ye shall be a peculiar treasure unto me above all people: for all the earth is mine:

6 And ye shall be unto me a kingdom of priests, and a holy nation. These are the words which thou shalt speak unto the children of Israel.

Exodus 20:2-4, 7, 8, 12-17

2 I am the LORD thy God, which have brought thee out of the land of Egypt, out of the house of bondage.

3 Thou shalt have no other gods before me.

4 Thou shalt not make unto thee any graven image, or any likeness of any thing that is in heaven above, or that is in the earth beneath, or that is in the water under the earth.

· · · · · · · · · · · ·

7 Thou shalt not take the name of the LORD thy God in vain: for the LORD will not hold him guiltless that taketh his name in vain.

8 Remember the sabbath day, to keep it holy.

· · · · · · · · · · · ·

12 Honor thy father and thy mother: that thy days may be long upon the land which the LORD thy God giveth thee.

13 Thou shalt not kill.

14 Thou shalt not commit adultery.

15 Thou shalt not steal.

16 Thou shalt not bear false witness against thy neighbor.

17 Thou shalt not covet thy neighbor's house, thou shalt not covet thy neighbor's wife, nor his manservant, nor his maidservant, nor his ox, nor his ass, nor any thing that is thy neighbor's.

GOLDEN TEXT: If ye will obey my voice indeed, and keep my covenant, then ye shall be a peculiar treasure unto me above all people.—Exodus 19:5.

From Slavery to Conquest
Unit 1: Exodus and Covenant
(Lessons 1-4)

Lesson Aims

After this lesson students should be able to:

1. Tell what God intended Israel to be and how He intended them to live, according to the covenant given at Sinai.

2. Explain how God's intentions for Israel apply to the church.

3. Determine to be a "kingdom of priests" and "a holy nation" by practicing what Jesus called the "greatest" commandments (Matthew 22:38-40).

Lesson Outline

INTRODUCTION
  A. Primitive Travel
  B. Lesson Background
  I. GOD'S COVENANT (Exodus 19:3-6)
    A. What God Has Done (vv. 3, 4)
    B. What Israel Must Do (v. 5a)
    C. What Israel Must Be (vv. 5b, 6)
  II. DUTIES TO GOD (Exodus 20:2-4, 7, 8)
    A. Exclusive Worship (vv. 2-4)
    B. Reverence (v. 7)
    C. Sabbath Observance (v. 8)
     In Memory of . . .
  III. DUTIES TO ONE ANOTHER (Exodus 20:12-17)
    A. Honoring Parents (v. 12)
    B. Forbidden Acts (vv. 13-16)
    C. Forbidden Thoughts (v. 17)
     "Guilty" of the Christmas Spirit
CONCLUSION
  A. Loving God
  B. Loving Your Neighbor
  C. Prayer
  D. Thought to Remember

Introduction

"1-2-3 TOURIST HOME." So read the sign by the roadside; for this was seventy-five years ago, and the name *motel* had not yet been invented. Behind the sign was a row of tiny cabins, spaced to leave room for cars to park between them. The numbers on the sign were significant. For one dollar you rented a cabin with a table, two chairs, and a bed; but you had to bring your own bedding. For two dollars you got a similar cabin with bedding. For three dollars you got all that and a kitchenette too. There was no running water in the cabins. Bathroom facilities were shared with guests in other cabins. A shower was twenty-five cents extra if you brought your own soap and towel. In each cabin a placard on the wall displayed the following rules:

No drunkenness.
No noise to disturb neighbors.
Keep this home as clean as your own.
Put refuse in the container provided.
Vacate cabin before noon or pay for another day.

A. Primitive Travel

Traveling from Egypt to the promised land, the people of Israel found no such tourist home. Indeed, modern New York or London could hardly provide hotel accommodations for such a throng. There were perhaps as many as three million men, women, and children, plus uncounted cattle, sheep, and donkeys. The barren desert they traveled had no inns of any kind, no shelter where the weary could stop and rest. They had to bring their own tents as well as everything else they needed.

Still, these travelers needed rules, as people always do when they live close together; and they did not bring their rules from Egypt. There the only rule had been to obey the slave driver or take a beating. So God provided laws for His people. For this lesson we consider the most famous group of those rules—the Ten Commandments, which were carved in stone and "written with the finger of God" (Exodus 31:18).

B. Lesson Background

After crossing the Red Sea, the people of Israel continued to move southeast instead of toward the promised land. God continued to lead the way with a pillar of cloud and a pillar of fire. When food supplies were gone, He provided daily manna from Heaven (Exodus 16). When no water was found, He produced an ample supply from a rock (Exodus 17:1-7).

In the third month of their journey, the travelers came to Mount Sinai—the mountain from which the Lord had sent Moses to Egypt. It was also the place where God had told Moses that the liberated slaves would worship Him (Exodus 3:11, 12). The Israelites made their camp on the broad plain beside the towering mountain (Exodus 19:1, 2).

I. God's Covenant
(Exodus 19:3-6)

In the four verses of this section we shall see the basic terms of the covenant (agreement or contract) that God was making with His people as they began their life as an independent nation.

A. What God Has Done (vv. 3, 4)

3. And Moses went up unto God, and the LORD called unto him out of the mountain, saying, Thus shalt thou say to the house of Jacob, and tell the children of Israel.

Moses left the camp of the Israelites and *went up* the steep slope of Sinai (we are not told how far) to meet *God. The Lord called unto him out of the mountain*, speaking in an audible voice, just as He had called to Moses before from a burning bush (Exodus 3:4-10). This time the Lord's message was not for Moses alone. Moses was to relay it to *the children*, or descendants, *of Israel*, whose original name was *Jacob*. The expressions *children of Israel* and *house of Jacob* are parallel terms and refer to the nation of Israel or, specifically, to the Israelites.

4. Ye have seen what I did unto the Egyptians, and how I bare you on eagles' wings, and brought you unto myself.

First, Moses was to remind the people of what they knew very well. *On eagles' wings* is a graceful metaphor for the divine power that carried (the meaning of *bare*) Israel over all obstacles—the stubborn opposition of Egypt, the deep water of the sea, the weary and waterless miles of desert, and the assault of a hostile tribe—and had brought them to God Himself at Sinai, His holy mountain. After all this evidence of God's power and favor, His people should have been eager to do things His way. [See question #1, page 32.]

B. What Israel Must Do (v. 5a)

5a. Now therefore, if ye will obey my voice indeed, and keep my covenant.

This describes the part assigned to Israel in the *covenant* that God was making. Israel had no right to claim any of the blessings of that covenant unless the people would *obey* the commandments that God gave them.

C. What Israel Must Be (vv. 5b, 6)

5b. Then ye shall be a peculiar treasure unto me above all people: for all the earth is mine.

Peculiar in this verse does not mean odd or strange. It is an adjective used to describe someone's personal property. *All the earth* and all its *people* belong to God because He made them all; but if the people of Israel faithfully served Him, they would be His own possession in a different way, in a higher sense, in a closer relationship.

6. And ye shall be unto me a kingdom of priests, and a holy nation. These are the words which thou shalt speak unto the children of Israel.

This verse explains the unique role that would distinguish Israel from all other peoples. God is King; the people of Israel were to be His subjects, obedient to Him. One function of *priests* is to teach God's will and way. The people of Israel were to do that for other peoples, not by words only, but by lives lived in obedience to Him and blessed by His favor. If the Israelites would do their part, they would also be so prosperous and so happy that all the world would see that it is best to obey the Lord. *A holy nation* is a nation set apart, dedicated to God, and therefore just and righteous and good. Note that Christians are called to fulfill these same responsibilities today (1 Peter 2:9). [See question #2, page 32.]

This brief message ended as it had begun. God said that His *words* were not for Moses only; he was to deliver them to the multitude camped beside the mountain.

II. Duties to God
(Exodus 20:2-4, 7, 8)

Moses delivered the message found in the first part of our text. The people then promised to be obedient to all God said (19:7, 8). On the third day God came to the mountain amidst awesome sights and sounds (v. 16). At Moses' summons the people came out of their tents and gathered on the plain near the mountain. "And mount Sinai was altogether on a smoke, because the Lord descended upon it in fire: and the smoke thereof ascended as the smoke of a furnace, and the whole mount quaked greatly" (v. 18). We can imagine that the people were "quaking" just as much as the mountain, as the long blast of a trumpet grew louder and louder, and as the voice of God answered the voice of Moses (v. 19). In the midst of such awe-inspiring surroundings, God spoke the Ten Commandments (20:1).

A. Exclusive Worship (vv. 2-4)

2. I am the LORD thy God, which have brought thee out of the land of Egypt, out of the house of bondage.

With these opening words God announced who He was and reminded the people of what He had done for them.

3. Thou shalt have no other gods before me.

As we noted in our lesson two weeks ago, the Lord is the only God who really exists; there are *no other gods*. Of course, man has been inventing pretend gods for many years, but the Lord's

---

How to Say It

SINAI. *Sigh*-nye or *Sigh*-nay-eye.

people must not insult Him and disgrace themselves by offering any part of their worship to anyone or anything else.

4. Thou shalt not make unto thee any graven image, or any likeness of any thing that is in heaven above, or that is in the earth beneath, or that is in the water under the earth.

This verse is often cited by itself for the sake of brevity, but it really needs to be read with verse 5: "thou shalt not bow down thyself to them, nor serve them." God's people are forbidden to make images and worship them. They are not forbidden to make sculptures or paintings or photographs to remember attractive objects or to admire their beauty. We know this because not long afterward, God ordered His people to adorn the tabernacle with representations of various items: cherubim (25:18); almonds and flowers (25:33, 34); and pomegranates and bells (28:33, 34). Each of these was a likeness of something, but none was ever to be considered an object of worship.

B. Reverence (v. 7)

7. Thou shalt not take the name of the LORD thy God in vain: for the LORD will not hold him guiltless that taketh his name in vain.

According to one lexicon, the Hebrew word translated *in vain* can have three meanings: (1) evil or wickedness; (2) falsehood; (3) emptiness, nothingness. So it seems that this Commandment is broken when God's name is used (1) in connection with any wrong purpose; (2) in swearing to a lie; (3) lightly, frivolously, and without respect for its real meaning.

C. Sabbath Observance (v. 8)

8. Remember the sabbath day, to keep it holy.

Verses 9-11 explain how the *sabbath day* was to be kept *holy*, or set apart: no work was to be done on that day, the seventh day of the week. It should be noted, however, that the people of Israel understood that some exceptions were allowable. Jesus defended His work of healing on the Sabbath, and pointed out that even meticulous Pharisees did a certain amount of necessary work on that day (Matthew 12:9-13).

Concerning Sabbath observance by Christians, there are three views that are commonly held:

1. Some say that the Sabbath is based on the pattern of creation (Genesis 2:1-3), and therefore it ought to be observed by all creation until this creation is no more (2 Peter 3:10). Opponents reply that there is neither command nor example of Sabbath observance before the Jewish nation began, that the law was given to Israel only, and that there is neither command nor example of Sabbath observance by the church.

2. Others believe the Sabbath restrictions have been transferred from the seventh day of the week to the first, which is sometimes referred to as the "Christian Sabbath." Opponents reply that the Bible does not say this; it is only a man-made interpretation. Besides, they say, the word *Sabbath* means "seventh," so its restrictions cannot be made to apply to the first day of the week.

3. Still others claim that Christians are not under the law (Romans 6:14; Galatians 5:18). They are guided by Christian teaching recorded in the New Testament. Many things commanded in the law are also taught in the New Testament, but Sabbath observance is not. Opponents reply with one of the two views described above.

It may be noted that a number of both Christians and non-Christians agree that it is good for workers to have a weekly day off, with or without a law. In fact, many workers have two days off each week. [See question #3, page 32.]

IN MEMORY OF . . .

How should we remember a significant person in our lives? The friends of "Wild Bill" Cottom found a way that they thought was perfectly appropriate. Wild Bill was an inveterate motorcyclist; he started riding when he was twelve years old. At various times in his life he was a racer, mechanic, and dealer, but almost always a friend to anyone on two wheels.

A stroke at age seventy ended Wild Bill's riding days. He spent the next sixteen years working in his shop, where he bought and sold used motorcycles, specializing in antique and British machines.

When Wild Bill died at the age of eighty-six, his body was cremated, and his ashes were placed in the gas tank of an antique Vincent motorcycle. On the day this unusual urn was placed on the wall of Cottom's shop, some fifteen hundred motorcyclists whom he had befriended at one time or another came to pay their respects.

When God asked Israel to honor Him and respect the memory of how He had befriended them, He gave more specific instructions: they were to serve Him only, refrain from worshiping representations of any creatures He had made, use His name reverently, and reserve one day a week for rest as a symbol of their identification with their Creator. Not too much to ask of Israel if they really loved God, was it?

We who are God's new creation in Christ can show our respect for God in much the same way. Not too much to ask of us either, is it?

—C. R. B.

Visual for lesson 3

The visual for today paraphrases the Ten Commandments in a rhyme, which may help your students to memorize the Commandments.

III. Duties to One Another (Exodus 20:12-17)

The first four of the Ten Commandments speak of those duties to God that have been discussed above. The final six Commandments instruct us in how we are to relate to our fellow human beings.

A. Honoring Parents (v. 12)

12. Honor thy father and thy mother: that thy days may be long upon the land which the LORD thy God giveth thee.

Children must honor their parents with respect and obedience. Parents must diligently teach God's law to their children (Deuteronomy 6:6, 7). When this was done, children who honored and obeyed their parents would also honor and obey God. God would then bless them with peace and prosperity in the *land* of promise (Deuteronomy 11:8, 9). [See question #4, page 32.]

B. Forbidden Acts (vv. 13-16)

13. Thou shalt not kill.

Some versions translate this verse, *You shall not murder*, and that seems to be the actual meaning of this Command. The Hebrew word translated *kill* is never used of legal or justifiable killing. We know that God did not mean to forbid all killing, for His law also provided the death penalty for a number of crimes ranging from murder to cursing a parent (Exodus 21:12, 17). God also told His people to "utterly destroy" entire groups of depraved heathen (Deuteronomy 7:1, 2).

14. Thou shalt not commit adultery.

Pagans of many eras, including those of our own time, have looked on adultery as "good clean fun"; but God's law made it one of the transgressions to be punished with death (Deuteronomy 22:22-24).

15. Thou shalt not steal.

A person has a right to whatever he earns honestly, or buys honestly, or receives as a gift. It is wrong to take it from him without his consent, whether by force, by stealth, or by deceit. Hardly anyone will deny this principle; but so many violate it that we are forced to spend millions for locks on bicycles and security systems for homes, cars, and banks, not to speak of theft insurance for many possessions. Other millions of dollars provide for police and courts and jails. Think what a difference it would make if everyone would put what is right above what is profitable!

16. Thou shalt not bear false witness against thy neighbor.

Of course it is wrong to commit perjury in court; we punish it with fines and imprisonment if it is detected. But what about out-of-court slander, such as the spiteful remark we make about someone we don't like? What about the derogatory gossip we repeat without checking or thinking? If we repeat a false report, do we really escape guilt by saying, "I heard . . ."? My grandmother's rule was: "Don't say anything bad about anyone, even if it's true." She said that made it unnecessary to find out whether any gossip was true or not.

C. Forbidden Thoughts (v. 17)

17. Thou shalt not covet thy neighbor's house, thou shalt not covet thy neighbor's wife, nor his manservant, nor his maidservant, nor his ox, nor his ass, nor any thing that is thy neighbor's.

At times this Commandment is abbreviated to *thou shalt not covet*. In that form it misses the point. To covet is to desire, to want. There's nothing wrong with wanting a good reputation, or new shoes, or even a wife. What's wrong is wanting *any thing that is thy neighbor's*. If your neighbor has something good, you should be happy about it. You wouldn't take it from him if you could. You may feel a longing for many good things, but not that thing.

"GUILTY" OF THE CHRISTMAS SPIRIT

In Pennsylvania a few years ago, the Mercer County Common Pleas Court closed down for two weeks during the Christmas holidays. Prosecutors didn't like to hold trials at that time of year because, as one said, "The holiday spirit lends itself more to not-guilty verdicts." On the other hand, defense lawyers love to have their cases come up at Christmastime!

Perhaps it isn't all to the good that the Christmas spirit interferes with the workings of the justice system, especially if the defendant is guilty! However, it is refreshing to hear of some tangible evidence that people actually do think more of the welfare of others at least for a few weeks a year.

The point of the last six Commandments is exactly this: to encourage us to think of the well-being of others rather than of ourselves. In a fashion typical of Old Testament culture, the Commandments are expressed as negatives. However, the New Testament—time and again—turns these same principles into positives. Thus, Christians not only abstain from doing harm to their neighbors; they actively seek their good.

—C. R. B.

Conclusion

The last Commandment of the ten turns our thinking in a new direction. Let's go on in that direction for a while. God wants to control our thinking as well as our doing. And really, doesn't our thinking control our doing?

Coveting a neighbor's good looks or popularity or influence can be a potential cause of bearing false witness against him, can't it? Coveting his wife can lead to adultery, coveting his wealth can lead to stealing, and all these covetings can lead to murder. Let's turn to the New Testament for more about this. One who hates his brother is a murderer at heart (1 John 3:15). One who lusts is an adulterer at heart (Matthew 5:27, 28). So let's turn our hearts away from ourselves. Let's love ourselves less, love our neighbors more, and love God most of all.

A. Loving God

The law said to love God with all your being (Deuteronomy 6:5). Jesus said that this was the greatest commandment (Matthew 22:37, 38). If you obey it, you will have no other gods. You will give no shred of worship to anyone or anything else—not the ancient idols of wood and stone, not the modern idols of materialism and pleasure, not even yourself.

If you love God completely, you will never think of using His name in vain. You will hold it in reverence and awe.

If you love God with all that is in you, you may conclude that His Sabbath law was for Israel only (Exodus 31:16, 17); but in any case you will hold every day holy to the Lord, and yourself holy every day. "Whatsoever ye do in word or deed, do all in the name of the Lord Jesus" (Colossians 3:17). [See question #5, page 32.]

B. Loving Your Neighbor

When we read God's commandments about love, instantly we know that they are not about the kind of love in which young people are said to "fall" every spring without trying. They are about the kind of love that God's people climb into by earnest effort. This love is a heartfelt concern for the welfare of someone else—a concern that moves us to help, even if helping is costly to us.

The law said to love your neighbor as yourself (Leviticus 19:18). Jesus said this too (Matthew 22:39). Your neighbor's place in your heart is below God's, but on a level with your own.

If you love your neighbor as you love yourself, you certainly will not murder him, nor steal from him, nor bear false witness against him, nor commit adultery with his mate. You will not even covet anything he has. Paul summed it up thus: "Love worketh no ill to his neighbor: therefore love is the fulfilling of the law" (Romans 13:10). And Jesus said, "On these two commandments hang all the law and the prophets" (Matthew 22:40).

God Himself inscribed the Ten Commandments on stone, but the two commandments of love are greater than them all. He wrote the love commandments on your heart (Jeremiah 31:33). Let them rule your life.

C . Prayer

We love You, Father, because You first loved us. For us You delivered Your only begotten Son to death. For You we would give up every selfish thought and wish. Help us, Father; please help us to purify our hearts, and guide our lives by Your love. Amen.

D. Thought to Remember

God is first; my neighbor is second; I am third.

Home Daily Bible Readings

Monday, Sept. 13—Israel Camps at Mount Sinai (Exodus 19:1-9)

Tuesday, Sept. 14—Israel Meets God at Mount Sinai (Exodus 19:16-25)

Wednesday, Sept. 15—Honor God, and Keep the Sabbath (Exodus 20:1-11)

Thursday, Sept. 16—Commandments for Life in Community (Exodus 20:12-21)

Friday, Sept. 17—Observe God's Statutes and Ordinances (Deuteronomy 4:1-8)

Saturday, Sept. 18—Teach Obedience to Generations That Follow (Deuteronomy 4:9-14)

Sunday, Sept. 19—Commandments, a Gift of God's Love (Deuteronomy 4:32-40)

Learning by Doing

This page contains an alternate lesson plan emphasizing learning activities.
Classes desiring such student involvement will find these suggestions helpful.

Learning Goals

After this lesson students should be able to:

1. Tell what God intended Israel to be and how He intended them to live, according to the covenant given at Sinai.

2. Explain how God's intentions for Israel apply to the church.

3. Determine to be a "kingdom of priests" and "a holy nation" by practicing what Jesus called the "greatest" commandments (Matthew 22:38-40).

Into the Lesson

While we often speak of the Ten Commandments, you may be surprised how few of your class members can actually repeat all of them from memory. To review them together, divide the class into groups of four to six, giving each group a stack of ten large index cards. Give them a few minutes to work together with instructions to write one Commandment on each card.

To review the correct answers, first read the Commandments out loud in incorrect order, and have the groups revise any they wrote incorrectly and/or write ones they missed. When all the groups have complete and accurate sets, ask each one to place the cards in the order the Commandments were given in Exodus 20.

Into the Word

To review the results and to move into the Bible study, have someone read Exodus 19:3-6; 20:2-4, 7, 8, 12-17 aloud. As each Commandment is read, post a card with that Commandment on a wall in the classroom at about head height. Keep them spaced fairly evenly around the room. (These ten cards will be useful later.)

Note that God describes His people as a kingdom of priests and a holy nation (Exodus 19:6). Challenge the class to consider ways that faithfully obeying these ten Commands will distinguish a person or a group of people from the culture around them that does not. To do this, bring several copies of the Sunday newspaper with you to class. Distribute them to the small groups formed earlier, and ask each group to find examples of ways our world is living in violation of the Ten Commandments (stories, articles, advertisements, etc.). As the groups find examples in the newspaper, have them clip the stories and place them on the wall under the card with the corresponding Commandment.

Highlight several of the examples found to share discoveries between the groups. Then ask, "How would life be different in specific areas if everyone were obeying that Commandment? How is being radically different from the surrounding culture related to your ability to serve as a 'kingdom of priests' and a 'holy nation'? How would faithful obedience to these Commands encourage others to turn from sin and toward God?"

Observe that people often think of the Ten Commandments as being only negative in orientation—simply prohibitions against things we should not do. Jesus, however, said that the entire law could be summarized by two clear, positively stated guidelines. Ask a volunteer to look up and read Matthew 22:37-40.

It is important to realize that fulfilling the Commandments is more than avoiding certain activities. It includes a positive pursuit of attitudes and actions that demonstrate the spirit and intent of the Commandments. As a class, discuss how these Ten Commandments could be stated in positive terms. (The following are provided as possible suggestions: 1. Trust in God alone. 2. Worship God wholeheartedly and exclusively. 3. Live in a way that honors God's character and reputation. 4. Take time to rest and focus on God. 5. Respect and honor your parents. 6. Value and protect human life. 7. Be faithful to your spouse. 8. Respect the property of others. 9. Live a life of honesty and integrity. 10. Be content with what is your own and pleased for the success of others.)

Into Life

As a class, identify practical things that could be done in each of the above areas to fulfill the true spirit of God's law. Look at the positive statement of individual Commands, and ask, "What should we be doing to show our love for God or our fellow man in this area?"

Which of the Commandments do the students think are the most difficult to obey? Are certain Commands harder to obey today than they would have been twenty years ago? a hundred years ago? during the time they were given to the Israelites?

Challenge class members to evaluate their lives to identify areas that need attention. Students should look for ways their obedience will enhance their testimony to the surrounding culture by demonstrating love for God and other people.

Let's Talk It Over

The questions on this page are designed to encourage review of the lesson Scriptures and to promote discussion of the lesson by the class. The answers provided are only discussion starters. Let your class talk it over from there.

1. God reminded Moses that He had carried the Israelites "on eagles' wings," enabling them to soar past all their problems. How has God enabled you to "soar"? Over what problems has He carried *you* "on eagles' wings"?

God has enabled us to soar above the guilt of our sins because the blood of Jesus has cleansed us of all sin (1 John 1:7). God has lifted us up above the awful dread of death. He has elevated us to a life of righteousness we may have once regarded as impossible. He has freed us from attitudes and habits that bound us like heavy chains. Now we experience freedom and power, because Jesus Christ Himself lives in us (Galatians 2:20). Members of the class may share specific problems and struggles over which God has granted victory, or your discussion may remain in general terms. Be alert for one who does not feel he or she is "soaring" in the Christian life. This one may need some special encouragement.

2. Israel was to be "a kingdom of priests." We Christians are likewise to be "a royal priesthood" (1 Peter 2:9). What is significant about the role of the priest that you find helpful in following the Lord today?

If your students do not have at least a rudimentary understanding of the role of the priest in the Old Testament, they may not have much to say in this "discussion."

The priests in Old Testament Israel taught God's laws to the people, led them in worship, and offered sacrifices on their behalf. We Christians bear a responsibility to communicate the will of God to people from all races and nations. They are not likely to learn how to trust and obey Him or how to worship and praise Him unless we fulfill our priestly responsibility.

Another implication is that, as priests, we do not need any other but Christ to mediate between us and God (1 Timothy 2:5). We can come boldly to the "throne of grace" (Hebrews 4:14-16).

3. Several views regarding the Christian's responsibility concerning "the Sabbath" were expressed in today's lesson. What do you think is the proper way for Christians to apply the fourth Commandment? Why?

As noted in the lesson, views on this subject range from a belief that we are bound to all the Sabbath regulations (usually applied to Sunday) to the view that we need not recognize a distinction (short of attending a worship service) at all. It would be wise to keep Romans 14 in mind here—especially verses 5 and 6. This is an issue on which we can hold different points of view and still be a part of the church for which the Lord gave His life. Yet each believer should think through the issue and "be fully persuaded in his own mind" (Romans 14:5).

4. What do you think it means to "honor" one's parents? If it's a matter of obedience (see Ephesians 6:1-3), does it apply to adults as well as children? Why or why not? If there is more to it than obedience, then what does it mean?

Ephesians 6:1-3 makes clear that obedience is at least part of what this Command requires, though it by no means limits the Command to obedience. One honors his parents by showing respect in various ways or looking after their needs when they are sick or aged.

Some believers feel the duty to obey one's parents never ends; others will contend that the need to obey ceases when one becomes an adult or when he or she leaves the parents' home. Even those who hold the latter view, however, will agree that one should give serious consideration to the counsel or wishes of his or her parents and refuse only if there is a compelling reason.

5. What can we do to develop whole-hearted love for God as commanded in Matthew 22:37?

Romans 5:5 informs us that "the love of God is shed abroad in our hearts by the Holy Ghost which is given unto us." In our public worship and our private devotion we must practice an openness to the Spirit, so that He can perform this work. When we pray, we should take time to ask God for a deeper awareness of His love and a stronger capacity to love Him in return. Also, Jesus taught His disciples, "If you love me, you will obey what I command" (John 14:15, *New International Version*). An intimate connection exists between obedience and love. Not only is it true that love leads to obedience—it is also accurate to say that obedience leads to love. The more we commit ourselves to perfect adherence to God's will, the more we will experience a loving communion with Him.

The Tabernacle and Obedience

DEVOTIONAL READING: Psalm 84.

BACKGROUND SCRIPTURE: Exodus 40:1-33; Leviticus 26.

PRINTED TEXT: Exodus 40:1-9; Leviticus 26:2-6a, 11-13.

Exodus 40:1-9

1 And the LORD spake unto Moses, saying,

2 On the first day of the first month shalt thou set up the tabernacle of the tent of the congregation.

3 And thou shalt put therein the ark of the testimony, and cover the ark with the veil.

4 And thou shalt bring in the table, and set in order the things that are to be set in order upon it; and thou shalt bring in the candlestick, and light the lamps thereof.

5 And thou shalt set the altar of gold for the incense before the ark of the testimony, and put the hanging of the door to the tabernacle.

6 And thou shalt set the altar of the burnt offering before the door of the tabernacle of the tent of the congregation.

7 And thou shalt set the laver between the tent of the congregation and the altar, and shalt put water therein.

8 And thou shalt set up the court round about, and hang up the hanging at the court gate.

9 And thou shalt take the anointing oil, and anoint the tabernacle, and all that is therein, and shalt hallow it, and all the vessels thereof: and it shall be holy.

Leviticus 26:2-6a, 11-13

2 Ye shall keep my sabbaths, and reverence my sanctuary: I am the LORD.

3 If ye walk in my statutes, and keep my commandments, and do them;

4 Then I will give you rain in due season, and the land shall yield her increase, and the trees of the field shall yield their fruit.

5 And your threshing shall reach unto the vintage, and the vintage shall reach unto the sowing time: and ye shall eat your bread to the full, and dwell in your land safely.

6a And I will give peace in the land, and ye shall lie down, and none shall make you afraid.

. . . .

11 And I will set my tabernacle among you: and my soul shall not abhor you.

12 And I will walk among you, and will be your God, and ye shall be my people.

13 I am the LORD your God, which brought you forth out of the land of Egypt, that ye should not be their bondmen; and I have broken the bands of your yoke, and made you go upright.

GOLDEN TEXT: Ye shall keep my sabbaths, and reverence my sanctuary: I am the LORD.—Leviticus 26:2.

Lesson Aims

After this lesson students should be able to:

1. Describe the tabernacle that Israel was commanded to construct in the wilderness.

2. Tell what the establishment of the tabernacle teaches Christians about how obedience to God is important to the one who would dwell in God's presence.

3. Praise God for making His dwelling among His people.

Lesson Outline

INTRODUCTION

    A. Laws for a Nation

    B. Tabernacle for a Nation

    C. Lesson Background

 I. SETTING UP THE TABERNACLE (Exodus 40:1-9)

    A. The Time (vv. 1, 2)

    B. The Most Holy Place (v. 3)

    C. The Holy Place (vv. 4, 5)

    D. The Court (vv. 6-8)

    E. The Dedication (v. 9)

II. OBEDIENCE AND ITS REWARDS (Leviticus 26:2-6a, 11-13)

    A. Call to Obedience (vv. 2, 3)

    B. Rewards of Obedience (vv. 4-6a)

    No Accidental Fixes

    C. The Crowning Reward (vv. 11-13)

CONCLUSION

    A. The Holy Place

    B. The Most Holy Place

    C. Prayer

    D. Thought to Remember

Introduction

In the third month of their journey out of Egypt, the people of Israel set up camp at the foot of Mount Sinai (Exodus 19:1, 2), where they stayed for nearly a year. At Sinai God gave the laws that were to govern His people for centuries; and at Sinai the people constructed an elegant tabernacle according to God's detailed instructions.

A. Laws for a Nation

Last week we considered the Ten Commandments, which God Himself inscribed on tablets of stone (Exodus 31:18). We considered also the two great commandments of love, on which "hang all the law and the prophets" (Matthew 22:40). Besides these, God also gave a multitude of other commandments, which Moses later wrote in a book (Deuteronomy 31:24-26). We find them, along with much historical material, in the books of Exodus, Leviticus, Numbers, and Deuteronomy.

B. Tabernacle for a Nation

Our English word *tabernacle* is used to translate two Hebrew words that are used quite frequently in the Old Testament. One of the words means "tent." The tabernacle was thus called because it was a temporary structure, made mostly of fabrics and leathers that could be folded or rolled and taken to another campsite. The other word means "dwelling place." The tabernacle was given that name because it was the special place signifying God's presence in the midst of His people.

At Sinai the people were asked to donate materials for the tabernacle, including lumber, fabrics, animal skins, gold, silver, and brass (Exodus 25:1-9; 35:4-9). They responded so generously that Moses had to tell them to stop giving (Exodus 35:20-29; 36:2-7).

God appointed two skilled artisans, Bezaleel and Aholiab, to supervise the project. Other skilled men went to work under their direction (Exodus 35:30—36:1). Many women also assisted in this effort. Using raw materials brought from Egypt, they spun the yarn and wove it into fabrics (Exodus 35:25, 26), which were then used to make the curtains of the tabernacle (36:8). Various parts of the tent and its furnishings are described in Exodus 36:8—38:31.

C. Lesson Background

After months of work the various sections of the tabernacle were completed, along with the specific items to be placed within it. Probably these were stacked near the place where the tabernacle was to stand. Moses inspected the work, declared it well done, and blessed those who had contributed to the task (Exodus 39:32-43). Now it was time to assemble the parts so that the tabernacle could be used.

I. Setting Up the Tabernacle (Exodus 40:1-9)

The roofed tent or tabernacle is described in Exodus 26. It was about forty-five feet long and fifteen feet wide. The sides were fifteen feet high, made of "ten curtains of fine twined [or twisted] linen" (Exodus 26:1) and supported by a wooden framework. The ceiling was made of "curtains of goats' hair" (v. 7), with a leather covering to keep it dry in the infrequent rain. Some students think that there must have been a ridgepole to support a sloping roof so the rain would run off, but there is no mention of this in the Bible. The Bible's silence is no proof that there was none, but there is no compelling reason to believe there was such a pole, either. The roof may well have been flat.

Inside this tabernacle were two rooms. At the west end was the Most Holy Place, also called the Holy of Holies. It was in the shape of a cube, fifteen feet long and wide and high. This was the inner shrine, the very place of God's presence. Here the high priest entered once a year, on the Day of Atonement, to make atonement for the sins of the people (Leviticus 16:11-14, 34). The other room measured fifteen by thirty feet. This was the Holy Place, entered only by priests.

Around this structure was a courtyard approximately 150 feet long and 75 feet wide. It was surrounded by curtains made of additional "fine twined linen." The entrance at the east end was covered with curtains when not in use.

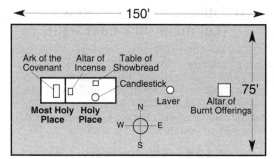

Plan of the Tabernacle Complex

In today's text we read of the various objects that were placed in the tabernacle.

A. The Time (vv. 1, 2)

1. And the LORD spake unto Moses, saying.

Thus we are reminded that *the Lord* was directing the construction of this tabernacle. He had given specific instructions for each part of it (chapters 25–27), and now He was directing the assembling of those parts. [See question #1, page 40.]

2. On the first day of the first month shalt thou set up the tabernacle of the tent of the congregation.

The Israelites had begun to measure time by the date of the exodus, which marked God's deliverance of His people. That was considered *the first day of the first month* (Exodus 12:2). Now,

one year later, they were celebrating the beginning of the system of worship that God had outlined for them. The first occasion of erecting the tabernacle was to occur on what we might call "New Year's Day." Israel had come to this camping place by Sinai in the third month of the previous year (Exodus 19:1, 2), so they had been there between nine and ten months at this point.

B. The Most Holy Place (v. 3)

3. And thou shalt put therein the ark of the testimony, and cover the ark with the veil.

The one piece of furniture to be placed within the Most Holy Place was *the ark of the testimony*, more often called the ark of the covenant. It was a wooden chest covered inside and outside with gold. This chest received its name because it held the Ten Commandments—the first and foundational part of God's *testimony* or covenant with His people. The rest of the covenant, written in a book, was to be kept beside the ark (Deuteronomy 31:24-26). Placed on top of the ark were two golden cherubim, and between them was the exact spot from which God promised to speak to Moses. For a fuller description of the ark, see Exodus 25:10-22.

The veil was the curtain that separated the Most Holy Place from the Holy Place. Moses was to *cover the ark with the veil*, not by laying the veil upon the ark, but by hanging the veil in its place so that the ark was not visible from the Holy Place.

C. The Holy Place (vv. 4, 5)

4. And thou shalt bring in the table, and set in order the things that are to be set in order upon it; and thou shalt bring in the candlestick, and light the lamps thereof.

Within the Holy Place were three articles of furniture. *The table* of showbread (see Exodus 25:23-30) stood in the north part of the room. As the Lord provided daily manna for His people, it was fitting that their offerings provided bread continually for His tent among them. Twelve loaves, one for each of Israel's twelve tribes, were displayed continually on the table. Each Sabbath Day they were replaced by new loaves. The old ones then became food for the priests, as did some of the other offerings of the people.

The candlestick stood in the south part of the Holy Place. It is more accurately called a lampstand, for it consisted of oil-burning lamps rather than candles. Its seven lamps in a straight row provided light for the room even in daytime. The tent had no windows, and the doorway was closed by a hanging curtain that shut out the daylight. See Exodus 25:31-40 for a description of the candlestick.

5. And thou shalt set the altar of gold for the incense before the ark of the testimony, and put the hanging of the door to the tabernacle.

The third piece of furniture in the Holy Place was *the altar of gold*, a small altar on which *incense* was burned. *The ark of the testimony*, the symbol of God's presence, remained out of sight in the Most Holy Place; the golden altar was placed in front of it with only the veil between. The fragrant smoke rising from the incense was a symbol of the people's prayers rising to God. This golden altar was made of wood covered with gold. Thus it was lighter than a solid gold altar would be, and easier to carry when the people moved to a new campsite. See the precise description of this altar in Exodus 30:1-10.

It should be noted that Hebrews 9:4 describes the golden altar as part of the items in the Most Holy Place, not the Holy Place. This may be due to its close association with the ministry that took place in the Most Holy Place on the Day of Atonement (Leviticus 16:12, 13, 18-20). [See question #2, page 40.]

The door to the tabernacle was located in the east end. It was closed with a *hanging*, or curtain. When Moses put these in place, the structure was complete. Now our attention is turned to the enclosed court surrounding the tabernacle, and to the two articles placed in this court.

D. The Court (vv. 6-8)

6. And thou shalt set the altar of the burnt offering before the door of the tabernacle of the tent of the congregation.

Outside the doorway of *the tent* was *the altar of burnt offering*, where the bodies of animals were burned in sacrifice to the Lord. This altar had to be strong enough to support a load of firewood and animal flesh, yet light enough to be easily moved. God prescribed a wooden frame seven and a half feet square, covered with brass to protect it from the fire. Inside the frame was suspended a brass grate to support the fire. Read more about it in Exodus 27:1-8.

7. And thou shalt set the laver between the tent of the congregation and the altar, and shalt put water therein.

The laver was a brass basin at which the priests washed their hands and feet before entering the Holy Place (Exodus 30:17-21). Its size is not mentioned.

8. And thou shalt set up the court round about, and hang up the hanging at the court gate.

Here *the court* designates the curtains set up to enclose the outer court. They were five cubits (about seven and a half feet) high, made of linen, and supported by posts five cubits apart. The *King James Version* indicates that the posts

were made of brass; however, the *New International Version* describes only the "bases" or sockets into which the posts were placed as brass. Perhaps the posts were made of wood, and each one was inserted in a heavy brass socket that held it upright. The posts were fitted with silver hooks by which to attach them to the linen curtains.

At the east end of the court the *gate*, or entrance, was thirty feet wide. The *hanging*, or curtains, that enclosed it were richly embroidered. See the description of the courtyard in Exodus 27:9-19 and 38:9-20.

E. The Dedication (v. 9)

9. And thou shalt take the anointing oil, and anoint the tabernacle, and all that is therein, and shalt hallow it, and all the vessels thereof: and it shall be holy.

Anointing with *oil* was a feature of ancient ceremonies of dedication, whether of people or of objects. Thus the *tabernacle* and its furnishings were to be set apart ("hallowed" or made *holy*) and consecrated to their intended use. [See question #3, page 40.]

II. Obedience and Its Rewards (Leviticus 26:2-6a, 11-13)

Now the tabernacle was complete—dedicated, holy, and ready for use. The priests likewise were dedicated and ready for their service. But what about the people? Were they also dedicated, ready to do God's will? In a few verses taken from Leviticus, we see God's call to obedience and His promise of rich rewards.

A. Call to Obedience (vv. 2, 3)

2. Ye shall keep my sabbaths, and reverence my sanctuary: I am the LORD.

Verse 1 forbids God's people to make and worship idols, thus repeating the second of the Ten Commandments. Now verse 2 turns to the positive side, mentioning what God's people ought to do in obedience to Him. *Keep my sabbaths* repeats the fourth of the Ten Commandments. God's people must also *reverence* His *sanctuary*. This phrase ties the latter part of our printed text to the first part. God's sanctuary is

---

How to Say It

AHOLIAB. Uh-*ho*-lih-ab.
BEZALEEL. Bih-*zal*-ee-ull.
DEUTERONOMY. Due-ter-*ahn*-uh-me.
LEVITICUS. Leh-*vit*-ih-kuss.

Visual for lesson 4

This visual shows the tabernacle set up amidst the camps of the tribes of Israel. The inset shows the floor plan and furnishings of the tabernacle.

His holy tabernacle that we have been considering. God's obedient people should approach it with reverence and awe because it is the special place of His residence among them.

3. If ye walk in my statutes, and keep my commandments, and do them.

Here is the call for God's people to obey His *commandments*: the Ten studied in last week's lesson and all the rest that are recorded in Exodus, Leviticus, Numbers, and Deuteronomy.

B. Rewards of Obedience (vv. 4-6a)

4. Then I will give you rain in due season, and the land shall yield her increase, and the trees of the field shall yield their fruit.

An abundance of produce is the first reward promised for obedience. If God's people were faithful to Him, He would give them rain when it was needed, and enough of it to produce good crops in the grainfields and fruit orchards. In contrast, disobedience would result in drought and crop failure (vv. 18-20).

5. And your threshing shall reach unto the vintage, and the vintage shall reach unto the sowing time: and ye shall eat your bread to the full, and dwell in your land safely.

Reaping normally began in May; but if God's people were obedient to Him, the harvest (*vintage*) would be so abundant that they would hardly be able to finish the *threshing* of grain in time to start picking grapes in August. Then the grapes would be so abundant that the people would hardly finish making and storing the wine in time to start planting grain around the end of October for the following year's crop. The people of Israel would have all the food they could eat.

The end of verse 5 introduces the second reward of obedience: the people would enjoy peace in their *land*. They would be kept safe from invasion and war.

6a. And I will give peace in the land, and ye shall lie down, and none shall make you afraid.

The promise of *peace* continued. If God's people obeyed Him, they would be able to lie down and sleep with no fear of an attack from enemies during the night. [See question #4, page 40.]

NO ACCIDENTAL FIXES

We expect natural disasters to destroy property and injure people, and this is what normally happens. We expect machines and other objects that aren't functioning to require the help of technicians or handymen to make them work properly again. Usually this is so.

However, consider what happened early one morning in January of 1994, when an earthquake measuring 6.6 on the Richter scale struck Los Angeles, California. In the darkness, many people stumbled out of bed fearing for their lives. Then, as a result of this tremor, some strange things happened. A woman whose home was severely damaged owned a pendulum clock that hadn't run for months. It worked after the earthquake. Another woman's refrigerator had sounded "like a diesel truck" before the quake, but afterward it "purred like a kitten." In one place of business, a repairman had tried on numerous occasions to fix the photocopier, but without success. After the earthquake, it worked perfectly!

On the human side of things, a man who had awakened every morning for the past ten years with an aching back found that, after the earthquake, he no longer had any pain.

All of these blessings are simply quirks of circumstance, nothing more than accidental fixes. However, God offered Israel a more certain way to a life of blessedness. If they would follow in His way and keep His commandments, He would bless their land. They could lie down in peace and not be afraid.　　—C. R. B.

C. The Crowning Reward (vv. 11-13)

11. And I will set my tabernacle among you: and my soul shall not abhor you.

Here our word *tabernacle* represents the Hebrew word for "dwelling place." God would live among His obedient people. This was the crowning promise. His people would have prosperity and peace (vv. 4-6), but above all they would have God's presence. If they faithfully obeyed Him, they would be good, and so He would *not abhor* them in the depth of His being, or His *soul*.

That God is described as having a *soul* (like humans) is no different from other Scriptures that assign Him other human characteristics, such as hands, eyes, a face, and a mouth. Such terminology is what both God and the Biblical writers use to describe Someone infinite in terms that finite human beings can grasp.

12. And I will walk among you, and will be your God, and ye shall be my people.

God's residence among His people was symbolized by the elegant tabernacle, but He would not be confined to it. He would *walk among* them: He would be active outside the tabernacle. He would be their *God*, providing for their every need. The people of Israel would be God's *people*, obeying Him, trusting Him, and depending upon Him. [See question #5, page 40.]

13. I am the LORD your God, which brought you forth out of the land of Egypt, that ye should not be their bondmen; and I have broken the bands of your yoke, and made you go upright.

Who was asking Israel to obey? He was *the Lord*—the only God who actually exists, the Almighty Creator and Keeper of Heaven and earth. To the people of Israel He had demonstrated His power and goodness by rescuing them from slavery in *Egypt*. Now, looking to the future, He offered them rich rewards for obeying Him. Knowing His power and goodness, how could they fail to obey?

Conclusion

For a long time the tabernacle was God's tent among the tents of His people. Later they replaced God's tent with a temple of stone. When that temple was destroyed, they replaced it with one that stood until it was improved and enlarged by King Herod toward the beginning of the Christian era. But not long after Herod's work was done, that temple was destroyed by the Romans in A.D. 70.

By that time God was building His own replacement for the ancient tent. He was building

Home Daily Bible Readings

Monday, Sept. 20—God's Command Regarding Tabernacle and Priests (Exodus 40:1-15)

Tuesday, Sept. 21—Building the Tabernacle (Exodus 40:16-20)

Wednesday, Sept. 22—Equipping the Tabernacle (Exodus 40:21-33)

Thursday, Sept. 23—Rewards for Obedience (Leviticus 26:1-13)

Friday, Sept. 24—Consequences of Disobedience (Leviticus 26:14-26)

Saturday, Sept. 25—Further Punishments (Leviticus 26:27-39)

Sunday, Sept. 26—Confession Will Bring Renewal (Leviticus 26:40-46)

"a greater and more perfect tabernacle, not made with hands" (Hebrews 9:11). The law provided only "a shadow of good things to come" (Hebrews 10:1). The old tent was only a "figure," a parable, an illustration (Hebrews 9:8, 9) of that "greater and more perfect tabernacle." Let's see how the prophetic figure compares with the reality.

A. The Holy Place

The Holy Place pictures the church. Only priests are allowed to enter there, and Christians constitute a "holy priesthood" (1 Peter 2:5). One task of priests is to teach God's will and way, and that is what we are to do for the world.

In the Holy Place is the table of showbread. Naturally we think of Jesus, "the bread of life" (John 6:35). The ancient priests ate the showbread, and as priests all of us Christians take of the bread that is the Lord's body (Luke 22:19).

In the Holy Place is also the candlestick, or lampstand. We think of Jesus, "the light of the world" (John 8:12); and we think of the Bible, through which the light of Jesus comes to us. This is the light that the church must shine in the midst of a dark world.

The third piece of furniture in the Holy Place is the altar of incense, which stands close to the Most Holy Place, the place of God's presence. The smoke of incense symbolizes the prayers of God's people. From the church such prayers rise continually to the very presence of God.

B. The Most Holy Place

The Most Holy Place is the earthly symbol of Heaven. It housed the ark of the covenant, which was the visible symbol of the presence of the invisible God. Once every year the high priest went into the Most Holy Place, carrying the blood of a sacrifice that was made to atone for the sins of Israel. Once for all Jesus carried into the real Heaven His own blood, offered to atone for our sins. There He appears before God for us (Hebrews 9:24-26) and continues to make intercession for us (Hebrews 7:25).

C. Prayer

Our Father in Heaven, it is awesome to think that You are also here on earth, that we ourselves are Your tabernacle, Your dwelling place. Accept the homage of our hearts, we pray, shape us according to Your will, and show us how to serve You better. Amen.

D. Thought to Remember

As a living stone in God's spiritual house, I must be shaped by His Word and active in His service.

Learning by Doing

This page contains an alternate lesson plan emphasizing learning activities.
Classes desiring such student involvement will find these suggestions helpful.

Learning Goals

After this lesson students should be able to:

1. Describe the tabernacle that Israel was commanded to construct in the wilderness.

2. Tell what the establishment of the tabernacle teaches Christians about how obedience to God is important to the one who would dwell in God's presence.

3. Praise God for making His dwelling among His people.

Into the Lesson

Bring to class pictures of several different homes from some home decorating magazines. Include several different types of architecture and styles of decorating. Ask the class to try to describe the owners of the homes by what they observe. What do the furniture, decorating, and landscaping tell you about the owners? Is there a statement they might be trying to make about themselves? About their families? About the importance of having guests? Is there anything else the decor and structure may suggest about the owners and their values?

Into the Word

Today we will examine the tabernacle, described as God's dwelling place among the Israelites. It will help us understand something about God, ourselves, and our worship.

Form three task groups from the students present and give the following instructions: "Today you will be preparing copy for a special issue of an architectural or decorating magazine dedicated to the tabernacle described in the Old Testament. Work with the others in your task group to prepare a brief diagram and description of the area you have been assigned. [See below.] Describe and explain the purpose for each of the furnishings in that area. Write your material as if for a decorating magazine."

Group 1. The Most Holy Place (Exodus 40:3), including the ark of the covenant (Exodus 25:10-22; Deuteronomy 31:24-26).

Group 2. The Holy Place (Exodus 40:4-5), including the table of showbread (Exodus 25:23-30), the candlestick (Exodus 25:31-40), and the altar of incense (Exodus 30:1-10).

Group 3. The court (Exodus 40:6-8), including the altar of burnt offering (Exodus 27:1-8) and the laver (Exodus 30:17-21).

Allow time for the groups to work; then ask for reports. Draw a composite diagram of the tabernacle and its furnishings on a large poster or on the chalkboard as the groups provide information. Fill in details and explanations from the commentary section as needed.

Have a volunteer read Leviticus 26:2-6a, 11-13. Note that in verses 2 and 3 God commanded the Israelites to "keep my sabbaths, and reverence my sanctuary." Clearly worship must be approached with a sense of great respect and awe. Discuss how the design of the tabernacle, as well as the furnishings, communicated this truth. How do we apply this truth in our own church and our own worship services?

Note that the demand for holiness was not just for worship. It applied to all of life and was linked with obedience to God's statutes (v. 3). Review the rewards promised for obedience to God (vv. 4-6). What rewards can Christians expect for such holiness and commitment to obeying God's commands?

Into Life

Read several New Testament passages that describe the dwelling place of God as within Christians (e.g., Acts 2:38; Romans 8:10-12; 1 Corinthians 3:16; 6:19; 2 Timothy 1:14).

Reflect on the lessons learned concerning the respect and care given to the tabernacle as the dwelling place of God, and discuss what those same principles suggest about the need for personal holiness by God's people. If God's tabernacle (later, temple) was to be kept holy, and if we are God's temple today, what kind of demand for holiness does that place on us?

Review the demand for obedience in all areas of life, and discuss the importance of such obedience to Christians. Some believers feel that grace releases us from the demands of obedience. What is wrong with that assumption? How are holiness and obedience related for the Christian?

Have someone read Hebrews 9:1-10 to identify how the work of Christ fulfilled the picture presented of the tabernacle. Then read together as a class the remainder of the chapter (Hebrews 9:11-28). This could be used as a closing prayer, a collective statement of praise for the work of Jesus Christ in providing salvation fully and completely.

Let's Talk It Over

The questions on this page are designed to encourage review of the lesson Scriptures and to promote discussion of the lesson by the class. The answers provided are only discussion starters. Let your class talk it over from there.

1. The lesson writer points out that the instructions regarding the tabernacle came from the Lord. What do you find significant about the fact that the construction of the tabernacle was according to God's specific plan? How do you think that applies to Christians or to the church today?

One of the common misconceptions about religion—and Christianity in particular—is that it represents man's search for God. The Bible repeatedly affirms that in the Old Testament and the New, God was revealing Himself to mankind. If the tabernacle were no more than a human attempt to create a shrine for God, it would not warrant the attention we pay to it today. But if it was, as the Bible claims, built by God's express design, then it teaches us something of God. Each piece of furniture can teach us something about relating to God. Furthermore, the book of Hebrews points out that the furnishings of the tabernacle/temple are a shadow of the realities to be found in Heaven.

2. The smoke of the incense burned on the tabernacle's altar of incense was to rise continually toward Heaven. What can we do to make certain our church's prayers are rising continually toward Heaven?

Many churches keep prayer lists that detail certain needs among their members and, perhaps, the missionaries that the church supports. But what is done to encourage use of the prayer list? Discuss ways to improve the prayer life of the church and of individual members in the areas of the frequency of prayers, the time spent in prayer, and the breadth of subject matter in our prayers. (For the latter see 1 Timothy 2:1, 2; Ephesians 6:18-20; Colossians 4:3, 4.) The early church was noted for prayer (Acts 2:42), and the church today needs to restore prayer to its primary role.

3. Anointing the tabernacle and its furnishings demonstrated its holiness and consecration to God's use. How can we emphasize the holiness of the church and its work and worship?

Sometimes the church is all too human, and we tend to forget its divine character. In an effort to be "seeker friendly" we sometimes make our worship services very casual. In the process, we might be conveying a very common and ordinary—even human—picture of God. Somehow we need to balance a friendly welcome with a sense of the holiness that Moses confronted in the burning bush.

We can also become too enamored with the ways of the world in our church programming. When we rely too heavily on marketing strategies and sociological data instead of working through the power of the Holy Spirit, we have secularized the church. Marketing and sociology have their place, but the Spirit must always come first.

4. According to Leviticus 26:6, one of the rewards of obedience to God is worry-free sleep. How does this promise apply to us today?

If an Old Testament believer could claim such a promise, how much more should Christians be able to do so! We have greater evidence of God's love for us and of His power to meet our needs. Jesus pointed out that we have no cause for anxiety (Matthew 6:25-34). Paul spoke of the peace that we can experience when we subject our worries to prayer (Philippians 4:6, 7). Peter urged us to cast on God our anxiety (1 Peter 5:7).

What, then, of occasions when we await a report from an oncologist or an ER doctor? What of times when our children get into trouble with the law? Is it wrong for Christians in these and similar situations to have trouble sleeping? We do need to keep in mind that God's promises to us can be claimed by each of us only for himself or herself. While we can rest assured of our own salvation, there will always be those for whom we are praying and hoping that they, too, will choose to accept Christ. Some anxiety in their behalf is sometimes appropriate.

5. God promised to walk among His obedient people. What encouragement do you find in this promise for today?

A New Testament parallel to this promise is found in Revelation 1:12, 13; 2:1. There Christ is depicted as walking among His churches. As One who walks among us, He is occupying His role as leader. He is our protector and our comforter. And when we, like the churches of Asia, need reproof (cf. Revelation 2:4, 5), He is walking among us to administer that as well.

The Cloud and the Fire

DEVOTIONAL READING: Psalm 107:1-9.

BACKGROUND SCRIPTURE: Exodus 40:34-38;
Numbers 9:15-23.

PRINTED TEXT: Exodus 40:34-38; Numbers
9:15-23.

Exodus 40:34-38

34 Then a cloud covered the tent of the congregation, and the glory of the LORD filled the tabernacle.

35 And Moses was not able to enter into the tent of the congregation, because the cloud abode thereon, and the glory of the LORD filled the tabernacle.

36 And when the cloud was taken up from over the tabernacle, the children of Israel went onward in all their journeys:

37 But if the cloud were not taken up, then they journeyed not till the day that it was taken up.

38 For the cloud of the LORD was upon the tabernacle by day, and fire was on it by night, in the sight of all the house of Israel, throughout all their journeys.

Numbers 9:15-23

15 And on the day that the tabernacle was reared up the cloud covered the tabernacle, namely, the tent of the testimony: and at even there was upon the tabernacle as it were the appearance of fire, until the morning.

16 So it was alway: the cloud covered it by day, and the appearance of fire by night.

17 And when the cloud was taken up from the tabernacle, then after that the children of Israel journeyed: and in the place where the cloud abode, there the children of Israel pitched their tents.

18 At the commandment of the LORD the children of Israel journeyed, and at the commandment of the LORD they pitched: as long as the cloud abode upon the tabernacle they rested in their tents.

19 And when the cloud tarried long upon the tabernacle many days, then the children of Israel kept the charge of the LORD, and journeyed not.

20 And so it was, when the cloud was a few days upon the tabernacle; according to the commandment of the LORD they abode in their tents, and according to the commandment of the LORD they journeyed.

21 And so it was, when the cloud abode from even unto the morning, and that the cloud was taken up in the morning, then they journeyed: whether it was by day or by night that the cloud was taken up, they journeyed.

22 Or whether it were two days, or a month, or a year, that the cloud tarried upon the tabernacle, remaining thereon, the children of Israel abode in their tents, and journeyed not: but when it was taken up, they journeyed.

23 At the commandment of the LORD they rested in their tents, and at the commandment of the LORD they journeyed: they kept the charge of the LORD, at the commandment of the LORD by the hand of Moses.

GOLDEN TEXT: For the cloud of the LORD was upon the tabernacle by day, and fire was on it by night, in the sight of all the house of Israel, throughout all their journeys.—Exodus 40:38.

From Slavery to Conquest
Unit 2: Wandering in the Wilderness
(Lessons 5-9)

Lesson Aims

As a result of this lesson, your students should be able to:

1. Tell how God led the Israelites by a pillar of cloud by day and of fire at night.

2. Recall significant moments in their lives when God's guidance sustained them.

3. Stay alert to indications of God's guidance through people and circumstances, and thank Him for His guidance.

Lesson Outline

INTRODUCTION
   A. Life at Sinai
   B. Lesson Background
 I. FACTS FROM EXODUS (Exodus 40:34-38)
   A. Presence of the Cloud (vv. 34, 35)
   B. Movement of the Cloud (vv. 36-38)
     A Protecting Presence
II. FACTS FROM NUMBERS (Numbers 9:15-23)
   A. The Tabernacle and the Cloud (vv. 15, 16)
   B. The Cloud and the Journey (vv. 17-23)
     Knowing When It Is Time
CONCLUSION
   A. Your Faultless Guide
   B. Blessed Assurance
   C. Prayer
   D. Thought to Remember

Introduction

A. Life at Sinai

The Israelites began an entirely new way of life when they left Egypt as a free people. Part of that newness was reflected in the way the Israelites started to measure time. The date of the exodus was considered the first day of the first month (Exodus 12:2). They encamped at Sinai "in the third month" (Exodus 19:1) and stayed there the rest of that year. On the first day of the next year they set up the tabernacle, as we saw in last week's lesson (Exodus 40:2). It appears that they then had a month during which to relax after all the work of making the tabernacle, and to observe the week-long feast of Passover in the middle of the month. That was the first anniversary of the Passover in Egypt (Numbers 9:1-14).

B. Lesson Background

The next month was busy with several matters of organization. The men available for military service (age twenty or older) were counted, totaling 603,550 (Numbers 1:44-46). The Levites, who were to take care of the tabernacle, were counted, organized, and ceremonially cleansed and dedicated (Numbers 1:47; 3:1-39; 4:1-49; 8:5-26). Each tribe was assigned a certain place in camp for its tents, and a certain position in the order of travel (Numbers 2). Thus prepared, the people were ready to leave Sinai on the twentieth day of the second month of the second year of their journey (Numbers 10:11, 12).

From the beginning of Israel's journey out of Egypt, "the Lord went before them by day in a pillar of a cloud, to lead them the way; and by night in a pillar of fire" (Exodus 13:21). This week we will read more about those visible signs by which the invisible God guided His people.

I. Facts From Exodus (Exodus 40:34-38)

Our text presents facts from Exodus and then facts from Numbers. These facts are so much alike that we may wonder why Moses recorded them twice. Two considerations should lessen our surprise. First, every teacher knows how important it is to repeat facts so that students will remember them. Moses is to be credited with repetition for memory retention. Second, the same facts may be used with different purposes and in different settings. Here again we see Moses' purpose in repeating the information. In Numbers he uses these details as the prelude to the story of the continuing journey from Sinai (Numbers 10:11, 12). In Exodus he uses them as the conclusion to the record of constructing and setting up the tabernacle. We'll consider them in that context first.

A. Presence of the Cloud (vv. 34, 35)

34. Then a cloud covered the tent of the congregation, and the glory of the LORD filled the tabernacle.

Notice that there is no gap between this passage and the text from Exodus in last week's lesson. There we read that "Moses finished the work" of erecting the tabernacle (Exodus 40:33). For months the people of Israel had worked on this project—shaping the wooden pieces, weaving the fabrics, making the articles of gold and silver and brass—all to provide a *tent* for the Lord in the midst of the tents of His people. Now that tent was completed. From Egypt to Sinai the Lord had gone before them in a cloud (Exodus 13:21). Now that cloud settled on the tent constructed for the Lord, and *the glory of the Lord* showed that He was in His tent. We have never seen that glory, but most suppose that it resembled a brilliant light. The Bible tells of one night when it "shone" around some shepherds near Bethlehem (Luke 2:9).

35. And Moses was not able to enter into the tent of the congregation, because the cloud abode thereon, and the glory of the LORD filled the tabernacle.

Here, as in verse 34, the *King James Version* calls this *the tent of the congregation,* but that reading seems to be a problem because the congregation would never enter that tent. We should understand the *tent of the congregation* as meaning the "tent where the congregating or communing [between God and Moses] was to take place" (Exodus 25:22). Thus the *New International Version* calls it "the Tent of Meeting."

Some time before this, Moses had hidden his face because he was afraid to look at the burning bush from which God spoke to him (Exodus 3:6). Now he found himself in awe before the radiant *glory* that filled the new tabernacle. [See question #1, page 48.]

B. Movement of the Cloud (vv. 36-38)

36. And when the cloud was taken up from over the tabernacle, the children of Israel went onward in all their journeys.

When the cloud was taken up, that was the signal for departure. The Levites took the *tabernacle* apart, rolled or folded its fabric and leather, and prepared everything for travel. The people took down their tents, packed their goods, and prepared to move on. If flocks were out grazing, they were brought in quickly. Probably the cloud hovered nearby until the packing was finished. Then it moved away across the desert. The Lord's people followed, each tribe taking its assigned place in the huge caravan.

37. But if the cloud were not taken up, then they journeyed not till the day that it was taken up.

The resting cloud was the signal for the people to rest. No doubt it remained still every Sabbath day. We are not told if any other special days were considered as occasions when the people did not travel.

38. For the cloud of the LORD was upon the tabernacle by day, and fire was on it by night, in the sight of all the house of Israel, throughout all their journeys.

All their journeys would last forty years, nearly thirty-nine of those after they left Sinai. Never would they have to ask when to break camp or which way to go; never would they have to ask when to stop or how long to stay.

The guiding *cloud* was with them all the way, day after day and year after year. When darkness fell the cloud turned to *fire,* providing light for the entire camp. [See question #2, page 48.]

A PROTECTING PRESENCE

If you live in a large city (and perhaps even if you don't), you have become used to hearing the sound of car alarms going off. The first alarms were simple affairs, flashing the car's headlights and honking its horn. However, false alarms caused people to ignore these warnings.

So the technology battle between thieves and car owners escalated. Next came alarms with sirens, then alarms with two different sirens. Then came "proximity alarms" that sensed a possible felon approaching the car and uttered a verbal command not to come any closer. Failure to stop would result in all manner of noise to call attention to the disregard for such authority.

One of the more whimsical alarm systems was the Security Bear—a teddy bear to be placed in a spot such as the car's back window. When it sensed changes in the car's internal air pressure (as would be the case if a window were broken or the door opened), it would trigger an alarm "comparable to having a fire engine in your car," according to its manufacturer.

Israel needed no electronic alarm for protection while on its way to the promised land. The sign of Israel's security was more spectacular than any that humans have ever dreamed up. The pillars of cloud and fire comprised the certain symbol of God's presence wherever the Israelites were. In fact, it really didn't matter where the people were; *God* was there with them. —C. R. B.

II. Facts From Numbers (Numbers 9:15-23)

In our text from Numbers we see the same facts that were found in our text from Exodus. As noted earlier, the details are set in different surroundings: in Exodus they provide the grand finale for the lengthy story of constructing the tabernacle; in Numbers they are the prelude to the story of the continuing journey from Sinai, which would be announced by the sounding of silver trumpets (Numbers 10:1-10) as well as by the sight of the rising cloud.

A. The Tabernacle and the Cloud (vv. 15, 16)

15. And on the day that the tabernacle was reared up the cloud covered the tabernacle, namely, the tent of the testimony: and at even there was upon the tabernacle as it were the appearance of fire, until the morning.

The day that the tabernacle was reared up was the first day of the new year (Exodus 40:1, 2). The first eight and a half chapters of Numbers tell of other events that followed, including the week-long Passover celebration that began on the fifteenth day of the month. Now comes a flashback to the first day of the month. On that day *the cloud covered the tabernacle*, as we have seen from Exodus. However, note that here the tent is called by another name: *the tent of the testimony*, because it held the foundation of God's testimony, or covenant, with Israel—the Ten Commandments (Hebrews 9:4).

16. So it was alway: the cloud covered it by day, and the appearance of fire by night.

Either the *cloud* or the *fire* was always present, as we saw in Exodus. But here Moses speaks of *the appearance of fire* rather than fire itself. This sight looked like fire, but it was no ordinary fire. Perhaps it was similar to that fire in a bush from which God had spoken to Moses when He first called him to go to Egypt. That fire had not burned the bush; this fire on the tabernacle did not burn the tabernacle. But each apparent fire indicated the presence of God.

B. The Cloud and the Journey (vv. 17-23)

17. And when the cloud was taken up from the tabernacle, then after that the children of Israel journeyed: and in the place where the cloud abode, there the children of Israel pitched their tents.

This is very clear, both here and in the text from Exodus.

18. At the commandment of the LORD the children of Israel journeyed, and at the commandment of the LORD they pitched: as long as the cloud abode upon the tabernacle they rested in their tents.

The children of Israel were not merely following a cloud and a fire; they were obeying *the commandment of the Lord*. Obviously the Lord had told Moses at some point that He Himself would direct the movement of the cloud and the fire and that the Israelites were to follow when the cloud moved and remain when it was stationary. Thus, every occasion of the cloud's moving or stopping became a *commandment of the Lord*. The Israelites obeyed.

Moses emphasizes that fact twice in this one verse. Then in the rest of our text he emphasizes it repeatedly. It is as if Moses knew that unbelievers in future times (such as ours) would scoff at the idea that God was really leading those people. Of course, even if Moses did not know that such scoffers would come, God knew and He inspired what Moses wrote. Says a scoffer, "Those people followed wind-driven clouds. It's no won-

der a short trip took them forty years!" But that cloud was not driven by the wind, and that fire was not the glow of the moon on the roof of the tent. God moved both cloud and fire according to His will, and God's people obeyed accordingly. [See question #3, page 48.]

19. And when the cloud tarried long upon the tabernacle many days, then the children of Israel kept the charge of the LORD, and journeyed not.

The emphasis of verse 18 is repeated. *The children of Israel kept the charge* (or command) *of the Lord*. That charge was to hold *when the cloud tarried*, and to move when it moved. Perhaps they were impatient when the cloud *tarried long* and hung motionless for *many days*. However, if the cloud remained still, the people *journeyed not*.

20. And so it was, when the cloud was a few days upon the tabernacle; according to the commandment of the LORD they abode in their tents, and according to the commandment of the LORD they journeyed.

We understood this well enough from the verses before this. Why does Moses emphasize it again? Perhaps he wanted to impress on our minds the weary monotony of those days in the desert. Travelers eager to be on their way to reach the promised land may have groaned when the cloud did not move in the morning. At other times, footsore travelers may have moaned when it did rise and lead them onward. Still, all of them waited or moved *according to the commandment of the Lord*. By doing so they were wise as well as obedient. Without the Lord and His cloud they would have been lost in a trackless desert—and most of them had never been in such country before.

21. And so it was, when the cloud abode from even unto the morning, and that the cloud was taken up in the morning, then they journeyed: whether it was by day or by night that the cloud was taken up, they journeyed.

Today's visual demonstrates that we do not need a pillar of cloud or of fire for God to lead us today. He gives us guidance through His Word, the Bible.

Visual for lesson 5

How to Say It

LEVITES. *Lee*-vites.
SINAI. *Sigh*-nye or *Sigh*-nay-eye.

Sometimes the cloud let the people sleep through the night, then led them on their way in the *morning*. That seems sensible; it's what we do when we're driving thousands of miles across country. But sometimes the *cloud* took off in the *night*, and we wonder why. Consider how, before cars were air-conditioned, motorists in desert country sometimes drove at night, because it was cooler, and then slept by day in air-conditioned motels. But Israel's tents were not air-conditioned. (Have you ever tried to sleep by day in a tent heated by a broiling sun?) Still, resting would expend less energy than traveling; so even if it was not very comfortable, it may have been wiser to rest in the day and to travel in the cool of the night. Whether the people of Israel could understand or not, they obeyed God. [See question #4, page 48.]

22. Or whether it were two days, or a month, or a year, that the cloud tarried upon the tabernacle, remaining thereon, the children of Israel abode in their tents, and journeyed not: but when it was taken up, they journeyed.

Now comes a hint that some of the stops must have seemed unreasonably long to impatient travelers. The people had stayed nearly a year at Sinai, where many of them had been busy preparing different sections of the tabernacle; but now, without such a project to occupy their time, even a month would seem tedious. People who led sheep or goats to pasture would have that leisurely occupation to pass the time, but what would the others do with their time? They had no spare time in Egypt. Could they have known anything about games or other forms of recreation? No doubt they eventually invented some activities to pass the time. Yet whether a stop lasted a night, a *month*, or a *year*, the people obeyed the Lord.

23. At the commandment of the LORD they rested in their tents, and at the commandment of the LORD they journeyed: they kept the charge of the LORD, at the commandment of the LORD by the hand of Moses.

Thus once more Moses repeats what he has been emphasizing in verse after verse. [See question #5, page 48.]

KNOWING WHEN IT IS TIME

The *Old Farmer's Almanac* has been published for more than two hundred years, having had only four owners in all that time. Its cover hasn't been changed since 1851. This implies a respect for the old ways of doing things. No doubt, this is one of the reasons for its popularity. The *Almanac* has long been treasured by its readers as a repository of arcane information: for example, how to build a bat house (to attract these efficient mosquito eaters), and the three best ways to hypnotize your chickens!

We may be amused or amazed by such stuff, but the information for which the *Almanac* is most famous is contained in its weather predictions and its tables of tides and astronomical phenomena. Among those who value these data are sailors, fishermen, and people who plant their gardens by the phase of the moon.

When Israel was encamped in the wilderness, they did not need an almanac to tell them when to move on. God's pillar of cloud and pillar of fire were the sign to them of the divine timing for either continuing or stopping their travels.

Unlike Israel, we are not able to tell with such absolute assurance what God's timing is; however, He has given us His Word so that we can know what He wants us to do. Wisdom suggests that Christians give the same careful scrutiny (and more!) to Scripture as some people do to the *Old Farmer's Almanac*.   —C. R. B.

Conclusion

Do you sometimes envy the people of Israel? Beset by a problem without an answer, or needing a decision and feeling indecisive, do you long for a cloud to guide you by day, or a fire to give light in the darkness?

A. Your Faultless Guide

You do have a faultless guide. Dressed modestly in black leather, or perhaps more brightly in cloth, it lies on the coffee table in your home or stands quietly on the bookshelf. What it is you will find written on the outside: *Holy Bible*.

"I know, I know. The Bible is God's Word. It's always right. I believe it. But the Bible doesn't give specific answers to specific questions."

Sometimes it does. Many of our problems involve choices between truth and falsehood, honesty and deception, generosity and greed, kindness and malice, or helpfulness and selfishness. In such cases you know the Bible's answer without even opening its covers. Yet so often the Bible stands quietly on the shelf, while selfish human nature shouts. Seduced by your own lust or desire (James 1:14), you turn away from the guiding cloud. When you find yourself lost in the desert, you say the Bible has failed you. No, you failed the Bible.

"But I'm trying to decide whether to marry this person or not. The Bible doesn't tell me that."

Maybe it does. Perhaps it doesn't use the exact words of the ceremony, but the Bible does picture marriage as a commitment to love, honor, and cherish a person in sickness and in health, in wealth or in poverty, for better or for worse, as long as you both shall live. If you are not ready to make such a commitment to a certain person wholeheartedly and joyfully, the answer is no. If you see that the other person is not ready to match your commitment, the answer again is no.

"I've been thinking about a job that pays a lot more. The Bible doesn't say yes or no to that."

Maybe it does. If the new job would involve you in anything illegal, anything deceptive, any cheating, or any greedy cruelty to customers or competitors, the answer is no. If the new job would open the way to more unselfish service to God and mankind, the answer may be yes. But even then you have other things to consider. If this attractive job would be so all-engrossing that you would have no time for church, your spouse, or your family, the answer is no.

"Why is it so hard to follow the leading of God's Word?" Two reasons are easily seen.

First, the Bible does not lead unless you listen. You need to spend long hours with the Bible, to make it your friend. You need to read it until the reading is a joy and not a duty, until you pick it up with eagerness and lay it down with regret.

Second, the Bible will not lead unless you follow. It only leads; it does not carry you against your will. It says, "Whosoever hateth his brother is a murderer" (1 John 3:15); but you yourself must pry the hatred from your heart and fill its place with love, love even for an enemy (Matthew 5:44). Clearly the Bible calls you to forgive (Matthew 6:14, 15), but the devil clamors, "Get even! Get even!" You have to choose.

B. Blessed Assurance

"Where was God when my loved one died?"

"Where was God when my mate left me?"

"Where was God when I lost my job?"

Every disaster gives rise to questions like these. When agony at midnight will not let you sleep, wouldn't you love to lift the flap of your tent and see the glow of God's fire telling you He is there?

He is there, if you are trusting Him. His Word tells you that, too, and His Word is as trustworthy as His fire. "He hath said, I will never leave thee, nor forsake thee" (Hebrews 13:5; also Deuteronomy 31:6, 8). Jesus said, "If a man love me, he will keep my words: and my Father will love him, and we will come unto him, and make our abode with him" (John 14:23).

In our grief, our weakness, our fear, God not only is there; He understands. He knows how we feel. "Where was God when my son died?" So wailed a grieving mother, and a wise counselor replied, "He was right where He was when His own Son died." None of our distress is hidden from Him. He knows and He cares.

"Then why doesn't God do something? Why does He allow terrible things to happen to good people?" His Word reminds us, "We know that in all things God works for the good of those who love him" (Romans 8:28, *New International Version*). Like Joseph in the Old Testament, we may not be able to realize how He has worked until some time has passed (Genesis 45:4-8; 50:20). But let's think about our own attitude. Do we have to know all God's reasons? Shall we demand an explanation of everything He does or doesn't do? Or shall we trust Him? If so, we can join in David's confident song to the Lord:

> If I go up to the heavens, you are there;
>   if I make my bed in the depths, you are there.
> If I rise on the wings of the dawn,
>   if I settle on the far side of the sea,
> even there your hand will guide me,
>   your right hand will hold me fast.
>   —Psalm 139:8-10, *New International Version*

C. Prayer

How good it is to know You are with us, Father! Though You are "the high and lofty One that inhabiteth eternity" (Isaiah 57:15), our joys are more delightful and our sorrows are less oppressive because You are here with us. Thank You, Father. In Jesus' name. Amen.

D. Thought to Remember

God is here with us.

Home Daily Bible Readings

Monday, Sept. 27—God's Glory Fills the Tabernacle (Exodus 40:34-38)

Tuesday, Sept. 28—Led by God's Cloud and Fire (Numbers 9:15-23)

Wednesday, Sept. 29—Journeying Away From Mount Sinai (Numbers 10:29-36)

Thursday, Sept. 30—God Keeps His Covenant Forever (Psalm 105:1-15)

Friday, Oct. 1—God Provided for Israel in Egypt (Psalm 105:16-25)

Saturday, Oct. 2—God Sent Plagues Upon Egypt (Psalm 105:26-36)

Sunday, Oct. 3—God Delivered Israel From Egypt (Psalm 105:37-45)

Learning by Doing

This page contains an alternate lesson plan emphasizing learning activities.
Classes desiring such student involvement will find these suggestions helpful.

Learning Goals

As a result of this lesson, your students should be able to:

1. Tell how God led the Israelites by a pillar of cloud by day and of fire at night.

2. Recall significant moments in their lives when God's guidance sustained them.

3. Stay alert to indications of God's guidance through people and circumstances, and thank Him for His guidance.

Into the Lesson

Begin by writing "GOD LEADS US" on the board. That will be the focal point for the lesson.

Probably most of your students will agree that God leads us. However, they may not all agree on the ways that God provides that leadership. Some may say that often it is difficult to tell whether we are following God's leading or our own ideas.

Introduce this lesson on God's leadership by asking each student to select the statement below that most nearly matches how he or she feels about God's leadership in his or her life. (This activity is included in the student book.)

• "I sense God's leadership every day in every phase of my life."

• "I go to God for guidance and leadership whenever I must make a big decision."

• "Most of the time I have a hard time knowing what God wants me to do."

• "I don't need God; I make out okay on my own."

• "I feel a real lack of God's leadership."

Some students may want to talk about God's leadership, but don't push. This lesson will help those who have trouble following God's leadership to move toward a more positive view.

Into the Word

Give half the class a handout that contains the text of Exodus 40:34-38 and the other half one that contains Numbers 9:15-23. Students are to read their texts and underline every phrase that gives information about God's leadership and direction. Suggested responses follow:

• Exodus 40:36—underline the entire verse. God told the Israelites when to go.

• Verse 37—underline the entire verse. God told the Israelites when to stop and how long to stay.

• Verse 38—underline "throughout all their journeys." God's direction continued as long as the Israelites needed it.

• Numbers 9:17—underline the entire verse. God told the people when and where to stop.

• Verse 18—underline the entire verse. God told the people how long to stay where they were.

• Verse 19—underline "when the cloud tarried." God demonstrated His continual presence and leadership. The people did not have to wonder if God was still with them and leading them.

• Verse 20—nothing to underline. This verse emphasizes the people's obedience.

• Verse 21—nothing to underline. This verse also emphasizes obedience to God's leadership, with the added idea that the Israelites followed that leadership whether it was by day or by night.

• Verse 22—underline "whether it were two days, or a month, or a year, that the cloud tarried." The Israelites had to wait for God's direction, and waiting can be difficult.

• Verse 23—underline "at the commandment of the Lord by the hand of Moses." This verse reemphasizes the people's obedience to God's leadership, with the added idea that Moses was involved in communicating God's direction to the people.

Into Life

Use that last idea—that people may be involved in communicating God's direction to us—in order to open the door to a consideration of the means that God uses to tell us what to do and when. We don't have a cloud or a pillar of fire. So what does God use?

Below is a list of suggested ways that God uses to communicate His guidance and direction to us. Ask the students to talk about a time when God used each method in their lives. (You may want to add your own ideas to this list.)

• The Word of God—the Bible.

• A particularly timely sermon.

• The advice of a trusted Christian friend.

• An open door or a closed door.

• A personal disaster or tragedy.

• A hymn or gospel song.

• A Sunday school lesson.

• A book or an article in a Christian magazine.

In closing, challenge your students to thank God for the guidance and direction that He gives.

Let's Talk It Over

The questions on this page are designed to encourage review of the lesson Scriptures and to promote discussion of the lesson by the class. The answers provided are only discussion starters. Let your class talk it over from there.

1. Moses was not able to enter the tabernacle when the "glory of the Lord" filled it. Similarly Isaiah (Isaiah 6) and Peter (Luke 5:8) were overwhelmed by divine glory and felt unworthy of being in the Lord's presence. What occasions or events make you particularly aware of God's glory and make you most appreciative of His grace, without which we could not stand in His presence?

Memories of the time one first came to believe in the Lord—that He is truly the Son of God— surely continue to fill that one with awe. Perhaps some of the members of your class can also tell of times when God revealed His power through some act of providence—a rescue from serious danger or an interruption of plans that turned out to be the best thing that could have happened. Maybe you have your own story to tell to get the discussion started.

2. The cloud or pillar of fire remained above the tabernacle "in the sight of all the house of Israel, throughout all their journeys" to assure the Israelites of God's presence. What assures you of God's presence today? How can you reassure a fellow believer who may doubt the Lord's presence?

How can we doubt God's presence when we can turn at any time to His eternal Word? Jesus and the New Testament writers frequently offered assurance to those who may feel alone. See Matthew 18:20; 28:20; Hebrews 13:5; Revelation 3:20. Many of your students can probably tell of additional assurances provided through experiences when God's presence sustained them through grief or danger or some other problem.

3. The lesson writer points out, "The children of Israel were not merely following a cloud and a fire; they were obeying the commandment of the Lord." How would you support that position if an unbeliever challenged the notion that God had led the Israelites?

More and more the Bible's position on historical facts is being challenged. As with other Biblical miracles, unbelievers seek naturalistic explanations for this one. It is easy for them to imagine the Israelites being so impressed by an enormous cloud formation ahead of them that they fancied it to be a sign from God. But natural clouds do not fit with the Biblical description. They do not move, rest, and later move again, as the pillar of cloud did. They do not turn into a pillar of fire at night. If one accepts that the Israelites followed a cloud at all, then he or she is forced to accept the Biblical explanation. So many will dismiss the entire notion of a cloud, suggesting the whole story was made up later. But then the rest of the Bible's veracity testifies. Again and again archaeology and secular history confirm so much of the Bible that its unconfirmed testimony must also be accepted. No Biblical statement has ever been proven to be false!

4. The lesson writer points out that the Israelites must have found long delays and nighttime travel hard to understand. Still they obeyed. When do you find God's leading or His commands confusing or troubling? What helps you to obey even when you do not fully understand where God is leading?

There is a real danger in obeying only the commands of God that we understand or like. More and more believers seem able to rationalize blatant disobedience by saying, "I know God wants me to be happy, so I know this course of action is okay." In your discussion, be sure you reaffirm the need to obey what we know of God's will even when we do not understand or like what God wants—especially when His will is clearly revealed in His Word.

5. The movement of the pillar of cloud forced the Israelites to depend on God's timing. What do you find difficult about waiting on God's timing? How do you attempt to meet this challenge?

When we pray for a certain blessing, we sometimes tend to set up our own timetable as to the arrival of the answer. Then we fret and fume when our chosen deadline passes. But when the answer at last comes, we see that God's timing was better all along. Remembering such occasions will help us when we find ourselves waiting once again.

Similarly, in our work for the Lord we sometimes think the results of our efforts are not coming. We may complain that God is not blessing those labors in the way we hoped. But again, when His blessing comes, we are able to appreciate how He knows best.

The People's Rebellion

DEVOTIONAL READING: Numbers 14:5-19.

BACKGROUND SCRIPTURE: Numbers 12:1—14:25.

PRINTED TEXT: Numbers 13:1-3, 32—14:4, 20-24

Numbers 13:1-3, 32, 33

1 And the LORD spake unto Moses, saying,

2 Send thou men, that they may search the land of Canaan, which I give unto the children of Israel: of every tribe of their fathers shall ye send a man, every one a ruler among them.

3 And Moses by the commandment of the LORD sent them from the wilderness of Paran: all those men were heads of the children of Israel.

.   .   .   .

32 And they brought up an evil report of the land which they had searched unto the children of Israel, saying, The land, through which we have gone to search it, is a land that eateth up the inhabitants thereof; and all the people that we saw in it are men of a great stature.

33 And there we saw the giants, the sons of Anak, which come of the giants: and we were in our own sight as grasshoppers, and so we were in their sight.

Numbers 14:1-4, 20-24

1 And all the congregation lifted up their voice, and cried; and the people wept that night.

2 And all the children of Israel murmured against Moses and against Aaron: and the whole congregation said unto them, Would God that we had died in the land of Egypt! or would God we had died in this wilderness!

3 And wherefore hath the LORD brought us unto this land, to fall by the sword, that our wives and our children should be a prey? were it not better for us to return into Egypt?

4 And they said one to another, Let us make a captain, and let us return into Egypt.

.   .   .   .

20 And the LORD said, I have pardoned according to thy word:

21 But as truly as I live, all the earth shall be filled with the glory of the LORD.

22 Because all those men which have seen my glory, and my miracles, which I did in Egypt and in the wilderness, and have tempted me now these ten times, and have not hearkened to my voice;

23 Surely they shall not see the land which I sware unto their fathers, neither shall any of them that provoked me see it:

24 But my servant Caleb, because he had another spirit with him, and hath followed me fully, him will I bring into the land whereinto he went; and his seed shall possess it.

GOLDEN TEXT: If the LORD delight in us, then he will bring us into this land, and give it us; a land which floweth with milk and honey. Only rebel not ye against the LORD.—Numbers 14:8, 9.

> *From Slavery to Conquest*
> Unit 2: Wandering in the Wilderness
> (Lessons 5-9)

Lesson Aims

After this lesson a student should be able to:

1. Describe Israel's failure at the border of the promised land, and the tragic result of their failure.

2. Cite examples, from Scripture and their own experience, of both the triumph of living by faith and the tragedy of living in unbelief.

3. Maintain a firm faith in God that is not affected by difficult or challenging circumstances.

Lesson Outline

INTRODUCTION
    A. Tedious Tasks
    B. Lesson Background
  I. FINDING THE FACTS (Numbers 13:1-3, 32, 33)
    A. Chosen Scouts (vv. 1-3)
    B. Fearful Report (vv. 32, 33)
      Toying With the Truth
 II. FAILURE OF FAITH (Numbers 14:1-4)
    A. Mourning (v. 1)
    B. Murmuring (vv. 2, 3)
    C. Rebellion (v. 4)
III. PARDON AND PUNISHMENT (Numbers 14:20-24)
    A. God's Assurance (v. 20)
    B. God's Glory (v. 21)
    C. Failure for the Faithless (vv. 22, 23)
      The Cost of Failing the Test
    D. Success for the Faithful (v. 24)
CONCLUSION
    A. Our Own Migration
    B. Stories of Tragedy and Triumph
    C. Prayer
    D. Thought to Remember

Introduction

A. Tedious Tasks

Are you old enough to remember what a great day it was when the circus came to town? It arrived in its own private train, and everyone who could leave his work went to watch the unloading. That free show was almost as good as the costly one later in the big top.

Wide-eyed we gazed at sleek lions and tigers resting or pacing in huge crates, monkeys leaping and climbing in smaller ones, great plodding elephants supplying power for the derricks that lifted tall poles into place and spread acres of canvas for the low walls and high roof of a tent bigger than Grandpa's barn.

What an equally busy scene there must have been when Israel's caravan came to a camping place! Can you imagine tents being set up all at once to shelter three million people, including shepherds and herdsmen trying to keep their sheep and cattle out of the way, and Levites carefully assembling the tabernacle in the middle of the camp?

You and I might have found it exciting to watch that busy scene a few times; but those doing the work must have found it monotonous and tiresome, particularly when they had to do it on several consecutive days. But if the cloud guiding them moved, that was their signal to move. No doubt they were grateful for some mornings when the guiding cloud did not stir from the Lord's tent, and the people did not have to stir from theirs.

B. Lesson Background

The people of Israel had been at Sinai for nearly a year. Probably there was joy in the camp when the cloud rose in the air, indicating that it was time to move on. Better still, the cloud led them north, toward the promised land! They left Sinai on the twentieth day of the second month (Numbers 10:11); and when they came to Kadesh at the other side of the desert, the grapes were beginning to get ripe (Numbers 13:20). That may have been somewhere in the fifth month, thus making a three-month trip for the Israelites.

From the camp in Kadesh the people could look northward into Canaan. This was the promised land, the land flowing with milk and honey. This was the home for which they had endured months of grueling travel in the desert. But now, with the promised land closer than ever, the people hesitated.

I. Finding the Facts
(Numbers 13:1-3, 32, 33)

At this point, the adventurers grew cautious. They came to Moses with a request that spies be sent to study the land so that the people could be better prepared for the task ahead of them (Deuteronomy 1:19-23).

A. Chosen Scouts (vv. 1-3)

1. And the LORD spake unto Moses, saying.

The idea of studying the land and planning how to take it sounded good to Moses (Deuteronomy 1:23), but apparently he did not want to give his approval without asking *the Lord*. Now we will read the Lord's answer.

2. Send thou men, that they may search the land of Canaan, which I give unto the children of Israel: of every tribe of their fathers shall ye send a man, every one a ruler among them.

The Lord told Moses to do what the people asked—to send a team of *men* to *search the land* that they hoped to call their home. Usually these men are referred to as "spies," since their primary purpose was "to spy out the land" (v. 16). Capturing that land was a project for the entire nation, so every *tribe* was to appoint a representative to be part of the team of spies. Each representative was to be a recognized leader (literally, the Hebrew word translated *ruler* means "one lifted up," thus, a prominent man in his tribe). [See question #1, page 56.]

3. And Moses by the commandment of the LORD sent them from the wilderness of Paran: all those men were heads of the children of Israel.

Having received divine approval for this plan, Moses, *by the commandment of the Lord*, now dispatched the men who had been selected as spies. Here they are called *heads*, a term that again highlights their leadership role.

Verses 4-31, omitted from our printed text, tell about the expedition. The spies' names are given in verses 4-16. They were to see if the defenders of Canaan were strong or weak and few or many, if the land was productive or barren, if the people lived in tents or in fortified cities, and if there was "wood" (trees) to be found in the land (vv. 17-20). In forty days they traveled approximately two hundred miles northward and searched the land thoroughly (vv. 21, 22).

When the men returned from their expedition, they brought good news and bad news. First, the land was indeed rich and fruitful. They brought samples of its produce to prove so (vv. 23-27). That was encouraging. Second, the defenders of the land were many and strong, and their cities were fortified. That was frightening (vv. 28, 29). One of the spies (Caleb) was bold and confident: "Let us go up at once, and possess it; for we are well able to overcome it" (v. 30). But most of the group had a different opinion: "We be not able to go up against the people; for they are stronger than we" (v. 31).

B. Fearful Report (vv. 32, 33)

32. And they brought up an evil report of the land which they had searched unto the children of Israel, saying, The land, through which we have gone to search it, is a land that eateth up the inhabitants thereof; and all the people that we saw in it are men of a great stature.

An evil report means an unfavorable report. True, the land was fertile and productive (v. 27), but the spies said that other factors made it undesirable. They claimed that *the land . . . eateth up the inhabitants thereof*. Most likely they were referring to the gigantic men living there, who were accustomed to overpowering and destroying weaker peoples who lived near them.

Such a negative report as this came from a frightened, faithless imagination. In addition, the spies' claim that **all** *the people* were *men of a great stature* was wildly exaggerated, if not utterly false. The spies had gone through the territory of several peoples. It is hard to believe that *all* the people they saw were giants.

33. And there we saw the giants, the sons of Anak, which come of the giants: and we were in our own sight as grasshoppers, and so we were in their sight.

It is quite possible that the spies did see a tribe with men who appeared to be *giants*; but the wild exaggeration of scared men is clear once again in the words, *We were in our own sight as grasshoppers*. [See question #2, page 56.]

TOYING WITH THE TRUTH

Marxist Communism gained a reputation for rewriting history to suit its political or social agenda. For example, when Nikita Khruschev was ousted from power in a bloodless coup in 1964, his name was quickly removed from history books and his face was even removed from official photographs. Then in the middle 1980s, when *perestroika* ("openness") became the new program in Russia, Khruschev's name and face were restored to history because his existence now served official government policy. Other Soviet notables experienced the same fate.

Perhaps it should not surprise us that ten of Israel's spies, for reasons rooted in lack of trust in God, gave a false report about the promised land. They probably could rationalize their falsifications to their own satisfaction, but a good cause is never served by this kind of behavior.

How to Say It

ANAK. *Ay*-nack.
CANAAN. *Kay*-nun.
KADESH. *Kay*-desh.
KADESH-BARNEA. *Kay*-desh-*bar*-nee-uh (strong accent on *bar*).
KHRUSCHEV. *Kroosh*-eff.
LEVITES. *Lee*-vites.
PARAN. *Pair*-un.
PERESTROIKA. pair-ih-*stroy*-kuh.

In Western society today, government officials, political action groups, advertisers, and even Christian ministries have been known to "massage" the truth. More than anyone else, *Christians* should be known for their careful, truthful handling of the facts. —C. R. B.

II. Failure of Faith
(Numbers 14:1-4)

At this point Caleb seemed to stand alone against all the other spies (Numbers 13:30, 31), but later we are told that Joshua was as firm and fearless as Caleb (14:6-9). Thus ten frightened men stood against two confident ones. It is not surprising to see that the people agreed with the frightened majority.

A. Mourning (v. 1)

1. And all the congregation lifted up their voice, and cried; and the people wept that night.

What a disappointment! These people had traveled many weary miles to find a land flowing with milk and honey. But now it appeared that they could not enter it after all.

Such grief as this could not be kept silent. The Israelites *lifted up their voice, and cried.* Darkness fell, but no one slept in Israel's camp. *The people wept that night.*

B. Murmuring (vv. 2, 3)

2. And all the children of Israel murmured against Moses and against Aaron: and the whole congregation said unto them, Would God that we had died in the land of Egypt! or would God we had died in this wilderness!

Soon the people's mourning was mixed with anger. Who was to blame? Why, *Moses* and *Aaron,* of course! They had enticed the people out of Egypt with promises of bliss, only to have their hopes dashed. They would have been better off if they had *died in the land of Egypt* or somewhere along that tiresome *wilderness* route than to be slaughtered by giants in Canaan!

Note that these words would later come back to haunt the people, for they indeed *died in this wilderness* because of their unbelief (vv. 28, 29).

3. And wherefore hath the LORD brought us unto this land, to fall by the sword, that our wives and our children should be a prey? were it not better for us to return into Egypt?

On second thought, the angry people could see that there was too much blame to be borne by Moses and Aaron alone. *The Lord* had enticed them out of Egypt. His cloud and fire had drawn them over those weary miles to this terrible end. Now the men of Israel would be butchered by the swords of giants, and their *wives* and *children*

would be forced into abject slavery. Ironically, however, God later declared that those children, whom they thought faced certain doom, would enter the land (v. 31).

Negative thinking seldom stops with one discouraging thought. Especially within a group, it is easy for such thoughts to "snowball" and become worse. Here, as the people's thinking became more and more dismal, they began to entertain another thought: wouldn't it be *better for us to return into Egypt?*

C. Rebellion (v. 4)

4. And they said one to another, Let us make a captain, and let us return into Egypt.

Driven by fear, the people's thinking rushed on into even greater folly. "Wouldn't it be better?" became "Let's do it!" A plot was hatched to replace Moses with another leader and to go back over all those weary miles to the slavery from which they had fled. [See question #3, page 56.]

According to verses 11-19 (not in our printed text), the Lord suggested a simple way of dealing with the rebels. He could destroy them all, and make Moses the father of a new nation that would carry out His plan. Immediately Moses protested. That plan would severely damage the Lord's own reputation. All the world knew that He had brought the people of Israel out of Egypt to lead them to Canaan. If He destroyed them now, all the world would think that He was unable to do what He had planned. Moses pleaded for pardon for the rebels.

III. Pardon and Punishment
(Numbers 14:20-24)

A. God's Assurance (v. 20)

20. And the LORD said, I have pardoned according to thy word.

The Lord *pardoned* the rebels: that is, He did not execute them for their treason. That did not

TEN + FEAR = FAILURE
TWO + FAITH = VICTORY

Today's visual demonstrates that "majority rule" is not always right; faith alters the equation. Discuss how we can stand up for our faith even when a vocal majority opposes us.

Visual for lesson 6

mean that their faithlessness and disobedience would make no difference.

B. God's Glory (v. 21)

21. But as truly as I live, all the earth shall be filled with the glory of the LORD.

As we read this verse in the *King James Version*, it seems to say that the Lord would not let the rebellion rob Him of His *glory*. He still would carry out His plan of bringing His people to the land He had promised them. *All the earth* would see it and give Him honor. More than that, His people living in the promised land would do what He had chosen them to do. They would bring into the world the Savior who would offer salvation to the whole world, thus fulfilling God's promise to Abraham, "In thee shall all families of the earth be blessed" (Genesis 12:3).

The *New International Version* interprets the verse in a different way: "As surely as I live and as surely as the glory of the Lord fills the whole earth." This means that God's declaration in verse 23 is as certain as are His existence and the presence of His glory in the earth.

C. Failure for the Faithless (vv. 22, 23)

22. Because all those men which have seen my glory, and my miracles, which I did in Egypt and in the wilderness, and have tempted me now these ten times, and have not hearkened to my voice.

The *men* of Israel had shown caution when they asked Moses to send spies to explore the promised land, but their caution had turned to cowardice when they refused to advance into the land and take possession of it. Their cowardice was inexcusable because they had *seen* God's *glory* in the cloud that led them (Exodus 16:10), on Mount Sinai (Exodus 24:16), and in

the tabernacle in the midst of their camp (Exodus 40:34). In addition, the people had *seen* His *miracles*, which had demonstrated both His unconquerable power and His favor toward His people. Still, they did not have faith enough to move into the land God had given them, trusting Him for safety and victory.

Each time the people had *tempted* the Lord (that is, tested Him), they had shown their lack of faith. Sometimes the phrase *ten times* seems to mean many times (repeatedly) rather than an exact number. Whether the number is literal or figurative here, it illustrates the repeated faithlessness of Israel. The incidents of the Israelites' testing God are recorded in Exodus 15:22—17:7. They are mentioned in Psalms 78:40, 41; 95:8-11; 106:13-33; 1 Corinthians 10:1-11; Hebrews 3:8, 9.

23. Surely they shall not see the land which I sware unto their fathers, neither shall any of them that provoked me see it.

The men of Israel had tested God often. Now, all those twenty years or older, who were earlier counted in the census, would never be allowed to live in the promised *land* (vv. 29, 30).

THE COST OF FAILING THE TEST

There seems to be no end to the schemes people come up with to make money at the expense of others. A business known as Test-A-Mate is a good example. If you think your husband or wife could be tempted into being unfaithful to you, for $250 you can hire Test-A-Mate to "test your mate."

Here's how it works: the suspicious mate looks at a photo album of attractive models for the person to whom he (or she) thinks his mate might be attracted. This person is then sent to the mate's favorite restaurant, health club, or other place where he or she socializes. The decoy does not initiate any conversation; but if the mate does, Test-A-Mate will report on whatever degree of unfaithfulness develops.

Suppose a husband or wife succumbs to the temptation, but later is sorry for having done so. The seeds of doubt have already been sown and may flower into a divorce. Or suppose the mate does not succumb, but finds out about the other's lack of confidence in him or her. What then? The result may still be a broken marriage, even though the suspicious mate may regret having ever initiated such foolishness.

We often forget that sorrow for sin or stupidity may be genuinely felt and expressed, but there are always consequences to our attitudes and actions. Israel discovered this fact of life to its deep regret. The people's lack of faith cost a whole generation the opportunity to enjoy the land that God had promised them.   —C. R. B.

D. Success for the Faithful (v. 24)

24. But my servant Caleb, because he had another spirit with him, and hath followed me fully, him will I bring into the land whereinto he went; and his seed shall possess it.

Caleb had not doubted, feared, or rebelled. Trusting the Lord, he had strongly urged the people to go on into the promised *land* without delay (Numbers 13:30). Therefore, he would be allowed to enter that land, to possess a share of it, and to pass it on to his children (*his seed*). Joshua had been as faithful and obedient as Caleb had (Numbers 14:6-9), and he, too, would find a home there (v. 30). [See question #4, page 56.]

But all of that was yet to occur. For now, rebellious Israel must turn back into the wilderness, and wander there until all the adults twenty years and older were dead. Of that faithless generation, only faithful Caleb and Joshua would survive to see the land conquered. The next generation, matured and toughened in the arid desert, would finally receive the promised land. With God's help they would make it their own.

Conclusion

A. Our Own Migration

Chapter 10 of 1 Corinthians (verses 1-11) points out that Israel's migration is a picture of our own. God has liberated us from the bondage of sin to lead us home to everlasting joy. Our journey leads through this world's wilderness. It, too, is a land of many hardships, but God is leading all the way. He will not fail us nor forsake us. Will we fail Him?

Some Christians lose their nerve when hardships come. They test God with reckless and repeated disobedience, and they die in the wilderness. Others find God's power for overcoming hardship, and they become stronger (James 1:2-4). [See question #5, page 56.]

B. Stories of Tragedy and Triumph

Sam manages a supermarket in our town. He does it well, and his salary provides a good living for him and his family. But Sam is not happy. Ten years ago he owned a bigger store in a bigger town, but that store burned down. Too late, Sam realized that he had let the insurance lapse. He was penniless until he found a job in our town.

Sam was a deacon in the church in that other town, but now he is furious whenever the minister goes to visit him. "Don't talk to me about church!" he storms. "I'm through with God! What did He ever do for me?"

Sam is prosperous now, but how will his story end? Will his final tragedy be worse than the loss of his store?

Holding a "middle management job" with a big firm, Mark was comfortable and happy. He was popular at work, at church, and at the tennis club. Then the firm "downsized," and Mark found himself unemployed. Jobs were available, but they were minimum-wage jobs. Mark scorned them. He had no one but himself to support; he figured he could live on unemployment compensation and his savings. When those resources were exhausted, Mark still scorned minimum-wage work. He took his gun to the next town and robbed a bank; but he was careless about it, and soon he was caught with the loot.

In prison, Mark feels abused. "I didn't do anything wrong," he says. "Not till I had to. Why is the Lord doing this to me?"

What kind of an ending do you foresee for Mark's story? Is there anything he can do to provide a happier one?

Martha is fifty-five years old. Her thirty-year-old son is seriously ill with tuberculosis. The doctor told her that a dry climate might help him, so the two of them drove to Arizona. They were nearly out of gas and money when they came to a little town at the edge of the desert. Martha left her sick son sleeping at the motel while she went to church. Then wonderful things began to happen. Friendly Christians helped Martha find a job. The only vacant house in the little town was too decrepit to be lived in, but men of the church gave it a new roof while women cleaned the inside. With a laugh, the owner said that their work had paid the rent for a year. He himself contributed an old refrigerator, and the women stocked it with food. The newcomers moved in, and neighbors heard Martha singing, "Praise God from whom all blessings flow," as she prepared breakfast.

That's a happy story, yet Martha's son remains very ill. Trouble and grief surely lie ahead—but don't you predict a glorious ending?

You write your own story by what you do while traveling through the deserts of life. Do you want a happy ending?

C. Prayer

Forgive us, Father. Too often we have failed You. Through laziness, selfishness, or fear, we have ignored Your leading. Forgive us, please, and continue to lead us. In Jesus' name. Amen.

D. Thought to Remember

Will my life have a happy ending? I must begin *now* to see that it will.

Learning by Doing

This page contains an alternate lesson plan emphasizing learning activities.
Classes desiring such student involvement will find these suggestions helpful.

Learning Goals

After this lesson a student should be able to:

1. Describe Israel's failure at the border of the promised land, and the tragic result of their failure.

2. Cite examples, from Scripture and their own experience, of both the triumph of living by faith and the tragedy of living in unbelief.

3. Maintain a firm faith in God that is not affected by difficult or challenging circumstances.

Into the Lesson

Begin by telling the adults in your class to imagine they are on a safari. Late one afternoon their vehicle has engine trouble and stops. Since it is too dangerous to camp out in the wild, the guide wants to push ahead on foot to the next station. Even though the road ahead passes through rough and hazardous terrain, he is confident that the entire group can make it. The others in the group want to go back. They would like to go forward, but they are afraid.

If your students were in that safari group, what would they do? At Kadesh-barnea, God challenged the Israelites to go forward in faith and enter the promised land. He set before them a choice: overcome obstacles by faith, or shrink back in unbelief.

Into the Word

Divide the class into three-person groups. Tell each group to compare and contrast the two accounts of the sending out of the spies in Numbers 13:1-3 and Deuteronomy 1:19-24. How are the two accounts alike? How are they different?

(They are alike in that both accounts report there were twelve spies, one from each tribe, and that the spies were sent to check out Canaan. The biggest difference is that the Numbers account reports that God told Moses to send the spies, but in Deuteronomy the plan originated with the people.) Observe that the accounts in Numbers and Deuteronomy have a different perspective, but they are not contradictory. The people could have suggested the plan, and God commanded Moses to go along with them.

Note that there is a significant difference in perspective from the two groups of spies. The ten faithless spies were looking at the conquest of Canaan from a human perspective—they knew they could not defeat the Canaanites in

their own strength. Caleb and Joshua were looking at the conquest from God's perspective.

Divide the class into three groups, and assign each group one of these passages: Numbers 14:1-4; 14:20-23; 14:24. The members of each group should look for the "key idea" in their passage.

• Verses 1-4: Faithlessness is contagious and infectious. Faithlessness opens the door to discontent and despair. We often want to blame someone else for the results of our own choices.

• Verses 20-23: Wrong choices bring negative consequences.

• Verse 24: Right choices bring rewards.

Into Life

Many adults are influenced by the opinions of others and are reluctant to go against the crowd. It is not necessarily wrong to do something simply because everyone else is doing it, but rebelling against God and shirking back from the challenges He places before us is always wrong no matter who else is doing it.

Discuss the following situations. Ask the students how they would classify the person's actions in each situation: rebellion against God's will, going along with the crowd, accommodation for the sake of convenience, compromise, or some other.

• A. Charlie is invited out to lunch with some guys at work. When he finds out they are going to a place that has exotic dancers, he wants to say no. But he's afraid of what the guys will think of him. So he keeps quiet and goes along.

• B. Some ladies from church get together every Tuesday for a Bible study. Grace used to enjoy the fellowship, but for the past few weeks one of the ladies has been making hateful comments about a family who just moved into the neighborhood. Grace wants to say something, but she's reluctant to confront the other woman. So she says nothing.

• C. The man with whom Frank carpools to work has no use for God or religion. He knows Frank is a believer, and early on said he would tolerate no talk of Christ or religion. In spite of that, Frank feels he should talk to this man about Christ. However, he doesn't want to risk losing his ride to work, so he says nothing.

In closing, challenge the adults to have the courage to trust God and do the right thing in difficult situations.

Let's Talk It Over

The questions on this page are designed to encourage review of the lesson Scriptures and to promote discussion of the lesson by the class. The answers provided are only discussion starters. Let your class talk it over from there.

1. God consented to the people's wishes to investigate the land of Canaan before invading it—even though, by divine foreknowledge, He surely knew what would result. What does that suggest to you about the way God allows us to choose our own course—even when we are wrong? How do we know when God is opening a door and when He is allowing a wrong course of action?

It is easy to look at circumstances that are favorable to our own chosen course of action and decide that God is opening a door for us. But circumstances are not a clear indicator of God's leading. Our own faith is a major factor—the faithless Israelites were looking for a guarantee of ease, which they did not find. Learning the way would be challenging, they withdrew. If our "open door" is also the easy way, we may simply be going the way of sight and not of faith.

2. In their unbelief the ten spies seemed to exaggerate the size and strength of Canaan's inhabitants. How are we similarly tempted to exaggerate the magnitude of our problems? How can we keep things in perspective?

Even the best of us may exaggerate our problems. The prophet Elijah, in the time of King Ahab and Queen Jezebel, lamented that he was the only faithful one left alive. God informed him that seven thousand other faithful followers remained in Israel (1 Kings 19:14-18). Such exaggeration is an example of failure of faith, and only faith can put things back into perspective. Let your students share some Bible verses that help restore their faith, or let them volunteer other ways they regain perspective, like talking with a person of faith or getting involved in a ministry activity that takes their focus off themselves and their problems.

3. The Israelites were ready to replace Moses with another leader and return to their slavery in Egypt. That seems ridiculous to us today, but many believers do essentially the same thing. Some may forget that they are saved by grace and stray back into the attitude of trying to earn their place in Heaven. (See Galatians 2:16-21; 5:1-6.) Some succumb to the temptation to return to a sinful habit that they had forsaken for Christ. Some believers give up their freedom

in Christ when they allow themselves to be dominated by a cult leader's personality and align with his cult. What can we do to maintain our freedom and to resist the lure of these and other rivals?

Perhaps some of your students will recount the kind of slavery from which they have found deliverance and how they cling to their freedom in Christ. Others may have confronted cults or other forms of false doctrine, and they can tell how they stood firm. The truth of the Word of God will be significant in these stories, as the believers were able to compare the false doctrines with the truth of the Word. Support from other true believers must surely have helped them also.

4. Caleb and Joshua are famous for their unpopular minority report. When have you had to make such an unpopular stand for God and His Word? How can we prepare ourselves to make such a stand?

It is important that we learn to value God's approval far above that of our fellow human beings. We must avoid the error of those Jewish leaders in Jesus' time who "loved the praise of men more than the praise of God" (John 12:43). Furthermore, we must approach life with a view toward the eternal more than the temporal.

Allow your students to describe how they have taken a stand at their places of work, in political discussions, at school, or even at home. Encourage those who may be making such a stand on a regular basis.

5. How can we learn to take a positive view of hardships so that we may grow stronger through them?

A review of past experiences will probably be helpful. We are almost certain to find that periods of hardship have been occasions of our most significant growth. When life is trouble-free, we tend to become complacent. But God gives us hardships to force us into His Word and onto our knees.

In addition to our own experiences, those of Bible people are also helpful. We remember Paul and his famous "thorn in the flesh." Through it he discovered that God's power could work best through his human weakness (2 Corinthians 12:7-10).

The Desert Years

October 17
Lesson 7

DEVOTIONAL READING: Isaiah 35.

BACKGROUND SCRIPTURE: Deuteronomy 1:26—2:25.

PRINTED TEXT: Deuteronomy 1:41—2:8.

Deuteronomy 1:41-46

41 Then ye answered and said unto me, We have sinned against the LORD, we will go up and fight, according to all that the LORD our God commanded us. And when ye had girded on every man his weapons of war, ye were ready to go up into the hill.

42 And the LORD said unto me, Say unto them, Go not up, neither fight; for I am not among you; lest ye be smitten before your enemies.

43 So I spake unto you; and ye would not hear, but rebelled against the commandment of the LORD, and went presumptuously up into the hill.

44 And the Amorites, which dwelt in that mountain, came out against you, and chased you, as bees do, and destroyed you in Seir, even unto Hormah.

45 And ye returned and wept before the LORD; but the LORD would not hearken to your voice, nor give ear unto you.

46 So ye abode in Kadesh many days, according unto the days that ye abode there.

Deuteronomy 2:1-8

1 Then we turned, and took our journey into the wilderness by the way of the Red sea, as the LORD spake unto me: and we compassed mount Seir many days.

2 And the LORD spake unto me, saying,

3 Ye have compassed this mountain long enough: turn you northward.

4 And command thou the people, saying, Ye are to pass through the coast of your brethren the children of Esau, which dwell in Seir; and they shall be afraid of you: take ye good heed unto yourselves therefore:

5 Meddle not with them; for I will not give you of their land, no, not so much as a foot-breadth; because I have given mount Seir unto Esau for a possession.

6 Ye shall buy meat of them for money, that ye may eat; and ye shall also buy water of them for money, that ye may drink.

7 For the LORD thy God hath blessed thee in all the works of thy hand: he knoweth thy walking through this great wilderness: these forty years the LORD thy God hath been with thee; thou hast lacked nothing.

8 And when we passed by from our brethren the children of Esau, which dwelt in Seir, through the way of the plain from Elath, and from Ezion-gaber, we turned and passed by the way of the wilderness of Moab.

Oct 17

GOLDEN TEXT: For the LORD thy God hath blessed thee in all the works of thy hand: he knoweth thy walking through this great wilderness: these forty years the LORD thy God hath been with thee; thou hast lacked nothing.—Deuteronomy 2:7.

From Slavery to Conquest
Unit 2: Wandering in the Wilderness
(Lessons 5-9)

Lesson Aims

After this lesson students should be able to:
1. Tell why the children of Israel were punished with wandering in the wilderness, and summarize their experience there.
2. Relate an example (from Scripture or from personal experience) that illustrates the tragic consequences of disobeying God.
3. Commit themselves to more consistent involvement in the work of the church so that God's kingdom can go forward.

Lesson Outline

INTRODUCTION
  A. No Irrigation Needed
  B. Lesson Background
  I. THE WANDERING BEGINS (Deuteronomy
    1:41—2:1)
  A. Warning Given (vv. 41, 42)
  B. Warning Ignored (v. 43)
  C. Tragic Consequences (vv. 44-46)
    Failing to Reach the Goal
  D. Further Travels (2:1)
    Condemned to Wander
 II. THE WANDERING ENDS (Deuteronomy 2:2-8)
  A. God's Instructions (vv. 2-6)
  B. God's Guidance (v. 7)
  C. On to Canaan (v. 8)
CONCLUSION
  A. God's Time Is Best
  B. Counting the Cost
  C. Counting the Resources
  D. Prayer
  E. Thought to Remember

Introduction

A. No Irrigation Needed

"The desert shall rejoice, and blossom as the rose" (Isaiah 35:1). Proudly the guide leading our tour of the Holy Land quoted this prophecy, pointing to wide green fields of wheat where only desert had been not long before. When the nation of Israel was reborn in the twentieth century, soon its people were pumping water from the Sea of Galilee in the north and transporting it through miles of canals to irrigate the desert of the Negev in the south.

As the Israelites stood on the brink of entering the promised land, Moses told them that this land was very different from Egypt, where they had lived so long in bondage. Whereas in Egypt the land was watered "with thy foot" (probably a reference to irrigation channels that were dug by foot), the promised land required no irrigation whatsoever (Deuteronomy 11:10, 11). The people would have so much land that they would not need to cultivate the desert of the Negev. Their country would be a place of abundance, "a land flowing with milk and honey" (Exodus 3:8).

B. Lesson Background

Near the end of their wandering in the desert, the people of Israel came again to the border of the promised land. This time they camped east of the Jordan River. There Moses made a lengthy speech to the nation (Deuteronomy 1:3). He reviewed their forty years in the desert; he repeated the laws God had given; he urged the people to be obedient to God. We take a portion of that speech for today's printed text. We begin with Moses' review of what happened following the events that were the subject of our lesson last week.

I. The Wandering Begins (Deuteronomy 1:41—2:1)

The Israelites had expressed fear, not faith, after they heard the spies' report concerning the land of promise. Because of their unbelief, all the adults twenty years and older (except for faithful Caleb and Joshua) were sentenced to death in the wilderness. Only their children (who they had claimed would perish) would be allowed to enter the land. Deuteronomy 1:40 records these tragic words of the Lord following the people's rebellion against Him: "But as for you, turn you, and take your journey into the wilderness by the way of the Red sea."

A. Warning Given (vv. 41, 42)

41. Then ye answered and said unto me, We have sinned against the LORD, we will go up and fight, according to all that the LORD our God commanded us. And when ye had girded on every man his weapons of war, ye were ready to go up into the hill.

At first the rebels admitted their wrongdoing. They had *sinned* in refusing to advance at the Lord's command, they said. However, they then proceeded to disobey God yet again by refusing to follow His command to turn back into the wilderness. Instead, they determined to *go up and fight*, as they should have done earlier. Apparently they thought the prospect of dying in the desert was worse than the prospect of being killed by the giants in the promised land. So they *girded on* (tied around the waist) their swords and prepared to go *into the hill* (meaning the higher country).

42. And the LORD said unto me, Say unto them, Go not up, neither fight; for I am not among you; lest ye be smitten before your enemies.

God gave His answer through Moses. This latter disobedience was no better than the former one. The rebels should obey God's latest command and turn back into the wilderness. It was too late to obey the earlier order that they had refused to obey—the command to go forward and *fight* for the promised land. God would no longer be *among* them in such an effort, so they would be *smitten before* their *enemies*.

B. Warning Ignored (v. 43)

43. So I spake unto you; and ye would not hear, but rebelled against the commandment of the LORD, and went presumptuously up into the hill.

Moses delivered God's message; however, as one might expect by now, the rebels paid no attention. They ignored God's latest directive, and instead obeyed the earlier one that He had now countermanded. *Presumptuously*—choosing their own way in defiance of God's clear command—they went *into the hill* country to battle the residents of the promised land.

C. Tragic Consequences (vv. 44-46)

44. And the Amorites, which dwelt in that mountain, came out against you, and chased you, as bees do, and destroyed you in Seir, even unto Hormah.

Here the word *mountain* describes a highland region rather than a single peak (much as "hill" in verses 41 and 43 actually refers to hill country). The men of Israel proceeded to enter the territory north of their camp. *The Amorites* who lived there were one of the peoples whom God had commanded the Israelites to destroy once they entered the promised land (Deuteronomy 7:1, 2). But here the Amorites *came out* and *chased* the Israelites *as bees do*. This presents a vivid picture to anyone who has seen a panic-stricken man running madly, hands flailing wildly at a swarm of hostile bees buzzing around his head. It suggests that the men of Israel panicked and took to their heels, hotly pursued by a swarm of Amorites who struck down as many as they could.

We do not know exactly where *Hormah* was. It appears to have been located northeast of Kadesh-barnea, within approximately ten miles of Beersheba. Most significant to note here is that rebellious Israel suffered a quick and disastrous defeat. [See question #1, page 64.]

45. And ye returned and wept before the LORD; but the LORD would not hearken to your voice, nor give ear unto you.

When the Amorites stopped chasing the Israelites, the survivors *returned* to their camp and *wept before the Lord*. We are not told just what feelings made them weep. Were they merely grieving for their comrades killed by the Amorites? Were they angry with themselves, weeping with shame and sorrow because they had run away rather than fight? Were they angry with the Lord because He had not helped them, even though He had told them plainly that He would not (v. 42)? Were they weeping tears of repentance and promising not to disobey again? Or were several or all of these feelings mingled in their grief? Whatever their feelings were, the facts are plain. They had turned their backs on God, and now His back was turned on them. [See question #2, page 64.]

We must remember that Moses was telling of this tragedy approximately thirty-eight years after it happened. He said *ye* and *you*, meaning the men of Israel; but the men actually involved in that tragedy were no longer living. They had died in the desert. Some of Moses' hearers had been children when that attack had failed; some had been born since that time. Now they were coming to the border of the promised land. From the disaster of their fathers, they could learn that it is better to obey God: to advance when He commands, and not to advance when He forbids. This is why Moses' review of the people's history at this time was so important.

How to Say It

AMORITES. *Am*-uh-rites.
AQABA. *Ock*-uh-buh.
ARABAH. *Air*-uh-buh.
BEERSHEBA. Beer-*she*-buh.
DEUTERONOMY. Due-ter-*ahn*-uh-me.
EDOM. *Ee*-dum.
EDOMITES. *Ee*-duh-mites.
ELATH. *Ee*-lath.
EZION-GABER. *Ee*-zee-on-*gay*-ber (strong accent on *gay*).
HORMAH. *Hor*-muh.
KADESH-BARNEA. *Kay*-desh-*bar*-nee-uh (strong accent on *bar*).
MOAB. *Mo*-ab.
NEGEV. *Neg*-ev.
SEIR. *See*-ir.

46. So ye abode in Kadesh many days, according unto the days that ye abode there.

Perhaps those *many days* were days of mourning for the men who had been killed. Perhaps they were days of indecision. It is not likely that anyone wanted to try another attack, but perhaps some wanted to return to Egypt. Perhaps the Lord's guiding cloud hung motionless, because the Lord wanted His people to have time to think. In that campsite the people had twice disobeyed Him. Perhaps those many days of thinking produced a resolution not to disobey God again.

FAILING TO REACH THE GOAL

"You can live to be one hundred!" Promises of long life are the standard pitch for many fad diets. Dr. Stuart Berger was a nutritionist who developed the "Immune Power Diet" and wrote a book titled *Forever Young.* He claimed he could treat cancer and other serious ailments with proper diet and vitamins. But just a few years ago, Dr. Berger died in his sleep at age forty. It seems he could not follow his own dietary advice: he weighed 365 pounds when he died.

J. I. Rodale, a publisher of magazines devoted to health, claimed that he would live to be a hundred; but he died of a heart attack at age seventy-two. Many others, both legitimate doctors and "quacks," have promised that their diet, vitamin combination, exercise regimen, or brand of secret-formula elixir would help one to live longer and better than would normally be expected.

Living to be one hundred is a "promised land" of sorts. Yet most people will not reach it, in part because they don't live up to what they know about good nutrition and a healthy lifestyle.

In that respect, most of us are like the Israelites: they knew what it would take to reach the promised land, but lacked the self-discipline to make it happen. The promised land was a reachable goal, and God would have helped them attain it; but they were disappointed because they failed to accept the challenge.   —C. R. B.

Visual for lesson 7

The visual for today's lesson recalls several events from Israel's experience. Discuss what the people ought to have learned from each event.

D. Further Travels (2:1)

2:1. Then we turned, and took our journey into the wilderness by the way of the Red sea, as the LORD spake unto me: and we compassed mount Seir many days.

As we look at the Red Sea on the map (page 5), we see that the north end of it is divided into two narrow arms. The west arm is called the Gulf of Suez. That is the part of the Red Sea that the people of Israel crossed as they were leaving Egypt (see lesson 2, page 19). In the first part of this week's text, Israel was encamped at Kadesh, near the southern boundary of the promised land. Now, in the latter part of our text, we read that the people *turned* and went back toward the south, but not to Sinai. They went *by the way of the Red sea*—that is, toward that small east arm of the Red Sea, the Gulf of Aqaba. We know this is the direction they traveled, because *Seir* is the country between that gulf and the Dead Sea. It is about a hundred miles long from south to north.

For the people to have *compassed mount Seir* means that they traveled about in the high country of Seir. In other words, they lived as nomads, moving about to find pasture for their livestock in a region where pasture was scanty. That continued for *many days,* thus completing the Israelites' time of wandering in the desert after leaving Kadesh. [See question #3, page 64.]

CONDEMNED TO WANDER

Fourteen-year-old Jeff Thornton loved to ride his snowboard in the ski areas of the mountains above Los Angeles. As he started his snowboard run on the afternoon of February 7, 1998, fog was beginning to settle in. He became disoriented, lost sight of the signs marking the snowboarding trail, and was soon wandering in the uninhabited mountain wilderness. For six days Jeff stumbled aimlessly in seventy-mile-an-hour winds, subfreezing cold, and snowfall so heavy that rescuers had to call off their search because of "whiteout" conditions.

Then (ironically on Friday the 13th) Jeff was found alive, but with lowered body temperature and severe frostbite. Family and friends rejoiced at the "miracle" and prayed for Jeff's recovery. But as often happens in such cases, his frozen body tissue caused an infection that spread throughout his body. One week after he was found, Jeff died of respiratory problems and heart failure. The wilderness had claimed its victim after all.

The Israelites' lack of faith in God caused them to lose their way spiritually, and they were condemned to wander in another kind of wilderness—the desert of Sinai. Many of them never got out of that wilderness alive. Their wanderings were the direct result of their failure to see the signs that would have kept them "on the trail" to the promised land.   —C. R. B.

II. The Wandering Ends (Deuteronomy 2:2-8)

A. God's Instructions (vv. 2-6)

2, 3. And the LORD spake unto me, saying, Ye have compassed this mountain long enough: turn you northward.

The Lord had declared that Israel must live in the desert forty years, because the people had refused to take the promised land when He first had led them to it (Numbers 14:33, 34). That time was now drawing to a close. It was time to move *northward* toward the promised land. [See question #4, page 64.]

4. And command thou the people, saying, Ye are to pass through the coast of your brethren the children of Esau, which dwell in Seir; and they shall be afraid of you: take ye good heed unto yourselves therefore.

The Israelites were to *pass through the coast* (the territory along the border) *of* their *brethren the children of Esau*, whose descendants (the Edomites) now lived in Seir (Genesis 36:8, 9). Esau was nicknamed Edom, which means "red," because he was fond of red lentil stew (Genesis 25:29, 30). The nation descended from him is usually called Edom, and his descendants are called Edomites (Genesis 36:9). At this time the heathen tribes living in the promised land had become intolerably wicked. The Lord ordered Israel to "utterly destroy" them (Deuteronomy 7:1, 2; 20:16, 17). But the people of Esau (Edomites) were not included in that sentence of destruction. Israel must continue to regard them as *brethren* and show no hostility toward them.

5. Meddle not with them; for I will not give you of their land, no, not so much as a footbreadth; because I have given mount Seir unto Esau for a possession.

The land promised to Israel did not include a single foot of the *land* of the Edomites. Israel must pass through that territory, but they must take care not to disturb its people.

6. Ye shall buy meat of them for money, that ye may eat; and ye shall also buy water of them for money, that ye may drink.

In the *King James Version*, *meat* means food of any kind. The people of Israel had been living on manna for nearly forty years; likely they would be happy to eat something else for a change. They could *buy* it from the Edomites for a fair price, but they must not take it by force or by threat of force. They must pay even for the *water* they would *drink*, for water was scarce in that country. The people of Israel could afford to pay for these items, for they had taken large amounts of silver from the Egyptians as they were leaving that country (Exodus 12:35, 36).

B. God's Guidance (v. 7)

7. For the LORD thy God hath blessed thee in all the works of thy hand: he knoweth thy walking through this great wilderness: these forty years the LORD thy God hath been with thee; thou hast lacked nothing.

The Lord had *blessed* His people during all those years in the *wilderness*. They had *lacked nothing* because He had provided manna every day and had brought water from a rock when it was needed. Their clothes had not worn out in forty years (Deuteronomy 8:4). Surely they could trust the Lord to provide for them in the present and the future. [See question #5, page 64.]

C. On to Canaan (v. 8)

8. And when we passed by from our brethren the children of Esau, which dwelt in Seir, through the way of the plain from Elath, and from Ezion-gaber, we turned and passed by the way of the wilderness of Moab.

This verse indicates that the Israelites obeyed the Lord's instructions: they *passed by . . . the children of Esau* in a friendly way. They traveled over *the way of the plain* ("the Arabah road" in the *New International Version*) which ran northward from *Elath* and *Ezion-gaber*, located at the northern edge of the Gulf of Aqaba. They then approached *Moab*, which lay east of the Dead Sea. There again they avoided conflict. Instead of entering Moab, they passed by *the way of the wilderness of Moab*, which followed the eastern border of Moab. In this way they reached the Jordan River north of the Dead Sea, where they prepared to cross into their new home.

Conclusion

There is a tide in the affairs of men,
Which, taken at the flood, leads on to fortune;
Omitted, all the voyage of their life
Is bound in shallows and in miseries.

In Shakespeare's imagination, those words expressed Brutus's thinking as he planned a crucial battle; and those same words express a truth that is seen in many other enterprises:
There is an opportune time!

A. God's Time Is Best

It appeared that the turning point of Israel's migration toward Canaan came at Kadesh. The desert was behind them; the promised land was before them; the Lord was with them. This was the time God had chosen for them to sweep onward like a flood, to overwhelm their enemies, and to take possession of the land He had given them. But in their timid minds the fear of giants conquered their faith in God. The men of Israel let a golden opportunity slip away, and lived the rest of their lives in the desert.

God's time is always best, but it is not always so easy to see. Do we need more room in our auditorium, our Sunday school classrooms, or our parking lot? Do we need a youth minister, an assistant minister, or a special minister to senior members? How do we know when God would have us supply any or all of these needs?

If more room would enable us to win more people to Christ and to salvation, isn't that a clear indication that now is the time to provide more room? If a youth minister can turn more young people from darkness to light and from the power of Satan to God, doesn't God want that to happen now? If a minister of education can devise a program that will speed Christian growth in all of us, what are we waiting for? If we see a capable person available for any needed ministry, that is an added indication that God's time is now.

B. Counting the Cost

Most of us are practical people and cautious about undertaking any big enterprise. We recall that Jesus spoke of counting the cost. If we begin a great work and can't finish it, we invite the contempt of our neighbors instead of their respect. That is clear in Luke 14:25-33.

What does it cost to follow Jesus? It costs all you have. Some of the multitude heard that and said it was too much, but others decided to pay it. Countless others have been willing to do so

---

Home Daily Bible Readings

Monday, Oct. 11—Moses Reminds Israel About Horeb (Deuteronomy 1:1-8)

Tuesday, Oct. 12—Tribal Leaders Are Appointed (Deuteronomy 1:9-18)

Wednesday, Oct. 13—Israel Refuses to Obey God (Deuteronomy 1:19-23)

Thursday, Oct. 14—Israel Is Punished for Disobedience (Deuteronomy 1:34-45)

Friday, Oct. 15—Israel Wanders in the Wilderness (Deuteronomy 1:46—2:15)

Saturday, Oct. 16—A Generation of Warriors Passes Away (Deuteronomy 2:16-25)

Sunday, Oct. 17—Israel Begins the Conquest of Canaan (Deuteronomy 2:26-37)

---

since then, and that is why the Christian enterprise is still growing. It is still worth the price one pays.

The men of Israel pretended to count the cost of invading the promised land. They claimed that such a venture would cost the lives of all of them, plus the freedom of their wives and children (Numbers 14:3). But that was not really a count; it was a wild exaggeration born of terror. We need an honest count.

C. Counting the Resources

The frightened men of Israel exaggerated the cost and underestimated their resources. They seemed to think that they had nothing but their own strength. God was with them, but they ignored Him. They appeared to forget that He still had the power that had overcome Egypt, the Red Sea, and all the dangers of the desert. God continues to do marvelous things through those people who are fully committed to Him.

Members of one church extended themselves to enlarge their meeting place, only to find that the added space was useless because there was no room in the parking lot. Some of them were in despair; but after much thought and prayer, the elders proposed the following:

"We're giving all we can to keep up the payments on our bigger place of worship. Now we have to have a bigger parking lot. Obviously we have to give more than we can. Let's think—every person, every family—think of some sacrifice, something we can do without."

One family decided their old station wagon could last another year, and then they found that it lasted *two* years. Another gave up a long-planned trip to Washington, DC. A single man took a part-time job in addition to his regular work. Youngsters gave up movies and candy and snacks, and found lawn-mowing and baby-sitting jobs.

As a result, the parking lot was doubled, and the church grew so rapidly that the loans were paid off in half the expected time. A little later the church employed its very own missionary in a distant land. The pain of sacrifice was forgotten in the joy of accomplishment.

D. Prayer

Teach us to put away our selfishness, Father. As You continually give to us, help us to give more of our time, more of our energy, more of our money, and more of ourselves in doing what You want us to do, and in doing it now. In our Master's name. Amen.

E. Thought to Remember

You can do more than you think you can.

Learning by Doing

This page contains an alternate lesson plan emphasizing learning activities.
Classes desiring such student involvement will find these suggestions helpful.

Learning Goals

After this lesson students should be able to:

1. Tell why the children of Israel were punished with wandering in the wilderness, and summarize their experience there.

2. Relate an example (from Scripture or from personal experience) that illustrates the tragic consequences of disobeying God.

3. Commit themselves to more consistent involvement in the work of the church so that God's kingdom can go forward.

Into the Lesson

Ask your students to review their lives over the past year. Then ask, "What is one thing you did in the past twelve months that you would like to be able to go back and do differently?" Discuss things they did that they would like not to have done, or that they did not but wished they had. What choices or decisions would they make differently?

Remind your students of the choices that the Israelites made at Kadesh-barnea. (We learned about those choices in last week's lesson.) They decided to rebel against and disobey God. No doubt during the thirty-eight years they spent in the desert they wished many times for an opportunity to go back and relive those decisions.

Into the Word

In today's lesson the Israelites were again at the threshold of the promised land. Moses reviewed past failures and challenged his people to go forward in faith this time.

Ask a student to read Deuteronomy 1:41—2:8 while the rest of the class listens for things the Israelites did wrong the first time at Kadesh-barnea. After the reading, ask, "What mistakes did the Israelites make?"

- They disobeyed and rebelled against God (v. 26).
- They spoke evil against the Lord (v. 27).
- They failed to listen to God, again rebelled, and acted presumptuously (v. 43).
- Because of their disobedience, they were defeated in battle (v. 44).

Now tell the students to suppose that the Israelites could have gone back and relived what they did at Kadesh-barnea. What do your students think they would have done differently? How would Israel's history have been changed?

Write the following clichés on the chalkboard. Ask your students to describe incidents in today's Bible passages that illustrate each cliché.

- "We reap what we sow." *(When the Israelites sowed rebellion at Kadesh, they reaped thirty-eight years of wandering in the desert.)*
- "We don't want something until we are told we cannot have it." *(When God told the Israelites to turn back into the desert, they suddenly wanted to invade Canaan.)*
- "Doing the right thing at the wrong time is the same as doing the wrong thing." *(When God said "Go," the people said "No." When God said "No," the people said "Let's go.")*

Into Life

To apply today's lesson, say, "At one time or another, we all go through desert experiences. Do you agree? If so, describe some of your desert experiences and what you have learned from them."

After some discussion, point out that we all suffer for our mistakes. Some of those mistakes are honest errors of judgment, but many of our mistakes are sparked by a rebellious and selfish attitude. For example, an unfaithful husband may come to regret the affair that broke up his marriage; a dishonest worker will likely regret the petty thievery that cost him his job; a tongue-wagging neighbor soon regrets the gossip that ruined a friendship; and a self-absorbed son will eventually regret the vicious and hateful words that drove a spike into his relationship with his father.

As the Israelites looked back on the thirty-eight years they had spent in the desert, they realized that God had been with them and taken care of them. Even though the sin of rebellion had sent them into the desert, God had not abandoned them.

In closing, ask your students where they are in relation to the desert. Are they bitter at God and blaming Him for their desert experience? Are they suffering from the heat and sandstorms, but learning and growing? Or are they at the edge of the desert, praising God for His care and deliverance in bringing them through?

Challenge your students to thank God during the coming week for His presence, even when circumstances are difficult and they must spend time in the desert.

Let's Talk It Over

The questions on this page are designed to encourage review of the lesson Scriptures and to promote discussion of the lesson by the class. The answers provided are only discussion starters. Let your class talk it over from there.

1. Having been rebuked for not going up into the land of Canaan, the Israelites attempted too late to obey the Lord and to take the land. They were soundly defeated. What are some modern examples when delayed obedience may fail? If we have been slow to obey, is it better not to? Why or why not?

The Israelites' failure was actually one of continued disobedience. Having failed when God told them to take the land, the Israelites were then told not to go up; but they disobeyed the latter command as they had the former.

The commands we find in the Bible are more general than the specific command God gave the Israelites. For example, we have been commanded to make disciples (Matthew 28:19, 20). If we have been slow to obey that command, we need to seek to obey it as soon—and as often—as possible. We may find, however, that in specific cases slow obedience may result in the loss of opportunity. If a neighbor is receptive to the gospel message and we fail to tell him or her, we may find later that the receptivity is gone and our opportunity for obedience is lost with it.

2. The Israelites wept before the Lord after their defeat at the hands of the Amorites, but He did not respond to their tears. Suppose a young Christian read this and said, "I am afraid that is how God will respond to my prayers—that He will not listen. How can I be sure He will listen to my prayers?" How would you answer?

God refused to listen to the Israelites because they refused to listen to Him. They were sorry they were defeated in battle; they were sorry they were punished for their sin; they were not sorry they had disobeyed. Like a loving Father, God is always moved by the penitent prayers of His children. But, also like a good parent, God will not be manipulated by His children when they wail about the consequences of their own actions but are unwilling to change their behavior.

3. The Israelites experienced years of wandering as a result of their disobedience. If a person or church seems to be "wandering"—just maintaining, showing no obvious signs of growth—is that evidence of disobedience? Why or why not? What should a "wandering" person or church do to make progress?

We must be careful not to judge by outward appearances. A person or church may appear not to be growing because the growth is internal, spiritual, or otherwise not obvious. Eventually, this kind of growth will break forth in observable growth, but it may take a while. Sometimes a person or church endures trials that some might mistake for punishment. Only the person or church involved can determine why growth is not more obvious. If sin is the problem, then repentance is called for. On other occasions, however, endurance may be what is needed.

4. After years of "going nowhere," the Israelites were told, "Turn you northward." Of course, there is nothing special or spiritual about the direction north, but for Israel it meant going in the right direction to reach their goal. In what way do you need to "turn you northward"? How can you do that?

Perhaps there are some who attend your class who have not given due consideration to making a commitment to the Lord. They need to stop going nowhere and turn to the Lord. Others have been in the church for a long time but have never got involved in ministry. It's time they became useful as a part of the Lord's body. Whatever a person's need, he or she must start with an honest evaluation of where he or she is in relation to the Lord. Then a combination of Bible study and counsel with a good Christian friend will help the person to do what he or she needs to do to start making progress toward the goal.

5. In spite of Israel's disobedience God provided for their physical needs throughout the years of wandering. How can we use the fact of God's continual provision for the physical needs of our unsaved friends to lead them to Christ?

We can note that Jesus said the heavenly Father "maketh his sun to rise on the evil and on the good, and sendeth rain on the just and on the unjust" (Matthew 5:45). We can observe that Christians and non-Christians alike share God's blessings as well as the pain and sorrows associated with this life. But Christians have a hope for the future that helps them to see God's grace even in the hard times. Having an answer for the hope that is within us may be just what it takes to lead one of our non-Christian friends to the Lord.

The Great Commandment

DEVOTIONAL READING: Deuteronomy 30:11-20.

BACKGROUND SCRIPTURE: Deuteronomy 6.

PRINTED TEXT: Deuteronomy 6:1-9, 20-25.

Deuteronomy 6:1-9, 20-25

1 Now these are the commandments, the statutes, and the judgments, which the LORD your God commanded to teach you, that ye might do them in the land whither ye go to possess it:

2 That thou mightest fear the LORD thy God, to keep all his statutes and his commandments, which I command thee, thou, and thy son, and thy son's son, all the days of thy life; and that thy days may be prolonged.

3 Hear therefore, O Israel, and observe to do it; that it may be well with thee, and that ye may increase mightily, as the LORD God of thy fathers hath promised thee, in the land that floweth with milk and honey.

4 Hear, O Israel: The LORD our God is one LORD:

5 And thou shalt love the LORD thy God with all thine heart, and with all thy soul, and with all thy might.

6 And these words, which I command thee this day, shall be in thine heart:

7 And thou shalt teach them diligently unto thy children, and shalt talk of them when thou sittest in thine house, and when thou walkest by the way, and when thou liest down, and when thou risest up.

8 And thou shalt bind them for a sign upon thine hand, and they shall be as frontlets between thine eyes.

9 And thou shalt write them upon the posts of thy house, and on thy gates.

. . . .

20 And when thy son asketh thee in time to come, saying, What mean the testimonies, and the statutes, and the judgments, which the LORD our God hath commanded you?

21 Then thou shalt say unto thy son, We were Pharaoh's bondmen in Egypt; and the LORD brought us out of Egypt with a mighty hand:

22 And the LORD showed signs and wonders, great and sore, upon Egypt, upon Pharaoh, and upon all his household, before our eyes:

23 And he brought us out from thence, that he might bring us in, to give us the land which he sware unto our fathers.

24 And the LORD commanded us to do all these statutes, to fear the LORD our God, for our good always, that he might preserve us alive, as it is at this day.

25 And it shall be our righteousness, if we observe to do all these commandments before the LORD our God, as he hath commanded us.

Oct 24

GOLDEN TEXT: Hear, O Israel: The LORD our God is one LORD: and thou shalt love the LORD thy God with all thine heart, and with all thy soul, and with all thy might.—Deuteronomy 6:4, 5.

From Slavery to Conquest
Unit 2: Wandering in the Wilderness
(Lessons 5-9)

Lesson Aims

After completing this lesson students should be able to:

1. Memorize the "great commandment" as found in Deuteronomy 6:4, 5.

2. Tell how the principles for teaching God's Word that are found in today's text apply to modern life.

3. Suggest a plan by which God's will can be communicated more effectively within their homes and to other family members.

Lesson Outline

INTRODUCTION
  A. Israel's Government
  B. Lesson Background
I. ISRAEL AND GOD'S LAW (Deuteronomy 6:1-9)
  A. Results of Obedience (vv. 1-3)
  B. Loving God and His Laws (vv. 4-6)
  C. Teaching God's Laws (vv. 7-9)
    The Tragedy of Neglect
II. FOR ALL GENERATIONS (Deuteronomy 6:20-25)
  A. Future Question (v. 20)
  B. God's Mighty Acts (vv. 21-23)
  C. God's Righteous Laws (vv. 24, 25)
    Keeping a Memory Alive
CONCLUSION
  A. Loving God and His Word
  B. Obeying God's Word
  C. Teaching God's Word
  D. Prayer
  E. Thought to Remember

Introduction

For years the western world has attempted to live by the system of government known as democracy (rule of the people) rather than monarchy (one-man rule). One-man rule is deemed unsatisfactory because the person in power too often becomes greedy and corrupt. In 1215 the English barons forced King John to approve the Magna Carta, which limited the king's power and protected the rights of the barons. Later developments limited the power of the monarch even more, and protected the rights of common people as well as barons.

When the United States came into being near the end of the eighteenth century, its people were determined to be their own rulers. They devised a Constitution for that purpose, and then added ten amendments to protect the rights of the people even more from despotic government. In this new country every man had a part in ruling; it was the very opposite of one-man rule. Through more than two hundred years that nation has been, for the most part, successful; but we all know that its success has been marred many times because ruling commoners can become as corrupt and greedy as ruling kings.

A. Israel's Government

When Israel came out of Egypt to begin its life as a nation, its government was neither one-man rule nor government by the people. It was one-God rule. The Lord gave the laws; the duty of the people was to obey. History shows both the strength and the weakness of such a nation. Its strength lay in God. His wisdom was flawless. The nation prospered whenever the people obeyed the laws He made. Its weakness lay in the people. Often they did not obey, and poverty and disaster were the result.

It seems that no form of government can work very well without good people.

B. Lesson Background

After living for forty years in the desert, the people of Israel came toward the border of the promised land. This was the second time they had approached this good land, for they had failed in their first opportunity to take possession of it. They camped east of the Jordan River, where Moses talked with them for a lengthy period of time. Last week we considered his brief review of their life in the desert and of God's instructions to them when it was time for them to resume their journey toward Canaan. Today we come to a bit of what he said about the law and about the people's responsibility to keep it and to pass it on to their children. Such teaching was essential if the promised land was to remain their home.

I. Israel and God's Law
(Deuteronomy 6:1-9)

The book of the Bible from which we are reading is called Deuteronomy. That title means "second law" or "repeated law." Chapter 5 tells us that Moses repeated the Ten Commandments, which we studied last month from Exodus 20. Deuteronomy 5 also records that Moses urged the people to obey God's commandments. Chapter 6 continues that exhortation and also encourages the people to think about the obedience of the next generation as well as the present one.

A. Results of Obedience (vv. 1-3)

1. Now these are the commandments, the statutes, and the judgments, which the LORD your God commanded to teach you, that ye might do them in the land whither ye go to possess it.

At Mount Sinai the people had been terrified by the awesome signs of God's presence on the mountain. They had begged that God would not speak to them directly, but would let Moses relay His commands. So the Lord had given the rest of His laws through Moses (Deuteronomy 5:22-31). Now, some forty years later, Moses was repeating those laws. Some of his hearers had been children when the laws first were given; others had been born later.

2. That thou mightest fear the LORD thy God, to keep all his statutes and his commandments, which I command thee, thou, and thy son, and thy son's son, all the days of thy life; and that thy days may be prolonged.

Why did God order Moses to give those laws to the people? Three reasons are given: first, so they would *fear the Lord*; second, so they would *keep* (obey) the laws, not only in that generation, but in all generations to come; and third, so their lives would be *prolonged*. God's laws prescribed a healthful and righteous way of living, and that would result in longer life. Long life is specifically tied to the command to honor one's father and mother (Deuteronomy 5:16).

3. Hear, therefore, O Israel, and observe to do it; that it may be well with thee, and that ye may increase mightily, as the LORD God of thy fathers hath promised thee, in the land that floweth with milk and honey.

Fervently Moses urged his people to obey God's laws, and he continued to relate the beneficial results of obedience. It would *be well* with obedient people: they would have peace, prosperity, good health, and long life. They would *increase mightily* in numbers, in wealth, and in power. The promised land was before the Israelites, *the land that floweth with milk and honey;* but it would withhold its plenty if the people were disobedient.

B. Loving God and His Laws (vv. 4-6)

4. Hear, O Israel: The LORD our God is one LORD.

Notice the word *is* in your Bible. In many editions it will appear in italics. That means the word is not found in the original Hebrew; it is inserted by the translators. Hebrew writers often left out the linking verb *is* or *are*. In most cases

the meaning is easily understood without it. For example, when a child just learning to talk says, "Milk good," we know he means, "Milk *is* good." But sometimes a different meaning is found by inserting *is* in a different place. In text and footnotes, the *New International Version* lists four possible translations of the second part of verse 4:

The Lord our God, the Lord is one.
The Lord our God is one Lord.
The Lord is our God, the Lord is one.
The Lord is our God, the Lord alone.

Each of these statements is true, and each is appropriate in this context; so which one did Moses have in mind? Perhaps all of them! Remember, the linking verb was not left out accidentally, as if by a child. Moses wrote with full understanding of the dynamics of the Hebrew language. The omission of the linking verb allows a fuller meaning than if we try to insert the verb and limit the meaning to that conveyed by one English construction. Surely all believers will agree with the truths expressed in all of these statements: the Lord is Israel's God, He is one God, and He is the only God.

5. And thou shalt love the LORD thy God with all thine heart, and with all thy soul, and with all thy might.

Since there is only one God, His people should give Him their total devotion. They should *love* Him, and love Him with all that is in them. It is not that *heart* and *soul* and *might* describe separate parts of an individual; rather, all of them together designate the whole person, and *all* of all of them are devoted to the Lord. When this is true, serving the Lord is a joy rather than a burden; obeying His commands is a happy choice rather than a dismal duty. [See question #1, page 72.]

6. And these words, which I command thee this day, shall be in thine heart.

Moses' voice was speaking *these words*, but they were the Lord's words (v. 1). When the Lord occupies one's whole heart, the Lord's words are there with him. One wholly devoted to the Lord finds delight in hearing them, learning them, and obeying them.

C. Teaching God's Laws (vv. 7-9)

7. And thou shalt teach them diligently unto thy children, and shalt talk of them when thou sittest in thine house, and when thou walkest by the way, and when thou liest down, and when thou risest up.

Everyone who has children should give careful attention to this verse. It says much about how to teach God's Word. Such teaching cannot be limited to a few minutes of family devotion, or to a daily half hour of Bible study. It cannot be left to the Sunday school. Even a Christian day school cannot take the place of the parents' teaching. Consider the various "classrooms" described in this verse:

The first is *when thou sittest in thine house.* How many of the children's quarrels can be resolved by a careful application of "Thou shalt not covet" (Exodus 20:17) or "Thou shalt love thy neighbor as thyself" (Leviticus 19:18)?

The second is *when thou walkest by the way.* A roadside tavern may provide an opportunity to teach what God says about the evils of drunkenness. Or if the child recognizes a friend's bicycle parked several houses away from where it belongs, that is a good time to teach a child that God does not endorse the "finders keepers" philosophy, but says we must return the lost property to its owner (cf. Exodus 23:4).

When thou liest down at night is a good time to recall any laws that have been broken by children or parents, and to ask forgiveness.

When thou risest up is a good time to sing, "This is the day which the Lord hath made; we will rejoice and be glad in it" (Psalm 118:24). That was first sung long after Moses' time, but it has been adapted to a happy chorus in our time and our language. Do you ever sing it in the morning before going to work?

THE TRAGEDY OF NEGLECT

Tragic stories began to come out of Eastern Europe soon after the breakup of the Soviet Union. Tales of government abuse, corruption, and malfeasance in office told us how hypocritical were the claims that Marxist Communism was the means to creating a "workers' paradise."

There were perhaps no more heart-rending stories than those that told of children in the state-run nurseries of Communist Romania. Children in these nurseries showed abnormally high levels of stress hormones and demonstrated terrible physical and mental retardation.

Such a scenario is not surprising. Even laboratory experiments with animals have shown us that separation of babies from their mothers and neglect by their caregivers causes an abnormal number of their brain cells to "commit suicide," in the chilling words of one science commentator. The lifelong effect is seen in serious behavior problems, apathetic spirits, learning difficulties, and patterns of chronic illness.

God, of course, knew the effects of parental neglect when He told the Israelites to give special attention to their children, especially when it came to teaching them the laws of God. Parental failure to attend to a child in his or her spiritual development can have even more tragic effects than physical deprivation. —C. R. B.

8. And thou shalt bind them for a sign upon thine hand, and they shall be as frontlets between thine eyes.

Pious Jews of later times took this literally, putting short passages of Scripture in small leather cases tied to their hands and foreheads. These "phylacteries" (cf. Matthew 23:5) may have been better reminders than strings tied on fingers, but surely the Lord's real intent is that His laws should guide all the doing of the *hand*, all the seeing of the *eyes*, and all the thinking of the head. [See question #2, page 72.]

9. And thou shalt write them upon the posts of thy house, and on thy gates.

This too was taken literally in later times. Even today some homes have on the doorposts small leather or metal cases with Scripture verses inside. These too may be useful reminders, but again the figurative meaning is greater: in the morning go out your door to be honest and generous in all your dealings, as God's law demands; in the evening come in to kind and loving family relationships. [See question #3, page 72.]

II. For All Generations
(Deuteronomy 6:20-25)

The laws that Moses was repeating were not only for the people who heard him; they were for all the coming generations of Israelites.

A. Future Question (v. 20)

20. And when thy son asketh thee in time to come, saying, What mean the testimonies, and the statutes, and the judgments, which the LORD our God hath commanded you?

In time to come looks to the future, to the time when Israel would be settled in its new home. It speaks of the continual need for faithful parental training. The fact that the child is the one who initiates this conversation about spiritual matters implies that the parents have been diligent in making such matters a priority. They have created a desire in their children to know more.

The word *mean*, like the *is* in verse 4, is printed in italics in many editions of the Bible. It is not in the Hebrew text, but is supplied by the translators. The answer that follows suggests that the question is not really a request for an explanation of meaning, but asks for general

---

How to Say It

DEUTERONOMY. Due-ter-*ahn*-uh-me.
EGYPTIANS. Ee-*jip*-shuns.
PHYLACTERIES. fih-*lack*-ter-eez.

Today's visual illustrates the important practice of teaching God's Word to our children. Discuss creative ways parents can do this.

Visual for lesson 8

information. A boy of our time and language might ask, "What about those laws? Where did they come from? Why are they so important?" Such concerns are addressed in the answer.

B. God's Mighty Acts (vv. 21-23)

21. Then thou shalt say unto thy son, We were Pharaoh's bondmen in Egypt; and the LORD brought us out of Egypt with a mighty hand.

The parent's answer should begin with a lesson in history. *The Lord* had rescued the people of Israel from slavery *in Egypt* and had led them to freedom. *A mighty hand* describes His tremendous power in action—power enough to overwhelm great Egypt, and power enough to open a path through the sea. Parents could fill in those details and more for inquiring children.

22. And the LORD showed signs and wonders, great and sore, upon Egypt, upon Pharaoh, and upon all his household, before our eyes.

Again the parents could supply details, describing the ten plagues that had driven *Egypt* and *Pharaoh* to surrender. Only God could do such *signs and wonders.*

23. And he brought us out from thence, that he might bring us in, to give us the land which he sware unto our fathers.

The Lord not only brought Israel *out from* slavery to freedom; He also brought them *in* to a marvelously fruitful *land* that could supply all their needs. From all these facts it was evident that Israel was greatly indebted to the Lord. [See question #4, page 72.]

C. God's Righteous Laws (vv. 24, 25)

24. And the LORD commanded us to do all these statutes, to fear the LORD our God, for our good always, that he might preserve us alive, as it is at this day.

These statutes came from *the Lord*—the One to whom Israel was deeply indebted. Simple gratitude should motivate every Israelite to obey. If that were not enough, God's people ought to *fear*

Him and be afraid to disobey. They knew about the plagues that had afflicted the disobedient Egyptians (Exodus 7:14—11:10). Surely they did not want to experience such affliction.

Another truth that should never be forgotten is expressed here: fearing and obeying God is for our good always. God's obedient people are the ones He keeps *alive.* That had been vividly illustrated in the sight of those who were listening to Moses. More than six hundred thousand men of Israel had been disobedient thirty-eight years earlier, refusing to enter the promised land (Deuteronomy 1:19-40), and all those disobedient men had died. Their sons and daughters stood at the border of the promised land. Couldn't they see how important it was to obey God and to teach all future generations to obey Him?

KEEPING A MEMORY ALIVE

During the 1950s James Dean was a popular film star. He was also a rebellious idol of many teenagers. Dean was only twenty-four years old when he died tragically in 1955. He was driving his Porsche sports car north from Los Angeles to Salinas, California, when, at about the halfway point of his trip, another car turned left into his path. Dean died instantly in the collision.

Three days after Dean's death, Warner Brothers released "Rebel Without a Cause"—a film in which he had starred—and a rather peculiar fascination with James Dean resulted. Even today, more than four decades later, Dean's memory is renewed annually when his fans trace the route Dean took the day he died. On the anniversary of his death, participants in the "Rebel Run" drive old cars from the 1950s and stop for a few moments at the places where Dean stopped on that fateful day: a gas station, a snack bar, and a country store. Their drive ends at the corner where Dean's life ended.

Much less bizarre (and far more useful) is the tradition initiated by the words of our text today. When children of the Israelites would ask why they kept the words of God, they would be told, not of a drive to death, but of an escape to life. God had set their ancestors free from slavery in Egypt, and the laws and customs of their nation were a timeless reminder of God's goodness. The people were to focus on the victorious beginning of their nation, not on the end of a short but rebellious life.   —C. R. B.

25. And it shall be our righteousness, if we observe to do all these commandments before the LORD our God, as he hath commanded us.

It shall be our righteousness. To right-thinking people, this is very persuasive. Obeying God is right, and that is reason enough to do it. It does please God, yes; and it is *for our good always* (v. 24). But even if doing right brings loss or injury, God's people must still do it.

Conclusion

Clearly our text presents three great themes: loving God and His Word, obeying God's Word, and teaching God's Word. Adapted to the New Covenant, these are as important to Christians today as they were to the Israelites in Moses' day.

A. Loving God and His Word

This lesson is titled "The Great Commandment." That title focuses our attention on verse 5 of our text: "Thou shalt love the Lord thy God with all thine heart, and with all thy soul, and with all thy might." Jesus said, "This is the first and great commandment" (Matthew 22:38). To it verse 6 of our text adds, "And these words, which I command thee this day, shall be in thine heart." God's people not only love God; they also love the words He speaks. Through what He does we know of His power, His greatness, and His majesty; through what He says we learn of His will.

When two people fall in love, all of us notice how they like to be together. They make appointments to meet; they part reluctantly. So when we love God and His words, we spend much time with them, and we do it gladly. If your Bible reading is no more than five minutes before breakfast, you reveal that His words have not taken possession of your heart. [See question #5, page 72.]

B. Obeying God's Word

When people are in love, selfishness fades. Each one wants to please the other. When we love God, we do what He wants us to do. Serving Him is not a burden, but a joy (1 John 5:3). If we find obedience distasteful, we need to examine our love.

We build on a solid foundation when we listen to Jesus and do what He says to do (Matthew 7:24-27). James urges, "Be ye doers of the word, and not hearers only" (James 1:22). When Jesus said that the first and great command is the command to love God, He added that a second and similar command is this: "Thou shalt love thy neighbor as thyself" (Matthew 22:39; Leviticus 19:18). One who loves God must love his brother also (1 John 4:21). Such love is expressed in helpfulness, and loving helpfulness is part of the path to a blessed eternity (Matthew 25:31-40). This does not mean that we earn Heaven by doing good on earth; but God prepares Heaven for those who love Him, and He gives Heaven to those who show their love by their obedience.

C. Teaching God's Word

If you don't teach God's Word to your children, who will? The public school will not, and that means that for the children who go there a large part of the day is closed to Christian teaching. The public school supervisor of the playground may teach something about fair play and sharing, but she is not likely to mention God. Other children on the street will not help your children learn God's Word. Most TV programs will not help. Who will be talking about God's Word "when thou sittest in thine house, and when thou walkest by the way, and when thou liest down, and when thou risest up"?

Most children will never get such constant teaching except from parents and others whom parents thoughtfully provide. If you employ sitters, do you choose those capable of Christian teaching? If your children are in day care, is Christian teaching done there?

Do you search your Christian bookstore for books that will help your children know God? Or what workable plan can you yourself devise for teaching God's Word "diligently unto thy children"?

D. Prayer

Please help us, Father. There are so many things we have to do! We do love You. We do want the children to know You and to be glad in Your daily presence. We're trying, Father. Please help us. In Jesus' name. Amen.

E. Thought to Remember

You cannot teach another about God and His Word until *you* know God and His Word.

Home Daily Bible Readings

Monday, Oct. 18—God's Great Commandment to Israel (Deuteronomy 6:1-9)

Tuesday, Oct. 19—Do Not Follow Other Gods! (Deuteronomy 6:10-19)

Wednesday, Oct. 20—Tell of God's Mighty Acts! (Deuteronomy 6:20-25)

Thursday, Oct. 21—Chosen by God's Love and Grace (Deuteronomy 7:6-11)

Friday, Oct. 22—Blessing of Obedience (Deuteronomy 10:12-22)

Saturday, Oct. 23—A Land of Milk and Honey (Deuteronomy 11:8-12)

Sunday, Oct. 24—Love God and Teach Your Children (Deuteronomy 11:13-21)

Learning by Doing

This page contains an alternate lesson plan emphasizing learning activities.
Classes desiring such student involvement will find these suggestions helpful.

Learning Goals

As a result of this lesson, your students should be able to:

1. Memorize the "great commandment" as found in Deuteronomy 6:4, 5.

2. Tell how the principles for teaching God's Word that are found in today's text apply to modern life.

3. Suggest a plan by which God's will can be communicated more effectively within their homes and to other family members.

Into the Lesson

If there are parents in your class, introduce this lesson on teaching spiritual truths to children by asking, "What do you say when one of your children asks you, 'Mom/Dad, why do we do it this way?'" In the question, "it" could refer to any custom, tradition, or practice.

How many students are willing to admit that they have given one of the following "explanations"?

"Because that's the way we do it."

"Because I say so."

"Don't ask so many questions."

"Because that's the way my parents did it."

"Because this is what our church teaches."

"Just because."

(This activity is in the student book.)

We teach our children by what we do. But it's essential that we explain the reasons behind the things we do and the way we do them. Today's lesson highlights both teaching religious traditions to children and explaining those traditions.

(If there are no parents in your class, ask your students to talk about times when they questioned *their* parents' customs, traditions, and practices.)

Into the Word

Deuteronomy 6:1-3 says that God gave His people a set of laws. Discuss this question: "Why did God give the laws?" *(For the people's good; so they would know what He expected of them, etc.)*

Tell your students to read Deuteronomy 6:1-9, 20-25 and mark each verse with one or more of the following symbols, as explained below:

+ Every verse that talks about teaching God's commandments (vv. 1, 7, 21-25).

= Every verse that talks about obeying God's commandments (vv. 1, 2, 3, 6, 24, 25).

✔ Every verse that talks about fearing God (vv. 2, 24).

♥ Every verse that talks about loving God as the basis for obedience to His commandments (v. 5).

▲ Every verse that talks about parents teaching their children about God's laws (v. 7).

♦ Every verse that talks about parents teaching their children about the meaning of their religious heritage (vv. 20-25).

(This activity is in the student book.)

After the students have done their individual Bible study, read every verse aloud and discuss which category or categories best describe each one.

Into Life

Deuteronomy 6:6-9 focuses on handling the Word of God. Which descriptive phrase below would your students use to describe how they handle the Word?

• Coffee table decoration.

• Paper weight.

• Dust gatherer.

• Trusted friend.

• Well-worn weapon.

• Sunday-morning special.

• Family heirloom.

(This activity is in the student book.)

Divide the class into three-person groups. Tell your students to translate the contexts for teaching God's Word to children in Deuteronomy 6:7 into contemporary settings:

• "when thou sittest in thine house." *(Example: at the dinner table.)*

• "when thou walkest by the way." *(Example: driving in the car.)*

• "when thou liest down." *(Example: at bedtime prayers.)*

• "when thou risest up." *(Example: during family devotions.)*

(This activity is in the student book.)

In closing, hand out index cards and ask each student to write out a Bible verse that he or she would like to keep with him or her. Urge your students to post their cards where they will see them frequently until they are able to keep the verses in their minds without the visual reminders.

Let's Talk It Over

The questions on this page are designed to encourage review of the lesson Scriptures and to promote discussion of the lesson by the class. The answers provided are only discussion starters. Let your class talk it over from there.

1. Like the Jews, we Christians stand firmly for the doctrine of one God. We, too, seek to love Him with all our heart, soul, and might. (See also Matthew 22:34-38.) How would you respond if a visitor to your home challenged your worship of Jesus as a violation of this command in Deuteronomy 6?

There are many who would seek to set Jesus apart from God as a good teacher, a prophet, or something less than the incarnate Word—God in the flesh. We know that Jesus Christ is God, but He is not *another* God. John affirmed this relationship in the prologue to his Gospel, John 1:1-5. Jesus affirmed His oneness with God in John 10:30. Jesus accepted worship (Matthew 8:2; 9:18; 14:33; 15:25; 18:26; 28:9, 17, etc.), something good men and even angels refuse (Acts 10:25, 26; Revelation 19:10; 22:8, 9). Jesus must be worshiped as God or rejected as a blasphemer. The "good man" option is not open!

2. We do not literally write Bible verses on our hands and foreheads. But what are some practical ways in which we can keep portions of God's Word with us? Why is this important?

Anyone who carries a purse or wears a garment with pockets can keep a New Testament handy. It is certainly wise for every Christian to carry a New Testament, not only for personal devotion, but also for teaching opportunities. In this computer age one can even keep God's Word handy on a laptop computer.

More important than carrying printed or electronic versions of the Bible, however, is the practice of carrying the Bible in one's heart (Psalm 119:11). Bible memorization seems not to be popular today, but it is the Christian's best defense against temptation and best resource for sharing his faith.

3. We do not write Bible verses on the doors or walls of our homes, but what are some practical ways in which we can keep God's Word before us in our homes?

Many Christian homes feature a devotional center. This may be little more than a small table with an open family Bible on it, but it clearly demonstrates the importance of God's Word in that home. In quite a few Christian homes wall plaques or paintings of Jesus or of other Bible scenes present the truth of God's Word. Families often keep Christian books and magazines on prominent display in their homes. They may affix Scripture verses to mirrors, refrigerator doors, desktops, family bulletin boards, and elsewhere. Doing so reminds the home's residents of the place God's Word must occupy there and provides a vital witness to visitors as well. More important than the *display* of the Bible, however, is the *use* of the Bible. If the open family Bible is never picked up and read, it is little more than an idol or good-luck charm.

4. Lessons from Israel's history were to be an important aspect of teaching in Jewish homes. How important do you think it is to teach Biblical and secular history in Christian homes?

Perhaps we feel that the teaching of secular history should be left to the public schools. One problem with that is that many current history texts present a distorted, politically-correct view of the past. Children and young people need to know that all history is "His story." In both Biblical history and human history in general we can perceive God's working. Ideally the study of history should guide us in avoiding the mistakes of past nations and individuals. Parents need to impress these truths on their children.

5. How can we promote the love of God's Word in the home and the church?

Too many people view the Bible as a rule book, full of *dos* and *don'ts* designed to restrict their activities and limit their fun. We need to cultivate an appreciation for the Bible as a love letter from God, a communication from the Originator of life and Source of every good and perfect gift.

In our Sunday school classes, in our worship services, and in our homes we need to demonstrate our own love for God's Word. We comply with its commands because we believe they were written "for our good always" (Deuteronomy 6:24), not simply because we *have* to. We read and study the Bible, not merely out of habit, but because it offers us victory over fear, sadness, discouragement, jealousy, bitterness, and other negative emotions. We teach and preach from the Bible because it is the timeless Word from the eternal God. When we as leaders love God's Word, those who follow us will love it, too.

A Warning

DEVOTIONAL READING: Psalm 85.

BACKGROUND SCRIPTURE: Deuteronomy 8.

PRINTED TEXT: Deuteronomy 8:6-20.

Deuteronomy 8:6-20

6 Therefore thou shalt keep the commandments of the LORD thy God, to walk in his ways, and to fear him.

7 For the LORD thy God bringeth thee into a good land, a land of brooks of water, of fountains and depths that spring out of valleys and hills;

8 A land of wheat, and barley, and vines, and fig trees, and pomegranates; a land of oil olive, and honey;

9 A land wherein thou shalt eat bread without scarceness, thou shalt not lack any thing in it; a land whose stones are iron, and out of whose hills thou mayest dig brass.

10 When thou hast eaten and art full, then thou shalt bless the LORD thy God for the good land which he hath given thee.

11 Beware that thou forget not the LORD thy God, in not keeping his commandments, and his judgments, and his statutes, which I command thee this day:

12 Lest when thou hast eaten and art full, and hast built goodly houses, and dwelt therein;

13 And when thy herds and thy flocks multiply, and thy silver and thy gold is multiplied, and all that thou hast is multiplied;

14 Then thine heart be lifted up, and thou forget the LORD thy God, which brought thee forth out of the land of Egypt, from the house of bondage;

15 Who led thee through that great and terrible wilderness, wherein were fiery serpents, and scorpions, and drought, where there was no water; who brought thee forth water out of the rock of flint;

16 Who fed thee in the wilderness with manna, which thy fathers knew not, that he might humble thee, and that he might prove thee, to do thee good at thy latter end;

17 And thou say in thine heart, My power and the might of mine hand hath gotten me this wealth.

18 But thou shalt remember the LORD thy God: for it is he that giveth thee power to get wealth, that he may establish his covenant which he sware unto thy fathers, as it is this day.

19 And it shall be, if thou do at all forget the LORD thy God, and walk after other gods, and serve them, and worship them, I testify against you this day that ye shall surely perish.

20 As the nations which the LORD destroyeth before your face, so shall ye perish; because ye would not be obedient unto the voice of the LORD your God.

**Oct
31**

GOLDEN TEXT: Beware that thou forget not the LORD thy God, in not keeping his commandments, and his judgments, and his statutes, which I command thee this day.—Deuteronomy 8:11.

From Slavery to Conquest
Unit 2: Wandering in the Wilderness
(Lessons 5-9)

Lesson Aims

After participating in this lesson, your students should be able to:

1. Summarize the warning given to Israel in today's text.

2. List ways in which it is possible for someone to "forget the Lord thy God."

3. Begin a practice or routine that will keep them mindful of God's daily blessings and less inclined to forget His goodness.

Lesson Outline

INTRODUCTION
    A. Promises and Warnings
    B. Lesson Background
 I. PRECIOUS PROMISES (Deuteronomy 8:6-10)
    A. Call to Obedience (v. 6)
    B. Promises to the Obedient (vv. 7-9)
    C. Call to Gratitude (v. 10)
II. SOLEMN WARNINGS (Deuteronomy 8:11-20)
    A. Beware! (v. 11)
    B. Peril of Prosperity (vv. 12-17)
      Rewriting History
    C. Call to Remembrance (v. 18)
    D. Penalty to the Disobedient (vv. 19, 20)
      A "Freeze-dried" God
CONCLUSION
    A. Israel's Failure
    B. Our Commission
    C. Samples of Salt
    D. Prayer
    E. Thought to Remember

Introduction

"The Lord our God is one Lord." So we read last week, and we believe it as firmly as the ancient Israelites did. One evidence of God's unity is the universe He created. It, too, is a unit. Its parts fit together marvelously. For example, gravity and centrifugal force are neatly balanced so that the earth circles around the sun. It does not fall into the sun to be burned, nor does it sail away in space to be frozen. Another example is provided by plants and animals. The animals need oxygen. They take it from the air, and give it back laden with carbon—a waste material. The trees take the carbon and use it to build their trunks and branches. They give back the oxygen for reuse by animals.

Though the problem is often overstated, we humans do sometimes disturb the wonderful balance God built into the world. With automobiles and industries we pollute the air with wastes no living thing can use. With other wastes we pollute the river so that it is not fit for drinking or bathing. Worse still, and this problem is usually understated, we pollute human relationships with enmity and strife.

The Bible is the Manufacturer's manual for all our relationships. It tells us to love God with a passion above all passions and to love our neighbors as ourselves. If all of us would follow its instructions, our relationships would be ideal. But we produce pollutants—and our relationships are poisoned. Thus by our own thinking and acting we rob ourselves of the good things God has provided.

A. Promises and Warnings

How we love the promises of God! Truly they are "exceeding great and precious" (2 Peter 1:4). Yet all through the Bible God's promises are balanced by His warnings. Thus far, in our lessons for September and October, we have seen a bright promise held before Israel, the promise of a land "flowing with milk and honey." Along with this promise we have seen the frequent warning that this land is for obedient people, not for those who disobey, and there are many more warnings than we have seen in these lessons. For a notable example, read Deuteronomy 28. Verses 1-14 of that chapter detail precious promises for God's obedient people; verses 15-68 give nearly four times as much space to warnings of terrible disaster for those who disobey. This week our text brings us a shorter example of both promise and warning.

B. Lesson Background

Deuteronomy 8 begins with a call to obedience—the same call that we have seen again and again in recent lessons. The frequent repetition emphasizes its importance, and we see the call repeated again in the very first verse of our text.

I. Precious Promises (Deuteronomy 8:6-10)

A. Call to Obedience (v. 6)

6. Therefore thou shalt keep the commandments of the LORD thy God, to walk in his ways, and to fear him.

Obedience to God involves our actions: we are *to walk in his ways*. It involves also our attitude: we are *to fear him*. Fearing God does not mean running away or hiding; it means staying close to Him, but with reverence and awe. We are not afraid to be with God, but we are afraid to disobey Him. [See question #1, page 80.]

B. Promises to the Obedient (vv. 7-9)

7. For the LORD thy God bringeth thee into a good land, a land of brooks of water, of fountains and depths that spring out of valleys and hills.

Some of those listening to Moses had been teenagers when they left Egypt. They remembered a flat country where the Nile River served as the primary water source. They also remembered the desolation of the vast wilderness where they had wandered for forty difficult years. Now God was leading them to a very different country, a land of *valleys and hills*. They would find many *brooks of water* fed by springs. The *King James Version* calls them *fountains*, but today that name is usually given to man-made fountains. Here it means natural springs. *Depths* probably describes the kind of streams that gushed forth from beneath the ground.

8. A land of wheat, and barley, and vines, and fig trees, and pomegranates; a land of oil olive, and honey.

Egypt was a fruitful land where it was irrigated. The promised land was no less fruitful, yet it needed no irrigation. *Wheat* and *barley* would provide bread, and Israel would move into the land just in time to harvest the grain planted by the former inhabitants. Grapes (the produce from *vines*), figs, *pomegranates,* and olives would ripen after the grain harvest. Bees were busy laying up stores of *honey* from the flowers of spring and summer.

9. A land wherein thou shalt eat bread without scarceness, thou shalt not lack any thing in it; a land whose stones are iron, and out of whose hills thou mayest dig brass.

Food supplies would be abundant in the promised land; there would always be enough to eat. The region of Palestine has never been noted for mining, but it did have deposits of iron and copper in the northern part and in some of the more mountainous terrain east of the Jordan River. *Brass* here translates the Hebrew word that was used for copper, brass (a copper-zinc alloy), and bronze (a copper-tin alloy). The raw material it signifies is copper. [See question #2, page 80.]

C. Call to Gratitude (v. 10)

10. When thou hast eaten and art full, then thou shalt bless the LORD thy God for the good land which he hath given thee.

To *bless the Lord* is to praise and thank Him, as all people ought to do for the food they eat.

Even now some people see no reason to thank God for food grown and processed by human labor. Skeptics like to tell of the preacher who complimented a farmer by saying, "You and the Lord produced a fine crop on that field."

"Yes," the farmer replied, "but you should see that field when the Lord had it all to Himself. It was nothing but a weed patch."

The skeptics, however, forget what the field would be like if the farmer had it all to himself. All his work would be useless if the Lord did not provide sunshine, rain, and air. Not even weeds would grow without the Lord.

II. Solemn Warnings
(Deuteronomy 8:11-20)

Close on the heels of the promises come the warnings. That arrangement is seen often, for that is where the warnings are most needed. Doesn't it seem absurd that the abundance of God's gifts makes people forget the Giver? Yet the history of Israel seems to show exactly that. People in desperate need cried in their misery to the Lord; and when He gave them all they needed and more, they forgot where their relief came from.

A. Beware! (v. 11)

11. Beware that thou forget not the LORD thy God, in not keeping his commandments, and his judgments, and his statutes, which I command thee this day.

Beware means be aware, be alert, be watchful. When we have all we need and are "full" (v. 10), we are comfortable, relaxed, and at ease. We have time on our hands. If we think of some activity that would be pleasant, we might not stop to think whether it would be right or not. Not maliciously, but carelessly, we ignore the commands that God has given.

B. Peril of Prosperity (vv. 12-17)

12, 13. Lest when thou hast eaten and art full, and hast built goodly houses, and dwelt therein; and when thy herds and thy flocks multiply, and thy silver and thy gold is multiplied, and all that thou hast is multiplied.

These verses picture the prosperity that would be the norm in the promised land. The people would have all the food they could eat, and would live in fine (*goodly*) *houses.* Their *herds* of cattle and *flocks* of sheep would be constantly increasing. They would have an abundance of *silver* and *gold.* Nothing would be exempt from God's blessing: *all* they had would be *multiplied.*

14. Then thine heart be lifted up, and thou forget the LORD thy God, which brought thee

forth out of the land of Egypt, from the house of bondage.

This verse pictures the peril of prosperity. People who have everything are apt to forget how much help they had in getting it and to become *lifted up* with pride. Moses was speaking these words near the end of the forty years Israel had spent in the wilderness. Those who were under forty years of age had never been slaves in *Egypt*. They knew the oppression of that *bondage* only by hearsay. It would be easy to forget how deeply they were indebted to the Lord because He had rescued them. [See question #3, page 80.]

15. Who led thee through that great and terrible wilderness, wherein were fiery serpents, and scorpions, and drought, where there was no water; who brought thee forth water out of the rock of flint.

Rescue from Egypt was only the beginning of God's benefits to this emerging nation. He had also sustained His people for forty years in the *wilderness,* a desert that is described as *great and terrible.* He protected them from poisonous *serpents* and *scorpions* in the desert. He brought *water out of the rock* when people and livestock would have died without it.

16. Who fed thee in the wilderness with manna, which thy fathers knew not, that he might humble thee, and that he might prove thee, to do thee good at thy latter end.

The *wilderness* soil provided no food for human travelers, but God provided *manna.* That and all the other helps mentioned in verse 15 kept the people alive. They also yielded a spiritual benefit as well by serving to *humble* the people. They could see that they were helpless and had to depend on God. Those years of God's provision also served to *prove* the people—that is, to test them and show whether they would obey God or not.

The result of all these blessings was that in the *latter end* of their journey God would do them *good* by giving them the promised land. There such want as they had known in the desert would never be known again—if they would obey God. [See question #4, page 80.]

17. And thou say in thine heart, My power and the might of mine hand hath gotten me this wealth.

The years of scarcity in the desert had made the people humble, showing them that they needed to depend on God for daily bread to eat, water to drink, and guidance through an unknown land. Now they were about to move into the promised land, where there would be no scarcity. The scarcity had made them humble; abundance had the potential to produce the opposite effect. The people themselves would plow the fields, plant the seed, and harvest the abundant grain. They themselves would lead their sheep to green pastures and refreshing waters. They themselves would sell bread and meat to passing caravans and store up the silver and gold from their sales.

Amid such prosperity, the people might drift carelessly into the habit of thinking that they themselves produced their wealth. They might forget that they were still depending on the Lord just as much as they had depended on Him for manna in the desert. They could no more produce rain than they could make a spring flow from desert rock. They could no more produce sunshine than they could produce manna from the sky. But in a land of plenty it would be easy to forget that God's hand was responsible for all that they enjoyed, and instead attribute their success to their own *power.*

REWRITING HISTORY

One of the great controversies to come out of World War II was whether the Japanese nation should acknowledge its guilt in starting the war. For understandable reasons, the post-war government of Japan has been reluctant to acknowledge the unpleasant facts of the nation's wartime past.

None of us likes to admit the wrong we have done. But even more is at stake in this case. Japanese culture places great value in "saving face," and to admit to wartime wrongdoing would violate that principle. So, for more than fifty years, the Japanese government censored school textbooks, deleting accurate descriptions of Japan's unprovoked attack on Pearl Harbor and wartime atrocities such as the Nanking massacre during the invasion of China and medical experiments on human guinea pigs. Finally, in 1997, the Japanese Supreme Court settled the issue by ruling that history should not be rewritten. Truth should be known, no matter how embarrassing it might be.

In later years, Israel would be tempted to say, "All the blessings of the promised land have come because of our own strength." In so doing, they would be "rewriting history," and fooling only themselves. The goodness of their land and their right to it came from the gracious hand of the God whom they all too often forgot.

—C. R. B.

How to Say It

BABYLON. *Bab*-uh-lun.
DEUTERONOMY. Due-ter-*ahn*-uh-me.

This chart cites important events from Israel's history and New Testament references to those events. Use it to initiate a discussion of the importance of studying the Old Testament today.

Visual for lesson 9

C. Call to Remembrance (v. 18)

18. But thou shalt remember the Lord thy God: for it is he that giveth thee power to get wealth, that he may establish his covenant which he sware unto thy fathers, as it is this day.

God was calling His people to be thoughtful, not careless. He was urging them to *remember* Him and all the things that He was doing and how much they depended on Him. He would do more than they would to produce their success in the promised land. If their efforts resulted in a bountiful harvest, then it would come about because He gave them the *power* to do what they were able to do. How foolish it would be for the people of Israel to forget Him and give themselves all the credit for their success! How foolish it is for people today to do the same! [See question #5, page 80.]

D. Penalty to the Disobedient (vv. 19, 20)

19. And it shall be, if thou do at all forget the LORD thy God, and walk after other gods, and serve them, and worship them, I testify against you this day that ye shall surely perish.

Forgetting God was a serious matter—it was a matter of life and death. In the promised land the people of Israel would depend on God for their living just as surely as they had been depending on Him in the wilderness. However, in the promised land they would not see His cloud every day and His fire every night. They would not see His manna lying fresh on the ground every morning.

In half a century there would be a new generation of Israelites, who had never seen these more obvious signs of God's presence. People of that new generation would be able to see and hear the loud religious celebrations of the pagan peoples around them. There would be plenty of food, plenty of wine, and plenty of music and dancing. Eager young people of Israel would begin to ask, "Why not join the fun?"

So as they stood at the border of the promised land, God had Moses tell them why not—bluntly and honestly: if you join that kind of "fun," *ye shall surely perish!*

A "FREEZE-DRIED" GOD

Your faithful dog Rover is a wonderful companion. He greets you happily when you come home after a hard day's work, he barks to warn of strangers approaching the house, and he is a suitable repository for an abundance of "leftovers" and morsels slipped quietly from the family table by his younger "masters" while Mom and Dad aren't looking.

However, as the saying goes, "Every dog has his day"; and when Rover's days are over, then what? A new way has been found to deal with Rover's remains when he can no longer bring happiness to his human "family." A Florida entrepreneur has developed a technique for freeze-drying family pets so that their owners can have a tangible, physical reminder of the joy-filled days and years their pets once brought them. The cost for this service varies from several hundred dollars to a few thousand.

A freeze-dried pet allows you to keep your pet with you without having to feed it, let it outside, bathe it, or otherwise care for it. Of course, the disadvantage is that you don't really have your pet after all.

God warned Israel that they dare not forget Him. If they maintained only some distant memories of Him, then the land of plenty that He had given them would be lacking in its most important quality: the presence of the true God in their midst. God will not be a "freeze-dried" memory.

—C. R. B.

20. As the nations which the LORD destroyeth before your face, so shall ye perish; because ye would not be obedient unto the voice of the LORD your God.

The Lord had judged the pagan *nations* then living in the promised land and determined they were too wicked to live. He was sending the men of Israel to execute His judgment and destroy them (Deuteronomy 7:1, 2).

If the men of Israel did not follow these orders, those pagans remaining would entice them to serve other gods (Deuteronomy 7:4). If Israel gave in to this temptation, it too would be judged and would *perish* (Numbers 33:55, 56).

Conclusion

Our upcoming lessons for November will deal with the conquest of the promised land under Joshua. We will see that God's people fought valiantly, and God gave them victory. Israel possessed the land and remained true to the Lord, as long as faithful Joshua was at the helm.

A. Israel's Failure

Sadly, Israel failed to destroy all the pagans as God commanded, and the remnant of them did indeed entice the people of Israel (Judges 2:1-3). After Joshua died, many Israelites took up pagan practices, and Israel suffered (Judges 2:11-15). Later the nation was divided, and idol worship became the state religion of the northern part (1 Kings 12:26-30). In due time the north was destroyed (2 Kings 17:5, 6). Paganism influenced the southern kingdom as well, and it grew until Jerusalem was destroyed and its survivors became captives in Babylon for a time (2 Kings 25:8-11).

B. Our Commission

As Christians we have a commission different from that of Israel in the promised land. They were sent to destroy the pagans; we are sent to convert them. Our task is to make them disciples of Jesus and teach them to obey Him (Matthew 28:18-20).

We undertake our commission with the solemn warning of Jesus ringing in our ears. "Ye are the salt of the earth," He said, "but if the salt have lost his savor, wherewith shall it be salted? it is thenceforth good for nothing, but to be cast out, and to be trodden under foot of men" (Matthew 5:13). If we do not keep the true character of Christianity, we can be destroyed as though we were pagans.

We must see our mission as twofold. First, we are to keep ourselves "salty" (pure and holy). Second, we are to make disciples of all nations.

C. Samples of Salt

Stephen spoke up for Jesus so clearly that Jesus' enemies stoned him to death (Acts 7:54-60). How many of us have been silenced by a snicker?

Christians in Jerusalem were so enthusiastic in praise of Jesus that non-Christian officials drove them out of town. Then they went everywhere preaching the word (Acts 8:1-4). How long has it been since you spoke up for the Lord in the workplace or at a party or at school?

Sitting on padded pews, some of us find it hard to endure a service an hour long. Meanwhile we read of Christians in Asia who walk ten hours and then sit joyfully on the floor for a four-hour meeting. Early Christians met in the temple every day (Acts 2:46), and they didn't have padded pews, either. Is it possible that our grandchildren will see missionaries come from Thailand to our country and find themselves as unwelcome as western missionaries now are in Moslem countries?

Saul combed Jerusalem to find Christians and put them in jail (Acts 8:3). If you were arrested for being a Christian, could the prosecutor find enough evidence to convict you?

The first Christians "sold their possessions and goods, and parted them to all men, as every man had need" (Acts 2:45). This year a statistician reported that the average church member contributes two-and-a-half percent of his income to the church and to Christian causes.

The Israelites were warned not to forget God, but to remember all the good things He had done for them. But what about we who know that Jesus died and rose again for us? It seems that though we have so much more for which to praise God, we too have forgotten Him and have become less dependent on Him. If this were not the case, wouldn't our world be more Christlike? Wouldn't the average church member be giving much more than two-and-a-half percent of his income to Christian work?

What do you think? Is the salt keeping its savor in our country, in our church—in you? What can you personally do to make it saltier?

D. Prayer

Our Father in Heaven, thank You for trusting us to be the salt of the earth—both to show the true nature of Christianity in our own way of living and to give Your gospel to the whole world. Forgive our failures, we pray, and help us to do better. In Jesus' name we ask. Amen.

E. Thought to Remember

Heed God's warnings now while there is still time.

Home Daily Bible Readings

Monday, Oct. 25—Don't Let Prosperity Spoil You (Deuteronomy 8:1-10)
Tuesday, Oct. 26—You Are Not Self-made People (Deuteronomy 8:11-20)
Wednesday, Oct. 27—You Were a Rebellious People (Deuteronomy 9:6-14)
Thursday, Oct. 28—God Listens to Moses on Your Behalf (Deuteronomy 9:15-21)
Friday, Oct. 29—Moses Intercedes for Israel Again (Deuteronomy 9:25-29)
Saturday, Oct. 30—Beware of False Prophets (Deuteronomy 13:1-5)
Sunday, Oct. 31—Purge Those Who Worship False Gods (Deuteronomy 13:6-11)

Learning by Doing

This page contains an alternate lesson plan emphasizing learning activities.
Classes desiring such student involvement will find these suggestions helpful.

Learning Goals

After participating in this lesson, the students should be able to:

1. Summarize the warning given to Israel in today's text.

2. List ways in which it is possible for someone to "forget the Lord thy God."

3. Begin a practice or routine that will keep them mindful of God's daily blessings and less inclined to forget His goodness.

Into the Lesson

Begin by writing PARADISE on the board. Ask the students to say what they think of when they see that word. What images does it call to their minds? What kind of place is a *paradise?*

Observe that the Israelites had been living in a barren and arid region for forty years. Now they were about to enter a land of abundance—"a land flowing with milk and honey" (Exodus 3:8). In comparison to what they had been experiencing for the past forty years, it would seem like a paradise! But the very bounty and prosperity of the land could be hazardous to the Israelites.

Into the Word

Deuteronomy 8:6-20 is filled with warnings. Moses gave these warnings to his people at the threshold of the promised land. They were to remember the warnings when they had conquered and settled in the land.

Divide the class into four groups, and give each group a different Bible-study assignment based on Deuteronomy 8:6-20. Allow about ten minutes; then call for reports from each group.

Group 1 should look for descriptions of the promised land. (See verses 7-9.)

Group 2 should look for predictions of the Israelites' success and prosperity in the promised land. (See verses 9, 10, 12, 13, and 17.)

Group 3 should look for examples of God's goodness to the Israelites. (See verses 14-16.)

Group 4 should look for warnings. (See verses 11, 14, 17-20.)

Deuteronomy 8:6-20 presents challenges. Ask the students to identify at least five challenges cited in the passage. Here are some suggestions.

• Verse 6: A challenge to keep the Lord's commandments and to fear Him.

• Verse 10: A challenge to thank God for His goodness.

• Verses 11 and 14: A challenge to remember the Lord. ("Forget not" is a more intensive way of saying, "Remember.")

• Verses 17 and 18: A challenge to give God the credit when things go right.

• Verses 19 and 20: A challenge to learn from the failures of others.

Into Life

Write the following open-ended statements on the chalkboard, and ask the students to provide completions:

"When things go wrong, I usually. . . ."

"When things go right, I usually. . . ."

If your students are honest, they probably will complete the first statement with something similar to ". . . ask God for help" and the second statement with something like ". . . take the credit myself." Expand on that point by asking the students, when something good happens in their lives, are they more likely to say "Look what I did" or "Look what God did"? Discuss ways to keep the role of God in mind and to be more ready to give Him the credit.

Moses warned the Israelites about the hazards of prosperity. Use the following situations to lead a discussion of the danger of prosperity:

• When Jim first became a Christian, he felt totally dependent on the Lord. He spent a lot of time reading the Bible, praying, and asking for help and direction. Now that he is a "mature" believer, Jim doesn't feel the need for an intensive devotional life. What happened?

• Ten years ago George started his own business. In spite of his best efforts, the business failed. George became bitter and blamed God for letting him down. He finally was able to start another business. This one is a big success, and George is taking all the credit. What happened?

If your students could spend one minute with each person described above, what would they say? What do they think Jesus would say?

In closing, challenge your students to think of ways they can be more mindful of God's blessings and not forget His goodness. Do they need to set aside a special time of Bible reading and meditating on what God has done? Can some of them start a small group that will encourage them in this direction? Encourage them to think of a specific manner in which they can frequently be reminded of God's goodness.

Let's Talk It Over

The questions on this page are designed to encourage review of the lesson Scriptures and to promote discussion of the lesson by the class. The answers provided are only discussion starters. Let your class talk it over from there.

1. The lesson writer says that obedience to God involves both our actions and our attitudes. In the New Covenant, which do you think is more important—or are they equally important? Explain why you think the way you do.

Many people believe that obedience to commands has no place in the New Covenant. Indeed, we are saved by grace and not by works (cf. Ephesians 2:8, 9). But works remain important—see Ephesians 2:10. Jesus Himself said that not all those who acknowledge Him as Lord will enter the kingdom, but only those who do His Father's will (Matthew 7:21).

It is impossible, however, to list all the things that one should *do* as a Christian, so the New Covenant focuses instead on attitude. James sums it up: "If ye fulfil the royal law according to the Scripture, Thou shalt love thy neighbor as thyself, ye do well" (James 2:8). The right attitude—love—will lead to the right actions.

2. The promises cited in verses 8 and 9 of our text are extremely appealing to those in an agrarian economy. How do you think God might express His love to us in our technological age?

Of course, the blessing of having enough good food to eat translates into any economy. As for the well-watered fields producing abundant grain and fruit, however, most of us today— since most of us are not farmers—would not know how to reap the benefit of such a blessing. We might prefer computers that boot up instantly and never crash, or stock options in a farming corporation that enjoys the agricultural benefits described here, or job security in an industry with unlimited sales potential. Whatever our own line of work, we need to look for the manner in which God is blessing us in that work—even when the crop fails or our computers crash or the sales lag behind their "potential." More importantly, we need to remember that God expressed His love to us in a manner that transcends time and economies when He gave His Son on the cross!

3. The lesson writer uses the phrase, "the peril of prosperity." How should Christians deal with material prosperity so as to avoid the peril?

Jesus warned about the danger of wealth, and we must take His warnings seriously (Matthew 6:19-21, 33; 19:23-26). We need to order our priorities, becoming good stewards when we have relatively little, so that we will be good stewards if and when God blesses us with much (Luke 16:10). Wealth must be viewed as a means of extended service for the Lord. By giving more to the church, to missions, and to benevolent causes, we can master our wealth for His glory. Proverbs 30:8, 9 is also helpful in this discussion.

4. Moses said that prosperity might cause the Israelites to forget the great things God had done for them. How can we avoid forgetting God and His blessings?

One way to keep God's blessings in mind is to give frequent thanks and praise for them. We can do this in private, or we can tell others what God has done for us. Every time we share the gospel and what it has meant in our lives, we not only touch the hearts of our hearers—we celebrate afresh God's goodness to us.

A major purpose in attending services with the church should be to gain regular reminders of God's blessings. This is the reason Jesus instituted the Lord's Supper. He said, "This do in remembrance of me" (Luke 22:19). The singing of hymns also serves as a reminder, as does the preaching and teaching of God's Word.

5. According to Deuteronomy 8:18, God "giveth thee power to get wealth." How important do you think it is for people to know that today? How can we keep that truth known?

If we would recognize God as the giver of "every good gift and every perfect gift" (James 1:17), then we must recognize Him as the One who makes us able to obtain wealth. It is He who gave us the talent to do what we do on the job, no matter how much we have honed that skill through education and training. It is He who gave us the ability to learn what we have learned in school and in job training.

Christian stewardship recognizes God not only as the *giver* of every good gift, but its *owner* as well. He gives it to us so that we may use it in His behalf. We need to teach that truth at a very early age if we want the next generation of Christians to practice Biblical stewardship.

Joshua Succeeds Moses

DEVOTIONAL READING: Numbers 27:12-23.

BACKGROUND SCRIPTURE: Deuteronomy 31:1-8; 34.

PRINTED TEXT: Deuteronomy 31:1-8; 34:5-9.

Deuteronomy 31:1-8

1 And Moses went and spake these words unto all Israel.

2 And he said unto them, I am a hundred and twenty years old this day; I can no more go out and come in: also the LORD hath said unto me, Thou shalt not go over this Jordan.

3 The LORD thy God, he will go over before thee, and he will destroy these nations from before thee, and thou shalt possess them: and Joshua, he shall go over before thee, as the LORD hath said.

4 And the LORD shall do unto them as he did to Sihon and to Og, kings of the Amorites, and unto the land of them, whom he destroyed.

5 And the LORD shall give them up before your face, that ye may do unto them according unto all the commandments which I have commanded you.

6 Be strong and of a good courage, fear not, nor be afraid of them: for the LORD thy God, he it is that doth go with thee; he will not fail thee, nor forsake thee.

7 And Moses called unto Joshua, and said unto him in the sight of all Israel, Be strong and of a good courage: for thou must go with this people unto the land which the LORD hath sworn unto their fathers to give them; and thou shalt cause them to inherit it.

8 And the LORD, he it is that doth go before thee; he will be with thee, he will not fail thee, neither forsake thee: fear not, neither be dismayed.

Deuteronomy 34:5-9

5 So Moses the servant of the LORD died there in the land of Moab, according to the word of the LORD.

6 And he buried him in a valley in the land of Moab, over against Beth-peor: but no man knoweth of his sepulchre unto this day.

7 And Moses was a hundred and twenty years old when he died: his eye was not dim, nor his natural force abated.

8 And the children of Israel wept for Moses in the plains of Moab thirty days: so the days of weeping and mourning for Moses were ended.

9 And Joshua the son of Nun was full of the spirit of wisdom; for Moses had laid his hands upon him: and the children of Israel hearkened unto him, and did as the LORD commanded Moses.

GOLDEN TEXT: And the LORD, he it is that doth go before thee; he will be with thee, he will not fail thee, neither forsake thee: fear not, neither be dismayed.—Deuteronomy 31:8.

Lesson Aims

After this lesson, students should be able to:

1. Describe the transfer of leadership in Israel from Moses to Joshua, according to today's text.

2. Tell why godly leadership is essential to the accomplishment of God's work.

3. Express their appreciation for Jesus' leadership in their lives, and for the leadership of someone in their church.

Lesson Outline

INTRODUCTION

  A. Three Leaders

  B. Lesson Background

 I. ENCOURAGEMENT FOR ISRAEL (Deuteronomy 31:1-6)

  A. Moses' Leadership Ends (vv. 1, 2)

  B. God's Leadership Continues (v. 3a)

  C. Joshua's Leadership Begins (v. 3b)

  D. Promise of Victory (vv. 4, 5)

  E. Call to Courage (v. 6)

 II. ENCOURAGEMENT FOR JOSHUA (Deuteronomy 31:7, 8)

  A. Moses' Challenge (v. 7a)

  B. Words of Assurance (v. 7b)

  C. God's Promise (v. 8)

   Encouragement Needed

III. CHANGE OF LEADERS (Deuteronomy 34:5-9)

  A. Death of Moses (vv. 5-7)

  B. Month of Mourning (v. 8)

   Honoring a "Living Memory"

  C. New Leader (v. 9)

CONCLUSION

  A. The Real Leader

  B. Follow the Leader

  C. Prayer

  D. Thought to Remember

Introduction

Older Americans can never forget "the Roosevelt Years"—those twelve years when President Franklin Delano Roosevelt was in the news so constantly that headline writers shortened his name to FDR.

Those years began in the midst of the Great Depression and ended during the turmoil of World War II. Opposition to the President was always strong, but his own attitude was always confident. Cartoonists illustrated it by the jaunty upward tilt of his long cigarette holder.

Then FDR died, and America wondered: could anyone take his place? But a "little man from Missouri" stepped in with courage and determination. Harry Truman was not FDR. He was opposed and belittled, but the country still moved forward. The war ended in triumph; the postwar problems were managed with vigor.

It is traumatic to lose a great leader in troubled times. The years that follow test the mettle, not only of the new leader, but also of those who follow. So it was in Israel.

A. Three Leaders

The First Leader. The Moses years were difficult years for Israel. They began in the bitter bondage of Egypt and continued in the years of wandering in the wilderness. The people were frequently critical and disobedient, and sometimes openly rebellious; but for forty years the towering figure of Moses dominated the scene. Then Moses died.

The New Leader. Joshua had been Moses' helper during Moses' forty years of leadership and had proved himself quite capable. Moses had designated him as the next leader. Best of all, the Lord had chosen him for this responsibility. So Joshua assumed this role and did so at a critical time. The people stood at the border of the promised land. It was time to invade—the very point at which Israel had failed before. Would they repeat the mistakes of the past?

The Real Leader. The answer to this question depended on whether Israel would acknowledge its real leader. This, of course, was the Lord. Moses had led well because the Lord had been with him. Now the Lord would be with Joshua. The Lord would open a way through a flooded Jordan, reduce the walls of Jericho to rubble, and give victory in battle after battle. So Moses encouraged both the people and Joshua to trust the Lord and be strong.

B. Lesson Background

This is the fourth lesson that we have taken from Moses' lengthy talk to his people as they stood for the second time at the border of the promised land. He has reviewed the law that God gave the people, their failure to take possession of the promised land at the first opportunity, and their years of wandering in the desert. All of this serves as background for today's lesson. At this point, we are nearing the end of Moses' dramatic speech and nearing the end of his life. What will he say now?

I. Encouragement for Israel
(Deuteronomy 31:1-6)

A. Moses' Leadership Ends (vv. 1, 2)

1. And Moses went and spake these words unto all Israel.

All Israel had failed before; *all Israel* must now succeed. So *Moses* gave his word of encouragement to all the people.

2. And he said unto them, I am a hundred and twenty years old this day; I can no more go out and come in: also the LORD hath said unto me, Thou shalt not go over this Jordan.

Moses' life can be divided into three forty-year segments. The first forty years were spent in Egypt. Then he killed an Egyptian and was forced to flee Egypt to save his life. For the next forty years Moses worked as a shepherd in Midian. That period of Moses' life ended abruptly when God called him from out of the burning bush. Over the final forty years Moses led the Israelites out of Egypt's bondage and during their wandering in the desert.

Now he would lead no more. The Lord had told him his task was done. Israel must now *go over this Jordan,* but Moses was not to go. This part of the message was not encouraging at all; it was frightening. Israel was losing its leader. Could anyone take his place? [See question #1, page 88.]

B. God's Leadership Continues (v. 3a)

3a. The LORD thy God, he will go over before thee, and he will destroy these nations from before thee, and thou shalt possess them.

Who had been Israel's real leader for the past forty years? Not Moses, but *the Lord.* In forty years He had never failed His followers, and He would continue to guide them. How could courage falter under such leadership?

C. Joshua's Leadership Begins (v. 3b)

3b. And Joshua, he shall go over before thee, as the LORD hath said.

Often repeated is the story of a small boy who was afraid of the dark at bedtime. He wanted Dad to stay with him.

"Oh, you don't need me," Dad assured him. "God is right here with you."

"I know," the trembling lad replied, "but I need somebody with skin on."

Even with God leading them through the perils beyond the Jordan, the people of Israel needed someone with skin on—a human leader like Moses and like themselves, who would set before them a visible example of fearless faith in action. *Joshua* was to be that leader. *The Lord* had chosen him for that responsibility.

How to Say It

AMORITES. *Am*-uh-rites.
BETH-PEOR. Beth-*pea*-or.
CANAAN. *Kay*-nun.
DEUTERONOMY. Due-ter-*ahn*-uh-me.
JERICHO. *Jair*-ih-ko.
MIDIAN. *Mid*-ee-un.
MOAB. *Mo*-ab.
NEBO. *Nee*-bo.
SEPULCHRE. *sep*-ull-kur.
SIHON. *Sigh*-hun.

D. Promise of Victory (vv. 4, 5)

4. And the LORD shall do unto them as he did to Sihon and to Og, kings of the Amorites, and unto the land of them, whom he destroyed.

Sihon and *Og* were *kings of the Amorites* who had lived in the territory east of the Jordan, the very country where Israel now was camping. Those kings had refused to let Israel pass through their country in peace. But God had *destroyed* these two kings and their armies. He had done that by means of the hands and swords of Israel, but the victories had been so decisive that Israel knew they were from God (Deuteronomy 2:26—3:11). That *land* east of the Jordan was now safely in the possession of Israel. Moses promised that in the same way, God would destroy the hostile peoples west of the Jordan and give their land to Israel.

5. And the LORD shall give them up before your face, that ye may do unto them according unto all the commandments which I have commanded you.

The Lord shall give them up before your face. This repeats the assurance of verse 4, promising that the Lord would hand the enemy peoples over to Israel. Israel was to "smite them, and utterly destroy them" (Deuteronomy 7:1, 2). God was determined to wipe out the peoples inhabiting Canaan because of their wickedness, and Israel was the instrument in His hand to do it.

E. Call to Courage (v. 6)

6. Be strong and of a good courage, fear not, nor be afraid of them: for the LORD thy God, he it is that doth go with thee; he will not fail thee, nor forsake thee.

The encouragement to Israel ended with yet another assurance: the Lord would *go with* His people. Therefore, victory was sure if the men of Israel would do their part. Their part was to *be strong and of a good courage.* They must approach the task at hand vigorously and fearlessly, confident of victory. If they would do that, they would *not fail*. The Lord promised it. [See question #2, page 88.]

II. Encouragement for Joshua (Deuteronomy 31:7, 8)

As the newly appointed leader of the people, Joshua's weight of responsibility exceeded all others'. Moses had a special word of encouragement for him, and of course that word came from the Lord.

A. Moses' Challenge (v. 7a)

7a. And Moses called unto Joshua, and said unto him in the sight of all Israel, Be strong and of a good courage.

The challenge to *Joshua* was similar to that given to the people: *Be strong and of a good courage.* Later God Himself would repeat this command to Joshua (Joshua 1:6, 7, 9). Joshua carried a load vastly greater than anyone else did, and he was to carry it no less bravely and vigorously. Moses did not take Joshua aside for private instruction; he sounded this call *in the sight of all Israel*. Thus all the people would see that their commander was one of them, though he was being set apart from them. [See question #3, page 88.]

B. Words of Assurance (v. 7b)

7b. For thou must go with this people unto the land which the LORD hath sworn unto their fathers to give them; and thou shalt cause them to inherit it.

Thou shalt cause them to inherit it. Joshua's responsibility was great, and his task was difficult; but his effort would be crowned with success. Such assurance must have lifted his spirits. And before giving that assurance, Moses stated the basis of it: *the Lord* long before had *sworn* to give the promised *land* to Israel. Having received an assurance so soundly based, how could Joshua fail to be fearless?

Visual for lesson 2

The map on the visual for lesson 2 includes the entrance into Canaan (the conquest) as well as the exodus. Refer to that visual as you discuss the great task that lay ahead of Joshua and the Israelites.

C. God's Promise (v. 8)

8. And the LORD, he it is that doth go before thee; he will be with thee, he will not fail thee, neither forsake thee: fear not, neither be dismayed.

At the climax of this word of assurance came the comforting promise of God's presence. He is *the Lord*—the invincible, the unconquerable, the Almighty—and *he will be with thee!* Not only that, but also He *doth go before thee*. He leads the way; He bears the brunt of the battle. So *fear not, neither be dismayed!* [See question #4, page 88.]

ENCOURAGEMENT NEEDED

An "ultra-race" is what people call the annual 135-mile run/walk from Death Valley, California, to Mount Whitney. It starts at "Badwater," 282 feet below sea level—the lowest spot in North America. The race ends at Whitney Portals, 8,300 feet up the side of the mountain. In between are several mountain ranges that must be crossed. The race must be run in less than sixty hours of physical and emotional torture in temperatures as high as 118 degrees.

Family and friends drive alongside the runners to shout encouragement and to provide support for their physical and emotional needs. Runners have to deal with heat exhaustion, chills, dehydration, muscle cramps, abdominal distress, and hallucinations—and all for a first prize of five hundred dollars!

What did Joshua feel as he faced the battle for the promised land? He did not know the details of what lay ahead, but certainly Moses knew something of the rigorous self-control and the leadership abilities that the task ahead required. So Moses stood beside Joshua in the sight of the entire nation and offered him encouragement, assured him of God's presence, and challenged him to faithfulness. Apparently Moses' actions and words had an impact: Joshua successfully led the people into the promised land.

The question each of us should ask himself is: "Whom do I know who could use my support and encouragement today?"   —C. R. B.

III. Change of Leaders (Deuteronomy 34:5-9)

For some time we have been reading parts of Moses' speech to the people of Israel as they were camping on the east side of the Jordan River. He finished that message with a poetic blessing on the twelve tribes of Israel (Deuteronomy 33). Then he took leave of his people for the last time and climbed alone to a high peak (Mount Nebo) in the land of Moab. From there he could see a wide sweep of the promised land that he was not to enter (Deuteronomy 34:1-4).

A. Death of Moses (vv. 5-7)

5. So Moses the servant of the LORD died there in the land of Moab, according to the word of the LORD.

Through forty troubled years, Moses had been a faithful *servant of the Lord.* Almost all the men of Israel had rebelled against God, and had been condemned to die in the desert instead of living in the promised land (Deuteronomy 1:19-40). Moses had not shared in that rebellion; however, even his service had not been perfect. Once when thirsty Israel was clamoring for water, the Lord said to Moses, "Speak ye unto the rock before their eyes; and it shall give forth his water" (Numbers 20:8). Instead of speaking to the rock, Moses hit it with his rod. Instead of saying, "God will give you water," he said, "Hear now, ye rebels; must we fetch you water out of this rock?" (Numbers 20:10, 11).

Because he did not give God the glory, Moses too was sentenced to die in the desert instead of living in the promised land (Numbers 20:12; Deuteronomy 32:48-52). Thus we read in the verse before us that *Moses . . . died . . . according to the word of the Lord.* Aaron shared in Moses' guilt, and he died before Moses did (Numbers 20:22-29).

6. And he buried him in a valley in the land of Moab, over against Beth-peor: but no man knoweth of his sepulchre unto this day.

The Lord *buried* Moses *in a valley in the land of Moab.* We cannot know which valley, for there are many small valleys among the mountains of Moab. We cannot even locate *Beth-peor.* Even now it is true that *no man knoweth of his sepulchre unto this day.* The Lord Himself officiated at Moses' funeral. What an honor!

7. And Moses was a hundred and twenty years old when he died: his eye was not dim, nor his natural force abated.

Moses was strong enough to climb the mountain, perhaps the highest one in the vicinity. His eyes were good enough to look far across the Jordan, over the length and breadth of the promised land (vv. 1-3). He was not worn out and worthless at the age of *a hundred and twenty;* he was strong and active. He died because he had taken to himself and Aaron the credit that belonged to God, and therefore he was not allowed to enjoy the land toward which he had led his people so long and so well.

Although Moses' body lay in an unmarked grave, we can be certain that Moses himself soared from the mountains of Moab to the heights of Heaven, not to be seen again on earth until he would appear to talk about the death of a greater One, the Lord Jesus (Luke 9:28-31). That greater One also came on a mission that would not be completed until after His death.

B. Month of Mourning (v. 8)

8. And the children of Israel wept for Moses in the plains of Moab thirty days: so the days of weeping and mourning for Moses were ended.

Amid the hurried pace of our modern world, we do not take this much time for *mourning,* not even for a popular national hero. Most likely *the children of Israel* continued such daily activities as gathering manna and leading their flocks to pasture, but they did delay their advance into the promised land until *the days of weeping and mourning for Moses were ended.*

HONORING A "LIVING MEMORY"

Jeanne Calment died at 122 years of age on August 5, 1997. She survived all her relatives, including her only grandson. The oldest person in the world at the time of her death, she was an unusually robust individual in spite of her age. At 85 she began taking fencing lessons. At 120 she gave up sweets "for her health." At 121 she released a compact disc with her reminiscences accompanied by music.

Jeanne Calment's passing was mourned by the entire city of Arles, France, where she had lived. The deputy mayor of Arles said, "She was the living memory of our city. Her birthdays were a sort of family holiday."

Moses' death was followed by thirty days of mourning in Israel. Strong and vigorous to the end, Moses had been Israel's personal contact with their amazing past—the "living memory" of the nation. Joshua gave the best testimony to

Home Daily Bible Readings

Monday, Nov. 1—God Will Lead Israel Across Jordan (Deuteronomy 31:1-6)
Tuesday, Nov. 2—Read and Obey the Law (Deuteronomy 31:7-13)
Wednesday, Nov. 3—Joshua Is Commissioned to Succeed Moses (Deuteronomy 31:14-23)
Thursday, Nov. 4—Death of Moses in Moab (Deuteronomy 34:1-7)
Friday, Nov. 5—Moses Is Mourned and Remembered (Deuteronomy 34:8-12)
Saturday, Nov. 6—God's Promise and Command to Joshua (Joshua 1:1-9)
Sunday, Nov. 7—Israel Prepares to Cross the Jordan (Joshua 1:10-16)

Moses' outstanding leadership by following his faithful example.

How do we best honor the "living memory" of God's dedicated servants? By imitating their faithfulness.　　　　　　　　　　　　—C. R. B.

C. New Leader (v. 9)

9. And Joshua the son of Nun was full of the spirit of wisdom; for Moses had laid his hands upon him: and the children of Israel hearkened unto him, and did as the LORD commanded Moses.

Joshua was fully prepared and duly commissioned to take the place of leadership that had belonged to Moses. *Moses had laid his hands upon him,* indicating that he was passing on the *spirit of wisdom* that God had given to him. Since the Hebrew language has no system of capitalization, we cannot know if the word *spirit* should be capitalized. Whether it is or not, the verse makes clear that Joshua's wisdom came from the Lord. *The children of Israel* understood this, so they *hearkened* to Joshua and obeyed him. However, Joshua was only giving the instructions that God had given to Moses long before. The people actually obeyed *the Lord.* In the next two lessons, we will see examples of the wonderful way in which the Lord led them. [See question #5, page 88.]

Conclusion

A. The Real Leader

In previous lessons we have seen Moses leading a nation so disobedient, so rebellious, and so stubborn that it took forty years to make a trip from Egypt to the promised land that should have taken closer to a year and a half. Though it took forty years, Moses did at last bring to the edge of the promised land a nation disciplined, toughened, and courageous enough to take the land. Why was Moses successful? Because, with rare exceptions, he himself was obedient to the real leader—the Lord.

This week we see Joshua stepping into Moses' place of leadership. In the weeks ahead, we shall see Joshua leading his people across the Jordan, capturing Jericho, and sweeping on in victory to make the promised land the Israelites' own. Why were they successful? Because both Joshua and the people were following the real leader—the Lord.

In the promised land the people were secure and prosperous as long as Joshua lived to lead them, and longer. But when the leaders of the invasion died, the next generation of Israelites began to disobey their real leader. Without His protection, the people soon fell prey to their enemies (Judges 2:6-15).

Centuries later, God's people were so disobedient that God delivered them over to the power of Babylon for seventy years. And centuries after that, in a horrible climax of disobedience, the rulers of Israel crucified the Son of God. In so doing, the chief priests declared, "We have no king but Caesar" (John 19:15). They had rejected outright their real leader.

B. Follow the Leader

"I will build my church," said Jesus (Matthew 16:18). And He continues to build it. It rests on the foundation of the apostles and prophets who told us of God's will, but Jesus Himself is the chief cornerstone (Ephesians 2:19, 20).

Today are we following our real leader? How can we follow Him better? Two thoughts should be evident.

First, we must listen, or "hearken," as the *King James Version* has it (Deuteronomy 18:19). Jesus speaks to us through the pages of the New Testament. Some editions print the quoted words of Jesus in red ink so we can identify them at a glance, but we must not think that no other words tell us of Jesus' will. He speaks to us also through the writing of His inspired apostles and prophets: Matthew, Mark, Luke, John, Paul, Peter, James, and Jude. Do you know all these too well to be misled by someone who misrepresents them?

Second, we must be "doers of the word, and not hearers only" (James 1:22). Does the word of Christ "dwell in you richly" so that you obey it automatically (Colossians 3:16)? Do you do whatever you do "in the name of the Lord Jesus" (Colossians 3:17)?

Honestly, do you love God with all that is in you (Matthew 22:37, 38)? How have you shown it in the past week?

Do you really love your neighbor as yourself (Matthew 22:39)? How have you shown it?

More than this, do you "love your enemies, bless them that curse you, do good to them that hate you, and pray for them which despitefully use you, and persecute you" (Matthew 5:44)? Can you think of any recent examples where you have shown that kind of love?

This week, do you want to do more in obedience to our real leader—Jesus?

C. Prayer

O Father, how poorly we have been following You! How we need Your mercy and grace! Forgive us, we pray. We do want to do better this week. In our Master's name. Amen.

D. Thought to Remember

Follow the Leader.

Learning by Doing

This page contains an alternate lesson plan emphasizing learning activities.
Classes desiring such student involvement will find these suggestions helpful.

Learning Goals

After participating in this lesson, students should be able to:

1. Describe the transfer of leadership in Israel from Moses to Joshua, according to today's text.

2. Tell why godly leadership is essential to the accomplishment of God's work.

3. Express their appreciation for Jesus' leadership in their lives, and for the leadership of someone in their church.

Into the Lesson

Divide your class into three or four smaller groups. Give each group a newspaper and ask the members to scan the paper for articles featuring dynamic leaders or changes in leadership. (Obviously you will need to have collected newspapers during the days before this class session. The longer you have spent collecting them, the greater will be the variety of story lines.) If you don't have newspapers, ask each group to select a historical leader about whom they are knowledgeable (e.g., George Washington, Alexander the Great, Winston Churchill, a famous sports coach). Ask the groups to discuss among themselves what made these leaders so important.

Allow your students five minutes to work. Then ask a representative from each group to explain either why the featured leader is/was dynamic or what difficulties (if any) the change in leadership caused. What leadership qualities does/did the leader in question possess? What distinguishes this leader from others?

Stress to the class the importance of a good leader. Israel had one: Moses. In today's text we see the mantle of leadership passed to Joshua.

Into the Word

Begin by reading the printed text (Deuteronomy 31:1-8; 34:5-9). Ask your class, "Why was Moses not permitted to enter the promised land?" and "How do you think Moses felt about not completing the task after dedicating forty years of his life to it?" *(For the first question, refer to Numbers 20:8-12; Deuteronomy 32:48-52. The second question is more subjective and should evoke a variety of answers.)*

Ask, "How do you feel when a new leader assumes authority over our country?" *(The answer probably depends on the new leader's "politics," the popularity of the previous leader, the kinds of* turmoil the former leader caused or calmed, and similar issues.) Ask, "How do you think you would have felt about having someone replace Moses?" After a brief discussion you can probably conclude that most people would feel a bit uneasy. Ask the class to look in the text to find as many promises as they can that God gave Israel to reassure them at this critical time. *(God would go before them; God would destroy the enemy nations; Israel would possess the land; the Lord would not fail them; the Lord would not forsake them.)*

Ask, "How do you suppose Joshua felt? What reasons can you think of that might have left him apprehensive about his new role?" *(Following a popular leader is difficult, even in the best of circumstances. Joshua had not only Moses' "shadow" to think of, but he faced opposition from hostile forces and was leading a group with a history of mutiny.)* Ask the class to list God's promises to Joshua to reassure him. *(Moses reminded him that God had sworn to give Israel the land; Joshua would "cause them to inherit it"; the Lord would go before Joshua; He would be with Joshua, and He would not fail or forsake Joshua.)*

Into Life

Give a three-inch-by-five-inch index card to each member of your class. Say, "This lesson reminds us of leaders in our own lives. Often we understand how much responsibility such people carry, but we fail to show them the appreciation they deserve."

Remind your students that Jesus is the foremost authority in their lives, and a model leader at that. Discuss how they could better appreciate Jesus' authority in their own lives (prayer, devotion time, ministry, service).

Second, ask each student to think of a leader he or she respects in the church and write the leader's name on the note card. (No names should be spoken aloud.) Give these instructions: "Think of three ways you can express appreciation this week to the person whose name you have written. Such appreciation can range from verbal acknowledgments to services rendered. Write down the ideas you think of."

Challenge your students to follow through in the tasks they have written. Then close with a prayer of appreciation for the leaders in your church.

Let's Talk It Over

The questions on this page are designed to encourage review of the lesson Scriptures and to promote discussion of the lesson by the class. The answers provided are only discussion starters. Let your class talk it over from there.

1. Moses knew when to step down as Israel's leader because the Lord told him. How can we today know when we ought to give up a position of leadership and let another take up the reins?

In addition to the Lord's word, Moses cited his age as a reason for "retiring" from leadership. While the Lord does not require retirement at any set age, advanced age can play a role in one's deciding to step down from leadership. Along with age often comes failing health or a lack of the energy needed for leadership in some ministries. (Note, however, that in Moses' case this was not the issue; see Deuteronomy 34:7.)

Besides age, changes in the makeup of the church's membership may call for leadership skills that are different from those the current leader possesses. Opposition may or may not be a factor. Moses was opposed often, but his leadership was just what the Israelites needed in those times. Still, if the leader and those with whom he works often clash on philosophy or methodology, the leader may do himself a favor if he finds another area of service.

2. How important do you think it is to exhort believers to "be strong and of a good courage"? Why?

Many believers are easily discouraged by current events. Declining morality, public scandals, and unjust court decisions are just a few of the problems that lead to a feeling of general discouragement. Add to that specific cases of rejection or ridicule, and a healthy dose of encouragement becomes critical. Perhaps your class members can relate some of the factors that particularly discourage or even frighten them in their Christian walk, and then discuss how they can "be strong and of a good courage." Perhaps you'll want to have them look up such New Testament promises as those found in Matthew 18:20; 28:18-20; Ephesians 3:14-21; Philippians 2:12, 13; Colossians 1:27; Hebrews 13:5, 6; 1 John 4:4.

3. Joshua, as the new leader, was especially challenged to "be strong and of a good courage." What are some ways we can encourage Christian leaders today?

Some church members seem to think they have been divinely commissioned to criticize the leadership of the church. Far better it would be to build the leaders up with words of encouragement, notes, recognizing their birthdays, anniversaries, etc., and other tangible means of encouragement. Especially helpful is a word spoken publicly to encourage the leader and to express and rally support for the work the leader is trying to do. This does not suggest blind following of any and every idea a leader has, no matter how bizarre. But when the time comes to express concern about a program or to approach the leader with a word of advice, the habitual encourager will be heard much more readily than will the constant critic!

4. Moses knew he would not reach the goal of the Israelites' forty-year trek in the wilderness—even as a whole generation of his followers had not. He might well have been discouraged, but still he was the one who encouraged the others. How might you use Moses' example to encourage a leader who is discouraged about the lack of results he sees in his work?

By many standards, Moses could be considered a failure, but God rated him a great success. "He endured," the writer of Hebrews says, "as seeing him who is invisible" (Hebrews 11:27). We all know leaders who work in ministries that do not show great or obvious results, but we can encourage them to look beyond the obvious and tangible and to share the reward of Moses!

5. Suppose one of the Israelites had complained that Joshua just wasn't the leader Moses had been. If you had been there, how would you have responded? What if one of them had said, "Joshua is pushing ninety himself—we need a younger leader for this young nation"?

Joshua was God's man for the job—there was no question about that. Differences between his style and Moses' were just that—differences, not deficiencies. His age was inconsequential. Even Moses did not "retire" because of his *age.*

It's easy to say what we would have done when we were not there, but many of us need to be careful about the way we treat new leaders today. Do we make unfair comparisons between new and old leaders? Do we generalize about their age or experience, or do we allow them to prove themselves? Discuss how you can give new leaders a fair chance in their new roles.

Israel Crosses the Jordan River

DEVOTIONAL READING: Joshua 4:15-24.

BACKGROUND SCRIPTURE: Joshua 3.

PRINTED TEXT: Joshua 3:7-17.

Joshua 3:7-17

7 And the LORD said unto Joshua, This day will I begin to magnify thee in the sight of all Israel, that they may know that, as I was with Moses, so I will be with thee.

8 And thou shalt command the priests that bear the ark of the covenant, saying, When ye are come to the brink of the water of Jordan, ye shall stand still in Jordan.

9 And Joshua said unto the children of Israel, Come hither, and hear the words of the LORD your God.

10 And Joshua said, Hereby ye shall know that the living God is among you, and that he will without fail drive out from before you the Canaanites, and the Hittites, and the Hivites, and the Perizzites, and the Girgashites, and the Amorites, and the Jebusites.

11 Behold, the ark of the covenant of the Lord of all the earth passeth over before you into Jordan.

12 Now therefore take you twelve men out of the tribes of Israel, out of every tribe a man.

13 And it shall come to pass, as soon as the soles of the feet of the priests that bear the ark of the LORD, the Lord of all the earth, shall rest in the waters of Jordan, that the waters of Jordan shall be cut off from the waters that come down from above; and they shall stand upon a heap.

14 And it came to pass, when the people removed from their tents, to pass over Jordan, and the priests bearing the ark of the covenant before the people;

15 And as they that bare the ark were come unto Jordan, and the feet of the priests that bare the ark were dipped in the brim of the water, (for Jordan overfloweth all his banks all the time of harvest,)

16 That the waters which came down from above stood and rose up upon a heap very far from the city Adam, that is beside Zaretan; and those that came down toward the sea of the plain, even the salt sea, failed, and were cut off: and the people passed over right against Jericho.

17 And the priests that bare the ark of the covenant of the LORD stood firm on dry ground in the midst of Jordan, and all the Israelites passed over on dry ground, until all the people were passed clean over Jordan.

Nov
14

GOLDEN TEXT: Be strong and of a good courage; be not afraid, neither be thou dismayed: for the LORD thy God is with thee whithersoever thou goest.—Joshua 1:9.

Lesson Aims

After this lesson students should be able to:

1. Summarize the plan by which God led the children of Israel across the Jordan River.

2. Recall times in their lives when God's guidance saw them through difficult circumstances.

3. Suggest a way to "memorialize" these and future occasions so that they will not be forgotten.

Lesson Outline

INTRODUCTION
  A. Reflections on Rain
  B. Lesson Background
 I. GOD'S WORDS (Joshua 3:7-13)
  A. For Joshua (v. 7)
  B. For the Priests (v. 8)
  C. For the People (vv. 9-13)
    Against the "Laws of Nature"
II. GOD'S ACTIONS (Joshua 3:14-17)
  A. The Trusting Start (vv. 14, 15)
  B. The Opened Way (v. 16)
  C. The Safe Arrival (v. 17)
    History Repeats Itself
CONCLUSION
  A. Memorial Monuments
  B. Personal Memories
  C. National Memories
  D. Prayer
  E. Thought to Remember

Introduction

A. Reflections on Rain

"It never rains in summertime." So says an advertising sign in Tel Aviv, and nearly always it is true in Israel. Once, in the time of Samuel, there was a heavy rain during harvesttime, but everyone knew that it was a miracle (1 Samuel 12:16-18).

Do you remember learning about why such dry summers occur in that part of the world? When warm weather comes, the dry land is warmed much faster than the waters of the Mediterranean Sea. When moisture-laden sea air moves inland, it is warmed and dried by the warm earth, so there is no rain. In winter the same principle works the other way. The land

cools faster than the sea. When sea air moves inland, it is cooled by the cool earth. Its moisture condenses into rain or, on some occasions, snow.

B. Lesson Background

It appears that the rainy season had ended while the people of Israel were mourning the death of Moses (Deuteronomy 34:8). For weeks after that, the runoff from the tributaries to the north (which included the melting from the snows on higher elevations such as Mount Hermon) continued to pour into the Jordan. Soon the river flowed out of its banks, spreading over the valley floor that is sometimes called the plain of Jordan.

As we have observed in our previous studies from Deuteronomy, the people of Israel were camped on the east side of the Jordan. There appeared to be no way for them to get their families and goods and livestock across the river. They would have to wait for the high waters to recede. But God had other plans, and He revealed them to Joshua, who had taken Moses' place as the leader of Israel. The camp of Israel had been some miles from the river; now it was moved closer (Joshua 3:1). Then came the day when Joshua told the people to prepare for another move. "Tomorrow," he said, "the Lord will do wonders among you" (Joshua 3:5).

I. God's Words
(Joshua 3:7-13)

Like Moses before him, Joshua was the second in command in Israel. The first in command was the Lord. Joshua gave no order to Israel until he had received an order from God.

A. For Joshua (v. 7)

7. And the LORD said unto Joshua, This day will I begin to magnify thee in the sight of all Israel, that they may know that, as I was with Moses, so I will be with thee.

Ultimately the people of Israel owed their allegiance to *the Lord,* not to *Joshua* alone. They would accept Joshua as their leader if they knew the Lord was *with* him. All through the past forty years the Lord had been *with Moses* and had demonstrated that fact in unmistakable ways. For example, at one time there had been a rebellion against Moses. To show that the Lord was on Moses' side, the earth had swallowed the rebels (Numbers 16:1-33).

Now Joshua was beginning his leadership of Israel, and the Lord was about to show how He would be with Joshua just as He had been with Moses. He would do this, not by having rebels destroyed, but by enabling Joshua to foretell a great miracle (v. 13). This miracle would indicate that God was with all the people and would do great things for them (v. 10); Joshua's prediction would demonstrate that God was with Joshua. Thus God would *magnify* Joshua and make him great *in the sight of all Israel.* [See question #1, page 96.]

B. For the Priests (v. 8)

8. And thou shalt command the priests that bear the ark of the covenant, saying, When ye are come to the brink of the water of Jordan, ye shall stand still in Jordan.

The priests that bear the ark of the covenant were to lead the march straight into the flooded river. As they waded into the shallow water at the edge, they were to *stand still.* The water would then vanish before them (v. 13). Verse 17 adds that the priests carrying the ark would then go on to the middle of the river and remain standing there until all the people crossed over.

C. For the People (vv. 9-13)

9. And Joshua said unto the children of Israel, Come hither, and hear the words of the LORD your God.

Joshua wanted *the children of Israel to come* as close as they could so that all of them could hear him. He began by declaring that they would *hear the words of the Lord,* not merely the words of Joshua.

10. And Joshua said, Hereby ye shall know that the living God is among you, and that he will without fail drive out from before you the Canaanites, and the Hittites, and the Hivites, and the Perizzites, and the Girgashites, and the Amorites, and the Jebusites.

Seven warlike peoples lived in the country west of the Jordan—the land that the Lord had promised to Israel. It would take courage to march into that country—more courage than the fathers of those Israelites had exhibited thirty-eight years earlier. Intimidated by giants and high city walls, that previous generation had balked at the border of the promised land, refusing to capture the land God had given them.

Now, as the new generation of Israelites was gathered before the Jordan, the giants and the high city walls were still present. The seven peoples listed by Joshua were the same ones mentioned by Moses in Deuteronomy 7:1. The coming battle was not one for Israel to undertake alone. They would need *the living God* to be *among* them. Joshua proceeded to give the people a sign to prove that this was so.

11. Behold, the ark of the covenant of the Lord of all the earth passeth over before you into Jordan.

The *ark of the covenant* was a symbol of God's presence and favor. It held the Ten Commandments engraved on enduring stone—the symbol of God's enduring and unchanging authority. He was leading the way into the flooded *Jordan* and into the battles beyond it. Israel could confidently follow without fear. [See question #2, page 96.]

12. Now therefore take you twelve men out of the tribes of Israel, out of every tribe a man.

What these *twelve men* were to do is not described at this point, but it will be a part of the miracle that is soon to take place. We shall come back to them later in the lesson.

13. And it shall come to pass, as soon as the soles of the feet of the priests that bear the ark of the LORD, the Lord of all the earth, shall rest in the waters of Jordan, that the waters of Jordan shall be cut off from the waters that come down from above; and they shall stand upon a heap.

Now Joshua described the convincing sign promised in verse 10. Soon the *priests* would wade into the *Jordan,* carrying *the ark of the Lord.* At the touch of their feet, the water in front of them would be *cut off from the waters that come down from above.* The water in front of the Israelites would flow on down toward the Dead Sea, but the water upstream would rise up in *a heap,* forming a growing mountain of water somewhere to the north. In front of Israel would be a dry riverbed. The people would walk across it without getting their feet wet.

Can you imagine a more convincing proof of the presence and power of the Lord? The similarity of this miracle to the crossing of the Red Sea would assure the people that the Lord who had brought the previous generation safely out of Egypt would bring them safely into the promised land and allow them to possess it.

AGAINST THE "LAWS OF NATURE"

Ann Landers is a famous purveyor of advice on many issues. Occasionally she prints items purportedly taken from the tests and papers of grade-school children. A recent list included the following from some fifth- and sixth-graders:

• "The law of gravity says no fair jumping up without coming back down."

• "You can listen to thunder and tell how close you came to getting hit. If you don't hear it, you got hit, so never mind."

• "A vibration is a motion that cannot make up its mind which way it wants to go."

These childlike perceptions of how things work in the world are unsophisticated; but like adult hypotheses, they are attempts to apply some sense of regularity to what happens in

God's creation. We trust this regularity and call exceptions to it "miracles."

When Joshua prophesied what would happen when the priests stepped into the Jordan River, he was saying, in effect, "You should follow my leading, for God has told me that a miracle will take place. He will make things happen that could not happen except by the power of God. The God who led Moses and your parents across the Red Sea is leading us now." That same God will lead us here and now and into eternity!

—C. R. B.

II. God's Actions
(Joshua 3:14-17)

A. The Trusting Start (vv. 14, 15)

14. And it came to pass, when the people removed from their tents, to pass over Jordan, and the priests bearing the ark of the covenant before the people.

Slowly the huge caravan was formed. The *priests bearing the ark of the covenant* led the way. The *people* left their campsite and followed at a respectful distance (Joshua 3:4). All Israel *removed from their tents* and prepared to approach the flooded *Jordan*, though not one of them could possibly wade across it.

15. And as they that bare the ark were come unto Jordan, and the feet of the priests that bare the ark were dipped in the brim of the water, (for Jordan overfloweth all his banks all the time of harvest).

This was the crucial moment in the promised sign of God's presence and power. Once *the feet of the priests . . . were dipped in the brim of the water*, it was time for the miracle to begin (v. 13). The fact that the *Jordan overfloweth all his banks all the time of harvest* is mentioned to underscore the magnificence of the sign.

B. The Opened Way (v. 16)

16. That the waters which came down from above stood and rose up upon a heap very far from the city Adam, that is beside Zaretan; and those that came down toward the sea of the plain, even the salt sea, failed, and were cut off: and the people passed over right against Jericho.

What happened was so unusual and marvelous that it was hard to find words to describe it. Some details of the record are not clear, but the main facts are indisputable. The water that *came down from above* simply piled up in *a heap*. That heap was upstream from Israel, of course, but it is hard to tell just where. The Hebrew text describes "one heap, very distant, at Adam." In the *King James* rendering of the verse, it is best to see the words *very far* as describing

where the heap was in relation to the Israelites. The heap originated *from the city* of Adam, which was *beside Zaretan.*

All of this would be somewhat less confusing if we knew where Adam and Zaretan were, but their exact locations are uncertain. The scene becomes more dramatic if we suppose that the people could see the waters rising swiftly into a mountain north of them, but the record does not make it clear whether the mound was in sight. At the same time, the waters right in front of Israel were *cut off*, or separated, and kept on flowing down toward *the sea of the plain, even the salt sea.* (These are two ways of describing the body of water we usually call the Dead Sea.)

As a result of all of this, in front of the people of Israel was no water at all—only the empty bed of a river! Very easily the people *passed over* that waterless ground, going straight toward the city of *Jericho*, which was just a few miles west of the river. [See question #3, page 96.]

C. The Safe Arrival (v. 17)

17. And the priests that bare the ark of the covenant of the LORD stood firm on dry ground in the midst of Jordan, and all the Israelites passed over on dry ground, until all the people were passed clean over Jordan.

Carrying *the ark of the covenant of the Lord*, the priests proceeded forward until they came to the middle of the dry riverbed. There the priests *stood firm* while *all the Israelites passed over* and went on to the west bank of the river. The ark was the symbol of God's presence and authority. Positioned there in the middle of the *dry ground*, it pictured God holding back the flooded Jordan while His people crossed to the other side. [See question #4, page 96.]

How to Say It

ADAM. Uh-*dahm.*
AMORITES. *Am*-uh-rites.
CANAANITES. *Kay*-nuh-nites.
CINCINNATUS. Sin-sih-*nat*-us.
DEUTERONOMY. Due-ter-*ahn*-uh-me.
GIRGASHITES. *Gur*-guh-shites.
HITTITES. *Hit*-tites.
HIVITES. *Hi*-vites.
JEBUSITES. *Jeb*-you-sites.
JERICHO. *Jair*-ih-ko.
MEDITERRANEAN. *Med*-uh-tuh-*ray*-nee-un
    (strong accent on *ray*).
PERIZZITES. *Pair*-ih-zites.
SINAI. *Sigh*-nye or *Sigh*-nay-eye.
ZARETAN. *Zair*-uh-tan.

When all the Israelites were gathered safely on the high ground west of the river, Joshua called to the priests, and they too walked the rest of the way across. Then the mountain of water came down with a rush, filling the wide channel, covering the banks, and spreading over the plain; but it did not reach the spot that Israel had chosen for a new campground. Read about all of this in Joshua 4:15-18.

What happened to those twelve men mentioned in verse 12 of our text? One of them was from each of the twelve tribes of Israel, remember? Thus they formed a committee representing the entire nation, and they had a special job to do. They were to get twelve stones from the middle of the river and carry them to the west bank. There Joshua would build the stones into a monument in memory of the miraculous crossing (Joshua 4:1-7).

Over the course of many generations, that monument would be seen by travelers, including family groups who would eventually go to Jerusalem for the annual feasts. Parents would tell their children of the miraculous crossing, and those children would repeat the story years later to their children. That story would lead to others: the crossing of the Red Sea, the providing of manna in the desert, the miraculous supplying of water from dry rock, and the giving of the Ten Commandments from Sinai. Thus through many centuries this simple monument would help to perpetuate the knowledge of God's power and God's care for His people.

Joshua 4:9 adds that Joshua constructed a similar monument in the middle of the river. Stones for that memorial would not have to be carried far, so bigger, heavier stones could be used. Probably the top of this monument could be seen above the water during the dry season. It would be an added teaching help as travelers were fording the stream when it was shallow.

HISTORY REPEATS ITSELF

Some people believe that a spacecraft from outer space crashed near Roswell, New Mexico, in 1947, killing the extraterrestrial aliens aboard. "UFOlogists" refuse to accept the U.S. government's denial that an alien crash took place. In 1997, fifty years later, true believers placed a plaque on a ranch near the supposed site of the crash. It said, "We don't know who they were; we don't know why they came; we only know they changed our view of the universe."

The plaque was put in place as part of a weekend celebration. The owner of the land at the "crash site" charged fifteen dollars per person for a tour of the area. Campsites for the weekend cost ninety dollars. Hundreds of people attended the six-day festival. A comic later remarked, "As in the past, nothing happened, but this time there were more witnesses." In other words, history repeated itself when an alien spaceship didn't crash there this time either!

There was no doubt about what happened when the priests carrying the ark of the covenant stepped into the Jordan River. At the defining moment when Israel became a free people, leaving Egypt behind, the Red Sea had parted and they had walked across on dry land. Now, as God led them to the land they would call their own, history indeed repeated itself and they crossed the Jordan on dry ground.

When God is at work, history is under His control. —C. R. B.

Conclusion

Once they reached the west side of the Jordan, the people of Israel could never forget how they got there. For them the Lord had overcome the flooded river, and for them He could overcome the flood of pagan warriors that awaited them. Buoyed by that faith, the Israelites plunged into that pagan flood and moved on from victory to victory. And through the years that followed, a simple monument of uncut stones by the river told each new generation about God's power and care, and called each new generation to trust and obey Him. [See question #5, page 96.]

A. Memorial Monuments

Since I live in Cincinnati, I have seen beside the Ohio River a statue of Cincinnatus and his plow. It calls to mind that ancient hero who turned his back on fame and fortune and went home to cultivate his farm. To every thoughtful passerby it says that growing food for the hungry

Today's visual applies our Golden Text to trials we may face today. What trials confront your class today? How can you find courage to face them?

Visual for lesson 11

can be as noble as leading an army; and to me personally it says that writing Sunday school lessons can be noble too, if I do it well.

In downtown Cincinnati I see another memorial monument. It is a statue of James A. Garfield, a minister of the gospel who became President of the United States. In the course of that service he was assassinated. As I pause to meditate, that silent statue tells me that faithful service to God and man is dearer than life itself. That agrees with the words of Jesus: "If any man will come after me, let him deny himself, and take up his cross, and follow me" (Matthew 16:24).

Probably your town has a memorial monument, too. When you stop to think, what do you hear it saying?

B. Personal Memories

When I was a child I nearly drowned. I was unconscious under the water when a man rescued me. He laid me on the ground, limp and pale and apparently lifeless. Mouth-to-mouth resuscitation was unknown then, but the Lord restored my breathing.

As a teenager I had typhoid fever and nearly died. But one day the Lord took away the fever, and I am alive today.

When I was middle-aged, I was involved in a terrible crash on the highway. Seeing the mangled remains of my car afterward, people said, "Nobody came out of that one alive!" As a matter of fact, my whole family came out alive. How can that be explained unless the Lord had a hand in it?

Think of your own life. Haven't you seen some wonderful works of God? Don't they compel you to trust God and obey Him today, tomorrow, and forever?

C. National Memories

The nation of Israel remembered the crossing of the Jordan and other wonderful works that showed God's power and His favor to Israel.

With rare exceptions, that memory kept Israel faithful to God through their years of fighting for the promised land, and for years after the fighting was over and the land was won. However, within the next generation the memory grew dim, and national faithfulness began to wane (Judges 2:7-15). In that bit of history lies a warning for every nation.

People in the United States of America pause each year on the fourth day of July to remember how their forefathers declared their independence from Great Britain and then procured it "with a firm reliance on the protection of divine Providence." While they continue to exercise their independence, do U.S. citizens still continue that "firm reliance"?

On the same continent the citizens of Mexico observe a similar day of independence on the sixteenth day of September. But do they remember that "the Most High ruleth in the kingdom of men, and giveth it to whomsoever he will" (Daniel 4:17)?

On the first of July the citizens of the largest country in North America observe Canada Day. They pause to remember and celebrate the consolidation of four separate provinces into one nation. But do the people and the government remember to trust and obey the Lord who "ruleth in the kingdom of men"?

During the latter half of the nineteenth century, Great Britain's influence in the world reached its peak. On Queen Victoria's Diamond Jubilee in 1897, Britain's navies gathered to the homeland for a happy celebration. Then, as the great ships steamed away on their worldwide missions, a thoughtful poet, Rudyard Kipling, penned a prayer that is most relevant to our times:

> If, drunk with sight of power, we loose
>   Wild tongues that have not Thee in awe—
> Such boasting as the Gentiles use
>   Or lesser breeds without the Law—
> Lord God of Hosts, be with us yet,
>   Lest we forget—lest we forget!

D. Prayer

How great Thou art, our Father and our God! From the day when You created the heavens and the earth to this present day, Your power and Your goodness have been evident in every generation. Thank You for such a clear testimony, Father, and thank You for our memories. In Jesus' name, amen.

E. Thought to Remember

Lord God of Hosts, be with us yet,
Lest we forget—lest we forget!

Learning by Doing

This page contains an alternate lesson plan emphasizing learning activities.
Classes desiring such student involvement will find these suggestions helpful.

Learning Goals

After this lesson, students should be able to:

1. Summarize the plan by which God led the children of Israel across the Jordan River.

2. Recall times in their lives when God's guidance saw them through difficult circumstances.

3. Suggest a way to "memorialize" these and future occasions so they will not be forgotten.

Into the Lesson

If you are able to do so in your classroom, arrange the chairs in a "maze" before the students arrive. Ask for a volunteer at the beginning of class. Blindfold the volunteer and stand him at the start of the maze. Direct him through the maze with vocal commands only (e.g., "turn right," or "turn left, take two steps, and turn right"). If you have a small classroom, secure a larger room for this activity. One can also arrange the students in a maze and navigate the blindfolded student through a maze of his own classmates. The point is to show how leadership is needed in a time of difficulty. We need to follow God's guidance in life.

If the maze idea won't work, ask the students to think of a time when God's guidance led them through a difficult time in their lives. It need not be too personal. Ask your students to share some of their experiences. Prepare to share an experience or two of your own.

Observe that in our lesson today we'll see Israel at an extremely vulnerable time in its history. Not only did the people have to ford a swollen river, but they needed to conquer seven hostile peoples before finding rest in the promised land. Israel needed God's guidance now more than ever.

Into the Word

Ask a volunteer to read today's Scripture aloud (Joshua 3:7-17). Use the contents of the lesson commentary to give a brief lecture on this passage. If possible, provide a map of the area so students can visualize the Bible passage. (See the visual for lesson 2.)

Ask your students to construct a chronological occurrence of events. Ask the students to call out randomly some of the events mentioned in the text while you write them on the chalkboard or on a large poster. Then work together to determine the chronological order of the events.

Write numbers (1, 2, 3, etc.) next to the events to show which happened first, second, third, etc. A summary of the significant events follows:

God speaks to Joshua; Joshua tells the people what God said to do; the priests carry the ark into the river; the flow of water stops; Israel crosses on dry ground; twelve men collect stones for a memorial; the priests come out of the riverbed; the river resumes its normal flow.

Discuss the significance of the priests' carrying the ark into the waters first. *(It demonstrated that God was leading them into the new territory. How can we be sure God is leading today?)*

Ask a student to read the account of the Red Sea crossing (Exodus 14:15-31). What similarities exist between these two miracles? *(Both were signs from God to His people. Both involved a halt in natural occurrences. Each event signaled a dramatic change in the national situation of Israel. You may note other similarities.)*

Ask, "What was the first thing the Israelites did after each crossing?" *(They memorialized the event in some way—a song, Exodus 15, or a monument, Joshua 4.)* Ask, "Why is it important to memorialize God's guidance in our lives?"

Into Life

Ask your students to recall times when God helped them through difficult circumstances. Urge them to find ways to memorialize these events. Perhaps they can write songs or poems or stories of their events. Others might record the instances in prayer logs, or set aside specific times to pray and thank God for His guidance.

As a class, find some way of memorializing God's guidance in general. Perhaps you could write a skit about God's guidance and perform it for the rest of the church. If your class does not wish to perform the skit for the entire church, at least record the skit on video. If your class is more "hands-on," make a trophy or a plaque to display in the classroom. During the week prior to class, collect any craft items you feel might aid this exercise (e.g., construction paper, glue, shoe boxes, paint, balsa wood, Styrofoam, etc.). The final product may not be the most attractive specimen, but it will remind the students of today's lesson each time they see it.

To close, gather in a prayer circle and thank God for His guidance in the past and for His continued guidance throughout the coming week.

Let's Talk It Over

The questions on this page are designed to encourage review of the lesson Scriptures and to promote discussion of the lesson by the class. The answers provided are only discussion starters. Let your class talk it over from there.

1. One reason for the miraculous crossing of the Jordan was to give Joshua credibility as the new leader of Israel (to "magnify [him] in the sight of all Israel"). How does a Christian leader gain credibility today? What do you look for in a leader? Why?

In the Biblical period God used miracles to credential His servants the prophets and even His own Son, as Nicodemus recognized (John 3:2). Today we look for qualities like honesty, integrity, and character. We want to know that the leaders we follow are genuine and not hiding behind some pretense. We look for experience, for wisdom that comes from testing. Paul cautioned the church not to appoint a new Christian as either an elder (1 Timothy 3:6) or a deacon (v. 10). Surely we want a leader who first and foremost walks with God.

2. It was an encouragement to the nation of Israel to see the ark of the covenant—the symbol of God's presence—going before them. What encourages you in following the Lord? What reassures you that God Himself goes before you and with you?

The Bible gives us many assurances of God's presence. One of the most important is its assurance that Jesus Christ Himself has gone before us to show us the way and to encourage us. In Hebrews 4:15 and 16 we are told that Jesus our high priest "was in all points tempted like as we are, yet without sin," and that through Him "we may obtain mercy, and find grace to help in time of need."

Hebrews 10:24 and 25 remind us that the presence of fellow believers can encourage us to be faithful. By their words and faithful example, our brothers and sisters in the Lord can be a great help when we grow weary or discouraged.

3. When the Israelites obeyed, the Lord made a way for them to cross the flooded Jordan. How can that fact strengthen our faith in the Lord's power to make a way for us through difficult circumstances?

We often encounter problems that seem virtually impossible to resolve. Some of us may be facing financial crises. Perhaps someone in the class has a serious personality conflict with a fellow employee or even another member of the

church. Another may be confronted with a critical threat to his or her health through sickness or injury.

Whatever the problem, we need to focus on the Lord and on obeying Him. We cannot use our circumstances to excuse disobedience. Had Israel not obeyed and stepped out in faith into the flooded Jordan, they never would have seen what God could do for them! Jesus once said, "With God all things are possible" (Matthew 19:26). Some preachers have put it well in stating, "God specializes in the impossible."

4. Of course, it was the priests, not the people in general, who had their faith most sorely tested in the crossing of the Jordan. They were the ones who stepped into water—the others saw the waters cut off before they entered the riverbed. And the priests had to stand in the middle of the riverbed while the rest of the people hurried on by. What does this suggest to you about leadership?

Leaders have always had demands placed on them that are not applied to others. In the church, the faith of the congregation rarely exceeds the faith of its leadership. If the church is raising funds for a building or special project, often the leadership will make and publicize a special pledge in advance to inspire others to give. Leaders have an obligation to look to the Lord for their strength and direction, and to encourage others to do the same.

5. Joshua 4:1-8 tells how the twelve men selected in verse 12 of the text collected stones from the riverbed for a monument to commemorate the crossing of the Jordan. What can we do to fix firmly in our memories those occasions when God's guidance and help have been especially evident?

Many Christians keep journals as a way of recalling important events and circumstances in their lives. These can serve a worthwhile purpose as a record of God's blessings and providential guidance. As a church we may hold annual celebrations of important events in our history. As long as they are used to glorify God and do not become empty ritual, these can be very edifying and may help us to see God at work in other areas of our lives.

God Destroys Jericho

DEVOTIONAL READING: Psalm 47.

BACKGROUND SCRIPTURE: Joshua 6.

PRINTED TEXT: Joshua 6:1-5, 15-20.

Joshua 6:1-5, 15-20

1 Now Jericho was straitly shut up because of the children of Israel: none went out, and none came in.

2 And the LORD said unto Joshua, See, I have given into thine hand Jericho, and the king thereof, and the mighty men of valor.

3 And ye shall compass the city, all ye men of war, and go round about the city once. Thus shalt thou do six days.

4 And seven priests shall bear before the ark seven trumpets of rams' horns: and the seventh day ye shall compass the city seven times, and the priests shall blow with the trumpets.

5 And it shall come to pass, that when they make a long blast with the ram's horn, and when ye hear the sound of the trumpet, all the people shall shout with a great shout; and the wall of the city shall fall down flat, and the people shall ascend up every man straight before him.

. . . .

15 And it came to pass on the seventh day, that they rose early about the dawning of the day, and compassed the city after the same manner seven times: only on that day they compassed the city seven times.

16 And it came to pass at the seventh time, when the priests blew with the trumpets, Joshua said unto the people, Shout; for the LORD hath given you the city.

17 And the city shall be accursed, even it, and all that are therein, to the LORD: only Rahab the harlot shall live, she and all that are with her in the house, because she hid the messengers that we sent.

18 And ye, in any wise keep yourselves from the accursed thing, lest ye make yourselves accursed, when ye take of the accursed thing, and make the camp of Israel a curse, and trouble it.

19 But all the silver, and gold, and vessels of brass and iron, are consecrated unto the LORD: they shall come into the treasury of the LORD.

20 So the people shouted when the priests blew with the trumpets: and it came to pass, when the people heard the sound of the trumpet, and the people shouted with a great shout, that the wall fell down flat, so that the people went up into the city, every man straight before him, and they took the city.

GOLDEN TEXT: And it came to pass at the seventh time, when the priests blew with the trumpets, Joshua said unto the people, Shout; for the LORD hath given you the city.—Joshua 6:16.

Lesson Aims

After this lesson, each student will be able to:

1. Summarize how God delivered the city of Jericho into the hands of the Israelites.

2. Tell how Christians today are to face the wicked "Jerichos" around them.

3. Express the need for personal holiness in today's world, and tell how he or she will cultivate it through time with God each day.

Lesson Outline

INTRODUCTION

 A. An End, Yet a Beginning

 B. Lesson Background

 I. BATTLE PLAN (Joshua 6:1-5)

 A. Frightened City (v. 1)

  The Chill of God's Displeasure

 B. Promise of Victory (v. 2)

 C. Instructions (vv. 3-5)

 II. CARRYING OUT THE PLAN (Joshua 6:15-20)

 A. The Long March (v. 15)

 B. The Signal (v. 16)

 C. Further Instructions (vv. 17-19)

  Certain Disaster

 D. Victory (v. 20)

CONCLUSION

 A. God's Judgment

 B. Our Judgment

 C. Our Duty

 D. Prayer

 E. Thought to Remember

Introduction

A. An End, Yet a Beginning

Driving westward across the great plains of middle America, we come in sight of the Rocky Mountains. At first they are only a silhouette on the horizon, as if cut from cardboard and pasted on the distant sky. Then, as we drive on, we come to a breathtaking but bewildering arrangement of mountains. We find a pass and leave a summit behind, only to see another summit looming ahead.

Geographically, the Jordan River is situated in a valley. Yet in importance, the crossing of that river was a high peak in the migration of Israel. Dangerous peaks of battle still loomed ahead, but

in a sense that crossing brought the Israelites to the end of their journey. They were in the promised land! They pitched their camp in Gilgal, between the river and the city of Jericho.

B. Lesson Background

During their years in the desert the Israelites had been guilty of frequent criticism of Moses, and in some cases open rebellion. But the Lord had intervened decisively in favor of Moses. (See, for example, the account of Miriam and Aaron's criticism of Moses in Numbers 12.) At this point it seems that the new generation of Israelites had learned their lesson. They clearly understood that the Lord was in charge and that He was giving orders through Joshua, who had taken the place of Moses. Commands were obeyed without question or protest, even when it was hard to see the importance or usefulness of them.

In Gilgal the Israelites observed the Passover forty years after the first Passover—the one they had observed in Egypt. They used the produce of the promised land for their food, and never again did they find manna lying around their camp in the morning (Joshua 5:10-12). For a time they lay quietly in camp, awaiting further instructions.

I. Battle Plan
(Joshua 6:1-5)

In God's own time He gave the order for Israel to advance to battle. With the command He provided a battle plan. Joshua passed it on to the Israelites, and they obeyed—even though they must have been quite mystified. This was a strange plan for conquering a city.

A. Frightened City (v. 1)

1. Now Jericho was straitly shut up because of the children of Israel: none went out, and none came in.

Before the Israelites crossed the Jordan, their spies learned that the people on the west bank were terrified of them. People of that region had heard how Israel had crossed the Red Sea forty years earlier, and how they had recently destroyed two nations east of the Jordan (Joshua 2:9-11). The residents of *Jericho* must have panicked when another miracle brought the invaders across the Jordan, for it looked as if Jericho would be next.

The frightened inhabitants of Jericho took refuge in the city and kept the gates locked day and night. *None went out, and none came in.* They could only hope that the city walls would keep them safe.

THE CHILL OF GOD'S DISPLEASURE

The winter of 1988-89 covered much of North America with record-breaking cold. The cold wave came out of the Arctic, swept through Alaska and across Canada, and proceeded into the midwestern states of the U.S. Temperatures stayed bitterly cold for several days in a row.

In the Alaskan town of Coldfoot—an aptly named community fifty miles north of the Arctic Circle—the temperature was reported to have dropped to -82°, which was colder than the official North American record set in the Canadian Yukon some forty years earlier.

All across Alaska (and elsewhere throughout Canada and the United States), schools and businesses closed, and people stayed inside their homes to survive. Food supplies were disrupted, and in some cases heating fuel wouldn't burn!

When the threat of external danger is so great, the only wise action is to stay inside until the peril is past. So it was in Jericho when Israel began its ominous march around the city wall. The air temperature may have been warm, but an emotional chill of terrible proportions must have settled over the doomed city.

Israel's solemn march around Jericho indicated the awful chill of God's displeasure with the city's wickedness. Unlike a weather front moving across a region, this bitter "season" of judgment would not go away.   —C. R. B.

B. Promise of Victory (v. 2)

2. And the LORD said unto Joshua, See, I have given into thine hand Jericho, and the king thereof, and the mighty men of valor.

Already *the Lord* had determined the outcome of the battle of *Jericho*. Its *king* had *mighty men of valor* in his army, but all of them would be helpless before the onslaught of Israel. God had *given* them into Joshua's hand.

C. Instructions (vv. 3-5)

3. And ye shall compass the city, all ye men of war, and go round about the city once. Thus shalt thou do six days.

Having assured the Israelites of victory, the Lord proceeded to outline how that victory was to be achieved. For *six days* no blow was to be struck, either against the walls of stone or against a human enemy. The *men of war* (the fighting men of Israel) were simply to march *round about the city once* a day. [See question #1, page 104.]

This reference to a specific group of Israelites (the men of war) makes it doubtful that all the Israelites marched around the city (which would have involved around two to three million people). Verses 9 and 13 tell us that the "armed men"

along with a "rearward" (rear guard) marched around Jericho. According to one estimate, ancient Jericho would have covered no more than four or five acres.

4. And seven priests shall bear before the ark seven trumpets of rams' horns: and the seventh day ye shall compass the city seven times, and the priests shall blow with the trumpets.

The *ark* of the covenant was to be carried in the great procession. To call attention to the ark, *seven priests* were to march in front of it, blowing *trumpets* as they went. Perhaps the people of Jericho knew that it was the symbol of Israel's God—the God who had made the water of the Red Sea stand up like walls, and made the water of the Jordan pile up in a heap—or perhaps their pagan minds supposed that the ark actually was that God.

On the *seventh day*, that great procession would go around the city *seven times*. The frequency of the number *seven* in these instructions highlighted their sacred significance (*seven* often symbolizes completeness in the Bible).

What was the point of all this marching? God did not explain, but we might suppose that these actions served to create a sense of panic and foreboding within the residents of Jericho. Probably they would not sleep well at night, as they wondered about that army marching outside their walls each day. On the seventh day they would grow more apprehensive as the marching went on and on and on. By the time the walls came down, they would have been weakened by a week of fitful sleep and daily anxiety; so their defense was not what it might have been when the Israelite soldiers stormed the city.

Perhaps, too, it was a lesson to Israel. What good is marching around a walled city? None, if that is all there is. But when their marching was an act of obedience to God, it was extremely valuable. This method may have been chosen for the same reason God later chose to deliver Israel through Gideon and only three hundred men: "lest Israel vaunt themselves, . . . saying, Mine own hand hath saved me" (Judges 7:2).

5. And it shall come to pass, that when they make a long blast with the ram's horn, and when ye hear the sound of the trumpet, all the people shall shout with a great shout; and the wall of the city shall fall down flat, and the people shall ascend up every man straight before him.

We are not told what sound the trumpeters were making prior to the seventh circuit; but when that final round of the city was completed, they would sound *a long blast*. The marchers were to remain silent through the week (v. 10), but that long blast would be the signal for *all the*

How to Say It

ACHAN. *Ay*-can.
GIDEON. *Gid*-ee-un.
GILGAL. *Gil*-gal.
JERICHO. *Jair*-ih-ko.
MIRIAM. *Meer*-ee-um.
RAHAB. *Ray*-hab.

people to *shout with a great shout.* Such a deafening roar would alarm the frightened defenders even more. Then *the wall of the city* would *fall down flat,* and panic would seize all in Jericho as *every man* among Israel's fighting men would charge over the fallen stones *straight before him* into the city. Probably those men were numerous enough to reach all the way around small Jericho, so they could enter the city from all directions. [See question #2, page 104.]

II. Carrying Out the Plan
(Joshua 6:15-20)

Verses 6-14 tell how God's battle plan was carried out for six days. The armed men led the way in marching around Jericho. Then came seven priests blowing their trumpets, followed by other priests carrying the ark of the covenant in the middle of the marching column. The rest of the armed men (the "rearward" or rear guard) followed at the end. Our printed text leaps over those six days and brings us to the events of the critical seventh day.

A. The Long March (v. 15)

15. And it came to pass on the seventh day, that they rose early about the dawning of the day, and compassed the city after the same manner seven times: only on that day they compassed the city seven times.

We know the people of Jericho were afraid of the Israelites (Joshua 2:11). Their fears and anxiety must have escalated when the marchers did not stop after one circuit as they had done before, but *compassed the city seven times.*

B. The Signal (v. 16)

16. And it came to pass at the seventh time, when the priests blew with the trumpets, Joshua said unto the people, Shout; for the LORD hath given you the city.

Following the loud trumpet blast of the *priests, Joshua* repeated the command to *shout.* That shout was the Israelites' battle cry. When it was given, the wall would collapse and they would rush into the city (v. 5). Joshua assured

the people, *The Lord hath given you the city.* Victory would be quick and complete.

C. Further Instructions (vv. 17-19)

17. And the city shall be accursed, even it, and all that are therein, to the LORD: only Rahab the harlot shall live, she and all that are with her in the house, because she hid the messengers that we sent.

Now came additional instructions concerning the treatment of *the city* once it was captured. Jericho and all the people, animals, and objects in it were to be *accursed . . . to the Lord.* The *King James Version* uses the word *accursed* because everything was to be destroyed. The Hebrew term, however, is best rendered "devoted." Everything was to be *devoted to the Lord*—that is, to be set apart and designated as His property. Just as the firstfruits of every harvest belonged to the Lord (Deuteronomy 26:1-4), so this first city taken from the pagans on the west bank was to be the Lord's.

In the case of Jericho, the setting apart was not so that these people and items could be used in God's service; it was so that they could be objects of His righteous judgment. The peoples living in the promised land were ripe for such judgment because of their idolatry and their resultant wickedness. Israel, in contrast, was to be "holy," or set apart, in the sense of being God's obedient people. The difference between these two kinds of setting apart is clear from a study of Deuteronomy 7:1-6. [See question #3, page 104.]

Verses 18 and 19 tell more about these instructions concerning Jericho, but the last part of verse 17 tells of an exception to the destruction. *Rahab* and her family were to be spared because she had saved the lives of Israel's spies when they came to Jericho (Joshua 2).

CERTAIN DISASTER

"Asteroid May Hit Earth in 2028!" read the newspaper headlines on March 12, 1998. The International Astronomical Union had announced that a mile-wide asteroid was expected to get as close as thirty thousand miles from earth in the year 2028. The television news that evening featured computer-generated pictures of the devastation that would be caused worldwide if the asteroid were to hit the earth. Hope was expressed that within the thirty years before the event was to happen, science would figure out a way to save the human race.

However, even before the grocery store tabloids were able to rush into print with the news, on the following day other astronomers claimed that the asteroid would miss the earth by six hundred thousand miles. They had discovered more data that put the celestial event at a much more comfortable distance.

The citizens of Jericho had only seven days in which to await their destruction. There would be no escape from the judgment of God. When Israel's trumpets blew on the seventh day, Jericho's walls would come crashing down; and only one woman and her family would be saved. Her prior service to the Lord and His people resulted in her deliverance from divine judgment.

The testimony of Scripture is that God's judgment is certain. Only those whose righteousness is found in Him shall escape.   —C. R. B.

Today's visual pictures the collapse of the walls of Jericho, in fulfillment of God's promise in verse 16.

Visual for lesson 12

18. And ye, in any wise keep yourselves from the accursed thing, lest ye make yourselves accursed, when ye take of the accursed thing, and make the camp of Israel a curse, and trouble it.

No one in Israel was to be enriched by any of the wealth of Jericho; all of it was the Lord's. Anyone who violated this order would be *accursed* along with the city: he too would be doomed to destruction. In addition, he would bring a *curse* upon the entire *camp of Israel.* Read Joshua 7 to see how this tragically came to pass when one man (Achan) ventured to steal some of the spoil of the city.

19. But all the silver, and gold, and vessels of brass and iron, are consecrated unto the LORD: they shall come into the treasury of the LORD.

Every living thing in Jericho, human or animal, was to be killed (v. 21). The city was to be burned (v. 24), including the houses and their contents, in a huge sacrifice to the Lord. The metals that could not be destroyed by fire were to be put *into the treasury of the Lord.*

Eventually other cities in the promised land would be conquered. Then the children of Israel would be permitted to live in the houses, eat the wheat and barley, use the animals, and pocket the treasure. This first captured city, however, belonged to the Lord.

D. Victory (v. 20)

20. So the people shouted when the priests blew with the trumpets: and it came to pass, when the people heard the sound of the trumpet, and the people shouted with a great shout, that the wall fell down flat, so that the people went up into the city, every man straight before him, and they took the city.

The plan of battle was carried out exactly as God had given it. *The trumpets* sounded a long blast, *the people shouted* at the top of their voices, the city *wall* collapsed, the men of Israel swarmed into Jericho from every side, *and they took the city.*

The citizens of Jericho had been demoralized already by a week of fear. The collapse of the wall must have brought them to utter despair. Women and children were killed along with the men. So were oxen, sheep, and donkeys (v. 21).

We may shrink in horror from such genocide, the devastation of an entire city. Can there be any justice in the killing of an innocent baby in his mother's arms? Can it be possible that God ordered such destruction?

Yes, He could and He did. What conclusion can we draw from a lesson like this?

Conclusion

God's justice is as real as His mercy. His punishment is as real as His love. In bringing Israel to the promised land, God had two purposes. One was to provide a homeland for the people He had chosen to bring a blessing to all families of the earth. The other was to wipe out several peoples that were not fit to live.

But the children—even babies not yet old enough to talk—what justice could there be in their deaths?

Let's think about that for a minute. Was their death justice, or was it mercy? Was it cruelty, or was it an act of kindness? Which would be better for those children: to die in their innocence and live forever in Heaven, or to live and grow up in sinful Jericho and suffer the "second death" of Hell?

A. God's Judgment

In another age "God saw that the wickedness of man was great in the earth, and that every imagination of the thoughts of his heart was only evil continually" (Genesis 6:5). People like that were not fit to live, and God destroyed them with a great flood—innocent babies along with wicked parents (Genesis 6–8).

In a later time, God chose one man (Abraham) to be the father of a nation that He designated as

His chosen people. He destroyed the people of Jericho and other evil people and gave His own people a land flowing with milk and honey. But God's chosen people became so ungodly that God sent pagan armies to destroy Jerusalem and drag His people to captivity in Babylon.

"The Lord is merciful and gracious, slow to anger, and plenteous in mercy" (Psalm 103:8). But to those who spurn His mercy and persist in doing wrong, "our God is a consuming fire" (Hebrews 12:29). The meek and lowly Jesus, the loving Savior of mankind, will someday say to some, "Depart from me, ye cursed, into everlasting fire, prepared for the devil and his angels" (Matthew 25:41). He will also say, "Come, ye blessed of my Father, inherit the kingdom prepared for you from the foundation of the world" (Matthew 25:34). Because of His love and grace, we can choose which of these statements we will hear. [See question #4, page 104.]

B. Our Judgment

"Judge not." We can hardly say a word against obvious evil without hearing those words of Jesus quoted. But Jesus also said, "Judge righteous judgment." The first of these sayings is a warning that we can expect to be judged by the same kind of judgment we use (Matthew 7:1-5). The second is a call to make our judgment agree with God's (John 7:24).

Very clearly God's Word describes some things as bad. If we accept them as good, we contradict God's judgment. That puts us on the way to being like the people of Jericho, who were not fit to live.

Some popular television programs seem to have been made in Jericho! Perhaps you have seen on TV a story in which illicit sex seems to be the normal conclusion of a date, or a story

that glorifies homosexuals proudly coming "out of the closet." God says that fornicators and homosexuals "shall not inherit the kingdom of God." They belong in Jericho, along with idolaters, adulterers, thieves, coveters, drunkards, revilers, and extortioners (1 Corinthians 6:9, 10). It is not we who judge the wrongdoers; it is God. Wrong is condemned in His Word as plainly as it is glorified in some TV programs, movies, magazines, and newspapers.

Yet God also has a word of hope for the evil-doers. They do not have to stay as they are. They can be washed and sanctified and justified "in the name of the Lord Jesus, and by the Spirit of our God" (1 Corinthians 6:11). [See question #5, page 104.]

C. Our Duty

If we are to live as God's people today, we have a threefold duty.

First, we are to keep ourselves pure (1 John 3:2, 3). We are not to be contaminated by the sins of ancient Jericho that run rampant in the modern towns where we live. We must recognize evil, no matter how adroitly it is camouflaged, and resolutely turn away from it.

Second, we are not to destroy but to restore a brother who has drifted or has been enticed into the sins of Jericho. Gently, not angrily, we are to lead him back home. We are to watch ourselves lest we be tempted, too (Galatians 6:1).

Third, we are to take the good news of life to every Jericho in the world today (Mark 16:15, 16). The wages of sin is death; but we are commissioned to let every sinner know that he does not have to die—every sinner in Jericho, every sinner in our national capital, every sinner in our hometown. But we cannot and must not conceal the promise that he will die unless he trusts and obeys the Savior.

We are not called to take a sword, a rifle, or a bomb and kill all the sinners in any Jericho. We are called instead to be winsome, to carry good news, and to plead, "Be ye reconciled to God" (2 Corinthians 5:20).

What shall we do this week to fulfill our duty?

D. Prayer

Lord, lay some soul upon my heart,
    And love that soul through me;
And may I nobly do my part
    To win that soul for Thee.
          —Dr. Leon Tucker

E. Thought to Remember

We are to influence our Jerichos for good; we are not to be influenced by them for evil.

Home Daily Bible Readings

Monday, Nov. 15—The Passover Celebrated at Gilgal (Joshua 5:10-15)

Tuesday, Nov. 16—Israel Begins Conquest of Jericho (Joshua 6:1-7)

Wednesday, Nov. 17—Six-Day March Around Jericho's Walls (Joshua 6:8-14)

Thursday, Nov. 18—Destruction of Jericho by Israel (Joshua 6:15-20)

Friday, Nov. 19—Rahab and Her Family Are Spared (Joshua 6:22-25, 27)

Saturday, Nov. 20—Joshua Renews the Covenant (Joshua 8:30-35)

Sunday, Nov. 21—A Sacred Song of Remembrance (Psalm 44:1-8)

Learning by Doing

This page contains an alternate lesson plan emphasizing learning activities.
Classes desiring such student involvement will find these suggestions helpful.

Learning Goals

After this lesson, each student will be able to:

1. Summarize how God delivered the city of Jericho into the hands of the Israelites.

2. Tell how Christians today are to face the wicked "Jerichos" around them.

3. Express the need for personal holiness in today's world, and tell how he or she will cultivate it through time with God each day.

Into the Lesson

Ask a dramatically inclined person, preferably not one of your students, to dress as a person of Joshua's day and to come and relate the story of the fallen city of Jericho through the eyes of an average Israelite. His soliloquy should summarize the story and offer down-to-earth commentary (e.g., "It seemed a silly thing to do, but we'd seen God do some pretty amazing stuff!"). The soliloquy can be humorous or serious and should last two to three minutes.

Into the Word

Divide your class into two groups. Supply each group with paper, pencils, and any Bible helps you can. Assign Group 1 to read Joshua 6:1-16 and Group 2 to read Joshua 6:17-27. Each group should answer its assigned questions below. (Do not give the answers, which follow in italic type in parenthesis.) After a time of discussion, ask each group to summarize its passage and offer answers to the rest of the class.

Group 1:

1. How was Israel's method of the siege of Jericho different from those normally used? *(Most sieges of the day spanned a great length of time. Armies would attempt to destroy or scale city walls, or they would merely cut off the city from outside help, including food supplies, and starve the inhabitants. Needless to say, armies never toppled walls by yelling.)*

2. What were the advantages of this unusual siege method? *(Many cities were prepared for an ordinary siege and would have fought well against it. In the meantime, the Israelites might have lost patience in a siege that went on for weeks or even months. God's method gave a decisive victory in just a week.)*

3. Joshua 5:15 names the commander of the Lord's army. Who was this commander, and how was he glorified? *(God, of course, was the commander, and He was glorified by the miraculous defeat of Jericho.)*

Group 2:

1. What was to be saved and what was to be destroyed? *(Everything was to be destroyed except silver, gold, iron, and brass vessels, which were added to the treasury of the Lord.)*

2. How was this a just punishment, since it meant the deaths of innocent children? *(See the comments under "Conclusion," pages 101, 102.)*

3. What is the significance of Rahab's being saved from destruction? *(There is still redemption for those who turn from sin and embrace God's will.)*

Into Life

On a chalkboard write "Modern-day Jericho." Ask your students to list ways in which our society resembles Jericho (metaphorically). Examples include pornography, adultery, fornication, greed, abortion, idolatry, etc. What potential do these evils have to corrupt a Christian's life?

Ask your students how they feel they should respond to the following situations:

— Coarse talk in the workplace.

— A pornography shop in town.

— A Christian friend who is unfaithful to his or her spouse.

— A friend or a relative who is an alcoholic.

God does not command us to destroy all evil. There is redemption. Rahab's deliverance in today's text is an example of this. Because of her obedience to God's will, she did not suffer the punishment that the rest of Jericho did. Though we are called to flee from sinful acts, we are also called to share the gospel with the people who do them.

Give each member of your class a blank sheet of paper and a pencil. This activity is called, "A Seven-day Siege." The student is to write one aspect of modern Jericho that troubles him or her. (Keep this exercise confidential and encourage the students to choose items that trouble them because they are tempted by them.) Each day, starting today, the student should set aside five minutes to write a journal entry about such matters and pray for God's guidance. Use the remaining class time to complete the first day of this exercise.

Let's Talk It Over

The questions on this page are designed to encourage review of the lesson Scriptures and to promote discussion of the lesson by the class. The answers provided are only discussion starters. Let your class talk it over from there.

1. Sometimes in our service for the Lord, it may seem as if we're just "spinning our wheels" or "going in circles." How might the event in today's text encourage us in such times?

For six days the Israelites were just "going in circles," but then they saw God's promise fulfilled. We, too, have "exceeding great and precious promises" from God. If we are faithful, even when results seem hard to discern, He will be faithful to us and bring about His desired ends. We need to remember that God has called us to faithfulness and to obedience, not to spectacular "results." Perhaps one more visit with a family who has resisted our evangelistic efforts, then, will be the visit when they see the truth of God's message. Maybe just one more recruitment call after a series of unprofitable ones will be the call that gets a teacher for that new Sunday school class. Even when we're going in circles, if we're doing what God has commanded, then we're going in the right direction.

2. Some scoffers have suggested that the vibration created by the loud shout of all those Israelites is what caused the wall of Jericho to fall. How would you respond to such a claim?

In spite of the fact that amazing things are now done with sound waves, there is no evidence that shouting could have produced the destruction of such high and thick walls as surrounded Jericho. Even if it could, who would have thought so in Joshua's day except the Lord, who created both sound and the heavy stone used to construct the walls? It would be evidence for God and His creative work in the world if the fall of Jericho *did* happen in the manner suggested by the scoffers!

3. The Israelites were to take no spoil from the vanquished city of Jericho. The city and everything in it were devoted to the Lord as His own, a kind of "firstfruits" offering from the conquest of Canaan. How might we honor God with our firstfruits in whatever venture we undertake?

Certainly our tithes and offerings, even as Israel's firstfruits of their harvest, should come from our first income, not what is left over after we indulge ourselves. The city of Jericho was a special case, however, and perhaps we need to look beyond the routine as well. Refusing to take the spoil required the Israelites to turn away from some tempting booty. What tempting items in the world does our commitment to God require us to shun?

Similar articles were allowed to the Israelites in later battles, so it was not the booty itself that was wrong. Rather, it was a matter of giving God first place. Are there items or practices we might shun that in and of themselves are not wrong but are avoided simply to declare our desire to put God first? What are some of those items?

4. The Israelites faced godless Jericho and destroyed everyone and everything in it— except faithful Rahab and her family (v. 17, cf. Hebrews 11:31). Today we face a godless society, and what shall we do? We can't "wipe them out"! What lessons are here for us?

The Israelites could not have taken the city of Jericho if they had not obeyed the Lord. But they did obey God, and God gave them the city. We, too, need to be sure we are obeying God.

Israel was commissioned to execute God's judgment on Canaan, including Jericho. We, however, are commissioned to bring God's grace (Matthew 28:18-20). May we be as faithful in telling the good news of Jesus as Israel was in executing God's wrath!

5. Many critics today accuse Christians of being judgmental, intolerant, and hypocritical. How do we respond to such charges?

Unfortunately there are believers who elicit such charges by behavior that is out of harmony with the teaching and example of Christ. But often these charges are leveled at Christians who are merely taking a firm stand on the side of Biblical morality. In that case, we need to make sure of two things. First, we must boldly affirm that what the Bible calls evil is indeed evil, and that we refuse to condone what the Word of God condemns—whether it be committed by a politician, businessman, blue-collar worker, housewife, or church member. Second, we must lovingly declare that God loves sinners and has given His own Son to die in their place. While we do not condone sin, sinners can still find a place in the kingdom of God. They, as we, can be "washed. . . sanctified. . . justified in the name of the Lord Jesus" (1 Corinthians 6:11).

Israel Chooses to Serve the Lord

DEVOTIONAL READING: Joshua 24:14-24.

BACKGROUND SCRIPTURE: Joshua 24.

PRINTED TEXT: Joshua 24:1, 2a, 14-25.

Joshua 24:1, 2a, 14-25

1 And Joshua gathered all the tribes of Israel to Shechem, and called for the elders of Israel, and for their heads, and for their judges, and for their officers; and they presented themselves before God.

2a And Joshua said unto all the people,

. . . .

14 Now therefore fear the LORD, and serve him in sincerity and in truth; and put away the gods which your fathers served on the other side of the flood, and in Egypt; and serve ye the LORD.

15 And if it seem evil unto you to serve the LORD, choose you this day whom ye will serve; whether the gods which your fathers served that were on the other side of the flood, or the gods of the Amorites, in whose land ye dwell: but as for me and my house, we will serve the LORD.

16 And the people answered and said, God forbid that we should forsake the LORD, to serve other gods;

17 For the LORD our God, he it is that brought us up and our fathers out of the land of Egypt, from the house of bondage, and which did those great signs in our sight, and preserved us in all the way wherein we went,

and among all the people through whom we passed:

18 And the LORD drave out from before us all the people, even the Amorites which dwelt in the land: therefore will we also serve the LORD; for he is our God.

19 And Joshua said unto the people, Ye cannot serve the LORD: for he is a holy God; he is a jealous God; he will not forgive your transgressions nor your sins.

20 If ye forsake the LORD, and serve strange gods, then he will turn and do you hurt, and consume you, after that he hath done you good.

21 And the people said unto Joshua, Nay; but we will serve the LORD.

22 And Joshua said unto the people, Ye are witnesses against yourselves that ye have chosen you the LORD, to serve him. And they said, We are witnesses.

23 Now therefore put away, said he, the strange gods which are among you, and incline your heart unto the LORD God of Israel.

24 And the people said unto Joshua, The LORD our God will we serve, and his voice will we obey.

25 So Joshua made a covenant with the people that day, and set them a statute and an ordinance in Shechem.

GOLDEN TEXT: And the people said unto Joshua, The LORD our God will we serve, and his voice will we obey.—Joshua 24:24.

From Slavery to Conquest
Unit 3: Entering the Promised Land
(Lessons 10-13)

Lesson Aims

After this lesson students should be able to:

1. Summarize Joshua's challenge to the children of Israel that is found in today's text.

2. List some of the "gods" in today's world that clamor for us to choose them, thus turning our focus away from serving God.

3. Make every day a day in which they will choose to serve God above anything else.

Lesson Outline

INTRODUCTION
  A. The First Time
  B. Lesson Background
 I. A CALL TO CHOOSE (Joshua 24:1, 2a, 14, 15)
  A. For All the People (vv. 1, 2a)
  B. The Right Choice (v. 14)
  C. Wrong Choices (v. 15a)
  D. Joshua's Choice (v. 15b)
    Important Choices
 II. A REASONABLE CHOICE (Joshua 24:16-18)
  A. Israel's Response (v. 16)
  B. Basis for Israel's Choice (vv. 17, 18)
III. A CONCLUDING CHALLENGE (Joshua 24:19, 20)
  A. A Demanding Choice (v. 19)
  B. A Clear Warning (v. 20)
IV. A SOLEMN PLEDGE (Joshua 24:21-25)
  A. Pledge of Service (v. 21)
  B. Witnesses of the Pledge (v. 22)
  C. Keeping the Pledge (v. 23)
    Reminders of an Ungodly Past
  D. The Pledge Repeated (v. 24)
  E. The Pledge Recorded (v. 25)
CONCLUSION
  A. To Be Continued
  B. The New Covenant
  C. Prayer
  D. Thought to Remember

Introduction

On May 14, 1948, the Jews in Palestine boldly proclaimed that the nation of Israel was again established in its ancient homeland, where no nation of Israel had been for 1878 years (since the destruction of Jerusalem by the Romans). Other nations in the vicinity objected violently. Fierce fighting continued for about a year, and

was ended only by armistice rather than real peace. Today, fifty-one years later, the objectors are still objecting, sometimes with violence.

This was not the first time that the people of Israel had won or lost that land. They lost the northern part of it to Assyria in 722 B.C., and the southern part to Babylon in 586 B.C. By permission of the Persians, who later conquered Babylon, the Jews recovered part of it without war, though not without objection from nearby residents. In a violent and bloody war they lost it to the Romans in A.D. 70, not to reclaim it until this century.

A. The First Time

It was Joshua and his troops who established the nation of Israel in the promised land for the first time. God had first promised the land of Canaan to Abraham, but he and his family never possessed the land; instead they "sojourned in the land of promise, as in a strange country" (Hebrews 11:8, 9). Abraham's grandson Jacob moved the family to Egypt to escape famine, but there the family remained for more than four hundred years, until Moses led them out. Forty years after they had left Egypt, Joshua led the Israelites across the Jordan River. There they destroyed Jericho and then fought for some seven years to establish themselves in the land, dividing it up among their tribes. With the firm hand of Joshua at the helm, the nation stayed faithful to God, and prosperous.

B. Lesson Background

Like his predecessor Moses, Joshua could not be expected to lead the people forever. He grew old (Joshua 23:1), more than a century old (Joshua 24:29). He called together the leaders of all Israel for the assembly that is recorded in chapter 23. For today's lesson we bypass that gathering and go on to chapter 24, which records Joshua's farewell address to the entire nation.

I. A Call to Choose
(Joshua 24:1, 2a, 14, 15)

Shechem was an appropriate place for a national meeting. It was located near the center of Israel's territory, making it easier for people throughout the land to attend. In addition, Shechem had already played a significant part in Israel's history (Genesis 12:6, 7, where it is called *Sichem* in the *King James Version*).

Shechem was situated in a narrow valley between Mount Gerizim and Mount Ebal, where Moses had commanded the people to gather and renew their commitment to obey God (Deuteronomy 27:9-13). Israel gathered there earlier under

Joshua's leadership to do this (Joshua 8:30-35). The rising terrain on either side of the valley provided a natural amphitheater.

A. For All the People (vv. 1, 2a)

1. And Joshua gathered all the tribes of Israel to Shechem, and called for the elders of Israel, and for their heads, and for their judges, and for their officers; and they presented themselves before God.

All the tribes of Israel, a huge throng, met at *Shechem.* A special appeal was given to the prominent men of every tribe and clan and family. Perhaps they came forward and stood with *Joshua* as he spoke. Thus they would show that they agreed with what he was saying. Previously he had consulted them and enlisted their support (Joshua 23:2). Together *they presented themselves before God.* They understood that God was with them in this meeting, seeing what they did and hearing what they said. [See question #1, page 112.]

2a. And Joshua said unto all the people.

This part of a verse is included in our text to make it plain that Joshua spoke the words that we read in the rest of the printed text (vv. 14-25). Before giving that challenge, however, Joshua repeated a message that God had given him for the people. It is recorded in verses 2-13, where God reviewed the history of Israel from the time Abraham left Ur of the Chaldees to the time in which Joshua was speaking.

B. The Right Choice (v. 14)

14. Now therefore fear the LORD, and serve him in sincerity and in truth; and put away the gods which your fathers served on the other side of the flood, and in Egypt; and serve ye the LORD.

Verses 2-13 reminded the people that God had faithfully helped Abraham and his descendants and had brought them to this moment of triumph. *Therefore* these people ought to *fear* and *serve* Him, not in mere form and ritual, but *in sincerity and in truth.* To do that they must put away idols of all kinds. The real God must be the only God in their minds and hearts.

In this verse the word translated *flood* actually means "river" and refers to the Euphrates River. Abraham had come from Ur, *on the other side* of the Euphrates from Canaan. In that land Abraham's father had worshiped idols (v. 2). More recently the *fathers* of the Israelites had lived in *Egypt,* a land of many false *gods.* Joshua urged that no worship or service should be given to any god but *the Lord,* the true God—the One who had blessed and helped Israel so abundantly.

C. Wrong Choices (v. 15a)

15a. And if it seem evil unto you to serve the Lord, choose you this day whom ye will serve; whether the gods which your fathers served that were on the other side of the flood, or the gods of the Amorites, in whose land ye dwell.

Joshua realized that he could not compel his fellow Israelites to do what he was urging. *To serve the Lord* was costly. But they ought to remember that the Lord was the One who had helped and blessed them continually ever since the time of Abraham.

Here the word *Amorites* is a general name for all the hostile people who had lived in the promised land before the Israelites came. Not all of these peoples had been "utterly destroyed" at this point, as God had commanded (Deuteronomy 7:1, 2). There was still the possibility that their *gods* could seduce the Lord's people. [See question #2, page 112.]

D. Joshua's Choice (v. 15b)

15b. But as for me and my house, we will serve the LORD.

Joshua's choice was made, and he would never waver. Only the real God is worthy of worship. Joyfully Joshua announced that he and his family would *serve the Lord.* [See question #3, page 112.]

IMPORTANT CHOICES

Martha Van Sloten thought she had recovered from cancer surgery—but two years later she was dying. Lisa, her nineteen-year-old daughter, dropped out of college to help care for her sisters, who were only eight and four years old.

Shortly before Martha died, her husband, Richard, began to have seizures. He was found to have a very aggressive brain tumor. Knowing what the future held, the couple began to plan for their children's future. Their medical bills were increasing, they had only limited life insurance, and they wanted to find a way to keep

Visual for lesson 13

This visual is an attractive reminder of Joshua's pledge. It's one that more of us might hang on our walls to express our own commitment to the Lord.

the family intact. Few choices are more momentous than that last one. One other extremely significant choice was this one: how would they respond to God in such a crisis?

Richard's response was this: "I thank God for His blessings. I get to make arrangements for my wife and for me. I get to remind my little girls that I love them . . . I've tried to conduct myself in a way that will make my daughters proud of me."

Joshua held out to Israel a life-and-death choice: spiritual life or spiritual death. It is the same choice that all of us get; the circumstances of our lives are all that differ. Do we choose to face life's challenges in a way that makes others proud of us? Do we choose to respond to God in a way that brings glory to Him? —C. R. B.

II. A Reasonable Choice
(Joshua 24:16-18)

A. Israel's Response (v. 16)

16. And the people answered and said, God forbid that we should forsake the LORD, to serve other gods.

Four options had been presented: serve the Lord, worship the idols of Mesopotamia that Abraham had long ago rejected, worship the gods of Egypt that the Lord had soundly defeated not fifty years earlier, or worship the Canaanite idols as the defeated peoples around them were doing. Vigorously *the people* declared their choice: they agreed with Joshua. They too would serve *the Lord.*

B. Basis for Israel's Choice (vv. 17, 18)

17. For the LORD our God, he it is that brought us up and our fathers out of the land of Egypt, from the house of bondage, and which did those great signs in our sight, and preserved us in all the way wherein we went, and among all the people through whom we passed.

The people of Israel were indebted to *the Lord* for many things. They acknowledged all His

deeds that had been mentioned earlier (vv. 5-11). Simple gratitude ought to lead them to give all their worship to the One who had done so much for them.

18. And the LORD drave out from before us all the people, even the Amorites which dwelt in the land: therefore will we also serve the LORD; for he is our God.

As noted under verse 15, *Amorites* is a general name for all the hostile peoples who had *dwelt in the land* before the Israelites came. Joshua 9:1 names six groups who lived west of the Jordan; Deuteronomy 3:1, 2 names two kings who ruled east of the river. The Lord had given Israel victory over all of these. That was one more good reason for Israel to *serve the Lord.* It seems that there was no dissenting voice as the people expressed their desire to make the same choice that Joshua had made. [See question #4, page 112.]

III. A Concluding Challenge
(Joshua 24:19, 20)

The people made the right choice. But no doubt wise old Joshua could see that they had made it too lightly, not realizing all it implied. Instead of praising their choice, he issued a strong challenge.

A. A Demanding Choice (v. 19)

19a. And Joshua said unto the people, Ye cannot serve the LORD.

Can you imagine how this statement shook the complacent *people?* They had made the same choice *Joshua* had made, the one he obviously wanted them to make. Then Joshua told them, "You can't do it!" What in the world could he mean?

19b. For he is a holy God; he is a jealous God; he will not forgive your transgressions nor your sins.

God is *holy.* He is altogether good, separated from anything that is bad or even questionable. His word to the people was, "Ye shall be holy: for I the Lord your God am holy" (Leviticus 19:2). Were the people of Israel ready for that? Are we?

God is *jealous.* He will not tolerate a rival in the minds and hearts of His people (Exodus 20:3). He wants their total devotion. Were the people of Israel ready for that? Are we?

God *will not forgive your transgressions nor your sins.* That jolts us, and it must have jolted those who heard Joshua say it. The law describes in detail several offerings to atone for sin and bring forgiveness (Leviticus 4:1—6:7). What could Joshua mean?

How to Say It

AMORITES. *Am*-uh-rites.
ASSYRIA. Uh-*sear*-ee-uh.
BABYLON. *Bab*-uh-lun.
CANAAN. *Kay*-nun.
EBAL. *Ee*-bul.
GERIZIM. *Gair*-ih-zim or Guh-*rye*-zim.
JERICHO. *Jair*-ih-ko.
SHECHEM. *Shek*-em or *Shee*-kem.
SICHEM. *Sigh*-kem.

Perhaps he meant that God will not forgive a person's sins if that one treats lightly the issue of sin in his or her life. God will not forgive one's transgressions while that one keeps on transgressing, thus showing that he prefers to do wrong rather than right. Were the people of Israel ready to serve so demanding a God? Are we? [See question #5, page 112.]

B. A Clear Warning (v. 20)

20. If ye forsake the LORD, and serve strange gods, then he will turn and do you hurt, and consume you, after that he hath done you good.

For three months our lessons have dwelt on the *good* that God did for His people. But He would not always do them good, regardless of what they would do. They were promising to serve Him. If they broke that promise, then He would do them *hurt* (harm) instead of good— and it would be no trivial harm. God would *consume,* or destroy, them.

Were the people ready to pledge themselves to God under these conditions? Are we?

IV. A Solemn Pledge
(Joshua 24:21-25)

Too lightly, too easily the people of Israel had pledged to serve God (vv. 16-18). Joshua had made them stop and think. It was a demanding commitment, and failure to meet its demands would be tragic (vv. 19, 20). Were the people still ready to make that pledge?

A. Pledge of Service (v. 21)

21. And the people said unto Joshua, Nay; but we will serve the LORD.

Joshua had said, "Ye cannot serve the Lord" (v. 19). To that the people responded, *Nay:* it is not so. They said, *We will serve the Lord.* They were pledging to meet all the demands of such service, to be holy and obedient to God.

B. Witnesses of the Pledge (v. 22)

22. And Joshua said unto the people, Ye are witnesses against yourselves that ye have chosen you the LORD, to serve him. And they said, We are witnesses.

There were no disinterested parties present to witness the promise that was made, so Joshua said that the very *people* who made the promise would have to be *witnesses.* If they later failed to *serve* the Lord, they would have to testify against themselves. They would have to admit that they had made that promise and broken it.

The people agreed: *we are witnesses.* They were affirming that they had made a solemn pledge to serve the Lord.

C. Keeping the Pledge (v. 23)

23. Now therefore put away, said he, the strange gods which are among you, and incline your heart unto the LORD God of Israel.

Twice the people had promised to serve the Lord, to worship and obey Him (vv. 18, 21). Now they had to demonstrate, immediately and completely, their sincerity about this promise. Joshua challenged them to get rid of any pagan *gods,* or idols, that they still had.

During their recent years of war, the Israelites had destroyed several towns in the promised land and taken the possessions of those towns as booty. No doubt the spoils included some pagan idols. Also, the Israelites who had lived in Egypt had brought many things of value from that land (Exodus 12:35, 36). Perhaps some of the Egyptian idols were included. Every idol of any kind had to go, for the Lord said, "Thou shalt have no other gods before me" (Exodus 20:3).

REMINDERS OF AN UNGODLY PAST

Forty or fifty years ago, one of the finest gifts a college-bound high-school graduate could receive was a portable manual typewriter. But, as the saying goes, "That was then; this is now." Next came electric typewriters and then computers. Today, many college students take their class notes on "laptops." Colleges are wiring their dormitories for the Internet and local networks so that students can do research right in their rooms.

Typewriters are becoming outmoded reminders of a pre-electronic past. Many children have grown up on computers, not knowing what a typewriter is. A recent cartoon showed a child watching her mother using a typewriter. The child was saying, "Wow! Cool! A keyboard with a built-in printer!" Today, a typewriter may best be kept around as an ornament to embellish a home or office decorated with antiques!

Israel had some "decorations" on hand also: the idols that their ancestors had brought with them out of Egypt, as well as those that the people had collected as spoils from their conquest of Canaan. Joshua told the people to destroy them all. These were not mere "antiques" or harmless household decor; they were physical reminders of Israel's idolatrous past. Joshua wanted to make sure that even the slightest temptation to return to that past was eliminated.

Is there anything from our past that keeps us from making and living out a sincere commitment to God?   —C. R. B.

D. The Pledge Repeated (v. 24)

24. And the people said unto Joshua, The LORD our God will we serve, and his voice will we obey.

The *people* had made this pledge twice before (vv. 18, 21). Each time Joshua had responded by helping them understand what they were promising. Now, with a fuller understanding, they voiced their pledge the third time.

E. The Pledge Recorded (v. 25)

25. So Joshua made a covenant with the people that day, and set them a statute and an ordinance in Shechem.

The text of this lesson clearly shows the nature of the *covenant* (the agreement or contract) that was made *that day*. It was a reaffirmation of the covenant made at Sinai about half a century earlier; and it was to serve as a *statute* and an *ordinance* that would guide the conduct of *the people* in the promised land.

Verses 26 and 27 add that Joshua recorded the words of this covenant "in the book of the law of God." He also placed a stone as a monument—a perpetual reminder of the covenant reaffirmed at *Shechem*.

Conclusion

A. To Be Continued

Next September we shall return to this story at the point where we are leaving it now. We shall see the people of Israel failing to keep the covenant they made. We shall see their obedience turning to disobedience, and their peace and prosperity turning to constant harassment and impoverishment at the hands of their enemies. See Judges 2:11-15 for a preview of that dismal time. The covenant made at Sinai and reaffirmed at Shechem failed, not because there was anything wrong with it, but because the people failed to worship and obey God as they had promised to do.

B. The New Covenant

It is good, then, that in December we will turn our thoughts to Jesus, the mediator of a New Covenant. For three months our study will center on Him, focusing on Matthew's Gospel. Then for six months we will be looking at various New Testament epistles. We will be reminded of the marvelous blessings of the New Covenant, foretold in Jeremiah 31:31-34. It provides the only sufficient atonement for sins; thus it is able to offer the forgiveness of those sins.

As Christians we rejoice in what the New Covenant supplies. But still the call of Joshua comes to us today, and tomorrow, and every day of our lives: "Choose you this day whom ye will serve."

Almost everyone agrees that earning a living is important. In doing so we can serve God, for He encourages us to earn our living (2 Thessalonians 3:12), support our families (1 Timothy 5:8), and give to the needy (Ephesians 4:28). However, if our eagerness to make money compels us to give up worship at church, or Bible study at home, or time with our families, are we not serving mammon and not God (Matthew 6:24)?

Most of us spend some of our money and more of our time on recreation, fun, or simply relaxing. That is not necessarily disobedient to God. Paul says, "Bodily exercise profiteth little" (1 Timothy 4:8); yet it does profit. God's ancient Sabbath law offers clear evidence that every worker needs some time off, even if he prefers relaxation to exercise. But if our time off is filled with "works of the flesh" (Galatians 5:19-21), or if we become "couch potatoes" who do nothing but view salacious shows or magazines, or if "fun" crowds out worship and church work, are we not among those "whose god is their belly" (Philippians 3:19)?

Can you think of other choices that can be made instead of serving the Lord? Whatever they are, and whatever they offer, will you still serve the Lord?

C. Prayer

Father in Heaven, how sure is Your love, and how everlasting! Throughout history You have offered the best, and too often mankind has chosen the worst. Today we choose You, Father. We will worship and obey You. In Jesus' name we ask for wisdom and strength and courage to live by our choice. Amen.

D. Thought to Remember

We will serve the Lord!

Learning by Doing

This page contains an alternate lesson plan emphasizing learning activities.
Classes desiring such student involvement will find these suggestions helpful.

Learning Goals

After this lesson students should be able to:

1. Summarize Joshua's challenge to the children of Israel that is found in today's text.

2. List some of the "gods" in today's world that clamor for us to choose them, thus turning our focus away from serving God.

3. Make every day a day in which they will choose to serve God above anything else.

Into the Lesson

Before the students arrive, write the words, "Choose you this day," on the chalkboard. As the students arrive, engage them in conversation about choices. What choices did they have to make this morning? (What outfits to wear, what to have for breakfast—or whether to have breakfast! Did some have to decide whether to come to class?)

Observe that we make choices every day. Some are routine, and we scarcely even notice we have made a choice. Others are more significant, and we are sometimes hard-pressed to make "the right choice." In our lesson today, Israel was faced with a choice—a choice that would determine much about what kind of future they would have in the promised land!

Into the Word

To read today's text, prepare a handout with Joshua 24:1, 2a, 14-25 printed on it, with verses 16-18, 21, 22b, and 24 in bold type. Distribute the handout and announce that you will read the type that is not bold, and the class is to read together what is in bold.

After the text is read, divide the class into three groups. Give the first group a sheet of poster board and some markers. Ask the group to read verses 14-18 and make a poster that describes the choice Israel had to make. They may use words or simple pictures to illustrate Israel's choice to serve God instead of Mesopotamian, Egyptian, or Amorite (i.e., Canaanite) gods.

The second group should examine verses 19-22 and write a poem that describes the warning Joshua gave and the Israelites' response. Provide pens or pencils as needed and some paper.

Provide group three with a variety of craft supplies and ask them to make a visual reminder of Israel's promise based on verses 23-25. They might make a poster or plaque with the words of verse 24, or perhaps they will make a heart that leans ("inclined") with the words of verse 23. Let them be creative!

Allow the groups time to work; then take a few minutes to display the results of each group's efforts.

Into Life

In life we are constantly bombarded by other gods and other lifestyles. It is crucial that we decide in whom to put our faith. Many choose God without giving it any thought and, in turn, are unprepared for when another choice is offered.

Ask your students to name some of the "gods" that clamor for our attention. "Gods" can refer to anything from other religions (Islam, Judaism, Buddhism, New Age) to postmodern philosophies (humanism, pluralism) to possessions (cite specific objects) to activities (such as one's occupation, sports, or watching TV). Write these on the chalkboard as the class names them.

Explain to your students that we live in a world that seeks to fill a spiritual void. Some seek fulfillment in God, others seek it elsewhere—in one or more of the "gods" you have already listed. Even those who believe in the Lord are frequently challenged to give one of these "gods" first place in their lives.

Distribute paper and pencils or pens to the class. Ask each student to draw two lines across the page, dividing it into three equal sections.

At the top of each section the student is to write the name of one of the other "gods" that clamor for attention in his or her life. (These will be kept private.) Under the name of this rival "god" the student should write some of the ways this temptation appears. (For example, one of the rivals might be "materialism." This rival may vie for attention through slick advertisements on TV or in print, through a co-worker who frequently brags about new purchases he or she has made, or through a spouse who complains that the family doesn't have enough nice things because they give too much to the church.) Then have the student write an answer in each section showing why serving the Lord is superior.

Finally, ask the students to write the words of Joshua 24:23 across the page. Encourage the students to keep these papers as reminders to put the Lord first. Close the session with a prayer of commitment.

Let's Talk It Over

The questions on this page are designed to encourage review of the lesson Scriptures and to promote discussion of the lesson by the class. The answers provided are only discussion starters. Let your class talk it over from there.

1. The leaders of Israel "presented themselves before God." They recognized Him as their Sovereign Lord and made themselves accountable to Him. How might leaders today "present themselves before God"? What advantage do you think there would be to such a practice?

In formal ordination services for ministers, elders, deacons, etc. a statement of commitment and accountability is a part of the ceremony. Perhaps we could use some kind of ceremony for more positions of servant-leadership in the church, impressing on both the leaders and the rest of the congregation the commitment and accountability the new leader is taking on. We can also do this informally. Perhaps a leader can choose a colleague who will hold him accountable for his ministry. Together they can help and encourage each other in their given ministries.

2. Someone might say that Joshua had a very tolerant attitude: he offered the Israelites their choice of gods. They might paraphrase Joshua: "If you don't want to serve Jehovah, that's okay. Choose some of the Mesopotamian, Egyptian, or Amorite (i.e., Canaanite) gods!" How would you respond to such a suggestion?

It is true that Joshua mentioned these choices, but not on equal terms. Joshua knew the people would worship something—it is human nature to seek to fill what someone has called that "God-shaped hole" in the human spirit. His "options" came after a clear call to serve the Lord and to put away any idols the people had among them (v. 14).

We might actually see Joshua's offering "options" as sarcasm: "If you don't serve God, then whom will you serve—the Mesopotamian gods our father Abraham refused? The Egyptian gods that our God defeated and put to shame when He brought us out of Egypt? The Amorite gods that could not save their people from the power of our God as He gave us their land? Count me out! My family and I will serve Jehovah!"

3. Joshua said, "As for me and my house, we will serve the Lord." How important do you think it is for a Christian parent to make such a commitment on behalf of his or her children?

Certain experts in our society seem to feel that religious training in the home is a hindrance to youngsters growing up in an increasingly humanistic society. They say, "Let the child himself decide about religion when he is old enough." Of course, we cannot dictate to our children our religious beliefs and values—we know at some point they will have to make their own choices. We must, however, lay the foundation for them to make the right choice. We don't let young children choose for themselves whether to eat poison. We lock it away and insist they not touch even the cabinet where it is stored. We need to take similar precautions about those things that can poison them for eternity. We must point them in the direction of life!

4. The people pledged to serve the Lord, rehearsing many of the things God had done for them. What things has God done for you, for which you feel indebted to Him and are compelled to serve Him?

Certainly we could all mention our salvation, purchased at the cost of the blood of God's own Son! But each of your students may have additional reasons to feel indebted to God. (See page 94, "Personal Memories," for some reasons our lesson writer might suggest.) Try to involve everyone in this discussion, as the students consider specifically what God has done for them.

5. Joshua was careful to point out to the Israelites that serving the Lord would cost them something in terms of holy, godly living. How much do you think Christians need to be reminded of the cost of following Jesus Christ? What has it cost you?

It is easy to lapse into a comfortable Christian lifestyle. Our discipleship may consist of little more than attending worship services when it is convenient, giving an insignificant portion of our income, and engaging in occasional prayer. Jesus emphasized the cross-bearing aspect of following Him (Matthew 16:24-26). Each believer must determine what that will specifically involve in his or her own life, but for everyone it must entail some genuine sacrifice. Just as probably all your students could report what God has done for them, they can probably also cite what following Jesus has cost them. Often, however, a believer will not see the *cost* because he or she has *gained* so much in return!

Winter Quarter, 1999-2000

Immanuel: God With Us

(Matthew)

Special Features

Lessons

Unit 1: Beginnings: Birth and Ministry

Unit 2: Ministry: Wonderful Words and Works

Unit 3: Fulfillment: Atonement and Final Commission

About These Lessons

These lessons, all taken from the Gospel of Matthew, lead the reader to one inescapable conclusion: Jesus was indeed Immanuel ("God With Us"), and He demonstrated this through His matchless words and mighty works. Although Matthew's Gospel was written primarily for a Jewish readership, the good news of which he writes is meant to be told to "all nations."

Dec 5

Dec 12

Dec 19

Dec 26

Jan 2

Jan 9

Jan 16

Jan 23

Jan 30

Feb 6

Feb 13

Feb 20

Feb 27

Quarterly Quiz

The questions on this page may be used in several ways: as a pretest at the beginning of the quarter; as a review at the end of the quarter; or as a review after each lesson. The questions are based on the Scripture text of each lesson (King James Version). **The answers are on page 116.**

Lesson 1

1. What did John the Baptist say was "at hand"? *Matthew 3:2* KINGDOM OF GOD

2. The prophet ISAIAH spoke of John as one crying in the wilderness. (Isaiah, Jeremiah, Ezekiel?) *Matthew 3:3*

3. Jesus told John to baptize Him in order to FULFILL ALL Righteousness *Matthew 3:15*

Lesson 2

1. Who led Jesus into the wilderness to be tempted? *Matthew 4:1* THE SPIRIT

2. Who ministered to Jesus following the temptations? *Matthew 4:11* ANGELS

3. What had happened to John immediately before Jesus went to Galilee? *Matthew 4:12*

Lesson 3

1. Who told Joseph to call Mary's child Jesus? *Matthew 1:20, 21* ANGel GABRIEL

2. What is the meaning of the name Immanuel? *Matthew 1:23* GOD with US

Lesson 4

1. From where had the wise men traveled? *Matthew 2:1* /

2. What two groups did Herod convene in order to determine where the Christ was to be born? *Matthew 2:4*

Lesson 5

1. James and John were the sons of what man? *Matthew 4:21*

2. Jesus told the Pharisees that He had not come to call the righteous but SINNERS to repentance. *Matthew 9:13*

3. Name the twelve disciples. *Matthew 10:2-4*

John
James
ANDREW
PeTeR
SIMON
Philip
JUDAS
BARthol
MATthew
Thomas
THADDeus
James

Lesson 6

1. Jesus said that the hypocrites loved to pray standing in the synagogues and in the corners of the city. *Matthew 6:5*

2. Jesus told us to go into what place to pray? *Matthew 6:6* secret closet

Lesson 7

1. The woman who secretly touched Jesus' garment so that she might be healed had been suffering from her affliction for how long? *Matthew 9:20* 18 Years

2. Jesus saw the multitudes as sheep without a shepherd *Matthew 9:36*

Lesson 8

1. The Pharisees accused Jesus of casting out devils by whose power? *Matthew 12:24* DeViLS

2. Jesus gave the scribes and Pharisees the sign of what prophet? *Matthew 12:39* JONAH

3. Jesus said that the men of what city will one day condemn that generation? (Babylon, Nineveh, Damascus?) *Matthew 12:41* NiNeveh

Lesson 9

1. In Jesus' parable of the laborers in the vineyard, the owner of the vineyard promised to give his workers what was FAIR. (fair, reasonable, right?) *Matthew 20:4, 7*

2. The workers who had labored the entire day were satisfied with how the owner paid the "eleventh-hour" workers. T/F *Matthew 20:11, 12* F

Lesson 10

1. How many disciples did Jesus send to get the animal on which he would ride? *Matthew 21:1* 2

2. The multitude spread many of two items before Jesus. What were they? *Matthew 21:8* Psalms

3. Jesus told those whom he cast out of the temple that they had made it a DeN of thieves *Matthew 21:13*

Lesson 11

1. Unlike the foolish virgins, the wise virgins took OIL with their lamps. *Matthew 25:3, 4*

2. All the virgins slept while the bridegroom tarried. T/F *Matthew 25:5* F

3. At what time did the bridegroom come? *Matthew 25:6*

Lesson 12

1. What message was placed above Jesus' head when He was crucified? *Matthew 27:37* King of the Jews

2. Those who mocked Jesus claimed that they would believe Him if He did something. What was it? *Matthew 27:42* came DowN

Lesson 13

1. Who told the women, "He is not here: for he is risen"? *Matthew 28:5, 6* ANGEL

2. Quote Matthew 28:19, 20.

Sweetest Story Ever Heard

by Johnny Pressley

Tell me the story of Jesus,
Write on my heart every word;
Tell me the story most precious,
Sweetest that ever was heard.
—Fanny J. Crosby

ARE THERE THINGS IN YOUR LIFE that you especially enjoy because you have become accustomed to them? Your own bed and pillow? A comfortable pair of shoes? Your family's favorite home-cooked meals? Old, familiar songs? The company of family and friends?

Most of us like to try new products, sample new foods, and buy brand-new items. But have you noticed how we all have some old familiar favorites that we keep going back to because we enjoy them so?

The Gospel story of Jesus is one of those "old familiar favorites" that we love to keep going back to again and again. At the same time, some may think that a lesson series on the life of Jesus could be nothing more than a repetition of what we have heard many times already. How quickly this attitude can change when we dig into the Scriptures and witness again the richness of the Gospel texts, and the deeper insights waiting to be discovered! With each reading of familiar texts of Scripture, we see truths that we had not observed before; and our understanding and comprehension are enhanced. Old lessons yield new applications to our ever-changing lives.

Perhaps more wonderful than all of this is simply the opportunity to hear again the beloved stories we have cherished from our youth and to let them touch and bless our hearts once more. They never fail to fill us with peace and joy, kindling anew a burning passion to know Christ even more.

As Fanny J. Crosby declared, the story of Jesus is a story "most precious," the "sweetest that ever was heard." When that is our attitude toward the Gospel story of our Lord, we will long to hear it told again and again.

Beginnings

The lessons for this quarter are all taken from Matthew's account of the life of Jesus. They cover the full range of Jesus' days on this earth, from His birth in Bethlehem to His ascension back to Heaven. Some of the lesson texts focus upon what Jesus did while others call attention to what He taught. Together they present a well-rounded portrait of His life and ministry.

The first unit of lessons is entitled "Beginnings: Birth and Ministry." **Lesson 1**, "King's Herald and Baptism," tells the story of John the Baptist and his role as the forerunner of the promised Messiah. With his austere manner and rough attire, John "prepared the way of the Lord" by creating within the hearts of the Jewish people an expectation that the Messiah's long-awaited arrival was "at hand."

Lesson 2, "Temptations and Ministry," picks up Matthew's account immediately after the baptism of Jesus. Before His Messianic ministry began, Jesus was first tested by the subtle craftiness of the devil; and, like gold in a refiner's fire, His faith proved to be genuine. Each of the well-known temptations in the wilderness was cleverly designed to undermine Jesus' plans for ministry. By focusing upon God's will and relying upon His Word, Jesus won a crucial victory. Our study of Matthew 4 will remind us how we too can counter the deceptions of the devil.

Lesson 3, "Birth of Jesus," takes us back to the announcement of Jesus' birth to His earthly father Joseph. Matthew 1 presents a portrait of Joseph as a quiet man of faith, who, though rarely mentioned in Scripture, played a significant role in God's scheme of redemption.

Lesson 4, "Coming of the Wise Men," is taken from the account in Matthew 2 of the search for the Christ child by the wise men from the East. The familiar story of their homage to the child and the precious gifts they presented to Him will challenge us to keep an attitude of worship and adoration in all our Christmas activities.

Ministry

The second unit of lessons, entitled "Ministry: Wonderful Words and Works," presents five examples of the teaching and healing ministry of Jesus. It also affords us a glimpse of the twelve closest disciples of Jesus as well as a look at some of His bitterest enemies.

Lesson 5, "The Twelve Disciples," uses select verses from three different chapters in Matthew to show how Jesus selected, groomed, and then sent forth into service the group of twelve men we now know as His apostles. The challenge of discipleship and service that He presented to them will serve as a reminder of His calling to us.

Lesson 6, "Teachings on Prayer," gives us the opportunity to look again at what may be the most famous and beloved prayer in Scripture—Jesus' "model prayer" in Matthew 6. Jesus gave this prayer to His disciples as an example to guide them in their own prayer lives. And though many of us have already memorized this prayer and often repeat it in our Lord's day worship, we will seek some practical lessons from this prayer that will guide us as we construct our own personal expressions of prayer to God.

Lesson 7, "Miracles of Compassion," uses some of the incidents recorded in Matthew 9 to present a "typical day" in the healing ministry of Jesus. A woman who for twelve years had suffered from severe bleeding, a young girl who had died, two blind men, and an entire crowd of afflicted people all benefited from Jesus' compassion. Though His powers were beyond our abilities, His manner of compassion and concern will challenge us as we try to respond with mercy to the needs of people around us.

Lesson 8, "Opposition to Jesus," looks at the unpleasant side of Jesus' ministry. While great multitudes often flocked around Jesus, listening to His words with wonder and amazement, always lurking in their midst were groups such as the scribes and Pharisees. Matthew 12 illustrates the kind of critical barrage Jesus regularly faced from His enemies and the incisive response He was capable of giving.

Lesson 9, "Laborers in the Vineyard," presents one of the many memorable parables of Jesus. The concept of the grace of God in this parable was difficult for Jesus' audience to grasp; but then, it is a concept with which many today still struggle.

Fulfillment

The last unit of lessons, "Fulfillment: Atonement and Final Commission," focuses upon the climax of Jesus' life and ministry: His death and resurrection and His final words to the church.

Lesson 10, "Entry Into Jerusalem," celebrates Jesus' triumphal entry into Jerusalem. On that "Palm Sunday" beginning the week that was climaxed by His crucifixion, Jesus received some of the kind of praise and exaltation that He truly deserves. Our goal in studying Matthew 21 will be to seek ways to enrich our own expressions of worship to our triumphant Lord and Savior.

Lesson 11, "Anticipation of Christ's Return," reminds us that someday Jesus will return to earth to gather up His people and take them home to Heaven. Selected passages from Matthew 24 and 25 will emphasize Jesus' clarion call for readiness. While many today study second coming texts for clues and signs of the end, this lesson will demonstrate the real purpose of such texts: to challenge us to pursue godly living daily and actively so that we will be found ready on the day Jesus returns.

Lesson 12, "Death of Jesus," is perhaps the most moving lesson in this series, for it focuses on the description in Matthew 27 of the terrible suffering of Jesus on the cross. We sing of how we "love that old cross" as we reflect upon the salvation that Jesus' death brought about; but then we draw back in horror as we realize the depth of the pain that Jesus endured because of our sins. Calvary is the heart of the gospel and the key to our redemption from sin.

Lesson 13, "Resurrection and Commission," brings the story of Jesus to a fitting conclusion. The final chapter of Matthew's Gospel tells of the women's discovery that the tomb of their Master was empty. Through this lesson we will relive the excitement and joy of the good news that our Savior has conquered death. And we will be reminded of that to which the church must give top priority—Jesus' Great Commission to take the gospel to "all nations."

Without question, the story of Jesus bears repeating time and time again, for it is indeed the "sweetest that ever was heard."

Answers to Quarterly Quiz on page 114

Lesson 1—1. the kingdom of heaven. 2. Isaiah. 3. "fulfil all righteousness." **Lesson 2**—1. the Spirit. 2. angels. 3. John was cast into prison. **Lesson 3**—1. the angel of the Lord. 2. God with us. **Lesson 4**—1. the East. 2. the chief priests and scribes. **Lesson 5**—1. Zebedee. 2. righteous, sinners. 3. Peter, Andrew, James (son of Zebedee), John, Philip, Bartholomew, Thomas, Matthew, James (son of Alpheus), Lebbeus (Thaddeus), Simon the Canaanite, Judas Iscariot. **Lesson 6**—1. synagogues, corners, streets. 2. a closet. **Lesson 7**—1. twelve years. 2. sheep, shepherd. **Lesson 8**—1. Beelzebub. 2. Jonah. 3. Nineveh. **Lesson 9**—1. right. 2. false. **Lesson 10**—1. two. 2. their garments, branches from the trees. 3. Den of thieves. **Lesson 11**—1. oil. 2. true. 3. midnight. **Lesson 12**—1. This is Jesus the King of the Jews. 2. came down from the cross. **Lesson 13**—1. an angel. 2. "Go ye therefore, and teach all nations, baptizing them in the name of the Father, and of the Son, and of the Holy Ghost: teaching them to observe all things whatsoever I have commanded you: and, lo, I am with you alway, even unto the end of the world. Amen."

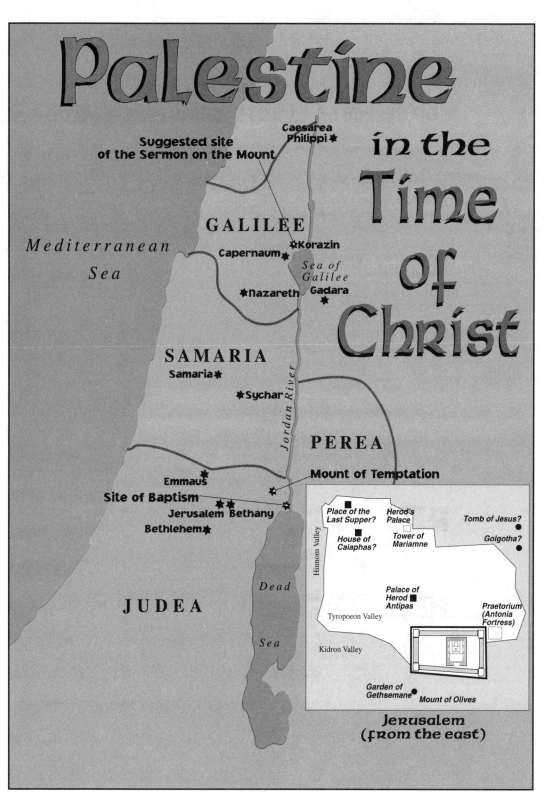

Palestine

in the Time of Christ

- Caesarea Philippi ★
- Suggested site of the Sermon on the Mount
- **GALILEE**
- *Mediterranean Sea*
- ★ Korazin
- Capernaum ★
- *Sea of Galilee*
- ★ Nazareth
- Gadara ★
- **SAMARIA**
- Samaria ★
- ★ Sychar
- *Jordan River*
- **PEREA**
- **Mount of Temptation**
- Emmaus ★
- Site of Baptism
- Jerusalem Bethany
- Bethlehem ★
- *Dead Sea*
- **JUDEA**

Jerusalem (from the east)

- Place of the Last Supper?
- Herod's Palace
- Tomb of Jesus?
- House of Caiaphas?
- Tower of Mariamne
- Golgotha?
- Hinnom Valley
- Palace of Herod Antipas
- Praetorium (Antonia Fortress)
- Tyropoeon Valley
- Kidron Valley
- Garden of Gethsemane
- Mount of Olives

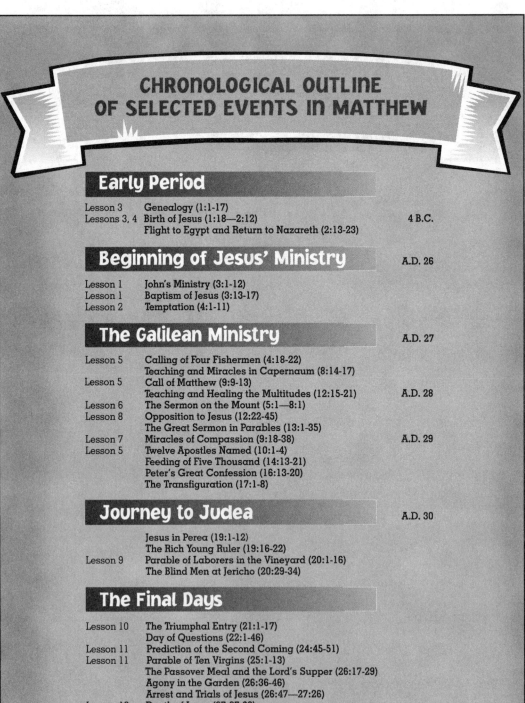

CHRONOLOGICAL OUTLINE OF SELECTED EVENTS IN MATTHEW

Early Period

Lesson 3	Genealogy (1:1-17)	
Lessons 3, 4	Birth of Jesus (1:18—2:12)	4 B.C.
	Flight to Egypt and Return to Nazareth (2:13-23)	

Beginning of Jesus' Ministry   A.D. 26

Lesson 1	John's Ministry (3:1-12)
Lesson 1	Baptism of Jesus (3:13-17)
Lesson 2	Temptation (4:1-11)

The Galilean Ministry   A.D. 27

Lesson 5	Calling of Four Fishermen (4:18-22)	
	Teaching and Miracles in Capernaum (8:14-17)	
Lesson 5	Call of Matthew (9:9-13)	
	Teaching and Healing the Multitudes (12:15-21)	A.D. 28
Lesson 6	The Sermon on the Mount (5:1—8:1)	
Lesson 8	Opposition to Jesus (12:22-45)	
	The Great Sermon in Parables (13:1-35)	
Lesson 7	Miracles of Compassion (9:18-38)	A.D. 29
Lesson 5	Twelve Apostles Named (10:1-4)	
	Feeding of Five Thousand (14:13-21)	
	Peter's Great Confession (16:13-20)	
	The Transfiguration (17:1-8)	

Journey to Judea   A.D. 30

	Jesus in Perea (19:1-12)
	The Rich Young Ruler (19:16-22)
Lesson 9	Parable of Laborers in the Vineyard (20:1-16)
	The Blind Men at Jericho (20:29-34)

The Final Days

Lesson 10	The Triumphal Entry (21:1-17)
	Day of Questions (22:1-46)
Lesson 11	Prediction of the Second Coming (24:45-51)
Lesson 11	Parable of Ten Virgins (25:1-13)
	The Passover Meal and the Lord's Supper (26:17-29)
	Agony in the Garden (26:36-46)
	Arrest and Trials of Jesus (26:47—27:26)
Lesson 12	Death of Jesus (27:27-66)
Lesson 13	Resurrection (28:1-15)
Lesson 13	The Great Commission (28:16-20)

Imitating Jesus' Inclusive Ministry
Including Persons With Disabilities in Your Teaching

by Jim Pierson

JAY JEFFRIES IS INCLUDED in his Sunday school class at the First Church of Christ in Covington, Indiana. "So what?" someone says. "Aren't most people included in their Sunday school classes?" What makes Jay's situation special is that Jay has mental retardation and physical disabilities. That, however, has not prevented him from being accepted by the members of his class. They take turns caring for him. They also call him each day, drive him to church activities, and take him to his doctor's appointments. They share in his life in these and many other significant ways.

Today there are some fifty-four million Jays living in the United States. In fact, in every community one will find people who have mental, sensory, physical, emotional, and communication disabilities, which may prevent their participation in many life functions. These people need to be included in the Sunday school, in the church, and in the lives of church members. Such inclusion mirrors Jesus' inclusive approach.

When Jesus was on earth, He regularly encountered people with disabilities. Matthew 9, from which lesson 7 in this quarter is taken, describes a series of such encounters. Jesus heals a man with a physical disability (v. 2). He cures a woman of a disease she had endured for twelve years (v. 20). He restores the sight of two men (vv. 29, 30). He encounters and rehabilitates a man with a speech problem (vv. 32, 33). Whatever the disability, Jesus made a difference.

Your adult Sunday school class can also make a difference in the lives of students with disabilities. Consider the following suggestions, which will assist in imitating Jesus' inclusive approach and applying it to your particular setting.

Sensory and Physical Disabilities

If a student's disability is deafness, find a volunteer interpreter to communicate the lesson. Ask the interpreter to conduct some sign language classes for the class members. Learning a few basic signs will make the student feel more a part of the group. If the student is not completely without hearing, other suggestions are in order. If the person lip-reads, he or she must have a clear view of the teacher's face. Instruct class members not to talk louder or shout to the individual, for doing so can interfere with his normal processes of communication.

If the disability is blindness, invite the person to the class. Orient him to the classroom and the path he will need to take to get there. Ask class members not to move furniture or other objects without telling the blind person. Provide a braille Bible and other materials. Address the person by name. Tell class members that it is important to let the person know who they are (also, remember that blind people may find it difficult to recall names, since they cannot match a face with a name). Give explanations of items being written on the chalkboard. If the person uses a guide dog, explain why other members of the class should not pet the dog. Be sure to offer transportation to the person if necessary.

It is also helpful to know some basic skills for guiding a person who is blind. For example, the folded arm provides the basic point of reference for the person. Moving the elbow back suggests that the person is to sit behind you. Stopping indicates that you are nearing a step or a curb.

The teacher may have special concerns about copying materials for a student who is not completely blind, but is visually impaired. You do not need special permission to enlarge the pages of one book for such a student. Whenever you need more than one copy of a page, contact the publisher for permission, unless the book is marked "reproducible."

If the disability involves other physical limitations, make the building and the classroom area accessible. When social activities are planned, consider the matter of accessibility and try to take care of the barriers ahead of time. Familiarize yourself with any special equipment such as wheelchairs and/or braces.

Often some of the physical problems that classes of older adults must address are those experienced by people who have had strokes. If someone who has had a stroke has been an active part of the class, keep him involved. Offer to provide transportation or assistance with activities that may now be difficult for the person to handle independently. Even if communication is difficult, continue to try. Look the person in the eye. Make statements instead of asking questions. Visit the person at home. Let him know he is still an important part of the group.

A friend of mine used to play golf every Thursday with three other men from his Sunday school class. Then he had a stroke, and his former golfing buddies withdrew from him. They weren't being rude; they simply didn't know what to do, and they were afraid of saying the wrong thing. At first my friend was devastated. But with a little creativity, the problem was solved. A new fourth person was added to the group; as for my friend, he continues to be a part of the Thursday gathering—only now he enjoys the action, along with the fresh air and sunshine, from his golf cart. He is back in Sunday school as well.

Other Types of Disabilities

If an individual's problem is emotional, be understanding and supportive—both of him and his family. Ask the family or the person about the nature of the problem, the treatment, and what the class can do to help. You may want to ask a mental health professional to come to a class function and discuss the nature of mental illness.

If the problem is a learning disability, be cautious and be sensitive to the person's needs. It may be good for a teacher of adults not to ask a visitor or new member to read aloud in class without checking with him or her ahead of time. Often poor reading is a noticeable symptom of a learning disability.

If the disability involves communication (and this is often a symptom of many disabling conditions), develop a successful means of communicating with the person. Never pretend that you understand. Ask the person to repeat a statement or say it in a different way. A home visit may lead to workable communication solutions involving both the classroom and class members. It might not hurt to have pencil and paper handy; if the person is able to read, he can indicate by nodding or by other signals whether or not his message is being understood.

If the disability is mental retardation, the process of inclusion will require more attention. If this involves only one or two people, include them in the regular class. Encourage class members to take turns sitting with them, assisting them with finding Scripture references, making interactions with other class members easier, looking out for them at class parties, and getting to know what nice people they really are.

Additional Avenues of Service

If more than two individuals with mental retardation are attending your church, the church should consider organizing a special class just for them. This class would have its own teacher and lesson, but the opening prayer time, refreshments, and social activities could be a joint endeavor. Such an arrangement provides an opportunity for mutual ministry and fellowship, while offering a program of Bible study and learning activities geared specifically to your special adults. Another possibility for this kind of ministry would be to sponsor a class for the residents of a nearby group home, for adults with special needs who live in your section of the community, or for any such adults who are known to your church family.

Class members may also want to begin doing volunteer work with organizations that help persons with disabilities. Many possibilities exist for this kind of service. A call to the appropriate organizations in your city or town will reveal a variety of needs.

Finally, the adult Sunday school class can minister by being sensitive to the needs of a family dealing with a disability. If such a family is part of your class, take time to learn their needs. If this disability involves a child in the family, keep in mind the four occasions when this family may require special attention: (1) when they learn the diagnosis, (2) when the child starts to school, (3) when the child leaves the school system (because the parents will no longer have access to the services provided by the school), and (4) when the parents realize that they can no longer provide care for their child. Often the most critical service parents need is respite care. In its simplest form, this means having an extra pair of hands to help with specific tasks. Parents will also appreciate the kindness of someone who will offer to watch their child so that they can go out for special occasions.

Be There!

Perhaps the best way to summarize all of this advice is to say, "Be there!" One Sunday our minister announced that the daughter of one of the women in our church would be moving to a residential facility on Tuesday. On Tuesday a member of this woman's Sunday school class arrived at her house. She said, "If my daughter were moving away from home, I would want someone to be with me. That is the reason I am here." She spent the day with the woman. After helping to arrange the furniture in the daughter's new residence, she drove the woman back to her apartment. Later that day, another member of the woman's Sunday school class took her out for dinner.

People such as this woman and Jay Jeffries (who was mentioned at the beginning of this essay) represent unique opportunities for your adult Sunday school class to mirror Jesus' compassion and His ministry of inclusion. By doing so, your class members will receive much more than they give; and they will be ministered to in ways they never imagined.

King's Herald and Baptism

December 5
Lesson 1

DEVOTIONAL READING: Matthew 21:23-27.

BACKGROUND SCRIPTURE: Matthew 3.

PRINTED TEXT: Matthew 3:1-17.

Matthew 3:1-17

1 In those days came John the Baptist, preaching in the wilderness of Judea,

2 And saying, Repent ye: for the kingdom of heaven is at hand.

3 For this is he that was spoken of by the prophet Isaiah, saying, The voice of one crying in the wilderness, Prepare ye the way of the Lord, make his paths straight.

4 And the same John had his raiment of camel's hair, and a leathern girdle about his loins; and his meat was locusts and wild honey.

5 Then went out to him Jerusalem, and all Judea, and all the region round about Jordan,

6 And were baptized of him in Jordan, confessing their sins.

7 But when he saw many of the Pharisees and Sadducees come to his baptism, he said unto them, O generation of vipers, who hath warned you to flee from the wrath to come?

8 Bring forth therefore fruits meet for repentance:

9 And think not to say within yourselves, We have Abraham to our father: for I say unto you, that God is able of these stones to raise up children unto Abraham.

10 And now also the axe is laid unto the root of the trees: therefore every tree which bringeth not forth good fruit is hewn down, and cast into the fire.

11 I indeed baptize you with water unto repentance: but he that cometh after me is mightier than I, whose shoes I am not worthy to bear: he shall baptize you with the Holy Ghost, and with fire:

12 Whose fan is in his hand, and he will thoroughly purge his floor, and gather his wheat into the garner; but he will burn up the chaff with unquenchable fire.

13 Then cometh Jesus from Galilee to Jordan unto John, to be baptized of him.

14 But John forbade him, saying, I have need to be baptized of thee, and comest thou to me?

15 And Jesus answering said unto him, Suffer it to be so now: for thus it becometh us to fulfil all righteousness. Then he suffered him.

16 And Jesus, when he was baptized, went up straightway out of the water: and, lo, the heavens were opened unto him, and he saw the Spirit of God descending like a dove, and lighting upon him:

17 And lo a voice from heaven, saying, This is my beloved Son, in whom I am well pleased.

GOLDEN TEXT: I indeed baptize you with water unto repentance: but he that cometh after me is mightier than I, whose shoes I am not worthy to bear: he shall baptize you with the Holy Ghost, and with fire.—Matthew 3:11

Immanuel: God With Us

Unit 1: Beginnings: Birth and Ministry

(Lessons 1-4)

Lesson Aims

After this lesson students will be able to:

1. Summarize the message of John the Baptist and how he fulfilled his role as the herald of Jesus.

2. Compare and contrast the reason Jesus was baptized with the reasons believers are baptized today.

3. Examine their lives and state changes they will make in order to "fulfil . . . righteousness."

Lesson Outline

INTRODUCTION

    A. Talkin' About Heaven

    B. Lesson Background

 I. HEED GOD'S CALL (Matthew 3:1-6)

    A. A Rugged Preacher (vv. 1-4)

    B. A Receptive Public (vv. 5, 6)

 II. PREPARE FOR JUDGMENT (Matthew 3:7-12)

    A. Fruits of Repentance (vv. 7-10)

    Only Human

    B. Wheat and Chaff (vv. 11, 12)

III. DO WHAT IS RIGHT (Matthew 3:13-17)

    A. Jesus' Obedience (vv. 13-15)

    The Critic

    B. God's Approval (vv. 16, 17)

CONCLUSION

    A. Time for a Change

    B. Prayer

    C. Thought to Remember

Introduction

A. Talkin' About Heaven

One of the old spirituals has the line: "Everybody talkin' about Heaven ain't goin' there." Jesus confirmed that it is true that many who think they are "on good terms" with God will be surprised to learn otherwise at the Judgment Day. Some will be turned away who, during their lives on this earth, claimed to be Christians. They will say, "But Lord, did we not prophesy in Your name, and cast out demons in Your name, and do many mighty works in Your name?" But they will be rejected because, "Not every one that saith unto me, Lord, Lord, shall enter into the kingdom of heaven; but he that doeth the will of my Father which is in heaven" (Matthew 7:21).

Most of us have heard the old expression that Christians ought to "practice what we preach." A more contemporary version of this principle is that we should "walk the talk." But no matter how one says it, the simple truth is that it is not enough just to talk about being a Christian—we need to live as though we mean it. After all, the old spiritual is right: not everyone talking about Heaven is going to be there.

B. Lesson Background

The Gospel of Matthew tells the story of the ministry of Jesus, moving from His baptism to His death and resurrection. However, as Matthew indicates, the ministry of Jesus actually began with the ministry of John the Baptist. John had been commissioned by God to prepare the Jews for the work that Jesus would do. He was to announce the imminent arrival of their long-awaited Messiah and to issue a call for all those who were ready to join the Messiah in establishing the kingdom of God. John was not one to mince words; he made it very clear that the joys of the Messianic kingdom are for only those who are willing to humble themselves before God and repent of their sins.

I. Heed God's Call (Matthew 3:1-6)

A. A Rugged Preacher (vv. 1-4)

1. In those days came John the Baptist, preaching in the wilderness of Judea.

John the Baptist conducted a ministry unlike that of anyone else in his day. The contents of his *preaching* were not of his own devising, but were given to him by God. John was not welcomed or accepted by the religious leaders of his day, and thus he withdrew from their jurisdiction to the *wilderness*, or less populated areas, of the province of *Judea*.

2. And saying, Repent ye: for the kingdom of heaven is at hand.

We can be certain that John's sermons were considerably longer than this one sentence. What Matthew has done is to record for us the essence of John's preaching. For centuries the Jews had waited for the fulfillment of the Messianic prophecies. John declared that the time of fulfillment was now *at hand*.

What is referred to in Matthew as the *kingdom of heaven* is described in the Gospel of Mark as "the kingdom of God." These are parallel phrases, as can be seen by comparing Matthew 13 and Mark 4. In neither case is the focus upon a place (a kingdom located in Heaven, or a territory on earth), but upon a relationship. We are in a *"kingdom* relationship" with *heaven* when God

Visual for lesson 1

This visual shows some of the sites where the events studied this quarter took place. Keep it on display throughout the quarter.

is our King and we are His servants. It is in this sense that John could say that the *kingdom of heaven* would appear on earth shortly. The anointed King had already been born and was about to begin His ministry. Then, after His resurrection, when "all power" would be given to Him (Matthew 28:18), Jesus would begin to summon all people through the gospel to enter into a kingdom relationship with Him by accepting Him as their Lord and King.

3. For this is he that was spoken of by the prophet Isaiah, saying, The voice of one crying in the wilderness, Prepare ye the way of the Lord, make his paths straight.

This quotation is taken from Isaiah 40:3, one of Isaiah's several prophecies of the coming Messiah. The imagery here is that of an "advance team" preparing for a visit from a royal dignitary. Roads are smoothed out (potholes are filled in), and people are made ready to greet their visiting king. John was the "advance team" for Jesus—the road builder who made *his paths straight,* and the *voice* (herald) who trumpeted the King's arrival.

4. And the same John had his raiment of camel's hair, and a leathern girdle about his loins; and his meat was locusts and wild honey.

John the Baptist is noted for his austere manner of living. He lived out in the wilderness areas away from the cities of Judea. His *camel's hair* clothing was rougher than other fabric, but also more durable and thus better suited for his outdoor lifestyle. The *leathern girdle,* or leather belt, held his robe together, and also allowed him to gather up the bottom of his robe so he could move freely when he traveled through rocky terrain or waded into the Jordan River.

John's *meat,* or food, consisted of *locusts and wild honey* (and probably anything else edible that he could take from the land). His choices were small and simple, but healthful. We should not imagine John to have been a sickly, malnourished man, but a healthy, vigorous outdoorsman

who made quite an impression upon all who ventured out to see this prophet of God.

B. A Receptive Public (vv. 5, 6)

5. Then went out to him Jerusalem, and all Judea, and all the region round about Jordan.

The ministry of John was extremely well received. Though the religious leaders despised him, the multitudes loved him. So great was their regard for John that the Pharisees hesitated to make public statements critical of John, for fear of agitating the crowds (Matthew 21:26). [See question #1, page 128.]

6. And were baptized of him in Jordan, confessing their sins.

As his nickname implies, John "the Baptist" (more literally, "the Baptizer") was well known for performing baptisms. Such a practice must have been rare or even non-existent in John's day for the title to have much meaning. First-century Judaism did devise a "proselyte baptism" to initiate Gentile converts into the Jewish faith, and the Jewish sect known as the Essenes used water baptism to symbolize their desire for spiritual cleansing. But there is no clear evidence that these pre-dated John's baptism. John's baptism was unique, both in its form and its purpose, and was intended to prepare the people spiritually for the arrival of the Messiah and the kingdom of God.

The baptism of John was like Christian baptism in its outward form, but not in its meaning. John's baptism was not linked to "the gift of the Holy Ghost" (Acts 2:38). His audience was not told that they would be "buried with Christ" (Romans 6:3-6) or experience a "putting on" of Christ (Galatians 3:27). John offered a "baptism of repentance" that anticipated the coming of the Messiah and His salvation (Acts 19:4). This is how the link between John's baptism and remission of sins (Mark 1:4; Luke 3:3) should be understood. His baptism looked forward to the time when remission of sins could be offered as a result of Jesus' death and resurrection, just as the sacrifices under the law of Moses had looked forward to Christ's perfect sacrifice. Note that believers in Jesus who had been baptized "unto John's baptism" were later challenged with the gospel to finish what they had started and to be "baptized in the name of the Lord Jesus" (Acts 19:1-5).

II. Prepare for Judgment
(Matthew 3:7-12)

A. Fruits of Repentance (vv. 7-10)

7. But when he saw many of the Pharisees and Sadducees come to his baptism, he said unto them, O generation of vipers, who hath warned you to flee from the wrath to come?

John's strange behavior and enticing message drew a diverse crowd. Along with the listeners who were genuinely interested, there were the curiosity seekers and the scoffers. The latter category included the *Pharisees and Sadducees*, the leaders of the Jewish community. They opposed John's ministry because he operated outside their oversight and disrupted the religious *status quo.* They came, not to grow in spirit, but to gather evidence that could be used to silence John.

Like one of the ancient prophets, John courageously challenged the malicious hypocrisy of the Pharisees and Sadducees when they attended his preaching. He called them a *generation of vipers,* using snakes as a symbol of evil and deception—an image that recalled the activity of the serpent in the garden of Eden. [See question #2, page 128.]

8. Bring forth therefore fruits meet for repentance.

Just as "faith without works is dead" (James 2:26), so likewise *repentance* that does not bear *fruits* is nothing more than empty words. Biblical repentance is more than remorse at getting caught or regret at how badly a situation turned out. It is an honest acknowledgment of having done wrong and a genuine desire to set things right as best we can.

One obvious fruit of repentance would be a verbal apology to someone we have wronged. Usually what we would rather do is to ignore a problem and hope it goes away; however, what we need to do is to muster the courage to face our friends and say, "I was wrong and I am sorry for what I did." Sometimes the obvious fruit of repentance is to offer to make restitution for the harm we have done, and perhaps, like Zaccheus, even add a bonus to underscore our sincerity (Luke 19:8). And, of course, nothing says "repentance" better than to change our behavior for the good and cease to do the sin in question.

In the case of deeply ingrained habits that do not easily go away, repentance may not be able to produce an immediate end to the sin. But a genuine desire to quit will seek out aggressive measures for effecting change, such as agreeing to work with counseling, setting up an accountability relationship, or staying away from people and places that tempt us to renew our sin.

A changed heart should result in a changed life. Neither standing in a crowd by the river Jordan nor sitting in a church pew will make us right with God unless our lives exhibit genuine fruits of repentance. [See question #3, page 128.]

ONLY HUMAN

Dr. Laura Schlessinger is the host of a popular talk radio program. She is frequently asked what question she most often receives from her radio audience. She answers, "The caller usually wants to know this: 'Now that I've done all these things I shouldn't have done, how can I avoid the consequences I knew about, but denied and just hoped wouldn't happen?'"

Dr. Schlessinger confesses that her pet peeve is the frequent protest that one is "only human."

"Only human?" she asks. "As if one's humanness were a blueprint for instinctive, reflective reactions to situations, like the rest of the animal kingdom. I see being 'human' as the unique opportunity to use our minds and wills to act in ways that elevate us above the animal kingdom."

Schlessinger then underscores her point with an illustration from the classic film, "The African Queen." Charlie, who is played by Humphrey Bogart, invokes the "only human" excuse to explain his drunkenness the evening before. Rosie, the missionary who is played by Katherine Hepburn, looks up from her Bible and sharply replies, "We were put on earth to rise above our nature."

Nothing says repentance better than change. When we truly repent, we "rise above our nature" and begin to live as our Creator meant for us to live.

—L. D. C.

9. And think not to say within yourselves, We have Abraham to our father: for I say unto you, that God is able of these stones to raise up children unto Abraham.

A genuine faith and repentance are required of all who would approach God, and that includes even His "chosen people." Though the Jewish people may be the natural heirs of the Messianic promises to *Abraham* their *father,* the blessings are actually bestowed upon those who imitate the faith of Abraham, and that regardless of ancestry (Galatians 3:26-29). There is no privileged

---

Home Daily Bible Readings

Monday, Nov. 29—John Preaches and Baptizes (Matthew 3:1-6)

Tuesday, Nov. 30—John Proclaims Jesus' Coming (Matthew 3:7-12)

Wednesday, Dec. 1—Jesus Is Baptized by John (Matthew 3:13-17)

Thursday, Dec. 2—John Sends Messengers to Question Jesus (Matthew 11:2-6)

Friday, Dec. 3—Jesus Praises John the Baptist (Matthew 11:7-11)

Saturday, Dec. 4—Jesus Admonishes the Crowd (Matthew 11:12-19)

Sunday, Dec. 5—John the Baptist Is Executed (Matthew 14:1-12)

VISUALS FOR THESE LESSONS

The small visual pictured in each lesson (e.g., page 123) is a small reproduction of a large, full-color poster included in the *Adult Visuals* packet for the Winter Quarter. The packet is available from your supplier. Order No. 292.

status when it comes to the grace of God—or the judgment of God. [See question #4, page 128.]

10. And now also the axe is laid unto the root of the trees: therefore every tree which bringeth not forth good fruit is hewn down, and cast into the fire.

As the woodsman holds the *axe* blade next to the *root* of a tree in order to prepare to strike it, so also the judgment of God is already being planned for those who fail to produce the *good fruit* of faith and repentance.

B. Wheat and Chaff (vv. 11, 12)

11. I indeed baptize you with water unto repentance: but he that cometh after me is mightier than I, whose shoes I am not worthy to bear: he shall baptize you with the Holy Ghost, and with fire.

John operated with a clear understanding of his relationship to Jesus. Desiring no glory for himself, all that he did was for the advancement of the Messiah's ministry. He knew that his was a temporary role that must soon "decrease," even as Jesus' role "must increase" (John 3:30). His humility was such that he did not consider himself worthy of even carrying the Messiah's *shoes*, or sandals. In the other Gospels John says he is not worthy to "unloose" the Messiah's shoes (Mark 1:7; Luke 3:16; John 1:27). No doubt these references to handling shoes were occasioned by the ancient practice of washing one's feet upon entering a home. This was a task for the lowliest household servant. John said he was unworthy to perform even this lowly task for the Messiah. [See question #5, page 128.]

Some believe that the fulfillment of John's words about the Messiah's baptizing *with the Holy Ghost, and with fire* came through what the apostles experienced on the Day of Pentecost (Acts 2:1-4). Others, noting that John's words were addressed to the multitudes, think it is more inclusive. Jesus seems to have referred to John's words here in Acts 1:5, when He told the apostles they would shortly "be baptized with the Holy Ghost," clearly a reference to Pentecost. In that instance, He did not mention baptism with fire, which this context explains is a reference to

judgment. All who resist the Spirit-led ministry of Jesus and His apostles after Him will experience this baptism of *fire*.

12. Whose fan is in his hand, and he will thoroughly purge his floor, and gather his wheat into the garner; but he will burn up the chaff with unquenchable fire.

After *wheat* was cut at the harvest, it was taken to the threshing *floor*, where the grain was separated from the straw, usually by having oxen trample it or drag a sled over it to break the grain out of the husks that surrounded it. The straw could then easily be removed, but the grain was still mixed with *chaff* (the husks and small, broken pieces of straw). So the grain, including the chaff, was then scooped up with a wide fork, or winnowing *fan*, and tossed into the air. The wind separated the light chaff from the heavier grain. The grain was then stored for later use, and the chaff was scooped up and burned.

John's picture of wheat and chaff clearly portrays the idea of a day of judgment when the saints will be separated from sinners. Just as God's "axe" is already being lined up against the unfruitful tree (v. 10), so also His *fan is in his hand*, ready to separate the useless chaff from the grain, and to *burn up the chaff* in the *unquenchable fire* of Hell.

III. Do What Is Right
(Matthew 3:13-17)

A. Jesus' Obedience (vv. 13-15)

13. Then cometh Jesus from Galilee to Jordan unto John, to be baptized of him.

Jesus was born in the southern province of Judea, in the town of Bethlehem, but He was raised at Nazareth in the northern province of *Galilee*. When He was thirty years old (Luke 3:23) and ready to begin His ministry, He traveled to the *Jordan* River to the location where *John* was baptizing.

14. But John forbade him, saying, I have need to be baptized of thee, and comest thou to me?

At this point, John had not yet received the divinely appointed sign that Jesus was indeed the Messiah. That would accompany Jesus' baptism (John 1:32-34). However, John may have known something about Jesus' miraculous birth and His exemplary character, which made him hesitant to baptize Jesus. The mothers of John and Jesus were related (Luke 1:36), and thus information about one may have become known by the other.

15. And Jesus answering said unto him, Suffer it to be so now: for thus it becometh us to fulfil all righteousness. Then he suffered him.

Jesus instructed John to *suffer*, or permit, Him to be baptized because doing so would *fulfil all righteousness*; that is, it would be the "right thing" before God. Jesus understood that John's baptism expressed more than just repentance from sin, but also a readiness for the kingdom of God. Thus Jesus thought it "right" that He submit to baptism in order to express before God His own readiness for the kingdom of God and His willingness to assume God's appointed role for Him in that kingdom as the Messiah who must suffer and die for the sins of the world (John 1:29).

THE CRITIC

When John F. Kennedy was President of the United States, newspaper columnists frequently wrote advising Kennedy how he could do a better job. In response to these critics, Kennedy told a story of a legendary baseball player. "He never failed to hit when at bat and never dropped a ball," Kennedy said. "Grounders never dribbled between his legs. He threw with unerring accuracy. In the field and on the bases he had the speed and grace of a leopard. He never tired or missed a signal. In fact, he would have been one of the all-time greats except for one thing—no one was ever able to get him to put down his soft drink and hot dog and come out of the press box to play."

Jesus did not simply command us to be baptized; Jesus *Himself* was baptized. Jesus was not a critic; He was a doer. What He instructed others to do He did. He set the ultimate example through a lifestyle that modeled the teachings that He gave. Though Jesus had no reason to repent (because He was without sin), He showed us what we are to do by being baptized. He not only taught us the right thing to do; He did what was right.   —L. D. C.

B. God's Approval (vv. 16, 17)

16. And Jesus, when he was baptized, went up straightway out of the water: and, lo, the heavens were opened unto him, and he saw the Spirit of God descending like a dove, and lighting upon him.

The Gospel of John explains this descent of *the Spirit of God* on Jesus *when he was baptized* as a sign to mark Jesus as the Messiah (John 1:32, 33). He did not receive the Spirit at this point, as

if He had not possessed the Spirit before. As God's Son, Jesus was one with the Father and the Spirit. The descent of the Spirit marked the beginning of Jesus' Spirit-empowered ministry. Immediately after that Jesus, "led up of the Spirit," defeated the devil in the wilderness (Matthew 4:1ff.). From that time on, He worked miracles by the power of the Spirit (Matthew 12:28).

17. And lo a voice from heaven, saying, This is my beloved Son, in whom I am well pleased.

God's *voice from heaven* confirmed that what Jesus had said to John was true. Baptism was the right thing for Him to do to start His Messianic ministry. The words *this is my beloved Son* were derived from the Old Testament prophecies that identified the Messiah as that person designated by God as "my Son" (Psalm 2:7). God was *well pleased* with what Jesus had done on this day.

Though our experience in Christian baptism is not identical to that of Jesus, our attitude should be the same as His. He knew what God wanted Him to do, and He took action to "fulfil all righteousness"—to do the right thing before God. Many today question whether or not they need to be baptized as long as they have a genuine faith in Christ. But since baptism is part of our Great Commission for evangelism (Matthew 28:18-20; Mark 16:15, 16), is stated in Scripture as a command (Acts 2:38; 22:16), and is the consistent practice of converted believers in the book of Acts, then there should be no debate. Faith does whatever God says to do because it is the right thing to do.

Conclusion

A. Time for a Change

How do you know when it is time to change the oil in your car? Many auto mechanics leave a sticker on the windshield to remind you when your next oil change should take place. Some may send a postcard notice as that time approaches. Some newer cars even have a red warning light to let you know it is time for a change.

Over and over through His messengers God has issued a call for repentance from sin. As we reflect on the ministry of John the Baptist, let us allow this story to serve as a spiritual "warning light," telling us that it is time for a change.

B. Prayer

Father, accept our humble admission of sin. Help us to change and grow in holiness through Jesus Christ, in whose name we pray. Amen.

C. Thought to Remember

"Be ye doers of the word, and not hearers only" (James 1:22).

How to Say It

ESSENES. *Eh*-seenz.
ISAIAH. Eye-*zay*-uh.
PHARISEES. *Fair*-ih-seez.
SADDUCEES. *Sad*-you-seez.
ZACCHEUS. Zack-*kee*-us.

Learning by Doing

This page contains an alternate lesson plan emphasizing learning activities.
Classes desiring such student involvement will find these suggestions helpful.

Learning Goals

After this lesson each student should be able to:

1. Summarize the message of John the Baptist and how he fulfilled his role as the herald of Jesus.

2. Compare and contrast the reason Jesus was baptized with the reasons believers are baptized today.

3. Examine his or her life and state one change he or she is willing to make in order to "fulfil . . . righteousness."

Into the Lesson

Purchase ten bananas. Write one letter of the word *repentance* on each. (Any felt-tip marker should work.) Hand a banana to each of the first ten students who arrive for your study. As class begins, ask those holding bananas to read their letters aloud, one at a time, at random. Direct the group to listen carefully and to guess what word the letters, if arranged properly, could spell. If they need help, have the letters read a second time or have the students with bananas to stand and show the letters.

Once the word *repentance* is seen, emphasize this as the theme of John's preaching and of today's lesson. Ask the banana holders to keep their fruit handy for later use.

Into the Word

As the class follows in their own Bibles (or in the student books), have a volunteer read Matthew 3:1-17. Divide the class into three groups. Ask one group to discuss John's relationship with the people, a second group to discuss his relationship with the religious authorities, and a third to discuss his relationship to Jesus.

If you or someone in your class has a talent for drama, plan an "interview of John the Baptizer." Give your John role player all the following references to read prior to today's class: Matthew 3:1-17; 14:3-12; Mark 1:1-11; 6:17-29; Luke 1:5-80; 3:1-22; 7:16-35; John 1:15-37; 3:23—4:1; 10:41. Prepare some interview questions on cards or slips of paper to be distributed randomly to class members. (Give the person playing John a copy of these questions.) Here are some samples that can highlight John's life and ministry. Allow the class members to ask additional questions based on their small group studies.

• How did your parents communicate to you regarding your God-given purpose?

• Describe your life in the Judean wilderness.

• Where did you get the idea of baptizing people as a symbol of cleansing?

• Matthew tells us only that you preached, "Repent, for the kingdom of heaven is at hand!" Please elaborate on the content of your sermons.

• How was the baptism you performed different from the baptism later demanded by the Christian evangelists?

• Why did you call the Pharisees and Sadducees "vipers"? Isn't that harsh and judgmental?

• You didn't feel worthy to baptize Jesus. Why didn't you simply refuse?

• You offended many important people in your preaching ministry. Wasn't some of your preaching foolishly risky?

• What did you mean by "fruits meet for repentance"?

At the end, you will want to discuss the accuracy and reasonable nature of "John's" answers, especially to those questions that call for answers not specifically found in the Scriptures.

Into Life

Have the class return to its small groups to discuss these questions. (You may give each group all the questions or divide the questions among the groups.)

1. Jesus' coming to John to be baptized is an example of a variety of righteous traits in the person of Jesus. What are some of those traits?

2. The imagery of baptism is a perfect symbol of its essence and meaning. How so?

3. John the Baptizer, as a servant of God, demonstrates some characteristics that are universal to God's servants and some that are peculiar to his specific ministry. Which are which?

After a brief statement by each of your discussion groups, return to the class members who held the bananas. Ask, "How is the banana a worthy symbol of the key word of today's text: *repentance?*" Accept various responses; anticipate someone noting that the banana is not useful . . . until it "makes a drastic change," until it "takes on a new appearance"; it must be peeled! If your personal budget permits, give each of the other members of your class a banana to carry home as a symbol and a reminder of today's key truth—and possibly a conversation starter.

Let's Talk It Over

The questions on this page are designed to encourage review of the lesson Scriptures and to promote discussion of the lesson by the class. The answers provided are only discussion starters. Let your class talk it over from there.

1. The people went to the wilderness in droves to hear a word from the Lord in the preaching of John the Baptist. Where do spiritually hungry people go for food in our modern world? How can we convince them that only in Jesus is there spiritual food to satisfy their need?

People in our society have not lost their spiritual appetite, but they do not always know where to find the truth. As has been the case for many years, some are led into cults with charismatic leaders who teach them bizarre philosophical views of reality. More recently, some have begun to create their own religions by piecing together elements of truth from a variety of sources.

Every age offers its own unique opportunities for communicating the gospel. We must ask, "What will capture the attention of irreligious people?" Some people will be more receptive far from the sanctuaries and fellowship halls of church buildings. What can the church do to meet people outside their own buildings with the saving message of Jesus' love?

2. Just as in John's day, people in our generation may not immediately embrace the good news of Jesus Christ. Negative experiences with Christianity and society's perception of the church have left a number of people very resistant to the gospel. How can Christians open the hearts of others to receive the gospel?

First, we must behave in a way that glorifies God and adds credibility to our message. Immoral acts and careless words dishonor the Lord and give unbelievers reason to disregard our efforts. John the Baptist's lifestyle was unusual, but his reputation as a man of God was unimpeachable.

Second, when we take note of others' needs and act with kindness, we demonstrate genuine love and concern. What are some ways we can communicate that we genuinely care for others?

An authentic faith can open hearts to the gospel. Authenticity cannot be contrived. It must flow naturally from a life fully devoted to the Lord Jesus. It demands an acknowledgment of our weaknesses and a humble attitude toward God who saves us.

3. How important do you think it was for John to emphasize repentance in preparation for Jesus' ministry? Why?

Jesus came to offer His life as a sacrifice on behalf of sinners everywhere. However, His sacrifice was meaningless to those who refused to admit their failures. Jesus Himself preached repentance as part of His ministry (Matthew 4:17). We cannot save ourselves by our own deeds or righteousness, so repentance in no way helps us to merit salvation. But repentance does open the door for Christ to change us. It is a part of accepting His grace. In Acts 2:38 repentance is connected with both forgiveness of sins and the gift of the Holy Spirit, who helps us do what we cannot do on our own.

4. The Sadducees and Pharisees were criticized for being self-righteous. How do religious people develop a self-righteous attitude?

The self-righteousness of the Sadducees and Pharisees was rooted in genealogical pride—they were children of Abraham—and the accuracy with which they, by their own accounting, had kept God's commandments. Some believers today have a sense of pride in what they or their families have done in the past, and they fail to keep their relationship with the Lord strong in the present. Some lose sight of grace and seem to think they have earned a place in God's kingdom. That kind of thinking is what causes unbelievers to view church members as self-righteous hypocrites.

5. John used a vivid illustration to demonstrate his view of his ministry. Jesus' role was so superior to his, he said, that he was not worthy even to carry Jesus' sandals. In an age that seems to worship "self-esteem," this kind of self-effacement sounds strange. How do you think one should balance self-esteem and humility?

John was not necessarily trying to devalue his own place in God's plan. Rather, he was trying to draw a contrast for his listeners. There were things Jesus was going to do that John could not do. He was going to offer His life as a blood sacrifice for sin. He was going to send His Holy Spirit to indwell believers and comfort them until His return. In the end, He would judge the world. While we can appreciate that we are "fearfully and wonderfully made" (Psalm 139:14), we must also keep in mind that the Creator is always greater than the creation. Submission to His purposes and plans gives meaning to our lives.

Temptations and Ministry

DEVOTIONAL READING: Luke 4:14-21.

BACKGROUND SCRIPTURE: Matthew 4:1-17.

PRINTED TEXT: Matthew 4:1-16.

Matthew 4:1-16

1 Then was Jesus led up of the Spirit into the wilderness to be tempted of the devil.

2 And when he had fasted forty days and forty nights, he was afterward ahungered.

3 And when the tempter came to him, he said, If thou be the Son of God, command that these stones be made bread.

4 But he answered and said, It is written, Man shall not live by bread alone, but by every word that proceedeth out of the mouth of God.

5 Then the devil taketh him up into the holy city, and setteth him on a pinnacle of the temple,

6 And saith unto him, If thou be the Son of God, cast thyself down: for it is written, He shall give his angels charge concerning thee: and in their hands they shall bear thee up, lest at any time thou dash thy foot against a stone.

7 Jesus said unto him, It is written again, Thou shalt not tempt the Lord thy God.

8 Again, the devil taketh him up into an exceeding high mountain, and showeth him all the kingdoms of the world, and the glory of them;

9 And saith unto him, All these things will I give thee, if thou wilt fall down and worship me.

10 Then saith Jesus unto him, Get thee hence, Satan: for it is written, Thou shalt worship the Lord thy God, and him only shalt thou serve.

11 Then the devil leaveth him, and, behold, angels came and ministered unto him.

12 Now when Jesus had heard that John was cast into prison, he departed into Galilee;

13 And leaving Nazareth, he came and dwelt in Capernaum, which is upon the seacoast, in the borders of Zebulun and Naphtali:

14 That it might be fulfilled which was spoken by Isaiah the prophet, saying,

15 The land of Zebulun, and the land of Naphtali, by the way of the sea, beyond Jordan, Galilee of the Gentiles;

16 The people which sat in darkness saw great light; and to them which sat in the region and shadow of death light is sprung up.

GOLDEN TEXT: Then saith Jesus unto him, Get thee hence, Satan: for it is written, Thou shalt worship the Lord thy God, and him only shalt thou serve.—Matthew 4:10.

Immanuel: God With Us

Unit 1: Beginnings: Birth and Ministry

(Lessons 1-4)

Lesson Aims

After this lesson each student will be able to:

1. Tell how Satan tempted Jesus and how Jesus resisted Satan in the wilderness.

2. Tell what principles for dealing with temptation can be drawn from Jesus' experience.

3. Devise a plan to overcome a personally troubling temptation by using Jesus' experience in the wilderness as a model.

Lesson Outline

INTRODUCTION

  A. Shameful Practices

  B. Lesson Background

 I. TRUSTING GOD'S WORD (Matthew 4:1-4)

  A. Not Motivated by Feelings (vv. 1-3)

    The Snake

  B. Relying on God (v. 4)

 II. SERVING GOD'S WILL (Matthew 4:5-7)

  A. Not Acting With Presumption (vv. 5, 6)

  B. Humble Before God (v. 7)

III. SEEKING GOD'S GLORY (Matthew 4:8-10)

  A. Not Thinking of Self (vv. 8, 9)

    The High Cost of Shortcuts

  B. Focused on God (v. 10)

IV. FULFILLING GOD'S PLAN (Matthew 4:11-16)

  A. Approved by God (v. 11)

  B. Ready for Service (vv. 12-16)

CONCLUSION

  A. The Worst for the Best

  B. Prayer

  C. Thought to Remember

Introduction

A. Shameful Practices

What kind of parents would kill their own children? The idea is almost unthinkable to most of us, for we like to think that all parents cherish their children as much as we do. And yet we know from news reports that this kind of shocking incident happens with increasing frequency.

How strange it is, then, to read in the Old Testament that sometimes parents would offer their children as burnt sacrifices to the pagan god Molech. How awful that some of the Hebrew parents began to join the pagans in this horrific practice! The prophet Ezekiel describes the

wrath of God against those from among His people who would cause their sons to "pass . . . through the fire" of the pagan altars (Ezekiel 23:37). And then, as if their sin were not great enough already, with utter hypocrisy they would enter the sanctuary of God with an offering *on the very same day* they had killed their own children (Ezekiel 23:38, 39).

However, let us not think that inconsistent behavior toward God is confined to the Old Testament age! Jesus rebuked the Pharisees of His day for their hypocrisy. They took great pains with small details such as setting aside a tithe of all their income, including the vegetables out of their gardens (Matthew 23:23). Yet they blatantly violated some of the greater demands of God's moral standard by such actions as defrauding widows and orphans out of the few possessions they had (Matthew 23:14).

We would do well to heed the Bible's warning that God is not pleased with a partial obedience that obeys only those portions of His Word that are agreeable to us. We must learn to put the will of God first above our own desires in *all* areas of our lives.

B. Lesson Background

Though the baptism of Jesus marked the official beginning of His ministry, He did not come before the public until weeks later. The first item on God's agenda was a private time of testing. Jesus was "led up of the Spirit" (Matthew 4:1) into a wilderness area. There Satan took the opportunity to try to distract Jesus from His divine calling, but Jesus firmly resisted all of Satan's temptations. In doing so He demonstrated the genuineness of the faith commitment that He had earlier declared through His baptism.

I. Trusting God's Word (Matthew 4:1-4)

A. Not Motivated by Feelings (vv. 1-3)

1. Then was Jesus led up of the Spirit into the wilderness to be tempted of the devil.

The precise location of Jesus' confrontation with the devil is not disclosed in any of the Gospels. However, the term *wilderness* conveys the idea of an area isolated from cities and villages. There were several such locations on both sides of the Jordan River, where Jesus could have gone following His baptism. The Gospel of Mark notes that Jesus was "driven" by the Holy Spirit into the wilderness (Mark 1:12). Jesus' time of testing was no coincidence; it was by God's design. (The visual for today's lesson pictures the site traditionally held to be the location of this testing. See page 131.)

2. And when he had fasted forty days and forty nights, he was afterward ahungered.

The fact that Jesus spent His *forty days and forty nights* in the wilderness *fasting* likely indicates that He was spending a significant amount of time each day in prayer and meditation. The issue for Jesus that would have been serious enough to warrant such intense prayer and fasting was the Messianic ministry that now lay before Him. Fasting is typically done for short periods of time, from one day up to a week. Thus Jesus' *forty days* of fasting was quite exceptional and somewhat risky. The human body can easily adapt to a few days without food. But with extended fasting there comes a point at which physical strength and health begin to decline. To say that Jesus *was . . . ahungered* at that point is quite an understatement.

Forty days of fasting is not humanly impossible, as some have contended. Modern-day protesters have often conducted "hunger strikes" for forty days and longer. But the result is always a physically weakened condition. [See question #1, page 136.]

3. And when the tempter came to him, he said, If thou be the Son of God, command that these stones be made bread.

In the three wilderness temptations, Satan demonstrates why he is to be acknowledged as a master of his craft, deserving of the title *the tempter*. Each temptation Jesus faced was carefully aimed at His present situation, striking where He was most vulnerable and in a manner that could actually have seemed reasonable and thus all the more tempting.

Satan's first temptation focused on Jesus' physical weakness and hunger. The devil knew that after forty days of fasting, Jesus would have a strong desire for food as well as a genuine need for nourishment. He also knew that when an enticing opportunity (temptation) matches a person's inner desires (lust), the conditions are right for sin to occur (James 1:14, 15). Our own experience with sin bears out this truth, for we can recall occasions when our moral judgment and good intentions were set aside because we felt overwhelmed by the desires of our flesh.

Satan also took care to package his temptation in the most appealing manner. *If thou be the Son of God*, he said, reflecting back on Jesus' baptism. Jesus had heard the voice from Heaven say, "This is my beloved Son" (Matthew 3:17), and He knew that He was "led . . . of the Spirit" (4:1); but He had yet to do anything truly Messianic or supernatural. So far He had simply been alone for forty days in a wilderness. Perhaps the devil was suggesting that Jesus attempt a miracle with the stones just to take advantage of His special

status as the Son of God. Or he may have proposed that Jesus use His powers to preserve His life so that He would be able to carry out His Messianic calling.

Whatever the intent of Satan's words, they constituted a subtle attempt to get Jesus to give up trusting in God for His needs and to take some initiative on His own. But since the Holy Spirit had directed Him into the wilderness, the Holy Spirit was the one who should tell Him what to do next. To move ahead of the Spirit would have been a sin. [See question #2, page 136.]

THE SNAKE

The story is told of a man who was walking through the woods on a cold winter day. As he was walking, he came upon a poisonous snake. Startled, he took a step back and noticed that the snake was freezing cold. The snake looked up at the man and said, "Please, sir, pick me up and warm me in your arms."

The man refused, saying, "No, if I pick you up, you will only bite me and I will surely die."

The snake replied, "But you would be helping me—why would I bite you?"

The man thought for a moment, while the viper continued to plead for the man to help him. Finally the man picked up the snake and put him inside his coat. As soon as the snake warmed up, he bit the man. As the man was dying, he asked the snake why he had bitten him. The snake responded, "You knew who I was before you picked me up; you just chose to see me in a different light."

This is how Satan wants us to treat sin. He wants us to see it in a different light, so that he can steer us into excuses and rationalizations. Satan glamorizes sin and makes it look delightful, when it is actually destructive. We must see sin as it really is, and we must see the one who tries to make us sin for who he really is—the deadliest of serpents.

—L. D. C.

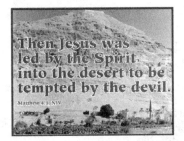

Visual for lesson 2

The visual for today's lesson shows the traditional site for the temptations of Jesus. Display it as you begin your study of the lesson text.

B. Relying on God (v. 4)

4. But he answered and said, It is written, Man shall not live by bread alone, but by every word that proceedeth out of the mouth of God.

Jesus responded to the devil's clever temptation with a resounding "no," quoting from Deuteronomy 8:3. Jesus could identify with the full context of this passage, which describes how the children of Israel wandered for forty years in another wilderness, living each day by the manna that fell from Heaven. Though their bodies longed for this miraculous bread, Moses cautioned them that their greater desire should always be for the Word of God. [See question #3, page 136.]

II. Serving God's Will (Matthew 4:5-7)

A. Not Acting With Presumption (vv. 5, 6)

5. Then the devil taketh him up into the holy city, and setteth him on a pinnacle of the temple.

The order of the second and third temptations in Matthew's account are the reverse of Luke 4:5-12. We assume that one of the Gospel writers was following a chronological order, while the other may have been telling the events according to the emphasis he wanted to make (perhaps desiring to end with what he considered the most pivotal of the three temptations).

The second temptation in Matthew's account of the testing of Jesus took place in *the holy city* of Jerusalem, at the top of one of the several towers built onto the roof of the temple complex to give it a look of grandeur. The text does not indicate how the devil took Jesus from the wilderness near the Jordan to this new location. He may have challenged Jesus to travel to Jerusalem and meet him at a designated *pinnacle of the temple*, but it is more likely that he used supernatural powers and transported Jesus there immediately.

6. And saith unto him, If thou be the Son of God, cast thyself down: for it is written, He

---

How to Say It

ANTIPAS. *An*-tih-pus.
CAPERNAUM. Kuh-*per*-nay-um.
DEUTERONOMY. Due-ter-*ahn*-uh-me.
EZEKIEL. Ee-*zeek*-yul or Ee-*zeek*-ee-ul.
ISAIAH. Eye-*zay*-uh.
MESSIANIC. Mess-ee-*an*-ik.
MOLECH. *Mo*-lek.
NAPHTALI. *Naf*-tuh-lye.
PEREA. Peh-*ree*-uh.
ZEBULUN. *Zeb*-you-lun.

---

shall give his angels charge concerning thee: and in their hands they shall bear thee up, lest at any time thou dash thy foot against a stone.

Showing his versatility in crafting temptations, Satan "fought fire with fire." Jesus had rebuffed the first temptation with a Scripture quotation; the tempter responded with his own text of Scripture. His quotation of Psalm 91:11, 12 was accurate, but, as we would expect, his application of it was misleading.

Psalm 91 is not really a Messianic prophecy. It is the testimony of a man who remained faithful to God under difficult circumstances and thus received God's protection because of his unfailing trust. Satan was suggesting that the promise of divine protection should apply to the Messiah most of all. After all, the Messiah is the faithful servant par excellence, and thus should be entitled to the help of *angels* if ever needed.

Once again, Satan was encouraging Jesus to exploit His relationship as *Son of God* and obligate the Father to intervene and rescue His Son. Perhaps the temptation here was to follow a different course of ministry from the one laid out for Him, which included service and the submission to death. Instead, Satan suggested that Jesus make a grandstand show to attract the crowds. Then Jesus could begin His Messianic ministry with a great following.

B. Humble Before God (v. 7)

7. Jesus said unto him, It is written again, Thou shalt not tempt the Lord thy God.

Jesus was not one to be outdone in a contest involving Scripture. Returning once again to the book of Deuteronomy, Jesus quoted a verse that effectively called the devil's bluff: *Thou shalt not tempt the Lord thy God* (Deuteronomy 6:16). No one, including the Messiah, should presume to tell God what to do. God was under no obligation to send angels to rescue Jesus, had He thrown Himself off the temple tower. Jesus' duty was to wait until God chose to act by His own initiative in His own time. [See question #4, page 136.]

III. Seeking God's Glory (Matthew 4:8-10)

A. Not Thinking of Self (vv. 8, 9)

8. Again, the devil taketh him up into an exceeding high mountain, and showeth him all the kingdoms of the world, and the glory of them.

For the third temptation the location shifted to an unnamed *mountain* peak. Of course, there is no mountain in the world from which one could actually see *all the kingdoms of the world*. Some suggest that Jesus may have been on a mountain from which He could see two or three large cities, which would have represented all civilizations. However, it is more likely that the devil used his supernatural powers and presented a vision of each of the major cities and kingdoms of the world. Luke's account speaks of Jesus' seeing the kingdoms "in a moment of time" (Luke 4:5). This brings to mind a rapidly moving vision with pictures in quick succession, or perhaps in some kind of montage with images overlapping one another. In any event, it would have been an impressive sight to behold.

9. And saith unto him, All these things will I give thee, if thou wilt fall down and worship me.

It might seem that Satan was losing his touch if he imagined for a moment that Jesus would *fall down and worship* him. However, when this temptation is understood properly, one is led to conclude that this may have been the most crucial test of the three. For what the devil appears to be offering Jesus is actually an attractive concession to His messiahship.

The Old Testament prophecies often foretold that the Messiah would eventually obtain the right to rule all nations in behalf of God. The devil was offering to step aside and let Jesus lay claim to the world right now, without any struggle or conflict. The one concession: allow the devil a moment to enjoy having his "sworn enemy," the Son of God, bow before him in submission. To put it another way, Satan was telling Jesus, "Let me win this one time, and then you can have it all."

Oh, the subtle strength of this temptation! Here was a shortcut to Jesus' Messianic destiny— a chance to bypass the horrible suffering of Calvary. The agony that awaited Him was so great that it "troubled" His spirit to even speak about it (John 12:27; 13:21). In Jesus' final moments before His arrest and crucifixion He prayed, "If it be possible, let this cup pass from me" (Matthew 26:39). He wanted to serve God faithfully in His role as Messiah, but He dreaded the price He had to pay. It had seemed as though there was no other way for Him to reign as Lord of creation except through His death—that is, no other way until now. [See question #5, page 136.]

THE HIGH COST OF SHORTCUTS

There was once an extremely wealthy man who employed a very devoted and responsible contractor. One day the wealthy man asked the contractor to build him a home. He gave the contractor the specific instructions that he wanted him to follow, and he told him to use only the finest materials. The man also gave the contractor all the money that building the house would require. Then the man left on a business trip, with the instructions that he wanted the house done by the time he returned.

The contractor had begun building the home, when he thought to himself, "I have worked for this man for many years. I have been dedicated and hard-working, yet I live in a small home and am barely able to put food on my plate—while this man lives in luxury and pays me next to nothing." So the contractor decided that he would make some money from his employer by taking certain shortcuts in his work. When he ordered the materials for the house, he bought cheaper items than the plan called for, especially in materials that would be covered up so checking on them would be difficult or impossible. Then he pocketed the rest of the money.

When the wealthy man returned from his trip, he came out to see the house. Then he said to the contractor, "You have been a hard-working, dedicated employee all these years, and I want to reward you." Then he handed the house key to the contractor and said, "Here, this is your house."

Satan tried to get Jesus to take a shortcut that would have bypassed the cross. Jesus, Satan claimed, would be able to rule over all the nations immediately, without having to suffer a horrible death. But Jesus refused to take any shortcuts. He stood His ground and remained obedient to the will of His Father.   —L. D. C.

B. Focused on God (v. 10)

10. Then saith Jesus unto him, Get thee hence, Satan: for it is written, Thou shalt worship the Lord thy God, and him only shalt thou serve.

Drawing for a third time from Deuteronomy, Jesus reminded the devil what our "jealous" God requires: *Thou shalt worship the Lord thy God, and him only shalt thou serve* (Deuteronomy 6:13). Jesus could not give to Satan that which is reserved exclusively for God, even though it would have benefited Him greatly. For Jesus there was no room for compromise with the plan laid out for Him by His Father.

IV. Fulfilling God's Plan (Matthew 4:11-16)

A. Approved by God (v. 11)

11. Then the devil leaveth him, and, behold, angels came and ministered unto him.

After his third defeat, Satan retreated to rethink his strategy and to watch for another opportune moment to tempt Jesus (Luke 4:13). He left behind a fragile form—one who had been weakened physically from the forty days of fasting, and was now also drained emotionally and spiritually as a result of His intense conflict with the devil. But now that He had proven Himself entirely faithful, God was pleased to fulfill the promise of Psalm 91:11, 12 and send *angels* to assist Jesus in the recovery of His strength.

B. Ready for Service (vv. 12-16)

12. Now when Jesus had heard that John was cast into prison, he departed into Galilee.

Soon after the time of tempting was completed, John the Baptist was arrested by Herod Antipas, who ruled as king of *Galilee* and Perea (Matthew 14:3). Perhaps because this arrest implied danger for Jesus as well, Jesus *departed* from the southern territory of the Jews where John had been ministering. The northern district of Galilee became the focal point of His ministry. From Matthew's Gospel we might think this move happened immediately after the wilderness temptations. John, however, records several events in an early Judean ministry (chapters 1-3), which must have lasted for a few months before Jesus departed for Galilee.

13, 14. And leaving Nazareth, he came and dwelt in Capernaum, which is upon the seacoast, in the borders of Zebulun and Naphtali: that it might be fulfilled which was spoken by Isaiah the prophet, saying,

The headquarters for Jesus' Galilean ministry was the city of *Capernaum*, located on the northwest shore of the Sea of Galilee. When Joshua allotted the promised land to the twelve tribes of Israel, this territory was given to the tribes of *Zebulun and Naphtali*. Though these tribal divisions no longer existed by Jesus' day, Matthew noted the old territorial names in order to show the fulfillment of an Old Testament prophecy from *Isaiah* (9:1, 2), which he proceeded to quote.

Home Daily Bible Readings

Monday, Dec. 6—Jesus Is Tempted by the Devil (Matthew 4:1-11)
Tuesday, Dec. 7—Jesus Begins His Ministry in Galilee (Matthew 4:12-17)
Wednesday, Dec. 8—Jesus in the Synagogue at Nazareth (Luke 4:14-19)
Thursday, Dec. 9—Jesus Is Rejected in Nazareth (Luke 4:20-30)
Friday, Dec. 10—Jesus Casts Out a Demonic Spirit (Luke 4:31-37)
Saturday, Dec. 11—Jesus Heals and Preaches (Luke 4:38-44)
Sunday, Dec. 12—Jesus Heals a Man With Leprosy (Luke 5:12-16)

15, 16. The land of Zebulun, and the land of Naphtali, by the way of the sea, beyond Jordan, Galilee of the Gentiles; the people which sat in darkness saw great light; and to them which sat in the region and shadow of death light is sprung up.

The *region* of *Zebulun* and *Naphtali* was never of any great significance in Old Testament history. Its location made it especially more vulnerable to the influence of the pagan peoples who lived to the north of Israel. Yet in spite of the presence of such spiritual *darkness*, this territory *saw great light*. Its *people* were blessed by the ministry of the one whom Isaiah proceeded to describe in chapter 9 as "Wonderful, Counselor, The mighty God, The everlasting Father, The Prince of Peace" (Isaiah 9:6).

Conclusion

A. The Worst for the Best

In *Mere Christianity*, C. S. Lewis writes that it is those who refuse to give in to temptations who face the greatest spiritual challenges. Those who give up, Lewis says, never know just how tough temptation can get. It is only those who fight to the end who know the full strength of the devil's craft. And as for Jesus Christ, "because he was the only man who never yielded to temptation, [he] is also the only man who knows to the full what temptation means."

Because of His strong dedication to the will of God, Jesus attracted the most powerful temptations Satan had to offer; and yet He was always "without sin" (Hebrews 4:15). It is to our benefit to study the Gospel accounts of the wilderness temptations so that we might learn from Jesus' success. We watch Him ignore the desires of the flesh that so readily lead us into sin (James 1:14, 15). We observe the way He used Scripture as a spiritual sword against the devil (Ephesians 6:17). We see how He set aside His own personal interests as He focused on God's will for His life (Philippians 2:3-8). Our fervent desire should be to imitate Jesus' faithfulness and thereby join Him in victory over the devil.

B. Prayer

Heavenly Father, when we are weak You are strong. So when we are tempted to sin, help us to "wait upon the Lord," knowing that You will renew our strength and provide the help we need. In Jesus' name. Amen.

C. Thought to Remember

"For I came down from heaven, not to do mine own will, but the will of him that sent me" (John 6:38).

Learning by Doing

This page contains an alternate lesson plan emphasizing learning activities.
Classes desiring such student involvement will find these suggestions helpful.

Learning Goals

After this lesson students should be able to:

1. Tell how Satan tempted Jesus and how Jesus resisted Satan in the wilderness.

2. Tell what principles for dealing with temptation can be drawn from Jesus' experience.

3. Devise a plan to overcome a personally troubling temptation by using Jesus' experience in the wilderness as a model.

Into the Lesson

As class begins, display the following list with the heading, "TODAY'S TOUGHEST TEMPTATIONS." Ask your class to take a few minutes and jot them down in order of "most common" to "least common" in contemporary society: tell a lie, commit fornication, practice gluttony, envy another's position, want to be rich and powerful, break governmental law, leave something important (and good) undone, elevate self above others, use foul or profane language, grumble about circumstances, gossip about another person.

After a few minutes, ask several to share what they put at the top and the bottom of their lists. Sample the class for uniformity and difference. Ask the class to suggest other temptations they could add to the list. Make the transition to Bible study by pointing out that in today's text, the Master Teacher teaches us all how to deal with "Today's Toughest Temptations."

Into the Word

Have Matthew 4:1-16 read aloud by three readers: one for Jesus' words, one for Satan's words, and one for the connecting narrative words.

Read the following generalizations about temptations and have the students agree or disagree with each, using elements of today's narrative and text to support their positions. Pause after each statement for learner response.

1. Temptations are always "reasonable."

2. Temptations always attack human weaknesses, that is, lusts.

3. Temptations are all "fathered" by the devil.

4. Temptations are persistent.

5. Temptations may be either blatant or subtle.

6. Temptations lose strength in the presence of Scripture.

7. Temptations always carry with them a doubt of God's power and care.

8. Temptations thrive in the company of stress.

9. Temptations are allowed by God, but never come from God.

10. Temptations do not have to "succeed."

As the class reacts and questions, introduce the following Scriptures at appropriate times: James 1:14, 15; Hebrews 4:15; Matthew 6:13; Luke 8:6, 13; 1 Corinthians 10:13; Galatians 4:13, 14; Revelation 3:10; James 1:2-4; 2 Peter 2:9; 1 Thessalonians 3:5. You may want to assign these texts to be found, held, and introduced appropriately, before beginning this activity.

Into Life

Introduce this activity by stating the key principle of dealing with temptations, as seen in today's text: *confront temptation with the power of God's truth!* Give each person in half of your class a blue index card with a text from the following list written on it. These students should find and read these texts.

Give each person in the other half of the class a red index card with one of the "temptations" from the list written on it. (There are two references for each temptation, so prepare two cards for each temptation.)

Ask your class to stand and circulate, exchanging cards without speaking until they come to a person who holds a "matching" card, that is, until a temptation is matched with a verse that could well be used to overcome it. When matches are made, those holding the two cards should be seated. The one who has read the verse should recognize the match; the one who held the temptation card should now keep the verse card, look up the Scripture, and read it. When all matches have been made, ask the group to share their matches.

Matthew 6:12 and Matthew 18:21, 22: **spirit of vengeance;** Proverbs 8:7 and Ephesians 4:15: **lying;** Leviticus 19:13 and Romans 12:17: **cheating;** 1 Corinthians 6:18 and 1 Peter 2:11: **sensual pleasure;** 2 Corinthians 9:7 and Acts 20:35: **greed, stinginess;** Hebrews 10:25 and 1 John 2:17: **indifference to godliness;** 1 Thessalonians 5:14 and Psalm 37:7, 8: **impatience;** Philippians 4:11 and 1 Corinthians 10:10: **grumbling.** (A similar activity can be found in the student book.)

Close with a prayer for strength to handle temptations.

Let's Talk It Over

The questions on this page are designed to encourage review of the lesson Scriptures and to promote discussion of the lesson by the class. The answers provided are only discussion starters. Let your class talk it over from there.

1. The Bible does not tell us what Jesus did during His forty-day fast, but we know a Jewish fast usually involved intense prayer and meditation. What do you think Jesus prayed about? What can we learn from this experience?

We can only speculate about Jesus' prayers, but the possibilities are intriguing. On a practical level, He could have prayed for personal safety. Mark tells us Jesus shared His habitat with wild animals (Mark 1:13). We, too, sometimes feel a need to pray about personal safety.

As Jesus contemplated His future role, He may have prayed for strength to endure hardships and persecutions. He was fully aware of why He had come and the fact that His words and actions would eventually lead Him to the cross. This journey would require patience, commitment, and courage. What challenging events in our lives can we predict with some certainty? What do we ask of God in regard to our own ministries?

2. Satan chose food for his first temptation. He knew Jesus had no moral weakness, but even the Son of God in human form had a need and a craving for food. What can we learn about temptation from this?

The immediate craving of the flesh is often the devil's entry point into our hearts. People who are caught in an embarrassing sin often say they fell in a "weak moment." When we are tired or hungry, we are an easier target for Satan. When a husband has been away from his wife for a time, he is more easily tempted with sexual sin.

Jesus needed food. But He also needed to depend on God. Satan tried to make it seem that meeting one of those needs would of necessity exclude the other, but Jesus proved him wrong. Whenever we say, "I know this is wrong, but I just need . . ." we have failed to follow Jesus' example. We need to maintain healthful routines to decrease the possibility of being tempted in our weakness. When we cannot, we need to take additional precautions to muster spiritual resources to make up for the physical weakness.

3. Jesus used Scripture to defend Himself against Satan. How is that significant to you? What does it suggest to you about how to deal with your own temptations?

By using Old Testament passages, Jesus was establishing that the truths expressed by God in the past were still valid. Times and circumstances may change, but God's Word stays the same.

The obvious implication of Jesus' use of Scripture is that we, too, can use Scripture to defend ourselves from the evil one. Of course, that means we have to know what the Bible says, and to know what it says we have to study it. What Bible study plans can your students suggest to help others who have not yet developed good habits of Bible study?

4. In his second temptation Satan challenged Jesus to test God to see whether He would keep His promises. How are Christians sometimes tempted to test God? How can we resist these temptations?

One of the most frequent ways we test God—though we usually do not see it as such—is in the matter of temptation itself. God has promised us that we will not be tested beyond what we can bear (1 Corinthians 10:13). Sometimes, however, we put ourselves in situations where we know we will be tempted, as if to test whether God will protect us. God will provide the way of escape, but if we fail to use it, we have only ourselves to blame if we fall.

5. Satan offered Jesus an easier path to glory. What kind of shortcuts does Satan offer us? How can we guard against his trickery?

One area in which Satan has a stranglehold on many people—including Christians—is in their finances. Our society is driven by a buy-and-spend mentality. Consumer debt is at an alarmingly high rate. Charitable giving, even by many Christians, is miniscule. People want to have all the conveniences without having to wait until they have saved for them. They believe such things will provide security, but many jeopardize their security with unmanageable debt.

Others are tempted with much the same temptations as Jesus faced: fame and power. In pursuit of these elusive goals, many will sacrifice integrity and good sense. To them, serving others is out of the question because they do not realize that Jesus' teaching on servant leadership was something He practiced as well as taught.

Birth of Jesus

DEVOTIONAL READING: John 1:1-14.

BACKGROUND SCRIPTURE: Matthew 1.

PRINTED TEXT: Matthew 1:1-6, 18-25.

Matthew 1:1-6, 18-25

1 The book of the generation of Jesus Christ, the son of David, the son of Abraham.

2 Abraham begat Isaac; and Isaac begat Jacob; and Jacob begat Judah and his brethren;

3 And Judah begat Pharez and Zerah of Tamar; and Pharez begat Hezron; and Hezron begat Ram;

4 And Ram begat Amminadab; and Amminadab begat Nahshon; and Nahshon begat Salmon;

5 And Salmon begat Boaz of Rachab; and Boaz begat Obed of Ruth; and Obed begat Jesse;

6 And Jesse begat David the king. And David the king begat Solomon of her that had been the wife of Uriah.

. . . .

18 Now the birth of Jesus Christ was on this wise: When as his mother Mary was espoused to Joseph, before they came together, she was found with child of the Holy Ghost.

19 Then Joseph her husband, being a just man, and not willing to make her a public example, was minded to put her away privily.

20 But while he thought on these things, behold, the angel of the Lord appeared unto him in a dream, saying, Joseph, thou son of David, fear not to take unto thee Mary thy wife: for that which is conceived in her is of the Holy Ghost.

21 And she shall bring forth a son, and thou shalt call his name JESUS: for he shall save his people from their sins.

22 Now all this was done, that it might be fulfilled which was spoken of the Lord by the prophet, saying,

23 Behold, a virgin shall be with child, and shall bring forth a son, and they shall call his name Immanuel, which being interpreted is, God with us.

24 Then Joseph being raised from sleep did as the angel of the Lord had bidden him, and took unto him his wife:

25 And knew her not till she had brought forth her firstborn son: and he called his name JESUS.

GOLDEN TEXT: And she shall bring forth a son, and thou shalt call his name JESUS: for he shall save his people from their sins.—Matthew 1:21.

Immanuel: God With Us
Unit 1: Beginnings: Birth and Ministry
(Lessons 1-4)

Lesson Aims

After this lesson each student will be able to:

1. Tell how the providence of God was active in the preparation of Joseph as the Messiah's earthly father.

2. Tell why a "behind-the-scenes" obedience, such as that of Joseph, is essential to the achievement of God's purposes.

3. Plan one or more acts of kindness during the Christmas season, which, though they may be done privately, will show Christ's love to others.

Lesson Outline

INTRODUCTION
   A. Small Parts
   B. Lesson Background
  I. ROYAL LINEAGE (Matthew 1:1-6)
   A. Son of Abraham (vv. 1, 2)
     The Truth of the Bible
   B. Son of David (vv. 3-6)
 II. GODLY MAN (Matthew 1:18-21)
   A. Difficult Situation (vv. 18, 19)
   B. Blessed Promise (vv. 20, 21)
III. OBEDIENT SERVANT (Matthew 1:22-25)
   A. Divine Plan (vv. 22, 23)
   B. Willing Obedience (vv. 24, 25)
     Accepting Your Role
CONCLUSION
   A. Quiet Service
   B. Prayer
   C. Thought to Remember

Introduction

A. Small Parts

"There are no small parts, just small actors." Such is the bold front often put up by actors and actresses who are assigned roles that they think are less than what their talents deserve. The words may appear to reflect a humble acceptance of one's circumstances, but in reality they may be nothing more than "sour grapes."

In the record of sacred Scripture, there are hundreds of "small parts," played by godly characters for whom we are given little information regarding their lives and service for God. Joseph, the earthly father of Jesus, is one such minor character, receiving far less attention in Scripture

than his wife Mary, John the Baptist's parents, or even the shepherds who traveled from their fields to Bethlehem. And yet, though Joseph's role in God's grand "drama of salvation" may seem small, he was faithful to his divine calling. He left behind an example worthy of our study and our imitation.

B. Lesson Background

The ministry of Jesus began with His baptism in the Jordan River and His testing in the wilderness. But the character and direction of His ministry was set some thirty years earlier at His birth. At that time several people received messages from God telling them what they could expect from this special child: His mother Mary (Luke 1:26-38), His earthly father Joseph (Matthew 1:20, 21), a group of shepherds (Luke 2:8-14), an old man named Simeon (Luke 2:25-35), and an aged widow and prophetess named Anna (Luke 2:36-38). The revelation each received was brief, but it included crucial information about the person and work of Jesus. Our lesson today will focus on that prophecy given to Joseph.

I. Royal Lineage
(Matthew 1:1-6)

A. Son of Abraham (vv. 1, 2)

1. The book of the generation of Jesus Christ, the son of David, the son of Abraham.

Matthew's Gospel, directed primarily to a Jewish readership, begins with a tracing of Jesus' roots back to two of the most prominent individuals in Jewish history. *Abraham* was the father of the Jewish nation, and *David* was her greatest king.

There are some peculiarities to note regarding Matthew's genealogy. First, it is not intended to be a comprehensive listing of all Jesus' paternal ancestors. Matthew has selected certain names to mention and has elected to skip others. He later notes (v. 17) that he has provided fourteen names from the patriarchal period (Abraham to David), fourteen from the monarchy (David to the Babylonian captivity), and fourteen from the post-exilic period (the captivity to the birth of Christ). One should keep in mind that it was not an uncommon practice among the Jews to selectively design a genealogy to accomplish a specific objective. Perhaps, in Matthew's case, this objective was to facilitate memorization of Jesus' ancestry.

In Jewish genealogies, *begat* does not necessarily imply a father-son relationship, because a man was considered the "father" of all of his descendants. Thus Jesus is identified as *the son of David* and *the son of Abraham*, though in fact He was many generations removed from both men.

Another significant point regarding Matthew's genealogy of Christ is that it does not match the genealogy provided in Luke's Gospel (Luke 3:23-38). The traditional explanation is still the most acceptable: Matthew is tracing Jesus' ancestry through Joseph, while Luke is tracing His lineage through Mary.

2. Abraham begat Isaac; and Isaac begat Jacob; and Jacob begat Judah and his brethren.

Matthew's genealogy of Christ begins with *Abraham*—the first and greatest of the patriarchs ("father rulers"). During the days prior to the establishment of formal government structures among the Jews, the patriarchs exercised authority over their family clans and all who lived within their boundaries. Abraham's position was handed down to his son *Isaac*, whose birth was a special gift from God to Abraham when he was old, and to his wife Sarah, who—until then—had been barren.

Isaac fathered twin sons, Esau and *Jacob*—the latter and younger of the two having been chosen by God before his birth to assume the patriarchal role of his grandfather and father. Jacob fathered twelve sons, from whom the twelve tribes of Israel were descended.

Passing over his first three sons because of offenses they committed against him, Jacob chose *Judah* to carry on the patriarchal tradition. And as Jacob on his deathbed made clear to Judah, this special blessing also included the privilege of being the "father" of the future kings of Israel as well as of the ultimate King, the Messiah (Genesis 49:10).

THE TRUTH OF THE BIBLE

Myron Augsburger tells of a young man from India who left his Hindu religion to become a Christian after reading the first chapter of Matthew. When he was asked what there was about the genealogy that led to his conversion, the man replied that for the first time in his life he had found a religion that is rooted in history. Hinduism and Buddhism are based on mythology, and the young man found Christianity's historicity a refreshing contrast.

Many people today try to disregard the Bible as a myth. They suggest that the authors of the books of the Bible simply made up the stories they record. In fact, however, the Bible is historically accurate. Matthew makes this point evident by accurately tracing the lineage of Jesus back to Abraham.

It is clearly demonstrated throughout the Bible that its authors were divinely inspired to be completely accurate. "All Scripture," Paul tells us, "is given by inspiration of God, and is profitable for doctrine, for reproof, for correction, for instruc-

tion in righteousness: that the man of God may be perfect, thoroughly furnished unto all good works" (2 Timothy 3:16, 17). From its history to its moral teaching to its claim to tell of the only way of salvation, the Bible is completely reliable and trustworthy.   —L. D. C.

B. Son of David (vv. 3-6)

3. And Judah begat Pharez and Zerah of Tamar; and Pharez begat Hezron; and Hezron begat Ram.

Most of the names that follow *Judah* identify obscure individuals for whom Scripture gives little if any biographical information. Judah once had an adulterous encounter with his daughter-in-law *Tamar*, resulting in the birth of twin boys (Genesis 38:27-30). The younger of the two was named *Zerah* (sometimes spelled Zarah). The firstborn, *Pharez* (sometimes spelled *Perez*), is known for slipping ahead of his brother during the time of birth, after his brother had thrust one hand out ahead of him then withdrew it. Pharez thus inherited the special royal lineage, which he passed along to his son *Hezron*, who did the same with his son *Ram*.

4. And Ram begat Amminadab; and Amminadab begat Nahshon; and Nahshon begat Salmon.

How to Say It

AHAZ. *Ay*-haz.
AMMINADAB. Uh-*min*-uh-dab.
BATHSHEBA. Bath-*she*-buh.
BOAZ. *Bo*-az.
EMMANUEL. Ih-*man*-you-el.
ESAU. *Ee*-saw.
GABRIEL. *Gay*-bree-ul.
HEROD. *Hair*-ud.
HEZRON. *Hezz*-ron.
HITTITE. *Hit*-ite.
IMMANUEL. Ih-*man*-you-el.
ISAIAH. Eye-*zay*-uh.
JERICHO. *Jair*-ih-co.
NAHSHON. *Nah*-shahn.
OBED. *O*-bed.
PEREZ. *Pair*-ezz.
PHAREZ. *Fair*-ezz.
RACHAB. *Ray*-kab.
RAHAB. *Ray*-hab.
SALMON. *Sal*-mun.
SHEOL. *She*-ol.
SIMEON. *Sim*-ee-un.
TAMAR. *Tay*-mer.
URIAH. Yu-*rye*-uh.
ZARAH or ZERAH. *Zair*-uh.

The royal lineage continued through *Amminadab*, the father-in-law of Moses' brother Aaron (Exodus 6:23). Amminadab's son *Nahshon* became the "captain" of the tribe of Judah during the forty-year march through the wilderness (Numbers 2:3; 10:14). The royal heritage was then passed on to his son *Salmon*.

5. And Salmon begat Boaz of Rachab; and Boaz begat Obed of Ruth; and Obed begat Jesse.

It is with *Salmon* that the first gap appears in Matthew's genealogy. The Old Testament provides no information regarding Salmon, making it difficult to know where to place him in Jesus' ancestry. It is only in Matthew that we learn that Salmon was married to Rahab (spelled here as *Rachab*), the harlot of Jericho who hid the Hebrew spies (Joshua 2). That information would place Salmon in the time of Joshua's conquest of Canaan. However, *Boaz*, who was David's great-grandfather, should be placed in the latter half of the period of the Judges, who ruled for some three hundred years (Judges 11:26). Salmon was thus a few generations removed from Boaz's actual father. In this case, Salmon *begat* Boaz in the sense that he "was the ancestor of" Boaz.

Boaz was a wealthy farmer who married *Ruth*, whose story of exceptional faith is told in the Old Testament book that bears her name. The lineage passed from Boaz to his son *Obed*, and then to his son *Jesse*, the father of King David. Boaz lived in Bethlehem (Ruth 2:1-4), which became known as the "city of David" and where centuries later Jesus was born (Luke 2:4, 11).

6. And Jesse begat David the king. And David the king begat Solomon of her that had been the wife of Uriah.

King *Solomon* was gifted by God with exceptional wisdom and was blessed with Israel's largest and wealthiest kingdom (2 Chronicles 1:7-12). His mother, Bathsheba, *had been the wife of Uriah* the Hittite, who was one of King David's military officers. Her adulterous affair with David led to a royal plot to have Uriah die in battle so that David could marry the widow and cover up her unexpected pregnancy. However, Nathan the prophet exposed the sin and told David that his and Bathsheba's child would die. Solomon, then, was the second child born to David and Bathsheba (2 Samuel 11:1—12:25).

David was the greatest king to rule Israel. Though his life and reign were not perfect, his heart was fully committed to God; and he became the standard by which future kings were measured (1 Kings 15:3, 11; 2 Kings 16:2; 18:1-3). David also became the symbol of the coming Messiah-King, who was acknowledged as the "Son of David" (Matthew 21:9; 22:41, 42). [See question #1, page 144.]

II. Godly Man
(Matthew 1:18-21)
A. Difficult Situation (vv. 18, 19)

18. Now the birth of Jesus Christ was on this wise: When as his mother Mary was espoused to Joseph, before they came together, she was found with child of the Holy Ghost.

The Gospel of Luke records the announcement to *Mary* by the angel Gabriel that she had been chosen by God to give birth to the promised Messiah (Luke 1:26-38). The *Holy Ghost* would use His supernatural power to cause Mary to become pregnant. With our modern, scientific understanding of reproduction and conception, we are often curious to know exactly what the Holy Spirit did. But all we know for certain is that the *birth of Jesus Christ* involved no intimacy with a man. The Holy Spirit truly performed a miracle.

Mary's pregnancy became known while she was still *espoused*, or engaged, to her fiancé *Joseph*. This could have been a scandalous discovery for Joseph and his family. The couple had at no time come *together* in sexual intimacy—in fact, Mary had been three months separated from Joseph in Judea (Luke 1:39, 56). Thus Joseph would have to assume that the child had been conceived as a result of intimacy with some other man. And since Mary had apparently not yet informed Joseph of Gabriel's message, he had no reason to believe anything other than that she had been unfaithful to her betrothal pledge.

19. Then Joseph her husband, being a just man, and not willing to make her a public example, was minded to put her away privily.

Joseph is here called Mary's *husband,* a term that emphasizes the serious nature of the betrothal. A couple who was betrothed were not to live together or sleep together, but they had entered a relationship as binding and as exclusive as marriage. Violations of this pledge were treated as violations of the marriage covenant, for which the law of Moses required the death penalty (Leviticus 20:10).

First-century Judaism did not have the legal authorization from Rome to carry out executions, and thus other measures were typically used to punish sexual infidelity. Anyone violating the betrothal pledge could be publicly denounced and humiliated, effectively shutting him or her out from any future marriage prospects (at least from any good ones). Furthermore, the violator's family could be assessed damages for bringing shame to the innocent party.

Regarding Mary, Joseph decided not *to make her a public example* by seeking punitive measures, but to *put her away privily* (quietly). Herein lies a testimony to the gracious character of Joseph. Even when he believed he had been wronged and shamed, there was a gentle and compassionate spirit in his response. As a *just*, or righteous, man he was prepared to seek justice, and yet his was a justice tempered by mercy. It is not difficult to understand why God selected Joseph to serve as one of the parents who would nurture and guide the young Messiah in His development. [See question #2, page 144.]

B. Blessed Promise (vv. 20, 21)

20. But while he thought on these things, behold, the angel of the Lord appeared unto him in a dream, saying, Joseph, thou son of David, fear not to take unto thee Mary thy wife: for that which is conceived in her is of the Holy Ghost.

Matthew's nativity account does not name the angel who appeared to Joseph at this time, then later following the visit by the wise men (Matthew 2:13), and again after the death of Herod (v. 19). The designation *angel of the Lord* could apply to any angel, but its parallel use for Gabriel in Luke's account (Luke 1:11) supports the idea that he was also Joseph's messenger from God.

Joseph was instructed not to break off the betrothal as he had intended to do, but to *take unto thee Mary thy wife*. He was then informed of the miraculous nature of Mary's pregnancy. This information would dispel any thought of infidelity by Mary, as well as indicate to Joseph the exceptional calling to which he and Mary were being summoned by God.

21. And she shall bring forth a son, and thou shalt call his name JESUS: for he shall save his people from their sins.

The *name Jesus* is the Greek form of the Hebrew word meaning "Jehovah is salvation" (from the Hebrew spelling comes the familiar name *Joshua*). The angel emphasized the spiritual nature of the Messianic mission when he declared

Today's visual pictures Joseph as the angel speaks to him in a dream, telling him that the Son to be born to Mary is the Savior: Jesus!

Visual for lesson 3

that *he shall save his people from their sins*. First-century Judaism did anticipate some spiritual blessings from the Messiah, but it focused more on the idea of a political ruler who would deliver the Jewish people from the domination of the Romans.

Jesus, however, understood His spiritual priority and never wavered from it. His friend and forerunner John the Baptist spoke of "the Lamb of God, which taketh away the sin of the world" (John 1:29). Jesus Himself passed over any talk of earthly kingdoms and simply declared that the Son of Man had come "to give his life a ransom for many" (Mark 10:45). [See question #3, page 144.]

III. Obedient Servant (Matthew 1:22-25)

A. Divine Plan (vv. 22, 23)

22. Now all this was done, that it might be fulfilled which was spoken of the Lord by the prophet, saying.

The prophecy *fulfilled* in this instance was not the appearance of an angel to the earthly father of the Messiah, for such is not predicted in the Old Testament. As the next verse indicates, the fulfilled prophecy was the child's miraculous conception by the Holy Spirit.

23. Behold, a virgin shall be with child, and shall bring forth a son, and they shall call his name Immanuel, which being interpreted is, God with us.

Matthew quotes one of the most famous Messianic prophecies of the Old Testament, found in Isaiah 7:14. This is a text cherished by Christians, especially during the Christmas season. Old Testament scholars often debate the meaning of this sentence in its original context, arguing over whether or not Isaiah meant to point to the pregnancy of a "young woman" in the days when the prophecy was spoken to King Ahaz of Judah, with Matthew then adding a Messianic implication to the passage centuries later.

While the issues involved can be quite complex, there are some simple observations that are worth noting. First, the "sign" Isaiah intended to give King Ahaz was to be "as deep as Sheol or high as heaven" (Isaiah 7:11, *New American Standard Bible*). This implies that Isaiah had in mind a supernatural event, such as would be the case with the miraculous conception of the Messiah. Also note that Matthew's interpretation of Isaiah 7:14 was given under the inspiration of the Holy Spirit. Whatever other applications to his own time Isaiah may or may not have had in mind when he spoke these words, Matthew assures us that the miraculous birth of Jesus was the fulfillment of Isaiah's prophecy.

The name *Immanuel* (also spelled "Emmanuel") literally means "with us is God," as Matthew tells his readers. This was sometimes used as a kind of "battle cry" by the Jews in times of trouble, expressing confidence that God was present with and fighting for the cause of His people. However, with the Son of God's incarnation on earth, *God with us* achieves its ultimate fulfillment. [See question #4, page 144.]

B. Willing Obedience (vv. 24, 25)

24. Then Joseph being raised from sleep did as the angel of the Lord had bidden him, and took unto him his wife.

True to the character we have earlier observed regarding *Joseph*, he obeyed the message from God. By doing so, he would have taken the shame of Mary unto himself. Observers would now wonder if he was in fact the man who had taken sexual liberties with this young lady, and, if not, why he would go through with the marriage plans. And certainly no one could be expected to believe a story about a supernatural conception. Joseph knew that his personal reputation might suffer from this decision, but he was fully committed to the will of God. [See question #5, page 144.]

ACCEPTING YOUR ROLE

Cheryl had been practicing for days—looking over her script, reading it out loud, and perfecting her delivery in front of a mirror. She was trying out for the high school play, and was hoping to be given the part of Dorothy in the school's presentation of *The Wizard of Oz*. Cheryl especially wanted to play the lead since this was her senior year. But Cheryl did not get the part; in

Home Daily Bible Readings

Monday, Dec. 13—The Genealogy of Jesus the Messiah (Matthew 1:1-11)

Tuesday, Dec. 14—Jesus' Genealogy Completed (Matthew 1:12-17)

Wednesday, Dec. 15—The Birth of Jesus the Messiah (Matthew 1:18-25)

Thursday, Dec. 16—Jesus Christ, God's Eternal Word (John 1:1-14)

Friday, Dec. 17—The Angel Gabriel Visits Mary (Luke 1:26-38)

Saturday, Dec. 18—Mary Visits Her Cousin Elisabeth (Luke 1:39-45)

Sunday, Dec. 19—Mary's Song of Praise (Luke 1:46-56)

fact, a freshman was assigned the role of Dorothy. Cheryl was understandably disappointed.

Later the director of the play approached Cheryl and told her that there were still a lot of minor roles to be filled, but not enough people to fill them. Would she accept one of these? Cheryl could have said, "You didn't need me when I wanted to play Dorothy, the main character; now you want me for a less important part." But she didn't. Instead, Cheryl accepted her new role and worked hard at the practices. The play would not have been the success that it was, if people such as Cheryl had not been available and willing to play the minor roles.

Joseph also had to accept a role that was far different from what he might have chosen for himself. Perhaps he looked forward to a happy, peaceful life in Nazareth with his new bride Mary. But God had another role for Joseph—as the earthly father of the Messiah. Joseph humbly accepted his role and faithfully carried out all the responsibilities that went with it.

When we are doing God's will, no role is minor or insignificant. —L. D. C.

25. And knew her not till she had brought forth her firstborn son: and he called his name JESUS.

For Matthew to say that Joseph *knew . . . not* Mary in an intimate way until after Jesus' birth implies that they did eventually establish a normal marriage relationship. Later references to Jesus' brothers and sisters confirm this (e.g., Matthew 13:55, 56).

Conclusion

A. Quiet Service

How many others in Jesus' ancestry could also give evidence, like Joseph, of faithful service to God, if only they had the opportunity to have their story told? How many servants of Christ over the course of church history have labored in obscurity—their devotion to duty known only to God? And how many of us are quietly doing our best to serve the Lord with the gifts and opportunities He provides, giving no thought to receiving recognition and applause?

B. Prayer

Father, teach us humility and obedience, and then use us in the service of Your kingdom. In Jesus' name we pray. Amen.

C. Thought to Remember

Let us be ever as prompt and willing to obey God as Joseph was.

Learning by Doing

This page contains an alternate lesson plan emphasizing learning activities.
Classes desiring such student involvement will find these suggestions helpful.

Learning Goals

After this lesson each student will be able to:

1. Tell how God's providence was active in preparing Joseph to be the Messiah's earthly father.

2. Tell why a "behind-the-scenes" obedience, such as that of Joseph, is essential to the achievement of God's purposes.

3. Plan one or more acts of kindness during this Christmas season, which, though they may be done privately, will show Christ's love to others.

Into the Lesson

Cut from poster board twenty-eight strips two inches by ten inches. Punch holes in the ends of all the strips. Pair the strips and then write on each pair the names of a father and son from Matthew 1:2-6: Abraham and Isaac, Isaac and Jacob, and so on until David and Solomon.

Connect the father-son pairs with string or yarn, about twelve to fifteen inches long. Position one name "upside down" to the other so you can hand each connected pair of strips to a class member to wear over his/her neck, one name (the father) showing to the front, the other name (the son) showing to the back.

Once the class assembles, ask the students to stand. Direct each student with father-son labels to find the person who carries a "son's" name that matches his or her "father's" name. (Students without labels may assist those who do.) As the students identify the proper matches, have the group line up in correct genealogical order.

Once finished, stress to your class the value that the Jews placed on such genealogical carefulness. Note also that many roles that seem unimportant or behind the scenes are actually of great value to God and His kingdom.

Into the Word

Read Matthew 1:1-6, 18-25. Give paper and pens to your class and ask them to write numbers 1 to 10 for the following true-false quiz about Joseph, based on the second half of today's text. Allow students to respond not only with T and F, but with D for "don't know" or P for "probably."

Read each statement carefully and slowly, repeating some as necessary. (1) Just as he had to Mary, the angel appeared to Joseph to reveal God's plan. (2) Joseph knew about Mary's pregnancy from the very beginning; she told him immediately. (3) Justice, in the Jewish scheme, would have allowed Joseph to call disgrace upon his wife-to-be. (4) Joseph, whom the text calls "just," could also be called Joseph the "kind." (5) Divorce was appropriate in the circumstances in which Joseph and Mary found themselves. (6) Joseph found out from the angel of the Lord that Mary was pregnant. (7) Joseph believed in the Holy Spirit of God. (8) Joseph called the Son given to Mary and him Jesus, because that was his father's name. (9) Joseph was familiar with the prophecy of Isaiah about a virgin giving birth to a son. (10) Joseph was a carpenter.

As you review the questions for answers and comment, consider the following. (1) False. Mary met the angel face to face; Joseph's encounter was in a dream. (2) False. Apparently Mary went to visit Elisabeth immediately after the angel spoke with her; see Luke 1:39. Joseph probably learned of her pregnancy after she returned. (3) True (Matthew 1:19). (4) True. Verse 19 labels Joseph "just," but also suggests his kindness in the matter. (5) True; betrothal was considered as binding as marriage. (6) False; Joseph already knew when the angel spoke to him (verses 18-20). (7) Probably; the Spirit is part of Old Testament revelation, not novel to the New. (8) False. Joseph named the child Jesus because the angel told him to; see verses 21, 25. (9) Probably; Joseph certainly had opportunity to know Old Testament Scripture, and there was a scroll of Isaiah in Nazareth; see Luke 4:16-20. (10) True. Not so identified in this text, but see Matthew 13:55.

Into Life

Some today are touting "Random Acts of Kindness"; encourage your class to perform "Private Acts of Kindness" after the order of Joseph's kindness. Give each member a small envelope and an index card. Ask each to write on that card a kindness he/she knows is needed by someone outside the class group. Have all the cards put into the envelopes; then collect the envelopes and drop them in a large grocery bag. Ask each member to draw a card from the bag on the way out of the class and to do the suggested kindness anonymously during this holiday season. Suggest a few possibilities: a family that needs food, a child who will be unlikely to receive gifts, a homebound person who needs a "shower" of cards. Tell the class to give clear, complete information on the cards they put into the bag.

Let's Talk It Over

The questions on this page are designed to encourage review of the lesson Scriptures and to promote discussion of the lesson by the class. The answers provided are only discussion starters. Let your class talk it over from there.

1. Four women are mentioned in the portion of Jesus' genealogy chosen for our printed text. Two were prostitutes (Tamar, Genesis 38:24, and Rachab—i.e., Rahab, Joshua 2:1), and one had an adulterous affair with King David (the wife of Uriah—i.e., Bathsheba). Ruth had a pagan past. What, if anything, does the presence of such characters in Jesus' ancestry suggest to you?

If nothing else, it reminds us that children ought not to be judged for the sins of their parents. Throughout history children have been tagged with unkind labels because of what their parents did. But children are innocent and ought not to be ostracized or punished for their parents' sin.

Some may observe that, by God's grace and through faith, we can rise above our circumstances. Children born to immoral relationships can be part of God's plan to work good for the world. People who reject their pagan past can become part of the community of the redeemed. A marriage relationship that never should have begun can become God's instrument of blessing to many.

2. Have you ever been in a situation in which you could have exacted revenge on a person— and most people would have believed you were entitled to it? How does one choose the "just" or "righteous" option of tempering justice with mercy?

People in Joseph's day, even as today, would have believed Joseph quite justified in making a public example of Mary. But Joseph rose above that and acted honorably.

Knowing God's grace in our own lives should lead us to act with grace toward others. Even when we have been wronged and humiliated, as Joseph believed he had been, we ought to follow Jesus' example and His teaching. We can turn the other cheek; we can pray, "Father, forgive them." It takes strong Christian character, but that is one of our goals as we grow in the Lord.

3. Both Mary and Joseph knew Jesus had come to bring salvation. They probably did not know, however, that He would die a sacrificial death to make salvation possible. Most people in Mary and Joseph's generation looked for a political

hero. **How can one participate in God's plan if he or she does not understand God's plan?**

Mary and Joseph most probably did not understand God's plan for the Messiah. Still, they could be faithful with what they did know. They could take Jesus to the synagogue on the Sabbath and to Jerusalem for the feasts. They could behave honorably and teach their children to do the same.

We today do not know what great things God may use our children—or ourselves—to do. But we can behave honorably. We can be faithful.

4. Many people have no concept of a personal relationship with God. God is too "otherworldly" in their thinking. Even if they acknowledge Jesus as the Son of God, His physical presence was experienced for a short time some two thousand years ago, and they are unable to appreciate any benefit for today. What do you find most significant to your own life about Jesus as "God with us"?

In your discussion, students should observe at least two benefits. First, Jesus is sympathetic with our trials because He has "been there." (See Hebrews 4:15, 16.) Though He is not physically *with us*, He has already been where we are and experienced what we experience. Second, He has made it clear that God is personal. He is not merely a "force" or abstract concept. He is a person, so we are able to have a personal relationship with Him. Christianity is more than an ethical code of conduct or a set of rituals, as many other religions are. It is a personal relationship with God Himself: God with us!

5. When you serve in a ministry that is largely unnoticed—as Joseph's role is often overlooked—what keeps you going? How do you maintain your desire to serve when no one seems to recognize the value of your service?

First, we remember why we are serving. We serve because Jesus is Lord of our lives, and we accept the responsibilities as well as the pleasures of that relationship. We must remember also that no act really goes unnoticed. We are confident that God knows the personal sacrifices we make for His sake. (See Hebrews 6:10-12.) We don't know how God will reward us. It does give us great satisfaction, however, to know we are pleasing Him.

Coming of the Wise Men

DEVOTIONAL READING: Psalm 98.

BACKGROUND SCRIPTURE: Matthew 2.

PRINTED TEXT: Matthew 2:1-12.

Matthew 2:1-12

1 Now when Jesus was born in Bethlehem of Judea in the days of Herod the king, behold, there came wise men from the east to Jerusalem,

2 Saying, Where is he that is born King of the Jews? for we have seen his star in the east, and are come to worship him.

3 When Herod the king had heard these things, he was troubled, and all Jerusalem with him.

4 And when he had gathered all the chief priests and scribes of the people together, he demanded of them where Christ should be born.

5 And they said unto him, In Bethlehem of Judea: for thus it is written by the prophet,

6 And thou Bethlehem, in the land of Judah, art not the least among the princes of Judah: for out of thee shall come a Governor, that shall rule my people Israel.

7 Then Herod, when he had privily called the wise men, inquired of them diligently what time the star appeared.

8 And he sent them to Bethlehem, and said, Go and search diligently for the young child; and when ye have found him, bring me word again, that I may come and worship him also.

9 When they had heard the king, they departed; and, lo, the star, which they saw in the east, went before them, till it came and stood over where the young child was.

10 When they saw the star, they rejoiced with exceeding great joy.

11 And when they were come into the house, they saw the young child with Mary his mother, and fell down, and worshipped him: and when they had opened their treasures, they presented unto him gifts; gold, and frankincense, and myrrh.

12 And being warned of God in a dream that they should not return to Herod, they departed into their own country another way.

GOLDEN TEXT: Where is he that is born King of the Jews? for we have seen his star in the east, and are come to worship him.—Matthew 2:2.

Immanuel: God With Us
Unit 1: Beginnings: Birth and Ministry
(Lessons 1-4)

Lesson Aims

This lesson is intended to help each student:

1. Retell the story of the visit of the wise men to see the child Jesus.

2. Tell what qualities shown by the wise men are worthy of imitation by Christians today.

3. Suggest a specific way to give of oneself more fully to the Lord and His work in the coming year.

Lesson Outline

INTRODUCTION

   A. "Anyone Can Play the Part"

   B. Lesson Background

  I. A NOBLE QUEST (Matthew 2:1-6)

   A. Starting in the East (vv. 1, 2)

   B. Stopping at Jerusalem (vv. 3, 4)

   C. Proceeding to Bethlehem (vv. 5, 6)

 II. A DEVIOUS KING (Matthew 2:7, 8)

   A. Plotting His Evil (v. 7)

   B. Preparing to Kill (v. 8)

    Funny, Isn't It?

III. A ROYAL CHILD (Matthew 2:9-12)

   A. Revealed by God (vv. 9, 10)

   B. Deserving of Worship (v. 11)

   C. Subject to Danger (v. 12)

    Honoring the Real King

CONCLUSION

   A. A Word to the Wise

   B. Prayer

   C. Thought to Remember

Introduction

A. "Anyone Can Play the Part"

"Anyone can play the part of a shepherd or a wise man." Such is the rule generally observed by all who direct boys and girls in church Christmas pageants, simply because (as is the case with many Bible stories) there are not a lot of female characters. Consider, for example, a dramatization of David and the Israelites against Goliath and the Philistines, Paul and Silas in prison, or Jesus and the apostles at the last supper in the upper room. Even in the nativity story the only female part is that of Mary. In order for many girls to have parts in these presentations, we usually hand a bathrobe to anyone who is interested

in acting and adopt the policy that "anyone can play the part of a shepherd or a wise man."

This practical rule conveys an important spiritual truth. The nativity accounts of Matthew and Luke portray the wise men and shepherds as noble individuals who, when confronted with Jesus Christ, humbled themselves before Him and gave Him their worship. Their example can be, and should be, imitated by all of us, no matter who we are. "Anyone can play the part of a shepherd or a wise man," especially the part of giving one's all to Jesus our Lord and King.

B. Lesson Background

The account of the birth of Christ in the Gospel of Matthew focuses on two events. As we noted last week, chapter 1 records an angel's message to Joseph that Mary was pregnant through the work of the Holy Spirit and that she would give birth to a Son who should be named Jesus. This week we will see that chapter 2 describes the visit of wise men from the East and King Herod's attempt to kill the Christ child. Located chronologically between the events of Matthew 1 and 2 is the familiar story of Luke 2.

During the final stage of Mary's pregnancy, Joseph and his fiancée traveled south from their hometown of Nazareth to Bethlehem, their ancestral home. The birth of Jesus occurred after the couple found temporary shelter, since there was "no room for them in the inn" (Luke 2:7). On the same day as the birth, angels appeared in the night sky to shepherds tending their flocks in a field. The angels directed the shepherds into town to locate the newly arrived Messiah.

For the next several weeks, Joseph and his new family apparently settled in Bethlehem. Whether this was a temporary arrangement to allow mother and child time to prepare for the long trip home to Nazareth or Joseph had decided to remain in Bethlehem is not clear. In any event, it was during this period that the wise men came to honor the one "born King of the Jews" (Matthew 2:2).

I. A Noble Quest
(Matthew 2:1-6)

A. Starting in the East (vv. 1, 2)

1. Now when Jesus was born in Bethlehem of Judea in the days of Herod the king, behold, there came wise men from the east to Jerusalem.

The Greek word used to describe these *wise men from the east* is a word that was the title used by religious wise men in several countries of the Middle East, notably Persia and Arabia. The wise men were renowned as "stargazers" who studied the night sky looking for divine clues to the future. Some believe they were proselyte converts to Judaism; others, that they were simply scholars interested in knowing more about the Jewish Messianic hope, a subject that people in all of the regions surrounding Jerusalem would have known something about. After all, many Jews had been dispersed throughout the known world centuries earlier by the Assyrians and Babylonians. Also, Jerusalem was located on a major trade route in the Middle Eastern world. Foreign travelers passing through could easily pick up bits and pieces of Jewish thought.

The wise men had more than a passing interest in the Messiah, however. They came to "worship" Him (v. 2), not just to greet Him. And they appear to have been more than mere astrologers, too, receiving direct communication from God (v. 12).

2. Saying, Where is he that is born King of the Jews? for we have seen his star in the east, and are come to worship him.

Matthew does not explain the nature of the *star in the east*. Some propose that the star was a bright meteor; others suggest a close alignment of two or more planets, at least one of which the wise men believed was linked to the fortune of Israel, or to the Messiah in particular. This appearance or alignment suggested to the wise men that something pivotal was about to happen. Some students think it very important that no movement is actually attributed to the star until after the visit of the wise men to Jerusalem (v. 9). To them, the fact that the wise men journeyed to Jerusalem rather than to Bethlehem suggests that the star was not yet guiding them to the birthplace; they were simply assuming that the *King of the Jews* would be born in the capital city of the Jews. [See question #1, page 152.]

Other students are quick to point out that while no earlier movement is mentioned, it remains quite possible that the star had been leading the wise men. If so, it probably would have led them along the normal trade route from the East, which would have taken them through Jerusalem. These students suggest that clouds may have obscured the star for a time, which would account for the wise men's premature assumption that they had arrived at the proper location when they reached Jerusalem and for their joy at seeing the star as they left the city (v. 10).

Whatever the precise nature of the star, it is clear that it was more than a natural phenomenon. God may have used a meteor or an alignment of planets to get the wise men's attention, or He may have created a special sign in the sky. But then He caused that heavenly light to move and to indicate the exact location where the wise men would find Jesus (v. 9). That is not natural. There is no reason to believe that the wise men's quest

---

How to Say It

ANTIPAS. *An*-tih-pus.
ASSYRIANS. Uh-*sear*-ee-unz.
BABYLONIANS. Bab-uh-*low*-nee-unz.
HERODIAN. Heh-*roe*-dee-un.
ISAIAH. Eye-*zay*-uh.
MICAH. *My*-kuh.
MYRRH. mur.
PEREA. Peh-*ree*-uh.
PHILISTINES. Fuh-*liss*-teens or *Fill*-us-teens.

---

was guided by mere assumptions based on astrology. The fact that God later spoke to the wise men (v. 12) suggests to some that He may well have spoken to them earlier, explaining the light in the sky. In any event, the star was a divine sign guiding the wise men on a divine mission.

B. Stopping at Jerusalem (vv. 3, 4)

3. When Herod the king had heard these things, he was troubled, and all Jerusalem with him.

The *Herod* of the nativity story was the first and most notable of the Herodian line of rulers. Known as Herod the Great, he ruled from approximately 37 B.C. to 4 B.C. over Galilee, Judea, and portions of the surrounding territory. (This is not the same Herod who would later be an antagonist of Jesus during His ministry. That was his son Herod Antipas, who ruled Galilee and Perea from 4 B.C. to A.D. 39.) [See question #2, page 152.]

Our knowledge of Herod the Great through sources outside the Bible enables us to approximate the date of Jesus' birth. Herod died in the latter half of March in the year 4 B.C., at which time Joseph and Mary returned home from Egypt, where they had gone to protect the baby Jesus (Matthew 2:15). Counting backward from this date, and allowing three to four months for the events noted in the Gospels—the forty-day wait until Jesus could be "presented" in the temple (Luke 2:22), the visit of the wise men, the journey to Egypt, and a short stay there—the birth of Jesus could have occurred anywhere between November of 5 B.C. and January of 4 B.C.

It should be evident from all of this that our modern Western calendar is three to four years in error. The "Gregorian Calendar," devised in 1582, was calculated to center on the birth of Christ. Thus, many Christians today assume that A.D. 1, for example, corresponds to Christ's first year on earth, and that His death at age 33 took place in A.D. 33. However, we now know from other research that these calculations were slightly off. Jesus' birth likely occurred in the winter of 5–4 B.C., and His death was in A.D. 30.

None of this should be of great concern to us because calendars are a human contrivance that have been modified frequently throughout the ages. What matters most to us is the historical reality that the Son of God "was made flesh" (John 1:14) and was born upon this earth.

4. And when he had gathered all the chief priests and scribes of the people together, he demanded of them where Christ should be born.

Herod the Great was noted for his political cunning, but not for his Old Testament scholarship. Thus he had to ask *the chief priests*, who administered the Jewish religious system, and the *scribes* or "writers," who were the leading Bible scholars, where the Messiah (*Christ*) was prophesied to be *born*.

C. Proceeding to Bethlehem (vv. 5, 6)

5. And they said unto him, In Bethlehem of Judea: for thus it is written by the prophet.

The town of *Bethlehem* was located approximately five miles southwest of Jerusalem. It was a small town in the hill country of *Judea*, and was generally considered to be of little importance except for two matters of note. Bethlehem could lay claim to being "the city of David," because it was the hometown of the shepherd boy who became king (1 Samuel 16:1). And it was, according to Old Testament prophecy, the future birthplace of the Messiah and thus destined one day for prominence. [See question #3, page 152.]

6. And thou Bethlehem, in the land of Judah, art not the least among the princes of Judah: for out of thee shall come a Governor, that shall rule my people Israel.

Micah 5:2 is the Old Testament prophecy that identified *Bethlehem* as the Messiah's birthplace. As noted last week regarding Isaiah 7:14 (quoted in Matthew 1:23), modern Old Testament scholarship often debates whether or not Micah was actually speaking of someone from his own day,

This visual pictures the wise men in Jerusalem looking for the King of the Jews. Discuss how we can direct people today to the Savior, even when they are looking in the wrong places.

Visual for lesson 4

with Matthew later reading into the text a Messianic meaning. However, the response of the chief priests and scribes to Herod indicates that even Jewish thinking already understood what Matthew recorded by inspiration of the Holy Spirit—that Micah predicted the birth of the Messiah in Bethlehem of *Judah* (or Judea).

Here we see a reason why the church has often used fulfilled prophecies as an important element of "apologetics," or the defense of the Christian faith. Jesus fulfilled all Messianic prophecies, even those that spoke of precise details outside of His control, such as the condition of His mother (a virgin) and the place of His birth (Bethlehem).

II. A Devious King
(Matthew 2:7, 8)
A. Plotting His Evil (v. 7)

7. Then Herod, when he had privily called the wise men, inquired of them diligently what time the star appeared.

The initial inquiries of the *wise men* may have been in public areas such as the temple, where crowds of people could hear their story and be *troubled* and perplexed (v. 3). But shortly thereafter they were summoned to a private meeting with *Herod*. The king wanted to know *what time the star appeared*, and apparently pressed the unsuspecting wise men for a precise date when they first noticed the heavenly sign.

Herod's subsequent actions reveal the motive behind his interest in the star. Assuming that the star first appeared on the day the new King was born, he calculated the age of the child in order to know the age of the person he should look for as he tried to have the new King killed. His order to kill all male children two years old and younger (v. 16) may indicate that the star had first appeared two years earlier, and thus much earlier than the actual birth of Christ. More likely, Herod was giving his soldiers a "margin for error" to make sure they did not miss the one boy he was after.

Matthew's description of King Herod's deceitful ploy with the wise men is consistent with other historical records. Throughout his reign Herod "distinguished" himself with his cunning and cruelty, but in the final year prior to his death his mental state was so greatly diminished that he experienced delusions of persecution accompanied by violent outbursts. His paranoia became so great that he killed anyone he suspected of plotting against him, including members of his immediate family. It was in this state of mind that he interrogated the wise men for information that would help him locate and destroy this child whom he suspected of being a new rival in Bethlehem.

B. Preparing to Kill (v. 8)

8. And he sent them to Bethlehem, and said, Go and search diligently for the young child; and when ye have found him, bring me word again, that I may come and worship him also.

Herod's subterfuge was set in motion. If the child was being hidden by His family for protection, the location was more likely to be revealed to foreign dignitaries seeking to honor the future King than to armed soldiers scouring the town. Herod would await the report of the wise men and then launch his deadly assault. [See question #4, page 152.]

FUNNY, ISN'T IT?

I recently received an e-mail that had a very thought-provoking message. It said, "Funny how ten dollars looks so big when we take it to church and so small when we take it to the store. Funny how big an hour serving God looks and how small it seems when spent playing golf, fishing, or playing bridge. Funny how laborious it is to read a chapter in the Bible and how easy it is to read a hundred pages of a best-selling novel. Funny how we believe what a person or newspapers say, but question what the Bible says. Funny how we can't think of anything to say when we pray, but don't have any difficulty thinking of things to talk about with a friend. Funny how we need two or three weeks to fit a church event into our schedule, but can adjust it at the last minute for a social event. Funny, isn't it?"

Well, obviously it isn't funny, and neither was the hypocritical attitude that King Herod displayed. He lied to the wise men and told them that he wanted to know the location of the Christ child in order to worship Him; but in reality he wanted to kill Him. Some Christians, though their attitude toward Jesus is not malicious as Herod's was, still demonstrate a disparity between their lives and their words. Jesus deserves more than our words. He gave up everything to save us. He humbled Himself and "was made in the likeness of men" (Philippians 2:7) so that we could be saved from the eternal punishment that we deserve for our sins.

Yet, like Herod, we want to be king—king of our own lives—and we do not want anyone else to have control over us. First Corinthians 6:19, 20 says that we are not our own, but "are bought with a price: therefore glorify God in your body, and in your spirit, which are God's." Jesus is worthy of our total devotion.   —L. D. C.

III. A Royal Child
(Matthew 2:9-12)
A. Revealed by God (vv. 9, 10)

9. When they had heard the king, they departed; and, lo, the star, which they saw in the east, went before them, till it came and stood over where the young child was.

The wise men now had the information they needed to locate the town where the new King was born, but they still did not know where in that town they would find the right child. However, in Bethlehem God provided another sign to assist the wise men. The *star* that had gone *before them . . . came and stood over* the place where the *young child* Jesus and His family were staying. Such movement by the star clearly suggests God's guidance and not merely a natural phenomenon.

10. When they saw the star, they rejoiced with exceeding great joy.

It has already been suggested that the *star* may have disappeared at some point when the wise men arrived in Judea, later to return after they departed from Jerusalem for Bethlehem. Another way to understand Matthew's statement is to read it in light of the previous verse: the wise men *rejoiced* upon seeing *the star* point to the location of the Messiah. They were pleased to have divine assistance hasten their search, and thrilled to reach at long last the goal of their long journey.

B. Deserving of Worship (v. 11)

11. And when they were come into the house, they saw the young child with Mary his mother, and fell down, and worshipped him: and when they had opened their treasures, they presented unto him gifts; gold, and frankincense, and myrrh.

Many modern portrayals of the visit of the wise men stray from the actual Biblical description. For example, the wise men did not kneel before a manger in a stable along with the shepherds; instead, they found the family settled in a *house.*

All of this makes sense when we examine the Biblical data. The wise men did not arrive with their expensive gifts until after Jesus' birth; otherwise at the forty-day presentation of their *child* in the temple, Joseph and Mary would have offered the required lamb sacrifice rather than the poor person's alternative of two turtledoves or pigeons (Luke 2:22-24). Also note that the Biblical text at no point indicates the number of wise men or that they held positions as "kings." It is the number of gifts and their royal flavor that suggest the popular idea of "we three kings."

The wise men treated Jesus in a royal manner, bowing before Him in worship and presenting to Him costly *gifts* suitable for a king. We recognize *gold* for the beautiful and expensive treasure that it is. The less familiar *frankincense* and *myrrh* were very expensive tree resins—the former derived from a type of balsam tree, the latter from something akin to a sturdy shrub. Frankincense was burned in a dish in order to release into the air a sweet-smelling smoke; it was also used in perfumes and medicines. Likewise myrrh was an ingredient in fragrances and medicines, and in addition was often used as an embalming agent (John 19:39).

All three of these gifts were befitting of royalty and served as genuine expressions of adoration and praise. While Herod deceitfully spoke of worship, the wise men truly offered it. [See question #5, page 152.]

C. Subject to Danger (v. 12)

12. And being warned of God in a dream that they should not return to Herod, they departed into their own country another way.

This time *God* spoke directly to the wise men *in a dream*. Herod's evil scheme was exposed, and the wise men discreetly returned to *their own country*, carrying with them the secret of their discovery. Matthew goes on to report that Herod became enraged when he realized his plans had been thwarted and ordered the execution of all male children two years of age and under (v. 16).

Like the wise men, Joseph was also warned in a dream of the imminent danger from Herod and was ordered to flee the king's jurisdiction and hide his family in Egypt (vv. 13, 14). There they remained for a short while until after the death of Herod the Great, at which time an angel instructed Joseph to return to his homeland (vv. 19-23) and nurture the child who would one day become Messiah and King.

HONORING THE REAL KING

Henry Ward Beecher was one of the most respected preachers in the United States during the latter part of the nineteenth century. He was so popular that people would travel from all over the country to listen to him preach. It was not uncommon for him to have more than three thousand people gather to hear him on a Sunday morning!

One Sunday, during the peak of his popularity, Beecher was away, so he asked his brother Thomas to preach for him. When Thomas Beecher got up to preach that morning, many in the congregation got up and headed for the door. Quickly he called out: "May I have your attention, please? All who came here this morning to worship Henry Ward Beecher may now leave. All who came to worship God may stay."

The wise men's purpose in traveling from the East was clear: they had come to worship King Jesus. They had not come to please King Herod. When God told them that Herod was being deceitful and intended to kill Jesus, the wise men followed God's instructions and traveled homeward by another route. They knew who the real King was.   —L. D. C.

Conclusion

A. A Word to the Wise

It is a popular refrain, often found on holiday cards: "Wise men still seek him." It reminds us of the diligence of the wise men in seeking the one "born King of the Jews" until they found Him. And it challenges us to follow their example: to seek after the One whom God sent to earth as Lord and King, to bow before Him in worship and homage, and to give Him the best gifts we have—our hearts committed to His will and our lives devoted to His service. The lessons learned from the story of the wise men are very much applicable in our modern times: wise men still seek Him.

B. Prayer

Father, help us to be eager students of Your Word, who are devoted fully to Your Son and committed to living a life of service and praise. In Jesus' name we pray. Amen.

C. Thought to Remember

Consider the difference between King Herod and King Jesus: Herod killed others so he could live; Jesus died so that others could live.

Home Daily Bible Readings

Monday, Dec. 20—The Birth of Jesus (Luke 2:1-7)

Tuesday, Dec. 21—Jesus' Birth Announced to Shepherds (Luke 2:8-20)

Wednesday, Dec. 22—Jesus Is Presented in the Temple (Luke 2:21-27)

Thursday, Dec. 23—Simeon and Anna Praise God (Luke 2:28-38)

Friday, Dec. 24—Wise Men Inquire About Jesus' Birth (Matthew 2:1-6)

Saturday, Dec. 25—Wise Men Visit and Honor Jesus (Matthew 2:7-12)

Sunday Dec. 26—Herod's Wrath Is Unleashed (Matthew 2:13-18)

Learning by Doing

This page contains an alternate lesson plan emphasizing learning activities.
Classes desiring such student involvement will find these suggestions helpful.

Learning Goals

After this lesson each student will be able to:

1. Retell the story of the visit of the wise men to see the child Jesus.

2. Tell what qualities shown by the wise men are worthy of imitation by Christians today.

3. Suggest a specific way to give of oneself more fully to the Lord and His work in the coming year.

Into the Lesson

As learners arrive, hand each one a card or note bearing either a **W**, **I**, **S**, or **E**. Ask the learners to assemble in four groups by matching letters with others: **W**'s together, **I**'s together, etc.

Direct each group to devise an alliterative title for these visitors to the child Jesus, using the key letter assigned to the group. Give this example: "If one of the letters were **M**, you might come up with something like 'Matthew's Mysterious Male, Meandering Messiah-seekers.'" Challenge them to get as many alliterative words into their titles as possible.

Here are some samples: **W**: Wise Wanderers Wanting to Worship the Worthy; **I**: Intelligent Inquirers Interested in the Immortal "I am"; **S**: Searching Scholars See Star and Seek Savior; **E**: Excellent Easterners Explore Evidence of the Eternally Existent.

Into the Word

One at a time, present these statements about the wise men to your class. Ask them to find support in Matthew 2 that indicates that each statement is true. (1) Wise men come prepared to worship. (2) Wise men tolerate difficulties in order to get to worship. (3) Wise men seek and value the company of other wise men. (4) Wise men give significant and costly gifts. (5) Wise men listen to all of God's directions. (6) Wise men do not hesitate to ask for help. (7) Wise men avoid trouble if they know about it and can. (8) Wise men know good, better, and best; they choose the best. (9) Wise men value inquiry and wonder. (10) Wise men do not hesitate to humble themselves in the presence of a greater One.

You may choose to write and use other statements you see as more relevant and important.

(Number 1 refers to the gifts the wise men carefully carried—and at great risk along the way—in order to present them to the new "King of the Jews." Number 2 relates to the long miles—perhaps hundreds of desert miles—that they suffered. Number 3 shows their studied consensus and mutual plan in coming. Number 4 is quite obvious. Number 5 pertains both to their following the star and to the dream given to save their lives. Numbers 6 and 7 are obvious. Number 8 relates to these wise men who were well studied and obviously prosperous, the good and the better, but they still chose to pursue the Messiah, the Best. Wise men [number 9] were the scientists and scholars of their day; they were joyous in knowledge, intrigued by possibility. Number 10 is the surest evidence of their wisdom; though no doubt honored in their homelands, they recognized their inferiority to Jesus.)

Into Life

Refer to the Introduction section of the commentary, where the writer says, "Anyone can play the part of . . . a wise man." Summarize the writer's description of the common practice of recruiting anyone for the role in a Christmas drama or pageant.

Then display several wardrobe items that a wise man might have worn. (You might borrow such items from the church's drama ministry—or, if your class has a good imagination, "fake" them by holding each up "invisibly," in the manner of "The Emperor's New Clothes"!)

As you hold up each item, ask your class members to suggest what attributes of the wise man's wardrobe it might represent. For example, hold up a tunic (sleeveless knee-length undergarment): "The wise person needs to hold certain things close to his heart, hidden from men, known only to God: his faith in God's directions for life and worship." Hold up a scarf that might have covered the wise man's face and neck: "The wise person always needs to know when to open his mouth and when to close it; this scarf can cover his mouth at all the right times—to avoid the harm that can come from having it open!" Let the class "imagine" and freely conjecture.

If it is possible—and affordable—present each class member with a clothes hanger to take home. Direct the students to attach little tags bearing the words, "What the Fashionable Wise Man/Woman is Wearing," and keep the hangers in their closets or dressing rooms as daily reminders of today's study.

Let's Talk It Over

The questions on this page are designed to encourage review of the lesson
Scriptures and to promote discussion of the lesson by the class. The answers
provided are only discussion starters. Let your class talk it over from there.

1. It seems reasonable to believe that the King of the Jews would be found in the capital city of the Jews; so the wise men looked for Him in Jerusalem. Where do people look for Jesus today? How can we help them to find Him when they look in our church or in our homes?

The concept of spirituality has been given many meanings in our world, so there is no assurance that people who are interested in "spiritual" things are at all interested in the God of the Bible. Many are looking in the wrong places because they are looking for the wrong "god."

Still, many people are seeking the true God. Some of them enter church buildings every Sunday, hoping to find Jesus. They expect to find Him in the words and actions of His people. They assume His people will reach out to them with sincere hearts. What can we do to make His presence felt more?

2. Herod was "troubled." And when Herod was troubled, someone has said, *everyone* was troubled! What "troubles" government officials today about the church or religion? How should Christians respond when government officials are troubled in this way—or when they trouble us?

Many government officials believe that there should be absolutely no Christian influence in the government—including courts, schools, and anything else funded by tax dollars. Thus they will seek to restrict or prohibit religious expression of any sort. Truth is made relative so it can be compartmentalized. "Religious" truth is to be kept in the churches or in the privacy of one's own home. Only "scientific" truth and other "secular" truth are acceptable in the public forum.

Christians need to take a stand for truth, period. Truth is truth; one truth is by definition consistent with all other truth. Whatever "rights" Christians may have or be granted within their society, they always have truth. And truth will make them free, indeed, in spite of anything government or government officials may do.

3. Bethlehem in the first century was considered to be of little importance. How has God used little-known people, places, and events to bless your life? What lessons, if any, do you see in that for us today?

It was in Bethlehem that the prophet Samuel met Eliab and thought to himself, "Surely the Lord's anointed is before him" (1 Samuel 16:6). But God told Samuel not to look on outward appearances, for it is the heart that matters. People still look at externals—size, worldly influence, and the like. But more precious to God is a heart devoted to Him—like the heart of the faithful Sunday school teacher who has taught a whole generation of children simply out of love for the Lord and for His little ones. What examples of pure hearts can your class name from your own church's membership and history?

4. Herod put on a show of pious sincerity while he was planning all along to murder the young Jesus! God warned the wise men of Herod's plan in a dream, but what about us? How can we see through the words of enemies who appear as friends? In what areas do we need to be especially alert for such duplicity?

Wouldn't it be nice if God told us in a dream every time a supposed friend had lied to us? Instead, we need to be cautious and wise, learning from every source available to us. If the wise men had been better acquainted with Herod and his past, they might have guessed he would not tolerate a rival. We need to take every opportunity to know the character and goals of those from whom we get information. A liberal media puts a particular spin on the news. The education lobby has more on its agenda than reading, writing, and arithmetic. Jesus' warning to His disciples is especially relevant today: "Be ye therefore wise as serpents, and harmless as doves" (Matthew 10:16).

5. What significance do you see in the wise men's humble attitude toward Jesus?

These were men of high reputation. While they may not have been worshiped by others, they were looked on with great favor. How strange to think of these travelers going to such expense and trouble to find the King of the Jews! It is stranger still to find them worshiping a child. Their attitude was clearly one of wonder and praise. They may not have understood everything about God's plan of redemption, but they seemed convinced they had found their King. Their example is one we ought to follow.

The Twelve Disciples

January 2
Lesson 5

DEVOTIONAL READING: Matthew 10:5-16.

BACKGROUND SCRIPTURE: Matthew 4:18-22;
9:9-13; 10:1-4.

PRINTED TEXT: Matthew 4:18-22; 9:9-13;
10:1-4.

Matthew 4:18-22

18 And Jesus, walking by the sea of Galilee, saw two brethren, Simon called Peter, and Andrew his brother, casting a net into the sea: for they were fishers.

19 And he saith unto them, Follow me, and I will make you fishers of men.

20 And they straightway left their nets, and followed him.

21 And going on from thence, he saw other two brethren, James the son of Zebedee, and John his brother, in a ship with Zebedee their father, mending their nets; and he called them.

22 And they immediately left the ship and their father, and followed him.

Matthew 9:9-13

9 And as Jesus passed forth from thence, he saw a man, named Matthew, sitting at the receipt of custom: and he saith unto him, Follow me. And he arose, and followed him.

10 And it came to pass, as Jesus sat at meat in the house, behold, many publicans and sinners came and sat down with him and his disciples.

11 And when the Pharisees saw it, they said unto his disciples, Why eateth your master with publicans and sinners?

12 But when Jesus heard that, he said unto them, They that be whole need not a physician, but they that are sick.

13 But go ye and learn what that meaneth, I will have mercy, and not sacrifice: for I am not come to call the righteous, but sinners to repentance.

Matthew 10:1-4

1 And when he had called unto him his twelve disciples, he gave them power against unclean spirits, to cast them out, and to heal all manner of sickness and all manner of disease.

2 Now the names of the twelve apostles are these; The first, Simon, who is called Peter, and Andrew his brother; James the son of Zebedee, and John his brother;

3 Philip, and Bartholomew; Thomas, and Matthew the publican; James the son of Alpheus, and Lebbeus, whose surname was Thaddeus;

4 Simon the Canaanite, and Judas Iscariot, who also betrayed him.

GOLDEN TEXT: Follow me, and I will make you fishers of men.—Matthew 4:19.

Immanuel: God With Us
Unit 2: Ministry: Wonderful Words and Works
(Lessons 5-9)

Lesson Aims

After this lesson a student should be able to:

1. Name the twelve apostles and tell a little of the background of some of them.

2. Tell how the calling of Jesus' first disciples instructs us today about responding to Jesus' call.

3. Express a commitment to being a disciple of Jesus.

Lesson Outline

INTRODUCTION
  A. Ready and Willing
  B. Lesson Background
 I. FOUR FISHERMEN (Matthew 4:18-22)
  A. Fishers of Men (vv. 18-20)
  B. Followers of Christ (vv. 21, 22)
    Obedience Without Question
 II. ONE TAX COLLECTOR (Matthew 9:9-13)
  A. Receptive Follower (vv. 9, 10)
    Evangelism—With No Strings Attached
  B. Resentful Pharisees (vv. 11-13)
III. TWELVE APOSTLES (Matthew 10:1-4)
  A. Set Apart for Service (v. 1)
  B. Selected as Apostles (vv. 2-4)
CONCLUSION
  A. Availability
  B. Prayer
  C. Thought to Remember

Introduction

A. Ready and Willing

When Pearl Harbor was bombed on December 7, 1941, that day became for Americans "a day that will live in infamy." But the following day, December 8, was a day of patriotic pride, which ushered in a period of vigorous American response to the bombing. For weeks after the bombing of Pearl Harbor, Americans volunteered in droves for military duty, ready and willing to stop the threat of world domination and to defend American honor.

Another recruitment call has been issued. It started on the shores of the Sea of Galilee with four fishermen, and continues today. Our Lord and Savior is looking for disciples to spread His gospel message to the uttermost parts of the earth, and then to teach and nurture those who respond. Our challenge as Christians is simply this: are we ready and willing to serve?

B. Lesson Background

Having taken a brief interlude to look at the birth of Christ, our study returns to the ministry of Jesus as recorded in the Gospel of Matthew. Following Jesus' baptism in the Jordan River and His testing in the wilderness (lessons 1 and 2), He was ready to begin three and a half years of teaching and preaching to the people of Israel.

One of Jesus' first tasks was to seek out some men who would assist Him in His ministry. Those who agreed to work with Him He called "disciples," from the Greek word referring to a student who followed his teacher around so that he could learn from him. (In ancient times a teacher would often leave the classroom setting and simply walk about, teaching as he walked.) Anyone who accepted the call to be a disciple of Jesus had to spend significant time with Him and had to be prepared to follow Him wherever and whenever He traveled.

At one point Jesus selected twelve from this group of disciples to serve in a more demanding role as "apostles." Our lesson today focuses on the calling of those men.

I. Four Fishermen
(Matthew 4:18-22)

A. Fishers of Men (vv. 18-20)

18. And Jesus, walking by the sea of Galilee, saw two brethren, Simon called Peter, and Andrew his brother, casting a net into the sea: for they were fishers.

The bulk of Jesus' ministry took place in the towns on the west side of *the sea of Galilee,* a large freshwater lake in the northern province of Galilee, about sixty miles north of Jerusalem. It was referred to as an inland "sea" because of its large size (thirteen miles long by eight miles wide), and because it exhibited wave movements and storm activity comparable to those of a typical coastal sea.

Jesus' ministry was headquartered on the west side of the Sea of Galilee in the city of Capernaum (Matthew 4:13). Not far from Capernaum was the smaller town of Bethsaida, identified in Scripture as the hometown of Peter, Andrew, and Philip (John 1:44). (Note that this is a different Bethsaida from the location on the northeast side of the Sea of Galilee, where, according to Luke 9:10-17, Jesus fed the five thousand.)

The most prominent of all the men Jesus summoned to follow Him as disciples or apostles was *Simon . . . Peter.* While *Simon* was his birth name, Jesus gave him the new name "Cephas" (Aramaic) or *Peter* (Greek), both of which mean "small stone" (John 1:42). Peter's brother *Andrew* was apparently the more reserved of the two men; but it is to his credit that Andrew introduced Peter to Jesus (John 1:40, 41), and later informed Jesus about some Greeks who wanted to see Him (John 12:20-22). It was also Andrew, who, in a crowd of five thousand men, discovered the little boy with five loaves of bread and two pieces of fish (John 6:8, 9).

19. And he saith unto them, Follow me, and I will make you fishers of men.

Luke (5:1-11) tells more details of this event, which likely culminated in Jesus' invitation: *Follow me, and I will make you fishers of men.*

20. And they straightway left their nets, and followed him.

One should not assume from Matthew's brief account that all Jesus had to do was to introduce Himself to men like Peter and Andrew, say "Follow me," and *straightway* (immediately) they would quit their fishing business to become full-time disciples. The men Jesus called into service were already well acquainted with Him.

Andrew first became acquainted with Jesus when he was a disciple of John the Baptist. When Jesus returned from the wilderness temptations, Andrew and an unnamed disciple began following Jesus, encouraged by John's testimony (John 1:35-40). Shortly thereafter, Andrew introduced his brother Simon to Jesus (vv. 41, 42). The two brothers lived and fished in Bethsaida near Capernaum (v. 44), which became the headquarters for Jesus' ministry. They would have had weeks, perhaps even months, to hear Jesus teach before He called them to travel with Him in full-time ministry. By the time He asked, they were ready to say yes.

B. Followers of Christ (vv. 21, 22)

21. And going on from thence, he saw other two brethren, James the son of Zebedee, and John his brother, in a ship with Zebedee their father, mending their nets; and he called them.

Peter and Andrew were partners in the fishing business with another pair of brothers, *James* and *John*, and their father *Zebedee* (Luke 5:10). Jesus likewise summoned these brothers to give up their fishing career and follow Him. Once again the groundwork for this call had likely been laid by Jesus' preaching and teaching during His early Judean ministry.

22. And they immediately left the ship and their father, and followed him.

We should not imagine that the two sets of brothers left the family business in a predicament by their departure. We know that Zebedee had hired servants to assist him (Mark 1:20). We can assume that the parents were pleased with their sons' decision to follow Jesus, for Zebedee's wife was one of several women from Galilee who supported Jesus' ministry (most likely in a financial way) and stood by the cross as He died (Matthew 27:55, 56). [See question #1, page 160.]

OBEDIENCE WITHOUT QUESTION

First Samuel 15 tells how God instructed King Saul of Israel to go to war against the Amalekites. Saul was instructed to "utterly destroy" them because of their past mistreatment of the Israelites (vv. 2, 3). Saul proceeded to defeat the Amalekites in battle; but instead of completely destroying the enemy, he kept their king and some of their livestock alive. The Lord told His prophet Samuel to confront Saul about his blatant disobedience. After Saul claimed that he kept the livestock alive to sacrifice them to the Lord, Samuel replied, "To obey is better than sacrifice" (v. 22).

The four fishermen whom Jesus called to be apostles had this factor in common: they were obedient. When Jesus invited them to come and follow Him, they followed. Their obedience is a great example to us today.

Mother Theresa once said, "There is no demand so unreasonable that God cannot make it of my life." This thought should be planted deeply in the thinking of each of us. Jesus said, "If ye love me, keep my commandments" (John 14:15). The acid test of the love that we sing about or talk about on Sunday morning is our daily obedience Sunday afternoon through Saturday night.
—D. R.

Home Daily Bible Readings

Monday, Dec. 27—Jesus Calls the First Disciples (Matthew 4:18-22)
Tuesday, Dec. 28—Jesus Calls Matthew (Matthew 9:9-13)
Wednesday, Dec. 29—Authority Conferred Upon the Disciples (Matthew 10:1-4)
Thursday, Dec. 30—The Twelve Proclaim God's Kingdom (Matthew 10:5-15)
Friday, Dec. 31—The Disciples Told of Coming Persecutions (Matthew 10:16-25)
Saturday, Jan. 1—The Disciples Told Not to Fear (Matthew 10:26-33)
Sunday, Jan. 2—Not Peace, but a Sword (Matthew 10:34—11:1)

II. One Tax Collector
(Matthew 9:9-13)

A. Receptive Follower (vv. 9, 10)

9. And as Jesus passed forth from thence, he saw a man, named Matthew, sitting at the receipt of custom: and he saith unto him, Follow me. And he arose, and followed him.

Some weeks or perhaps months after the calling of the four fishermen, Jesus enlisted *Matthew* into His service as a full-time disciple. Once again, the readiness with which he responded indicates that he had already met Jesus, listened to His message, and given serious thought to this decision. His *receipt of custom* (the location where he collected taxes) was located near the shore of the Sea of Galilee (Mark 2:13, 14). Thus he, like the four fishermen, was residing in the area where Jesus concentrated His preaching and teaching.

Matthew was also known as Levi (Mark 2:14; Luke 5:27), which was most likely his original name. Luke, who wrote not only the third Gospel but also the book of Acts, refers to him by the name Matthew, which means "gift of God," in Acts 1:13. Matthew's writing and recording skills, possibly developed in his position as a tax collector, later served him well; he wrote the longest of the four Gospels, and the one distinguished for its fuller summaries of the teachings of Jesus.

10. And it came to pass, as Jesus sat at meat in the house, behold, many publicans and sinners came and sat down with him and his disciples.

Luke's record indicates that *the house* where Jesus *sat at meat* was Matthew's own home, and that Jesus was his guest of honor (Luke 5:29). The place was filled with infamous outcasts of Jewish society—perhaps the only friends a tax collector could claim as his own, being an outcast himself. Matthew had invited other *publicans* or tax collectors, all of them despised by the

Jews for collaborating with the Roman government. They also had the reputation, usually well-earned, of being dishonest and coercive. (Recall the words of Zaccheus to Jesus in Luke 19:8.)

There were also other *sinners* present, which in this context usually refers to those who made their living in a disreputable manner, such as prostitutes (Matthew 21:31, 32). Matthew's joy at being accepted by Jesus knew no bounds, and thus he cared not with whom he celebrated. In fact, this banquet may have been intended as his first evangelistic effort.

EVANGELISM—WITH NO STRINGS ATTACHED

Evangelism needs to be a part of every Christian's life and needs to be the heartbeat of every church. Minister Steve Sjorgren (*Sor*-gren) tells the true story of Joe Delaney and his eight-year-old son Jared, who were playing catch in their backyard. Jared asked, "Dad, is there a God?" Joe explained that he wasn't really sure if God existed or not. "I'll be right back," Jared shouted as he ran into the house.

Moments later, he returned with a helium balloon from the circus, a pen, and an index card. "I'm going to send God an airmail message," Jared explained. "Dear God," he wrote, "if You are real and You are there, send people who know You to Dad and me."

"God, I hope You are watching," Joe thought as they watched the balloon and message sail away.

Two days later, Joe and Jared pulled into a car wash sponsored by Sjorgren's church. When Joe asked, "How much?" he was told, "It's free. No strings attached."

"But why are you doing this?" Joe asked.

"We just wanted to show God's love in a practical way," Sjorgren answered.

"Are you guys Christians—the kind of Christians who really believe in God?" Joe asked.

Sjorgren replied, "Yes, we're that kind of Christians." From that encounter, Steve led Joe to accept Christ.

When Matthew chose to follow Jesus, he found something that he wanted to share with his friends. That is the reason he invited them— and Jesus—to his house. Let us follow his example and develop a similar passion for caring about and reaching out to the lost.   —D. R.

B. Resentful Pharisees (vv. 11-13)

11. And when the Pharisees saw it, they said unto his disciples, Why eateth your master with publicans and sinners?

The *Pharisees* were one of the two most prominent of the Jewish religious groups. (The Sadducees were the other.) They exercised a powerful influence over the laws and rituals of

Visual for lesson 5

This chart will help your students to sort out the chronology of the events you will study this quarter. Display it throughout the quarter.

Judaism. They were the "sworn enemies" of Jesus throughout His years of ministry, ultimately becoming the group with the most influence in the Jewish Sanhedrin—the council that officially sentenced Jesus to death on the false charge of blasphemy. Of course, the other party that was represented on the Sanhedrin, the Sadducees, was equally hostile toward Jesus.

The Pharisees could not understand how any preacher who wanted to be taken seriously could participate in a gathering of people who were at odds with the high moral code of the Mosaic law. Their criticism of Jesus implied that He had compromised His convictions and was condoning the lifestyles of *publicans and sinners* by His presence with them. [See question #2, page 160.]

12. But when Jesus heard that, he said unto them, They that be whole need not a physician, but they that are sick.

What the Pharisees always failed to take into account was the evangelistic duty that God's people have toward those who are lost. They claimed that associating with sinners would tarnish their godly image and place them too close to dangerous influences.

While this may have been a ruse to justify the Pharisees' prejudices, there is a concern here with which Christians can identify. We enjoy being with people who share our religious convictions, and we are often troubled to be around sinful words and activities. Even so, the *sick* need to be visited by a *physician* if they are ever to recover their spiritual health and vitality. Thus the New Testament rule for Christians is that we develop relationships with the people of this world by which we can graciously challenge their sinful lives and bring them to salvation. Our role model is Jesus, who could eat with sinners and yet firmly say, "Go, and sin no more" (John 8:11).

13. But go ye and learn what that meaneth, I will have mercy, and not sacrifice: for I am not come to call the righteous, but sinners to repentance.

Jesus, the Master Teacher, suggested a homework assignment for these who presumed to know the full will of God: *learn* the meaning of Hosea 6:6. The prophet Hosea criticized Israel for its hypocrisy. The people correctly practiced the religious rituals and sacrifices of Judaism, but they did not apply the meaning of it to their hearts. Theirs was a religious formalism that concentrated on outward appearances but failed to grasp deeper spiritual truths.

A heart truly devoted to God must demonstrate *mercy* to all *sinners*. Even though we may be repulsed by the lifestyles of such individuals, the love of God should draw us near to them. We

must recognize that God could have been repulsed by our sins as well and could have left us to perish in them. Jesus' newest disciple was one who had quickly learned the spirit of genuine service to God. [See question #3, page 160.]

III. Twelve Apostles
(Matthew 10:1-4)

A. Set Apart for Service (v. 1)

1. And when he had called unto him his twelve disciples, he gave them power against unclean spirits, to cast them out, and to heal all manner of sickness and all manner of disease.

Of the many disciples who followed Jesus during His ministry, He selected twelve, "that they should be with him, and that he might send them forth to preach" (Mark 3:14). These twelve are known as the *twelve disciples,* reflecting Jesus' desire "that they should be with him." A disciple followed his teacher, learning from him in a variety of settings. They are also known as the twelve "apostles" (see verse 2), reflecting the latter part of the charge: "that he might send them forth to preach." The word *apostle* literally means "one sent out."

The apostles eventually served as the human agents who formed part of the foundation of Christ's church (Ephesians 2:20). They were commissioned to be the primary authors of the New Testament Scripture that guides the church (John

---

How to Say It

ALPHEUS. Al-*fee*-us.
AMALEKITES. *Am*-uh-leh-kites or Uh-*mal*-ih-kites.
ARAMAIC. Air-uh-*may*-ick.
BARTHOLOMEW. Bar-*thah*-luh-mew.
BETHSAIDA. Beth-*say*-uh-duh.
CANAANITE. *Kay*-nun-ite.
CAPERNAUM. Kuh-*per*-nay-um.
CEPHAS. *See*-fus.
DIDYMUS. *Did*-uh-mus.
ISCARIOT. Iss-*care*-ee-ut.
JOSES. *Joe*-sez.
LEBBEUS. Leh-*bee*-us.
NATHANAEL. Nuh-*than*-yull.
PHARISEES. *Fair*-ih-seez.
SADDUCEES. *Sad*-you-seez.
SANHEDRIN. San-*heed*-run or *San*-huh-drin.
THADDEUS. *Thad*-ee-us.
ZACCHEUS. Zack-*kee*-us.
ZEALOT. *Zel*-ut.
ZEBEDEE. *Zeb*-uh-dee.
ZELOTES. Zeh-*low*-teez.

14:26; 15:26, 27). They were the first recipients of the Great Commission to evangelize all peoples throughout the world (Matthew 28:18-20).

These twelve had been with Jesus for several months, learning from Him and serving with Him. Now they were ready for an assignment on their own. They had seen how Jesus taught and acted with authority. Now they would be empowered—at least temporarily—with miraculous gifts that they could use to establish their credentials as God's messengers (Matthew 10:5-15). [See question #4, page 160.]

B. Selected as Apostles (vv. 2-4)

2. Now the names of the twelve apostles are these; The first, Simon, who is called Peter, and Andrew his brother; James the son of Zebedee, and John his brother.

All four of the New Testament passages that list the twelve *apostles* (Matthew 10:2-4; Mark 3:16-19; Luke 6:13-16; Acts 1:13) begin with the four fishermen: *Peter, Andrew, James,* and *John.* As previously noted, they were among the earliest disciples called by Jesus. Also, in every list found in the Gospels, Peter appears first and Judas last.

3. Philip, and Bartholomew; Thomas, and Matthew the publican; James the son of Alpheus, and Lebbeus, whose surname was Thaddeus.

For most of the remaining apostles, little information about them (if any) can be found in Scripture. It was noted earlier that *Philip* was a native of Bethsaida (John 1:44). *Bartholomew* is apparently the apostle referred to in the Gospel of John as Nathanael (John 1:45-51; 21:2). Nathanael was introduced to Jesus by his friend Philip (John 1:45), and the two are listed side-by-side (as Philip and Bartholomew) in the listings of apostles found in the Gospels.

Thomas was also known as Didymus (John 11:16), which means "twin." *James the son of Alpheus* may have been the brother of *Matthew the publican,* since Matthew's father was also named Alpheus (Mark 2:14). Perhaps to distinguish him from James the brother of John (Acts 12:2), he is sometimes referred to as "James the less" (Mark 15:40) or "James the younger" (*New International Version*). James's mother's name was Mary, and he had a brother named Joses (Mark 15:40).

Thaddeus was also known as "Judas the brother of James" (Luke 6:16; Acts 1:13); however, the words "the brother" are not in the Greek text (thus they appear in italics in the *King James Version*). The translators of the *New International Version* have chosen to use the words "the son" to describe the relationship between Judas and James, but we cannot say with certainty how they were related.

4. Simon the Canaanite, and Judas Iscariot, who also betrayed him.

Luke's writings refer to *Simon the Canaanite* as "Simon called Zelotes" (Luke 6:15) and as "Simon Zelotes" (Acts 1:13). This is a reference to Simon's membership in a radical liberation party called the Zealots, which was known for the extreme and violent actions it took against Roman officials. Certainly the most interesting matchup among the apostles was a former anti-Roman Zealot (Simon) working with a former Roman tax collector (Matthew).

The name *Iscariot* probably referred to Judas's native town in southern Judea. *Judas* served as the "treasurer" of the apostles (John 12:6; 13:29), and probably started his service to Jesus with good intentions. But as almost everyone realizes, his ending was tragic, and he will always be known as "Judas the traitor."

It was this diverse group of men whom Jesus used to proclaim the message of His kingdom. Several of them were highly unlikely candidates for leadership in such an enterprise, yet all (except for Judas) left behind a legacy of faithful service to Jesus. [See question #5, page 160.]

Conclusion

A. Availability

When we try to recruit helpers for any project in the church, we sometimes use the expression: "The key is not ability, but availability." Christian service is enhanced by our gifts and abilities, education and experience, and personalities and attitudes. Certainly leadership positions must be limited to those who are Biblically qualified. But with God the key to effective ministry is a desire to serve. God seems to enjoy taking unlikely candidates—such as four fishermen, a tax collector, and a political radical—and making them a testimony to His grace and power.

Any of us can engage in some kind of meaningful service for Jesus' kingdom, if only we are willing to answer the call to discipleship.

B. Prayer

Father, help us to be ready and willing to serve, whenever and wherever You present the opportunity. In Jesus' name. Amen.

C. Thought to Remember

Jesus calls us: by Thy mercies,
    Savior, may we hear Thy call,
Give our hearts to Thy obedience,
    Serve and love Thee best of all.
        —Cecil F. Alexander

Learning by Doing

This page contains an alternate lesson plan emphasizing learning activities.
Classes desiring such student involvement will find these suggestions helpful.

Learning Goals

After this lesson a student should be able to:

1. Name the twelve apostles and tell a little of the background of some of them.

2. Tell how the calling of Jesus' first disciples instructs us today about responding to Jesus' call.

3. Express a commitment to being a disciple of Jesus.

Into the Lesson

As students arrive, put them in groups of three or four members each. (People who arrive a little later can join the existing groups, up to about six in a group.) Give each group a slip of paper on which you have written a task from the list below and this set of instructions: "If you were choosing a team to accomplish this task, what qualities would you look for among the participants? List four to six qualities." Assign these and/or other tasks: plant a garden, build a house, win a basketball game, develop a new ministry in your church.

After a few minutes, ask the groups to reveal their lists. Record the answers on a chalkboard or overhead transparency. Ask, "What common characteristics are listed?" (Integrity, vision, passion, detail-orientation.) "Why are some characteristics different?" (Tasks are different, individuals are different, skill levels are different.)

Next, ask, "How would you recruit people to be a part of your team?" Answers may include telephone calls, letters or notes, e-mail, or face-to-face meetings.

Note that today's study focuses on Jesus' calling of the twelve apostles. We will see how each came when Jesus called, characteristics of some of them, and how we can follow Jesus today.

Into the Word

Encourage members to complete the following activity in groups of three or four. Make sure that each has a copy. (This activity is also in the student book.) Give them ten to twelve minutes to complete the exercise, matching the letter with the correct name.

1. Peter	2. Andrew	3. James
4. John	5. Matthew	6. Philip
7. Bartholomew	8. Thomas	9. James
10. Thaddeus	11. Simon	12. Judas

(1, g; 2, k; 3, a; 4, h; 5, i; 6, b; 7, l; 8, d; 9, f; 10, c; 11, j; 12, e.)

a. One of two brothers, known for his temper and martyrdom (Luke 9:54; Acts 12:2).

b. A Galilean who brought a friend to Jesus (John 1:44, 45).

c. Referred to as "Judas the brother of James" (Luke 6:16; Acts 1:13).

d. The original "doubter," but first to confess Jesus as Lord (John 20:25, 28).

e. The keeper of the purse, or treasurer, of the Twelve (John 12:6; 13:29).

f. Also known as "the Less" or "the Younger" (Mark 15:40).

g. Fisherman who confessed his own sinfulness, yet stood like a rock (Luke 5:5-8; John 1:42).

h. Most beloved by Jesus (John 13:23; 19:26; 21:24).

i. Tax collector (Matthew 9:9; Mark 2:14).

j. A "Zealot," member of an anti-Rome faction (Luke 6:15).

k. Originally a follower of John the Baptist, brought his brother to Jesus (John 1:40-42).

l. Also named Nathanael, a man of honest motives (John 1:45-49).

When most of the students have finished, discuss their answers, explaining background information and details from the lesson commentary. Particularly note that Scripture indicates some prior knowledge of Jesus before this specialized call. Say, "We see that Jesus called a variety of people to be His first disciples. This unique group fulfilled a unique mission."

Into Life

Reflect back to the "Into the Lesson" section where we discussed qualities necessary for different tasks. Remind students that the church's mission is to seek and to save the lost. Distribute three-by-five index cards and instruct each student to list two or three qualities he or she possesses that can be used in this mission. (These could include: gregarious personality, communication skills, persistence, a winsome smile, as well as evangelism training or leadership skills.)

Ask one or two volunteers to read their lists to the class. Then have the class open their Bibles to Matthew 28:19, 20, and have a volunteer read it aloud. Say, "Jesus will use in His mission the qualities you have listed. Write, 'Matthew 28:19, 20' over your list of qualities. Silently pray a prayer of commitment to use your personal qualities in participating in the Great Commission."

Let's Talk It Over

The questions on this page are designed to encourage review of the lesson Scriptures and to promote discussion of the lesson by the class. The answers provided are only discussion starters. Let your class talk it over from there.

1. At least three factors were involved in Jesus' process of calling His "apostles": seeking men who would be willing to assist Him; giving limited exposure to the type of work they would do; and challenging them to follow Him. Do you think these same steps might be used to motivate people to discipleship today? If so, how?

There are some differences between Jesus' call to discipleship today and His call to the apostles. Disciples today often work from within their "secular" occupations to follow the Lord; the fishermen left their boats to follow Jesus even as Matthew and the others left their occupations.

Yet there are similarities. Following Jesus still requires a break with the past, as these disciples illustrate. We need to be honest about the level of commitment we ask people to make when we are discipling them, just as Jesus was. And for some, who choose ministry as their vocations, the similarities are even more pronounced. For them, perhaps an internship to give limited exposure to the type of work they would do would be helpful.

2. Jesus was criticized for associating with "sinners." Though He defended His actions, the Bible does warn us about our associations. (See 2 Corinthians 6:14-18.) At the same time, we are told to be "light" and "salt" in the world (Matthew 5:13-16). Where do we draw the line? How much contact do you think we as Christians should maintain with unbelievers? Why?

This is a difficult balancing act. Whenever people of different positions interact, one or both will be influenced. We need to be sure we are being influential for good while we resist being influenced by evil.

Jesus' example is instructive here. His answer included a clear statement of His purpose: "I am not come to call the righteous, but sinners to repentance." What is our purpose? Do we keep it clearly in mind *at all times*?

What other specific suggestions can your class offer? Certainly prayer is one; another is making sure that one is held accountable by other Christians. See how many the class can suggest.

3. How can we, as Jesus' disciples, avoid the tendency of the Pharisees to focus only on outward appearances? What steps would help us

exercise mercy toward others without condoning their sinful actions or lifestyle?

The beginning point should always be a constant awareness of our own sin and God's gracious forgiveness. The apostle Paul never forgot how God had rescued him from his past (1 Timothy 1:12-16). His deep appreciation for the grace of God helped him to preach and demonstrate grace in his own life, "speaking the truth in love," as he put it (Ephesians 4:15).

4. When asked to take positions of ministry in the church, some people refuse because they do not know how. In fact, Jesus did spend three years training His disciples. How much training and discipling do you think are necessary before a person can effectively serve in Christ's church? Why?

Some jobs require training and some do not. Remember that Jesus was training "apostles" or leaders, and not just "disciples"—followers. Different training is needed for leadership roles.

We should guide new believers in much the same way we give our children increasing levels of responsibility within the home. As they serve at one level, they can be trained to serve at another. The Twelve were trained in this way, as Matthew 10 records.

Most of all, we must educate the entire congregation to see that every Christian needs to serve in some type of ministry, and that every ministry is vitally important to the church's overall ministry. (See Ephesians 4:11-13; 1 Peter 4:10, 11.)

5. What does the wide diversity seen in Jesus' first disciples suggest to you about the makeup of the church? Can a church with similar diversity survive today? Why or why not?

God never intended for all His disciples to have the same appearance, abilities, interests, and roles in the church. Instead, our uniqueness helps strengthen the body of Christ (1 Corinthians 12). Jesus knew that His church needed Peters who are bold and forceful, Andrews who humbly and quietly minister among people without regard to who gets credit, and Thomases who will ask questions and refuse to take everything for granted. Most of all, God needs every disciple to serve in his or her unique way, while still growing in each area of the Christian life.

Teachings on Prayer

Devotional Reading: Luke 11:1-13.

Background Scripture: Matthew 6:1-15.

Printed Text: Matthew 6:1-15.

Matthew 6:1-15

1 Take heed that ye do not your alms before men, to be seen of them: otherwise ye have no reward of your Father which is in heaven.

2 Therefore when thou doest thine alms, do not sound a trumpet before thee, as the hypocrites do in the synagogues and in the streets, that they may have glory of men. Verily I say unto you, They have their reward.

3 But when thou doest alms, let not thy left hand know what thy right hand doeth:

4 That thine alms may be in secret: and thy Father which seeth in secret himself shall reward thee openly.

5 And when thou prayest, thou shalt not be as the hypocrites are: for they love to pray standing in the synagogues and in the corners of the streets, that they may be seen of men. Verily I say unto you, They have their reward.

6 But thou, when thou prayest, enter into thy closet, and when thou hast shut thy door, pray to thy Father which is in secret; and thy Father which seeth in secret shall reward thee openly.

7 But when ye pray, use not vain repetitions, as the heathen do: for they think that they shall be heard for their much speaking.

8 Be not ye therefore like unto them: for your Father knoweth what things ye have need of, before ye ask him.

9 After this manner therefore pray ye: Our Father which art in heaven, Hallowed be thy name.

10 Thy kingdom come. Thy will be done in earth, as it is in heaven.

11 Give us this day our daily bread.

12 And forgive us our debts, as we forgive our debtors.

13 And lead us not into temptation, but deliver us from evil: For thine is the kingdom, and the power, and the glory, for ever. Amen.

14 For if ye forgive men their trespasses, your heavenly Father will also forgive you:

15 But if ye forgive not men their trespasses, neither will your Father forgive your trespasses.

Golden Text: When thou prayest, enter into thy closet, and when thou hast shut thy door, pray to thy Father which is in secret; and thy Father which seeth in secret shall reward thee openly.—Matthew 6:6.

Lesson Aims

After this lesson students should be able to:

1. Summarize Jesus' teaching about prayer in this portion of the Sermon on the Mount.

2. Explain the difference between "letting your light shine" and "blowing your own horn."

3. Suggest specific steps that they can take to make their prayer lives conform to Jesus' teaching.

Lesson Outline

INTRODUCTION
   A. All the World's a Stage
   B. Lesson Background
 I. A HUMBLE GIFT (Matthew 6:1-4)
   A. Not for Show (vv. 1, 2)
   B. Given With Discretion (vv. 3, 4)
     Flint, Sponge, or Honeycomb?
 II. A GENUINE DEVOTION (Matthew 6:5-8)
   A. Focused Upon God (vv. 5, 6)
   B. Led by Faith (vv. 7, 8)
III. A MODEL PRAYER (Matthew 6:9-15)
   A. Respect for God (vv. 9, 10)
   B. Request for Needs (vv. 11-13)
     Plug In!
   C. Living by Grace (vv. 14, 15)
CONCLUSION
   A. Worship That Does Not Count
   B. Prayer
   C. Thought to Remember

Introduction

A. All the World's a Stage

"All the world's a stage, and all the men and women merely players." William Shakespeare penned this famous line (*As You Like It*, Act II, Scene 7) to illustrate the changes that we all experience throughout our lives. We work through different "stages" of life, from childhood to old age, like an actor changing roles from one play to the next until at the end we finally make our grand exit. Today this quotation is often used to make the claim that all of life is mere acting and pretending. We say and do what is required of us, whether we actually mean it or not.

While the latter idea was not Shakespeare's intent, it does describe the way too many people approach life, pretending to be genuine and putting on a show for others to see. And all too easily this can be the way we practice our Christianity—singing, praying, and giving—with more concern for outward form than for the inner attitude of worship and devotion.

B. Lesson Background

Most of Matthew's Gospel is concerned with Jesus' ministry in Galilee. This ministry included three major tours of Galilee, in which Jesus visited several cities, preaching and doing miracles (Matthew 4:23; Luke 8:1; Matthew 9:35). It was in connection with the third tour that Jesus called the Twelve together, gave them power to work miracles, and sent them out on a tour of their own, as noted in last week's lesson.

Today's lesson backs up to the time between the first and second tours, during the second year of Jesus' ministry. Jesus spent most of these months on the west side of the Sea of Galilee, in the vicinity of Capernaum and Bethsaida. His teaching and miracles attracted throngs of people (Matthew 12:15; Mark 3:9, 10).

In order to speak to crowds that must have numbered in the thousands, Jesus had to devise creative ways to be seen and heard. In today's lesson, for example, He took His place on the side of a small mountain in order to project His voice over the crowd (Matthew 5:1). It was from this location that Jesus preached what is known as His "Sermon on the Mount" (Matthew 5–7).

The Sermon on the Mount is the longest recorded sermon of Jesus, containing such familiar teachings as the Beatitudes, the admonition not to worry (because God takes care of the birds of the air and clothes the lilies of the field), and the parable of the wise and the foolish builders. In the middle of this are Jesus' instructions regarding worship and devotion, giving, and prayer. Its importance is suggested by the early placement Matthew gives it in his Gospel, even though several events in the eighth, ninth, and twelfth chapters actually occurred before Jesus preached this sermon.

I. A Humble Gift
(Matthew 6:1-4)

A. Not for Show (vv. 1, 2)

1. Take heed that ye do not your alms before men, to be seen of them: otherwise ye have no reward of your Father which is in heaven.

The law of Moses required the Jews to give tithes and offerings regularly to support the ministry of the Levites (Numbers 18:21-24), who in turn gave a tithe of what they received in order to provide for the priests (vv. 25-32). In addition to these offerings, those who had the means to provide for their own families were also expected to make charitable donations to the poor (Deuteronomy 15:11).

The Old English term *alms* refers to donations or acts of mercy that are meant to provide relief for the poor. The *New King James Version* clarifies this by using the phrase "charitable deeds" in place of *alms*.

Jesus is critical of those who make charitable contributions *before men, to be seen of them.* The Greek word translated *to be seen* is the source of our English word "theater." The idea is that of someone putting on a show, as if "on stage," with the desire to be noticed and applauded by observers.

2. Therefore when thou doest thine alms, do not sound a trumpet before thee, as the hypocrites do in the synagogues and in the streets, that they may have glory of men. Verily I say unto you, They have their reward.

The imagery of sounding a *trumpet* to announce the giving of a charitable donation is probably hyperbole—that is, an exaggeration to emphasize a point. There may not have been actual trumpets blowing near the treasury boxes in the local *synagogues* or in the Jerusalem temple, but hypocrites could always find a way to draw attention to themselves. In first-century Judaism it was not uncommon for the collection receptacles to be placed in prominent locations where individuals would walk in front of the crowd and deposit their gifts. On one occasion Jesus sat with His disciples and watched people come forward and give their money, aware of how much each one was giving (Mark 12:41-44).

The modern church is not exempt from Jesus' warning against doing good deeds in order to *have glory of men.* Some Christians long to receive public acknowledgment and appreciation for their gifts, to be included in a posted list of donors, or to be singled out in some other manner. And they are offended if not given their due. Some like to mention how much they give or do for others—in casual conversation, public testimonies, and even in lessons or sermons. How easy it is for any of us to set aside humility for a moment and to *sound a trumpet*, or, as we might say it today, "toot our own horn."

B. Given With Discretion (vv. 3, 4)

3. But when thou doest alms, let not thy left hand know what thy right hand doeth.

Here Jesus used the imagery of the human body to illustrate the concept of giving with discretion. Just as our *left hand* and our *right hand* can at the same time be holding two different objects or performing two different functions, so

each of us should be busy serving the Lord as best we can, without a concern for whether others notice how much we are doing.

Let us note that there *is* a place in Jesus' teaching for a desire that others see our good deeds—not that we might receive the praise of others (v. 2), but to set an example for them to follow. Earlier in this sermon Jesus said, "Let your light so shine before men, that they may see your good works, and glorify your Father which is in heaven" (Matthew 5:16). For those of us who serve as leaders in the church, it is good for others to see that we "practice what we preach" so that they can be encouraged to heed our teaching and imitate our godly example. We should speak of our spiritual activities in very general terms for the purpose of illustration and edification, and always with humility and moderation.

The key difference between "do not give your alms before men" (v. 1) and "let your light shine before men" (Matthew 5:16) is the intent of the heart. We can discover a proper balance when we start with a humble spirit.

4. That thine alms may be in secret: and thy Father which seeth in secret himself shall reward thee openly.

Here Jesus established a principle for all gifts and deeds of service. If we seek the notice and applause of men, then we forfeit a claim to heavenly blessings (v. 1). God gives us our "just deserts" by holding back the bounty He is able to bestow, because our heart is set on the *reward* of men (v. 2).

However, there is a positive side to this principle. If we are motivated by a devotion to God, with no thought for the praise of men, then God our *Father* will *reward* us *openly*. His blessings not only have eternal implications, but can result in the praise and appreciation of others—not because we sought it, but because God was pleased to give it. [See question #1, page 168.]

FLINT, SPONGE, OR HONEYCOMB?

There are three types of givers when it comes to stewardship—the flint, the sponge, and the honeycomb. To get anything out of the flint, you must hammer it. You hit it and hope you are coming from the right angle—and even then you get only chips and sparks. To get water out of a wet sponge, you squeeze it. The more pressure you exert, the more water you will get. But remove the lid from a jar of honey with the comb inside and take out a generous piece of the honeycomb. That piece of honeycomb will overflow with its own sweetness.

Jesus talked about our attitudes and our motives in personal stewardship. He tells us it is not only the gift we give, but also the condition of our hearts when we are giving, that is important to the Lord. Our attitude in giving counts!

Paul mirrors this very thought when he writes in 2 Corinthians 9:7 and tells us, "Every man according as he purposeth in his heart, so let him give; not grudgingly, or of necessity: for God loveth a cheerful giver." When we come to the place in our love for the Lord that we are giving from the purest of motives and from a spirit of joy, we are overflowing in a "honeycomb" style of giving.

Each one of us, then, must answer the question, "Am I flint, sponge, or honeycomb?" —D. R.

II. A Genuine Devotion
(Matthew 6:5-8)

A. Focused Upon God (vv. 5, 6)

5. And when thou prayest, thou shalt not be as the hypocrites are: for they love to pray standing in the synagogues and in the corners of the streets, that they may be seen of men. Verily I say unto you, They have their reward.

Jesus' description of the *hypocrites* sounds like the Pharisees, of whom He said on another occasion, "Ye devour widows' houses, and for a pretense make long prayer: therefore ye shall receive the greater damnation" (Matthew 23:14). To *love to pray* is certainly commendable; however, the Pharisees loved the opportunity that praying gave them to call attention to their high level of spirituality. Rather than seek out a prayer chamber in the temple or a quiet place of retreat, they preferred to stand and pray in the midst of public activity: in the *synagogues* and even on the *corners* of busy *streets*.

6. But thou, when thou prayest, enter into thy closet, and when thou hast shut thy door, pray to thy Father which is in secret; and thy Father which seeth in secret shall reward thee openly.

Instead of a public display of prayer, Jesus counseled that we withdraw from busy places for our personal prayer time. The idea of praying in a *closet* brings to mind an interesting scenario, if we think of trying to squeeze inside one of our cluttered closets. The Greek word actually refers to an inner room of a house, such as a bedroom, which is a more realistic picture of a place for prayer. Jesus was not requiring the use of a bedroom for prayer; He was simply illustrating the type of setting that is most appropriate.

Some have erroneously concluded that a public prayer in an assembly contradicts this text. However, Jesus Himself prayed aloud on several occasions, such as when He fed the multitude (Matthew 14:19) and when He approached the tomb of Lazarus (John 11:41, 42). Prayer was a regular part of the worship gatherings of the early church (Acts 2:42), and on special occasions was the main reason for a church to assemble (Acts 12:12).

Public prayer is appropriate when done in a manner consistent with Jesus' principle of humility and discretion. The person who prays aloud should speak directly to God, not for the ears of the assembly (though with a clarity that will allow the people to comprehend and then say a genuine "Amen!" or "So be it!"). The wording should reflect an eloquence befitting God, but not with the intent of impressing men.

When the thoughts of all assembled are directed heavenward, then a public prayer has been done well. [See question #2, page 168.]

B. Led by Faith (vv. 7, 8)

7. But when ye pray, use not vain repetitions, as the heathen do: for they think that they shall be heard for their much speaking.

The *vain repetitions* of the *heathen* or pagan religions included a chanting of key words and phrases over and over with the hope that such incessant repetition or *much speaking* would eventually win the favor of a deity. (Recall the cries of the prophets of Baal in 1 Kings 18:26-29.) Such prayer was not so much a conversation with God, or even a well-worded petition to God, as a verbal appeasement of God. The *New American Standard Bible* speaks of "meaningless repetition," while the *New International Version* says not to "keep on babbling."

We Christians, however, can also be guilty of repeating traditional prayer phrases without giving them careful thought. Our prayers before meals and at bedtime can easily become routine as we repeat familiar words. In addition, the public prayers in our worship services (especially the invocation, the benediction, and the prayers for the Lord's Supper and the offering) can seem like trite formulas when the same phrases are repeated time after time. Even the name of "God" or "Lord" can fall into the category of *vain repetitions* when routinely attached to every sentence,

---

How to Say It

BAAL. *Bay*-ul.
BETHSAIDA. Beth-*say*-uh-duh.
CAPERNAUM. Kuh-*per*-nay-um.
HYPOCRITES. *hip*-uh-krits.
ISAIAH. Eye-*zay*-uh.
LAZARUS. *Laz*-uh-rus.
LEVITES. *Lee*-vites.
MACEDONIANS. Mass-uh-*doe*-nee-unz.
SYNAGOGUES. *sin*-uh-gogs.

as if God's name were a magic formula. It is easy to understand why we repeat that which is familiar, and how difficult it is to be creative all the time. Nevertheless, our goal should be to put serious thought behind each word we use, even the familiar ones.

Some people think that reciting "the Lord's Prayer" (below) or reading aloud a written prayer contradicts Jesus' prohibition against *vain repetitions*. However, the key to Jesus' criticism is not repetition, but *vain* or meaningless repetition. As long as one's words are spoken with care and not repeated like a magical formula, the repetition itself is not a problem.

8. Be not ye therefore like unto them: for your Father knoweth what things ye have need of, before ye ask him.

Prayer should not be a religious ritual, but a loving communication between us and our *Father*. We were created by God for fellowship with Him, and thus He enjoys hearing us talk to Him in the expression of a personal relationship.

Of course, an omniscient God who knows all things does not need to hear our prayers in order to know our needs; He knows *before* we *ask him*. He expects us to speak our petitions in prayer because of the joy He experiences in the fellowship that occurs. Just because a parent understands the needs of his or her children does not mean that there should be no communication regarding these matters. [See question #3, page 168.]

III. A Model Prayer
(Matthew 6:9-15)

A. Respect for God (vv. 9, 10)

9. After this manner therefore pray ye: Our Father which art in heaven, Hallowed be thy name.

What we refer to as "the Lord's Prayer" is a beloved text often memorized and repeated by Christians, and regarded on a par with the Twenty-third Psalm and John 3:16. On another occasion, Jesus repeated this prayer in response to a request from His disciples that He teach them how to pray properly (Luke 11:1-4).

Prayer should begin with an address to God that expresses our highest respect for Him. There is a sense of familiarity in addressing God as *Our Father*, yet there is also a formality in noting that He is our heavenly Father, exalted far above His creation. His name is to be *hallowed*, or revered as holy and special. The Ten Commandments declare that God's name is not to be used "in vain," but always with great care and reverence (Exodus 20:7). We would do well in our prayers not to become too casual with God, thinking of Him as our "Daddy in the Sky" or the "Big Man

This display of the Lord's Model Prayer will be useful for your lesson today and on many occasions even after this quarter of study has concluded.

Visual for lesson 6

Upstairs," but to approach Him with all the adoration He so richly deserves.

10. Thy kingdom come. Thy will be done in earth, as it is in heaven.

What is this *kingdom* that Jesus told us to pray would *come*? Actually the Greek word for *kingdom* does not refer so much to a place or an organization as to a relationship with God. The "kingdom of God" describes God's authority and rule being exercised over those individuals who express their allegiance to His lordship. To pray *thy kingdom come* is to pledge submission to God, or, as the parallel phrase says, to declare that *thy will be done* in all that we do. The angels in *heaven* give God their total submission (Hebrews 1:6). May we on *earth* give Him the same respect and devotion. [See question #4, page 168.]

B. Request for Needs (vv. 11-13)

11. Give us this day our daily bread.

We should not be embarrassed when we use our prayer time to make requests for the items we believe we need. Certainly to focus our prayers exclusively upon our own needs would be out of balance. But if we first approach God with the reverence He deserves, then we can in good conscience proceed to our petitions. To ask for God's assistance is an expression of our dependence on Him; thus our requests honor Him as our Creator and Provider.

By mentioning something as routine as *our daily bread*, Jesus was indicating that any concern we have is appropriate to bring before God. The fact that God numbers the hairs on our heads (Matthew 10:30) shows that even the minor details of our lives are of interest to Him.

12. And forgive us our debts, as we forgive our debtors.

While it is proper to petition God for our physical needs, we should never forget our spiritual needs. It is especially helpful that Jesus gave us the example of praying for forgiveness. We are reminded that we must not take sin for granted;

rather, we must honestly acknowledge when we have sinned (1 John 1:8-10) and then must "bring forth . . . fruits meet for repentance" (Matthew 3:8; Acts 26:20). One of those fruits is our willingness to *forgive* others, which reflects our understanding of God's forgiveness toward us. This is brought out most clearly in Jesus' parable of the unforgiving servant (Matthew 18:21-35).

13. And lead us not into temptation, but deliver us from evil: For thine is the kingdom, and the power, and the glory, for ever. Amen.

"No temptation has seized you except what is common to man. And God is faithful; he will not let you be tempted beyond what you can bear. But when you are tempted, he will also provide a way out so that you can stand up under it" (1 Corinthians 10:13, *New International Version*). Paul's promise provides a helpful commentary on Jesus' prayer. When we express in prayer our complete trust and dependence upon God, we can be assured that He will look out for our spiritual well-being.

It should be noted that the second part of this verse (beginning with *For thine is the kingdom*) does not appear in the oldest manuscripts of Matthew, and is therefore omitted from some English translations. Nevertheless, the words offer a fitting conclusion to this model prayer, focusing on the majesty of God just as the prayer's opening words have done. [See question #5, page 168.]

PLUG IN!

A man popped his morning bagel into the toaster. He waited for the pleasant aroma he usually detected when the bagel was toasting, but even after several minutes there was no aroma. He looked inside the toaster, and the metal strips that were usually bright orange were cold and dark. Pulling the toaster away from the wall, he found that the toaster had not been plugged in after the counter had been cleaned the day before. He plugged the appliance in, and in just a few moments he was enjoying his toasted bagel. His lesson for the day: everything works better when it's plugged in!

At times we are tempted to allow several days to go by without prayer. When we do this, we realize that the power we need to confront temptation, to speak a good word for the Lord, and to carry out other spiritual disciplines is not with us as we would like.

Prayer is the Christian's source of power: no prayer—no power. Plug yourself in daily to the most exciting power source in the universe: our Savior, the Son of God!   —D. R.

C. Living by Grace (vv. 14, 15)

14. For if ye forgive men their trespasses, your heavenly Father will also forgive you.

God's grace is not deserved or earned, and yet there is a "fairness" to grace. That which we ask God to give to us without merit, we must also be willing to give to others on the same terms.

15. But if ye forgive not men their trespasses, neither will your Father forgive your trespasses.

Jesus confirms that what we say is in our hearts must also be translated into real life before God and man, or it is not genuine. Grace must become more than a point of theology; it must govern how we live and how we treat others.

Conclusion

A. Worship That Does Not Count

Jesus quoted the prophet Isaiah (29:13) in expressing His frustration with some of the people to whom He ministered: "This people draweth nigh unto me with their mouth, and honoreth me with their lips; but their heart is far from me. But in vain they do worship me . . ." (Matthew 15:8, 9). The lesson is clear. We can practice the required rituals and say the proper words, but if it is all outward display rather than conviction of the heart, then it is of no value.

B. Prayer

Father, cleanse our hearts from the pride and ego that seek the praise of men so we may devote ourselves to You alone. In Jesus' name. Amen.

C. Thought to Remember

"Take heed that you do not do your charitable deeds before men, to be seen by them. Otherwise you have no reward from your Father in heaven" (Matthew 6:1, *New King James Version*).

Home Daily Bible Readings

Monday, Jan. 3—A Call to Love Enemies (Matthew 5:43-48)

Tuesday, Jan. 4—Instructions About Alms and Prayer (Matthew 6:1-6)

Wednesday, Jan. 5—The Lord's Prayer (Matthew 6:7-15)

Thursday, Jan. 6—Ask, Seek, Knock: God Will Respond (Matthew 7:7-11)

Friday, Jan. 7—Persevere in Prayer (Luke 11:5-13)

Saturday, Jan. 8—A Parable on Perseverance in Prayer (Luke 18:1-8)

Sunday, Jan. 9—The Pharisee and the Publican (Luke 18:9-14)

Learning by Doing

This page contains an alternate lesson plan emphasizing learning activities.
Classes desiring such student involvement will find these suggestions helpful.

Learning Goals

After this lesson students should be able to:

1. Summarize Jesus' teaching about prayer in this portion of the Sermon on the Mount.

2. Explain the difference between "letting your light shine" and "blowing your own horn."

3. Suggest specific steps that they can take to make their prayer lives conform to Jesus' teaching.

Into the Lesson

Bring to class a flashlight, a blinking light, a bicycle horn or air horn, and a megaphone. (A megaphone can be made by rolling a sheet of paper into a cone, leaving openings at each end.)

Ask for volunteers each to take one of the objects and operate it in turn. Be sure that the flashlight is not waved around. Ask, "What is the reason for using this object?" Answers may vary: sound a warning, let your presence be known, draw attention to the operator.

Note that the flashlight can quietly point the way for someone who is lost or who is searching. Today's lesson warns us to check our motives in giving and praying. Are we trying to draw attention to ourselves for man's praise or to give glory to God? We will explore this issue in our lesson.

Into the Word

This lesson presents some of Jesus' teaching in a time when crowds followed everywhere to hear what He had to say. (See the "Lesson Background" in the commentary for information concerning the setting of this Scripture.) Emphasize that Jesus was challenging His would-be disciples to live differently from other people, even those who appeared religious.

Ask three volunteers to read the text for today. One reads Matthew 6:1-4; the second reads Matthew 6:5-8; the third reads Matthew 6:9-15. Use these discussion questions with the class. The commentary will help to complete the answers.

Matthew 6:1-4 (Group 1)

1. What is Jesus' concern? *(The showiness of gift-giving for the sake of the giver.)*

2. How does this contrast with genuine, compassionate giving to the poor? *(Genuine giving is the matter of a humble heart. Its intent is to bring glory to God.)*

3. What is the promise to each? What is meant by "reward"? *(Each will receive his reward. For*

some the craving of men's applause will wind up being empty. For the humble, God will give blessing with eternal implications.)*

Matthew 6:5-8 (Group 2)

1. What does hypocritical prayer look like? *(It is "me-focused," showy; often uses trite formulas.)*

2. What does sincere prayer look like? *(It is "God-focused." It is done out of the limelight. It is from the heart of the believer.)*

3. If God knows what we need, why should we pray? *(Prayer is loving communication with God. We pray because we wish to interact with Him and experience mutual joy.)*

Matthew 6:9-15 (Group 3)

1. What concerns for God are expressed in this prayer? *(His name be respected, His authority and rule be exercised, His purpose be accomplished.)*

2. What concerns for personal well-being are expressed? *(Our daily physical needs are met. Our daily spiritual needs are met: for forgiveness, guidance, and deliverance.)*

3. Why are personal forgiveness, forgiving others, and prayer linked? *(We need to recognize that God expects us to live out what we pray and to show grace toward others.)*

Into Life

It is often easy to fall into established patterns of worshiping and serving God—patterns and forms that are comfortable to us. We need to monitor our motives to be sure we are seeking to bring glory to God.

Prepare a poster, overhead transparency, or chalkboard with the following headings. "1. Pray Regularly"; "2. Pray in Secret"; "3. Pray With Your Heart"; and "4. Pray Intentionally." Ask the students to give specific ideas as to how one should accomplish the activity in each heading. Use the printed text and other ideas. Examples may include the following: 1. Mark your calendar for prayer time. 2. Have a special place for prayer. 3. Write out your prayers. 4. Use this model prayer as an example.

Have each student choose the one area of these four in which he or she most needs improvement. Ask each one to discuss with a neighbor one or two ways to improve. Then close the session with prayer, in these groups of two, for strength and resolve to obey Christ.

Let's Talk It Over

The questions on this page are designed to encourage review of the lesson Scriptures and to promote discussion of the lesson by the class. The answers provided are only discussion starters. Let your class talk it over from there.

1. In most churches Jesus' words about doing our alms "in secret" are applied very literally to financial giving. At the same time, when people give volunteer service, we have appreciation dinners, publish their names in the bulletin and newsletter, etc. Why do you think we don't take Jesus as literally about these "alms"?

Jesus' words include both our financial gifts and our gifts of service. If either kind of gift is given for the purpose of receiving praise from men, then it is wrong. So as much as our public recognition fosters a temptation to give "to be seen of men," then some might contend that we ought not to give recognition.

Some services cannot be hidden, however, and one's example of giving or serving may encourage others to participate. Paul encouraged the Corinthians to give by telling them of the Macedonians' generosity (2 Corinthians 8:1-5).

Jesus was not urging a policy one way or the other. He was addressing personal attitudes. Our policies about recognition and confidentiality are always second to our own responsibility to give and to serve from pure motives.

2. What guidelines would you suggest regarding public prayers?

The one who prays in public prays to the Father, not to "be seen of men." Still, the prayer is offered for the benefit of the other worshipers in that it is intended to lead them in prayer. A sincere private prayer life will enhance the sincerity of public prayers. One should pray without using impressive words that are not natural to his or her own vocabulary. Clichés and well-worn phrases should also be avoided. The subject of the prayer, however, should include all those assembled. Intensely personal prayers are usually not appropriate in the public setting. The position of the prayer in the worship service should also be considered. An invocation will differ from a benediction. A prayer at the Lord's table should focus—almost exclusively—on the Lord's Supper and its meaning.

3. How much thought should we give to our words before leading a public prayer?

On the one hand, there is a danger in preparing our words so carefully that we fall into the unhealthy pattern of trying to impress those who hear. Yet, if we give no thought to our choice of words, we run the risk of becoming casual or flippant with the Lord God of the universe.

While prayer is simply conversing with God, it is also an incredible privilege made possible through the blood of Jesus. Our goal should be to communicate in a clear, meaningful way that shows respect for God and also leads others to join in thoughtful conversation with Him.

4. The lesson writer says, "To pray 'thy kingdom come' is to pledge submission to God." If our prayer is sincere, what kind of actions would you expect to see demonstrating this submission?

(1) Personal submission: we take the first step toward God's kingdom by submitting our own lives to His authority. This will be seen in our faith and holiness.

(2) Personal example: When our lives are submitted to God's lordship, we become positive examples to others. We actively demonstrate what it means to be part of God's kingdom. Our homes become places where Jesus always feels at home.

(3) Personal evangelism: We reflect Jesus' light in the dark kingdom of this world (Matthew 5:14-16). We serve as active ambassadors for Christ's kingdom in our schools, offices, factories, and community events. Others can then see the hope, peace, and meaning of a life submitted to Jesus.

5. How closely do you think we should try to follow the format of Jesus' "model prayer" in each of our own prayers?

The danger of following a specific format is that we can become mechanical, focusing more on the logistics than on actually praying.

On the other hand, following Jesus' model for prayer will help us maintain the proper balance in our prayers. It will assure that we begin with a proper acknowledgment of who God is (6:9) and keep our focus on God's will instead of our personal desires (6:10). Only then should we voice our petitions for daily provision, forgiveness, and the power to overcome temptation.

It should be noted that in public prayers the setting or occasion will affect our prayer format and content. A prayer for Communion, offering, or even a meal will have a more singular focus.

Miracles of Compassion

**Jan
16**

DEVOTIONAL READING: Matthew 11:2-6.

BACKGROUND SCRIPTURE: Matthew 9:18-38.

PRINTED TEXT: Matthew 9:18-31, 35, 36.

Matthew 9:18-31, 35, 36

18 While he spake these things unto them, behold, there came a certain ruler, and worshipped him, saying, My daughter is even now dead: but come and lay thy hand upon her, and she shall live.

19 And Jesus arose, and followed him, and so did his disciples.

20 And, behold, a woman, which was diseased with an issue of blood twelve years, came behind him, and touched the hem of his garment:

21 For she said within herself, If I may but touch his garment, I shall be whole.

22 But Jesus turned him about, and when he saw her, he said, Daughter, be of good comfort; thy faith hath made thee whole. And the woman was made whole from that hour.

23 And when Jesus came into the ruler's house, and saw the minstrels and the people making a noise,

24 He said unto them, Give place: for the maid is not dead, but sleepeth. And they laughed him to scorn.

25 But when the people were put forth, he went in, and took her by the hand, and the maid arose.

26 And the fame hereof went abroad into all that land.

27 And when Jesus departed thence, two blind men followed him, crying, and saying, Thou Son of David, have mercy on us.

28 And when he was come into the house, the blind men came to him: and Jesus saith unto them, Believe ye that I am able to do this? They said unto him, Yea, Lord.

29 Then touched he their eyes, saying, According to your faith be it unto you.

30 And their eyes were opened; and Jesus straitly charged them, saying, See that no man know it.

31 But they, when they were departed, spread abroad his fame in all that country.

. . . .

35 And Jesus went about all the cities and villages, teaching in their synagogues, and preaching the gospel of the kingdom, and healing every sickness and every disease among the people.

36 But when he saw the multitudes, he was moved with compassion on them, because they fainted, and were scattered abroad, as sheep having no shepherd.

GOLDEN TEXT: But when [Jesus] saw the multitudes, he was moved with compassion on them, because they fainted, and were scattered abroad, as sheep having no shepherd.—Matthew 9:36.

Johnson + Johnson
Vision
care

www WJLA.Com

Immanuel: God With Us
Unit 2: Ministry: Wonderful Words and Works
(Lessons 5-9)

Lesson Aims

After this lesson each student will be able to:

1. Retell the miracles performed by Jesus and recounted in today's text.

2. Tell how these miracles show the compassion of Jesus.

3. Demonstrate Jesus' compassion this week to someone in need.

Lesson Outline

INTRODUCTION
  A. Birds of the Air
  B. Lesson Background
 I. ACT OF DESPERATION (Matthew 9:18-22)
  A. When All Else Fails (vv. 18-21)
    Ask Jesus
  B. God Is Able (v. 22)
 II. CHALLENGE TO REASON (Matthew 9:23-26)
  A. When All Hope Is Gone (vv. 23, 24)
  B. God Gives Life (vv. 25, 26)
III. CRY FOR MERCY (Matthew 9:27-31)
  A. When People Suffer (vv. 27, 28)
  B. God Makes a Way (vv. 29-31)
IV. HEART OF COMPASSION (Matthew 9:35, 36)
  A. When People Are Lost (v. 35)
  B. God Still Cares (v. 36)
    Acting With Compassion
CONCLUSION
  A. Ready to Call
  B. Prayer
  C. Thought to Remember

Introduction

A. Birds of the Air

A duck hunter hits his target as it flies overhead, and then sends out his bird dog to retrieve it. A cat crouches under a bush, preparing to make a dash toward the unsuspecting birds in the birdbath. A baby bird ventures out of its nest too soon and falls to the ground below. Numerous times each day the words of Jesus come true: "Are not two sparrows sold for a farthing? and one of them shall not fall on the ground without your Father" (Matthew 10:29). The Creator of all life notices everything He has created; nothing that happens escapes His watchful eye.

Jesus exemplified the compassion of God in His ministry as day after day He reached out to those around Him who were hurting. And it should come as no surprise that so much of His time was spent helping others. After all, if God notices even a tiny bird that falls, He will certainly take an interest in those created in His own image when they are in need. For as Jesus went on to explain, "Fear ye not therefore, ye are of more value than many sparrows" (v. 31).

B. Lesson Background

The Old Testament book of Isaiah is sometimes referred to as "the Fifth Gospel" because it contains so many detailed prophecies regarding the coming Messiah, particularly His birth, His suffering, and His death. The prophet even predicts the impact of the Messiah's daily ministry. In one place he writes: "Then the eyes of the blind shall be opened, and the ears of the deaf shall be unstopped. Then shall the lame man leap as a hart, and the tongue of the dumb sing" (Isaiah 35:5, 6).

Jesus invested much of His ministry in performing miracles of healing. And while these miracles fulfilled prophecy and provided supernatural evidence that Jesus was God's appointed Messiah (John 5:36; Acts 2:22), there was much more to His miracles than this. Jesus was motivated by compassion. He truly cared about the people He touched and healed. He sympathized with the families who grieved. He healed, not only because He needed to for the sake of His mission, but because He wanted to for the sake of the people.

I. Act of Desperation (Matthew 9:18-22)

A. When All Else Fails (vv. 18-21)

18. While he spake these things unto them, behold, there came a certain ruler, and worshipped him, saying, My daughter is even now dead: but come and lay thy hand upon her, and she shall live.

Each day crowds of people gathered around Jesus with requests for healing. As soon as one person had been helped, there would be many others waiting their turn. The appearance of a father with a request regarding his *daughter* was not unusual; what was unusual was the position this man held.

The man who approached Jesus on this day was a *ruler* named Jairus (Mark 5:22), a religious official in one of the local Jewish synagogues. Since he knew of Jesus' reputation, he may have been from the Capernaum area, where Jesus focused much of His ministry. His daughter was twelve years old (Luke 8:42), suffering from an unknown ailment. Both Mark and Luke note that the girl was dying (Mark 5:23; Luke 8:42), while Matthew says that she was *even now dead*. According to Mark's fuller account of the story, the girl was "at the point of death" when Jairus left home to seek out Jesus. Later, while they were walking toward his house, Jairus received word that the girl had since died (Mark 5:35). Apparently Matthew is giving an abbreviated version that emphasizes the condition of the child when Jesus arrived at her home.

The religious leaders in general had not given Jesus' ministry a friendly reception, and most of them remained adversaries until the day they crucified Him. We do not know whether Jairus had once been part of this official opposition, but there was no place for animosity now—not with his daughter dying, and with no one else to turn to. He *worshipped* Jesus and expressed great respect for Him, proclaiming his faith in Jesus' healing power. [See question #1, page 176.]

ASK JESUS

Jairus did the one thing that he believed was necessary to save his daughter: *he asked Jesus for help*. He recognized that no one else could do for his daughter what Jesus could.

A minister planted a new church, which proceeded to experience a surge of growth. After several months, three of the key couples, in terms of involvement and financial commitment, had to move out of town because of a change in employment or some other cause. While the church maintained its health, it began to struggle financially.

One Sunday during the traditional "summer slump," the offering came to $700, far short of the weekly need. There were also several other bills that had to be paid; all told, the church needed $2,200 by the following Friday to pay these bills and to meet other expenses.

The minister remembered Jairus and his boldness in approaching Jesus about his daughter. He got on his knees and laid the needs of the church before the Lord. Literally while he was praying, the phone rang. One of the relatively inactive members of the church asked the minister to come to his house that afternoon, saying that he wanted to make a donation to the church.

On the way to the gentleman's house, the minister prayed again and asked the Lord to make the gift at least $1,000 in order to help reach the needed $2,200. After receiving an envelope with the man's check inside, the minister drove back to the church and opened the envelope. It contained a check for $10,000! Not only did the gift supply this new church's immediate need, but it

also helped get the church through the remainder of the summer.

Ask Jesus. He heard Jairus. He heard the minister of the new church. And He will hear you, if you will ask.   —D. R.

19. And Jesus arose, and followed him, and so did his disciples.

Jesus did not hesitate to respond to Jairus's desperate need and humble spirit.

20. And, behold, a woman, which was diseased with an issue of blood twelve years, came behind him, and touched the hem of his garment.

The most we are told about the plight of this *woman*, even by the physician Luke, is that she had some kind of persistent internal bleeding that could not be healed (Luke 8:43). She had used all of her resources to pay for various medical treatments, but they had only made her situation worse (Mark 5:26). Note that her *twelve years* of suffering matches the girl's age of twelve years. It seems, perhaps, more than coincidental, but the Scripture makes nothing of the similarity. We, therefore, ought to be cautious about drawing conclusions from it.

21. For she said within herself, If I may but touch his garment, I shall be whole.

Here was a daring act of faith. At this point in the ministry of Jesus there is no record of someone's being healed by touching Jesus' clothing. How this woman arrived at this idea, we are not told. But "desperate times call for desperate measures." Since her situation seemed hopeless otherwise, she was willing to try. [See question #2, page 176.]

B. God Is Able (v. 22)

22. But Jesus turned him about, and when he saw her, he said, Daughter, be of good comfort; thy faith hath made thee whole. And the woman was made whole from that hour.

Not only was the woman *made whole from that hour*, but, more precisely, at the very moment she touched "the border of his garment" (Luke 8:44). The timing was so exact that there was no mistaking the source of her healing.

Mark notes that Jesus felt healing power leave His body when the woman touched His robe. The disciples were dumbfounded when Jesus asked, "Who touched my clothes?" because there were many people touching Him. But Jesus looked directly at those around Him until finally the woman confessed that she was the one who had touched Him and received healing (Mark 5:30-33). Jesus sought out her confession, not to rebuke her for an unauthorized action, but that He might receive credit for the blessing she had

---

How to Say It

CAPERNAUM. Kuh-*per*-nay-um.
ISAIAH. Eye-*zay*-uh.
JAIRUS. *Jye*-rus or *Jay*-ih-rus.
MESSIANIC. Mess-ee-*an*-ick.

---

received from God through His Messianic ministry. The testimony of this miracle to Jesus' power was not to be lost on this crowd.

Thy faith hath made thee whole, Jesus then said to the woman. She had exhausted the healing arts of mankind, but to no avail. Believing that God was her only recourse left and that Jesus was the way to approach God, she touched Him and was blessed for her faith.

II. Challenge to Reason
(Matthew 9:23-26)

A. When All Hope Is Gone (vv. 23, 24)

23. And when Jesus came into the ruler's house, and saw the minstrels and the people making a noise.

By the time Jesus arrived at Jairus's house, not only had his daughter died, but the mourners had assembled. As was typical for that culture, neighbors would quickly gather at the home of the deceased and put on a noisy display of emotions on behalf of the grieving family (who tended to remain secluded inside the home). *Minstrels* (musicians) would play sad funeral dirges, and people would publicly weep while uttering loud wailing sounds. Mark accurately describes the sound as a "tumult," or what we might call a "commotion" (Mark 5:38).

24. He said unto them, Give place: for the maid is not dead, but sleepeth. And they laughed him to scorn.

Jesus' statement *the maid is not dead, but sleepeth* was met with derisive laughter, for His words defied all reason and logic. But these scoffers would later remember what Jesus said, and how a dead girl came to life again as if she had only been sleeping.

B. God Gives Life (vv. 25, 26)

25. But when the people were put forth, he went in, and took her by the hand, and the maid arose.

Jesus cleared the house of all spectators except for the girl's parents and His three closest disciples—Peter, James, and John (Luke 8:51). The crowd was removed because their mocking attitude made them unworthy of taking part in the special event that was soon to occur.

Jesus *took* the girl *by the hand*, summoned her to arise (Mark 5:41), and *the maid arose*. Once again, there was no doubt that a miracle had occurred and that Jesus was the source of it.

26. And the fame hereof went abroad into all that land.

As He often did during His Galilean ministry, Jesus gave the parents of the girl strict orders not to broadcast this miracle (Mark 5:43). The persistent problem Jesus faced was that His miracles often drew larger crowds than He could manage. As thousands pressed in upon Him, they presented a danger to themselves and to His disciples (Luke 12:1).

In addition the crowds also wanted to manipulate Jesus' ministry by forcing Him to keep on healing when He wanted to preach (Mark 1:32-38) or to lead them as an earthly king (John 6:15). In some cases Jesus stayed away from the cities in order to avoid the huge crowds, yet they always seemed to find Him anyway (Mark 1:45). Here, in spite of what Jesus said, His *fame . . . went abroad into all that land*; because the joy of experiencing God's power when all hope is gone is too great to keep locked up inside.

III. Cry for Mercy
(Matthew 9:27-31)

A. When People Suffer (vv. 27, 28)

27. And when Jesus departed thence, two blind men followed him, crying, and saying, Thou Son of David, have mercy on us.

Raising the dead is such an extraordinary miracle that it would provide an appropriate occasion to stop and take a break for the remainder of the day. Actually, Jesus had had a full day of healing, including having to travel slowly through a massive crowd over whatever distance it took to reach the home of Jairus. It was apparently time for Him to retire for the day. Thus He did not stop to heal the *two blind men* (or apparently anyone else) who called out to Him along the way, but kept moving forward.

One of the hard truths for a compassionate heart to accept is that we do not have the time or energy to help everyone who calls out for us. Even as Jesus balanced healing with His preaching and teaching, so we must balance our service for Christ with our other work and family responsibilities. And, like Jesus, we must be disciplined enough to know when to quit and refresh ourselves in order to be prepared adequately for later tasks. [See question #3, page 176.]

28. And when he was come into the house, the blind men came to him: and Jesus saith unto them, Believe ye that I am able to do this? They said unto him, Yea, Lord.

The house that Jesus entered was not likely that of Jairus, but a place where He and His disciples could rest each evening. It may have been the home of a family member or friend of Jesus. It was probably the home that served as His "headquarters" whenever He was in Capernaum.

These *blind men* pleaded for a hearing with Jesus, driven as they were by the misery of darkness and alienation that they endured day after day. They cried out for mercy and drew the attention of Jesus by the faith and persistence that they demonstrated when they followed Him all the way home. This was no easy task for blind men on crowded streets, but they refused to abandon their cause.

B. God Makes a Way (vv. 29-31)

29. Then touched he their eyes, saying, According to your faith be it unto you.

Jesus enjoys distributing His blessings *according to* one's *faith*. However, this should not be understood to mean that possessing faith automatically results in a life of blessings. Many faithful saints will suffer much in this lifetime, and only after they have departed this world will they "rest from their labors" (Revelation 14:13). We are to give thanks in every situation (1 Thessalonians 5:18), acknowledging that even in the most trying of circumstances God is working for our good (Romans 8:28)—a perspective that can be grasped only *according to* one's *faith*.

30. And their eyes were opened; and Jesus straitly charged them, saying, See that no man know it.

Once again Jesus *straitly charged* (sternly warned) those whom He healed not to draw any more attention to Him. As this story illustrates, the crowd control problem was sometimes so great that Jesus could not even rest in a house without people seeking to get in. [See question #4, page 176.]

31. But they, when they were departed, spread abroad his fame in all that country.

The news of miraculous healing continued to *spread*, despite Jesus' best efforts to slow it down. If only Christians had the same enthusiasm today for publicizing the greater "healing" that has occurred in our souls—the forgiveness of our sins and life anew in the Spirit!

IV. Heart of Compassion (Matthew 9:35, 36)

A. When People Are Lost (v. 35)

35. And Jesus went about all the cities and villages, teaching in their synagogues, and preaching the gospel of the kingdom, and healing every sickness and every disease among the people.

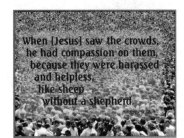

Visual for lesson 7

Today's visual challenges us to see the multitudes of today as Jesus saw the crowds in His day: as "sheep having no shepherd."

This verse provides a good summary of the priorities of Jesus' ministry. His first concern was His *teaching* and *preaching*, which He confirmed through His *healing* ministry.

The theme of Jesus' preaching was *the gospel of the kingdom*. Jesus taught that His kingdom was not something to be seen and touched, but something "within you" (Luke 17:21). He told Pilate that His kingdom was "not of this world" (John 18:36). For Jesus, the *kingdom* means a relationship with the King, not a geographical region. The kingdom of God exists wherever there is someone in total submission to the will of God, for when there is someone in charge (a king) and someone who serves (the subject), then there is a kingdom.

Thus when Jesus preached about the kingdom of God, He was preparing hearts for the challenge He would later issue through the Great Commission. The church is to go out and "make disciples" (Matthew 28:19, *New International Version*)—that is, recruit people who will commit themselves to Jesus as their Master, Lord, and King. While a "heavenly kingdom" awaits the faithful (2 Timothy 4:18), our kingdom relationship begins now when we make a faith commitment to the lordship of Jesus Christ.

Jesus was able to heal *every sickness and every disease among the people*. His ministry of healing stands in sharp contrast with the so-called faith healers of today. Whereas Jesus would take on any physical affliction (and even death), modern faith healers are selective. Generally avoiding congenital ailments and incurable diseases, they usually focus on internal conditions that are not easily or immediately substantiated. And, as we have already noted, Jesus' healings were instantaneous, occurring at the moment He acted or spoke, and never produced a failure. What a contrast to the modern healer who makes several attempts to cure, then blames any failure on the lack of faith of those who come to him. Whatever is actually going on with contemporary faith healers, it is no match for what Scripture tells us Jesus did.

B. God Still Cares (v. 36)

36. But when he saw the multitudes, he was moved with compassion on them, because they fainted, and were scattered abroad, as sheep having no shepherd.

Both the English word *compassion* and the Greek word behind it literally mean "to feel with" someone else. The spirit of compassion is to feel someone else's hurts and pains, then desire to relieve their misery.

Jesus was motivated by the spirit of compassion. Although there was a "theological necessity" for His healings, supplying divine proof for His Messianic claims, Jesus was also *moved with compassion*. His was a heart that could not look upon hurting people without longing to reach out and relieve their misery. [See question #5, page 176.]

ACTING WITH COMPASSION

Just as Jesus was "moved with compassion" in response to the needs of others, so we as His followers need to cultivate hearts of compassion.

A godly gentleman served as an elder in his church. He was active in many areas of the life of the congregation and was involved in several parachurch organizations as well. His commitment to the kingdom of God made him highly respected in his church and community.

One day, while the elder was doing some finishing touches on a house he was building, a young man from across the street, who was "high" on a heavy amount of illegal drugs, entered the house where the elder was working and took this man's life. He was caught, convicted of the crime, and eventually sent to prison for a lengthy term.

While the young man was awaiting trial, the wife of the elder began coming to the jail where he was kept and spending time with the man who had killed her husband. Displaying a tremendous heart of compassion, she took him cookies and gave him her husband's Bible to read. In time, the minister of the church where the man had been an elder baptized this young man into Jesus Christ.

The actions of this elder's wife truly demonstrated the compassion of Jesus to one of the "sheep having no shepherd." Her courageous witness illustrates an important principle: the world can never know the compassion of Jesus without experiencing it through His people.   —D. R.

Conclusion

A. Ready to Call

No one wants to have to make an emergency phone call. But check out the phone(s) in most of our homes and you will see that we are ready to call for help if necessary. Our speed dial buttons are set with the emergency numbers we need to summon the police and rescue squad, as well as to contact close family members. Perhaps there is an emergency sticker on the phone, reminding our children to dial 911. And for those occasions when we leave the children with a baby-sitter, there will be a note with special instructions for the evening. We hope we never need all of these numbers, but we are ready just the same.

Now for a spiritual inventory. Do we have God's "number" ready to call in times of need? Often, when problems come our way, we scramble to deal with them the best that we can, only to realize later that we forgot to support our efforts with prayer. Too often God is an afterthought; we come to Him only after we have exhausted our own resources, finally realizing that we need *His* help.

Oh, the unnecessary grief we bring upon ourselves when we do not think to call first upon the wise and understanding compassion of our Father in Heaven!

B. Prayer

Father, help us to draw near to You in times of trouble. Then help us to imitate our Lord and Savior by assisting those around us who are in need of acts of compassion. We ask in His name. Amen.

C. Thought to Remember

Others will never know of the compassion of Christ unless they see it in His followers.

Home Daily Bible Readings

Monday, Jan. 10—Jesus Continues His Healing Work (Matthew 8:1-17)

Tuesday, Jan. 11—Jesus Heals the Gadarene Demoniacs (Matthew 8:28—9:1)

Wednesday, Jan. 12—Jesus Heals a Paralytic (Matthew 9:2-8)

Thursday, Jan. 13—Jesus Gives Life and Healing (Matthew 9:18-26)

Friday, Jan. 14—Jesus Heals the Blind and Mute (Matthew 9:27-38)

Saturday, Jan. 15—Jesus Heals a Man's Withered Hand (Matthew 12:9-14)

Sunday, Jan. 16—The Faith of a Canaanite Woman (Matthew 15:21-31)

Learning by Doing

This page contains an alternate lesson plan emphasizing learning activities.
Classes desiring such student involvement will find these suggestions helpful.

Learning Goals

After this lesson each student will be able to:

1. Retell the miracles performed by Jesus and recounted in today's text.

2. Tell how these miracles show the compassion of Jesus.

3. Demonstrate Jesus' compassion this week to someone in need.

Into the Lesson

Today's lesson deals with Jesus' compassion, His motive for ministry and miracles. Call attention to the fact that one of the characteristics of a Christian is to be compassionate.

Prepare a chart or chalkboard with the acrostic COMPASSION written down the side. Say, "What are some words, beginning with these letters, that describe a person with compassion?" (Examples include Comforting, Openness, Motivated, Purposeful, Awareness, Sensitivity, Serving, Intense, Observant, Needs-oriented.) This activity is in the student book.

Many of us in this class today have experienced Christ's compassion in our lives. As we explore today's text, we will determine to show compassion to others.

Into the Word

Prepare a mini-lecture on Jesus' miracles in the New Testament. Use material in the commentary section of the lesson to talk about the purpose being apologetic, the motive being compassion, and the balance needed for ministry.

Distribute the following true/false quiz based on today's text. In groups of two to four, students are to read the Scripture (Matthew 9:18-31, 35, 36) and complete the quiz. Reasons for the answers are printed to help the teacher discuss the material further.

___1. The ruler asked Jesus to speak and his daughter would be healed. *(False, verse 18; the ruler asked Jesus to touch her.)*

___2. The woman with bleeding had been ill twelve years. *(True, verse 20.)*

___3. Jesus touched the woman to heal her. *(False, verse 20; the woman touched Jesus' clothing.)*

___4. Jesus told the woman that His faith had made her well. *(False, verse 22; Jesus said her faith had made her whole. See the commentary notes for a fuller treatment of this issue.)*

___5. Jesus told the people that the girl was asleep. *(True, verse 23. Of course, they knew that she was dead; the commentary gives additional notes concerning Jesus' challenge to the crowd.)*

___6. Jesus asked the blind men if they believed He could heal them. *(True, verse 28; even their behavior speaks of their belief.)*

___7. Jesus encouraged the men to speak freely of His miracle. *(False, verse 30; the commentary speaks of the intensity of the crowd.)*

___8. Jesus' miracles were instantaneous. *(True; see the comments on verse 35 to expand on this point.)*

___9. Jesus' compassion was for those without a shepherd. *(True, verse 36. Be sure to emphasize to your students that Jesus has compassion for them as well.)*

Into Life

Ask, "If you had been in the crowd for any of these miracles, what would you have felt? What would you have thought? How does this help you to understand the goodness of God? If you had been there, could you have kept quiet concerning these miracles?"

During the week, as you prepare for this lesson, collect newspaper and magazine articles showing the compassion of people toward others. Distribute these articles to your groups, asking them to identify the situation, the compassion shown, and the results. For example, you may find stories about a hospitalized child and individuals who raised money to help with the bills, bringing thanks from grateful parents.

We recognize a person's compassion by his or her actions. How did Jesus' actions show His compassion? *(He desired to reach out and relieve misery. He was willing to be "inconvenienced" to help. He met real needs.)*

Have each group make a list of issues people face today and the ways in which compassion can be shown. Be sure to involve each group by using its suggestions.

Have each class member choose a situation familiar to him or her in which compassion is necessary. Encourage each to list the need, the person involved, and the response the student will give. Have each student choose a prayer partner. Share the concern. Pray for strength to act. Establish a time when a checkup will be made on the commitment.

Let's Talk It Over

The questions on this page are designed to encourage review of the lesson Scriptures and to promote discussion of the lesson by the class. The answers provided are only discussion starters. Let your class talk it over from there.

1. How should we react today when a person who has been antagonistic toward Christ and the church begins attending church as a result of a crisis that has left him or her desperate?

Unfortunately, the tendency for many long-time church members is to feel skeptical and maybe even react negatively toward such a one. Rather than rejoice that God has opened a door for ministry and teaching, we sometimes question the person's sincerity and motives.

Even if such a one is not honestly seeking the proper way of life, we should still consider his or her attendance as an opportunity to reflect Jesus' compassion and offer a testimony of how God has met our own needs, especially when we faced certain crises. This person's desperate situation may provide our only opportunity to point him or her to Jesus. We dare not miss that opportune moment!

2. What are some situations that can seem hopeless to people today? What, if anything, does today's text offer to people in hopeless situations?

The situations faced by Jairus and the woman with the bleeding disorder typify two such situations: death of a loved one and long-term illness. There are many others—loss of a job, a failed marriage, a financial crisis, etc.

On the one hand, this passage may not seem to offer hope. After all, Jesus is not physically present to help as He did here. The dead stay dead; the terminally ill eventually join them; and even the situations that do improve only do so, it seems, over many weeks that seem even longer.

This passage does offer assurance that God is in control. Though He may not instantly reverse our misfortune, He can and will see us through it. His grace is sufficient (2 Corinthians 12:9).

3. As we try to help hurting people, how can we determine when it is time to withdraw for personal refreshment and renewal, and when we should stay and minister to one more person?

There will always be hurting people and undone work. Yet we must remember Jesus' example. He knew that if He did not regularly withdraw to be with God the Father, He would not be able to minister adequately to the multitudes clamoring for His attention.

We also need to understand our own limitations. At what point do we cease to think clearly and work effectively? Will we get more done with less effort after a good night's sleep?

We also must determine a person's level of need. Will waiting another day make much difference? Is this a life-threatening situation? Can someone else help the person?

4. In the case of the infirm woman, Jesus deliberately called attention to her so that, according to our lesson writer, "He might receive credit for the blessing she had received from God." But Jairus was told not to broadcast the miracle of raising his daughter (Mark 5:43) and the blind men were also charged, "See that no man know it." Why do you suppose Jesus wanted one miracle known but not the others? What difference does it make today?

This is puzzling. For the most part, Jesus was trying to play down the sensational aspects of His ministry to prevent a premature climax and showdown with the religious leaders. But occasionally He did tell the one healed to "return to thine own house, and show how great things God hath done unto thee" (Luke 8:39).

Perhaps we should simply conclude that Jesus has the answers even when we do not. For His own purposes He told some people to spread the news and others to refrain. He has told us to spread the news (Matthew 28:18-20). Our responsibility is to obey. Telling of these marvelous events is part of our obedience.

5. Jesus was moved with compassion for the people, seeing them "as sheep having no shepherd." What do you think would happen if all Christians began to see people with the same compassion Jesus had?

Surely we would respond as Jesus did. While we cannot work miracles, there is much we can do to relieve the suffering of the sick and the handicapped. Are we doing all we can? Are our services and facilities designed to assist them in worship? Could we make them more so?

Jesus' greater priority was preaching the good news. If we truly saw the lost as lost, with a full appreciation of how tragic that condition is, we would be less hesitant to share our faith and would urge others to accept Jesus.

Opposition to Jesus

DEVOTIONAL READING: Matthew 12:1-14.

BACKGROUND SCRIPTURE: Matthew 12.

PRINTED TEXT: Matthew 12:22-32, 38-41.

Matthew 12:22-32, 38-41

22 Then was brought unto him one possessed with a devil, blind, and dumb: and he healed him, insomuch that the blind and dumb both spake and saw.

23 And all the people were amazed, and said, Is not this the Son of David?

24 But when the Pharisees heard it, they said, This fellow doth not cast out devils, but by Beelzebub the prince of the devils.

25 And Jesus knew their thoughts, and said unto them, Every kingdom divided against itself is brought to desolation; and every city or house divided against itself shall not stand:

26 And if Satan cast out Satan, he is divided against himself; how shall then his kingdom stand?

27 And if I by Beelzebub cast out devils, by whom do your children cast them out? therefore they shall be your judges.

28 But if I cast out devils by the Spirit of God, then the kingdom of God is come unto you.

29 Or else, how can one enter into a strong man's house, and spoil his goods, except he first bind the strong man? and then he will spoil his house.

30 He that is not with me is against me; and he that gathereth not with me scattereth abroad.

31 Wherefore I say unto you, All manner of sin and blasphemy shall be forgiven unto men: but the blasphemy against the Holy Ghost shall not be forgiven unto men.

32 And whosoever speaketh a word against the Son of man, it shall be forgiven him: but whosoever speaketh against the Holy Ghost, it shall not be forgiven him, neither in this world, neither in the world to come.

. . . .

38 Then certain of the scribes and of the Pharisees answered, saying, Master, we would see a sign from thee.

39 But he answered and said unto them, An evil and adulterous generation seeketh after a sign; and there shall no sign be given to it, but the sign of the prophet Jonah:

40 For as Jonah was three days and three nights in the whale's belly; so shall the Son of man be three days and three nights in the heart of the earth.

41 The men of Nineveh shall rise in judgment with this generation, and shall condemn it: because they repented at the preaching of Jonah; and, behold, a greater than Jonah is here.

Jan 23

GOLDEN TEXT: He that is not with me is against me; and he that gathereth not with me scattereth abroad.—Matthew 12:30.

Immanuel: God With Us
Unit 2: Ministry: Wonderful Words and Works
(Lessons 5-9)

Lesson Aims

After participating in this lesson, each student will be able to:

1. Summarize the controversy between Jesus and the Pharisees described in today's text.

2. Tell how Jesus' acts and teachings answer those who oppose Christianity today.

3. Prepare a statement of faith that answers the criticisms he or she most often hears from unbelievers.

Lesson Outline

INTRODUCTION
   A. A Sign Opposed
   B. Lesson Background
 I. KINGDOM OF GOD (Matthew 12:22-30)
   A. Bold Challenge (vv. 22-24)
   B. Foolish Idea (vv. 25-27)
   C. Strong Stand (vv. 28-30)
 II. SIN AGAINST THE SPIRIT (Matthew 12:31, 32)
   A. Unpardonable Sin (v. 31)
   B. Eternal Consequences (v. 32)
 III. SIGN OF JONAH (Matthew 12:38-41)
   A. Closed Mind (v. 38)
   B. Sure Sign (vv. 39, 40)
   C. Clear Warning (v. 41)
    Get to the Heart
CONCLUSION
   A. I Know Too Much
   B. Prayer
   C. Thought to Remember

Introduction

A. A Sign Opposed

No matter how wrong the world may seem, all is forgotten when we hold a baby in our arms. For those few moments we see innocence, beauty, and hope for a brighter future. And when we return to the cares of this life, we always treasure our memories of that precious, innocent child.

As Mary, the mother of Jesus, held her special child in her arms, there was much that she could have "pondered . . . in her heart" (Luke 2:19). "What a glorious future must lie ahead for my Son!" she may have thought as she reflected on the words that the angel Gabriel had spoken to her months earlier (Luke 1:28-37). Yet how troubled her thoughts must have become when she and Joseph met an old man named Simeon in the temple and heard his prophecy that the child would be "a sign to be opposed" (Luke 2:34, *New American Standard Bible*). Simeon went on to tell Mary, "A sword shall pierce through thy own soul also" (Luke 2:35). The word *also* indicates that the sword would pierce Jesus as well—a veiled reference to His death.

In last week's lesson we noted how huge crowds often surrounded Jesus during His ministry—seeking His assistance, clinging to His every word. The "flip side" of this popularity is that Jesus' years of ministry were marked by severe opposition from start to finish, culminating in His crucifixion at Calvary.

B. Lesson Background

The first instance of opposition to Jesus during His public ministry occurred shortly after He had established His headquarters in Capernaum (Matthew 4:13). He made a brief trip to Jerusalem for the Passover (John 2:13). While He was there, He chased the merchants out of the temple (John 2:14-16). The hostile response from the religious leaders was only a foretaste of what Jesus would experience each time He returned to the city of Jerusalem.

In addition, opposition to Jesus was present even in His hometown of Nazareth. The first time He visited and identified Himself as the Messiah of prophecy, His former neighbors were so offended that they attempted to force Him off a cliff (Luke 4:16-29).

The encounter that is the subject of today's lesson was not as dangerous as the one in Nazareth, but it was more vicious. On this occasion the assault did not involve the threat of physical violence; instead, it came in the form of a most slanderous charge: that Jesus was actually an agent of Satan. The battle lines were clearly being drawn.

I. Kingdom of God
(Matthew 12:22-30)

A. Bold Challenge (vv. 22-24)

22. Then was brought unto him one possessed with a devil, blind, and dumb: and he healed him, insomuch that the blind and dumb both spake and saw.

One of the most impressive miracles a person could perform is to free another individual from the influence of a demonic spirit. While all supernatural healings are amazing events, this healing is special in that it involves a face-to-face confrontation with an evil and powerful enemy. Thus, when the seventy disciples reported to Jesus about the miraculous signs they had performed, their greatest thrill was in casting out demons (Luke 10:17). Our text speaks of an individual being *possessed with a devil*, though today we tend to refer to Satan as "the devil" and his associates as "demons."

One of the characteristics of demon possession revealed in Scripture is that demons tended to abuse their victims physically. The people Jesus confronted were often afflicted with ailments such as the lack of sight and speech (the man in our text is an example), or with torments such as causing the victim to cut himself with sharp objects (Mark 5:5) or to throw himself into a fire (Matthew 17:15).

23. And all the people were amazed, and said, Is not this the Son of David?

When Jesus challenged the power of Satan and cast out demons, some wondered if He might be *the Son of David*—one of several expressions for the Messiah (Matthew 22:42). This is not to say that any person who cast out demons had to be the Messiah, for Jesus' disciples could also do this. But miraculous signs served to confirm the claims made by the person working the miracles (John 3:2; 5:36; 10:38; 14:11). Thus Jesus' claim to be the Messiah was reinforced by His miraculous power over demons. [See question #1, page 184.]

24. But when the Pharisees heard it, they said, This fellow doth not cast out devils, but by Beelzebub the prince of the devils.

Beelzebub is a variant spelling of the ancient name "Baal-zebub," which was the title of one of the local Canaanite pagan gods in Old Testament times (2 Kings 1:2). Some Bible students believe that *Beelzebub* (meaning "lord of the flies") was a name meant to ridicule the actual name of the supposed deity, which was *Beelzebul* (meaning "lord of the house"). In fact, Beelzebul is the form of the name that appears in the Greek text of this passage. The significance of the name "lord of the house" is especially clear in the context of Jesus' response to the Pharisees' charge (see verse 29).

For now, let us note that by the first century, Beelzebul had become one of the titles that the Jews used for Satan. This means that the charge the Pharisees leveled against Jesus was the lowest form of slander against someone claiming to represent God. They were crediting Jesus' miraculous works to the power of Satan. The implication of such a charge was either that Jesus was Himself deceived regarding who was empowering Him, or that He was knowingly working in league with the devil and thus operating under false pretenses. Jesus could not allow such an accusation to go unchallenged.

B. Foolish Idea (vv. 25-27)

25. And Jesus knew their thoughts, and said unto them, Every kingdom divided against itself is brought to desolation; and every city or house divided against itself shall not stand.

These words constitute a principle that has stood the test of time. Any organization that allows internal conflicts to continue unchecked is destined for failure. [See question #2, page 184.]

26. And if Satan cast out Satan, he is divided against himself; how shall then his kingdom stand?

Jesus offered a very rational application of the "house divided" principle to the slanderous charge against Him. Suppose it were true that Jesus was operating by the powers of *Satan*. Considering the aggressiveness with which Jesus had attacked demonic spirits during His ministry thus far, did it make sense that Satan would support such a ministry? Only a fool would continue to supply the supernatural power that was being used against him. The logical conclusion is that Satan cannot be the source of Jesus' power, or he would have cut it off long ago.

27. And if I by Beelzebub cast out devils, by whom do your children cast them out? therefore they shall be your judges.

The next argument Jesus used also shows the foolishness (as well as the hypocrisy) of the Pharisees' accusation against Him. They taught their own disciples (*children*) how to *cast out devils*. Thus to argue that it requires a Satanic power to cast out demons would in effect be an indictment against themselves.

Jesus' incidental reference to the Pharisees' casting out demons raises the question of just

---

Home Daily Bible Readings

Monday, Jan. 17—Plucking Grain on the Sabbath (Matthew 12:1-8)

Tuesday, Jan. 18—Jesus Accused as Beelzebub's Partner (Matthew 12:22-32)

Wednesday, Jan. 19—Understand the Signs of the Times (Matthew 12:33-45)

Thursday, Jan. 20—Jesus Is Rejected at Nazareth (Matthew 13:54-58)

Friday, Jan. 21—Confrontation Between Jesus and the Pharisees (Matthew 15:1-9)

Saturday, Jan. 22—Jesus' Enemies Demand a Sign (Matthew 16:1-12)

Sunday, Jan. 23—Peter Declares That Jesus Is the Christ (Matthew 16:13-20)

what exactly these men were capable of doing, and by what means. We would not expect that the Pharisees were empowered by the Holy Spirit, given their opposition to the work of the Holy Spirit in Jesus Christ. Nor is it likely that they were empowered by Satan, using the same logic Jesus used to defend Himself. If they were successful in casting out demons, then perhaps they were doing it through the means that Jesus suggested His disciples use: "prayer and fasting" (Mark 9:29).

The difference between this approach and a supernatural gift such as the one Jesus and His disciples possessed is that the gift can effect an immediate release from the demon, with all the evidence of a miracle in the eyes of those who observe. Prayer and fasting, on the other hand, takes time to accomplish its objective. It may have been this difference that accounted for the crowds' being "amazed" at the manner in which Jesus cast out demons (v. 23). His work was a powerful, instantaneous miracle of God, not simply an eventual response to fervent and persistent prayer.

C. Strong Stand (vv. 28-30)

28. But if I cast out devils by the Spirit of God, then the kingdom of God is come unto you.

Jesus could not be operating by the power of Satan, since He continually assaulted the kingdom of Satan. He was obviously doing something bigger than what was achieved through prayer and fasting, since He obtained immediate and impressive results. By the process of elimination, Jesus had proven that He was empowered by the *Spirit of God*.

Now came the challenging implication for the Pharisees: the power of God within Jesus confirmed the claims being made by Jesus. He is the Messiah, the Son of David. *The kingdom of God is come unto you*, for the King Himself was standing before them.

29. Or else, how can one enter into a strong man's house, and spoil his goods, except he first bind the strong man? and then he will spoil his house.

Jesus provided a further application of His "house divided" principle. Each time He freed an individual from demonic influence, He took from Satan people whom Satan saw as his own "possessions." Consider how this language was, in effect, a response to the original charge of the Pharisees. If Satan is, as the Pharisees called him, *Beelzebul* (the "lord of the house"), then Jesus must be very powerful if He is able to enter into such a *strong man's house*, *bind* him, and then "loot" him by seizing his *goods* (people under his influence). There is only one power ca-

pable of meeting such a challenge: Jesus must possess the power of God.

30. He that is not with me is against me; and he that gathereth not with me scattereth abroad.

The battle lines were drawn. The Pharisees knew too much about the power of Jesus to take a neutral position with any kind of intellectual or moral integrity. The choice facing them was clear: either to support Jesus in His Messianic ministry, or, by default, to be rejected by Jesus and by God. [See question #3, page 184.]

II. Sin Against the Spirit (Matthew 12:31, 32)

A. Unpardonable Sin (v. 31)

31. Wherefore I say unto you, All manner of sin and blasphemy shall be forgiven unto men: but the blasphemy against the Holy Ghost shall not be forgiven unto men.

One of the most terrifying warnings in Scripture is this reference to a sin that is "unpardonable." There are many theories regarding the *blasphemy against the Holy Ghost*, but most have little to do with the incident that we have seen developing in this chapter. The key to interpreting this verse (or any verse of Scripture, for that matter) is to look at the context.

Since the Pharisees were being warned about this sin, they had apparently not yet crossed the line. Even so, it was their charge—that Jesus was empowered by Satan rather than the Holy Spirit—that led to this warning. With this understanding as our starting point, some reasonable conclusions can be derived from this text.

First, blasphemy against the Holy Spirit has something to do with denying the Spirit's powerful witness to Jesus Christ. Furthermore, it is a slander against the Holy Spirit; for when His divine powers are said to be Satan's powers, He is truly being "blasphemed." Blasphemy against the Holy Spirit also seems to involve a deliberate and willful rejection of the Holy Spirit's evidence on behalf of Jesus. Such an attitude is not an honest doubt that needs more time to reason through the data; it is a recognition of the truth and a refusal to accept it. This is the line the Pharisees were being warned not to cross.

Perhaps this sin can best be likened to the attitude of Satan himself. He knows the truth about Jesus; he and all his cohorts "believe" in Jesus (James 2:19). And yet Satan has willfully chosen to reject the authority of God and to oppose the ministry of Jesus. This is a perversion of the will so deep that one cannot recover from it, and therefore God cannot forgive.

Let us keep in mind that this is not a sin we would expect to see often, if ever. After all, even

Jesus' staunchest enemies, the Pharisees, had not yet reached this level of opposition. Thus, we should continue to evangelize all those who reject the gospel of Jesus Christ; because what we will likely confront is not the willful and final rejection of a truth that these individuals know, but the resistance of a truth of which they have not yet been persuaded. [See question #4, page 184.]

As for the Christian who is worried that he may have committed the unpardonable sin at some point in his past, the fact that he is troubled by this possibility suggests that he has never reached this level of perversion. He is to be encouraged to repent of the sins he has committed and renew his pledge of faith to Christ.

B. Eternal Consequences (v. 32)

32. And whosoever speaketh a word against the Son of man, it shall be forgiven him: but whosoever speaketh against the Holy Ghost, it shall not be forgiven him, neither in this world, neither in the world to come.

Why is speaking *against the Son of man* more tolerable than speaking *against the Holy Ghost*? Consider that Jesus made His exceptional claims while He was in His incarnate state, and it is always reasonable to be cautious when a man claims to be God. While preaching in human form, Jesus looked not unlike any other man who might make such an incredible claim—and there were many in His day who claimed to be great leaders (cf. Acts 5:34-39). There was nothing about Jesus' appearance that would have given Him an advantage over these other claimants—or over those who Jesus predicted would come after Him (Matthew 24:5).

Thus to "speak against Jesus" and doubt His claims would not be unreasonable—that is, until the Holy Spirit provided indisputable, supernatural witness to Christ through the apostles (John 14:26; 16:13, 14; 17:20). A rejection at this point would not be against the Son of Man, but against the Holy Spirit who testifies on His behalf.

Visual for
lesson 8

Today's visual is a timely reminder that we must choose to be either with Jesus or against Him. There truly is "No Middle Ground."

The consequences of blaspheming against the Spirit and His witness to Jesus are as severe as one can imagine: *it shall not be forgiven him, neither in this world, neither in the world to come.* The Spirit's word concerning Jesus is God's last word. One rejects it at his own eternal peril.

III. Sign of Jonah
(Matthew 12:38-41)
A. Closed Mind (v. 38)

38. Then certain of the scribes and of the Pharisees answered, saying, Master, we would see a sign from thee.

There was something less than honest about the demand of the *scribes* and the *Pharisees* for a *sign*. This becomes especially apparent when one notes that Jesus had just provided several such signs (vv. 15, 22). Apparently the scribes and Pharisees expected to set the terms for the sign they demanded and to name the type of miracle they wanted to see.

B. Sure Sign (vv. 39, 40)

39. But he answered and said unto them, An evil and adulterous generation seeketh after a sign; and there shall no sign be given to it, but the sign of the prophet Jonah.

The Pharisees and their compatriots were *an evil and adulterous generation*. They had committed spiritual adultery in failing to live as God's covenant people. And, like the adulterous husband who cheats on his wife, they were being malicious and dishonest in their discussion with Jesus. They said that if they were given the proper *sign*, they would believe Jesus' claims. Their opposition to Jesus remained so strong, however, that they would never have changed their minds, no matter how many signs He gave them.

Jesus was willing, however, to grant His critics a special sign—*the sign of the prophet Jonah*. What Jesus offered as the ultimate proof for His claims was a third-day resurrection (Matthew 16:21; John 2:18-22). Certainly a resurrection miracle in and of itself is extraordinary; but naming the day of the resurrection is even more impressive, and thus provides even stronger credentials for Jesus.

The key to this sign of the resurrection is that it would most assuredly be an act of God. Once Jesus was dead, He would be totally dependent upon the actions of God, because dead people do not perform miracles (or do any other works). If Jesus rose from the grave on the third day, there would be no other reasonable explanation except the hand of God. The third-day resurrection promise became the ultimate sign for Jesus and the test by which His word would be proven to be either genuine or false (Romans 1:3, 4). And it is the miracle upon which our faith stands firm today (1 Corinthians 15:12-20).

40. For as Jonah was three days and three nights in the whale's belly; so shall the Son of man be three days and three nights in the heart of the earth.

Some Christians are bothered by the Biblical account of Jesus' death on a Friday afternoon and His resurrection on a Sunday morning, because it does not comprise three days and three nights. The problem is resolved when we understand the Jewish practice of "rounding off" numbers when counting time, in adding, and (as we saw in lesson 3) in recording a genealogy. It is important to observe that the Jewish people who were present when the resurrection happened counted Sunday as the "third day" since the crucifixion of Christ (Luke 24:21; 1 Corinthians 15:4). Jesus fulfilled His third-day resurrection sign.

C. Clear Warning (v. 41)

41. The men of Nineveh shall rise in judgment with this generation, and shall condemn it: because they repented at the preaching of Jonah; and, behold, a greater than Jonah is here.

What greater shame could there be for the Jewish leaders than to have an evil, pagan nation like Assyria (whose capital was *Nineveh*) *condemn* them at God's final *judgment?* At least *the men of Nineveh* recognized their need to change their ways. The Pharisees were unwilling to do this, in spite of the fact that *a greater than Jonah is here.* [See question #5, page 184.]

GET TO THE HEART

A man working in his garden noticed a large, green, healthy-looking squash plant. The stems

---

How to Say It

ASSYRIA. Uh-*sear*-ee-uh.
BAAL-ZEBUB. *Bay*-ul-*zee*-bub (strong accent on *zee*).
BEELZEBUB. Bih-*el*-zih-bub.
BEELZEBUL. Bih-*el*-zih-bull.
CALVARY. *Cal*-vuh-ree.
CANAANITE. *Kay*-nun-ite.
CAPERNAUM. Kuh-*per*-nay-um.
GABRIEL. *Gay*-bree-ul.
MESSIANIC. Mess-ee-*an*-ick.
NAZARETH. *Naz*-uh-reth.
NINEVEH. *Nin*-uh-vuh.
PHARISEES. *Fair*-uh-seez.
SIMEON. *Sim*-ee-un.

---

appeared to be strong, and the leaves were large and full. A few days later, however, he noticed that the plant had wilted terribly. Within a few days it was completely dead. Pulling up the plant and examining its roots, the man discovered a bore worm, which could not be seen from the outside. That worm had eaten the heart out of the stem of the plant.

The religious leaders who confronted Jesus had allowed sin to penetrate their hearts to the place that they were attributing Jesus' miracles to Satan. This should alert us to the need to deal with temptation as soon as it appears. We must attack it early and refuse to allow it to get a foothold. Failing to do this can lead to disaster. In the case of the religious leaders, Jesus pronounced them ripe for God's judgment.

Three disciplines will prevent sin from "eating the heart out" of our relationship with Christ: (1) taking time daily for the Word of God; (2) empowering ourselves with prayer; and (3) seeking serious, significant fellowship with other believers. These disciplines will help us find the power and strength to keep sin from controlling our lives and to keep our walk with Christ alive and meaningful.   —D. R.

Conclusion

A. I Know Too Much

Imagine that you have committed a crime and that your conscience is racked with guilt. You believe that the only way to get a good night's sleep again is to admit your wrongdoing to someone and get it out of your system. So you confess what you have done to your friendly neighbor. If your neighbor is a professional counselor, he can hold your confession in confidence. But if your neighbor is a policeman, get ready to be arrested. In this case, your neighbor has sworn an oath to uphold the law, and he is honor bound to act on the information you gave him. He knows too much now to ignore your situation. He must do what is right.

The supernatural witness for Jesus Christ is overwhelming. The only honest recourse we have is to accept His claim to be our Savior and Lord. We know too much to ignore Him. Now we must do what is right.

B. Prayer

Father, we thank You for accrediting Jesus before us by Your power, and we readily claim Him as our Lord. In His name. Amen.

C. Thought to Remember

The evidence for Jesus is too overpowering to overlook.

Learning by Doing

This page contains an alternate lesson plan emphasizing learning activities.
Classes desiring such student involvement will find these suggestions helpful.

Learning Goals

After this lesson the student will be able to:

1. Summarize the controversy between Jesus and the Pharisees described in today's text.

2. Tell how Jesus' acts and teachings answer those who oppose Christianity today.

3. Prepare a statement of faith that answers the criticisms he or she most often hears from unbelievers.

Into the Lesson

A children's rhyme goes, "Sticks and stones may break my bones, but words will never hurt me." In groups of two or three, ask class members to critique that rhyme. Say, "Do you agree or disagree with this rhyme?" Ask each group to write two reasons for its chosen answer. Most will agree that words can, indeed, hurt—even if they do not cause *physical* injury.

Observe that words can also be helpful. While some are "fighting words," others are building words. Ask the class to suggest some building words and some fighting words. (Building words include: "Great job!" "I agree." "Keep it up." Fighting words include: "I disagree." "You are completely wrong!" "No way!") Discuss the difference between the two types of words. Can these words ever be confused? How does one disagree without using "fighting words"?

Make the transition to today's lesson by noting that today we will see how Jesus used some strong words to denounce the vicious attacks of His enemies.

Into the Word

Take about ten minutes to give a background lecture on the tension between Jesus and the Pharisees. Use the commentary's "Lesson Background" section (page 178).

Write four headings on the chalkboard: "Situation of the Demon-possessed Man"; "Crowd's Reaction"; "Pharisees' Rejection"; and "Jesus' Response." Have students search the text (Matthew 12:22-32, 38-41) to fill in data under each heading. Be sure to cover the reasons for the Pharisees' challenge to Jesus (public embarrassment and the questioning of His claims to be God). This was a highly charged atmosphere.

Divide the class into three groups. Give each group five to eight minutes for the following Bible study.

Group one is to survey the text and determine the central points of Jesus' answer to the Pharisees. (For example: Standing here, in your midst, is the King Himself!)

Group two is to create a list of ways by which Jesus answered His critics. Students could respond: His miracles (casting out the demon[s], healing, resurrection), His words (do not misrepresent the work of the Holy Spirit), and His warning (do not miss what I am doing or you will miss God).

Group three is to prepare a short list of implications from verse 30 for today. Responses could include: reaching out to the lost with the teachings of Jesus, seeking to relieve some of the physical problems people face, or encouraging those with broken hearts.

Into Life

Ask each group to report its findings, leading a group discussion on the points in each report. Emphasize the need to be sure about the teachings of Jesus on the need for strong faith.

Choose one or both of the following options to apply today's text.

1. Keep the students in their small groups, and ask each group to create a list of the most often heard criticisms of Jesus today. This list might include the following: "His miracles are fantasy"; "He did not rise from the dead"; "He has done nothing for me"; "This is nothing but a bunch of moralists taking away my fun!"

Next, answer the objections. Create a brief statement of faith that the student can carry with him or her. Emphasize that we do not substitute a statement of faith for Scripture, but the statement can be helpful for understanding.

2. Prepare several "bumper-sticker" sized strips of paper and give one to each student. (You may want to use colored paper.) Be sure to have a marking pen for each person.

Group the students in the same groups of two or three as at the beginning of the session. In these smaller groups encourage the students to create bumper stickers that will give testimony to the truth of Jesus as Lord. Have students display and explain their bumper stickers to the class. (There is a similar activity in the student book.)

Close the session in prayer for boldness to confront false images of Christ and for strength to face opposition.

Let's Talk It Over

The questions on this page are designed to encourage review of the lesson Scriptures and to promote discussion of the lesson by the class. The answers provided are only discussion starters. Let your class talk it over from there.

1. People in Jesus' day had differing views about His identity. What are some of the views people today have about Jesus' identity, and how can we help them to know Him for who He is?

People have many wrong views of Jesus: that He is merely a man who discovered a divine idea, that He is something similar to Michael the archangel (an important being created by God), that He is a "Son" of God, but not "God the Son," or that He was a prophet or even a mere man who was wrongly deified by His followers.

Any of these false teachings is dangerous because it presents less than the Biblical Jesus. C. S. Lewis's summary is still one of the best answers to the many differing opinions about Jesus: He is either the sovereign Lord, a terrible liar, or a confused lunatic. There are no other options. Making that point is the difficult part. In discussing methods, be sure to note the importance of living a life consistent with what we profess!

2. Some people apply Jesus' statement about a kingdom divided against itself to the church. Do you think this is a valid application? Why or why not? If so, what duties or responsibilities does it lay on us?

The truth of Jesus' words has been proven countless times throughout history in nations, civic organizations, sports teams, and the church. Dissension and division are devastating. Paul's first letter to the Corinthians strongly rebuked that church for its internal hostilities and called for them to unite. Jesus' high priestly prayer in John 17 was a passionate call for the oneness of His followers.

Satan and his evil forces will present a united front in their attacks on the church, so God's people must stand together as one body in purpose, doctrine, and mission to draw the world to the One who is Lord over all. We have a duty to work for unity in our own local church first, and for the church at large as much as we are able.

3. In what way did Jesus' call to make a decisive choice between His kingdom and the kingdom of this world become clear to you?

The Biblical evidence is clear as to who Jesus was, what He taught, and what He demands. Class members who grew up in the church may not remember a specific time when they first

began to appreciate the lordship of Jesus—it's something they "always" knew. Others, however, faced crisis situations that forced them to come to grips with the demands of the risen Christ. Discuss how their situations can be models to help others who arrive at those crisis situations to make the right choice.

4. If a Christian friend came to you and said he was afraid that he had committed the "unpardonable sin," what would you say?

This question will give you an opportunity to be sure the class is understanding the message of this text as well as seeking to apply it. Note some of the sins that have been called the unpardonable sin—adultery, divorce, suicide, and others. This passage says nothing about these issues!

Next, focus on how to counsel someone who is under conviction for sin. (This issue would not likely come up if a person were not feeling conviction.) Since it is the Spirit who convicts (or reproves) of sin (John 16:8), then the Spirit is still working in the person's life.

Finally, we must point the person to the amazing grace of God and the complete cleansing that comes through the blood of Christ. The first eight chapters of Romans are quite helpful, especially 5:6-11 and 8:1-4. First John 1:5–2:2 is also a blessed promise for repentant Christians.

5. Jesus said that the men of Nineveh would condemn those of His generation who rejected Him. Who do you think will rise up and condemn our own generation? Why? What can we do to help people avoid such condemnation?

Jesus' presence and miraculous works were such clear evidence that God was at work that people were without excuse for rejecting Him. Jesus said, however, that "greater works" would accompany His followers than even the works He did (John 14:12). Our generation, then, is similarly without excuse.

In the story of the rich man and Lazarus Jesus said His generation had "Moses and the prophets; let them hear them" (Luke 16:29). We have not only "Moses and the prophets," but the New Testament as well. Hebrews 2:1-4 points out that if the people under the Old Covenant were judged for failure to believe, "how shall we escape, if we neglect so great salvation?" (v. 3).

Laborers in the Vineyard

DEVOTIONAL READING: Matthew 20:20-28.

BACKGROUND SCRIPTURE: Matthew 19:16-20:16.

PRINTED TEXT: Matthew 20:1-16.

Matthew 20:1-16

1 For the kingdom of heaven is like unto a man that is a householder, which went out early in the morning to hire laborers into his vineyard.

2 And when he had agreed with the laborers for a penny a day, he sent them into his vineyard.

3 And he went out about the third hour, and saw others standing idle in the market place,

4 And said unto them; Go ye also into the vineyard, and whatsoever is right I will give you. And they went their way.

5 Again he went out about the sixth and ninth hour, and did likewise.

6 And about the eleventh hour he went out, and found others standing idle, and saith unto them, Why stand ye here all the day idle?

7 They say unto him, Because no man hath hired us. He saith unto them, Go ye also into the vineyard; and whatsoever is right, that shall ye receive.

8 So when even was come, the lord of the vineyard saith unto his steward, Call the laborers, and give them their hire, beginning from the last unto the first.

9 And when they came that were hired about the eleventh hour, they received every man a penny.

10 But when the first came, they supposed that they should have received more; and they likewise received every man a penny.

11 And when they had received it, they murmured against the goodman of the house,

12 Saying, These last have wrought but one hour, and thou hast made them equal unto us, which have borne the burden and heat of the day.

13 But he answered one of them, and said, Friend, I do thee no wrong: didst not thou agree with me for a penny?

14 Take that thine is, and go thy way: I will give unto this last, even as unto thee.

15 Is it not lawful for me to do what I will with mine own? Is thine eye evil, because I am good?

16 So the last shall be first, and the first last: for many be called, but few chosen.

Jan 30

GOLDEN TEXT: So the last shall be first, and the first last.—Matthew 20:16.

Immanuel: God With Us

Unit 2: Ministry: Wonderful Words and Works

(Lessons 5-9)

Lesson Aims

After this lesson a student should be able to:

1. Retell Jesus' parable of the laborers in the vineyard.

2. Explain the principle by which the owner of the vineyard dealt with his workers and how this applies to God's dealings with us.

3. Express gratitude for God's grace in his or her own life as well as for the demonstrations of God's grace in another's life.

Lesson Outline

INTRODUCTION
   A. I Would Do It for Nothing
   B. Lesson Background
 I. THE MASTER'S CALL (Matthew 20:1-7)
   A. Willing Workers (vv. 1, 2)
   B. Reinforcements (vv. 3-7)
     Growing Through Involvement
 II. THE WORKERS' PAY (Matthew 20:8-12)
   A. Surprise (vv. 8-10)
   B. Complaint (vv. 11, 12)
III. THE LORD'S GRACE (Matthew 20:13-16)
   A. Fairness (vv. 13, 14)
   B. Generosity (v. 15)
     A Picture of Grace
   C. Humility (v. 16)
CONCLUSION
   A. Team Play
   B. Prayer
   C. Thought to Remember

Introduction

A. I Would Do It for Nothing

Is there any kind of activity you enjoy so much that you would pay to do it? Of course there is. We pay admission fees all the time in order to participate in activities that entertain and amuse us. Is there a job you would gladly do because of the satisfaction it gives you, even if it did not offer the pay and benefits of other types of employment? Many of us, in fact, have the privilege of working in occupations we enjoy that much. Are there family and friends whom you would help when they were in need, with no thought of being paid for your services? For

Christians the answer should be a definite *yes*. The fact is that for most of us there are many things we will "do for nothing."

At the same time, when we are working for a living, we do expect reasonable pay. We want to be treated fairly, and we may leave a job if we are dissatisfied with our working conditions. This is all well and good where our job is concerned because our family responsibilities require that we give some concern for the income and benefits we can provide. However, these thoughts are out of place when considering our service for the Lord. This work we do because we ought to and because we want to, not because of any reward we hope to attain. The Christian service we do, we do "for nothing," and yet we receive an abundance of spiritual riches from the vast treasures of God's grace.

B. Lesson Background

The "Parable of the Laborers in the Vineyard," as recorded in Matthew 20, was spoken by Jesus within three or four months of the end of His ministry. (The reader can sense that the end is near by noting that next week's lesson from Matthew 21 covers Jesus' triumphal entry into Jerusalem a few days before His crucifixion.)

During the closing months of His three-and-a-half-year ministry, Jesus gave several parables and lessons on service and stewardship, perhaps in anticipation of the call for laborers that He would issue following His death and resurrection. The Great Commission would challenge His disciples to take on the task of spreading the gospel message throughout the world. Those who remembered the parable of the laborers in the vineyard and others like it would know the kind of response Jesus expected to see.

I. The Master's Call
(Matthew 20:1-7)

A. Willing Workers (vv. 1, 2)

1. For the kingdom of heaven is like unto a man that is a householder, which went out early in the morning to hire laborers into his vineyard.

This parable about *the kingdom of heaven* is not about the place we call Heaven, but about the principles established by Heaven's King and how they apply to our lives on earth.

The parable revolves around an unidentified *householder*, or, as other translations put it, "landowner" of a sizable estate. It is the time of year for harvesting his grape *vineyard*, and thus he is seeking *laborers* to *hire*. Naturally he would have his regular crew of hired hands and servants who assist him all year long; but for a brief period, while the grapes are ripe for picking, he needs all the help he can get.

Already one application of this parable to the work of *the kingdom of heaven* should be apparent. There is always before the church an urgency to take the gospel to the world as quickly as we can. Every day untold numbers of people die without Christ—and without hope. Our urgency is multiplied by the fact that there is so much work to be done and so few willing to serve.

2. And when he had agreed with the laborers for a penny a day, he sent them into his vineyard.

The word *penny* in our text can be misleading to the modern reader, for it seems like a wage far too small for any rational person to agree to. The actual coin referred to by Jesus is the "denarius." Though its equivalence in today's currency is always subject to change, the easiest way to appreciate the value of the denarius is to think in terms of one day's wages. This single coin was the typical daily pay for a common laborer with no professional skills, and it possessed a modest spending power adequate to supply a family's basic needs. The landowner in Jesus' parable was offering a fair wage for harvest labor.

B. Reinforcements (vv. 3-7)

3. And he went out about the third hour, and saw others standing idle in the market place.

Around mid-morning the landowner was still looking for workers. By the Jewish reckoning of time, this was *the third hour* after sunrise, approximately 9:00 A.M.

The men who were *standing idle in the market place* were probably not being lazy, but were simply waiting for someone to hire them. These were "day laborers" who gathered in this central location each day at this time of year. Landowners would know to come by in the early morning hours and choose as many workers as needed for that day. Those who worked well and impressed an owner would be asked to come directly to the fields each day until the harvest was completed. Whenever a landowner needed more laborers, he returned to the market place.

4. And said unto them; Go ye also into the vineyard, and whatsoever is right I will give you. And they went their way.

As noted earlier, the standard wage for this type of work was one denarius for a full day's labor. Since this second group of workers would not be working a full day, a typical landowner would calculate the appropriate percentage of a day's wage. It was not necessary that our owner declare the exact amount he would pay at this time; his statement *whatsoever is right* assured

the workers that he would *give* them a fair pay based on—they would reasonably suppose—the denarius.

5. Again he went out about the sixth and ninth hour, and did likewise.

It was unusual to be hiring day laborers as late as *the sixth hour* (12:00 noon) and *the ninth hour* (3:00 P.M.), but it could happen if unforeseen events occurred during the day (such as an approaching storm) that necessitated a faster pace than originally planned. This late-hiring scenario is quite appropriate, however, for our kingdom of Heaven lesson; because in our case there are never enough workers to "harvest" the whole world before the approaching "storm" of God's judgment arrives. God will always be seeking new laborers for His fields, even in the "late hours" of history.

6. And about the eleventh hour he went out, and found others standing idle, and saith unto them, Why stand ye here all the day idle?

With only one hour left in the working day, the landowner was still eager at *the eleventh hour* (5:00 P.M.) to hire anyone willing to work for him. Is this a realistic scenario from Biblical times? Perhaps only when the situation was most desperate. But then, when the analogy is made to a world racing toward an eternity of torment, the situation *is* most desperate.

7. They say unto him, Because no man hath hired us. He saith unto them, Go ye also into the vineyard; and whatsoever is right, that shall ye receive.

The final crew of workers for the day was sent into the *vineyard*. Their contribution could never be equal to those who had invested more time, but their labors would benefit the landowner just the same. Every person's contribution was appreciated by the landowner, whose greatest concern

Home Daily Bible Readings

Monday, Jan. 24—The Rich Young Man and Jesus (Matthew 19:16-22)
Tuesday, Jan. 25—All Things Are Possible With God (Matthew 19:23-30)
Wednesday, Jan. 26—Hiring of Laborers for the Vineyard (Matthew 20:1-7)
Thursday, Jan. 27—God's Grace Illustrated in a Parable (Matthew 20:8-16)
Friday, Jan. 28—Jesus' Death and Resurrection Foretold (Matthew 20:17-23)
Saturday, Jan. 29—Jesus Teaches About Servanthood (Matthew 20:24-28)
Sunday, Jan. 30—Jesus Demonstrates Servanthood (John 13:1-15)

was harvesting as much as possible while there was still time. Note once more his promise to pay the workers *whatsoever is right*. [See question #1, page 192.]

In our spiritual application of this parable, we realize that it is never too late to become actively involved in service for the kingdom of Heaven. Certainly the ideal situation is to "remember now thy Creator in the days of thy youth" (Ecclesiastes 12:1) and give a lifetime of devotion and service to our Lord. A good youth ministry or camp program will issue such challenges to our young people as early as possible. Our Bible colleges typically draw those who are recent high school graduates and are ready to be trained for service. Those who get serious about their faith commitment late in life may wonder sometimes if they have arrived too late to make any significant contribution to the Lord's work. Jesus' parable reminds us that God welcomes even the "eleventh-hour laborer" to serve in His fields. The task at hand is too important to turn away anyone who is willing to help. [See question #2, page 192.]

GROWING THROUGH INVOLVEMENT

Judy's minister had finished preaching a series of sermons on the topic, "Using Your Spiritual Gifts." After the last sermon, she went to see him. She wanted to serve the Lord, she said, but she had no spiritual gift. The minister told her that he was sure she had been gifted by the Lord in some way. Sensing that Judy was a lady of great compassion (and thus someone with the gift of mercy), he urged her to begin making weekly visits to one of the church's shut-ins, who was living in a nursing home.

After several visits, one of the attendants at the nursing home asked Judy if she had any Bible stories on video tape that she could show to the residents of the home. She replied that she did and would be glad to bring those the following week. Judy was very uncomfortable with the idea of teaching or leading discussions, however, and she told the attendant that she did not want to do that.

The next week she brought the tape and showed it to a few of the residents. After they had seen the video, one of the residents raised her hand and asked a question. There was no one there to give an answer except Judy, so she responded to the resident's question as best she could. Before long, Judy was conducting a weekly Bible study with several people in the nursing home. She then began teaching a women's class at the church, which has grown incredibly over the years. And all this from a woman who had "no spiritual gift!"

Whether we begin our labors for Christ early in life or much later, the Lord is always interested in our willingness to serve Him. It's never too late to get busy in His vineyard!   —D. R.

II. The Workers' Pay
(Matthew 20:8-12)

A. Surprise (vv. 8-10)

8. So when even was come, the lord of the vineyard saith unto his steward, Call the laborers, and give them their hire, beginning from the last unto the first.

At the end of the work day the landowner explained to his *steward* (we would probably refer to him as the manager or foreman) how he wanted the day's payments to be made. There was no standard procedure in Biblical times for the order in which to pay workers. For the sake of the lesson to be learned in this parable, Jesus had His owner pay *beginning from the last unto the first.*

9. And when they came that were hired about the eleventh hour, they received every man a penny.

The first surprise was the generous pay received by those who had worked for only one hour. No one, not even the "*eleventh hour* workers" themselves, would have imagined such a thing. Of course, none of the people in this group complained about their pay! All were thrilled to receive more than they had anticipated, and were probably eager to be hired for the next day.

10. But when the first came, they supposed that they should have received more; and they likewise received every man a penny.

The second surprise was not one of joy and astonishment, but of shock and disbelief. Those who had been hired *first* and had worked the full day received the very same pay as those who had worked only one hour! The workers who had previously benefited from the owner's generosity probably assumed that those who had worked the longest would receive more than they did. No one could believe what was happening.

B. Complaint (vv. 11, 12)

11. And when they had received it, they murmured against the goodman of the house.

How to Say It

DENARII. dih-*nair*-ee or dih-*nair*-eye.
DENARIUS. dih-*nair*-ee-us.
ECCLESIASTES. Ik-*leez*-ee-*as*-teez
　　(strong accent on *as*).

To say that those who were hired first *murmured* would likely be an understatement. This situation would have had all the makings of a riot. Most of us can identify with these workers' complaint. The vineyard owner appeared to treat his best workers unfairly.

12. Saying, These last have wrought but one hour, and thou hast made them equal unto us, which have borne the burden and heat of the day.

If one knows anything about Jesus' method of teaching, he knows that this story is leading toward an important spiritual lesson. Our thinking about fairness will probably be challenged. However, even before we reach the conclusion to this parable, there is something we should note. Those who grumbled did so only after they compared their situation with that of the other workers. If they had not known what the others had been paid, they would probably have been happy to receive their denarii. Their bitterness surfaced when they observed others being given an advantage they had not received. [See question #3, page 192.]

Keeping an eye on what others have or receive is a sure road to discontent. A child thinks it is unfair if he does not receive the same thing a brother or sister received. The oldest child grumbles when his younger siblings get to do something he was not permitted to do at their age. An employee is upset when he thinks that his salary and benefits are not comparable to those of his fellow workers. The church member is offended when others are publicly thanked for their service and he is not mentioned.

The complaint of the workers who had toiled the longest may seem reasonable at first; but when we realize that theirs was a judgment based on how they thought they should have been treated in comparison with others, we should be cautious about joining their cause.

III. The Lord's Grace
(Matthew 20:13-16)

A. Fairness (vv. 13, 14)

13. But he answered one of them, and said, Friend, I do thee no wrong: didst not thou agree with me for a penny?

No matter how unfair this situation might seem to us, the first group of laborers had not been cheated. The landowner had, in fact, upheld his original agreement with them. He had given them a *penny* (a denarius) for their day's labor—just as he had promised.

This story gives us a more Biblical view of fairness than what we sometimes assume. Fairness should not be judged on the basis of how

we are treated in comparison to others, but on whether or not the terms to which we agreed have been honored. The question should not be, "Did others receive any advantage over me?" but rather, "Has any agreement or promise to me been broken?"

Consider how God deals with us. We are not all given the same spiritual gifts, for the Holy Spirit distributes His gifts with much variety (1 Corinthians 12:4-6). Likewise, God's providence does not produce blessing and suffering among us in equal measure. The fact that we are treated differently by God is no basis for accusing God of being unfair to us, for He has never promised us equality of gifts and experiences. God has promised to love each one of us fully and to value all human life as a special creation made in His image. He has promised eternal blessings to every one who remains faithful to Him. But at no time has God ever been unfair to us, for God never violates a promise. Fairness does not require equal or comparable treatment of others, but simply that a person live up to his word.

14. Take that thine is, and go thy way: I will give unto this last, even as unto thee.

In this case, the landowner's decision was final. He had not been unfair to anyone, despite their expectations. Those who have a complaint should *take* what they have received and *go*. They have no basis for a charge against the landowner, except that which derives from their envy of the blessings received by others.

B. Generosity (v. 15)

15. Is it not lawful for me to do what I will with mine own? Is thine eye evil, because I am good?

Is there something familiar about the idea of giving someone more than what his effort deserves? There should be. After all, this is the meaning of grace.

Grace is a free gift that is given simply because the giver chooses to do so. Grace does not necessarily make sense, especially when we are on the sidelines watching others receive it. But grace is not bound by our sense of what is fair as we compare ourselves with others. Grace cannot be demanded or expected, nor is it regulated by our opinions of it. Grace does not answer to anyone except the heart of the giver himself.

We who are the beneficiaries of the greatest act of grace the world has ever known should not feel cheated when, in the daily circumstances of life, we see others experience a generosity not offered to us. We should be humbled by the vineyard owner's question regarding envy: *Is thine eye evil, because I am good?* [See question #4, page 192.]

A PICTURE OF GRACE

You are on your way to church, but running a bit late because of some delays at home. So you apply just a bit more pressure to the accelerator. All of a sudden, you see lights in your rearview mirror as a patrolman pulls up behind you. You pull off into a parking lot and get your license and registration ready. The officer comes to your window and tells you that you were doing fifty-five in a thirty-five miles-per-hour zone. Then he asks where you are going and you sheepishly tell him that you are on your way to church. He asks for your license and registration and tells you he will be back. As you sit there, you berate yourself for driving so fast. Before long the officer comes to your window to give you the "bad news."

At this point, what would grace look like? Would it be the officer's saying to you, "This time I'm going to give you just a warning"? This would certainly look like grace, but it would more accurately be called compassion.

Suppose the officer said, "I'm going to have to give you a ticket because you broke the law; you were exceeding the speed limit. However, I have decided to go to court with you and pay the fine myself." That would be grace. And that is exactly what our heavenly Father did when Jesus went to the cross for our sins. God paid the debt Himself.

The vineyard workers who had labored the entire day did not seem to understand that the owner had the right to extend all the compassion and grace that he wanted to extend, since he was the owner. It was his right and privilege to handle the situation as he desired.

May God's "amazing grace" keep us ever dependent on Him and genuinely grateful for His blessings—not only in our lives but in the lives of others.   —D. R.

C. Humility (v. 16)

16. So the last shall be first, and the first last: for many be called, but few chosen.

This haunting photo warns us not to take our privileged position for granted, for "the last shall be first, and the first last."

Visual for lesson 9

The first portion of this expression fits the parable quite well: *the last shall be first.* Those hired near the end of the work day were indeed treated as if they had been among those who had been *first* in service. This calls attention to a prominent Biblical theme: God takes great pleasure in lifting up the lowly and exalting those who are humble in spirit.

The latter statement is likewise an important lesson: *the first* (shall be) *last.* Some have misread these words, wondering if they mean that those who have given God their best will actually end up being slighted by God. Not at all. The intent of this latter expression is related to that of the former. Just as God exalts those who are humble, He will eventually humble those who are exalted in their own eyes. Those who compare themselves with others and think that they are more deserving of God's grace must learn that no one actually deserves grace.

God will not disregard those who give Him a "full day's labor." He will bless them richly, but only if they maintain a humble spirit in relation to others.

Conclusion

A. Team Play

Some games are designed to be played in teams, where people work together and use the strengths that each member is able to contribute. Other games are intended to be played "every man for himself." Such games have their place, but in team sports the every-man-for-himself attitude is a ticket to disaster.

The Christian life is meant to be conducted as a team effort rather than every man for himself. It was never God's intent that His people "go it alone," but that they work together for a common goal—the ministry of the gospel to a lost and dying world. We are not to envy one another, but to encourage and support one another in all circumstances, both good and bad. And while it is the bond of love that holds us together, it is the grace of God that humbles us and makes us suitable vessels for His service. [See question #5, page 192.]

B. Prayer

Father, may we never be so blinded by what we feel we deserve that we lose sight of the riches of Your grace toward us, given through Jesus our Lord. In His name we pray. Amen.

C. Thought to Remember

"For by grace are ye saved through faith; and that not of yourselves: it is the gift of God" (Ephesians 2:8).

Learning by Doing

This page contains an alternate lesson plan emphasizing learning activities.
Classes desiring such student involvement will find these suggestions helpful.

Learning Goals

After this lesson the student will be able to:

1. Retell Jesus' parable of the laborers in the vineyard.

2. Explain the principle by which the owner of the vineyard dealt with his workers and how this applies to God's dealings with us.

3. Express gratitude for God's grace in his or her own life as well as for the demonstrations of God's grace in another's life.

Into the Lesson

Ask every other student to turn to the person on his or her right and discuss the following: "What is the best job that you ever had? Why?"

Allow four to five minutes for discussion; then ask the pairs to report. List on a poster or chalk board the jobs cited. Ask, "Is it fair that some jobs pay more than others? Why or why not?"

After four minutes, make the transition to the lesson by saying, "The text we are studying today contains Jesus' parable of the laborers in the vineyard. The actions of the vineyard owner challenge many people's sense of fairness. We will see that the parable is about more than being fair; it's about being more than fair!"

Into the Word

Ask a volunteer to read today's text, Matthew 20:1-16. Then divide your class into three groups. Distribute the following outline to each group. (Allow about a third of a page under each point for students to make notes.)

A. The Call

B. The Complaint

C. The Conclusion

Give the following questions to Group A:

1. To whom is the call given? *(Laborers)*

2. What are the terms of the call? *(Work in my vineyard for a day's pay.)*

3. What is the master's response to the need for more workers? *(Hire more when needed.)*

Assign these questions to Group B:

4. How are the workers compensated? *(Each is paid a day's wage.)*

5. Who is the first compensated? *(The last hired.)*

6. What concerns are raised? *(It's not fair that some are paid the same as we for less work.)*

Give these questions to Group C:

7. What is the master's initial answer? *(I did nothing wrong.)*

8. Why did the master compensate as he did? *(Because that was the agreement made at hiring.)*

9. What principles are stated at the end of this parable? *(The last shall be first, and the first shall be last. Many are called, but few chosen.)*

Call the groups together after several minutes and discuss together their answers to the questions, filling in the outline. Use the lesson commentary to answer any questions or expand on any thoughts raised.

Make the transition to the application phase of the session by saying, "It is apparent that the early workers began to compare themselves with and to envy the latter workers. We want to explore how this concept carries over into the church today."

Into Life

Using today's text, have each group (from the three groups formed earlier) write a definition of *fairness* and of *grace*. After allowing the groups a few minutes to work, ask them to compare their definitions of *fairness* with this definition from the lesson commentary: "Fairness should not be judged on the basis of how we are treated in comparison to others, but on whether or not the terms to which we agreed have been honored." Discuss how this is seen in the text. Then discuss the definitions of grace, noting how the landowner was motivated more by grace (giving the workers who worked least what they needed, rather than what they deserved).

Ask the students to think of situations when they thought they were treated unfairly. Ask them to consider whether their standards of fairness were the same as the standards you have discussed today. Perhaps they need to see that grace was at work for another and to rejoice in that rather than feel slighted. And if they truly were treated unfairly, perhaps they need to practice grace toward the offending party.

Conclude this lesson by having five volunteers read the following Scripture passages: Romans 5:8; 1 Corinthians 12:4-6; Ephesians 1:3-14; Matthew 20:13; Matthew 20:15. Note the lesson writer's comments concerning God's promises and God's grace (page 189).

Close the session by asking each person to offer a silent prayer expressing gratitude for God's grace in his or her own life and thanking Him for another person's grace gifts.

Let's Talk It Over

The questions on this page are designed to encourage review of the lesson Scriptures and to promote discussion of the lesson by the class. The answers provided are only discussion starters. Let your class talk it over from there.

1. The lesson writer notes that the landowner's "greatest concern was harvesting as much as possible while there was still time." The workers may or may not have shared this concern. God is concerned that none "should perish, but that all should come to repentance" (2 Peter 3:9). What do you think distracts Christian workers from this view? How can we bring our view more into line with God's?

Many things distract us from God's vision, but most have to do with pride. I don't get along well with another believer; I did not get the recognition I deserved, so I quit; I can do better than so-and-so, but he always gets the job I want!

The Word of God reveals God's heart, especially when it records His dealings with people. The culmination, of course, is at the cross of Jesus. When the message of the cross becomes central in our lives, we begin to see other people and the kingdom harvest through God's eyes.

2. Where do you see yourself—as an early-morning worker, a third-hour worker, sixth-hour worker, ninth-hour worker, or eleventh-hour worker? Why? How does this view of yourself motivate you in Christian service?

It is likely that every adult class will have some early-morning workers—those who came to the Lord in their youth. But you should have some who came to the Lord in their adult years, perhaps new Christians even now. These may be third-, sixth-, ninth-, perhaps even eleventh-hour workers. They have missed serving the Lord in some of their most productive years, but they are serving Him now and can still make valuable contributions to the Lord's work!

Every worker in God's vineyard needs to look to the task ahead and serve faithfully without regard to how long anyone has been at the task. Those who began early can teach from experience those who joined late. Sometimes those who joined late can encourage the longtime workers with new enthusiasm. But we all work together for the common good.

3. What steps can we take to prevent the comparative spirit seen in the parable?

We must begin by seeking to please God instead of ourselves. When our focus is on His standard for us, we are seldom concerned about how we measure up with other people. Then we must learn or remind ourselves of the dangers of jealousy and envy. Another safeguard is developing the contentment exemplified by the apostle Paul (Philippians 4:10-13).

Most of all, we must remember that our concern is not who harvests the most, but whether or not we together are getting the harvest gathered before it is too late!

4. Jesus' parable demonstrates the astonishing grace and generosity of God toward the undeserving. How can we become better at showing that same grace in our treatment of others?

First, we should study again the subject of grace in the Bible and allow ourselves to be reminded in a fresh way of the magnitude of God's grace. That in turn will help us develop a humble awareness of our own sin and our need of God's forgiveness. The apostle Paul wrote about, preached, and demonstrated God's grace because he never lost the wonder of his own sin and forgiveness (1 Timothy 1:15, 16).

Once the grace of God fills our lives to that degree, we find it more natural to show patience toward others, and to forgive their failures and offenses toward us. We also are pleased to celebrate the blessings and successes of others, and to rejoice when God's grace changes the life of a longtime sinner who comes into the kingdom of God at the eleventh hour.

5. A good team spirit is crucial in any group endeavor. How can we build a spirit of unity and teamwork for the Lord's harvest?

First, we must affirm that harvesting souls for God is central to the church's existence so that believers will be unified in purpose. New Testament teaching regarding the uniqueness and importance of each member's role within the body must be stressed. That diversity can then be used to full capacity in winning the lost. The team spirit is further developed and enhanced through programs and events that bring people together in a variety of settings. People are more comfortable harvesting together when they have also laughed and cried together in other situations. We need one another, and God wants us to be working together with others in the kingdom.

Entry Into Jerusalem

DEVOTIONAL READING: Luke 19:29-44.

BACKGROUND SCRIPTURE: Matthew 21:1-17.

PRINTED TEXT: Matthew 21:1-13.

Matthew 21:1-13

1 And when they drew nigh unto Jerusalem, and were come to Bethphage, unto the mount of Olives, then sent Jesus two disciples,

2 Saying unto them, Go into the village over against you, and straightway ye shall find an ass tied, and a colt with her: loose them, and bring them unto me.

3 And if any man say aught unto you, ye shall say, The Lord hath need of them; and straightway he will send them.

4 All this was done, that it might be fulfilled which was spoken by the prophet, saying,

5 Tell ye the daughter of Zion, Behold, thy King cometh unto thee, meek, and sitting upon an ass, and a colt the foal of an ass.

6 And the disciples went, and did as Jesus commanded them,

7 And brought the ass, and the colt, and put on them their clothes, and they set him thereon.

8 And a very great multitude spread their garments in the way; others cut down branches from the trees, and strewed them in the way.

9 And the multitudes that went before, and that followed, cried, saying, Hosanna to the Son of David: Blessed is he that cometh in the name of the Lord; Hosanna in the highest.

10 And when he was come into Jerusalem, all the city was moved, saying, Who is this?

11 And the multitude said, This is Jesus the prophet of Nazareth of Galilee.

12 And Jesus went into the temple of God, and cast out all them that sold and bought in the temple, and overthrew the tables of the money changers, and the seats of them that sold doves,

13 And said unto them, It is written, My house shall be called the house of prayer; but ye have made it a den of thieves.

GOLDEN TEXT: Tell ye the daughter of Zion, Behold, thy King cometh unto thee, meek, and sitting upon an ass, and a colt the foal of an ass.—Matthew 21:5.

> ### Immanuel: God With Us
> Unit 3: Fulfillment: Atonement
> and Final Commission
> (Lessons 10-13)

Lesson Aims

After this lesson students should be able to:

1. Summarize the events surrounding Jesus' triumphal entry into Jerusalem.

2. Explain what made Jesus' triumphal entry so significant.

3. Take specific steps to eliminate something from their lives that keeps Jesus from ruling as Lord and King.

Lesson Outline

INTRODUCTION
  A. Impromptu Greetings
  B. Lesson Background
  I. OBEY THE MASTER (Matthew 21:1-6)
  A. Finding an Animal (vv. 1-3)
  B. Fulfilling God's Will (vv. 4-6)
  "All Creatures Great and Small"
 II. HONOR THE KING (Matthew 21:7-11)
  A. Bringing Him Glory (vv. 7, 8)
  B. Shouting His Praise (vv. 9-11)
  Who Doesn't Love a Parade?
III. RESPECT THE LORD (Matthew 21:12, 13)
  A. Cleansing the Temple (v. 12)
  B. Teaching the Truth (v. 13)
CONCLUSION
  A. Royal Highways
  B. Prayer
  C. Thought to Remember

Introduction

A. Impromptu Greetings

Do you remember the old expression, "If I knew that you were coming I would have baked a cake"? The line expresses both surprise and appreciation to unexpected guests. According to the statement our friends deserve special treatment; and we would gladly give it to them if we have sufficient notice to prepare that special treatment. Too often, though, we have to do the best we can with the situation we are given.

The Passover crowd gathered in Jerusalem on the first day of Jesus' final week had no idea when the day began that they would witness the arrival of the Messiah-King of prophecy. Had they known, surely they would have made grand preparations for His arrival. As it was, they did the best they could under the circumstances, and with palm branches and shouts of adoration they honored the King. So significant was Jesus' "triumphal entry" that it is recorded by all four Gospel writers.

B. Lesson Background

The twenty-first chapter of Matthew's Gospel begins his account of Jesus' final week, which culminated in His death at the end of the week and His resurrection on the first day of the following week. The events of this week actually began on Saturday evening with a dinner in Jesus' honor in the town of Bethany, about two miles southeast of Jerusalem. The host for these festivities was a man called "Simon the leper" (Matthew 26:6), probably so named because he had at some point been healed by Jesus. Also in attendance were Jesus' close friend Lazarus and his sisters Mary and Martha (John 12:1-3). Though this episode occurred before the events recorded in chapter 21 (cf. John 12:1, 2), Matthew saves the telling of it until chapter 26 (vv. 6-13). There he uses this incident in combination with two other events to recount Jesus' betrayal, as a prelude to his record of the death of Christ in chapter 27.

Following the dinner on Saturday evening, Jesus made His "triumphal entry" into Jerusalem on Sunday. The day we now call "Palm Sunday" commemorates that electrifying day when Jesus was given a royal welcome as He entered the city of Jerusalem in fulfillment of prophecy.

I. Obey the Master
(Matthew 21:1-6)

A. Finding an Animal (vv. 1-3)

1. And when they drew nigh unto Jerusalem, and were come to Bethphage, unto the mount of Olives, then sent Jesus two disciples.

The day after the dinner in Bethany, Jesus and His disciples began to walk the approximately two miles to *Jerusalem*. This road took them over the *mount of Olives*, down a steep descent, and into Jerusalem from the east side.

The Mount of Olives is a ridge running north-south just across the Kidron Valley from the city of Jerusalem. It is the highest peak on the east side, providing a strategic view of Jerusalem. Historical sources of Jesus' day indicate that a person could stand upon the top of the mount and see clearly into the temple courts. In ancient times the terrain was thick with olive groves, thus providing the origin of the mount's name.

Somewhere on the lower slopes of the Mount of Olives was a place known as Gethsemane, which means "olive press." We suppose it was one of the many olive groves on the mountain. John calls it a "garden" (John 18:1). Gethsemane was a favorite place of prayer for Jesus (John 18:2; Luke 22:39). He retreated there each evening of His final week (Luke 21:37), and it was there that His disciples slept as He prayed on the night that He was arrested (Matthew 26:36-46).

Somewhere on the Mount of Olives was the village of *Bethphage*, along—or a short distance from—the main road on which Jesus was walking. It was there that *two disciples* of Jesus obtained the donkey used for the triumphal entry.

2. Saying unto them, Go into the village over against you, and straightway ye shall find an ass tied, and a colt with her: loose them, and bring them unto me.

Jesus knew exactly what His two disciples would find when they entered the *village* of Bethphage. The focus of their search was the young *colt*, for that was the animal Jesus actually rode upon (and the only one mentioned in the accounts of Mark and Luke). While we normally think of a colt as a young horse, it is clear from this verse (and from the prophecy Jesus fulfilled) that this animal was a young donkey.

This particular colt was special in that he had not yet been ridden by any person (Mark 11:2). Perhaps the reason his mother was also brought along was to steady this young donkey during his first experience at being ridden. The task on this day was both his first and his most important ever—to transport the promised Messiah-King during His royal procession.

3. And if any man say aught unto you, ye shall say, The Lord hath need of them; and straightway he will send them.

In a small village such as Bethphage, one might expect that two strangers taking off with someone else's property would be challenged. Mark and Luke tell us that the disciples were, indeed, questioned about taking the animals (Mark 11:5; Luke 19:33). However, when informed that the animals would be used by Jesus, the owners were pleased to oblige.

It is possible that the use of the animals for this occasion had been prearranged. Or it may be that this request was just as impromptu as it appears in the Biblical text, and that the owners responded favorably out of respect for Jesus and a desire to assist in His ministry. In either case, their attitude is an example for us. When called upon by Jesus they were ready to serve, and we should be as well. [See question #1, page 200.]

B. Fulfilling God's Will (vv. 4-6)

4. All this was done, that it might be fulfilled which was spoken by the prophet, saying.

According to Matthew, the triumphal entry on the donkey was a fulfillment of the prophecy in Zechariah 9:9. In a chapter that speaks of God's judgment coming on Israel's enemies, Zechariah foretold the coming of the Messiah-King to Jerusalem, at which time He would establish among God's people a "peace" that would never come to an end (Zechariah 9:10).

5. Tell ye the daughter of Zion, Behold, thy King cometh unto thee, meek, and sitting upon an ass, and a colt the foal of an ass.

The precise details of this prophecy given centuries before the time of Jesus are amazing. The Messiah would publicly reveal Himself to the city of Jerusalem, referred to here as the *daughter of Zion*. The sign of the Messiah would be a grand and royal entrance—not by just any means, but specifically by riding on *a colt the foal of an ass*. This prophetic sign was so clear that the crowd who observed Jesus on this occasion immediately began to proclaim the coming of "the Son of David" (v. 9). What appeared to be very humble and unassuming was actually an unmistakable sign heralding the arrival of the long-awaited *King*.

The *meek* appearance of the Messiah-King was intended to symbolize the peace that He would establish upon the earth. For royalty to parade on a white horse symbolized military might and a readiness to do battle with the enemy—a most appropriate symbol for Jesus' second coming (Revelation 19:11). In contrast, the use of a gentle animal such as the donkey symbolized a reign of peace and security.

There are some today who interpret Zechariah 9 as predicting a political peace for the nation of Israel. The history of Israel since the days of Zechariah has been marked by foreign domination and by frequent conflicts with surrounding peoples. Thus some believe that this prophecy has not yet been fulfilled, and will not be fulfilled until the arrival of a future period of peace on earth for the Jews.

Visual for lessons 10 & 11

This visual contrasts Jesus' arrival in Jerusalem, "meek, and sitting upon an ass," with His awesome second coming in power and in glory.

Matthew, however, declares that Zechariah's prophecy was fulfilled at Jesus' triumphal entry into Jerusalem. Indeed, we know that through Jesus' death and resurrection, which occurred a few days later, peace has been established among God's people—a peace between sinners and God, as well as a peace between Jew and Gentile (Ephesians 2:11-22). If Zechariah's promise of peace is thus understood to be a spiritual peace, then we can join Matthew in proclaiming that Jesus has fulfilled this Old Testament Messianic prophecy.

"ALL CREATURES GREAT AND SMALL"

Have you ever thought about the prominence of animals in the Bible? Animals play an important role in many Bible stories, and are often used symbolically. Herbert Lockyer has compiled an entire book that lists and comments on *All the Animals in the Bible*—a volume with hundreds of entries!

It is not surprising that Jesus entered Jerusalem riding, rather than on foot. What was unusual was that He, the Messiah-King, sat astride a small and humble beast of burden rather than atop a great white horse. Though many in the crowd would have been familiar with the Zechariah prophecy that Matthew cites, they were likely confused by such a humble image—inappropriate, it seemed, for Israel's King and Deliverer.

Our understanding, however, is aided by the New Testament Scriptures, which elaborate on the humility of Christ and the non-political nature of His kingdom. (See Philippians 2:6-11.) The Suffering Servant reigns as a selfless, modest, and lowly prince. Thus the colt of a donkey was an appropriate animal for Jesus' "triumphal entry" into the holy city. The donkey is a fitting

Home Daily Bible Readings

Monday, Jan. 31—Jesus Sets His Face Toward Jerusalem (Luke 9:51-56)

Tuesday, Feb. 1—Jesus Enters Jerusalem Amid Hosannas (Matthew 21:1-11)

Wednesday, Feb. 2—Jesus Cleanses the Temple (Matthew 21:12-17)

Thursday, Feb. 3—Chief Priests and Elders Resist Jesus (Matthew 21:23-27)

Friday, Feb. 4—Parable of the Wicked Husbandmen (Matthew 21:33-46)

Saturday, Feb. 5—A Question About the Resurrection (Matthew 22:23-33)

Sunday, Feb. 6—The Greatest Commandment of All (Matthew 22:34-46)

symbol of the condescension that prompted the Son of God to leave a heavenly throne and die on a shameful cross.

Now re-exalted, the Messiah will return one day on a royal white horse, as "King of Kings, and Lord of Lords" (Revelation 19:11-16).

—R. W. B.

6. And the disciples went, and did as Jesus commanded them.

This story teaches a good lesson regarding our duty to the Lord, for it presents the worthy examples of individuals who were willing to be used in the service of Jesus. The two *disciples* were ready to do whatever *Jesus commanded them*, and the owners of the donkey were eager to offer what they had for Jesus' sake (even the donkey proved to be useful to our Lord). There is no better way to honor Jesus Christ than to offer Him our willing obedience in all things. [See question #2, page 200.]

II. Honor the King (Matthew 21:7-11)

A. Bringing Him Glory (vv. 7, 8)

7. And brought the ass, and the colt, and put on them their clothes, and they set him thereon.

Lacking a saddle, the disciples laid some of their *clothes*—likely their outer garments, or cloaks—on the backs of the animals. It seems strange that they thus equipped both animals, since Jesus could ride only one. Perhaps they put some cloaks on the larger animal, assuming Jesus could not ride an unbroken colt, but then Jesus insisted they cover the younger one. Or maybe one of the disciples—Peter, perhaps—thought he would ride one of the animals alongside Jesus! That, of course, did not happen.

8. And a very great multitude spread their garments in the way; others cut down branches from the trees, and strewed them in the way.

As the crowd along the road saw the "sign of Zechariah" approaching, they quickly caught the spirit of a royal procession. In a special gesture of homage, they placed their *garments* on the ground for Jesus to ride upon (see 2 Kings 9:13). Since the road passing over the Mount of Olives went through a heavily wooded area, many in the crowd *cut down branches from the trees* and *strewed* (spread) them in Jesus' path. The Gospel of John specifically refers to the use of palm branches (John 12:13). This is the source of our modern designation of "Palm Sunday."

While no estimate of the size of the crowd is given in the four Gospels, Matthew does mention *a very great multitude*. Given that this was the Passover season, Jerusalem would have had well over one hundred thousand guests, making Matthew's description quite accurate. As the Pharisees watched the proceedings, they remarked with envy and bitterness that "the world is gone after him" (John 12:19).

B. Shouting His Praise (vv. 9-11)

9. And the multitudes that went before, and that followed, cried, saying, Hosanna to the Son of David: Blessed is he that cometh in the name of the Lord; Hosanna in the highest.

The *multitudes* that gathered did not simply observe what transpired but joined in the procession. Many of them marched in front of Jesus and announced His coming. Others stood and watched Him pass, then fell in behind the parade. All were shouting Messianic tributes of praise. They celebrated the arrival of *the Son of David*, a reference to the Messiah-King who would literally descend from the family of David and establish a kingdom no less glorious than that of His father David. This King would come *in the name of the Lord*—that is, with the authority and power of God.

On this day the multitudes wished for Jesus nothing but God's finest blessings. They shouted *Hosanna*, from a Hebrew word meaning, "Save, we pray." It was their desire that God save and preserve the life of this King and grant Him success with His Messianic plans. How ironic that only five days later many in this same crowd would be crying, "Crucify him, crucify him" (John 19:6). [See question #3, page 200.]

WHO DOESN'T LOVE A PARADE?

Most people enjoy a parade—watching it on television or, especially, being along the parade route to see it firsthand. The floats, the bands, the sights, sounds, and crowds—all of it makes for a pretty exciting spectacle!

As Jesus came into Jerusalem, He too generated so much excitement that "multitudes" were soon taking part in the celebration. But all too soon the "oohs" and "aahs" turned into shouts of contempt. In just a few days, crowds of worshipers became an angry mob of self-appointed executioners, crying, "Crucify him!"

Some people love a parade only as long as the *crowd* loves a parade. A few disenchanted observers, if they are vocal enough, can quickly turn the mood of the masses toward hatred and violence. It's called "mob psychology"—a dark and scary side of human nature.

It may have appeared to some that Jesus' parade ended at Calvary. But that was only a pause in the action; by God's resurrection power, Jesus' parade became once again a march of triumph.
—R. W. B.

10. And when he was come into Jerusalem, all the city was moved, saying, Who is this?

As the crowd entered *Jerusalem,* it quickly became apparent to those inside the city that something unusual was happening. Such a crowd and commotion suggested that an important person was arriving, but apparently they could not tell who it was.

Who is this? they asked. Some of those asking probably were visitors in town who did not know anything about Jesus. Those who did know of Him may have joined the crowd as they learned that Jesus was in the middle of it. They would want to see this One who had been at the center of popular admiration and official controversy for the past three years.

11. And the multitude said, This is Jesus the prophet of Nazareth of Galilee.

Despite the Messianic overtones of the crowd's earlier accolades, they gave a moderate answer to the question of Jesus' identity. To describe Him as a *prophet* was far less controversial than to label Him the Messiah. Perhaps we are seeing already the fickle nature of this *multitude.*

The Gospel of Mark notes that it was near evening when Jesus arrived within the walls of Jerusalem (Mark 11:11). Thus, He did not stay long that day. The events reported later in this text took place on the following day.

Well before the time Jesus arrived in the city, at "the descent of the mount of Olives" (Luke 19:37), the Pharisees had urged Jesus to silence the crowd and dismiss them, for their jubilation was getting out of hand. Jesus refused, adding that, "If these should hold their peace, the stones would immediately cry out" (Luke 19:39, 40). It was not possible to contain the excitement being felt over the arrival of the long-awaited King of prophecy. One can imagine that this excitement fairly exploded once the crowd had entered the city. It was a day of unbridled celebration and praise, quite fitting for the One who is our Lord and King.

III. Respect the Lord (Matthew 21:12, 13)

A. Cleansing the Temple (v. 12)

12. And Jesus went into the temple of God, and cast out all them that sold and bought in the temple, and overthrew the tables of the money changers, and the seats of them that sold doves.

As noted above, the "cleansing of the temple" took place on the day following Jesus' triumphal entry (Mark 11:11-17). No doubt Jesus deliberately planned to separate the two events to allow the crowd to settle down. Had He immediately entered the *temple of God* and rid it of the abuses taking place there, the frenzied crowd might well have broken out in a riot. By waiting until the next day, Jesus was able to cleanse the temple in a manner that demonstrated His high authority as Messiah-King. This was no mob action, but wholly the act of Jesus.

By the time of Jesus, the chief priests and Pharisees had turned the temple into a religious marketplace. Initially their intentions may have been quite commendable. Those traveling to the temple from great distances for the Passover or other occasions would find it more convenient to buy their sacrificial lambs and birds at the temple rather than having to transport them to Jerusalem. Likewise, tithes and offerings had to be converted to acceptable Jewish coins by *the money changers.*

At some point, however, this convenience had turned into a racket. Some sources indicate that perfectly good animals were often rejected as inadequate in order to coerce travelers into purchasing from the temple market. The exchange fees charged by the money changers became exorbitant. The system had become corrupt and was badly in need of reform. The problem was that the spiritual leaders who should have sought reform needed to be reformed themselves.

In His role as Messiah, Jesus *cast out* the merchandisers and *overthrew* their *tables* of money. Furthermore, He would not allow pedestrians to take shortcuts across the temple grounds while they conducted their business (Mark 11:16). There is no indication that Jesus harmed anyone, but there was a clear expression of His anger against the defilement of God's holy temple. [See question #4, page 200.]

B. Teaching the Truth (v. 13)

13. And said unto them, It is written, My house shall be called the house of prayer; but ye have made it a den of thieves.

How to Say It
BETHANY. *Beth*-uh-nee.
BETHPHAGE. *Beth*-fuh-gee.
GETHSEMANE. Geth-*sem*-uh-nee.
HOSANNA. Ho-*san*-uh.
ISAIAH. Eye-*zay*-uh.
JEREMIAH. Jair-uh-*my*-uh.
KIDRON. *Kid*-ron.
LAZARUS. *Laz*-uh-rus.
MESSIANIC. Mess-ee-*an*-ick.
NAZARETH. *Naz*-uh-reth.
ZECHARIAH. Zek-uh-*rye*-uh.

The phrase *den of thieves* was taken from Jeremiah, who lamented the fact that the people who gathered for worship in his day were so evil to each other throughout the week that the temple became, whenever they were present, a "den of robbers" (Jeremiah 7:11). The situation was even worse in Jesus' day. The thievery that once had been practiced outside the temple was now actually being conducted, under priestly sanction, on temple grounds. Jesus' cleansing of the temple was intended to remove such corruption.

However, there was more to Jesus' actions. Using the language of the prophet Isaiah, Jesus then declared that the temple was meant to be a *house of prayer* (Isaiah 56:7) where people could remove themselves from the cares of this world and focus their attention upon God. The merchants within the temple interfered with the solemn and serene setting intended by God. Thus Jesus was able to "cleanse" the temple of both its corruption and its distractions. And though it is likely that the abuses resumed shortly after His death, He had at least established an ideal that thoughtful worshipers of God must keep in mind. [See question #5, page 200.]

Conclusion

A. Royal Highways

In announcing the coming of the Messiah, the prophet Isaiah used the imagery of a road crew, whose task was to prepare a royal highway for the grand arrival of a visiting dignitary. "The voice of him that crieth in the wilderness, Prepare ye the way of the Lord, make straight in the desert a highway for our God. Every valley shall be exalted, and every mountain and hill shall be made low: and the crooked shall be made straight, and the rough places plain: and the glory of the Lord shall be revealed, and all flesh shall see it together" (Isaiah 40:3-5).

The spirit of honoring the arrival of Jesus as King was present at His triumphal entry. May it ever be present in our hearts each time we gather in worship to celebrate our Lord Jesus Christ. May it be present each day as we seek to honor and serve Him before a dying world.

B. Prayer

Father, we thank You for sending Your Son to save us, and to reign over us as the Prince of Peace. Help us to be His humble and obedient servants. In Jesus' name we pray. Amen.

C. Thought to Remember

"Hosanna to the Son of David: Blessed is he that cometh in the name of the Lord" (Matthew 21:9).

Learning by Doing

This page contains an alternate lesson plan emphasizing learning activities.
Classes desiring such student involvement will find these suggestions helpful.

Learning Goals

After this lesson students should be able to:

1. Summarize the events surrounding Jesus' triumphal entry into Jerusalem.

2. Explain what made Jesus' triumphal entry so significant.

3. Take specific steps to eliminate something from their lives that keeps Jesus from ruling as Lord and King.

Into the Lesson

To open today's class, rent and play a clip from a video that shows a ticker-tape parade. (*The Right Stuff* or *The Spirit of America* with James Stewart would do nicely.) If you have a class member who is interested in videos, this would be a good time to invite this person to help. This person could rent the video and cue it to the appropriate section. He or she could also set up the equipment in the room.

Introduce the clip by saying, "Everyone loves a parade. As you watch this clip, see if you can identify the movie."

Make the transition to the Bible study by saying, "Our lesson today examines an event that was similar to a ticker-tape parade—the triumphal entry of Jesus into Jerusalem. As we study Matthew 21:1-13, look for similarities with this movie clip."

Into the Word

After a volunteer reads today's lesson text, Matthew 21:1-13, use one or both of the following activities to lead in a study of the text.

Parallel Passage Study

The triumphal entry is one of the few events recorded in all four Gospels. In addition to Matthew 21:1-13, it is found also in Mark 11:1-19; Luke 19:28-43; and John 12:12-19. Have your class study the parallel accounts by listing similarities and differences in the four accounts. For example, Matthew alone mentions the foal's mother, while John doesn't mention Jesus' sending two disciples to get the animal. Prepare a chart with four columns (headed with the names Matthew, Mark, Luke, and John), or use the chart provided in the student book. Put items that are the same in more than one Gospel on the same line. Unique items in a column should be on separate lines from anything in any other column.

Choral Reading

Matthew 21:1-13 lends itself well to a choral reading. Assign the parts of narrator, Jesus, the quotes from the Old Testament (Zechariah, Psalms, Isaiah, and Jeremiah), and the crowds. (Let the class help to decide which individuals or groups would be most appropriate for each part. For example, the Psalm 8 quote could be read by a chorus of mothers.) Encourage readers to read dramatically with exaggerated expression.

Invite the students to ask questions about the text, seeking to answer them with the help of the commentary section of this book.

Into Life

Choose one or both of the following activities to apply the message of today's text.

Praise Service

Depending on the time and equipment available, you may want to have a praise service to conclude today's class session. Palm fronds can be purchased from your florist without too much expense. Contact a florist ahead of time to make sure the palm fronds will be available. Have your class members select songs from church hymnbooks or song sheets. Tell your class to look especially for songs related to today's text, that is, with phrases like "Hosanna" or "Blessed is he who comes in the name of the Lord."

Cleansing Your Temple

Tell the class, "When Jesus visited the temple at the beginning of His final week, He cleansed it from activities and actions that had corrupted it. According to 1 Corinthians 6:19, 20, the believer's body is the temple of God today. Please bow your heads and prayerfully consider each of these questions based on today's Scripture."

Ask the following questions, allowing about fifteen seconds of silence after each one.

1. Are there any "money changers" that need to be removed from your temple of God today?

2. Are there any areas of greed that are corrupting your temple today?

3. Which description best applies to your temple of God today: a house of prayer or a den of robbers?

4. Are there activities that look religious to others but, in reality, interfere with God's spiritual purposes in your temple?

Let's Talk It Over

The questions on this page are designed to encourage review of the lesson Scriptures and to promote discussion of the lesson by the class. The answers provided are only discussion starters. Let your class talk it over from there.

1. When you are asked to take a responsibility or perform a task in the church, how do you decide what your response will be?

There seems always to be more things to do in the church than there are people to do them. Studies show that 80% of the work done is accomplished by 20% of the people. A few in the church are probably doing too much; many are doing little or nothing!

Sometimes our answer has to do with time. For many, "downsizing" at their workplace has multiplied their workload. If one is already heavily involved at church, finding time for an additional task may be difficult. For others, however, the excuse of not having time reflects their priorities more than their responsibilities.

Sometimes our answer depends on how the task matches our abilities or gifts. If everyone in the church looked for a ministry that matched his or her spiritual gifts, much more would be accomplished without anyone's being overburdened.

2. The disciples "did as Jesus commanded them." Why is it sometimes difficult for us to just do what God's Word instructs us to do? How can we make a better effort to do what the Lord commands?

Sometimes we disobey out of ignorance; we need a better knowledge of His will (Psalms 1:2; 119:34). Sometimes we accept a different authority—such as scientists, peers, or even parents. We need to be careful that we do not seek to please men more than God (cf. John 12:43). Complete obedience requires an emotional, intellectual, and volitional commitment (Colossians 3:1, 2, 5-9) to the Lord, which results in a person's being conformed to the image of Christ (Colossians 3:10).

3. Many in the crowd that shouted "Hosanna" on one day were, just a few days later, shouting "Crucify!" In what ways are we sometimes just as fickle? How can we resist the temptation to "change our tune" when the crowd shifts?

Aren't we all a bit inclined to be influenced by popular opinion? We may decide to buy a book because it is on the best-seller list. Or we go to see a movie because it received several academy awards. It's not easy to take a stand regardless of what others think, is it? For example, if a popular movie glamorizes immorality, are we willing to say so when our friends rave about how good the movie is?

We have a clear mandate from the Lord. He has not called us to be popular; He has called us to be faithful. Keeping that foremost in our minds will help us to follow the right path—no matter what course others may take.

4. If Jesus were to come into a contemporary church, what might He observe, if anything, that would cause Him to respond similarly to the way He reacted to what was going on at the temple?

Be careful that this question does not open the door for class members to complain about whatever they personally do not like in the worship service. Note that the actions of selling and exchanging money in and of themselves were not wrong, but the abuse and exploitation associated with them were. If Jesus came into our worship service, the things He would condemn are those things born of ill will, insincerity, and hypocrisy. Anything that was a barrier to true worship, or that distorted the nature of worship, would receive His censure. Sincere worship, through a variety of means, would be honored.

5. God's house, or temple, is not the church building, but the church—believers collectively (1 Corinthians 3:16, 17) and individually (1 Corinthians 6:19, 20). To what extent, then, do you think Jesus' words about honoring God's house apply to us today?

Certainly they apply to keeping ourselves pure (the issue in 1 Corinthians 6) and to preserving the unity of the church (1 Corinthians 3). But they might apply also to our care for the building.

The issue here is one of purpose. The Jewish leaders had abused the purpose of the temple. Our church buildings, while not "holy" in and of themselves, are dedicated to the holy purposes of sincere worship, Bible teaching, and Christian fellowship!

When people come to this place for worship that is what must occur. This demands a certain decorum and reverence. Even with a variety of worship styles, we need to take care that everything "be done decently and in order" (1 Corinthians 14:40).

Anticipation of Christ's Return

DEVOTIONAL READING: Matthew 24:36-44.

BACKGROUND SCRIPTURE: Matthew 24:1—25:13.

PRINTED TEXT: Matthew 24:45—25:13.

Matthew 24:45-51

45 Who then is a faithful and wise servant, whom his lord hath made ruler over his household, to give them meat in due season?

46 Blessed is that servant, whom his lord when he cometh shall find so doing.

47 Verily I say unto you, That he shall make him ruler over all his goods.

48 But and if that evil servant shall say in his heart, My lord delayeth his coming;

49 And shall begin to smite his fellow servants, and to eat and drink with the drunken;

50 The lord of that servant shall come in a day when he looketh not for him, and in an hour that he is not aware of,

51 And shall cut him asunder, and appoint him his portion with the hypocrites: there shall be weeping and gnashing of teeth.

Matthew 25:1-13

1 Then shall the kingdom of heaven be likened unto ten virgins, which took their lamps, and went forth to meet the bridegroom.

2 And five of them were wise, and five were foolish.

3 They that were foolish took their lamps, and took no oil with them:

4 But the wise took oil in their vessels with their lamps.

5 While the bridegroom tarried, they all slumbered and slept.

6 And at midnight there was a cry made, Behold, the bridegroom cometh; go ye out to meet him.

7 Then all those virgins arose, and trimmed their lamps.

8 And the foolish said unto the wise, Give us of your oil; for our lamps are gone out.

9 But the wise answered, saying, Not so; lest there be not enough for us and you: but go ye rather to them that sell, and buy for yourselves.

10 And while they went to buy, the bridegroom came; and they that were ready went in with him to the marriage: and the door was shut.

11 Afterward came also the other virgins, saying, Lord, Lord, open to us.

12 But he answered and said, Verily I say unto you, I know you not.

13 Watch therefore; for ye know neither the day nor the hour wherein the Son of man cometh.

Feb 13

GOLDEN TEXT: Watch therefore; for ye know neither the day nor the hour wherein the Son of man cometh.—Matthew 25:13.

Immanuel: God With Us
Unit 3: Fulfillment: Atonement
and Final Commission
(Lessons 10-13)

Lesson Aims

After this lesson students should be able to:

1. Tell what Jesus' teachings concerning the unfaithful servant and the ten virgins say about His second coming.

2. Explain the difference between being wise and foolish regarding Jesus' second coming.

3. List some specific steps they can take to prepare for the return of Jesus and to increase its impact on their daily living.

Lesson Outline

INTRODUCTION
    A. Charts for Sale
    B. Lesson Background
  I. FAITHFUL SERVICE (Matthew 24:45-47)
    A. Stewards of God (v. 45)
    B. Blessed and Exalted (vv. 46, 47)
  II. FOOLISH ACTIONS (Matthew 24:48-51)
    A. Evil Stewards (vv. 48, 49)
    B. Cursed and Tormented (vv. 50, 51)
     Are You Ready?
 III. FULLY PREPARED (Matthew 25:1-7)
    A. Important Duties (vv. 1-4)
    B. Ready When Called (vv. 5-7)
     The Bridegroom Cometh
 IV. FUTILE EFFORTS (Matthew 25:8-13)
    A. Desperate Request (vv. 8, 9)
    B. Kept From Entering (vv. 10-13)
CONCLUSION
    A. "Do Over"
    B. Prayer
    C. Thought to Remember

Introduction

A. Charts for Sale

"Bible Prophecy Chart for Sale—Used Only Once." What an amusing sign this would be at a garage sale for some Bible prophecy preachers, who have often attempted to guess the date of Christ's return by searching for clues in the Scripture. Church history records twenty centuries of such theorizing about the date of Christ's return, with none of the efforts having proved successful. Even so, every day new guesses replace the old failed ones, and time eventually takes its toll on additional prophecy speculators.

Today's lesson offers a more solid alternative to the study of the second coming of Christ. Rather than urging us to seek signs pointing to the time this event will take place, Jesus' words encourage us to stay ready at all times, always recognizing that today could be the day that He returns.

B. Lesson Background

Today's lesson material is part of the teaching that Jesus probably gave on Tuesday of His final week. Most of this day was spent in the temple, presenting lessons in parables to the Passover crowds, fielding difficult questions from His enemies, and rebuking the hypocrisy of the scribes and Pharisees. The evening was spent in a private setting with His closest disciples. The Gospel of Matthew devotes most of five chapters to this busy day of public and private teaching (Matthew 21:23—25:46).

As Jesus and the disciples were leaving the temple area at the end of the day, some of the disciples commented on the impressive stones of the temple buildings (Mark 13:1). Jesus startled them when He said that a day would come when the temple would be destroyed, with not one stone left upon another (Matthew 24:2).

Once they arrived at the seclusion of the Mount of Olives, the stunned disciples asked Jesus to elaborate on His statement. Their questions were simple enough. When will the temple be destroyed, and what will be the sign that the end of the age has arrived (Matthew 24:3)? Jesus' answer, recorded in Matthew 24, remains one of the most controversial passages in the Gospels.

Some Bible students maintain that Matthew 24 predicts the fall of Jerusalem, including the destruction of the temple, at the hands of the Roman army in A.D. 70. Others insist that it is focused exclusively on signs that will foretell the end of time and the second coming of Christ. Most students see both of these events—the fall of Jerusalem and the second coming—reflected in chapter 24. Of these, some see Jesus alternating back and forth in His discussion of the two, while others believe that Jesus is linking the two events, with the end of the temple as a foretaste of the end of the world.

Regardless of the approach one takes to this chapter, it seems obvious that by verse 36 Jesus is focusing attention on the day when He will return to earth. He speaks of "that day and hour" as being unknown to all but our heavenly Father (v. 36) and tells us to "watch" every day for His coming (v. 42). Thus begins a series of lessons on the theme of staying ready for Christ's return.

I. Faithful Service
(Matthew 24:45-47)
A. Stewards of God (v. 45)

45. Who then is a faithful and wise servant, whom his lord hath made ruler over his household, to give them meat in due season?

The phrase *ruler over his household* describes the individual whom the master has designated as a household "steward." He was the slave who supervised other slaves. His job included overseeing the performance of assigned duties, including the administration of discipline when needed. His job was to make sure everything was done in a manner pleasing to the master. He would also *give* the servants *meat in due season*—that is, he would see that all of them were properly fed, housed, and cared for.

We Christians likewise are "stewards" in the household of God. We are expected to take whatever spiritual gifts and service opportunities the Lord provides and do the best we can to please the Master (1 Peter 4:10, 11). Paul reminds us, "Moreover it is required in stewards, that a man be found faithful" (1 Corinthians 4:2).

B. Blessed and Exalted (vv. 46, 47)

46. Blessed is that servant, whom his lord when he cometh shall find so doing.

A wealthy landowner could be away from home for several days or weeks at a time, pursuing business dealings abroad or attending to political affairs. While he was gone he would expect his house to operate as if he were there personally overseeing it. If he returned to find everything in excellent order, the steward could expect to be *blessed* and rewarded by his *lord*. [See question #1, page 208.]

47. Verily I say unto you, That he shall make him ruler over all his goods.

Any servant in ancient times who did his job well and proved himself to be of special value would naturally be promoted to a position of greater responsibility, where his competence would bear even greater fruit for the master. That is how an ordinary servant could become a household steward, and how the steward in Jesus' illustration could move on to more important leadership duties.

While this parable refers primarily to our readiness for the second coming of Christ, it carries immediate application to our present service in the kingdom of God. Those who minister and serve in the church in a commendable manner are often encouraged to try more challenging areas of service. There is a real satisfaction we receive in being noticed and appreciated for our work and in being desired for other labors. [See question #2, page 208.]

II. Foolish Actions
(Matthew 24:48-51)
A. Evil Stewards (vv. 48, 49)

48. But and if that evil servant shall say in his heart, My lord delayeth his coming.

In contrast to the "faithful and wise" steward of verse 45, Jesus introduced an *evil* steward. This *servant* thought he could ignore his duties as long as he did not get "caught." Since he believed his master had been delayed and would not catch him in inactivity or abuse, he began to misuse his position of trust.

Many Bible teachers will use the idea that the Lord's return is upon us to motivate good behavior—lest the Lord "catch us" doing wrong when He returns! The fact of the matter is, we ought to do right whether the Lord's return is going to be today or is still far off in the future.

At the same time, if we believe the Lord's return is far off in the future, we may be tempted to treat spiritual matters with little or no urgency. We intend to do the things we ought, but later. We need to keep in mind that the Lord may return very soon; it is urgent that we do all we can as soon as we can—particularly when it comes to winning the lost.

As for the unsaved, they may view Christ's apparent delay in returning as proof that believing in His second coming is futile. By the time Peter wrote his second epistle (approximately thirty years after Jesus' resurrection and ascension) there were already "scoffers" making fun of the Christian hope of a second coming because of the "long" delay (2 Peter 3:3, 4). But Peter understood the concept of a "delay" based on God's timetable rather than our expectations (Acts 1:6, 7). He explains that "one day is with the Lord as a thousand years, and a thousand years as one day" (2 Peter 3:8). From God's perspective, Jesus has been gone only "a couple of days," and who knows how many more "days" the church is to wait? We would do well to learn patience and practice readiness. [See question #3, page 208.]

49. And shall begin to smite his fellow servants, and to eat and drink with the drunken.

"Dereliction of duty" is the official charge we would declare against this evil steward today. When he dared to *smite his fellow servants*, he

---

How to Say It

HYPOCRITES. *hip*-uh-krits.
PHARISEES. *Fair*-ih-seez.

was violating the trust that his master had placed in him. Also, when he began to *drink with the drunken*, he was shirking his assigned duty to carefully oversee the master's business at home. He would certainly not be "blessed" as the faithful steward was (v. 46) if he were caught participating in such activity.

B. Cursed and Tormented (vv. 50, 51)

50. The lord of that servant shall come in a day when he looketh not for him, and in an hour that he is not aware of.

The evil steward thought the same way many so often think—that they have plenty of time to take care of business. And yet who among us has not watched family and friends die sooner than expected and, for many, without adequate spiritual preparation?

One day some generation in this planet's history will experience the day of Christ's return. No doubt it will occur when least expected. Many will find themselves unprepared for the judgment to follow, because they assumed that they had plenty of time to get ready. Who knows? We could be that generation of people for whom the Lord comes *in an hour that* we are *not aware of.*

51. And shall cut him asunder, and appoint him his portion with the hypocrites: there shall be weeping and gnashing of teeth.

In Biblical times it was considered a serious threat to the social stability for servants not to perform their duties faithfully. Rebellious attitudes could become widespread among the servant population, bringing the whole societal structure to collapse. Thus landowners were legally permitted to take strong punitive measures against servants who needed to be disciplined. Imprisonment and even torture were permitted.

The horror of the imagery of Hell in this verse is designed to teach us a valuable lesson: as we await the return of our Lord for a day of accounting before God, we need to get ready and stay ready.

ARE YOU READY?

The lady picking strawberries in the row next to me—I'll call her Susan—was explaining how difficult it had been to move her father and mother out of their house in Cleveland and into an assisted-living facility in Cincinnati. They were in their nineties and had become unable to care for themselves. Now they were having trouble adjusting to their infirmities and to living in a new environment.

Susan (an only daughter) and her husband had insisted on and assisted with the move. When it was completed, they were exhausted

and "stressed out"; so they decided to take a "spring break." But on their way to Hilton Head, South Carolina—without symptoms or warning—Susan's comparatively young husband suddenly dropped dead, the victim of a heart attack.

Susan said she wasn't ready for that. Of course, she wasn't! But a more important question arises: was *he* ready? That is, was he ready to meet his Maker?

Another possibility should be of equal concern: are *you* ready to meet *your* Maker? Christ's return or your physical death is certain; the timing of either event is *uncertain*. Given those truths, "what manner of persons ought ye to be?" (2 Peter 3:11). —R. W. B.

III. Fully Prepared
(Matthew 25:1-7)

A. Important Duties (vv. 1-4)

1. Then shall the kingdom of heaven be likened unto ten virgins, which took their lamps, and went forth to meet the bridegroom.

The *virgins* of this parable were comparable to what we would call bridesmaids today. They themselves were not yet married, but were sending off one of their own to be married. They were to gather at the site of the wedding festivities, whether in the home of the bride or groom or in another location. Their assignment was to go out and greet the *bridegroom* and his entourage as they approached, and then usher them into the house in a stately manner. Not knowing the precise time of the bridegroom's arrival, the virgins needed to bring their *lamps* in case he did not come until dark.

2. And five of them were wise, and five were foolish.

Before Jesus even described the virgins' actions, He gave an assessment of their readiness for duty on behalf of the bride and groom. *Five* of them were called *wise*, while the other *five* were designated as *foolish*.

3. They that were foolish took their lamps, and took no oil with them.

When Jesus says that the *foolish* virgins *took no oil with them*, He means that they did not carry "vessels" of oil for refilling their lamps, as did the wise virgins (v. 4). Their lamps would have been filled and burning as soon as the sun set, but they would not have the means for replenishing their lamps if the bridegroom's coming was delayed.

4. But the wise took oil in their vessels with their lamps.

In contrast to the foolish virgins, the *wise* virgins did anticipate the possibility of a delay and brought along *vessels* with extra *oil*. The foolish

Visual for
lessons 10 & 11

Display the poster from last week's lesson to illustrate the lesson today. Discuss how different Jesus' return will be from His first coming.

virgins may have had good intentions, but they were short-sighted in their planning. Such a special event as a wedding deserved the kind of foresight demonstrated by the wise virgins.

B. Ready When Called (vv. 5-7)

5. While the bridegroom tarried, they all slumbered and slept.

The *bridegroom* could have been delayed by business dealings that needed to be completed before his attention could be given to his wedding activities. Or it may be, as some commentaries suggest, that he and his family and friends had their own preliminary celebration that had run late. Whatever the cause, this kind of delay would not have been uncommon where people were not as time conscious as Westerners are today. For an event like this, people would not so much have designated a time for it to begin as they would have appointed a particular day. The virgins would simply have been told that the bridegroom's party would arrive sometime that evening.

Some have concluded that it was wrong for the foolish virgins to have *slept*. But that was not the problem; after all, even the wise virgins *slumbered*. A watchman would awaken the entire household in plenty of time for people to take their positions (vv. 6, 7); thus resting was a reasonable thing to do.

6. And at midnight there was a cry made, Behold, the bridegroom cometh; go ye out to meet him.

The *cry* was sounded *at midnight*, approximately six hours after the lamps had been lit at sunset. By this time, probably all of the lamps had gone out or would soon do so.

7. Then all those virgins arose, and trimmed their lamps.

The *virgins* quickly *trimmed their lamps* by removing the burned portion of the wick and pulling out a fresh wick. It quickly became apparent to the foolish virgins that their oil supply

was inadequate. The five virgins who had thought to bring extra oil added it to their lamps and were fully prepared for the bridegroom's arrival.

THE BRIDEGROOM COMETH

A grandmother recently shared the account of her grandson's wedding reception, which was nearly a disaster. The caterer failed to bring even half enough food to feed the more than two hundred guests. (A "free-will" offering had to be received to order pizza!) The specially ordered cake, to be complete with a fountain in the center, was delivered "downsized" and *incomplete*— with no fountain. The audio tape intended to provide big-band sounds was mistakenly replaced by a recording of the Monkees! The bride was in tears most of the evening, and the groom was fuming.

Even the best-made plans can go awry on the most careful planners. Apparently none of the aforementioned mishaps was due to poor preparation on the part of the bride or the groom. But *someone* dropped the ball—or several someones, perhaps.

Weddings require enormous amounts of time and effort in preparation. The "marriage supper of the Lamb" (Revelation 19:9) also demands diligent planning. To be ready for the coming of our Bridegroom is our most important challenge. To ignore personal preparation for His return is most foolish. Proper attention to details, double-checking instructions, clear and frequent communication, and fulfilling responsibilities "to the letter" will enhance our readiness for the day when "the bridegroom cometh." —R. W. B.

IV. Futile Efforts
(Matthew 25:8-13)

A. Desperate Request (vv. 8, 9)

8. And the foolish said unto the wise, Give us of your oil; for our lamps are gone out.

The *foolish* virgins' request that the *wise* share their *oil* sounds reasonable to Christians who appreciate the Biblical idea of sharing what you have with others and helping your friends when they are in need.

9. But the wise answered, saying, Not so; lest there be not enough for us and you: but go ye rather to them that sell, and buy for yourselves.

The *wise* virgins realized that if they shared their limited supply of oil, then none of the attendants would have enough in their lamps to be certain that they could keep them lighted for the remaining six hours until morning. The wedding celebration would thus be spoiled. The wise virgins must have realized that five lamps capable of remaining lighted through the night were better than ten lamps shining brightly at first but later failing.

Though it is true that sharing with others is usually a good practice, in this case there was a greater principle to be considered. The first loyalty of the wise virgins was to their duty on behalf of the bridegroom. Their refusal to share was not based on a selfish spirit, but on a clear perception of their duty. [See question #4, page 208.]

B. Kept From Entering (vv. 10-13)

10. And while they went to buy, the bridegroom came; and they that were ready went in with him to the marriage: and the door was shut.

Had this been a real event and not a parable, the foolish virgins probably never would have found a shop owner willing to reopen his store after midnight. Their return was significant to the point Jesus was making, so after some delay, they did return with oil. In the meantime, however, the wedding party had entered the banquet hall and *the door was shut.* In such cases, a guard was often posted to keep any curious but uninvited neighbors outside.

11. Afterward came also the other virgins, saying, Lord, Lord, open to us.

Eventually the *other virgins* returned with fresh oil and trimmed lamps, ready to fulfill their duties. Perhaps it had been their intention to do a good job; they simply had failed to plan adequately. Now they were asking for a second chance.

12. But he answered and said, Verily I say unto you, I know you not.

The good intentions of the foolish virgins were worthless once the door was secured. For the bridegroom to say *I know you not* does not mean that he did not recognize these ladies, but that he had no use for their services now. After all, he had no reason to care for these who had given him so little care earlier. [See question #5, page 208.]

13. Watch therefore; for ye know neither the day nor the hour wherein the Son of man cometh.

The lesson from this parable should be obvious to all readers. The second coming of Christ will not be announced in advance so that we can plan on when to get our lives ready for the judgment. "Of that day and hour knoweth no man, no, not the angels of heaven, but my Father only," Jesus declared in this same passage (Matthew 24:36). Here is the one clear instruction He has given to all His disciples regarding the second coming: stay ready every moment of every day.

Conclusion

A. "Do Over"

Watch children playing a game that requires them to try out new skills, and you will often hear someone ask for a "do over." This means that, even though a child has failed at some part of the game and according to the rules should forfeit a turn to someone else, he is given a second chance. And since the other children would enjoy having that same privilege if they failed, a "do over" is generally granted.

Wouldn't it be great if life gave out a few "do overs" when we messed up? Unfortunately, we adults know from the classroom of experience that such is not often the case. God has given each of us a limited amount of time to accomplish whatever we wish to do with our lives, and He expects us to use our time and resources wisely. Missed opportunities are rarely repeated. Those who delay in addressing spiritual matters are making a mistake they will regret throughout eternity, unless they take steps to set their spiritual houses in order.

There is no better day for doing this than *today.*

B. Prayer

Father, help us to be more diligent in our pursuit of holiness and service. May we never take time for granted, knowing that it is a limited and precious resource. In Jesus' name. Amen.

C. Thought to Remember

"Behold, he cometh with clouds; and every eye shall see him, and they also which pierced him: and all kindreds of the earth shall wail because of him. Even so, Amen" (Revelation 1:7).

Home Daily Bible Readings

Monday, Feb. 7—Let No One Deceive You (Matthew 24:1-8)

Tuesday, Feb. 8—Jesus' Followers Will Be Persecuted (Matthew 24:9-14)

Wednesday, Feb. 9—Beware of False Messiahs (Matthew 24:15-28)

Thursday, Feb. 10—Coming of the Son of Man (Matthew 24:29-35)

Friday, Feb. 11—Be Watchful and Expectant (Matthew 24:36-44)

Saturday, Feb. 12—Call to Be Faithful Servants (Matthew 24:45-51)

Sunday, Feb. 13—Parable of the Ten Virgins (Matthew 25:1-13)

Learning by Doing

This page contains an alternate lesson plan emphasizing learning activities.
Classes desiring such student involvement will find these suggestions helpful.

Learning Goals

After this lesson students should be able to:

1. Tell what Jesus' teachings concerning the unfaithful servant and the ten virgins say about His second coming.

2. Explain the difference between being wise and foolish regarding Jesus' second coming.

3. List some specific steps they can take to prepare for the return of Jesus and to increase its impact on their daily living.

Into the Lesson

This lesson looks at character qualities and skills necessary to be a faithful and wise servant. To get into the lesson, ask your class members to write help-wanted ads that might appear if Jesus were advertising for disciples today in the "Help Wanted" section of the newspaper. Warm up for the writing period by identifying some qualities that Jesus expects in His servants. For example, He wants faithfulness, ability to work alone and in groups, perseverance, and the like. Ask for volunteers to read their ads to the class.

Make the transition to the Bible study by saying, "Jesus is actively seeking servants to work in His kingdom today. We've seen the qualities that we think He would want. Today's text tells us what He expects. Some of you may even have thought of the qualities identified in Matthew 24:45—25:13. Let's compare our ideas with what Jesus taught in this passage."

Into the Word

Ask a volunteer to read Matthew 24:45—25:13. Then choose one or more of the following activities to study the text. Or divide the students into three groups and assign one activity to each.

Concordance Study

These parables employ terms that Jesus used regularly. Understanding how Jesus used these terms in other places will broaden our understanding of this passage. Provide concordances for your students to use in class. Have them look up "weeping and gnashing of teeth," "evil servant," "hypocrites," and "watch."

Drama

Drama can be a powerful Bible study tool because it requires us to examine the text carefully to determine the characters, story line, tone of voice, etc. Ask your class members to act out the two parables in today's lesson. In the first parable they will need characters to represent Jesus, the wise servant, the foolish servant, and the other servants. In the second, they will need five foolish virgins, five wise virgins, the crier, the oil merchant, and the doorman.

Cartooning

Every class has members who like to doodle and draw. A cartooning activity will appeal to them and allow them a chance to use their skills. For this activity you will need to assemble pencils, paper, erasers, and a means of displaying the finished work, such as a clothesline and clips or masking tape and a blank wall.

Instruct the class to draw cartoon strips that will tell the two parables in this lesson. They may want to work in pairs or small groups to decide how many frames need to be drawn to tell the story completely. Then one frame could be assigned to each person. Assure them that the quality of the drawing is not the critical point, but a faithful telling of the story.

Into Life

The common thread in both parables is that Jesus' return will be delayed longer than expected, and some will not be prepared for His return. Give each person an index card and a pen. Ask each person to write down the name of a service or project that is not complete because of procrastination. Then ask him or her to set a date by when it will be completed and to select a partner who will agree to pray and/or help him or her complete the project. Close the class with a prayer time, with each pair praying for one another's project.

Option

Distribute several copies of older hymnbooks to your class members. Make sure the books include songs like, "Toiling On," "Work, for the Night Is Coming," or "There's a Place for Every Worker." Invite your class to do a hymn study. They will compare ideas from today's Bible passage with the ideas from these and other hymns. For example, "toiling on" is the basic message of Matthew 24:45-51. Close the class by singing one or more songs of commitment to be wise and faithful servants until Jesus comes again.

Let's Talk It Over

The questions on this page are designed to encourage review of the lesson Scriptures and to promote discussion of the lesson by the class. The answers provided are only discussion starters. Let your class talk it over from there.

1. These parables are about being ready to give an accounting of our service when the Lord returns. The "faithful and wise servant" is the one who has nothing for which to be ashamed on that day. Of course, we are asked to account for our actions in a variety of settings in this life as well. What application do you think this concept has for Christians at the workplace?

The "faithful and wise servant" is still the one who has nothing for which to be ashamed when called to give an accounting of his actions. He is the one who works steadily, whether the boss or foreman is watching or not. He is not worried about a surprise inspection because his work is first-rate with or without inspection. He is the one who keeps honest records, whether it's on his time sheet or the company ledger. He doesn't have to worry about someone's discovering fraud because there is none to find.

2. The lesson writer says, "There is a real satisfaction we receive in being noticed and appreciated for our work" in the church. But what if we work hard and are *not* noticed? What applications do you find in this parable for ministry in the church?

We have to remember who our Master is. Even if church leaders or others in the church fail to recognize our efforts, it is the Lord Jesus Christ whom we serve. Lack of recognition or appreciation is no reason to give up on service. It may help us decide where we will serve, but whether we will serve should already have been decided when we accepted the Lord's call. No matter what, we must be faithful to Him.

3. If I asked your spouse or best friend if you are patient, what would he or she say? Why? Why do you think we have so much difficulty being patient, individually and as a society?

Patience (i.e., long-suffering) is a fruit of the Holy Spirit (Galatians 5:22) that we are all expected to possess, yet many of us struggle to manifest it in our endeavors and in our relationships. Someone has said that the longest time known to man is the time it takes for the traffic light to turn green, and the shortest is the time it takes for the guy behind you to honk his horn when it does.

We live in a culture that is results oriented. We want things to happen and we want them to happen now. We pray "Lord, give me patience, NOW!" Whether it is physical improvement, career advancement, financial increase, or even spiritual development, we are looking for a faster way to get results.

So many of us have a need to be in control of things . . . even things that are beyond our control. As Christians our responsibility is to be faithful in whatever task our Lord gives us and let Him take care of the rest. That requires patience, and it may take a while for us to learn it and manifest it as we should.

4. Can you think of an instance in which you were asked to "bail out" someone who had failed to fulfill a responsibility or make adequate preparation? What did you do? How did you arrive at your decision?

Often, the excuse a person makes is, "I wasn't expecting ___, so I haven't had time to prepare." We seem to think that life consists of the circumstances we must face that we didn't or couldn't anticipate. When we have this perspective, it is easy to see ourselves as unfortunate victims of these circumstances. In fact, life is much more a matter of the choices we make even though we can't anticipate all the circumstances that may come. When those choices grow out of good work habits, self-discipline, and a commitment to excellence and faithfulness, then we are able to face unexpected circumstances much better.

There may be some instances when it is appropriate to "bail out" someone who has failed to prepare adequately for a responsibility, but there are other times when we should not or cannot do so, lest we fail to fulfill our own responsibility.

5. So often we intend to do better than we do! What can be said for good intentions? How can we turn good intentions into good actions?

Good behavior obviously starts with good intentions. We will not do many good things by accident; they must be planned. Unfulfilled intentions, however, can become a habit. We excuse ourselves, and others accept the excuse; then it's easier the next time to fail to follow through on our intentions. One of the best ways to turn our intentions into action is to have someone hold us accountable for our actions, and not to accept our excuses!

Death of Jesus

DEVOTIONAL READING: John 19:16-30.

BACKGROUND SCRIPTURE: Matthew 27:32-61.

PRINTED TEXT: Matthew 27:35-54.

Matthew 27:35-54

35 And they crucified him, and parted his garments, casting lots: that it might be fulfilled which was spoken by the prophet, They parted my garments among them, and upon my vesture did they cast lots.

36 And sitting down they watched him there;

37 And set up over his head his accusation written, THIS IS JESUS THE KING OF THE JEWS.

38 Then were there two thieves crucified with him; one on the right hand, and another on the left.

39 And they that passed by reviled him, wagging their heads,

40 And saying, Thou that destroyest the temple, and buildest it in three days, save thyself. If thou be the Son of God, come down from the cross.

41 Likewise also the chief priests mocking him, with the scribes and elders, said,

42 He saved others; himself he cannot save. If he be the King of Israel, let him now come down from the cross, and we will believe him.

43 He trusted in God; let him deliver him now, if he will have him: for he said, I am the Son of God.

44 The thieves also, which were crucified with him, cast the same in his teeth.

45 Now from the sixth hour there was darkness over all the land unto the ninth hour.

46 And about the ninth hour Jesus cried with a loud voice, saying, Eli, Eli, lama sabachthani? that is to say, My God, my God, why hast thou forsaken me?

47 Some of them that stood there, when they heard that, said, This man calleth for Elijah.

48 And straightway one of them ran, and took a sponge, and filled it with vinegar, and put it on a reed, and gave him to drink.

49 The rest said, Let be, let us see whether Elijah will come to save him.

50 Jesus, when he had cried again with a loud voice, yielded up the ghost.

51 And, behold, the veil of the temple was rent in twain from the top to the bottom; and the earth did quake, and the rocks rent;

52 And the graves were opened; and many bodies of the saints which slept arose,

53 And came out of the graves after his resurrection, and went into the holy city, and appeared unto many.

54 Now when the centurion, and they that were with him, watching Jesus, saw the earthquake, and those things that were done, they feared greatly, saying, Truly this was the Son of God.

GOLDEN TEXT: Truly this was the Son of God.—Matthew 27:54.

Lesson Aims

After this lesson students should be able to:

1. Relate the important details of Jesus' crucifixion according to today's text.

2. Tell how these details reveal the degree of shame and suffering that Jesus experienced on the cross.

3. Renew their love for and commitment to Jesus, recognizing that He endured the agony of the cross for them.

Lesson Outline

INTRODUCTION
  A. Cherished Symbols
  B. Lesson Background
I. PUBLIC SHAME (Matthew 27:35-38)
  A. Clothing Removed (vv. 35, 36)
    The Shame of It
  B. Treated Like a Criminal (vv. 37, 38)
II. HATEFUL SCORN (Matthew 27:39-44)
  A. From the Crowd (vv. 39, 40)
  B. From the Leaders (vv. 41-43)
  C. From the Thieves (v. 44)
III. JESUS' DEATH (Matthew 27:45-50)
  A. Cry of Agony (vv. 45, 46)
  B. Loss of Strength (vv. 47-49)
  C. Moment of Death (v. 50)
    Travesty of Justice—Miracle of Mercy
IV. GOD'S RESPONSE (Matthew 27:51-54)
  A. Atonement Accomplished (v. 51)
  B. Death Defeated (vv. 52, 53)
  C. Witnesses Speak (v. 54)
CONCLUSION
  A. The Old Rugged Cross
  B. Prayer
  C. Thought to Remember

Introduction

A. Cherished Symbols

We Christians have several religious symbols that speak volumes without ever having to be explained. We see a rainbow and immediately think of Noah and the great flood. We see a manger with straw and fondly recall the birth of Jesus, or the emblem of a dove descending and imagine our Lord's baptism in the Jordan River.

Of all of these symbols, perhaps none is more cherished than the cross. While for the Jew the cross was an offensive "stumblingblock" and for the Greeks it was a "foolishness" that they could not understand, for the Christian the cross speaks of "Christ the power of God, and the wisdom of God" (1 Corinthians 1:23, 24). In the cross the Christian sees an object in which he can rightfully "glory" as did Paul (Galatians 6:14).

B. Lesson Background

At the heart of the Christian faith is the death of Christ on the cross. "Good Friday," as we call it today, brought the culminating event of Jesus' final week. On Thursday evening Jesus ate His "Last Supper" with the apostles in an upper room, where He instituted the Lord's Supper. Later in the evening He prayed in the garden of Gethsemane while three of His disciples slept. There He was arrested by the temple guards and taken through a series of Jewish and Roman "trials" before finally being condemned to die by the Roman governor, Pontius Pilate.

Early Friday morning Jesus carried His own cross (most likely one of the beams, which weighed thirty to forty pounds) and made the slow march to a site outside Jerusalem known as Golgotha (Aramaic) or Calvary (Latin). It was there that our Lord and Savior was crucified.

I. Public Shame
(Matthew 27:35-38)

A. Clothing Removed (vv. 35, 36)

35. And they crucified him, and parted his garments, casting lots: that it might be fulfilled which was spoken by the prophet, They parted my garments among them, and upon my vesture did they cast lots.

Part of the "spoils" of guard duty at a crucifixion was the right to confiscate a condemned man's clothing. The usual band of four soldiers would divide the *garments* four ways, with each soldier getting a fair share. The prize among Jesus' clothing was His seamless *vesture*, a soft undergarment worn beneath His outer robe. This was a valuable item that would be rendered worthless if torn into four pieces. Thus the soldiers *cast lots* (the equivalent of rolling dice) to determine which one of them could claim the whole garment (John 19:23, 24). All of this fulfilled the prophecy in Psalm 22:18, which is part of a Messianic Psalm that foretells several of the indignities to be experienced by the Messiah at the hands of His enemies.

36. And sitting down they watched him there.

There was no concern that a crucifixion victim might break free from his cross and escape, for his hands and feet were securely nailed to the cross (in some cases they were tied). The guards were posted in order to prevent anyone from rescuing the victim.

THE SHAME OF IT

There is something hideous and bloodthirsty in the human condition. Consider the popularity of movies with gore, horror, and violence. Consider also the "rubbernecking" of motorists passing a highway accident and slowing to a snail's pace to see the wreckage. A morbid curiosity lurks just beneath the surface of their facade of sophistication. One wonders how many today would turn out to watch a public execution—too many, perhaps, from a supposedly civilized, "polite" society.

The same morbid curiosity likely drew many to the scene at Golgotha where three men were crucified. The crowd looked and leered, they taunted and jeered, as these nearly-naked men suffered unspeakable indignities. Jeremiah certainly was right when he declared, "The heart is . . . desperately wicked" (Jeremiah 17:9).

The crucifixion of Christ marked a shameful day for the human race. Thankfully, He "endured the cross, despising the shame, and is set down at the right hand of the throne of God" (Hebrews 12:2).   —R. W. B.

B. Treated Like a Criminal (vv. 37, 38)

37. And set up over his head his accusation written, THIS IS JESUS THE KING OF THE JEWS.

In a typical crucifixion, a placard was posted on the cross to inform observers of the criminal charges against the victim. The sign *over* Jesus' *head* gave the identity of the accused, *This is Jesus*, and the charge, *the King of the Jews*. The *accusation* against Jesus was treason, for His claim to be a King was twisted to imply that Jesus wanted to usurp the authority of the Roman emperor.

The phrase *King of the Jews* was added by Pilate to poke fun at the Jewish leaders, because he knew that it would offend them to speak of this man they hated as being their king (John 19:21, 22). The sign was written in Hebrew (or Aramaic), Greek, and Latin (John 19:20) so that all passersby (including the many travelers who were present for the Passover) could read it and know why this man was being put to death.

38. Then were there two thieves crucified with him; one on the right hand, and another on the left.

It was the practice of the Romans to hold condemned criminals in prison until there were several who could be crucified at the same time, thereby requiring only one set of guards (rather than a set for each victim). Because the Jewish leaders insisted that Pilate execute Jesus without delay, the soldiers had to work with the number they had available at that time—in this case, only *two thieves*. It would have been bad enough for Jesus to be crucified alone, but for a righteous and innocent man it was an agonizing shame to be associated with common criminals. [See question #1, page 216.]

II. Hateful Scorn
(Matthew 27:39-44)

A. From the Crowd (vv. 39, 40)

39. And they that passed by reviled him, wagging their heads.

The Romans designed crucifixion to be a public spectator event. Crosses were placed next to major highways, often up on a hill, for all to see. The intent was to draw a large crowd who would witness an excruciating and humiliating death for the worst kind of criminals. The crowd itself was encouraged to participate through mocking and derision. All of this was designed, not only to torment the criminal, but also to teach the people a lesson: do not violate the laws of Rome and risk putting yourself in this same situation.

40. And saying, Thou that destroyest the temple, and buildest it in three days, save thyself. If thou be the Son of God, come down from the cross.

Near the beginning of His ministry, Jesus had spoken the prophetic words, "Destroy this *temple*, and *in three days* I will raise it up" (John 2:19). Though He was not understood at the time, even by His own disciples, the apostle John explains that Jesus was referring to the "temple" of His body being destroyed by His enemies and then resurrected by God (vv. 21, 22). These words were perverted by the false witnesses who came forward at Jesus' trial (Mark 14:57, 58).

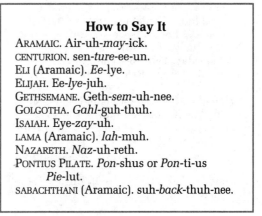

How to Say It

ARAMAIC. Air-uh-*may*-ick.
CENTURION. sen-*ture*-ee-un.
ELI (Aramaic). *Ee*-lye.
ELIJAH. Ee-*lye*-juh.
GETHSEMANE. Geth-*sem*-uh-nee.
GOLGOTHA. *Gahl*-guh-thuh.
ISAIAH. Eye-*zay*-uh.
LAMA (Aramaic). *lah*-muh.
NAZARETH. *Naz*-uh-reth.
PONTIUS PILATE. *Pon*-shus or *Pon*-ti-us *Pie*-lut.
SABACHTHANI (Aramaic). suh-*back*-thuh-nee.

How Jesus' enemies must have relished the scenario before them! *If thou be the Son of God, come down from the cross,* they cried. Jesus could only bear these indignities in silence—for the cross was the very reason that He, the Son of God, had come to earth.

B. From the Leaders (vv. 41-43)

41. Likewise also the chief priests mocking him, with the scribes and elders, said.

The *chief priests, scribes, and elders* had been bitter enemies throughout Jesus' ministry. Jesus had warned His disciples that these three groups of leaders would be instrumental in putting Him to death (Matthew 16:21). What pleasure they must now have experienced in being able to deride Jesus without fear of a reprisal! Finally, they thought, they were getting the last word.

42. He saved others; himself he cannot save. If he be the King of Israel, let him now come down from the cross, and we will believe him.

He saved others; himself he cannot save. With these words Jesus' enemies scorned His ministry of healing and His claim to be the Savior sent from Heaven. The one who promised and provided salvation to others was now unable to provide it for Himself. [See question #2, page 216.]

On more than one occasion the Pharisees had demanded that Jesus give them a "sign" to validate His Messianic claims (Matthew 12:38). They had witnessed dozens of miracles by Jesus, but they wanted to be able to name their own miracle as a "test case" that they believed would be impossible for anyone but God. Now they saw their opportunity to name the "sign." They would *believe* Jesus, they declared, if He would *come down from the cross.* But He had already announced the one "sign" that He would give:

Home Daily Bible Readings

Monday, Feb. 14—Jesus Delivered to Pilate; Judas's Suicide (Matthew 27:1-10)

Tuesday, Feb. 15—Jesus Before Pilate (Matthew 27:11-18)

Wednesday, Feb. 16—The Crowd Agitates for Barabbas's Release (Matthew 27:19-23)

Thursday, Feb. 17—Jesus Is Handed Over for Crucifixion (Matthew 27:24-31)

Friday, Feb. 18—Jesus Is Crucified (Matthew 27:32-44)

Saturday, Feb. 19—Jesus Dies (Matthew 27:45-56)

Sunday, Feb. 20—Jesus Is Buried (Matthew 27:57-61)

the "sign of . . . Jonah" (Matthew 12:39, 40). He must remain on the cross and die, so that in three days He could provide the true sign that He is the Son of God (Romans 1:3, 4).

43. He trusted in God; let him deliver him now, if he will have him: for he said, I am the Son of God.

Of all the derision that Jesus endured on the cross, these words may have hurt the most. His whole life had been spent devoted to God's will. He had been faithful in all His duties. If anyone deserved to be spared this suffering, He did. [See question #3, page 216.]

C. From the Thieves (v. 44)

44. The thieves also, which were crucified with him, cast the same in his teeth.

As if the insults of His enemies were not enough, Jesus was also verbally attacked by strangers who had no reason to dislike Him. There should have been a common bond between Jesus and *the thieves* as they faced this horrible death together; yet they too *cast the same in his teeth*—that is, they mocked Jesus with the same kind of ridicule. (Luke notes, however, that one of the thieves later reconsidered and repented—Luke 23:39-43.)

III. Jesus' Death
(Matthew 27:45-50)

A. Cry of Agony (vv. 45, 46)

45. Now from the sixth hour there was darkness over all the land unto the ninth hour.

According to Mark's Gospel, the crucifixion of Jesus began, by Jewish reckoning, at "the third hour" (Mark 15:25) after sunrise, which was approximately 9:00 in the morning. This unusual *darkness* set in at *the sixth hour* (12:00 noon) and lasted for three hours.

46. And about the ninth hour Jesus cried with a loud voice, saying, Eli, Eli, lama sabachthani? that is to say, My God, my God, why hast thou forsaken me?

Jesus died at *about the ninth hour* (3:00 P.M.), after six agonizing hours on the cross. In His final moments He *cried* out (in Aramaic) the lament from Psalm 22:1: *My God, my God, why hast thou forsaken me?* Many Christians have wondered how Jesus could have spoken such words. Surely He knew that God would never abandon Him. And yet the prophet Isaiah did speak of a tension between Father and Son at Calvary, as the Messiah "carried our sorrows" and was "stricken, smitten of God, and afflicted" in our place (Isaiah 53:4). There was a sense in which Jesus was being *forsaken* and punished by God as the substitutionary atonement for our sins.

Perhaps, however, Jesus was thinking about more than just the opening verse of Psalm 22, and would have quoted the rest of the passage had He had the strength to do so. After David described the misery he was suffering at the hands of men and voiced his despair with God for not responding quickly, he still expressed his belief that God would eventually rescue him (vv. 22-25). In the midst of His agony on the cross, Jesus still knew that God would "rescue" Him in due time on the third day. [See question #4, page 216.]

B. Loss of Strength (vv. 47-49)

47. Some of them that stood there, when they heard that, said, This man calleth for Elijah.

At this point in the crucifixion, Jesus would have been extremely weak. His tongue was likely swollen and His throat dry. His lungs would have been struggling for air, making it difficult for Him to speak. His words *Eli, Eli* ("my God, my God") were probably spoken in such whispered tones that they sounded to the crowd like the name *Elijah*. The onlookers assumed that Jesus was calling for the prophet Elijah to descend from Heaven and rescue Him.

48. And straightway one of them ran, and took a sponge, and filled it with vinegar, and put it on a reed, and gave him to drink.

The *drink* offered to Jesus at this time was quite different from that which He had refused earlier that day. As the Roman soldiers prepared to drive the spikes through His hands and feet, they offered Him a mixed drink of wine, gall, and myrrh (Matthew 27:34; Mark 15:23). Each of the ingredients acted to numb a person temporarily, much as an anesthesia would do, so that the victim would not die prematurely of shock when His body was pierced and thus avoid the hours of agony on the cross. Since Jesus came to the cross with the intent of suffering as an atoning sacrifice, He refused to drink anything that would diminish what He had agreed to do before God.

The drink offered six hours later was a mild wine *vinegar*. It would not have the numbing effect of the earlier drink, but it would ease the pain of Jesus' throat enough for Him to speak clearly His final words before He died.

49. The rest said, Let be, let us see whether Elijah will come to save him.

The mistaken idea that Jesus was calling for *Elijah* to *come* and *save* Him merely added to the mocking and derision that Jesus had experienced from His first moments on the cross.

C. Moment of Death (v. 50)

50. Jesus, when he had cried again with a loud voice, yielded up the ghost.

Now that His throat was moistened enough for Him to speak for a moment, Jesus *cried again with a loud voice*, "It is finished" (John 19:30), and then, "Father, into thy hands I commend my spirit" (Luke 23:46). When these words were spoken, Jesus' spirit departed from His body.

TRAVESTY OF JUSTICE—MIRACLE OF MERCY

A young man sits in a Southern prison for signing a check he was not authorized to sign. He didn't forge the check; he didn't steal the money. He simply was not licensed to receive investments on behalf of his brother's firm.

To many, the punishment seems excessive; his accusers seem to carry a vendetta. Lesser charges could have been filed, or a minimal sentence imposed. Thus far the parole board has been inflexible—some would say unreasonable. This prisoner, who has a wife and three children, may be incarcerated for as long as fifteen years! It has been called by many a travesty of justice.

Jesus of Nazareth, at age thirty-three, was arrested late one night in a garden where He went to pray. He was dragged before an illegally convened court, charged with blasphemy for merely telling the truth, and hauled off to the governor's palace to be tried and sentenced without "due process." Even the governor proclaimed this respected preacher and compassionate healer innocent, then later succumbed to mob pressure and ordered Him to be executed. Jesus had committed no crime yet paid the supreme penalty. It was by all standards a travesty of justice!

But God, in His incomprehensible grace, turned the crucifixion of Christ into a miracle of mercy. He "made him to be sin for us, who knew no sin; that we might be made the righteousness of God in him" (2 Corinthians 5:21). —R. W. B.

IV. God's Response
(Matthew 27:51-54)

A. Atonement Accomplished (v. 51)

51. And, behold, the veil of the temple was rent in twain from the top to the bottom; and the earth did quake, and the rocks rent.

The main portion of the *temple* consisted of two central rooms. The outer chamber, known as the Holy Place, was serviced by priests each day. The inner chamber was the Holy of Holies, the place that symbolized the presence of God. Only the high priest could enter this room and did so only once a year on the Day of Atonement.

Between these two rooms was a curtain or *veil* that barred admission into the Holy of Holies. Each year the high priest carried the blood of an animal sacrifice into the inner room and presented it to God. The fact that he had to do this year after year indicated that this sacrifice was imperfect (Hebrews 10:1-4). Full atonement for sin was not yet accomplished.

However, at the moment Jesus died this veil was *rent in twain* (torn in two) *from the top to the bottom*. That the tearing originated from the top indicated an act of God, announcing that on the cross an acceptable sacrifice had finally been offered—that of the sinless Lamb of God. God now declares that anyone may "draw near" to Him and "enter into the holiest" through the atoning blood of Jesus (Hebrews 9:11, 12; 10:19-22).

B. Death Defeated (vv. 52, 53)

52. And the graves were opened; and many bodies of the saints which slept arose.

The previous verse mentions a great earthquake that occurred the moment Jesus died. Its primary impact was to crack open some of the *graves* outside the city of Jerusalem. These graves were not like our Western burial places, six feet underground, but caves sealed with large stones. Many of these stones were cracked by the earthquake, with the pieces falling to the side and creating a means of exit. All of this was a prelude to the resurrections that followed.

53. And came out of the graves after his resurrection, and went into the holy city, and appeared unto many.

These resurrections did not occur at the time of the earthquake on Friday; they occurred in conjunction with Jesus' *resurrection* on Sunday, or, as Matthew says, *after his resurrection*. No details are given regarding who these people were, how long they lived this second time, and what happened when they *appeared* to people in Jerusalem. We can assume that these were godly people (they are called "saints" in verse 52) who had anticipated the coming of the Messiah and were now beneficiaries of His power. Whatever the case, their brief reprieve from death was a God-given symbol of an even greater miracle. Death had been defeated through the work of Jesus Christ—not just for a short while, but for eternity.

C. Witnesses Speak (v. 54)

54. Now when the centurion, and they that were with him, watching Jesus, saw the earthquake, and those things that were done, they feared greatly, saying, Truly this was the Son of God.

The *centurion* was the officer in charge of the shifts of soldiers who stood guard duty around the crosses. He and *they that were with him* (probably some of his men) must have been deeply moved by the manner in which Jesus humbly died in the face of great ridicule and scorn, and by the supernatural phenomena that accompanied His death. Our English translation makes it seem that these witnesses now believed in the deity of Jesus. However, the Greek text is more accurately rendered, "This was a son of God," the equivalent to Luke's expression, "This was a righteous man" (Luke 23:47). The centurion was declaring that Jesus was a godly man, undeserving of the treatment He had received. Perhaps he interpreted the darkness and the earthquake as indicators that some god in Heaven was obviously not pleased with the way Jesus had been treated.

We can hope that this very rudimentary faith eventually matured in this centurion, as well as in the others at the cross that day, leading them to a saving commitment to Jesus as the promised Christ and the true Son of God. [See question #5, page 216.]

Conclusion

A. The Old Rugged Cross

What is the best way to conclude this study after reflecting so intensely upon the death of Christ? Perhaps the classic words of George Bennard can provide a fitting closing thought.

On a hill far away stood an old rugged cross,
  The emblem of suffering and shame;
And I love that old cross where the dearest and best
  For a world of lost sinners was slain.

B. Prayer

Father, help us never to lose our love for the cross of Calvary or for the One who died there so that we might live with You forever. It is in His name that we pray. Amen.

C. Thought to Remember

"He was wounded for our transgressions, he was bruised for our iniquities: the chastisement of our peace was upon him; and with his stripes we are healed" (Isaiah 53:5).

Truly this was the Son of God.

Visual for lesson 12

Today's visual captures the dramatic moment when the centurion at the cross realized the death of Jesus was unlike any other crucifixion he had ever seen.

Learning by Doing

This page contains an alternate lesson plan emphasizing learning activities.
Classes desiring such student involvement will find these suggestions helpful.

Learning Goals

After this lesson students should be able to:

1. Relate the important details of Jesus' crucifixion according to today's text.

2. Tell how these details reveal the degree of shame and suffering that Jesus experienced on the cross.

3. Renew their love for and commitment to Jesus, recognizing that He endured the agony of the cross for them.

Into the Lesson

The account of the last hours of Jesus' life is familiar to most Bible students. Give them the following "true-false-maybe" quiz to reveal how fuzzy they may be on the details, to raise questions, and to motivate them for study. (Answers with references are provided in parentheses to aid you in discussing the quiz after the students complete it.)

1. The final hours of Jesus' life are recorded in all four Gospels. (True; Matthew 27, Mark 15, Luke 23, John 19)

2. Jesus said He could have called ten thousand angels to His rescue. (False; twelve legions—some 72,000 angels, Matthew 26:53)

3. Jesus refused wine mixed with gall. (True; Matthew 27:34)

4. It was dark from noon until three o'clock on the day Jesus died. (True; Matthew 27:45)

5. Jesus accepted a sponge soaked in wine vinegar. (True; Matthew 27:48)

6. Jesus died at about 6:00 P.M. (False; 3:00 P.M., Matthew 27:45-50)

7. The centurion at the crucifixion expressed his faith in Jesus. (Maybe; Matthew 27:54)

Into the Word

If you can, rent or borrow a video of the crucifixion, particularly if you can find one based solely on Matthew's account. (Visual Entertainment has such a video.) This is a good opportunity to recruit some help from a class member who has video interest and equipment. Have him or her cue the video to the appropriate parts of the text. This person can also be sure the equipment is set up and ready for the class time.

After the viewing, have a volunteer read the text, Matthew 27:35-54. Compare the video with the text for accuracy. Then use one or more of the following options to explore the text.

Interview

The intense drama of the final hours of Jesus' life can best be understood by considering them from the perspective of the participants. Divide your class into groups to prepare interviews with the following characters: the centurion, one of the robbers crucified with Him, someone standing nearby who heard what Jesus said, and one of the women who watched (verses 55, 56).

Diary or Journal Entry

The centurion who was in charge of the crucifixion is a fascinating character. Did his comment at the death of Jesus mean he was a convert? Or was he simply observing that Jesus was an innocent man unjustly condemned? We cannot tell for sure, but it is interesting to speculate based on what is recorded. Have your class write a journal or diary entry that the centurion might have written that day.

Group Discussion

Assign a group to discuss various aspects of the suffering of Jesus in His death. Read through the passage looking for indications (stated or implied) of each of these kinds of suffering: physical, emotional, mental, volitional, and spiritual.

Into Life

Choose one of the following activities to make application and to conclude today's session.

Communion Devotion

The events in this lesson often come to mind as we observe the Lord's Supper. Conclude today's lesson by asking your students to write a meditation or devotional thought to be used in preparation for the Lord's Supper. Ask if it might be used in your church services today or soon.

Write a Song

Have your class write new words to a familiar melody. Let the first stanza tell about the events, the middle stanzas deal with the emotions of the participants, and the final stanzas call for us to respond to these events in life application. Assign these three sections to three groups from your class. If time is too short for songwriting, write prose paragraphs following the same guidelines.

If the class does write a song, sing it together and close with prayer.

Let's Talk It Over

The questions on this page are designed to encourage review of the lesson Scriptures and to promote discussion of the lesson by the class. The answers provided are only discussion starters. Let your class talk it over from there.

1. Shame was a major part of the punishment of crucifixion. The victim's clothing was taken, he was verbally assaulted, and he was made a public spectacle. Surely nothing we suffer even comes close, but in what ways do Christians sometimes suffer shame for their faith? How can we maintain our faith in the face of ridicule?

These days, anyone who believes in absolute truth is considered narrow or even bigoted. The concept of the inspiration of Scripture has long been discounted—sometimes even by professing Christians! Many Christians have been ridiculed for believing things that science has supposedly proven to be false. If you have college students or graduates in your class, many of them may recall harassment by professors and fellow students alike.

The example of Jesus should encourage us to remain faithful. When ridiculed, we ought to consider ourselves blessed (Matthew 5:11, 12).

2. Ironically, the chief priests, scribes, and elders were right when they said, "He saved others; himself he cannot save." Jesus could have saved Himself, but then He would not have been the atoning sacrifice for our sins. If He would save others, He had to refuse to save Himself to do it. Under what circumstances would you be willing to sacrifice yourself for the sake of another?

Jesus said, "Greater love hath no man than this, that a man lay down his life for his friends" (John 15:13). A parent would scarcely flinch to make such a sacrifice. Nor is it uncommon to see a soldier sacrifice himself for his squad—and, at the same time, for his country.

Consider also that Paul urges us to submit our bodies as "living sacrifices" to God (Romans 12:1). Discuss how this sacrifice imitates the example of Jesus on the cross.

3. Of all who mocked Jesus—the passersby, the religious leaders, and the thieves—whose taunts do you suppose hurt Jesus the most? Why? Whose criticism hurts you the most? How do you deal with that in a manner consistent with Jesus' example?

Was it the fickleness of the crowd that a week earlier cheered Jesus during the triumphal entry and now jeered Him that hurt most? Or was it the rejection of the leaders—who should have known better? Of course, we'll never know. But we all have experienced conflict that was especially grievous because of its source. Perhaps there is a father in your class whose son has rejected the faith and made hurtful remarks to his dad. Perhaps there is a woman whose husband has abandoned her, making unkind remarks about her faith as he left. In all these situations—as well as others—we need to remember Jesus, "who, when he was reviled, reviled not again; . . . but committed himself to him that judgeth righteously" (1 Peter 2:23).

4. How do you respond to people who question your faith and trust in God when you experience circumstances that suggest to them that God has abandoned you?

It depends on who is asking the questions. If another believer is questioning our faith, we may wonder if that one has the mistaken notion that faith should immunize us from the consequences of sin in this world. We should remind such a one that God has promised never to forsake us (Romans 8:38, 39), and that Jesus Himself warned us there would be tribulation in this life (John 16:33).

If the one raising the questions is an unbeliever, then our example of consistent faith in spite of the circumstances may be what eventually leads that person to Christ!

5. There are many reasons that people become convinced that Jesus is "the Son of God." What was the primary reason that brought you to this belief?

Some come to this truth by intellectual means. They study the Scripture, read the arguments on both sides, and reason themselves to this conclusion. Their belief is grounded in reason.

Others are moved more by their emotional attraction to the life and ministry of Jesus. While He was on this earth, He drew people to Him because of His kindness and compassion. Their decision grows out of feelings.

Most often, however, belief begins when one notices a consistent example in the life of a believer. As Jesus' example led the centurion to a level of faith, so our example can lead others to faith—or it can drive them away!

Resurrection and Commission

DEVOTIONAL READING: John 20:19-31.

BACKGROUND SCRIPTURE: Matthew 27:62—28:20.

PRINTED TEXT: Matthew 28:1-10, 16-20.

Matthew 28:1-10, 16-20

1 In the end of the sabbath, as it began to dawn toward the first day of the week, came Mary Magdalene and the other Mary to see the sepulchre.

2 And, behold, there was a great earthquake: for the angel of the Lord descended from heaven, and came and rolled back the stone from the door, and sat upon it.

3 His countenance was like lightning, and his raiment white as snow:

4 And for fear of him the keepers did shake, and became as dead men.

5 And the angel answered and said unto the women, Fear not ye: for I know that ye seek Jesus, which was crucified.

6 He is not here: for he is risen, as he said. Come, see the place where the Lord lay.

7 And go quickly, and tell his disciples that he is risen from the dead; and, behold, he goeth before you into Galilee; there shall ye see him: lo, I have told you.

8 And they departed quickly from the sepulchre with fear and great joy; and did run to bring his disciples word.

9 And as they went to tell his disciples, behold, Jesus met them, saying, All hail. And they came and held him by the feet, and worshipped him.

10 Then said Jesus unto them, Be not afraid: go tell my brethren that they go into Galilee, and there shall they see me.

. . . .

16 Then the eleven disciples went away into Galilee, into a mountain where Jesus had appointed them.

17 And when they saw him, they worshipped him: but some doubted.

18 And Jesus came and spake unto them, saying, All power is given unto me in heaven and in earth.

19 Go ye therefore, and teach all nations, baptizing them in the name of the Father, and of the Son, and of the Holy Ghost:

20 Teaching them to observe all things whatsoever I have commanded you: and, lo, I am with you alway, even unto the end of the world. Amen.

GOLDEN TEXT: Go ye therefore, and teach all nations, baptizing them in the name of the Father, and of the Son, and of the Holy Ghost: teaching them to observe all things whatsoever I have commanded you: and, lo, I am with you alway, even unto the end of the world.—Matthew 28:19, 20.

Feb
27

Lesson Aims

After this lesson each student will be able to:

1. Summarize Matthew's record of Jesus' resurrection and the commission He gave His disciples.

2. Tell why the Great Commission must remain a priority for today's church, in spite of other concerns that the church is often asked to address.

3. Think of a specific individual who needs to hear the good news about Jesus, and plan to tell that person this week.

Lesson Outline

INTRODUCTION
    A. A Fitting Ending
    B. Lesson Background
  I. GOOD NEWS (Matthew 28:1-7)
    A. God Has Acted (vv. 1-4)
    B. Christ Is Risen (vv. 5-7)
      "Out-of-Tomb" Experience
 II. GLORIOUS SIGHT (Matthew 28:8-10)
    A. Mixed Emotions (v. 8)
    B. Blessed Encounter (vv. 9, 10)
III. GREAT COMMISSION (Matthew 28:16-20)
    A. Lord's Authority (vv. 16-18)
    B. Church's Priority (vv. 19, 20)
      Who's Your Boss?
CONCLUSION
    A. Moving Experience
    B. Prayer
    C. Thought to Remember

Introduction

A. A Fitting Ending

What a disappointment it is when an otherwise good movie concludes with a bad ending! Sometimes the ending is anticlimactic and not nearly as exciting as the action that led up to it. At other times a movie critic will express dismay at what is often called a "Hollywood ending," where the hero or heroine experiences a somewhat farfetched turn of events just so the movie can have a happy ending. It leaves us yearning for something more realistic, more fitting with the story line. Or perhaps the story line takes a sudden turn for the worse, and we leave feeling grief for a character we had come to like but who made an unfortunate choice or met an untimely end at the conclusion of the film.

Matthew draws his Gospel to a conclusion with what is indeed a fitting ending to his account of the life of Jesus Christ. Matthew does not leave us with an anticlimactic or grievous finish with Jesus' body lying dead in the grave. Nor does he create some dramatic rescue attempt by the disciples of Jesus. What he records is truly a "grand finale" well suited for the story he has told: the power of Almighty God reaches down to earth to complete the plan He began in His Son Jesus Christ by raising Him from the dead. In this case, the truth is better by far than any fiction Matthew might have dreamed up!

B. Lesson Background

Shortly after Jesus died on the cross, a secret disciple named Joseph of Arimathea asked the Roman governor Pilate for permission to bury the body (John 19:38). Assisted by Nicodemus, a Pharisee who had visited Jesus by night during the early months of His ministry (John 3:1, 2), Joseph quickly placed Jesus' body in a tomb. (He had less than three hours to move the body and seal the tomb before the Sabbath began at sundown.) Joseph used a "new sepulchre," one "hewn out in the rock" (Matthew 27:60) for his own family, because it was near the vicinity of the crucifixion (John 19:41, 42).

As Joseph closed the tomb with a "great stone," some of the women who had supported Jesus throughout His ministry stood nearby and watched. They then returned to their quarters to prepare spices and other materials that they would use to complete the burial process on Sunday, after the Sabbath was over (Luke 23:55, 56). The day after the crucifixion, the chief priests and Pharisees persuaded Pilate to station Roman guards at the tomb, in order to keep Jesus' disciples from stealing the body and then spreading news of an alleged "resurrection" (Matthew 27:62-66). The scene was being set for a most astonishing discovery.

I. Good News
(Matthew 28:1-7)

A. God Has Acted (vv. 1-4)

1. In the end of the sabbath, as it began to dawn toward the first day of the week, came Mary Magdalene and the other Mary to see the sepulchre.

Matthew names two of the women who went to Jesus' *sepulchre* (tomb) early on Sunday morning. *Mary Magdalene* was the most prominent of the several women who supported Jesus' ministry, having become a follower after Jesus cast seven demons out of her (Mark 16:9). *The other Mary* was the mother of one of Jesus' disciples, "James the less," and his brother Joses (Mark 15:40; 16:1).

Mark notes that the two Marys were accompanied by a woman named Salome (Mark 16:1), who may well have been the same woman Matthew identifies as the mother of two other disciples, James and John (Matthew 27:56). Luke adds the name of Joanna (24:10). Having served Jesus faithfully while He was alive and having witnessed His horrible crucifixion and His burial (Matthew 27:55, 56, 61), these women—and perhaps others—were now about to pay due respect to their Master. [See question #1, page 224.]

The women came to the tomb around *dawn* on *the first day of the week.* As they neared it, they suddenly realized that they would need help rolling the large stone away from the entrance (Mark 16:3). But God had a means of entry already planned for them.

2. And, behold, there was a great earthquake: for the angel of the Lord descended from heaven, and came and rolled back the stone from the door, and sat upon it.

The precise timing of Jesus' resurrection is not indicated in any of the Gospel accounts, but we have traditionally assumed that the *great earthquake* occurred at the moment He arose and departed the tomb. According to Matthew, the earthquake occurred when *the angel of the Lord came and* moved the heavy *stone* to the side. The stone was not moved to let Jesus out; He later demonstrated that He could pass through walls (John 20:19, 26). Instead, it was moved to let the witnesses in so that they could testify that the tomb was empty.

3. His countenance was like lightning, and his raiment white as snow.

The angel's *countenance*, or face, shone with the unearthly brilliance of a blinding, *white* light. It is not likely that the radiant glory was that of the angel himself; rather, it was a reflection of the glory of God. It is common in Scripture for angels sent by God to be characterized by His radiance, just as "the glory of the Lord shone round about them" when an angel announced the birth of Jesus to the shepherds (Luke 2:9). The radiant glory displayed at the tomb was intended to declare, along with the earthquake, that God's power had raised Jesus to life.

4. And for fear of him the keepers did shake, and became as dead men.

The sight of the angel terrified the Roman guards (*keepers*), who for a moment froze like *dead men.* However, they must have regained their composure quickly and fled; because the other Gospel accounts indicate that the tomb was unguarded when the women arrived. The power of God had provided, not only the removal of the heavy stone, but also unobstructed access to the tomb.

B. Christ Is Risen (vv. 5-7)

5. And the angel answered and said unto the women, Fear not ye: for I know that ye seek Jesus, which was crucified.

By the time *the women* arrived at the tomb, the Gospel accounts indicate that *the angel* was no longer sitting on the stone. Luke simply states that they found the stone removed, entered the tomb, and discovered that the body of Jesus was missing (Luke 24:2, 3). It was then that "two men" in "shining garments" were observed in the darkness of the tomb (Luke 24:4). Matthew and Mark mention only the one who did the speaking and who was "sitting on the right side" (Mark 16:5). This angel told the women that he knew why they had come: to locate the body of *Jesus, which was crucified.* He must have piqued their curiosity when he asked, "Why seek ye the living among the dead?" (Luke 24:5).

6. He is not here: for he is risen, as he said. Come, see the place where the Lord lay.

The message of what is often called "Easter" Sunday is succinctly expressed in these words of the angel: *He is not here: for he is risen.* It was time to make known the glorious news, although the full impact of the angel's words was not grasped by the women or the disciples until later that day.

The resurrection of Jesus happened *as he said.* The angel reminded the women that Jesus had taught His disciples during His ministry in Galilee that "the Son of man must be delivered

Home Daily Bible Readings

Monday, Feb. 21—Pilate's Soldiers Guard Jesus' Tomb (Matthew 27:62-66)
Tuesday, Feb. 22—The Resurrection of Jesus (Matthew 28:1-10)
Wednesday, Feb. 23—Jesus Commissions His Disciples (Matthew 28:11-20)
Thursday, Feb. 24—Jesus and Travelers on the Emmaus Road (Luke 24:13-27)
Friday, Feb. 25—The Travelers Recognize Jesus (Luke 24:28-35)
Saturday, Feb. 26—Jesus Appears to His Disciples (Luke 24:36-43)
Sunday, Feb. 27—Jesus Blesses the Disciples and Ascends (Luke 24:44-53)

into the hands of sinful men, and be crucified, and the third day rise again" (Luke 24:6, 7). The women then "remembered his words" (v. 8).

There was great significance in having an opportunity to *see the place where the Lord lay*. Not only did it confirm that the tomb was empty, but to the observant eye it provided evidence of a miracle. When the apostle John later inspected the tomb, he noticed that the linen strips that had been wrapped around the body of Jesus were still lying in the tomb undisturbed. The cloth or "napkin" that had been tied around Jesus' head was lying separate from the linen cloths, in the place where the head had been. It appeared as if the body of Jesus had not been taken, but had simply vanished, leaving the burial clothing still in place.

When John saw this, he believed in the resurrection of Jesus (John 20:6-8). Perhaps seeing the place where Jesus' body had been laid had a similar effect on the women. [See question #2, page 224.]

"OUT-OF-TOMB" EXPERIENCE

In recent years, much has been written by and/or about people who claim to have had "out-of-body" experiences. Many individuals receive such reports with a good bit of skepticism. Most of the accounts include similar elements, such as "hovering above one's body" or "passing through a long tunnel toward a bright light." Could these simply be personalized versions of someone else's experience? Is it possible that impressionable people are pre-programmed to dream or visualize what others have described?

Make no mistake—Jesus had a *"real*-death, out-of-*tomb"* experience. He really died on the cross, and His body lay on a stone shelf in a grave for three days. On the third day, God raised Him from the dead and miraculously ushered Him out of that tomb.

At first the reports of Jesus' "out-of-tomb" experience were received with skepticism and doubt. But no one has ever invalidated the Gospel accounts of Christ's resurrection. Jesus' experience will one day be ours, according to His promise: "Because I live, ye shall live also" (John 14:19).

—R. W. B.

7. And go quickly, and tell his disciples that he is risen from the dead; and, behold, he goeth before you into Galilee; there shall ye see him: lo, I have told you.

The women were sent by the angel to *tell* Jesus' *disciples* that he had *risen from the dead*. Mark reports that Jesus especially mentioned telling Peter (Mark 16:7). Perhaps Jesus intended to let Peter know that his denials of Jesus could

be forgiven. They need not separate him from fellowship with the risen Lord.

The angel's message also included instructions for the disciples to meet Jesus in *Galilee*. During His last supper in the upper room, Jesus had told His disciples to meet Him there following His resurrection (Matthew 26:32). But since they had not yet grasped the truth of Jesus' resurrection, they did not sense the urgency of going to Galilee. Now, however, it was time for them to proceed there.

The reason for going to Galilee is not stated. Perhaps it was for safety. (The disciples were certainly in fear of the Jews in Jerusalem, as seen in John 20:19.) Whatever the reason, the angel's command served as a test of the disciples' faith. Would they travel to Galilee simply on the women's claim that they had seen an angel of God, or would their limited faith require a resurrection appearance of Jesus to them? We are told that they did not believe the women, nor the testimony of others that Jesus was alive (Mark 16:11-13). Later Jesus rebuked the disciples for their refusal to accept such testimony (Mark 16:14). [See question #3, page 224.]

II. Glorious Sight
(Matthew 28:8-10)

A. Mixed Emotions (v. 8)

8. And they departed quickly from the sepulchre with fear and great joy; and did run to bring his disciples word.

After seeing an angel and hearing his message that Jesus was alive, the women were not sure what to think. They experienced *great joy* at such good news, yet they were beset by *fear*. Nevertheless, the women faithfully reported what they had seen and heard.

B. Blessed Encounter (vv. 9, 10)

9. And as they went to tell his disciples, behold, Jesus met them, saying, All hail. And they came and held him by the feet, and worshipped him.

Although Mary Magdalene came to the tomb with the other women, at some point she apparently became separated from them. John's account indicates that when Mary saw that the stone had been rolled away from the tomb, she immediately ran to tell Peter and John the news (though incorrect) that someone had taken the body of Jesus (John 20:1, 2). Thus Mary did not see the angel at the tomb and was not present at the appearance of Jesus recorded by Matthew.

Having summoned Peter and John, Mary returned alone to the tomb, where Jesus appeared to her (John 20:11-18). Mark 16:9 tells us that

Jesus appeared to Mary Magdalene *first*. So Mary had returned to the tomb and had seen Jesus before His appearance to the women reported by Matthew in this account.

Once these women saw the resurrected Jesus, they fell prostrate before Him and *held him by the feet*. This was an act of humility and worship. The touch also served to verify that the women were not hallucinating, but were indeed seeing Jesus alive.

10. Then said Jesus unto them, Be not afraid: go tell my brethren that they go into Galilee, and there shall they see me.

Jesus repeated the instruction for the women to tell the disciples to *go into Galilee* and meet Jesus (v. 7). No doubt the women relayed the command faithfully, but the disciples viewed the women's claims as "idle tales, and they believed them not" (Luke 24:11). Apparently it was not until after Thomas had the opportunity to see the resurrected Jesus and voice his belief (John 20:26-29) that the eleven departed for Galilee as they had been instructed (Matthew 28:16).

Though it would have been commendable for the disciples to believe in the resurrection without hesitation, their reluctance serves to confirm the truth of the resurrection for us. Contrary to the skeptics who suggest that the disciples were so eager to believe in a resurrection that they imagined seeing Jesus alive, the Gospel accounts indicate that their minds were not at all predisposed for such a hallucination. They had to be convinced by solid evidence, thus providing us with a firm basis for believing their witness to the resurrected Christ.

III. Great Commission
(Matthew 28:16-20)

A. Lord's Authority (vv. 16-18)

16. Then the eleven disciples went away into Galilee, into a mountain where Jesus had appointed them.

The *eleven disciples* (minus Judas) finally gathered in *Galilee* as instructed by Jesus. The designated *mountain* is not identified in the Gospels. It may be that Jesus called His disciples back to a mountain that had played a prominent role during His Galilean ministry.

17. And when they saw him, they worshipped him: but some doubted.

The eleven had come to believe in Jesus' resurrection while in Jerusalem, thus they were prepared to worship Him when He appeared before them on the mountain. Apparently other disciples from Jesus' Galilean ministry were permitted to join the eleven on the mountain, for Matthew

How to Say It

ARIMATHEA. *Air*-uh-muh-*thee*-uh (strong accent on *thee; th* as in *thin*).
JOSES. *Joe*-sez.
MAGDALENE. *Mag*-duh-leen or Mag-duh-*lee*-nee.
NICODEMUS. Nick-uh-*dee*-mus.
PHARISEE. *Fair*-ih-see.
PILATE. *Pie*-lut.
SALOME. Suh-*lo*-me.
SEPULCHRE. *sep*-ul-kur.

says that there were *some* present who *doubted*. The apostle Paul notes that following His resurrection Jesus once appeared to as many as five hundred believers at one time (1 Corinthians 15:6). Perhaps this gathering was that occasion.

18. And Jesus came and spake unto them, saying, All power is given unto me in heaven and in earth.

The word *power* can mean might or strength, or it can mean authority. It is the latter that is intended here, as Jesus was about to issue orders that would establish the first priority for every disciple from then until the end of time. Only on the basis of His authority as the Lord of *heaven* and *earth* could He give such a command!

This is the same authority Jesus demonstrated again and again throughout His ministry. His disciples were amazed when He stilled the storm, marveling, "What manner of man is this, that even the winds and the sea obey him!" (Matthew 8:27). When Jesus healed the palsied man, He demonstrated that He had "power [authority] on earth to forgive sins" (Matthew 9:6).

Yet there was something climactic about Jesus' announcement here. He was about to return to "the glory which [He] had with [the Father] before the world was" (John 17:5). Jesus' time on earth was a time of submission, of being a "servant" (Philippians 2:6-8). He and His authority were about to be exalted by God the Father (Philippians 2:9-11). When He ascended to Heaven forty days after His resurrection (Acts 1:3, 9), He was seated on the throne of Heaven at the right hand of God (Acts 2:32, 33). Jesus' identity as "Lord and Christ" (Acts 2:36) now takes on an even greater significance than when the disciples called Him "Lord" (John 13:13) or when Peter confessed Him as the "Christ" (Matthew 16:16).

That Jesus possesses all authority has a practical and daily application to our lives. [See question #4, page 224.] It challenges us to look within to see if in our hearts we truly honor Jesus as Lord and King. Saving faith is not just believing facts about Jesus, but accepting Jesus as the supreme authority in our lives.

B. Church's Priority (vv. 19, 20)

19. Go ye therefore, and teach all nations, baptizing them in the name of the Father, and of the Son, and of the Holy Ghost.

We call Jesus' instructions for evangelizing the world the "Great Commission," for it represents the "marching orders" for the church. The other three Gospel writers also record the Great Commission, though in different contexts with different wording (Mark 16:15, 16; Luke 24:46-49; John 20:21-23). This repetition implies that evangelizing the world was considered a top priority by Jesus and should be viewed as such by His followers.

We are to *teach all nations*, or, to bring out the meaning of the Greek more fully, "make disciples" or followers of Christ of as many people as we can. Those willing to make such a commitment are to be immersed in water, which is the actual meaning of the Greek word rendered *baptizing*. When applied to a believer, it washes away sins (Acts 22:16) and then empowers him for Christian living with the sanctifying "gift of the *Holy Ghost*," or Holy Spirit (Acts 2:38; Romans 8:11-13).

Though the theological world loves to debate the subject of baptism, for most believers all that needs to be said is that, in His Great Commission, Jesus commanded that it be done. Since He has all authority, our obedience to Him in this matter should be unhesitating and without question. [See question #5, page 224.]

20. Teaching them to observe all things whatsoever I have commanded you: and, lo, I am with you alway, even unto the end of the world. Amen.

Our task of evangelism is not complete when a person rises from the waters of baptism. There remains a lifetime of *teaching*, for the Word of God has a depth that is never exhausted; and our

Visual for
lesson 13

This visual illustrates six actual mission works in different parts of the world. Use it to challenge your students to take Christ's commission seriously.

lives are always in need of constant challenge and growth. As the church performs its dual task of evangelism and nurturing, Jesus promises to be *with* us and thus to support us, *even unto the end of the world*.

WHO'S YOUR BOSS?

Our four-year-old grandson has been taught by his mother that whenever grandparents are baby-sitting him, they are "in charge." He has never questioned nor challenged our authority. Rarely has he protested our instructions or prohibitions. Never has he said, "You can't tell me what to do; you're not my boss!"

Jesus prefaced His final commission by claiming "all power . . . in heaven and in earth." Christians may rarely, if ever, openly question Christ's authority, yet many believers have not taken seriously all of His commandments. Isn't ignoring the clear instructions of someone in authority the same as saying, "You're not my boss!"?

The Great Commission is so called because it defines the "supreme task of the church: world evangelization" (Oswald Smith). Though millions of Christians are aware of what it says, dozens of people groups and countries have not yet been told the good news of salvation.

Personal evangelism continues to be one of the "bugaboos" of Christian discipleship. Though Christ has earned the right to send us into our own "spheres of influence" and even unto the ends of the earth with the gospel, many fail to honor His authority and comply with His command. We must recognize His lordship before we will trust and obey Him.

Who's *your* boss?   —R. W. B.

Conclusion

A. Moving Experience

A study of the life of Christ should be a moving experience. We are moved to admiration as we observe the manner in which Jesus ministered and as we listen to His words of teaching. We are moved to wonder and awe as we watch Him die the horrible death of the cross. And now may we be moved to devotion and service as He stands before us as our risen Savior and Lord.

B. Prayer

Father, we thank You for the many lessons we have learned about Jesus through the Gospel of Matthew. May our lives be fully devoted to You and to Your Son. In His name. Amen.

C. Thought to Remember

The final command of Jesus (the Great Commission) should be the church's first priority.

Learning by Doing

This page contains an alternate lesson plan emphasizing learning activities.
Classes desiring such student involvement will find these suggestions helpful.

Learning Goals

After this lesson each student will be able to:

1. Summarize Matthew's record of Jesus' resurrection and the commission He gave His disciples.

2. Tell why the Great Commission must remain a priority for today's church, in spite of other concerns that the church is often asked to address.

3. Think of a specific individual who needs to hear the good news about Jesus, and plan to tell that person this week.

Into the Lesson

Use one or both of the following activities to introduce today's lesson.

Believe It or Not

Ripley's Believe It or Not is a collection of incredible facts. Borrow a copy from your library. Select some samples to introduce today's lesson.

Make the transition to the Bible study by saying, "These are incredible accounts of astonishing events. We probably would have to see some of them to believe them. In the disciples' thinking the resurrection of Jesus was an unbelievable event. In fact, they refused to believe until they examined the evidence firsthand. Let's look at the evidence for ourselves."

Circle Response

Seat the class or a small group in a circle. Go around the circle and have each person complete the following sentence. (In a circle response, each person gets a chance to respond once before anyone gives a second response.) The sentence is this: "I believe the purpose of the church is. . . ." You may want to list responses on a chalkboard or poster.

Into the Word

Ask a volunteer to read Matthew 28:1-10, 16-20. Work together to develop an outline of the text. Ask class members to call out significant facts from the text. Then work together to arrange them into an outline. Group several events together under heads that tie them together. Use the lesson outline on page 218 as an example.

Ask the class, "Can you imagine the drama of seeing the risen Lord and hearing Him give the Great Commission?" Briefly discuss what that must have been like. Then ask each class member to write a diary entry that one of the apostles might have written the night after Jesus gave the Great Commission.

Into Life

Conducting an interview is a non-threatening way for your class members to involve others in a discussion about Christ and Christianity's basic message. Challenge your class members to interview ten people this week asking questions about the resurrection of Jesus. They should take notes recording people's responses and bring them to class next week. Here are two questions to get your class started. They can add to them as necessary.

1. Do you believe that Jesus rose from the dead? Why or why not?

2. What difference does it make in your life?

If there is time remaining in the class session, use one or both of the following additional application exercises.

Write a Letter

Much of the New Testament is composed of letters written to encourage and strengthen believers. Probably several young people from your church are away from home at college or in military service. These people need your class members' support to stand firm and true against attacks on their faith.

Ask each class member to select one of these and write him or her a letter of encouragement. Some of the insights from this lesson on the resurrection and Great Commission should be shared. Be sure to have names and addresses, zip codes, stationery, envelopes, pens, and stamps available for your class members.

Evangelism Training

Many Christians know that they should share their faith and make disciples, but they lack the skills and experience to be effective. Ask your church leaders to sponsor a course in witnessing and disciple making. This class should include classroom instruction, observation of others, and practical experience. If it is certain that such a course will be available, conclude today's class by inviting and urging your class members to enroll!

Let's Talk It Over

The questions on this page are designed to encourage review of the lesson Scriptures and to promote discussion of the lesson by the class. The answers provided are only discussion starters. Let your class talk it over from there.

1. The lesson writer says that the women went to the tomb with spices "to pay due respect to their Master." But if they had believed what Jesus told them about His death and resurrection, what would they have done differently? In what ways are we sometimes guilty of appearing to "pay due respect," when really we are guilty of not acting in faith?

Like Israel before us, the church is sometimes guilty of going through the motions of worship without acting in obedience to the Lord the rest of the week. When we pay respect with our lips but not with our lives, we dishonor the Lord and act as if He never arose.

Again and again surveys show that many people who claim to be Christians demonstrate very little real difference in lifestyle from that of non-Christian people. Our faith should make a difference in our values and our behavior.

2. The lesson writer says, "There was great significance in having an opportunity to see the place where the Lord lay." What else do you find especially significant in the resurrection account—something that demands belief in the resurrection?

There is physical evidence: the grave clothes and the empty tomb. There is eyewitness evidence, as many people saw Jesus alive. There is character evidence, as the disciples were dramatically changed in their demeanor after the resurrection. Perhaps the most significant fact of all is that the cumulative evidence is overwhelming.

As for alternative views, each of them pales in comparison with the truth. The presence of armed Roman guards rules out a theft of the body. The failure of the Jewish leaders to produce the body of Jesus rules out the idea that the women somehow went to the wrong tomb. Desperate for an alternative, some have even suggested that Jesus was not really dead—that He regained consciousness in the coolness of the tomb, single-handedly moved the stone and overpowered the guards, and then escaped! And they call the resurrection unbelievable!

3. The resurrection was, at first, a test of faith for the disciples. Would they believe the women? Would they go to Galilee? Would they recall and believe Jesus' own predictions?

In what ways is the resurrection a test of our own faith today?

Probably some of the adults in your class have lost parents, spouses, or even children to death. In such instances the resurrection is a test of their faith, with the ability to turn the fear of death into the hope of life eternal. For others, the test of faith comes when critics challenge their belief in the resurrection as "unscientific." On the opposite side of the coin are those who promote a mystic concept of "reincarnation" instead of the Biblical doctrine of resurrection.

For most of us, the choice to render simple obedience to the Lord, even in the small matters of life, is a resurrection test of faith. If we believe He rose from the dead, then we believe Him to be Lord (cf. Romans 10:9), so we must obey Him.

4. If it is true that all authority in Heaven and earth has been given to Jesus, how ought this reality to affect the daily conduct of our lives?

The simple answer is that we should obey Him in all things and serve Him faithfully. Wearing "WWJD" ("What Would Jesus Do?") on a wristband or necklace has become a popular way of reminding ourselves that we should always do what Jesus would do. But we are not Jesus and cannot always do what He would do. Perhaps a better question to ask is, "What would Jesus have *me* do?"

Too often we seek the opinion of friends, or we check out the prevailing popular practice, or what is "politically correct" to determine what we ought to do. If we acknowledge Jesus' authority, then we must be prepared to seek His wisdom rather than the wisdom of the world.

5. How can we assure that our focus is clearly on making "disciples of all the nations"?

Many churches have "Mission Statements" or "Vision Statements" that are intended to focus the local church's efforts. But Jesus has given us the mission statement for every church. Every ministry, every program, every activity, every budget, every facility expansion must be tested against this question: "How will this help us make disciples or teach disciples to obey Jesus?"

Our Lord has entrusted this mission to no other body of people, and no other organization or institution will seek to fulfill it.

Spring Quarter, 2000

Helping a Church Confront Crisis (1 & 2 Corinthians)

Special Features

Lessons

Unit 1: Christ, the Basis for Unity

Unit 2: Unity in Human Relationships

Unit 3: Unity Expressed in Ministry

About These Lessons

This quarter finds us in some of the most practical material in the New Testament. Within five years of its establishment, the church at Corinth was having profound problems, which Paul addressed in his letters to the Corinthian believers. His help for that church will bless your class and your church as you study Paul's Corinthian letters this quarter.

Mar 5
Mar 12
Mar 19
Mar 26
Apr 2
Apr 9
Apr 16
Apr 23
Apr 30
May 7
May 14
May 21
May 28

Quarterly Quiz

The questions on this page may be used in several ways: as a pretest at the beginning of the quarter; as a review at the end of the quarter; or as a review after each lesson. The questions are based on the Scripture text of each lesson (King James Version). **The answers are on page 228.**

Lesson 1

1. Paul mentions four individuals around whom the Corinthians had formed divisions. Name the four. *1 Corinthians 1:12*
2. What two individuals in Corinth did Paul baptize? *1 Corinthians 1:14*
3. Paul recalled that he had also baptized the household of _____. (Aquila, Stephanas, Apollos?) *1 Corinthians 1:16*

Lesson 2

1. Paul said he determined to know only one thing when he came to Corinth. What was it? *1 Corinthians 2:2*
2. Paul wanted the Corinthians' faith to rest not in the _____ of _____ but in the _____ of _____. *1 Corinthians 2:5*

Lesson 3

1. What did Paul say is "required in stewards"? *1 Corinthians 4:2*
2. According to Paul, what group had been "appointed to death"? *1 Corinthians 4:9*

Lesson 4

1. The immoral act that Paul wanted the Corinthians to address was one of which the Gentiles approved. T/F *1 Corinthians 5:1*
2. Paul told the Corinthians to deliver the immoral man to _____. *1 Corinthians 5:5*

Lesson 5

1. Of which groups did Paul say, "It is good for them if they abide even as I"? *1 Corinthians 7:8*
2. Paul said that the unbelieving spouse is _____ by his or her Christian mate. *1 Corinthians 7:14*

Lesson 6

1. According to Paul, what puffs up? What edifies? *1 Corinthians 8:1*
2. Paul did not want a Christian's liberty to become a _____. *1 Corinthians 8:9*
3. Paul said that to wound a weak Christian's conscience is to sin against Christ. T/F *1 Corinthians 8:12*

Lesson 7

1. "There are diversities of _____, but the same _____." *1 Corinthians 12:4*

2. By one Spirit we are all _____ into one _____. *1 Corinthians 12:13*

Lesson 8

1. By His resurrection Christ has become the _____ of those who slept. *1 Corinthians 15:20*
2. What is the last enemy that shall be destroyed? *1 Corinthians 15:26*

Lesson 9

1. What two objects did Paul say he would be like if he spoke with the tongues of men and of angels but did not have love? *1 Corinthians 13:1*
2. Love does not rejoice in _____ but in the _____. *1 Corinthians 13:6*
3. What three items did Paul say "abide"? *1 Corinthians 13:13*
4. Which is the greatest? *1 Corinthians 13:13*

Lesson 10

1. Of whom did Paul say, "We are not ignorant of his devices"? *2 Corinthians 2:11*
2. Paul said that a door of ministry had opened in a certain city. What city was it? (Philippi, Lystra, Troas?) *2 Corinthians 2:12*
3. Paul was deeply concerned that he had not found whom? *2 Corinthians 2:13*

Lesson 11

1. Paul described his treasure as being in _____ _____. *2 Corinthians 4:7*
2. Things that are seen are _____; things that are not seen are _____. *2 Corinthians 4:18*

Lesson 12

1. Paul had boasted of the Corinthians' giving to the Christians in another region. Was it Galatia, Macedonia, or Judea? *2 Corinthians 9:2*
2. What kind of giver does God love? *2 Corinthians 9:7*

Lesson 13

1. Paul said that he was prepared to visit the Corinthians for the _____ time. (second, third, fourth?) *2 Corinthians 13:1*
2. God had given Paul the power to work for the Corinthians' _____, not their destruction. *2 Corinthians 13:10*
3. With what did Paul tell the Corinthians to greet one another? *2 Corinthians 13:12*

Not Another Crisis!

by John W. Wade

EVERY TIME WE PICK UP a newspaper or listen to the TV news, the word *crisis* leaps out at us. From day to day, even hour to hour, it seems that we are confronted with another crisis. Now we have to deal with another one in our Sunday school lessons, for this quarter's lessons are entitled, "Helping a Church Confront Crisis."

The word *crisis* comes from the Greek word *krisis*, which in turn is derived from a verb meaning to "judge," "separate," or "select." A dictionary definition of *crisis* is "a time of great danger or trouble, whose outcome decides whether possible bad consequences will follow." The Chinese symbol for *crisis* consists of a combination of two symbols—one meaning "danger" and the other meaning "opportunity." That seems an appropriate way to describe the lessons in this quarter, which are based on 1 and 2 Corinthians. Each lesson deals with an issue that posed a serious threat to the young church at Corinth. At the same time, each issue also offered the opportunity for growth toward maturity.

Because of the frequency and intensity of the crises around us today, we may be inclined to think that no other period in history has ever encountered the problems we are facing. However, every period has had its share of problems. The church in Corinth was certainly no exception.

We need to remember that the church of Jesus Christ has lived its entire history in a crisis, because Christians have always been engaged in a spiritual warfare with Satan and his hosts. We can be sure that this conflict will continue until God finally triumphs over Satan. If this is the case, we must ask how the crises experienced by the Corinthian church are relevant to us today. The lessons of this quarter will provide answers to that question. They will show how the problems troubling the Corinthian church—including divisiveness, worldliness, proper use of spiritual gifts, personal ambitions, and pettiness—are surprisingly contemporary.

Unit 1: Christ, the Basis for Unity

In **lesson 1** Paul, who had learned of divisions that had formed among the Corinthian Christians, makes an earnest plea for unity. This first lesson does not touch on all the causes for the lack of unity; later lessons will examine some of these. Paul's plea for unity is based on the person and work of Christ. "Is Christ divided?" he asks. "Was Paul crucified for you? Were you baptized

in the name of Paul?" In the face of all the divisions that exist within the church today, these are still important issues to raise.

Lesson 2 deals with "The Holy Spirit as Teacher." Other activities of the Holy Spirit will be treated in later lessons. The focus in this lesson is His work in revealing truth to Paul and other inspired leaders.

Leadership is the theme of **lesson 3**. Few factors are more important to the growth of the church than dedicated leadership. Paul deals with some aspects of this issue in 1 Corinthians 4. The key qualification of leaders is that they must consider themselves "ministers," or "servants." They must also be good "stewards of the mysteries of God." Humility and integrity form the foundation upon which any effective leadership in Christ's church must be built.

Lesson 4 deals with a serious moral problem within the Corinthian church. Such a circumstance was perhaps more apt to surface in a city like Corinth, since so many of the Corinthian Christians came to Christ out of a paganism that included frequent sexual promiscuity. How timely this lesson is in our culture, where moral standards once accepted without question have been seriously eroded by the corrosive winds of secularism! Combine this with the rampant "meism" of our times, and the result is a situation not greatly different from the one Paul faced in Corinth.

Unit 2: Unity in Human Relationships

First Corinthians 7:1-16, which deals with marriage and related matters, is the basis for **lesson 5**. Few today have any doubts that marriage and the home are under siege in our society. Nor does anyone deny that unless we find ways to make our homes more stable, our nation faces a devastating future. The standards that Paul lays down—sexual fidelity in marriage and a serious commitment to the marital vows—are not popular with many today, but they remain God's standards. As a teacher you will need to handle this lesson with sensitivity and compassion.

Our culture puts a great deal of emphasis upon education and knowledge. These certainly are important; however, in **lesson 6** Paul points out that intellectual superiority can create an arrogance that disregards the sensitivities of others. He emphasizes the importance of showing love and concern to weaker brethren, even to the point of limiting some of one's own freedoms for the sake of others.

In **lesson 7** Paul answers some of the questions that had been raised in the Corinthian church about "spiritual gifts." This issue is quite controversial in many churches today. It is important to keep in mind that "the manifestation of the Spirit is given to every man to profit withal" (1 Corinthians 12:7). Whatever gifts and abilities an individual has should be put to use for the "profit" of the entire church.

The printed text for **lesson 8**, taken from 1 Corinthians 15, is an appropriate study for Easter Sunday. The resurrection story needs to be retold, not only for those who have never heard it or do not understand it, but also for faithful saints who never tire of it.

"Love's Better Way," the subject of **lesson 9**, leads us through 1 Corinthians 13, the "love chapter" of the Bible. The lessons of this chapter are not difficult to understand, but they can be difficult to implement, even for mature believers. Young Christians must learn these lessons, but mature saints need to relearn them and apply them to new situations. Christians must never take for granted that they already know all there is to know about love.

Unit 3: Unity Expressed in Ministry

Lesson 10 introduces the third unit in this quarter. It is also the first lesson based on a text from 2 Corinthians. We might note here that some students believe this was actually the third or even the fourth letter Paul wrote to the Corinthians, with one or two epistles having been lost. Theories advanced to explain the Corinthian correspondence are varied and complicated; they are best left to more technical studies. Suffice it to say we have the message the Spirit wanted us to have from Paul's Corinthian correspondence.

In this lesson we find a reference to one who had done some earlier wrong but had repented. This is probably the man mentioned in 1 Corinthians 5. This lesson gives us, then, "the rest of the story" begun in lesson 4, and tells us the discipline exercised by the church was successful.

No one ever promised that being a follower of Christ and living the Christian life would be easy, especially the apostle Paul. In **lesson 11** we consider his teaching on the "Trials and Triumphs of Christian Ministry." Paul's experiences as a messenger for Christ made him an "expert" on the pain and agony of ministry. While many in our world today endure physical suffering—beatings, imprisonment, and even death—for their faith, we in the Western world may never experience such opposition. However, in certain situations our faith and how we live it out may produce

emotional pain in the form of ridicule and discrimination. When these occasions arise (and they are likely to if we take our faith seriously), we can look to the example of Paul, whose faith empowered him to triumph over anything Satan could throw at him.

One important area of Christian ministry is our use of the material resources that God has entrusted to us. **Lesson 12**, "Collection for Jerusalem Christians," will give you an opportunity to stress several facets of Christian stewardship. Giving should never be approached as a legalistic requirement, so that it is done "grudgingly, or of necessity." Rather, we should rejoice that we have the opportunity to share our blessings with others; for "God loveth a cheerful giver" (2 Corinthians 9:7).

Lesson 13 concludes this series of studies from the Corinthian letters. It is also a fitting conclusion for this quarter's final unit, which emphasizes ministry. During his ministry to the Corinthians, Paul had come under sharp criticism from some within the church. Any person who becomes a leader will face some degree of criticism. How one handles it will go a long way in determining how successful he will be as a leader. Paul set the example of dealing both firmly and yet gently with criticism. As an apostle he had the authority to deal firmly with any troublemakers; but he chose to act with humility and gentleness, desiring to work for the Corinthians' edification, not their destruction (2 Corinthians 13:10).

May God help us do likewise in addressing similar situations in the body of Christ today.

Answers to Quarterly Quiz on page 226

Lesson 1—1. Paul, Apollos, Cephas, Christ. 2. Crispus and Gaius. 3. Stephanas. **Lesson 2**—1. Jesus Christ and Him crucified. 2. wisdom, men, power, God. **Lesson 3**—1. that they be found faithful. 2. the apostles. **Lesson 4**—1. false. 2. Satan. **Lesson 5**—1. the unmarried and widows. 2. sanctified. **Lesson 6**—1. knowledge, love. 2. stumblingblock. 3. true. **Lesson 7**—1. gifts, Spirit. 2. baptized, body. **Lesson 8**—1. firstfruits. 2. death. **Lesson 9**—1. sounding brass, tinkling cymbal. 2. iniquity, truth. 3. faith, hope, charity. 4. charity. **Lesson 10**—1. Satan. 2. Troas. 3. Titus. **Lesson 11**—1. earthen vessels. 2. temporal, eternal. **Lesson 12**—1. Macedonia. 2. cheerful. **Lesson 13**—1. third. 2. edification. 3. a holy kiss.

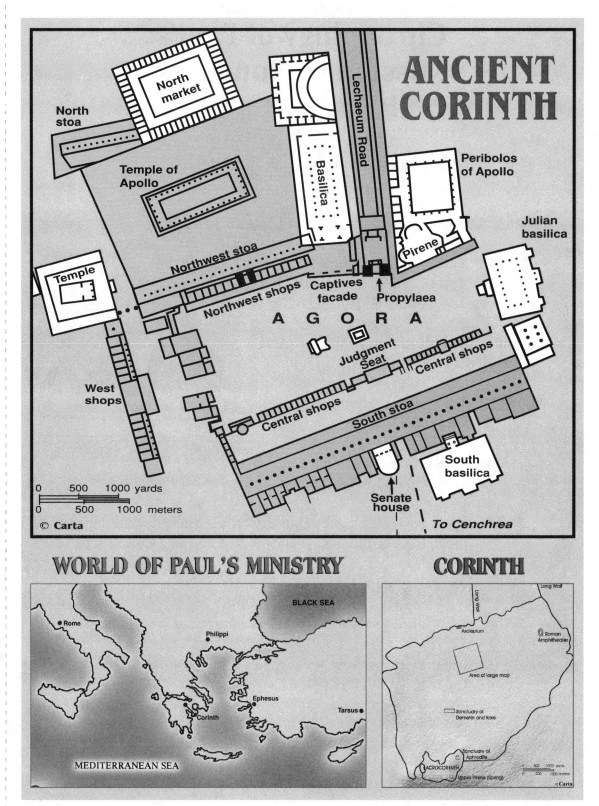

ANCIENT CORINTH

North market

North stoa

Temple of Apollo

North stoa

Basilica

Lechaeum Road

Peribolos of Apollo

Julian basilica

Pirene

Northwest stoa

Temple

Northwest shops

Captives facade

Propylaea

A G O R A

Judgment Seat

Central shops

West shops

Central shops

South stoa

South basilica

0   500   1000 yards
0   500   1000 meters

© Carta

Senate house

To Cenchrea

WORLD OF PAUL'S MINISTRY

BLACK SEA

Rome

Philippi

Ephesus

Corinth

Tarsus

MEDITERRANEAN SEA

CORINTH

Long Wall

Long Wall

Asclepium

Roman Amphitheater

Area of large map

Sanctuary of Demeter and Kore

Sanctuary of Aphrodite

ACROCORINTH

Upper Pirene (Spring)

© Carta

Chronology of Paul's Missionary Journeys

(And of Epistles Written at the Same Time)

Date

A.D. 47-49 **First Missionary Journey (Acts 13:1—14:28)**

A.D. 52-54 **Second Missionary Journey (Acts 15:40—18:22)**

52 Thessalonian epistles written (from Corinth, 1 Thessalonians 3:1-6; Acts 18:5)

A.D. 54–58 **Third Missionary Journey (Acts 18:23—20:38)**

54/55-57 Three-year ministry in Ephesus (Acts 20:31)

56 1 Corinthians written (from Ephesus, 1 Corinthians 16:8, 9)

56/57 Possible second trip by Paul to Corinth, since he mentions coming to the Corinthians for the "third time" in 2 Corinthians 13:1

57 Arrival in Macedonia (Acts 20:1-6)

57/58 2 Corinthians written (from Macedonia, 2 Corinthians 2:12, 13; 7:5-7)

58 Galatians written (from Macedonia, or possibly from Corinth)

58 Romans written (from Corinth, Romans 16:23; 1 Corinthians 1:14) in anticipation of Paul's visiting Rome

A.D. 58 **Paul Arrested in Jerusalem (Acts 21:17-33)**

Ugly Words, Ugly Reality

Using Discussion and Debate Effectively

by Ronald G. Davis

IT IS AN UGLY WORD—*SCHISM*—and it is an even uglier reality. *Crisis* compounds the dark picture. And where *schism* and *crisis* are, *confront* must enter. Christ's church is on the line in Corinth. The question is not, "Will the church thrive in Corinth?" but "Will the church *survive* in Corinth?" The Christians there were letting their differences overwhelm their basic similarity: they were all sinners saved by grace. Some were using sin as a basis for division. Some were using division as an occasion for sin. Paul, by the Holy Spirit, confronted those devilish attitudes with strong words and strong authority.

The differences causing divisions in Corinth were both shallow and deep, both minor and major, both doctrinal and practical (that is, if any division in the church can be called "shallow," "minor," or "non-doctrinal"!). The fulfillment of Jesus' prayer "that they all may be one" (John 17:21) was being threatened by those divisive elements that separated and threatened to undo the Corinthian church. How could their witness to their pagan world be successful if they showed no unity through a lifestyle of holiness and love?

This was Paul's concern in the first century, and it must be ours in the twenty-first. We must be as unrelenting against disunity in the body of Christ as Paul was. This series on his two epistles to the Corinthians offers a marvelous opportunity to focus on this goal.

Differences need resolution. Doctrines need uniformity. Discussion and debate are teaching strategies that resemble the processes of such resolution and uniformity. Discussion and debate, therefore, are ideal ways to approach a number of the studies in this quarter.

Discussion is not idle rambling. Nor is it a "mutual exchange of ignorance," as one educator suggested to characterize what usually happens. Discussion is a planned and prepared-for consideration of issues in which all participants are invited to share personal knowledge, experience, and insights.

Debate, likewise, needs to shed its negative image. In true debate, well-studied speakers address the two opposing sides of a topic. Debate should never consist of attacks on the opponent—only on the weaknesses of his or her proposition and argument.

Christians have nothing to fear about honest discussion and debate. Standing on the right side of moral and ethical issues is the only place to be, and that is where Christians must stand. But we also need an awareness of and a familiarity with the best arguments of those who stand with the devil. Although he is "a liar, and the father of it," as Jesus said (John 8:44), he can be most persuasive. Ask Eve. Ask Peter.

Discussion Delights

The Corinthian letters feature marvelous blends of the kinds of doctrinal and practical elements that many individuals relish talking about. 1 Corinthians 7 and 8 (lessons 5 and 6) are just such studies, beautifully combining doctrine and life.

Paul's simple caution, "Take heed lest by any means this liberty of yours become a stumblingblock to them that are weak" (8:9) raises several issues. What adult could resist responding to such a proposition as this: "Stumblingblock arguments are only a thin veil used to cover legalistic faces"? Consider dividing a class into two or more groups to discuss such questions as, "Should the immature influence the decisions of the mature?" "What do love and knowledge have to do with Paul's stumblingblock declaration?" "How is such inappropriate behavior a 'sin against Christ' (8:12)?" "How long should we let another's ignorance keep us from benefiting from our own knowledge?" "How far does Paul's principle, 'If _____ causes my brother to fall into sin, I will never _____,' go?"

Insisting that the groups apply the text of chapter 8 to their deliberations will encourage them to examine what the Spirit says and to express an understanding of the principles involved. (Better yet, assign some of the relevant questions to various class members the Sunday before.) Some will certainly have lesser understanding than others, but that is the very core of Paul's affirmations: how can we find unity amid our differing levels of understanding and maturity?

Likewise, no matter whether your class is one of singles or couples, old or young, who can ignore a proposition such as this one from 1 Corinthians 7, "The single life is the better life"? As Paul discusses marriage, he boldly declares, "I say therefore to the unmarried and widows, It is good for them if they abide even as I" (v. 8). The obvious questions surface immediately: "In what ways is the single life to be preferred?" "Is Paul stating an absolute of God or a purely personal view?" "God's design from the beginning was 'Therefore shall a man leave his father and his mother, and shall cleave unto his wife'; how does Paul's teaching relate to that?" "How do some of Paul's other affirmations about marriage and divorce in 1 Corinthians 7 relate to contemporary culture?"

Discussion will enliven the class, if the questions asked are personally and culturally relevant. The teacher's task is to write the questions and to invite class members to give them some thought before the discussion takes place. Whether that is accomplished by distributing a copy of all the questions (and/or an outline) ahead of time or simply by asking various members to be "primed" to deal with one particular question, the method of preparation is unimportant. That the preparation happens is critical.

Debate Dichotomies

Debate is a form of discussion, but it is more formalized. Control is exercised over time, order of speakers, and opportunity for audience participation. Whether it involves one individual versus another or one team versus another team, debate produces a clear-cut division between the parties involved. In a certain sense, one might say that *debate* could characterize what was happening within the Corinthian church: the "Paul" group versus the "Apollos" group, or the "Cephas" group versus the "Christ" group (1 Corinthians 1:12). A debate has the potential, as it unfolds, to raise some hackles (but should not to the point that it did among the Corinthians!). Debate, to be fully effective, needs to elicit some emotion—the emotion of strongly held belief, realizing what is at stake in peoples' lives.

Lesson 9, "Love's Better Way," is a good lesson to use to highlight the difference between a cynical perspective and a godly one. To many in the modern world, the loving lifestyle is a foolish, even fatal, one. Think what could ensue if you divided your class into "Cynics" and "Believers" and asked them to prepare arguments for and against this proposition: "Resolved: the loving lifestyle, as beautiful as it sounds, will not work in the contemporary workplace, play place, or living space!" You may want to give the class a week to prepare for this debate. Consider using the lesson writer's outline to help them in their preparation, or develop your own and distribute it.

When the class session begins, give the two sides a brief time to meet and to compile their "arguments." Have each select a spokesperson

(or two) for its position. Give each speaker a limited time (two to three minutes), alternate, allow class participation orally at the end, then summarize the issues raised and the conclusions drawn.

Lesson 2, "The Holy Spirit as Teacher," can also be used to create a debate. The role of the Spirit in daily living and in the revelation of truth has been deliberated from the first century to the year 2000. Such a resolution as the following could lead to an edifying debate: "The inspiration of the Spirit in the preparation of infallible documents is at the core of my faith." Some believe that inspiration of Scripture is a fuzzy doctrine for fuzzy minds. Even more avow that infallibility is meaningless, and thus unimportant, without original manuscripts.

As your class arrives for the study, hand out "Inspired" and "Uninspired" labels alternately. (Consider also distributing a list of Scriptures that the lesson writer mentions in lesson 2, along with other appropriate references.) Again, let each group meet and develop its statements. This time you may want to alternate thirty-second statements from the two sides, asking members to stand and be recognized before they speak. (This will work better if you seat the two groups so that they are facing each other.)

Sometimes, to encourage clarity in thinking, it is good to let groups or individuals prepare for one side, then present the other side's arguments! (They will need a brief period of time to consider the *written* notes of the other side.)

Now take a look at lesson 10, "Christian March of Triumph," from 2 Corinthians 2:4-17. Which of the following resolution statements do you believe could best be debated in your class?

1. The best way to deal with troublemakers is forgiveness and encouragement.

2. Confrontation is sometimes necessary, even when it brings grief.

3. The Christian must serve as a "sweet savor" to those who are saved, but as a "savor of death" to the unsaved.

What arguments or questions would you suggest to your debaters in order to examine the statement to be debated? How would you organize the classroom and the procedure for your debate?

The Corinthian church could be characterized as one with ugly words and ugly behaviors. What Paul wanted (and what God wanted) was the beauty of holiness, the beauty of unity. What could be better goals for today's church? For our church? Will we let cracks become canyons? Will we let fences become fortresses? Or will we work for that holiness and unity for which Christ prayed and died?

Appeal for Unity

March 5
Lesson 1

DEVOTIONAL READING: 1 Corinthians 1:18-25.

BACKGROUND SCRIPTURE: 1 Corinthians 1:1-17.

PRINTED TEXT: 1 Corinthians 1:2-17.

1 Corinthians 1:2-17

2 Unto the church of God which is at Corinth, to them that are sanctified in Christ Jesus, called to be saints, with all that in every place call upon the name of Jesus Christ our Lord, both theirs and ours:

3 Grace be unto you, and peace, from God our Father, and from the Lord Jesus Christ.

4 I thank my God always on your behalf, for the grace of God which is given you by Jesus Christ;

5 That in every thing ye are enriched by him, in all utterance, and in all knowledge;

6 Even as the testimony of Christ was confirmed in you:

7 So that ye come behind in no gift; waiting for the coming of our Lord Jesus Christ:

8 Who shall also confirm you unto the end, that ye may be blameless in the day of our Lord Jesus Christ.

9 God is faithful, by whom ye were called unto the fellowship of his Son Jesus Christ our Lord.

10 Now I beseech you, brethren, by the name of our Lord Jesus Christ, that ye all speak the same thing, and that there be no divisions among you; but that ye be perfectly joined together in the same mind and in the same judgment.

11 For it hath been declared unto me of you, my brethren, by them which are of the house of Chloe, that there are contentions among you.

12 Now this I say, that every one of you saith, I am of Paul; and I of Apollos; and I of Cephas; and I of Christ.

13 Is Christ divided? was Paul crucified for you? or were ye baptized in the name of Paul?

14 I thank God that I baptized none of you, but Crispus and Gaius;

15 Lest any should say that I had baptized in mine own name.

16 And I baptized also the household of Stephanas: besides, I know not whether I baptized any other.

17 For Christ sent me not to baptize, but to preach the gospel: not with wisdom of words, lest the cross of Christ should be made of none effect.

GOLDEN TEXT: Now I beseech you, brethren, by the name of our Lord Jesus Christ, that ye all speak the same thing, and that there be no divisions among you; but that ye be perfectly joined together in the same mind and in the same judgment.—1 Corinthians 1:10.

Helping a Church Confront Crisis
Unit 1: Christ, the Basis for Unity
(Lessons 1-4)

Lesson Aims

After participating in this lesson, each student should be able to:

1. Explain what was causing division within the church at Corinth.

2. Tell why division is so destructive to the church and its message.

3. Tell how a divided church can find oneness in Christ.

Lesson Outline

Introduction

A. Saddened, Yet Encouraged

In the days when the Soviet Union was a world power, an American minister spent some years visiting and preaching among congregations behind the Iron Curtain. When he went there, he expected to find the churches united. After all, they were facing the common enemies of Communism and militant atheism. He pictured them like the pioneers of the American West, drawing their wagons into a circle to support each other in the face of danger. Instead, he was shocked to find the same kinds of disagreements, divisions, power struggles, and personality conflicts so common within the churches of the free world.

At first the minister was quite depressed by his discovery, but then he came to realize that the devil is not creative. Only God is creative. The devil uses the same tactics all over the world, in every place and in all generations. Sadly, these methods almost always work.

When we become the cause of division in the family of God, we do not advance God's cause but Satan's. When we work for peace and unity in the body of Christ, we help to advance the cause for which He died.

B. Lesson Background

The city of Corinth was one of the great commercial centers of the first-century world. It was located on a very narrow strip of land that connected the two land masses of Greece. The city had harbors on two seas, the Aegean to the east and the Adriatic to the west. Rather than go around the great stretch of southern Greece (called the Pelopenessus), ships unloaded in one harbor, carried their goods overland, and reloaded on another ship in the other harbor. This gave Corinth many opportunities for employment and for the accumulation of wealth through the taxation of any items that passed through its harbors.

Like many seaport cities Corinth was also the center of frequent immorality. Two temples in particular dominated the city: that of Apollo (the sun god) and that of Aphrodite (the goddess of love and beauty). The latter housed more than a thousand temple prostitutes. Corinth's reputation for immorality was so widespread that it became a byword for vice: the verb "to Corinthianize" was coined to mean "to engage in sexual immorality." It is easy to see why Corinth was an especially challenging place to start a church, and why it appeared to present more problems for Paul than any other church with which he was associated.

Paul came to Corinth from Athens during his second missionary journey. Acts 18:1-18 records his initial visit there. Aquila and Priscilla were among his first contacts in Corinth (it is not clear from Scripture whether they were led to Christ through Paul's efforts or were already Christians when Paul met them). A close bond developed since, like Paul, Aquila and Priscilla were tentmakers.

Paul stayed in Corinth for about eighteen months (Acts 18:11). Eventually his success became so great that he encountered serious opposition. Jewish leaders brought him before Gallio, an official of the province of Achaia (where Corinth was located), but Gallio refused to hear the case. Paul then traveled to Ephesus, where he made a brief stop, then proceeded on to Jerusalem. He returned to Ephesus on his third missionary journey and stayed there for three years (Acts 20:31). It was from Ephesus that he wrote 1 Corinthians, in approximately A.D. 56.

I. Winsome Greeting (1 Corinthians 1:2, 3)

A. Two Terms to Understand (v. 2)

2. Unto the church of God which is at Corinth, to them that are sanctified in Christ Jesus, called to be saints, with all that in every place call upon the name of Jesus Christ our Lord, both theirs and ours.

The word *church* is used to translate the Greek word *ekklesia*, which, in New Testament times, referred to a meeting or assembly. Literally the word means, "called-out ones." It described the gathering of the citizens of Greek cities to discuss affairs of government (something comparable to a town hall meeting). The term became an appropriate one to apply to those "called . . . out of darkness into [God's] marvelous light" (1 Peter 2:9).

The word *sanctified* means set apart for a holy purpose. In the Bible the word is used of buildings, objects, and people. It does not imply a higher level of Christian commitment. Similarly, the word *saints*, which comes from the same root as *sanctified*, is a reference simply to Christians, not to people who are known for extraordinary commitment to God.

The followers of Jesus are known by many names. "Believers" and "disciples" describe their relationship to the Lord. "Brethren" pictures their relationship to one another. *Saints* highlights a dual relationship: they are set apart from the world and set apart to the Lord, in whose *name* they serve. Such devoted followers of the Master are needed *in every place* to serve as His ambassadors. [See question #1, page 240.]

Today's visual will give your students a better understanding of the location and features of the city of Corinth. Post it before the session begins.

Visual for lesson 1

B. Two Gifts to Receive (v. 3)

3. Grace be unto you, and peace, from God our Father, and from the Lord Jesus Christ.

Paul uses this same greeting of *grace* and *peace* in all of his letters, and it is always in the same order: *grace* then *peace*. This is important, for until one has experienced the grace of God he cannot hope to experience the peace of God. Both are gifts from *God our Father*, not personal achievements. The use of the word *peace* is particularly significant in this letter to a congregation where there was so little peace.

II. Word of Gratitude (1 Corinthians 1:4-9)

A. Paul's Practice (v. 4)

4. I thank my God always on your behalf, for the grace of God which is given you by Jesus Christ.

While Paul was aware of the many problems troubling the Corinthians, he began his remarks to them with words of commendation, not criticism. With the exception of Galatians, all of Paul's letters in the New Testament begin with words of encouragement similar to *I thank my God.* [See question #2, page 240.]

How often do we thank God for other believers? Do we thank Him for believers who are imperfect, immature, and struggling (as Paul did here)? Do we thank Him for the believers we have known who have taught us, inspired us, and encouraged us in our walk with Christ?

B. Spiritual Riches (vv. 5, 6)

5, 6. That in every thing ye are enriched by him, in all utterance, and in all knowledge; even as the testimony of Christ was confirmed in you.

Some believe that the words *utterance* and *knowledge* refer to the related gifts of the Spirit—speaking in tongues and the "word of knowledge" (1 Corinthians 12:8, 10). Others think that they refer to spiritual blessings given to all the Corinthians. The significance of Paul's mentioning these blessings lay in the fact that the Greek world placed great emphasis on wisdom and on eloquence in speech—points to which Paul will refer shortly in this letter (1:19-30; 2:1-5). Here he affirms that the Corinthians, through God's grace, had nothing to be ashamed of in these important areas.

TWO KINDS OF RICHES

Lottery fever has taken over America. It is a disease for which there is neither a vaccine to prevent it nor an antibiotic to cure it. In recent years, most states in the nation have legalized gambling in lotteries, casinos, or riverboats.

In May of 1998, an Illinois couple won the Iowa "Power Ball" lottery. It was a record prize at the time. The couple chose to receive the lump sum of more than $104 million, rather than 25 annual payments totaling $196 million. They must have thought that 104 million "birds in the hand" were worth 196 million "birds in the bush"!

The odds against winning that lottery were eighty million to one. Think of it this way: suppose you laid a continuous row of quarters, touching each other, from Washington, D.C., to Tulsa, Oklahoma. Picking the right quarter would have won the Iowa "Power Ball" lottery!

After winning such a prize, the individuals often say, "It's not going to change the way we live." Later, however, a high percentage of such winners find that their wealth has brought them far more grief than happiness.

Not so with the riches of which Paul writes! The gracious gifts of God's Spirit bring us peace and satisfaction. One who has been enriched in this way knows what true wealth is.   —C. R. B.

C. Spiritual Gifts (v. 7)

7. So that ye come behind in no gift; waiting for the coming of our Lord Jesus Christ.

The term *gift* may refer to the miraculous gifts of the Spirit listed in 1 Corinthians 12:8-10. However, the word has a broader meaning and is also used of gifts that are not miraculous (Romans 12:6-8; Ephesians 4:11-13). The possession of such gifts was not to be an occasion of personal

---

How to Say It

ACHAIA. Uh-*kay*-uh.
ADRIATIC. Ay-dree-*at*-ik.
AEGEAN. Ay-*jee*-un.
APHRODITE. Af-ruh-*dite*-ee.
APOLLO. Uh-*pahl*-o.
APOLLOS. Uh-*pahl*-us.
AQUILA. *Ack*-wih-luh.
ARAMAIC. Air-uh-*may*-ik.
CEPHAS. *See*-fus.
CHLOE. *Klo*-ee.
CORINTH. *Kor*-inth.
CORINTHIANIZE. Kor-*in*-thee-un-ize.
CORINTHIANS. Kor-*in*-thee-unz.
CRISPUS. *Kris*-pus.
EKKLESIA (Greek). ek-lay-*see*-uh.
EPHESUS. *Ef*-uh-sus.
GAIUS. *Gay*-us.
GALLIO. *Gal*-ee-o.
PELOPENESSUS. *Pell*-uh-puh-*nee*-sus (strong accent on *nee*).
PRISCILLA. Prih-*sil*-uh.
STEPHANAS. *Stef*-uh-nass.

---

pride. When exercised by individuals, gifts are to be used to benefit the entire congregation and to prepare people *for the coming of our Lord Jesus Christ*. Clearly the Corinthians were not deficient in the possession of spiritual gifts; they were deficient in the attitude required to use those gifts as the Giver intended.

D. The Faithful God (vv. 8, 9)

8, 9. Who shall also confirm you unto the end, that ye may be blameless in the day of our Lord Jesus Christ. God is faithful, by whom ye were called unto the fellowship of his Son Jesus Christ our Lord.

The word *confirm* means "strengthen." *That ye may be blameless* is rendered in one translation in these words: "so that nobody can accuse you of anything." While we are called to good works (Ephesians 2:10), it is only God's grace and not our personal goodness that will allow us to plead "not guilty" when we stand in the judgment before God *in the day of our Lord Jesus Christ*. That day will be the time when final judgment is rendered (Matthew 25:31, 32).

III. Call for Agreement (1 Corinthians 1:10-12)

A. Paul's Plea (v. 10)

10. Now I beseech you, brethren, by the name of our Lord Jesus Christ, that ye all speak the same thing, and that there be no divisions among you; but that ye be perfectly joined together in the same mind and in the same judgment.

Paul urged that the Corinthians *all speak the same thing*. This does not mean that he expected individuals to have no differing viewpoints. There was—and is—room for private opinions. However, Paul wanted believers to say that which would work for the common good of all believers (Romans 15:6; Ephesians 4:29). He was urging a unity of purpose in Christ.

Paul's challenge to be *perfectly joined together in the same mind and in the same judgment* may seem to present an unattainable standard. However, the word *perfectly* means "completely." As Christians we do not have to agree on everything, but our disagreements must not be allowed to divide the church. We should all seek to have the mind of Christ, which means being "likeminded, having the same love, being of one accord, of one mind" (Philippians 2:2). [See question #3, page 240.]

B. Chloe's Report (v. 11)

11. For it hath been declared unto me of you, my brethren, by them which are of the house of Chloe, that there are contentions among you.

We do not know who *Chloe* was, nor what members of her *house* (household) went to see Paul in Ephesus with the news about the *contentions* (quarrels or dissension) within the Corinthian church. They were a credible source, however, and Paul took their allegations seriously. [See question #4, page 240.]

C. Divided Loyalties (v. 12)

12. Now this I say, that every one of you saith, I am of Paul; and I of Apollos; and I of Cephas; and I of Christ.

People in the Corinthian church had become closely attached to different leaders. This was the primary cause of the friction that had developed within the church.

Apollos had come to Ephesus, apparently after Paul's first visit (Acts 18:24—19:1), and had then proceeded to Corinth. *Cephas* was the Aramaic name for the apostle Peter. The specific factors leading to the formation of these groups are not mentioned. Perhaps some included Jewish Christians (particularly Peter's group), while the others (such as the followers of Apollos) tended to draw Gentile Christians. Those claiming loyalty to Christ may have claimed to belong to Christ in some exclusive sense, or perhaps took some measure of pride in refusing to be labeled by the names of human leaders.

Jesus prayed that all who believed in Him might be one, "that the world may believe that thou hast sent me" (John 17:21). He knew that the world would believe the message of a united church more readily than that of a divided church. The schisms in Corinth were working against the desires of the Head of the church.

A DIVIDED FAMILY

A couple who had filed for divorce three times went to see a Fresno, California, minister. They supposedly wanted to try once more to patch things up. The counseling session came to an abrupt end, however, when the couple started shooting at each other!

When the woman started to walk out of the counseling session, her husband pulled out a gun and shot her. Not mortally wounded, she reached into her purse, turned, and shot him in the shoulder. The couple went outside, where the wife fell to the ground and the husband fired several more shots at her. Both survived, and both were charged with attempted murder. It would be a gross understatement to say that this was not a happy family.

Just as God intends for marriage and family life to provide contentment and mutual support for all concerned, this is also what He intends for His spiritual family—the church. The church in Corinth, however, was not "one big, happy family." Instead of contentment there was contention over personal loyalties—loyalties that were a symptom of some deeper spiritual problems to which Paul would later call their attention.

This is typical of troubled families and troubled churches—usually their problems consist of several overlapping layers of disturbing issues. But God wants *all* families—both ours and His— to live in peace and unity.   —C. R. B.

IV. Persuasive Argument (1 Corinthians 1:13-17)

A. Three Important Questions (v. 13)

13. Is Christ divided? was Paul crucified for you? or were ye baptized in the name of Paul?

The sin of division is highlighted in Paul's question, *Is Christ divided?* Just as Christ had only one physical body, so the church is to be His one spiritual body (1 Corinthians 12:12; Ephesians 4:4). The obvious answer to Paul's question is *no*.

Next, Paul asked a question with an equally evident answer: *was Paul crucified for you?* Clearly not—Christians must hold allegiance to only one Person, and that is the Person who gave His life for them at the cross. No human preacher or teacher, however brilliant or prominent, could ever do for us what Jesus did.

The third question raised by Paul was, *Were ye baptized in the name of Paul?* This raises the issue of the One by whose name or authority baptism takes place. Baptism is an act commanded by Christ (Matthew 28:18, 19; Mark 16:16) and brings a person "into Christ" (Romans 6:3; Galatians 3:27). Baptism joins a person only to Christ, not to Peter, Paul, Apollos, or whoever does the baptizing.

Home Daily Bible Readings

Monday, Feb. 28—Paul Greets the Corinthian Christians (1 Corinthians 1:1-9)
Tuesday, Feb. 29—Divisions Among Corinthian Christians (1 Corinthians 1:10-17)
Wednesday, Mar. 1—God's Power and Wisdom in Christ (1 Corinthians 1:18-25)
Thursday, Mar. 2—Christ Jesus, Source of Our Life (1 Corinthians 1:26-31)
Friday, Mar. 3—Paul Encourages Timothy (2 Timothy 1:3-14)
Saturday, Mar. 4—Serve Jesus Christ Faithfully (2 Timothy 2:1-13)
Sunday, Mar. 5—The Ways of God's Servant (2 Timothy 2:14-26)

These were three powerful arguments intended to persuade the Christians at Corinth to think seriously about the divisions they had created. They had become sidetracked from the doctrines that really mattered. [See question #5, page 240.]

B. Paul's Recollection (vv. 14-16)

14-16. I thank God that I baptized none of you, but Crispus and Gaius; lest any should say that I had baptized in mine own name. And I baptized also the household of Stephanas: besides, I know not whether I baptized any other.

The mention of baptism in the previous verse led to Paul's further consideration of this topic. He kept no records of people whom he had baptized; he depended on his memory. *Crispus* was the ruler of the synagogue at Corinth (Acts 18:8). *Gaius* may have been the same man mentioned in Romans 16:23 as Paul's host when he wrote the letter to the Romans (since Paul most likely wrote Romans from Corinth). *The household of Stephanas* is described as Paul's "firstfruits [or first converts] in Achaia" (1 Corinthians 16:15).

Paul was not diminishing the importance of baptism. He was simply expressing his gratitude that others had done most of the baptizing, in view of the divisions that had developed over individuals.

C. Paul's Commission (v. 17)

17. For Christ sent me not to baptize, but to preach the gospel: not with wisdom of words, lest the cross of Christ should be made of none effect.

Again, Paul's intent was not to disparage baptism; if anything, these words and those of verse 16 show how important baptism is. Baptism is meant to be the common experience of all Christians and, thus, a point of unity for them. To focus on who does the baptizing draws attention away from baptism's real significance. When one considers how much Paul had to say about baptism in his letters (Romans 6:3-6; 1 Corinthians 12:13; Galatians 3:27; Ephesians 4:5; Colossians 2:12; Titus 3:5), it is clear that he did not consider it an unimportant topic nor an insignificant act.

VISUALS FOR THESE LESSONS

The small visual pictured in each lesson (e.g., page 235) is a small reproduction of a large, full-color poster included in the *Adult Visuals* packet for the Spring Quarter. This packet is available from your supplier. Order No. 392.

In most cases, it seems that Paul's primary concern in his evangelistic efforts was to *preach the gospel*, while others baptized the converts. If we consider Paul's poor health (apparently alluded to in 1 Corinthians 2:3; 2 Corinthians 12:7-10; Galatians 4:13), we can see why others would have done the physical work of baptizing whenever possible. In addition, knowing the way that some people can become attached to certain personalities, we can see the wisdom of someone other than Paul doing the actual baptizing. With the Corinthians, Paul could use the argument that he had baptized very few people to make his case for unity in Christ, not division based on loyalty to human teachers.

Conclusion

A. Stick With the Fundamentals

It is so easy to be sidetracked into issues that are tangents, thus losing sight of the "big picture." The heart of the gospel is that Christ died for us, was buried, and rose again (1 Corinthians 15:3, 4). Keeping focused on those fundamentals will give us a sense of perspective when we evaluate other issues.

However, with the church at Corinth, doctrine was not the primary issue that divided the Christians (it seldom is, even today). Often believers divide over power struggles or personality conflicts. Because we do not want to admit that these quarrels are really the consequence of our sinful attitudes, we sometimes hide behind an alleged controversy over what is a very minor issue. We do not want to admit that *we* are at fault, so we magnify the differences of opinion that exist and present ourselves as "defending the faith."

Yes, we must be true to the fundamental doctrines of our faith. But we must also keep in mind that those fundamentals include keeping "the unity of the Spirit in the bond of peace" (Ephesians 4:3) and practicing the "more excellent way" of love (1 Corinthians 12:31).

B. Prayer

Dear Lord, we have often been foolish in dividing the body of Christ over our own opinions. We have often been jealous of our own power. We have often been too attached to human personalities. We ask Your forgiveness for the times we have failed You, and we ask for strength to work for unity in the body of Christ. We pray in His name. Amen.

C. Thought to Remember

To work for Christian unity is to heed the prayer of Jesus and the plea of Paul. To divide the body of Christ is to ignore the prayer and the plea.

Learning by Doing

This page contains an alternate lesson plan emphasizing learning activities.
Classes desiring such student involvement will find these suggestions helpful.

Learning Goals

After today's lesson, each adult will be able to:

1. Explain what was causing division within the church at Corinth.

2. Tell why division is so destructive to the church and its message.

3. Tell how a divided church can find oneness in Christ.

Into the Lesson

Before class, ask two or three pairs of class members, or other adults, to prepare brief (one minute or less) skits that show people being divisive about a church situation. You might suggest that a pair discuss the minister's sermon, a change in the worship service, or the choice of color for the new carpet in the fellowship hall. Tell them to exaggerate and add humor if they like, but to make the spirit of divisiveness obvious. (You may want to caution the pairs about avoiding any "sticky" issue in your church.)

Begin the class by playing a recording of the first verse of "They'll Know We Are Christians by Our Love" and then letting your first pair perform their skit. Without comment, play the chorus again and let the second pair present its skit.

Say, "Did any of these scenes sound or look familiar? Unfortunately, divisiveness does happen sometimes in our churches. This is not a new problem arising in our time. In the first century the apostle Paul learned about problems in the church in Corinth. This quarter we will be studying what he wrote to confront those crises."

Into the Word

Begin with a lecture by yourself or a student on the background information for today's study. (See pages 234, 235 in the commentary.) Half of your students are probably people who learn best by "seeing" the information, so illustrate the lecture. Use a map showing Corinth and the other cities mentioned in the background material. Display some teaching pictures of Paul preaching in Athens, working with Aquila and Priscilla, and teaching in Ephesus.

Have a volunteer read 1 Corinthians 1:1-9. Use the commentary to explain some of the key terms, such as *church of God, sanctified, saints,* and *grace and peace.*

Read 1 Corinthians 1:10-17. Use the following questions to help students analyze these verses.

(They are also in the student book.) This can be done with the class as a whole, or divide into smaller groups for discussion and have the groups report their results after a short time.

• What is Paul's attitude toward the division and the Christians at Corinth? *It is serious, but the Corinthians are still brethren; he is glad he didn't baptize more people to add to the problem.*

• What seems to be the cause of the division? *People are claiming allegiance with one of the leaders to the point of forming parties/cliques.*

• Why might a Corinthian believer want to be associated with one of the men listed—Paul, Apollos, Cephas, Christ? *Status because of who taught and/or baptized them, devotion to the person.*

• Note the three questions with the obvious answer, "No." Why do you think Paul asks them? *To persuade the believers to think seriously about the things they were doing; to divert attention from human leaders to the Christ.*

Into Life

Draw lines on a large poster or overhead transparency to divide it into four quadrants. Label the top quadrants: *Phrases That Contribute to Division* and *Phrases That Contribute to Unity.* Label the lower quadrants: *Actions That Contribute to Division* and *Actions That Contribute to Unity.*

Let groups of four or five people brainstorm answers for the chart. As a group completes its work, tell members to discuss why division is so destructive to a church and its mission to win people to Christ.

Let groups report two ideas for each category. Write their ideas on the chart for all to see.

Ask, "What destruction did your group describe as the result of division in a church?" Write down key phrases so that they become part of the total picture in front of the students.

Review the suggestions. Close the class session by asking the students to write specific actions they can take to promote unity within the local church. When most students have stopped writing, play the recording of the entire song, "They'll Know We Are Christians by Our Love." If you cannot find a recording, read the words of the song (all the verses) to the class. Pray for unity, asking God for help to carry out the specific ideas suggested in class.

Let's Talk It Over

The questions on this page are designed to encourage review of the lesson Scriptures and to promote discussion of the lesson by the class. The answers provided are only discussion starters. Let your class talk it over from there.

1. According to the New Testament, we are saints, disciples, and brethren. How can we use these titles to promote and preserve unity?

Our status as *saints* means that God has called us all to lives of holiness, and we should all be progressing in holiness. None of us has achieved complete holiness, however, so we need one another's support in continuing our growth. *Disciples* are learners. Here again we should all be involved in the continual process of learning about God and Christ and how we may live a fruitful Christian life. As *brethren* we understand that we belong to the same spiritual family. In Christ we are all children of the same Father.

2. Paul characteristically thanked God for the believers to whom he wrote. What benefits do you think would result if we all developed the habit of thanking God for all our brothers and sisters in Christ?

Thanking God for fellow Christians encourages us to look at the positive aspects of their character. Too often we focus on the negative: this person talks too much; that person tends to be boastful; these individuals engage in hypocritical behavior. When we thank God for them, we pay more attention to their faithfulness in attendance and service, their efforts at winning others to Christ, or their willingness to use their talents for the Lord. Also, thanking God for them can be the prelude to asking Him to help them overcome some of the negative aspects in their character. Our prayers for them will be more effective when we maintain a balance between thankfulness and intercession. Finally, when we thank God for them and pray for them, we will be more likely to respond to them with love and compassion.

3. Differing opinions and disagreements regarding minor matters are inevitable in any congregation. What principles can we follow to keep such opinions and disagreements from becoming divisive?

In Galatians 5:13 Paul urged his readers to serve one another in love. If we master this approach to our life in the church, we can avoid an insistence on getting our way and having our opinion exalted above others. In Romans 14:19 Paul set forth this principle: "Let us therefore make every effort to do what leads to peace and to mutual edification" (*New International Version*). Of course, we must not allow our quest for peace to keep us from objecting to any deviation from clear Biblical doctrine. But where opinions are concerned, we should be peacemakers, meekly giving each brother and sister an opportunity to voice what is on his or her mind. And when we make it a priority to edify, or build up, one another, we will be less likely to permit disagreements to tear down what we are building up.

4. Word of the contentions in the Corinthian church had reached Paul in Ephesus. It seems that bad news regarding a congregation spreads rapidly. How much does that bother you? What is most troubling to you about that?

Paul's hearing of the trouble in Corinth was different from the spread of bad news in most cases. Concerned church members reported the difficulties to Paul in order to enlist his help. Too often bad news spreads through gossip and slander. When the unsaved hear about wrangling in a local church, they use that as a justification for avoiding any church. News of conflicts within the church obscures the fact that it is Jesus' church and that it testifies to His salvation. Of course, the bad news also reaches other congregations. It then produces some discouragement in them, and it may also stir up crippling doubts in the minds of young, immature believers. How much better it is to work through conflicts before they can become fast-spreading bad news!

5. Christian leaders must take care to prevent those they influence from forming a divisive faction within a church. How can they do this?

One of the factions in the Corinthian church was centered around Paul's name. But Paul frequently discouraged this in his writings. He referred to himself as a servant of God and man (Romans 1:1; 2 Corinthians 4:5; Philippians 1:1; Titus 1:1). Even as an apostle, he viewed himself as a mere "steward" of something entrusted to his care (1 Corinthians 4:2). In word and in deed, he attempted to point people beyond himself and to the Christ (1 Corinthians 11:1). Even so, one of the factions took his name, suggesting that in spite of our best efforts there will be some who overemphasize a leader's role. Still, the leader must make the effort to point them to Christ.

The Holy Spirit as Teacher

DEVOTIONAL READING: 1 Corinthians 3:1-9.

BACKGROUND SCRIPTURE: 1 Corinthians 2, 3.

PRINTED TEXT: 1 Corinthians 2:1-16.

1 Corinthians 2:1-16

1 And I, brethren, when I came to you, came not with excellency of speech or of wisdom, declaring unto you the testimony of God.

2 For I determined not to know any thing among you, save Jesus Christ, and him crucified.

3 And I was with you in weakness, and in fear, and in much trembling.

4 And my speech and my preaching was not with enticing words of man's wisdom, but in demonstration of the Spirit and of power:

5 That your faith should not stand in the wisdom of men, but in the power of God.

6 Howbeit we speak wisdom among them that are perfect: yet not the wisdom of this world, nor of the princes of this world, that come to nought:

7 But we speak the wisdom of God in a mystery, even the hidden wisdom, which God ordained before the world unto our glory;

8 Which none of the princes of this world knew: for had they known it, they would not have crucified the Lord of glory.

9 But as it is written, Eye hath not seen, nor ear heard, neither have entered into the heart of man, the things which God hath prepared for them that love him.

10 But God hath revealed them unto us by his Spirit: for the Spirit searcheth all things, yea, the deep things of God.

11 For what man knoweth the things of a man, save the spirit of man which is in him? even so the things of God knoweth no man, but the Spirit of God.

12 Now we have received, not the spirit of the world, but the Spirit which is of God; that we might know the things that are freely given to us of God.

13 Which things also we speak, not in the words which man's wisdom teacheth, but which the Holy Ghost teacheth; comparing spiritual things with spiritual.

14 But the natural man receiveth not the things of the Spirit of God: for they are foolishness unto him: neither can he know them, because they are spiritually discerned.

15 But he that is spiritual judgeth all things, yet he himself is judged of no man.

16 For who hath known the mind of the Lord, that he may instruct him? But we have the mind of Christ.

GOLDEN TEXT: Now we have received, not the spirit of the world, but the Spirit which is of God; that we might know the things that are freely given to us of God.
—1 Corinthians 2:12.

Helping a Church Confront Crisis
Unit 1: Christ, the Basis for Unity
(Lessons 1-4)

Lesson Aims

After participating in this lesson, students should be able to:

1. Explain the Holy Spirit's role in revealing the gospel message.

2. Tell why it is important to base one's faith on the Spirit-given message of Christ and not on man-made wisdom.

3. Express faith in Christ, as revealed by the Spirit's wisdom.

Lesson Outline

INTRODUCTION
    A. Paul's Eloquence
    B. Lesson Background
  I. PAUL'S TESTIMONY (1 Corinthians 2:1-5)
    A. The Method (v. 1)
    B. The Message (v. 2)
    C. The Messenger (v. 3)
    D. The Motive (vv. 4, 5)
 II. TRUE WISDOM (1 Corinthians 2:6-13)
    A. Not of This World (v. 6)
      The Cure That Really Works
    B. Ordained of God (v. 7)
    C. Unknown by Rulers (v. 8)
    D. Beyond Man's Thinking (v. 9)
    E. Taught by God's Spirit (vv. 10-13)
III. RECEIVING WISDOM (1 Corinthians 2:14-16)
    A. The Natural Man (v. 14)
    B. The Spiritual Man (vv. 15, 16)
      Two Kinds of People
CONCLUSION
    A. Turn Your Eyes Upon Jesus
    B. Prayer
    C. Thought to Remember

Introduction

A. Paul's Eloquence

One need only read 1 Corinthians 13 to know that the apostle Paul was an eloquent man. It would be hard to find words in any of the world's literature that are more expressive than those found in this chapter. However, Paul did not want the Corinthians to be moved simply by eloquence. He wanted them to be moved by his message—"Jesus Christ, and him crucified"—and not by the manner of its delivery.

B. Lesson Background

As we noted in last week's Lesson Background (page 234), Paul came to Corinth from Athens during his second missionary journey. Some Bible students believe that Paul left Athens with a sense of having failed there. Pointing to 1 Corinthians 2:2—"I determined not to know any thing among you, save Jesus Christ, and him crucified"—they suggest Paul thought he had tried too hard to appeal to the philosophical thinking of his audience in Athens, at the expense of diminishing the power of the gospel. This verse, they say, signals a change in Paul's method. Other students think such a conclusion reads too much into this verse. They believe Paul's words should be seen in contrast to the Corinthians' own overemphasis on human wisdom rather than in contrast to an earlier method tried by Paul.

Whatever we conclude about Paul's evaluation of his work at Athens, there is no mistaking the determination he expresses in today's lesson text. Every Christian would do well to cultivate this same passion for making Christ known to others.

I. Paul's Testimony
(1 Corinthians 2:1-5)

A. The Method (v. 1)

1. And I, brethren, when I came to you, came not with excellency of speech or of wisdom, declaring unto you the testimony of God.

Paul was a highly educated man. He could have used this training to draw attention to himself. But people might have gone away saying, "What a great man Paul is!" Paul wanted them to go away saying, "What a great Savior Jesus is!" *Excellency of speech* and of *wisdom* are powerful tools for those who seek a following for themselves. Paul, however, was seeking a following for the Lord. Thus he was determined to focus his hearers' attention on the *testimony of God*— that is, what God did, through Jesus, at the cross.

It would be wrong to use this passage to claim that excellence is not important in Christian work. We should never put forth haphazard or shoddy efforts in serving the Lord. However, no one should use his gifts in such a way as to call attention to the gifts and not to the gospel. Paul did not want to come to Corinth with overpowering oratory or impressive demonstrations of wisdom. Such methods may have drawn a crowd, but the results would not last.

B. The Message (v. 2)

2. For I determined not to know any thing among you, save Jesus Christ, and him crucified.

Paul had already emphasized the centrality of *Jesus Christ, and him crucified* to the Christian message (1:17-24). He did so knowing that many would be offended by such preaching (1:18, 23). The Greeks at Corinth could not imagine a deity who died for men. They thought that only criminals died on crosses. But Paul refused to tailor his message to suit the sensitivities or prejudices of his audience. Too much was at stake! [See question #1, page 248.]

C. The Messenger (v. 3)

3. And I was with you in weakness, and in fear, and in much trembling.

Many artists have painted self-portraits, including Michelangelo, van Gogh, and Rembrandt. It is estimated that Rembrandt painted between fifty and sixty self-portraits. Many of these are quite realistic and not very flattering. Paul's verbal self-portrait in today's lesson text is not a flattering one. He describes himself as a man who came to the Corinthians *in weakness, and in fear, and in much trembling*. Sometimes we tend to draw the apostle Paul larger than life. We picture him as a man who was always bold and confident, and never timid, hesitant, or afraid. This verse tells us exactly the opposite. Paul felt quite inadequate to proclaim properly so great a message as the gospel.

All Christians have felt this inadequacy, and it is right that they should. No one is really qualified to handle so sublime a message. All must say with Paul, "Who is sufficient for these things?" (2 Corinthians 2:16).

D. The Motive (vv. 4, 5)

4. And my speech and my preaching was not with enticing words of man's wisdom, but in demonstration of the Spirit and of power.

We have various words to describe speakers who use *enticing words* to appeal to people, including demagogue, rabble-rouser, and propagandist. These individuals usually employ deception or distortion rather than truth to get their message across. Paul believed that the truth of the gospel can stand on its own merits without being promoted by such devious means. To use such tactics smothers the *demonstration of the Spirit and of power* that is central to the gospel (Romans 1:16; 1 Thessalonians 1:5). [See question #2, page 248.]

5. That your faith should not stand in the wisdom of men, but in the power of God.

Here is the reason Paul refused to use "excellency of speech or of wisdom" (v. 1) or "enticing words" (v. 4) in presenting the gospel to the Corinthians. He did not want their *faith* to rest in the method of presentation, which was based on *the wisdom of men*, but in the content of the gospel, which magnifies *the power of God* to save lost sinners through His Son's death on the cross.

This verse is a helpful warning to us to examine whatever methods we use in presenting the gospel, lest those methods draw attention away from the crucified Christ.

II. True Wisdom (1 Corinthians 2:6-13)

A. Not of This World (v. 6)

6. Howbeit we speak wisdom among them that are perfect: yet not the wisdom of this world, nor of the princes of this world, that come to nought.

Paul had already noted the futility of *the wisdom of this world* in attempting to know God (1 Corinthians 1:18-21). Often the *princes*, or rulers, *of this world* are governed by such wisdom, and find themselves frustrated that their policies and laws fail to accomplish their desired ends. Those who are *perfect* (mature or complete) in Christ should turn away from such false wisdom and embrace the higher, spiritual wisdom "that is from above" (James 3:17).

THE CURE THAT REALLY WORKS

Emily Rosa was just eleven years old when she became the youngest person ever to author a scientific paper published in the *Journal of the American Medical Association*. Her article was the result of a fourth-grade science project. It was heralded as "brilliant" by a physician whose specialty is bringing medical fraud to light.

"Therapeutic touch healers" practice their "art" by moving their hands above their patients' bodies, asserting that they are realigning the "energy fields" that illness has disturbed. They have claimed that their method is helpful in treating AIDS, cancer, and other illnesses.

Emily tested twenty-one such therapeutic touch healers and demonstrated that they could *not* reliably sense their patients' energy fields—a claim on which rests their supposed ability to heal. As you would expect, the practitioners of the technique have cried, "Foul!"

Human wisdom often uses strange ideas and deceptive techniques to tell us how to cure our souls' diseases, unlike the revelation of God that we have in Scripture. The Bible gives us truth that does not depend on either human wisdom or human folly. It comes from the One who made us and knows us better than anyone. It will always serve as an accurate standard by which to measure any rival claims. —C. R. B.

B. Ordained of God (v. 7)

7. But we speak the wisdom of God in a mystery, even the hidden wisdom, which God ordained before the world unto our glory.

Today we use the word *mystery* much differently from how it is used in the New Testament. Usually we mean something that is unknown, or cannot be explained or comprehended by human reasoning. Often the word describes a riddle or secret for which an answer has not been found.

In the New Testament, however, *mystery* means something that once was secret but has now been revealed. Pagan religions in the Greek world were often referred to as "mystery religions" because they claimed to offer their adherents knowledge and insights available from no other source. New converts were initiated in secret ceremonies.

Here Paul put a different twist on the idea of *mystery*. He states that *the wisdom of God* (meaning His plan to save the world through the crucified Christ) was something He *ordained*, or determined, *before the world*—meaning before the world was created. (See 1 Peter 1:18-20.) Though parts of this plan were outlined in the Old Testament, their fulfillment did not occur until the New Testament era. God's plan embraces the future of His people as well, promising them that they will share His *glory* (John 17:24). [See question #3, page 248.]

C. Unknown by Rulers (v. 8)

8. Which none of the princes of this world knew: for had they known it, they would not have crucified the Lord of glory.

Earthly rulers are called, as in verse 6, *princes of this world*. The reference to those who *crucified the Lord of glory* indicates that these *princes* include Pilate, Herod, and the religious leaders in Jerusalem whose efforts resulted in the death of Jesus. These men did not recognize the wisdom that Jesus represented and that guided God's plan concerning Jesus. This did not exonerate them, of course. (See Romans 3:5-8.) They had many opportunities to learn of that wisdom, but they rejected those opportunities.

Here, as elsewhere in the New Testament, the cross is linked with *glory* (John 12:23, 28; Galatians 6:14; Philippians 2:8, 9; Revelation 5:12). It is remarkable that the cross, which was a symbol of shame and humiliation, should in Christian

How to Say It

ATHENS. *Ath*-unz.
CORINTH. *Kor*-inth.
CORINTHIANS. Kor-*in*-thee-unz.
ISAIAH. Eye-*zay*-uh.
MICHELANGELO. My-kull-*an*-jell-o.
REMBRANDT. *Rem*-brant.
VAN GOGH. van *Go*.

thought be turned into an emblem of glory. Today we do not think it at all strange to sing, "In the Cross of Christ I Glory." However, we should never forget that the way of the cross can still be marked by occasions of humiliation and persecution for the followers of Jesus.

D. Beyond Man's Thinking (v. 9)

9. But as it is written, Eye hath not seen, nor ear heard, neither have entered into the heart of man, the things which God hath prepared for them that love him.

Isaiah 64:4, from which this quotation is taken, does not include the line *neither have entered into the heart of man*. Apparently Paul was paraphrasing this text, yet providing, under the inspiration of the Holy Spirit, a correct understanding of its meaning.

Given the context, *the things which God hath prepared* comprise the mystery of the gospel. It is not something invented by natural means, something the *eye* could observe or the *ear* could hear. It was not conceived in *the heart of man*, but was, instead, revealed by God's Spirit (v. 10). [See question #4, page 248.]

Christians through the years have also seen this promise as a reference to future blessings and to Heaven in particular. That application is justified—though with some limitation. Just as no one in Isaiah's day could have imagined the grandeur of the Christian religion, so no one in our day can imagine the grandeur of Heaven. God has revealed something of that glory to us, but the images are sketchy and the details few. We know it will be a great and marvelous experience to be with the Lord in Heaven, but we cannot imagine just how awesome it will be.

Charles L. Allen used to explain our lack of information about Heaven in this manner. He said that you cannot imagine setting a dish of ice cream in front of a little boy and then saying, "Eat your spinach." He believed that if God had told us everything about Heaven, it would have ruined earth for us!

E. Taught by God's Spirit (vv. 10-13)

10, 11. But God hath revealed them unto us by his Spirit: for the Spirit searcheth all things, yea, the deep things of God. For what man knoweth the things of a man, save the spirit of man which is in him? even so the things of God knoweth no man, but the Spirit of God.

The word *searcheth* does not mean that the *Spirit* has difficulty finding out *the deep things of God*. It describes His access, as part of the "Godhead" (Acts 17:29; Colossians 2:9), to these deep truths. The Spirit comprehends these truths and is thus able to reveal them to us.

The visual for today's lesson illustrates the source of Paul's teaching. Post it as you begin to discuss verse 12 of the lesson text.

Visual for lesson 2

When Paul says that God *hath revealed* these matters to us, he is linking the preceding verse about eye and ear and heart to the truths we now know. No man could have discovered these truths by his own effort or through the use of the five senses. The initiative had to come from God. If He had not revealed these truths, they would have remained unknown.

In verse 11 Paul uses the illustration of the human *spirit* to give us insight into the mind of God. No other human can know what a person is thinking; that person must reveal the content of his thoughts. In the same way, only the *Spirit of God* has insight into *the things of God.* They cannot be known by human beings except through revelation. This is the reason the Holy Spirit was given to the apostles (John 14:26; 16:13).

12. Now we have received, not the spirit of the world, but the Spirit which is of God; that we might know the things that are freely given to us of God.

The use of the word *we* suggests that Paul is talking about the apostles, not about Christians in general. (Earlier in the text, as in vv. 1-5, he uses "you" and "your" when speaking of all believers.) The apostles certainly received a measure of the Spirit that far exceeds that of any other human being, then or now. Paul observed to the Corinthians that he could speak in tongues "more than ye all" (1 Corinthians 14:18). The apostles' ability to impart gifts by the laying on of hands was so extraordinary that Simon the sorcerer tried in vain to purchase it (Acts 8:14-19).

In the phrase *the spirit of the world*, the *world* may refer to those influences in our surroundings that lure us from God. Perhaps Paul is thinking of one of the "spirits" of whom Christians are warned in 1 John 4:1-3. Whatever the phrase may mean, it is undoubtedly linked to "the wisdom of this world" mentioned in verse 6. The greater emphasis should be on the word *world.* The Spirit who inspired Paul was not of the world, but *of God.* [See question #4, page 248.]

13. Which things also we speak, not in the words which man's wisdom teacheth, but which the Holy Ghost teacheth; comparing spiritual things with spiritual.

Paul insisted that the content of his message was not to be found in *man's wisdom,* just as he contended in the previous verse that the power behind the message was not of this world. Paul's message was not the product of human creativity or skill. It consisted of words from God Himself—*which the Holy Ghost teacheth.*

The only way we humans can understand anything is by means of words, so it was necessary that the divine revelation be given to Paul in words and that those words be taught by the Holy Spirit. This is in keeping with Jesus' promise of what the Spirit would do for the apostles (John 14:26; 16:13). To know this should bolster our confidence in the words of Scripture. While the personalities of the Biblical writers and their purposes in writing come through in their choice of words, we can affirm without hesitation that God governed their words so that they were prevented from error.

The verse ends with a difficult phrase to interpret: *comparing spiritual things with spiritual.* The Greek text simply reads "comparing spiritual with spiritual," so it is hard to know what nouns should be added to accompany each adjective. In addition, the verb rendered "comparing" can also mean "interpret," "combine," "express," or "explain." Based on the previous verse, one might choose to read, "expressing spiritual truths in spiritual words." Others suggest, "interpreting spiritual truths to spiritual men." One can make a case for either of these explanations.

III. Receiving Wisdom (1 Corinthians 2:14-16)

A. The Natural Man (v. 14)

14. But the natural man receiveth not the things of the Spirit of God: for they are foolishness unto him: neither can he know them, because they are spiritually discerned.

Paul said "we" (that is, the inspired apostles) did receive the message from *the Spirit of God.* The *natural man,* who *receiveth not the things of the Spirit,* must be seen, then, in contrast to the apostles. Such a one is limited to physical means of receiving information, such as the eyes and ears (v. 9). These are inadequate to receive the mysteries of God, which are *spiritually discerned.* [See question #5, page 248.]

B. The Spiritual Man (vv. 15, 16)

15. But he that is spiritual judgeth all things, yet he himself is judged of no man.

He that is spiritual, in this context, is one who is inspired by the Spirit. No one can pass judgment on the apostles' message; it comes from the Holy Spirit. The inspired messenger was able to judge or discern (it is the same Greek word here as in verse 14) *all things* by the standard of truth as taught by the Spirit.

As verse 9 has a dual application, we also see a secondary application in verses 14 and 15. There is a noticeable difference between the Christian, especially a mature Christian, and one who has no interest in spiritual matters. The indwelling Spirit in the Christian's life makes a difference! One who has ordered his or her life according to "the things of the Spirit of God" (v. 14) is equipped with the spiritual wisdom needed to be discerning in life. Such wisdom comes from God's Word, which "is profitable for doctrine, for reproof, for correction, for instruction in righteousness" (2 Timothy 3:16). The natural man, or the unbeliever, considers the things of God "foolishness" (v. 14); he cannot discern or understand the thinking of one who is spiritual. Things that are obvious to believers mystify the unsaved.

TWO KINDS OF PEOPLE

As the saying goes, "There are two kinds of people in the world." In this case, I'm thinking of those who find mathematics fascinating, as opposed to the rest of us who have been out of school for a few years and have forgotten much of what we once knew about math. We may still be able to use πr^2, but quick—do you recall what a prime number is? (Answer: it is a number divisible only by itself and 1.)

A fascination with prime numbers was the driving force guiding Roland Clarkson, a nineteen-year-old college student who, two years ago,

found the largest prime number yet discovered. It is 909,526 digits long, would fill a four-hundred-page book, would stretch for more than a mile if written out in one line, and would take 277 hours to say! Roland's "natural curiosity about math," as he describes it, led him to search for the number on a computer. He ran his computer part-time for forty-six days before coming up with the record-setting prime number.

There is another distinction, however, that is far more important than mathematicians and non-mathematicians. That is the distinction between natural and spiritual. The natural person lives life on the surface, content with the material things of this present world. The spiritual person has a deep interest in the real values in life—the things that *really* make a difference.

Which kind of person are you? —C. R. B.

16. For who hath known the mind of the Lord, that he may instruct him? But we have the mind of Christ.

Here Paul takes his thought from Isaiah 40:13. No one can know *the mind of the Lord* unless He chooses to reveal His thinking to us. No one can *instruct* God, but we can (and must) be instructed by Him. Because God has revealed the truth to us in Scripture, we are able to know *the mind of Christ* and how He wants us to live.

Conclusion

A. Turn Your Eyes Upon Jesus

Paul wanted the Corinthian Christians to keep their focus on Jesus—not on him, not on clever words, not on eloquent phrases, but on the Lord Jesus Christ. He knew that only through the crucified Lord could one know "the power of God, and the wisdom of God" (1 Corinthians 1:24).

Certainly spreading the good news deserves the use of our best gifts and abilities, but we must never forget that the power is always in the gospel itself. That gospel came from God and not from human wisdom. It carries within it "the power of God unto salvation" (Romans 1:16). It has changed lives throughout the years, and it will continue to do so until Jesus comes.

B. Prayer

Lord, forgive us when we trust in human personalities and the power of human eloquence, and do not trust wholly in Jesus Christ. We pray in His name. Amen.

C. Thought to Remember

Without God's revelation of truth to us in the Scriptures, we are left alone to grope in spiritual darkness.

Home Daily Bible Readings

Monday Mar. 6—Proclaiming Christ Crucified (1 Corinthians 2:1-5)
Tuesday, Mar. 7—The True Wisdom of God (1 Corinthians 2:6-16)
Wednesday, Mar. 8—Put Away Quarrels and Jealousies (1 Corinthians 3:1-9)
Thursday, Mar. 9—Build on the Foundation of Jesus Christ (1 Corinthians 3:10-15)
Friday, Mar. 10—We Belong to God Through Jesus Christ (1 Corinthians 3:16-23)
Saturday, Mar. 11—Life in the Spirit (Romans 8:1-8)
Sunday, Mar. 12—We Are Children of God (Romans 8:9-17)

Learning by Doing

This page contains an alternate lesson plan emphasizing learning activities.
Classes desiring such student involvement will find these suggestions helpful.

Learning Goals

After today's lesson each adult will be able to:

1. Explain the Holy Spirit's role in revealing the gospel message.

2. Tell why it is important to base one's faith on the Spirit-given message of Christ and not on man-made wisdom.

3. Express faith in Christ, as revealed by the Spirit's wisdom.

Into the Lesson

Before class, prepare a collection of objects that would be recognized by people familiar with their subject or category, but not easily recognized by those who are not. For example, when people are asked what kind of car a person was driving, some people can name the model, make, and year. Another person might say, "Well, it was white." From dealers' showrooms you could collect pictures of cars that are very similar in appearance and blot out the identifying names.

To begin class, show the pictures—perhaps posted on a wall where people can look at them as they arrive. Ask class members to identify the make and model of each car. After they have had some fun with this, say, "Those of you who are familiar with cars probably had no trouble distinguishing one car from another. But some of you did have trouble because you don't know enough about the subject. In today's lesson, we will learn from Paul that we need to be able to distinguish God's wisdom from man-made wisdom."

Into the Word

Today's lesson is vital for Christians. Man's "wisdom" presents a message or value structure quite different from the timeless principles given through the Spirit in God's Word. In fact, it varies from culture to culture and from generation to generation. Such an important lesson can best be learned through a lecture of important content, followed by lots of time to apply it to life.

Read 1 Corinthians 2:1-16 to the class, clarifying the content with the material in the commentary as you read. Make an overhead transparency of the lesson outline (page 242) and reveal each point as you go.

When you talk about verse 7, hold up a mystery novel. "When we read a good mystery, we consider many answers to the question, 'Who did it?' But we don't know the *real* answer until the author tells us. In the same way, we can make up all the answers we want to the mysteries of life, but we don't know the real answers until the Author of life tells us. And we find those answers in His Word—the Bible."

Into Life

When talking about basing one's faith on the Spirit-given message rather than man-made wisdom, there are some issues on which many Christians are agreed. For example, man-made wisdom asserts that a person is born with his/her sexual orientation, so practicing one's homosexuality is not sin. The first chapter of Romans makes it clear, however, that God's timeless principle says that such practice is sin. (See vv. 26, 27.)

Ask your students to form groups of four or five. Have each group consider one of the following venues and contrast what man's wisdom says with what God's wisdom says.

Workplace: *Man says, "Get ahead at any cost." "Watch out for number one." "The end justifies the means." God's Word says, "Do unto others what you would have them do unto you." "You shall not steal." "You shall not give false testimony." "Serve wholeheartedly, as if you were serving the Lord. . . . Masters, treat your slaves in the same way."*

Neighborhood: *Man says, "Nice guys finish last." "I have my rights." "You can take only so much." God's Word says, "Do unto others what you would have them do unto you." "If someone strikes you on the right cheek, turn to him the other also." "Love your neighbor." "Love your enemies." "You shall not covet your neighbor's. . . ." "If you forgive men when they sin against you. . . ."*

Family: *Man says, "Quantity of time doesn't matter as long as it is 'quality' time." "One parent is as effective as two." "Who needs marriage? True love is more important than a piece of paper." "You need to meet my needs." God says, "Do not commit adultery." "Do not store up treasures on earth . . ." "Do not worry about your life." "Honor your father and your mother." "Do everything without complaining."*

If reports stimulate discussion about how difficult it is to live such a life, remind students that Christians have the help of the Holy Spirit to do what is difficult. Guide them to make specific plans of how to let the Holy Spirit work in their lives and how they can help one another to live such lives. Let students pray in their small groups.

Let's Talk It Over

The questions on this page are designed to encourage review of the lesson Scriptures and to promote discussion of the lesson by the class. The answers provided are only discussion starters. Let your class talk it over from there.

1. In order to draw crowds, some churches and evangelists have begun to emphasize positive thinking and "feel-good" messages. This is in contrast to Paul's emphasis on "Jesus Christ, and him crucified." What dangers do you see in the contemporary practice?

Contemporary thought puts much value in self-esteem and self-acceptance. But if sinners are led to accept themselves as they are and to feel good about their condition, what will lead them to salvation? Our purpose is to make unsaved people feel sorrow over their sin, fear as they contemplate facing a holy God in judgment, and humility of mind in realizing they must surrender to the Lord. Even telling people that God accepts them as they are is not enough; we must tell them that He accepts them as they are in order to make them what they ought to be. If the emphasis on change (i.e., repentance) is not there, then we are not preaching the gospel.

2. Paul's preaching was "in demonstration of the Spirit and of power." Of course, Paul spoke by the inspiration of the Spirit, and he worked miracles by the power of the Spirit. How can modern preaching and teaching exhibit a "demonstration of the Spirit and of power"?

In Ephesians 6:19, 20 Paul asked for prayer that he would be able to declare the gospel boldly and fearlessly. In today's climate of religious compromise it is well to ask God for bold and fearless preachers.

In 2 Timothy 4:1-5 Paul counseled Timothy to "Preach the word." Since the Word is inspired by the Spirit (2 Timothy 3:16, 17) and the gospel is "the power of God unto salvation" (Romans 1:16), then our preaching—if it is faithful to the message of the Bible—is supported by the power of the Spirit. (See also question #5.)

3. What are some specific contrasts you see between "the wisdom of this world" and the "wisdom of God"?

James 3:13-18 contrasts wisdom that is "earthly, sensual, devilish" with "the wisdom that is from above." The characteristics of the earthly wisdom include its inciting people to envy, selfish ambition, disorder, and every evil practice. (See James 3:16 in the *New International Version.*) Its emphasis on selfishness contrasts with Christ's sacrifice

for us and the sacrificial service we are called to practice. Its tendency to envy others their success is the opposite of the gospel's call to love and compassion. Its stress on using any means to get ahead is far removed from the righteousness and truth God expects from His people. The disorder and confusion it generates contrasts with the peace that is a fruit of heavenly wisdom.

4. The lesson writer says the gospel message could never have been invented by human creativity. How would you answer a skeptic who contended that it was?

In Romans 5:6-8 Paul demonstrated how Christ's death went against the normal course of human thinking. It was extremely rare for a person to give up his life, Paul noted, for someone who was righteous or good. But "Christ died for the ungodly." He died for us "while we were yet sinners." Further, Christ's death did not appear heroic. He perished like a common criminal—a victim of a form of execution that was regarded as particularly shameful. The Gentiles tended to dismiss it as foolishness. As for the Jews, their law declared, "He that is hanged [upon a tree] is accursed of God" (Deuteronomy 21:23). So "Christ crucified" was a stumbling block to them.

5. Paul said, "The natural man receiveth not the things of the Spirit of God" (1 Corinthians 2:14). Yet Jesus promised that the Holy Spirit would "convict the world of guilt in regard to sin and righteousness and judgment" (John 16:8, *New International Version*). How would you resolve this apparent contradiction?

A contradiction exists only when one statement affirms what another denies. That is not the case here. That the natural man cannot "receive" the message of the Spirit simply points out the need for spiritual (inspired) men to receive that message. Once received, the message is delivered, both orally and in writing, to others.

The Holy Spirit may convict the unbeliever by providentially arranging for him or her to hear or read the gospel. He works through the Word itself when it is read or heard. He uses the witness of a believer's own Spirit-filled life to reach out to the lost one. In these and other ways the Spirit is active in "convict[ing] the world of guilt in regard to sin and righteousness and judgment."

The Church and Its Leaders

DEVOTIONAL READING: 1 Peter 5:1-11.

BACKGROUND SCRIPTURE: 1 Corinthians 4:1-13.

PRINTED TEXT: 1 Corinthians 4:1-13.

1 Corinthians 4:1-13

1 Let a man so account of us, as of the ministers of Christ, and stewards of the mysteries of God.

2 Moreover it is required in stewards, that a man be found faithful.

3 But with me it is a very small thing that I should be judged of you, or of man's judgment: yea, I judge not mine own self.

4 For I know nothing by myself; yet am I not hereby justified: but he that judgeth me is the Lord.

5 Therefore judge nothing before the time, until the Lord come, who both will bring to light the hidden things of darkness, and will make manifest the counsels of the hearts: and then shall every man have praise of God.

6 And these things, brethren, I have in a figure transferred to myself and to Apollos for your sakes; that ye might learn in us not to think of men above that which is written, that no one of you be puffed up for one against another.

7 For who maketh thee to differ from another? and what hast thou that thou didst not receive? now if thou didst receive it, why dost thou glory, as if thou hadst not received it?

8 Now ye are full, now ye are rich, ye have reigned as kings without us: and I would to God ye did reign, that we also might reign with you.

9 For I think that God hath set forth us the apostles last, as it were appointed to death: for we are made a spectacle unto the world, and to angels, and to men.

10 We are fools for Christ's sake, but ye are wise in Christ; we are weak, but ye are strong; ye are honorable, but we are despised.

11 Even unto this present hour we both hunger, and thirst, and are naked, and are buffeted, and have no certain dwelling place;

12 And labor, working with our own hands: being reviled, we bless; being persecuted, we suffer it:

13 Being defamed, we entreat: we are made as the filth of the world, and are the offscouring of all things unto this day.

GOLDEN TEXT: Let a man so account of us, as of the ministers of Christ, and stewards of the mysteries of God.—1 Corinthians 4:1.

Helping a Church Confront Crisis
Unit 1: Christ, the Basis for Unity
(Lessons 1-4)

Lesson Aims

After this lesson each student will be able to:

1. Summarize how Paul viewed his apostolic ministry according to this text.

2. Tell why the concept of being a "steward" is appropriate for any leader in the church.

3. Speak or write a message of appreciation and encouragement to the leaders of his or her church.

Lesson Outline

INTRODUCTION
  A. Leading and Serving
  B. Lesson Background
 I. SERVANTS AND STEWARDS (1 Corinthians 4:1, 2)
  A. We Are Servants (v. 1a)
  B. We Are Stewards (v. 1b)
  C. We Must Be Faithful (v. 2)
 II. HUMAN AND DIVINE JUDGMENT (1 Corinthians 4:3-5)
  A. Others' Viewpoint (v. 3)
  B. God's Perspective (vv. 4, 5)
  The Power of Perception
III. PAUL AND APOLLOS (1 Corinthians 4:6, 7)
  A. Concrete Examples (v. 6)
  B. Sobering Questions (v. 7)
IV. PRIDE AND HUMILITY (1 Corinthians 4:8-11)
  A. From Sarcasm to Tenderness (v. 8)
  B. The Apostles' Shame (v. 9)
  C. A Touching Comparison (v. 10)
  D. Suffering for Christ's Sake (v. 11)
 V. WORKING AND ENDURING (1 Corinthians 4:12, 13)
  A. Toiling On (v. 12a)
  B. Facing Opposition (vv. 12b, 13)
  Treated Like Dirt
CONCLUSION
  A. Always Work for Jesus
  B. Prayer
  C. Thought to Remember

Introduction

A. Leading and Serving

A minister once related that he was asked to come to a certain church and speak on leadership. He agreed; however, when he stood to speak, he surprised the congregation by announcing that his topic would be, not leadership, but servanthood.

There are many ways to serve in the Lord's church. Being a leader should be considered one of them. In Romans 12:8 Paul describes leadership (the work of "he that ruleth") as a gift given by God. Just as some have the gift of preaching and some the gift of encouragement, some have the gift of leadership. Those who have been given this gift should not see it as an occasion of pride nor as an opportunity to exercise power, but as a calling to glorify God and minister to others. Every leader is a servant. Leadership is one way of serving the Lord!

It is natural that we are drawn to some personalities more than others. That is unavoidable. We will feel a kinship with some leaders that we will not sense with other leaders. However, we should never permit this to lead to conflict. We should never assume that the person we like is always right nor that the person we don't like is always wrong. The head must rule the heart here.

B. Lesson Background

Paul established the church at Corinth in approximately A.D. 52. After he left there, Apollos, who had been preaching in Ephesus, then traveled to Corinth (Acts 18:24—19:1). Apollos was a native of Alexandria (in Egypt), which was one of the most renowned centers of learning in the world at that time. He was undoubtedly highly educated. He possessed a thorough knowledge of the Scriptures and was very effective as an evangelist, being "an eloquent man" (Acts 18:24-28).

It was only natural that people would be drawn to such a highly educated and articulate speaker as Apollos. In Corinth, as we noted in lesson 1, the church had divided into factions, one of which declared its allegiance to Apollos and another to Paul (1 Corinthians 1:12). Perhaps the original converts in Corinth were those who were attached to Paul, while newer converts were drawn to Apollos. (Often people feel a special bond to the person who led them to Christ.)

Of course, Paul and Apollos themselves could not have cared less about who "liked" either of them better than the other. It had become clear, however, that such loyalties were producing conflict that was having a devastating effect on the Corinthian church. Some were becoming "puffed up for one against another" (1 Corinthians 4:6). Paul had already told the church that individuals such as he and Apollos were simply "laborers together with God" (3:9) and that the Corinthians should not "glory in men" (v. 21). In today's text Paul elaborates on this point.

I. Servants and Stewards
(1 Corinthians 4:1, 2)

A. We Are Servants (v. 1a)

1a. Let a man so account of us, as of the ministers of Christ.

When Paul says *us,* he means to include primarily himself, Peter (Cephas), and Apollos, since they are mentioned at the end of the previous chapter (3:22) and were the leaders around whom the various groups in Corinth had formed (1:12). We will see, however, that Paul's words convey an important message to all leaders in the church.

The word *ministers* is better translated "servants." The literal meaning of the Greek word is "under-rowers." In New Testament times, this word was used to describe the slaves who pulled the oars and moved a ship forward. These under-rowers were confined to the dark, smelly hold of the ship. Such a picture of humble, unnoticed service provided the image Paul wanted us to have of himself and of all leaders in Christ's church.

B. We Are Stewards (v. 1b)

1b. And stewards of the mysteries of God.

Many *stewards* were slaves, just as the under-rowers of a ship were slaves. But stewards often held very responsible positions. A steward was the manager of a large household and was given the responsibility of the care of other servants. The task of such a person is described in Matthew 24:45-51.

The word *mysteries* was discussed in last week's lesson (see the comments under 1 Corinthians 2:7). There it was noted that God has revealed, not hidden, His mysteries. Christians are the stewards of this revealed truth.

C. We Must Be Faithful (v. 2)

2. Moreover it is required in stewards, that a man be found faithful.

So then, men ought to regard us as servants of Christ and as those entrusted with the secret things of God.

1 Corinthians 4:1, 2

Visual for
lesson 3

Today's visual reminds us that we who have the Word of God so available are also "servants of Christ . . . entrusted with the . . . things of God."

There is a necessary quality *required* of all *stewards.* It is *that a man be found faithful.* If you go to the bank, you will find there a person known as a trust officer. That individual is entrusted with the care and investment of other people's money. Thus he must be someone of dependable character, or *trust*worthy.

The same qualification must be found in those who are entrusted with God's eternal truth. They must never forget that they are Christians only because someone else took his or her calling as a steward seriously. [See question #1, page 256.]

II. Human and Divine Judgment
(1 Corinthians 4:3-5)

A. Others' Viewpoint (v. 3)

3. But with me it is a very small thing that I should be judged of you, or of man's judgment: yea, I judge not mine own self.

When Paul says *it is a very small thing,* he is referring to the evaluation some in Corinth had of his work. Apparently, they had *judged* Paul and attempted to disparage his work and his ministry. Perhaps they claimed that Apollos was a better preacher than Paul, or that Peter—as one of the original twelve apostles—was more important than Paul. Paul did not want the Corinthians to put any stock in such futile comparisons.

This verse does not suggest that the judgment of others is of no significance. Certainly it is important what others think of us as Christians. We must set a good example. It is no "small thing" when what we are or what we do causes people to turn a deaf ear to the gospel. It is a small matter if someone thinks another is a more capable worker than we are. [See question #2, page 256.]

Paul's words *I judge not mine own self* mean that he is not wasting time comparing his effectiveness or his popularity with others. As he earlier stated, "Who then is Paul, and who is Apollos, but ministers by whom ye believed, even as the Lord gave to every man?" (3:5).

B. God's Perspective (vv. 4, 5)

4. For I know nothing by myself; yet am I not hereby justified: but he that judgeth me is the Lord.

The phrase *I know nothing by myself* is more accurately rendered, "I know nothing against myself." Paul is saying that his conscience is clear, yet he knows that he is not *justified* by his own self-examination. In his own mind he believed that he had been a faithful steward at Corinth; however, *the Lord* alone is the One capable of judging such matters.

5. Therefore judge nothing before the time, until the Lord come, who both will bring to light

the hidden things of darkness, and will make manifest the counsels of the hearts: and then shall every man have praise of God.

Paul urged the Corinthians not to *judge* anything prematurely—that is, *before the time* of final judgment comes. Apparently some had already made a decision about Paul's faithfulness as a steward of Christ. They had rendered a verdict the trial was over! Paul told them that they must not do this. All of us must wait for the time appointed for judgment, which will take place when *the Lord* returns.

Paul adds some details regarding the final judgment. On that day the Lord *will bring to light the hidden things of darkness.* Only God knows all the facts. He will bring into the open both our secret sins and our secret virtues. In addition, He knows *the counsels of the hearts.* He will reveal not only what we did, but why we did it. It is His *praise*, or approval, that Paul seeks. [See question #3, page 256.]

THE POWER OF PERCEPTION

If you were told you had to live on Iceland or Greenland—and you knew nothing about the two islands except their names—which would you choose? In spite of its name, Iceland is famous for its volcanoes, and its winters are no more harsh than those of the New England coast.

Greenland, on the other hand, is covered by a permanent ice cap. In A.D. 984 the Norse explorer, Eric the Red, was trying to entice settlers to leave the relative warmth of Iceland and Scandinavia and move to a land he had discovered, which is the largest island on the planet. Both Scandinavia and Iceland benefit from the warm Gulf Stream current, so Eric had to exercise some creative thinking if his goal of populating his new land was to be realized. He was equal to the task: he called the island "Greenland." (Modern advertising executives should think of Eric as their patron saint!)

We are sometimes greatly misled by our perception of what is valuable, and advertisers play on our weakness. They keep telling us that if we had a better house or a nicer car or finer clothes, others would have a better image of us.

How to Say It

ALEXANDRIA. Al-ex-*an*-dree-uh.
APOLLOS. Uh-*pahl*-us.
CEPHAS. *See*-fus.
CORINTH. *Kor*-inth.
CORINTHIANS. Kor-*in*-thee-unz.
EPHESUS. *Ef*-uh-sus.

Paul tells us otherwise: the person who truly pleases God is the one who willingly seeks to be a servant—a faithful, trustworthy steward of what his Master has entrusted to him. The world may consider this a waste of time and effort; however, we serve a cause "not of this world."

Which perception are we more concerned about? —C. R. B.

III. Paul and Apollos
(1 Corinthians 4:6, 7)
A. Concrete Examples (v. 6)

6. And these things, brethren, I have in a figure transferred to myself and to Apollos for your sakes; that ye might learn in us not to think of men above that which is written, that no one of you be puffed up for one against another.

Paul now *transferred*, or applied, the principles he had just stated to himself *and to Apollos*. The Corinthians' loyalties were not to be divided among different *men*, but united in following *that which is written*—most likely a reference to Scripture. If all submit to the authority of Scripture, then it is far less likely that individuals will become *puffed up* in their efforts to set one teacher above another.

B. Sobering Questions (v. 7)

7. For who maketh thee to differ from another? and what hast thou that thou didst not receive? now if thou didst receive it, why dost thou glory, as if thou hadst not received it?

In cases where members of God's family *differ from another* in gifts and abilities, the differences should not become a source of contention (as they had in Corinth). Instead, they should be used to further the work of the kingdom.

One of the most humbling questions we should ask ourselves is, *What hast thou that thou didst not receive?* We are simply stewards—nothing more. [See question #4, page 256.]

IV. Pride and Humility
(1 Corinthians 4:8-11)
A. From Sarcasm to Tenderness (v. 8)

8. Now ye are full, now ye are rich, ye have reigned as kings without us: and I would to God ye did reign, that we also might reign with you.

Occasionally we find touches of irony and sarcasm in the Bible. It is obvious that the meaning of the speaker's words is just the opposite of what he says. We do the same today, as when we spill something and say, "Oh, that was smart!" Biblical examples can be found in 1 Kings 18:27 and Amos 4:4.

Here, when Paul describes the Corinthians as *full* and *rich* and as those who have *reigned as kings*, his language reflects the conceit that had come to characterize the Corinthians' attitude and that had resulted in their divisions. In their own estimation, they had attained spiritual maturity. But in reality, they had a long way to go!

Paul then moved quickly from this strong tone of irony to more tender words that reflected his sincere concern for the Corinthians. He loved them and truly wished that their evaluation of themselves were accurate—that they did indeed *reign* as they desired. But did they really understand what it meant to reign with Christ? Paul proceeded to elaborate on this point.

B. The Apostles' Shame (v. 9)

9. For I think that God hath set forth us the apostles last, as it were appointed to death: for we are made a spectacle unto the world, and to angels, and to men.

While we often think of the apostolic office as an exalted one, Paul described it in very different terms. Did the Corinthians want to "reign" as the apostles did? Then here is Paul's personal experience of "reigning": being *appointed to death* and being *made a spectacle*. The Greek word rendered *spectacle* here is the word from which we get our English word "theater." The picture behind this word was a familiar one in Paul's world. At the end of the gladiatorial contests, those gladiators who were doomed to die were stripped of their armor, led before the crowd, and then taken to the coliseum to be killed by wild animals. In the same way, the apostles suffered shame, suffering, and even death for Christ (Acts 12:1, 2; 2 Corinthians 1:9; 4:11).

The Corinthians' understanding of serving Christ seems similar to that of James and John. We are told how they approached Jesus about "reigning" with Him by being given the chief seats in His kingdom. Jesus responded by challenging them to drink the cup He was going to drink and be baptized with the baptism He would experience (Mark 10:35-40). They would indeed reign with Christ, but only on His terms, not theirs. The Corinthians needed to learn this same lesson.

C. A Touching Comparison (v. 10)

10. We are fools for Christ's sake, but ye are wise in Christ; we are weak, but ye are strong; ye are honorable, but we are despised.

Here Paul continues his ironic tone. People in the world saw individuals such as Paul as *fools* because they chose to forsake all and follow Jesus. In contrast, many at Corinth thought themselves *wise, strong,* and *honorable.* But in

their perceived wisdom, strength, and honor, had they lost sight of what it meant to follow Jesus? The contrast is both striking and touching. It was meant, not to shame the Corinthians, but to warn them (v. 14). It is easy to see how deeply Paul loved these people and how concerned he was for their spiritual welfare.

D. Suffering for Christ's Sake (v. 11)

11. Even unto this present hour we both hunger, and thirst, and are naked, and are buffeted, and have no certain dwelling place.

We do not know of any specific occasions when Paul experienced *hunger* and *thirst.* He later wrote to the Philippians that he had known such need and appreciated their giving to supply that need (Philippians 4:10-13). The word *naked* simply means poorly clothed.

Acts 14:19 and 16:22-24 record occasions Paul may have been thinking of when he writes that he had been *buffeted,* or beaten. (The instances in Acts 21:30-32 and 23:2 took place after Paul wrote the Corinthians.) A partial summary of Paul's sufferings for Christ is found in 2 Corinthians 11:23-28. Like Abraham, who "sojourned in the land of promise" (Hebrews 11:9), and Jesus, who had no place to lay His head (Matthew 8:20), Paul had *no certain dwelling place.* His true citizenship was in Heaven (Philippians 3:20, *New International Version*).

V. Working and Enduring (1 Corinthians 4:12, 13)

A. Toiling On (v. 12a)

12a. And labor, working with our own hands.

Paul supported himself throughout most of his ministry (Acts 20:34), though he did on some occasions receive outside support (Philippians 4:14-18). Generally he preferred to be self-supporting as an example of how Christians ought to conduct themselves (1 Corinthians 9:15; 1 Thessalonians 2:9; 2 Thessalonians 3:8, 9). But he vigorously defended his right and the rights of fellow Christian workers to be supported by other believers (1 Corinthians 9:1-14).

B. Facing Opposition (vv. 12b, 13)

12b, 13a. Being reviled we bless; being persecuted, we suffer it: being defamed, we entreat.

Paul's words about *being reviled* should call our attention to Jesus' teaching in the Sermon on the Mount. He taught His followers to respond to verbal abuse and slander by rejoicing, blessing the persecutors, and praying for them (Matthew 5:10-12, 44; cf. Luke 6:28). Peter reminds us that Jesus Himself responded in this way to those who mistreated Him (1 Peter 2:23).

To speak of *being persecuted* reminds us of the teaching in 1 Peter 2:19-21 and 4:12-16 that Christians who suffer should bear their suffering patiently. *Being defamed* means to be slandered and falsely accused. To *entreat* in the face of such treatment means to speak kindly.

If the Corinthians really want to reign in Christ and become wise, strong, and honorable (v. 10), here is the path they must take. What an example we have both in Jesus and in Paul!

13b. We are made as the filth of the world, and are the offscouring of all things unto this day.

The word *filth* is rendered by some translators as "scum." We occasionally refer to someone who is particularly despicable as "the scum of the earth." Paul notes that this is the way some have treated him and his fellow apostles.

A word of similar meaning is the term *offscouring*. This refers to the scrapings from a pan or other utensil that are discarded because they have no value whatsoever. In the eyes of the world, this is how Paul and the apostles were viewed. Today, in many parts of the world, Christians are looked at with an equal degree of scorn. However, it is not the world's approval that we seek, for we are "dead to the world" (Galatians 6:14). Only one view matters, and that is Christ's.

TREATED LIKE DIRT

Throughout most of modern history, great art has usually represented the world fairly accurately (that is, as most observers saw it). However, the twentieth century witnessed a revolution in artistic expression. Some very bizarre forms of "art" have become commonplace.

In New York City a few years ago, "conceptual artist" Walter DeMaria created a work that gave new meaning to the term, the "field" of art. DeMaria's work was entitled "Earth Room." That's just what it was: a room containing 3,600 square feet of dirt, two feet deep. Bill Dilworth, curator of the gallery where DeMaria's work was displayed, claimed that the work "has more of an emotional range than the 'Mona Lisa' or the Sistine Chapel." (Dilworth seems to have missed something there.)

It's a strange world where dirt is treated as if it were art, and art is treated as if it were dirt! But that's really not too different from Paul's description of how he and the other apostles were viewed: "as the filth of the world, and . . . the offscouring of all things" (1 Corinthians 4:13). For all of the mistreatment that Paul suffered and all of the effort that he expended, for all of the good that he did and the blessings he brought to others, many people still "treated him like dirt." But he had a clearer vision of reality than his enemies did. He wasn't fooled by their idle talk, nor did he try to see value in their delusions.

—C. R. B.

Conclusion

A. Always Work for Jesus

The verse that follows today's printed text reveals Paul's purpose in writing to the Corinthians as he has. He tells them, "I write not these things to shame you, but as my beloved sons I warn you" (1 Corinthians 4:14). He does not write to get even with those who have mistreated him. He writes to warn them that they must not be too fascinated with receiving earthly glory for their spiritual service.

If we receive praise and appreciation for our service to the Lord, that is fine. We should be grateful for such appreciation, but we should not work for it. Our primary calling is to work for Jesus, serving Him in a sinful world. Our chief recognition will be in the world to come. Jesus said that the smallest act of service done in His name will not be overlooked. Even a cup of cold water will be rewarded (Matthew 10:42). [See question #5, page 256.]

B. Prayer

O Lord, help us to keep on working, even when we are ignored, misunderstood, or criticized. Help us to keep our eyes on our heavenly reward rather than on earthly praise. In the name of Jesus we pray. Amen.

C. Thought to Remember

We do well to recognize the good work that others do. We do better when we seek no recognition for the work that we do.

Learning by Doing

This page contains an alternate lesson plan emphasizing learning activities.
Classes desiring such student involvement will find these suggestions helpful.

Learning Goals

After this lesson each student will be able to:

1. Summarize how Paul viewed his apostolic ministry according to this text.

2. Tell why the concept of being a "steward" is appropriate for any leader in the church.

3. Speak or write a message of appreciation and encouragement to the leaders of his or her church.

Into the Lesson

Before class, create two piles on the floor or on a table. In one pile place items that represent riches and honor (such as a crown, a trophy, and a purse); in the other pile place rags and trash.

Begin class by asking, "If you could possess everything in one of these piles, which one would you choose?"

Comment on the fact that it is natural that we would select the riches and symbols of honor. Note the irony, then, in Paul's assessment of himself as "the filth of the world" and "the offscourings [refuse] of all things" (1 Corinthians 4:13).

Into the Word

Provide some background for today's lesson by noting the cliques that had formed in Corinth when the believers put too much emphasis on human leaders (1 Corinthians 1:12). Note that Paul tells us how we ought to view Christian leaders in 1 Corinthians 4. Say, "Paul uses himself and Apollos to illustrate how the people should view their leaders. Let's analyze the chapter to discover what he says and then pull out principles that apply to all leaders in the church today." If your students completed the exercise in their student books, let them report their findings. If your students use the student books in class, assign them to complete the chart now in small groups or individually.

Read the chapter aloud. (Let your voice reveal the sarcasm of verses 8-10.) Then have the class make two lists: "Paul's View of Himself" and "Principles for Leaders in Any Age." They can do this in small groups or as a class. Have someone write the group's ideas on the chalkboard or a large poster. (A similar activity appears in the student book.)

Paul's View of Himself: *servant of Christ, entrusted with secret things of God, obligated to prove faithful, has clear conscience, spectacle to whole universe/scum of the earth, father through the gospel, consistent in his teaching of the gospel.*

Principles for Leaders in Any Age: *God will judge all people's motives, don't take pride over one another, all that we have we received, we may become a spectacle or scum of the earth, we should respond as the apostles did (verses 12, 13).*

Into Life

After reading the list of principles for leaders of all ages, ask pairs to describe when they have experienced or observed another church leader or teacher carrying out any of the principles on the list. (Letting people talk in pairs will allow shy people to feel comfortable answering. They often give excellent answers that will now be heard by a partner who can later urge the quiet person to tell a good example to the whole class.)

Ask for two or three volunteers to describe positive examples of leaders who have followed the principles.

Observe that Paul and the apostles lived in the way he described without expecting praise or appreciation, and we know from our study that leaders today should do the same. But it is hard to live that way, so it is always good to encourage leaders and let them know that we recognize their willingness to bear the hardships of leadership.

Distribute envelopes and stationery. Tell students to write to any leaders in your church. To avoid having a few people get all the letters, you might post a list of categories of leadership on the wall or chalkboard, or post a list of leaders and teachers. If appropriate, you could let people check off the name of the person to whom they are writing so that each leader will get at least one note.

Some people may not feel comfortable trying to express their thoughts on paper. Let them work with others to write a group letter or prepare a different way to show appreciation. (For example, some might bake a pie for a leadership meeting or volunteer to help carry out a task.)

Close with directed prayer. Name a category of leaders (ministers, elders, deacons, ministry team leaders/committee chairmen, superintendents, teachers, coordinators, music directors, etc.) and allow at least a minute of silence for the students to pray for these leaders. Then name another category and allow a minute of prayer, etc.

Let's Talk It Over

The questions on this page are designed to encourage review of the lesson Scriptures and to promote discussion of the lesson by the class. The answers provided are only discussion starters. Let your class talk it over from there.

1. Paul stresses that a steward must be faithful or trustworthy. How can regarding ourselves as stewards help us to be faithful and trustworthy?

As stewards we recognize that the gospel and the church are not ours. They are entrusted to us by the Lord so that we can work with them as He wills. It is easy for us to become distracted by the humanness of the church. If we neglect our duties or perform them in careless fashion, it may seem unimportant. After all, other leaders and workers may treat their responsibilities in the same way. But when we keep in mind that it is *His* church and that we are accountable to *Him*, the picture changes. Only faithful, conscientious, diligent effort is acceptable from a steward serving under the one Lord and Leader of the church.

2. To what extent should we be concerned about what other people think of us as Christians? Why?

What we do and say reflects on our reputation as Christians, on our church, and on Jesus Christ Himself. We must make it our goal that other people will see each of us as a person of faith— honest, dependable, patient, and charitable. Our concern that they hold such a viewpoint must not be based on pride or the mere wish to be admired, but on the hope that we can influence the unsaved for Christ. We need not be concerned, however, about people's idly comparing us with other Christians. A preacher should not be troubled over unfavorable comparisons of his preaching with that of another proclaimer of God's Word. An elder should not fret if he is told that someone else offers more inspiring prayers at the Lord's table. A soloist should not experience wounded pride if her singing is said to be inferior to someone else's.

3. Why is it important that we engage in frequent self-examination over our motives for service? How can we change unworthy motives?

Jesus on several occasions condemned the Jewish religious leaders for their unspiritual motives. (See Matthew 6:1, 2, 5, 16; 23:1-7; John 5:41-44.) Obviously we do not want to put ourselves under the same condemnation.

The religious leaders were eager for human praise. If that is a temptation for us, we must recognize it as dangerous. It can cause us to compromise our convictions and soften our stance regarding sin. If we discern that our motives are a mixture of pride, self-advancement, a lust for power, a tendency to lord it over other believers, and the like, we should treat these as sins. That means subjecting them to prayers of penitence. It means earnestly seeking the help of the Holy Spirit in replacing unspiritual motives with godly ones.

4. Why is it important that we acknowledge frequently that our talents and gifts have been given to us by God?

It is easy to forget the divine source of our gifts. We can be tempted to imagine that our speaking or singing or writing ability is our own creation. That in turn may lead us to regard our ability as something over which we have control. Then we may use our gifts in a selfish manner, seeking only financial profit or personal praise rather than the glory of God. When we view the gifts as God-given, we will be more inclined to seek God's guidance in utilizing them. And we will be more likely to use them for God's glory. Peter spoke in 1 Peter 4:10, 11 of some of the gifts Christians receive. He urged his readers to employ their gifts in such a way "that God in all things may be glorified through Jesus Christ."

5. How can we express our appreciation to workers in the church who labor without thought of earthly rewards?

Some congregations set aside special days to honor elders, teachers, musicians, and other workers. This is good, but it should not replace frequent personal expressions of gratitude. We should make a special effort to thank these people for specific blessings they bring to us. An elder's meditation at the Lord's table may deeply touch us—tell him so. A teacher's lesson may clear up a misunderstanding regarding Biblical truth—tell him or her so. A choir's anthem may stir in us a richer worship experience—tell them so. Our expressions of gratitude may be more meaningful if we put them in written form. A worker can reread a card or note of appreciation at a time of discouragement and be blessed anew by it. The above suggestions are also applicable to ministers. They may receive financial rewards for their labors, but they also need the encouragement that comes from expressions of gratitude.

Need for Church Discipline

DEVOTIONAL READING: James 3:13-18.

BACKGROUND SCRIPTURE: 1 Corinthians 5:1—6:11.

PRINTED TEXT: 1 Corinthians 5.

1 Corinthians 5

1 It is reported commonly that there is fornication among you, and such fornication as is not so much as named among the Gentiles, that one should have his father's wife.

2 And ye are puffed up, and have not rather mourned, that he that hath done this deed might be taken away from among you.

3 For I verily, as absent in body, but present in spirit, have judged already, as though I were present, concerning him that hath so done this deed,

4 In the name of our Lord Jesus Christ, when ye are gathered together, and my spirit, with the power of our Lord Jesus Christ,

5 To deliver such a one unto Satan for the destruction of the flesh, that the spirit may be saved in the day of the Lord Jesus.

6 Your glorying is not good. Know ye not that a little leaven leaveneth the whole lump?

7 Purge out therefore the old leaven, that ye may be a new lump, as ye are unleavened. For even Christ our passover is sacrificed for us:

8 Therefore let us keep the feast, not with old leaven, neither with the leaven of malice and wickedness; but with the unleavened bread of sincerity and truth.

9 I wrote unto you in an epistle not to company with fornicators:

10 Yet not altogether with the fornicators of this world, or with the covetous, or extortioners, or with idolaters; for then must ye needs go out of the world.

11 But now I have written unto you not to keep company, if any man that is called a brother be a fornicator, or covetous, or an idolater, or a railer, or a drunkard, or an extortioner; with such a one, no, not to eat.

12 For what have I to do to judge them also that are without? do not ye judge them that are within?

13 But them that are without God judgeth. Therefore put away from among yourselves that wicked person.

GOLDEN TEXT: Therefore let us keep the feast, not with old leaven, neither with the leaven of malice and wickedness; but with the unleavened bread of sincerity and truth.
—1 Corinthians 5:8.

Helping a Church Confront Crisis
Unit 1: Christ, the Basis for Unity
(Lessons 1-4)

Lesson Aims

After this lesson a student should be able to:
1. Tell why discipline was needed in Corinth and how Paul said it should be administered.
2. Explain the purpose of church discipline, and tell how that purpose would influence the administration of discipline.
3. Cultivate personal holiness with greater dedication, and support his or her church's efforts on the rare occasions when discipline may be necessary.

Lesson Outline

INTRODUCTION
  A. One Tough Chapter
  B. Lesson Background
 I. TAKING SIN SERIOUSLY (1 Corinthians 5:1, 2)
  A. An Unusual Sin (v. 1)
  B. An Unusual Reaction (v. 2)
    How Much Sin Should We Tolerate?
 II. MAINTAINING PURITY (1 Corinthians 5:3-8)
  A. A Verdict Reached (v. 3)
  B. An Action Jointly Taken (v. 4)
  C. An Objective Sought (v. 5)
  D. An Old Testament Example (vv. 6, 7)
  E. A Practical Application (v. 8)
III. WATCHING FRIENDSHIPS (1 Corinthians 5:9-11)
  A. Proper Contact (vv. 9, 10)
  B. Improper Contact (v. 11)
IV. JUDGING CORRECTLY (1 Corinthians 5:12, 13)
  A. The Church's Responsibility (v. 12)
  B. God's Responsibility (v. 13)
CONCLUSION
  A. A Closing Caution
  B. Prayer
  C. Thought to Remember

Introduction

A. One Tough Chapter

There are some chapters in 1 Corinthians that we genuinely enjoy reading. Chapter 13 is pure poetry. Chapter 15 may be the greatest commentary on the resurrection of Jesus ever written.

First Corinthians 5, however, is quite another story. It reflects a sternness about a delicate situation that may make us uncomfortable. But it, too, is a part of God's Word and merits our study

and consideration. All of the book was meant to be taken seriously by those to whom it was first sent, and all of it has value for Christians today.

B. Lesson Background

As noted in the Lesson Background of the first lesson in this quarter (see page 234), the church at Corinth was located in a very sinful city. Like many seaport cities, prostitution was rampant there. In Corinth, however, there was a particularly evil side to it; for many prostitutes were affiliated with the pagan temples. Thus one could easily combine vice with "worship."

Such a corrupt atmosphere certainly provided a challenging environment for the Christian message, which emphasized personal purity. The church there was an island of holiness in a sea of evil—at least, it ought to have been.

I. Taking Sin Seriously
(1 Corinthians 5:1, 2)

A. An Unusual Sin (v. 1)

1. It is reported commonly that there is fornication among you, and such fornication as is not so much as named among the Gentiles, that one should have his father's wife.

The words *reported commonly* suggest that Paul's information about the situation in Corinth had come from more than one source. This sin was common knowledge—not just a piece of private gossip. It seems to have been flaunted before both the public and the church. [See question #1, page 264.]

We usually understand *fornication* to mean sexual relations between two people who are not married. The Greek word is *porneia*, from which comes our word "pornography." It possesses a wide range of meaning and includes sexual immorality of any kind. The immoral act that Paul cited was *that one should have his father's wife.* Such language indicates that Paul was most likely describing an incestuous relationship between this man and a woman whom we would call his stepmother.

Various questions may arise regarding the details of this relationship. Was this woman's husband dead? Was she divorced from her husband? Were they merely separated? The same questions could be asked regarding the man involved in this immorality. However, such details are not provided. The shame of the sin called for the action that Paul later recommended, not for additional, and unnecessary, details.

In any case, this relationship was regarded as incest by Greeks, Romans, and Jews. (See the Old Testament teaching on this subject in Leviticus 18:8.) That a sin so widely condemned by even the *Gentiles* (better rendered as "pagans") should be condoned by Christians was unthinkable. Even the excessively pagan environment in Corinth, which was not noted for its sexual purity, frowned on such an act.

B. An Unusual Reaction (v. 2)

2. And ye are puffed up, and have not rather mourned, that he that hath done this deed might be taken away from among you.

In the previous chapter (from which part of last week's text was taken), Paul spoke of the Corinthians' pride and used the same phrase *puffed up* (vv. 6, 18, 19). Here he points out how inappropriate such pride is in dealing with a situation that should have concerned them greatly. Apparently their pride had led them to tolerate this situation instead of take action to correct it. They sound like people in our own day—proud that they can tolerate what others condemn!

The Corinthians should have *mourned* over the sin in their presence. Note that the proper response is not anger. We can easily get angry when we are disappointed in someone's behavior, but the proper response is one of sorrow and heartache. Apparently caught up in their pride in their own supposed spiritual attainments, the Corinthians had chosen to ignore a situation that should have troubled them deeply.

When Paul expresses his desire that the man *might be taken away from among you*, he clearly means that this individual should be put out of the church. Why does Paul say nothing about the woman involved? Perhaps she was not a member of the church. If so, she was outside the church's jurisdiction—a point with which Paul concludes his discussion of this issue (vv. 12, 13).

HOW MUCH SIN SHOULD WE TOLERATE?

An Ohio man drove for years without his driver's license after numerous convictions for drunk driving. Although convicted eighteen times, it had no effect on his behavior.

After conviction number eighteen, a judge handed down a sentence that brought shocked responses. A representative of MADD (Mothers Against Drunk Driving) denounced the sentence as being too lenient. A sheriff called it "very squirrely!" And what was the sentence that brought such responses?

There were three parts to it: the judge ordered the man to spend the first week of each of the ensuing five years in jail; when he rides in a car, he must either be handcuffed to the door on the passenger side or have someone sit between him and the driver; and he must move within easy walking distance of a liquor store so he isn't tempted to drive while drunk.

From what Paul says about the immoral member of the Corinthian church, it would appear that his sin involved unrepentant, habitual behavior similar to that of the Ohio drunk driver. The reason for the shocked reactions to the judge's sentence is that people have started to realize the need to get serious about punishing drunk driving. The Corinthian church, however, appears to have had no limit to the amount of sinful behavior they were willing to tolerate!   —C. R. B.

II. Maintaining Purity (1 Corinthians 5:3-8)

A. A Verdict Reached (v. 3)

3. For I verily, as absent in body, but present in spirit, have judged already, as though I were present, concerning him that hath so done this deed.

Since Paul was *absent* from Corinth, how could he be involved in the verdict concerning the guilty man? The answer is that this matter did not involve some unsubstantiated rumor or idle bit of gossip that may or may not have been true. It would have been a great mistake to rush to judgment merely on the basis of idle talk. Situations can be misunderstood and people can be misrepresented. But that was not the case here. There was no question of the truth of the reports that Paul had heard. [See question #2, page 264.]

The term *judged* does not mean that Paul was condemning the man for eternity at this point. He was expressing his decision regarding how this critical matter should be handled *as though* he *were present*.

B. An Action Jointly Taken (v. 4)

4. In the name of our Lord Jesus Christ, when ye are gathered together, and my spirit, with the power of our Lord Jesus Christ.

To invoke *the name of our Lord Jesus Christ* is to place in the most solemn of categories the occasion when the church will be *gathered together* to address the situation at hand. Not only the name but the *power* of Jesus was to be acknowledged in this assembly. This is not to say that the name and power of Jesus were not present at other assemblies of the church. Paul is simply emphasizing these factors because of the grave situation confronting the Corinthians.

How to Say It

CORINTH. *Kor*-inth.
CORINTHIANS. Kor-*in*-thee-unz.
HYMENEUS. High-meh-*nee*-us.
PORNEIA (Greek). por-*nye*-uh or por-*nay*-uh.

Was this a meeting called for the very purpose of dealing with the immoral man? Or was this part of a regular gathering of the church? It is difficult to tell. If the latter, were any visitors dismissed before discussing a matter such as this? Perhaps they were allowed to remain in the assembly so that they could see a demonstration of the church's commitment to purity.

While Paul would not be at this gathering, he told the Corinthians that his *spirit* would be there. This does not suggest some miraculous presence, but rather the need to recognize Paul's authority as an apostle and his role as a spiritual father to the Corinthians (1 Corinthians 4:14, 15). Paul had founded this church and certainly possessed some influence because of that. But he also recognized that the congregation had some authority, too, as well as a grave responsibility to deal correctly with the matter at hand.

C. An Objective Sought (v. 5)

5. To deliver such a one unto Satan for the destruction of the flesh, that the spirit may be saved in the day of the Lord Jesus.

From a spiritual standpoint, there are two rulers and two kingdoms. Satan is "the prince of this world" (John 12:31; 16:11), and Jesus is the Head of the church (Ephesians 1:22, 23; 4:15, 16). To *deliver such a one unto Satan* simply means to put him out of the church so that he may return into the world, or Satan's kingdom. It is sometimes called "withdrawing fellowship" from the guilty one. [See question #3, page 264.]

What is indicated by the phrase *for the destruction of the flesh*? Certainly Paul was not telling the Corinthians to punish this man physically in any way, nor was he allowing Satan to kill him! The term *flesh* should be understood as describing the kind of perspective that lives in defiance of God's authority and in pursuit of one's own desires. One who thus lives is said to "live after the flesh" (Romans 8:12, 13). However, those who "are Christ's have crucified the flesh with the affections and lusts" (Galatians 5:24). It is this kind of *destruction of the flesh* that Paul desires so that the man in question will no longer live by immoral standards.

We should not overlook the objective of putting this man out of the church. It was *that the spirit may be saved*—in other words, that the spirit may be delivered from the control of the flesh and that the willingness of the spirit may triumph over the weakness of the flesh (to use Jesus' words in Matthew 26:41). The church's action was meant to be a kind of "shock treatment" to the man. It was not merely a means of punishment; it was intended as a wake-up call. Its goal was that the man would repent and would thus be saved. And,

from what we read in 2 Corinthians 2:5-11, it worked! There we find that the man did repent, and Paul ordered him restored to the fellowship of the church. When congregations today exercise church discipline, it must be for this very same purpose.

The day of the Lord Jesus refers to the return of Christ and to the judgment that will take place at that time. Paul's desire was that whatever discipline the church administered now would prepare the person being disciplined for that day. Any discipline he undergoes now will be worth it if by so doing he escapes the eternal punishment of Hell.

D. An Old Testament Example (vv. 6, 7)

6. Your glorying is not good. Know ye not that a little leaven leaveneth the whole lump?

Again Paul cites the pride and boasting (*glorying*) of the Corinthians. In view of the many problems about which Paul writes in this letter, they had very little reason to boast. But this matter was especially troubling. They were taking sin far too lightly. The church itself was being put in danger. [See question #4, page 264.]

In a day when most families baked their own bread, the image of *leaven* was an appropriate one. Leaven was the yeast that made the bread raise. As most know, when *a little leaven* is introduced into the dough, it soon spreads through *the whole lump.*

7. Purge out therefore the old leaven, that ye may be a new lump, as ye are unleavened. For even Christ our passover is sacrificed for us.

While *leaven* can be used in a positive sense (Matthew 13:33), it usually carries a negative connotation in Scripture (Matthew 16:6, 12; Mark 8:14, 15; Galatians 5:7-9). Here the *passover* ritual of purging the house of leaven is invoked to illustrate the removal of evil influences—*the old leaven.* At the time of the exodus from Egypt, the Jews were instructed to remove all leaven from their houses (Exodus 12:14-20). This purging became an annual custom in preparation for Passover. The custom was to sweep one's house thoroughly before preparing the Passover meal so that even the crumbs of leavened bread would be discarded. Such a cleansing is used here as an analogy to the spiritual cleansing that the Corinthians needed to undergo.

The presence of the immoral relationship in the church was dangerous. If this sin were tolerated, then other sin would also be tolerated—the leaven would spread. The Corinthians needed to *purge out* these influences from their midst and become *a new lump* of dough, free of the leavening influence. Individually we all need to go through the same process of spiritual renewal

Visual for
lessons 4 & 6

Ruins are all that remain of the pagan temples where many in ancient Corinth were seduced into immoral behavior. Discuss the lures Satan uses in our own culture.

from time to time: to examine ourselves, purge whatever sin is present from our lives, and renew our commitment to purity.

Paul's description of *Christ our passover* calls to mind another important Old Testament link to the New Testament. Just as a lamb was killed at the time of the first Passover (and annually at the celebration of the feast by the Israelites), so Jesus the Lamb of God was crucified at the time of the Passover. The lamb slain in Egypt died to mark the Israelites' freedom from bondage there; the Lamb of God died for our freedom from sin (John 1:29). With this parallel in mind we should, like the Corinthians, get rid of the old leaven, or evil influences, that have the potential of keeping us in bondage to sin.

E. A Practical Application (v. 8)

8. Therefore let us keep the feast, not with old leaven, neither with the leaven of malice and wickedness; but with the unleavened bread of sincerity and truth.

That Paul is not referring to an obligation to *keep the feast* literally is clear from his reference to *the unleavened bread of sincerity and truth.* Paul is not referring to the Lord's Supper or to any kind of religious observance. He is continuing his challenge to the Corinthians to rid themselves of the *old leaven* mentioned in the previous verse. All *malice and wickedness* must be purged from the thoughts, words, and acts of the people so that they may reflect the holiness God desires in His church (Ephesians 5:27).

III. Watching Friendships (1 Corinthians 5:9-11)

A. Proper Contact (vv. 9, 10)

9. I wrote unto you in an epistle not to company with fornicators.

Some students believe that Paul refers here to an earlier *epistle*, or letter, from himself to the Corinthians—one that has not been preserved.

Such a conclusion is not necessary, however. The expression can also be translated, "I have written you in my letter," referring to the letter Paul was writing at that time. Paul used the same construction with the verb "sent" in Ephesians 6:22; Philippians 2:28; and Colossians 4:8.

Paul had written in verse 2 of the present chapter that the brother guilty of fornication should "be taken away from among you." Now, lest some assume he meant Christians were not *to company,* or associate, *with* any *fornicators,* Paul will clarify his instructions.

10. Yet not altogether with the fornicators of this world, or with the covetous, or extortioners, or with idolaters; for then must ye needs go out of the world.

If we separated ourselves *altogether* from *this world* and from worldly people, there would be no evangelism of the lost. We have not been called to *go out of the world*; instead, we are to "go . . . into all the world" (Mark 16:15). We dare not shun those who need the witness of Christians the most. We must build a bridge of friendship to win them. However, in the process of doing this, we must always be cautious as to who is influencing whom. [See question #5, page 264.]

In addition to the *fornicators,* Paul speaks of the *covetous.* While this term is usually applied to material greed, it can refer to all forms of desire for self-indulgence. *Extortioners* are more than "swindlers," as the word is sometimes translated. The Greek word conveys the idea of seizing something by force. *Idolaters* were common in Corinth, given its numerous pagan temples.

B. Improper Contact (v. 11)

11. But now I have written unto you not to keep company, if any man that is called a brother be a fornicator, or covetous, or an idolater, or a railer, or a drunkard, or an extortioner; with such a one, no, not to eat.

There is a difference between the kind of association one has with an evil person whom he is trying to win to Christ and the kind of association one has with a *brother* who persists in sin and refuses to repent. The former situation is acceptable, for it is part of the Christian's obedience to Christ. The latter situation is what had developed in Corinth, and it was totally unacceptable.

It is important to distinguish between the circumstance in Corinth and that described by Paul in Galatians 6:1: "Brethren, if a man be overtaken in a fault, ye which are spiritual, restore such a one in the spirit of meekness; considering thyself, lest thou also be tempted." Here Paul is presenting a case involving someone who has yielded to temptation in a particular instance and needs assistance and encouragement. All of us are imperfect in this regard, and when these situations occur, we need to help one another. We must not shoot our own wounded. The problem in Corinth, however, involved a person who wanted to continue in sin (cf. Romans 6:1) and still be considered a brother in Christ.

To *keep company* with such an individual would have a devastating effect on the church's influence on its surroundings. If the Corinthians did not address the immorality, they would give the impression that the church approved of such behavior. Their laxness would lead others into similar sins. Note that the four sins listed previously by Paul are repeated in this verse, and two more are added. A *railer* is one who slanders or speaks evil of others. Also added is the *drunkard*.

With *such a one* they were *not to eat*. This probably is not a direct reference to the Lord's Supper. Eating together constituted an expression of kinship between those who shared a meal, so Paul told the Corinthians to withhold such expressions from the immoral brother.

IV. Judging Correctly (1 Corinthians 5:12, 13)

A. The Church's Responsibility (v. 12)

12. For what have I to do to judge them also that are without? do not ye judge them that are within?

Neither Paul nor the church was to apply his counsel to those *that are without*, or, those outside the congregation. The congregation itself should take responsibility for its own—for those *within* the church.

It is not to be expected that non-Christians will behave like Christians. We should not be surprised that people outside of Christ do not try to live like Christ. But we can expect people who

---

Home Daily Bible Readings

Monday, Mar. 20—Sexual Immorality Defiles the Church (1 Corinthians 5:1-8)

Tuesday, Mar. 21—Stay Away From Sexual Immorality (1Corinthians 5:9-13)

Wednesday, Mar. 22—Resist Lawsuits Among Believers (1 Corinthians 6:1-11)

Thursday, Mar. 23—Watch Your Tongue! (James 3:1-12)

Friday, Mar. 24—Choose Wisdom That Is From Above (James 3:13-18)

Saturday, Mar. 25—Submit to God's Will and Way (James 4:1-10)

Sunday, Mar. 26—Seek Humility and Avoid Judging (James 4:11-17)

---

are Christians to live like Christ, and we should be very saddened when they do not.

B. God's Responsibility (v. 13)

13. But them that are without God judgeth. Therefore put away from among yourselves that wicked person.

The church is not to take the kind of actions with *them that are without* (outside the church) that it takes in disciplining a member. God has instituted civic authorities to discipline wrongdoers in the world (Romans 13:1-5). The final judgment of the world will, of course, be left to God Himself (Romans 2:16).

Conclusion

A. A Closing Caution

We make a great mistake if we isolate this passage in 1 Corinthians from the rest of the book. In the church at Corinth there were many people committing many wrong acts.

There were divisive people.

There were people taking Christian brothers to court.

There were people conducting themselves improperly in worship.

Yet Paul did not say to put any of these out of the church! The incident found in today's text is the only example of church discipline recorded in the New Testament. In fact, besides the incident recorded in today's text, the only other reference to a similar act of church discipline is found in 1 Timothy 1:19, 20. There Paul writes that he has "delivered unto Satan" Hymeneus and Alexander, "that they may learn not to blaspheme."

If this kind of action occurred rarely in the New Testament church, we should not be surprised that it occurs rarely today. It is likely that no more than once in a lifetime would a congregation face a situation that demanded such radical action. It was rare then and it should be rare now. Two factors in particular seem to call for discipline in a given situation: if there is widespread knowledge of the sin and if there is a refusal to repent.

B. Prayer

O Lord, keep us from the sins of the flesh. Keep us also from the sin of self-righteousness. Give us hearts that care about sinners and grieve over their sin. Give us courage to apply discipline if it is ever needed. In Jesus' name. Amen.

C. Thought to Remember

The church is a hospital for those who are sick, not a rest home for those who are well.

Learning by Doing

This page contains an alternate lesson plan emphasizing learning activities.
Classes desiring such student involvement will find these suggestions helpful.

Learning Goals

After today's lesson each adult will be able to:

1. Tell why discipline was needed in Corinth and how Paul said it should be administered.

2. Explain the purpose of church discipline, and tell how that purpose would influence the administration of discipline.

3. Cultivate personal holiness with greater dedication, and support his or her church's efforts on the rare occasions when discipline may be necessary.

Into the Lesson

Write the following statement on the chalkboard or a large poster: *"Church leaders should not remove fellowship from a member."*

Distribute half-sheets of paper and ask each student to write whether he agrees or disagrees and to write one reason he believes as he does. Then collect the papers and notice how many agree and how many disagree. Read one or two reasons on each side.

Make your transition into the Bible study with a statement like, "Let's find out what Paul said about the goal and process of church discipline in his first letter to the Corinthians."

Into the Word

Use an overhead transparency, a poster, or the chalkboard to display three headings: *A Problem, A Timeless Principle,* and *An Application.* Ask the students to read through the text and suggest what should be cited under each heading. (The student book has an activity to assist in this.)

Problem: *It was commonly known in Corinth (and obviously beyond) that a man within the church was committing fornication with his father's wife. Instead of mourning the behavior, the church was ignoring it!*

Principle: *We always want the sinner to repent and be saved.*

Application: *Ignoring the sin was having two negative consequences: the other members of the church were in danger of becoming dull so that they would be more likely to sin, and the man was not being challenged to repent so that he could be saved. Paul wants the church to withdraw close fellowship from him.*

Read 2 Corinthians 2:6, 7 and 7:9-12 to reinforce the fact that the goal of the church discipline was achieved. The man repented!

Form two groups of students. Ask each group to prepare a list of "Guidelines for Church Discipline" from its assigned text. Assign one group to work with 1 Corinthians 5; the other with Matthew 18:15-17. Summarize the results of the groups' efforts on a chart that all can see.

Guidelines from 1 Corinthians 5

• Take seriously sin by a Christian, especially sin that is publicly known.

• Recognize that failure to take responsibility can lead others to sin.

• Act with the goal of saving the person.

• Withdraw close fellowship so that the church is purified.

• When the person repents, restore the person to fellowship.

Guidelines from Matthew 18:15-17

• Admonish privately the person who sins. If he listens, you have been successful.

• If he does not repent, take one or two others with you.

• If he still refuses to repent, get the church leaders involved.

• If he still refuses to repent, treat him as a pagan.

Into Life

Distribute copies of a handout on which is written the following:

A local man has been convicted of embezzling funds from a local business. Some investigation reveals that he was fired from his last job for the same reason. He, his wife, and children have been active members of your congregation for over ten years.

Applying the guidelines listed above, prepare a step-by-step plan for the leaders. Be ready to explain why you will take each step.

Allow time for the class, working in small groups, to develop a plan. Then ask one group to volunteer to describe its plan. Ask any others who differed in any way to add their insights and tell why they proposed what they did.

Summarize all the discoveries made during the class session so that students can hear one more time the purpose and the process of discipline. Then read 1 Corinthians 5:6-8—Paul's admonition to live a life of personal holiness.

To close the session, lead the class in a time of silent personal introspection and prayer.

Let's Talk It Over

The questions on this page are designed to encourage review of the lesson Scriptures and to promote discussion of the lesson by the class. The answers provided are only discussion starters. Let your class talk it over from there.

1. The sin Paul dealt with in 1 Corinthians 5 was apparently a matter of public knowledge. Why did this make it particularly serious?

The churches of that time were existing in a society plagued with sexual immorality. In order to remain pure, Christians needed mutual encouragement. If news of the sin in Corinth, and especially of the church's toleration of it, was widely known among the churches, how many other believers would be tempted to lower their moral standards? Even more serious was the effect on unbelievers. Paul noted that the sin was of a type that was "not so much as named among the Gentiles." If the pagans looked down on the church for its lax moral standards, how could the message of the gospel be advanced? The church—both in Corinth and beyond—would have lost its integrity and its ability to speak to the issues of concern to the people in the area.

2. Anyone who has dealt with problems in the church knows it can be difficult to separate facts from rumors, opinions, and speculations. What principles would you suggest that leaders can follow in ascertaining the facts?

Jesus once spoke about the importance of "the testimony of two or three witnesses" (Matthew 18:16, *New International Version*). Certainly any reported sin or conflict in a church should be investigated on the basis of a plurality of witnesses. Paul's counsel in Galatians 6:1, 2 is also applicable here. Leaders must take a "spiritual" approach. That suggests much time in prayer and study of the Word while dealing with the problem. They are to be meek and gentle, not harsh and judgmental. They are to be bearers of burdens and not merely couriers of condemnation.

3. If a person in our church were being disciplined by the same standard as described in our text, how would you do it?

Putting one out of the church does not involve physically restraining the individual from entering the church building. Nor would it require that we sit in a pew as far as possible from the offender or go out of our way to avoid speaking to him. To some extent, we would treat the person as we would a visitor—a non-Christian. As Jesus said, "Treat him as you would a pagan or a tax collector" (Matthew 18:17, *New International*

Version). Our goal for the person, as it is for an unbeliever, is to lead him or her to repentance. But Paul makes clear in this passage that the separation is even greater than that between Christians and non-Christians (vv. 9-11). Still, the message we want to convey is one of love and assurance that when the person turns back to the Lord, he or she will have our support.

4. If a congregation is lax in disciplining members guilty of sexual sin, what kind of message does that send to members in general?

Some may be tempted to think, "Perhaps cheating on my husband or wife is not such a serious matter after all." The unmarried members may decide that it is not absolutely wrong to engage in sexual relations outside of marriage. We human beings are always looking for "loopholes." It is tempting to view our circumstances as being the exception to the rule. Anything that supports such a tendency to self-deception is quite dangerous. That makes it essential that preachers in their pulpits and teachers in their classrooms consistently sound forth the Biblical warnings against adultery, fornication, and other sexual sins. And church leaders must act in accordance with such preaching and teaching by taking prompt action in regard to such sins in the congregation.

5. What are some principles we can utilize to guide us in our association with unbelievers?

Jesus' emphasis on loving our neighbor (Luke 10:25-37) is of primary importance. It is obvious that our neighbor is anyone we have contact with and are in a position to help. That includes the people we work with; those who live near us; and those we encounter while taking care of personal business, shopping, and participating in recreational activities. While we are likely to disapprove of many of their habits and attitudes, we must still demonstrate love to them. Of course, the most loving action we can perform is sharing our faith in Christ with them. We should be alert for opportunities to do this gracefully. But the lesson writer wisely points out that "we must always be cautious as to who is influencing whom." If we find that an unsaved associate is negatively affecting our thinking in regard to spiritual or moral values, we must curtail that association.

Marriage

DEVOTIONAL READING: 1 Corinthians 7:25-35.

BACKGROUND SCRIPTURE: 1 Corinthians
6:12—7:16.

PRINTED TEXT: 1 Corinthians 7:1-16.

1 Corinthians 7:1-16

1 Now concerning the things whereof ye wrote unto me: It is good for a man not to touch a woman.

2 Nevertheless, to avoid fornication, let every man have his own wife, and let every woman have her own husband.

3 Let the husband render unto the wife due benevolence: and likewise also the wife unto the husband.

4 The wife hath not power of her own body, but the husband: and likewise also the husband hath not power of his own body, but the wife.

5 Defraud ye not one the other, except it be with consent for a time, that ye may give yourselves to fasting and prayer; and come together again, that Satan tempt you not for your incontinency.

6 But I speak this by permission, and not of commandment.

7 For I would that all men were even as I myself. But every man hath his proper gift of God, one after this manner, and another after that.

8 I say therefore to the unmarried and widows, It is good for them if they abide even as I.

9 But if they cannot contain, let them marry: for it is better to marry than to burn.

10 And unto the married I command, yet not I, but the Lord, Let not the wife depart from her husband:

11 But and if she depart, let her remain unmarried, or be reconciled to her husband: and let not the husband put away his wife.

12 But to the rest speak I, not the Lord: If any brother hath a wife that believeth not, and she be pleased to dwell with him, let him not put her away.

13 And the woman which hath a husband that believeth not, and if he be pleased to dwell with her, let her not leave him.

14 For the unbelieving husband is sanctified by the wife, and the unbelieving wife is sanctified by the husband: else were your children unclean; but now are they holy.

15 But if the unbelieving depart, let him depart. A brother or a sister is not under bondage in such cases: but God hath called us to peace.

16 For what knowest thou, O wife, whether thou shalt save thy husband? or how knowest thou, O man, whether thou shalt save thy wife?

GOLDEN TEXT: What! know ye not that your body is the temple of the Holy Ghost which is in you, which ye have of God, and ye are not your own?—1 Corinthians 6:19.

Helping a Church Confront Crisis
Unit 2: Unity in Human Relationships
(Lessons 5-9)

Lesson Aims

After completing this lesson, each student should be able to:

1. Recite the standards Paul set for both married and single persons in our text.

2. Tell how today's society illustrates the folly of abandoning God's guidelines for marriage.

3. Take steps to promote and model these guidelines in the family, the church, and the community.

Lesson Outline

INTRODUCTION
  A. A Ninety-Ten Marriage
  B. Lesson Background
 I. CONCERNING MARRIAGE (1 Corinthians 7:1-7)
  A. Not Required of All (vv. 1, 2)
  B. Conjugal Obligations (vv. 3-5)
    A Moral Earthquake
  C. Qualifying Statements (vv. 6, 7)
    "If Only . . ."
 II. OTHER CIRCUMSTANCES (1 Corinthians 7:8-16)
  A. The Unmarried and Widows (vv. 8, 9)
  B. Separation (vv. 10, 11)
  C. Those Married to Unbelievers (vv. 12-16)
CONCLUSION
  A. Hard Teachings
  B. Prayer
  C. Thought to Remember

Introduction

A. A Ninety-Ten Marriage

Many years ago I was visiting an older couple who had experienced more than half a century of happy married life together. "I'm sure the secret to your long marriage is that both of you accepted it as a fifty-fifty partnership."

"No, son," the husband quickly replied. "Our marriage has always been a ninety-ten partnership."

"You mean you got your way ninety percent of the time, and she got her way only ten percent of the time?" I asked in surprise.

"No! What I mean is that each of us was willing to go ninety percent of the way in any matter, and as a result the other never had to go more than ten percent of the way."

Heeding that wise advice from an older generation would go a long way toward solving many marital problems today.

B. Lesson Background

Today's lesson introduces the second unit in this quarter's study from Paul's letters to the Corinthians. Unit 1 dealt with Christ as the basis for unity. Unit 2 shows how Christ provides a basis for unity in human relationships.

Our lesson today deals with one of the fundamental institutions in any society—marriage. Marriage provides the cement that holds a society together and helps it function in a healthy, positive way. It is no empty truism that as the homes go, so goes the nation.

We have already noted that Corinth was a city steeped in paganism, making it an especially challenging location to plant a church. Throughout the city were numerous symbols of blatant sexuality, including the temple of Aphrodite, where more than a thousand sacred prostitutes plied their trade. When the Corinthians became Christians, no doubt it was difficult for many of them to rid themselves of all of their pagan values and beliefs. For example, it appears that some began to question whether or not a married person should share physical intimacy with his or her spouse. Such intimacy had always been linked with pagan deities and practices.

The Corinthians expressed their concerns about these matters in a letter to Paul, as verse 1 of today's text indicates ("Now concerning the things whereof ye wrote unto me"). Paul then addressed not only these questions, but several other marriage issues.

I. Concerning Marriage
(1 Corinthians 7:1-7)

A. Not Required of All (vv. 1, 2)

1. Now concerning the things whereof ye wrote unto me: It is good for a man not to touch a woman.

In the verses immediately preceding our printed text (6:12-20) Paul had raised the issue of fornication, warning the Corinthians of its disastrous consequences. Now, in chapter 7, he begins to suggest some ways that the people could guard themselves against the polluting forces around them and uphold God's standards in all their relationships.

Some believe that Paul's statement *It is good for a man not to touch a woman* quotes the letter the Corinthians have written Paul and describes what some in the church were teaching. More likely, Paul was introducing his teaching on the value—at least in certain situations—of celibacy (cf. verses 26, 32-35). Paul himself was unmarried (note verse 7), though it is not clear whether he never married or was a widower. [See question #1, page 272.]

The word *touch* is literally "lay hold of." It may refer to sexual relations, but the word was commonly used by the Greeks to refer to marriage. The *New International Version* translates, "It is good for a man not to marry." Paul himself had chosen to remain unmarried in order to give himself completely to his strenuous and dangerous ministry. Those who make a similar choice have exercised their "proper gift of God," as Paul states in verse 7.

2. Nevertheless, to avoid fornication, let every man have his own wife, and let every woman have her own husband.

Even though Paul commended celibacy, he recognized that it was not typical and that not everyone would be able to live within such limits. Surrounded as the Corinthians were with sexual symbols, language, and acts, it is not surprising that many would find living the celibate life an unbearable burden. Paul knew it was not reasonable to expect everyone to live as he lived.

Given such conditions, it was appropriate for many of the Corinthians that they enter marriage in order *to avoid fornication*. We should understand that this seemingly negative view of marriage does not present the total picture of the marital state or the sole reason for marriage. The fact that God instituted marriage in the garden of Eden and gave His highest blessing to it (Genesis 2:24; Matthew 19:4, 5) should make it obvious that marriage is much more than simply a protection against the temptation of fornication. [See question #2, page 272.]

B. Conjugal Obligations (vv. 3-5)

3. Let the husband render unto the wife due benevolence: and likewise also the wife unto the husband.

The *due benevolence* mentioned here refers to the physical intimacy of marriage. The Greek word literally means "debt" (the *New International Version* translates the phrase as "fulfill his marital duty"). This obligation is not one-sided, falling upon either spouse alone, but must be shared equally by both *husband* and *wife*.

4. The wife hath not power of her own body, but the husband: and likewise also the husband hath not power of his own body, but the wife.

In marriage a man and a woman become "one flesh" (Genesis 2:24). This expression has a broad application, covering many aspects of the marriage relationship, but it certainly includes conjugal relations. Each member of the marriage partnership must be sensitive to the needs of the other. Difficulties arise when one partner makes selfish demands without considering the other. As our culture increasingly encourages persons to be self-centered, it should not surprise us that marriage problems are multiplied. [See question #3, page 272.]

A MORAL EARTHQUAKE

In January of 1994, the Northridge earthquake hit Southern California, toppling freeway overpasses, collapsing parking garages, and demolishing many businesses. Thousands of church buildings and homes were severely damaged, and many people died or were injured.

Ironically, California's largest egg farm (producing one million eggs every day) lay just five miles from the epicenter of the quake. The egg farm suffered a broken water line and *one broken egg!* One manager at the farm told his workers, "We had a 6.6 earthquake that broke fewer eggs than you guys do when we're working!"

A far more lethal moral earthquake shook Western civilization in the last half of the twentieth century. The so-called "sexual revolution" caused our society to view marriage as a quaint relic of the past. The idea that some people (for moral reasons) would remain celibate outside of marriage was no longer seen as self-discipline; it was "repression"—something to be mocked by the cultural "movers and shakers." The moral quake of the sexual revolution shattered lives, destroyed families, caused the indiscriminate death of millions of babies, and promoted irresponsible behavior among innumerable teenagers and adults.

The long-term damage from this shaking of the Biblical norms for sexual behavior has been far greater than all the damage done by any mere earthquake.   —C. R. B.

5. Defraud ye not one the other, except it be with consent for a time, that ye may give yourselves to fasting and prayer; and come together again, that Satan tempt you not for your incontinency.

Here Paul stresses just how vital conjugal obligations are: one who is not willing to accept such responsibilities is said to *defraud* his or her spouse. At the same time, Paul recognized that there may be occasions when sexual relations are to be forsaken, but only *with consent* and *for a time*—that is, by mutual agreement and temporarily. Paul cites a specific situation that may occur when one involves himself or herself in a special period of *fasting and prayer*. But this period should be brief, lest *Satan* use this time apart to *tempt* one to sacrifice his or her *incontinency*, or self-control, and be unfaithful.

Some students have noted that the word *fasting* does not appear in most of the ancient Greek manuscripts. However, fasting does qualify as an occasion of special spiritual need during which one might choose to abstain from sexual relations.

Paul's statement does not address many modern situations that may require the temporary separation of husband and wife. While many of these circumstances may be considered secular rather than spiritual (for examples, military service or employment far from home), they can create similar problems. Most of us know of situations where such separations have opened the door for Satan to gain a foothold and wreak havoc in a marriage. [See question #4, page 272.]

C. Qualifying Statements (vv. 6, 7)

6. But I speak this by permission, and not of commandment.

To what does *this* refer? Most likely it refers to what Paul has just stated in the previous verse. He is granting *permission* for abstinence from sexual relations during times of prayer or other serious spiritual activities. But this teaching is not a *commandment* (it is not found in the teachings of Jesus or elsewhere in Scripture)—only a "concession" (*New American Standard Bible*, *New International Version*).

Since such abstinence is permitted but not commanded, some have questioned whether such a statement carries the kind of divine authority that we associate with the Scriptures. We must understand that the apostle Paul, even in this case, was a divinely inspired messenger of God, and that what he speaks as a "concession" is still communicated under the inspiration of God's Holy Spirit.

7. For I would that all men were even as I myself. But every man hath his proper gift of God, one after this manner, and another after that.

The Greek word *men* in this verse is generic, including both men and women. Paul's desire was that *all* Christians remain celibate *even as* he himself. The extreme demands of Paul's ministry made celibacy almost an absolute must in his case. However, he readily acknowledged that not every Christian has been given this *gift*.

"IF ONLY . . ."

"If only . . ." is a game played by many of us. Life would be better—maybe even *perfect*—if only this or that were different. The most popular form of the game is probably "If only I were rich. . . ." Numbers two and three on the list may be, "If only I were married . . ." and "If only I hadn't married. . . ."

Gregg Warren claims to have a solution for all these problems. If you are distraught over being single or having married the "wrong person," Warren says, you no longer have to be troubled about it. Write out your problem, burn the paper, and send him the ashes (along with five dollars). He will carry the ashes aloft in his plane—cleverly named "Worry Free"—and dump them out over Carefree, Arizona. Warren is a Buddhist, and his idea is a technological adaptation of an ancient Buddhist practice. In the first six months after he began this service, Warren handled some five thousand requests!

God's way, however, is better than the Buddhist way. Paul wrote that one should consider his or her marital status a "proper gift of God" (1 Corinthians 7:7). Worrying about such a matter is not productive. Trusting and being faithful to the Lord will have a profoundly positive effect—whatever our status.   —C. R. B.

II. Other Circumstances (1 Corinthians 7:8-16)

A. The Unmarried and Widows (vv. 8, 9)

8, 9. I say therefore to the unmarried and widows, It is good for them if they abide even as I. But if they cannot contain, let them marry: for it is better to marry than to burn.

Paul next considered those who were *unmarried* or were *widows*. While he does not specifically include widowers, it seems reasonable to suppose that they would be covered by his advice. Once again he states his preference that those not presently married should *abide*, or remain, in that state. At the same time, he recognized that remaining celibate would be extremely difficult for some persons. Many of those in the Corinthian church to whom Paul was writing were recent converts, and they had not yet developed the spiritual strength to resist sexual temptations. Those with stronger sex drives or who were surrounded by especially enticing temptations would likely be

Visual for lesson 5

The visual for today's lesson is a reminder that love, purity, and unity are required for the kind of marriage that Paul urges in our text.

overwhelmed. For them, Paul conceded, *it is better to marry than to burn.* Most commentators hold that this burning refers to the flames of one's passion rather than to the fire of Hell.

B. Separation (vv. 10, 11)

10. And unto the married I command, yet not I, but the Lord, Let not the wife depart from her husband.

Paul's words *yet not I, but the Lord* indicate that the teaching in these verses reflected what *the Lord* (Jesus) had taught concerning marriage and divorce. (The Greek word rendered *depart* refers to divorce, not simply to separation.) At this point in time, Paul may have had access to some of the Gospel accounts of how Jesus dealt with the matter of divorce. But even without these written records, Paul spoke with the authority of an inspired apostle, echoing Christ's teaching in this matter (Mark 10:2-12).

11. But and if she depart, let her remain unmarried, or be reconciled to her husband: and let not the husband put away his wife.

In the event that someone should *depart* from his or her spouse, the Christian should *remain unmarried* or else *be reconciled* to the mate. A commitment to stay unmarried would keep open the possibility of eventual reconciliation. Paul did not raise the issue of adultery as an acceptable reason for divorce (see Jesus' teaching in Matthew 5:32), but what he says here does not contradict that teaching.

C. Those Married to Unbelievers (vv. 12-16)

12, 13. But to the rest speak I, not the Lord: If any brother hath a wife that believeth not, and she be pleased to dwell with him, let him not put her away. And the woman which hath a husband that believeth not, and if he be pleased to dwell with her, let her not leave him.

As Christianity reached out into the pagan society of the first century, it would not have been unusual for a person to become a Christian while his or her spouse remained a pagan. We can readily imagine some of the conflicts that must have arisen in some of those households.

In dealing with the issue of divorce in the previous verses, Paul presented the word of the Lord Jesus. However, in dealing with the problem of a Christian married to an unbeliever, he says *to the rest speak I, not the Lord.* This should not be taken to mean that Paul's teaching on this subject did not reflect the will of Christ or that he was not inspired at this point. He was simply saying that Jesus did not address the issue of a Christian married to an unbeliever during His earthly ministry. Now, under the inspiration of the Holy Spirit, Paul provided counsel not previ-

Home Daily Bible Readings

Monday, Mar. 27—Jesus Teaches About Divorce (Mark 10:1-9)
Tuesday, Mar. 28—Strive for Moral Purity (1 Corinthians 6:12-20)
Wednesday, Mar. 29—Be Faithful to Your Spouse (1 Corinthians 7:1-7)
Thursday, Mar. 30—Directions for Single and Married Life (1 Corinthians 7:8-16)
Friday, Mar. 31—Remain With God Above All Else (1 Corinthians 7:17-24)
Saturday, Apr. 1—Married or Not, the Time Is Short (1 Corinthians 7:25-31)
Sunday, Apr. 2—Does Marriage Hinder Discipleship? (1 Corinthians 7:32-40)

ously given on this subject. He did so as a divinely inspired apostle (1 Corinthians 7:40), making his words authoritative.

Paul taught that a Christian is to remain in the situation of a "mixed marriage" with an unbeliever, no matter how inconvenient it might be, as long as the unbeliever is *pleased,* or willing, to abide in it. In dealing with this problem, Paul did not suggest a double standard—one for men and another for women—as that which existed in the pagan world.

Perhaps a more common situation today occurs when a Christian marries an unbeliever. We need to teach our young people to seek their marriage partners among those who are Christians (2 Corinthians 6:14-18). Yet, in spite of our best efforts, some will marry outside the faith. When this occurs, we need to encourage them to build a solid marriage without compromising their commitment to the Lord. [See question #5, page 272.]

14. For the unbelieving husband is sanctified by the wife, and the unbelieving wife is sanctified by the husband: else were your children unclean; but now are they holy.

Paul now explained why a Christian should remain in a marriage with an unbeliever as long as possible: *the unbelieving husband is sanctified by the wife,* while *the unbelieving wife is sanctified by the husband.* Bible students have held various views about what this statement means. It certainly does not mean that an unbeliever will come to enjoy the blessings of salvation simply because he or she happens to be married to a Christian. Salvation always requires the sinner to make a personal commitment to the Lord and cannot be gained by mere contact with a Christian.

Paul probably means that a Christian marriage partner has a unique opportunity to present the claims of the gospel to his or her mate by word and, even more important, by deed. Most of us can think of persons who patiently and graciously witnessed to their mate and after many years finally led him or her to the Lord. In this sense the unbeliever who has become a Christian is thus *sanctified*, or set apart to the Lord.

Not only does a Christian marriage partner have an opportunity to witness to his or her mate, but also to rear the *children* to become Christians. The children of such a marriage are *unclean* in the sense that they are not Christians and will not become Christians unless they are properly taught. The home, even when one partner is not a Christian, is still the best place for a child to learn about the Lord.

15. But if the unbelieving depart, let him depart. A brother or a sister is not under bondage in such cases: but God hath called us to peace.

If the unbelieving depart—if he or she chooses not to live with the Christian spouse—the *brother or sister is not under bondage* and is released from all attempts to keep the marriage together. Some believe that, since the marriage bonds are thus broken, the Christian is free to remarry. According to this interpretation, Paul has added abandonment to adultery (Matthew 5:32) as a Biblical basis for divorce and remarriage.

Other Bible students oppose this view, insisting that the *bondage* Paul mentions only frees the Christian from the obligation of trying to maintain a marriage with a partner who has left. They point out that remarriage is not mentioned here and that we have no right to infer that it is included as a part of Paul's teaching.

One thing is certain: *God hath called us to peace.* God wants us to have harmony, not discord, in our marriages. No Christian should intentionally foster strife in a marriage and thereby pressure the unbelieving spouse to seek to end the marriage.

16. For what knowest thou, O wife, whether thou shalt save thy husband? or how knowest thou, O man, whether thou shalt save thy wife?

A Christian married to an unbeliever may think that the chances of converting his or her unbelieving spouse are remote indeed. But even in situations that seem hopeless, we must never underestimate the power of a believer's consis-

tent, compassionate witness. Christians who are married to non-Christians should find strength and hope in this verse. And certainly they need the prayers and support of other Christians.

Conclusion

A. Hard Teachings

The teachings of Christ and the apostle Paul concerning marriage and divorce are not easy to accept in our modern culture. Keep in mind, however, that down through history those who have tried to follow the teachings of the Bible have often found themselves at odds with their culture. All too often Christians, when faced with such confrontations, have compromised their convictions and surrendered to the culture.

Divorce is one of the major problems facing our homes today; and because the home is the foundation of the nation, it is therefore a major problem facing our nation. Within two generations we have moved from a situation in which divorces were rather rare to the point where nearly half of all marriages end in divorce. Even among professing Christians, divorces are distressingly common. As a result we have seen the rapid growth of single-parent families, frequently resulting in impoverished homes and psychologically scarred children.

Given the attitudes current in our society, there is no easy solution to this problem. As Christians, however, we must not surrender to the values of our society. We must teach our children the Biblical standards for marriage both by word and by example. We need to start when they are young and keep repeating these teachings at every opportunity.

The church must also provide help for those whose marriages are in trouble. It isn't enough just to preach and condemn. Fortunately, there are many Christian marriage counselors available who can help people whose marriages are struggling. Even those of us who are not professional counselors can often give helpful advice to such couples. Above all we can pray for them.

B. Prayer

We come to You, Father, who instituted marriage in the garden of Eden, because our hearts are heavy with the burden of what is happening to marriages in our land. Give us a fuller understanding about what the Bible teaches concerning marriage. Then give us the strength to live up to those teachings. In our Master's name, amen.

C. Thought to Remember

"What therefore God hath joined together, let not man put asunder" (Mark 10:9).

How to Say It

APHRODITE. Af-ruh-*dite*-ee.
CORINTH. *Kor*-inth.
CORINTHIANS. Kor-*in*-thee-unz.
INCONTINENCY. in-*con*-tih-nen-see.

Learning by Doing

This page contains an alternate lesson plan emphasizing learning activities.
Classes desiring such student involvement will find these suggestions helpful.

Learning Goals

After this lesson students should be able to:

1. Recite the standards Paul set for both married and single persons in our text.

2. Tell how today's society illustrates the folly of abandoning God's guidelines for marriage.

3. Take steps to promote and model these guidelines in the family, the church, and the community.

Into the Lesson

As your students arrive, give them copies of the following agree/disagree exercise, or direct their attention to the student book, where it is reprinted. Allow two minutes to complete the exercise and five more to discuss their answers.

1. Under no circumstances should Christians divorce. Agree or disagree?

2. Every preacher should have a family to relate better to his congregation. Agree or disagree?

3. Single Christians are better situated than married ones to deal with this sinful world. Agree or disagree?

4. Christians compromise their faith when they are married to unbelievers. Agree or disagree?

5. Christians are commanded by God (Genesis 1) to marry and have children. Agree or disagree?

After the discussion, tell your students that today's lesson addresses each statement.

Into the Word

Many of the topics in 1 Corinthians were occasioned by a letter addressed to Paul. The seventh chapter contains the first such topic. Ask your students to work in pairs to read each passage indicated below and compose the question they think Paul was answering. Possible questions are indicated in parentheses. As the pairs report, use the additional questions cited after each one to further your class discussion of these issues.

7:1-6 (With all the sexual immorality in Corinth, should we abstain from sex entirely?)

According to Paul, what is the proper view of marital intimacy for husbands and wives? What potential problems face married couples if they avoid intimacy? When is it permissible for couples temporarily to cease sexual relations?

7:7-9 (Should unmarried believers be discouraged from marrying?)

Why did Paul wish all were unmarried, as he was? What advantages might a single Christian have over a married one? When might it be better for a Christian to marry than to remain single?

7:10-16 (To protect his faith, should a believer divorce his unbelieving spouse?)

What is the Lord's view of divorce between believers? When is divorce allowed? If believers divorce for any other reason, what can they do? What can they not do? What is Paul's teaching on mixed marriages between believers and unbelievers? How is an unbeliever sanctified by a believing spouse? What does Paul mean about their children being either "unclean" or "holy"? What breaks the marriage bonds between a believer and an unbeliever? Is the believer then free to remarry? Compare verse 15 with verse 39, where Paul uses similar language of widows.

Into Life

Ask each pair of students who completed the previous exercise to write a brief response to one of the situations below. Assign every situation to at least one pair of students to make sure that all are covered. Each situation is based on an agree/disagree statement from the opening activity.

1. Bruce and his wife Beth, both Christians, have been having marital problems over money and in-laws for several years. Bruce has decided to file for divorce. What would you tell him?

2. You serve on the pulpit committee of your congregation. A great prospect for the minister's position has applied, but he is single and some of the committee members think that his marital status would hinder his work. What would you say to the committee?

3. Tom, a forty-something bachelor, would love to settle down to be a family man, but he has yet to meet the right woman. He is deeply depressed because he feels he is past his prime and his chances for happiness are gone. What would you write to reassure him?

4. George's wife, Patricia, cannot understand what he sees in Christianity. Though she is a good wife and mother, George feels that they have less in common every day. Some of his Christian friends have suggested that he would be better off without her. How would you counsel him?

5. Luke believes that now is the right time to have children, but his wife is afraid to raise a child in today's violent, pagan society. What would you tell them?

Let's Talk It Over

The questions on this page are designed to encourage review of the lesson Scriptures and to promote discussion of the lesson by the class. The answers provided are only discussion starters. Let your class talk it over from there.

1. Paul's recommendation of the celibate life seems to have hinged on current circumstances (see 1 Corinthians 7:26). Under what conditions today might it be advisable for a Christian to shun marriage?

From God's notation that it was not good for the man to be alone (Genesis 2:18) to the recognition in the book of Hebrews that marriage is honorable (Hebrews 13:4), the Bible is pro-marriage. But there have always been situations when marriage is not the better choice. Many engaged couples will put off marriage until one or the other of them completes schooling. One serving in the military might decide not to marry until after his tour of duty. People whose jobs require frequent travel might choose to remain single rather than be separated from their families. Christian leaders who live in areas where Christians are persecuted might opt for singleness rather than jeopardize the lives of family members.

2. Paul noted that sexual temptations in Corinth were strong enough that some should marry to avoid fornication. What similarities to this situation do you see in our society?

In many ways sexual temptations are even more pervasive today than in ancient Corinth. If we own a television set, we may try to monitor our viewing habits, but it is difficult to avoid material with a strong sexual content. Many commercials, for example, utilize sex to gain viewers' attention. We purchase newspapers and magazines for information and amusement. These frequently include photographs and features that can stimulate sexual desire. And the wealth of news that comes our way often describes the sexual misbehavior of politicians, entertainers, leaders in business and industry, and other prominent people.

3. A husband's and wife's bodies belong to one another. How can the recognition of this truth contribute to a successful marriage?

Paul's observation in Ephesians 5:29 is applicable here: "For no man ever yet hated his own flesh; but nourisheth and cherisheth it. . . ." A husband and wife should be deeply concerned about the health, comfort, and security of each other's bodies. In connection with our present lesson it is clear that marriage partners will focus not only on their own sexual fulfillment, but that

of their mates as well. The concept is not intended to justify exploitation of one mate by the other—as if the one owns the other and can do what he or she pleases. Rather, it is a mutual recognition that each one is not his or her own, but has an obligation to assist and edify the other.

4. Suppose a friend told you he was considering taking a job in a far-off city, but that his wife could not leave her job until she was vested—eighteen months from now. In light of today's text, how would you advise your friend? Why?

Considering what Paul says about marriage's being a hedge against fornication, and his warning not to "defraud" one's spouse, one might well urge caution here. Working out of town will probably require him to stay in the other town most of the time, perhaps being home only on weekends. Separation and the ready availability of cable TV in hotel rooms have wrecked many marriages. Is the wife's retirement pension worth risking the marriage? Is the higher pay of the new job? If the couple believes the marriage is strong enough to handle the difficulty, one might recommend some safeguards: occasional visits, frequent phone or e-mail contact, and accountability partners—especially one for the man—who can help the couple to remain faithful.

5. How can Christian parents prepare their children for successful marriage?

Some significant family Bible study should be dedicated to those passages that contain God's principles for marriage. Even very young children can begin to learn about the love, trust, and mutual respect and service that are essential to marriage. For pre-teens and teenagers it is important to make books available that will guide them through the years of physical and emotional change, dating, sexual temptations, courtship, and marriage. Parents need to make themselves available for private discussions of these matters. And, of course, parents must keep in mind that they are always teaching by example. Children can learn disrespect and selfishness in this way, or they can learn how two people continue to cherish each other's companionship throughout life. They can learn dissension and conflict, or they can learn how love works to resolve disagreements and other problems.

Love and Knowledge

DEVOTIONAL READING: 1 Corinthians 10:23—11:1.

BACKGROUND SCRIPTURE: 1 Corinthians 8.

PRINTED TEXT: 1 Corinthians 8.

1 Corinthians 8

1 Now as touching things offered unto idols, we know that we all have knowledge. Knowledge puffeth up, but charity edifieth.

2 And if any man think that he knoweth any thing, he knoweth nothing yet as he ought to know.

3 But if any man love God, the same is known of him.

4 As concerning therefore the eating of those things that are offered in sacrifice unto idols, we know that an idol is nothing in the world, and that there is none other God but one.

5 For though there be that are called gods, whether in heaven or in earth, (as there be gods many, and lords many,)

6 But to us there is but one God, the Father, of whom are all things, and we in him; and one Lord Jesus Christ, by whom are all things, and we by him.

7 Howbeit there is not in every man that knowledge: for some with conscience of the idol unto this hour eat it as a thing offered unto an idol; and their conscience being weak is defiled.

8 But meat commendeth us not to God: for neither, if we eat, are we the better; neither, if we eat not, are we the worse.

9 But take heed lest by any means this liberty of yours become a stumblingblock to them that are weak.

10 For if any man see thee which hast knowledge sit at meat in the idol's temple, shall not the conscience of him which is weak be emboldened to eat those things which are offered to idols;

11 And through thy knowledge shall the weak brother perish, for whom Christ died?

12 But when ye sin so against the brethren, and wound their weak conscience, ye sin against Christ.

13 Wherefore, if meat make my brother to offend, I will eat no flesh while the world standeth, lest I make my brother to offend.

GOLDEN TEXT: If any man think that he knoweth any thing, he knoweth nothing yet as he ought to know. But if any man love God, the same is known of him.
—1 Corinthians 8:2, 3.

Lesson Aims

After this lesson students should be able to:

1. Summarize Paul's teaching about love and knowledge as it applies to the issue of eating meat sacrificed to idols.

2. Compare the issue Paul addressed with disputable matters that concern Christians today.

3. Determine to make choices based on love for Christ and His church more than on personal freedom.

Lesson Outline

INTRODUCTION
  A. Haymow Theology
  B. Lesson Background
I. LIVING BY KNOWLEDGE (1 Corinthians 8:1-8)
  A. The Danger of Knowledge (vv. 1-3)
  B. The Truth About Idols (vv. 4-6)
    "The King Is Dead; Long Live the King"
  C. A Weak Christian's Conscience (vv. 7, 8)
II. LIVING BY LOVE (1 Corinthians 8:9-13)
  A. Not Misleading Others (vv. 9, 10)
  B. Considering Christ (vv. 11, 12)
  C. Willing to Adapt (v. 13)
    How Much Is a Person Worth?
CONCLUSION
  A. I-Strain
  B. Our Brothers' Keepers
  C. The Weaker Brother
  D. Prayer
  E. Thought to Remember

Introduction

A. Haymow Theology

Some teenage boys often played in the neighbor's barn. From the top of the barn they had suspended a long rope. On it they would swing from the haymow on one side of the barn across the open area in the middle to the haymow on the other side, landing safely on the loose hay.

This game, which seemed safe enough for the older boys, went on for several weeks. Then one day a younger brother, seeing the older boys swinging on the rope, decided to try it. Before the older boys could stop him, he grabbed the rope and jumped. But he lost his grip, fell to the floor below, and was seriously injured.

The next day the older boys, without any urging from their parents, took down the rope. They realized that what was safe for them posed serious dangers for one not so strong or experienced. This illustrates what Paul was talking about when he stated that he was willing to give up any activities that might cause a weaker brother to stumble and fall into sin.

B. Lesson Background

Today's lesson, which includes all of 1 Corinthians 8, continues Paul's discussion of practical problems facing the church at Corinth. Apparently one of the issues that had been raised in the Corinthians' letter to Paul was whether or not a Christian could eat meat that had been sacrificed to idols. There were primarily two ways to handle this matter, and they are found within today's lesson title: "Love and Knowledge." According to Paul, knowledge may make some people puffed up and arrogant. Those who see debatable issues, such as eating meat offered to idols, from the perspective of knowledge alone often insist on their freedom of behavior, even though the exercise of that freedom might be harmful to some of their fellow Christians. Love, on the other hand, seeks to help and encourage other Christians, especially those who are weaker in the faith.

I. Living by Knowledge (1 Corinthians 8:1-8)

A. The Danger of Knowledge (vv. 1-3)

1. Now as touching things offered unto idols, we know that we all have knowledge. Knowledge puffeth up, but charity edifieth.

The phrase *now as touching* indicates that Paul was addressing a question that the Corinthians had raised in their letter to Paul (see 7:1). While the specific subject involved is not an issue in our society today, the principle that Paul lays down to deal with the matter certainly applies to many issues that modern Christians face.

The specific problem troubling some of the Corinthians was whether it was right to eat meat that had been sacrificed to *idols*. Part of such a sacrifice was consumed on the altar, some was eaten by the priests, and what was left over was commonly sold in the meat markets (called the "shambles" in 1 Corinthians 10:25). Persons who only recently had been converted from paganism understandably had some reservations about eating such meat.

Apparently some of the more mature Christians, recognizing that the pagan idols were nothing, had no qualms about eating this meat. Paul, however, pointed out that this knowledge can sometimes be dangerous. *Knowledge puffeth up;*

that is, it can cause a person to become arrogant and domineering over others and to believe that everyone should think as he does. On the other hand, *charity*, or love, *edifieth*; it builds up others in the faith. It seeks to work with people and help them, regardless of their level of knowledge.

It is important to note that Paul was not commending ignorance. His quarrel was with the exercise of the kind of knowledge that is self-centered. Love, by contrast, is always concerned about others first. Love is the attitude that will help us to use our knowledge in a way pleasing to God. It would be better that we all have love rather than that *we all have knowledge*.

2. And if any man think that he knoweth any thing, he knoweth nothing yet as he ought to know.

One can be knowledgeable about many things; but if this knowledge leads a person to become vain and conceited, then that individual *knoweth nothing* about the things *he ought to know*—the things that really matter. [See question #1, page 280.]

3. But if any man love God, the same is known of him.

Rather than desiring knowledge, we should seek to be *known* of God. This happens when we *love God,* thereby fulfilling "the first and great commandment" (Matthew 22:37, 38). As Paul will state in verse 4, some of the Corinthians were correct in their knowledge that the idols were nothing and that the meat sacrificed to them was in no way contaminated. However, it is not enough for one to hold correct views about certain matters. One who truly knows God and loves Him will express his love to God by caring for the weaker believers around him. Most of us have known people who were sound in the faith but expressed their faith in an arrogant and

unloving fashion. Others were driven away from Christ, not drawn to Him.

B. The Truth About Idols (vv. 4-6)

4. As concerning therefore the eating of those things that are offered in sacrifice unto idols, we know that an idol is nothing in the world, and that there is none other God but one.

Paul agreed with those who knew that the *idols* were *nothing.* Although many of them had come from pagan backgrounds steeped in polytheism (the worship of many gods), they had come to the mature understanding that there was *none other God but one.*

5, 6. For though there be that are called gods, whether in heaven or in earth, (as there be gods many, and lords many,) but to us there is but one God, the Father, of whom are all things, and we in him; and one Lord Jesus Christ, by whom are all things, and we by him.

Paul is not affirming that the *gods many* and *lords many* of other peoples (such as the ancient Greeks and Romans) actually existed alongside the true God. He is simply stating that there are many supposed entities that are *called gods* and worshiped and treated as though they were gods; however, *there is but one God.* In addition, He is *the Father*, indicating His warm personal relationship with those who serve Him. He is the Creator of *all things* and the source of all that is necessary for man's livelihood. In contrast to the many lords of the pagans, there is but *one Lord Jesus Christ.* Through Him has come God's plan for human redemption.

"THE KING IS DEAD; LONG LIVE THE KING"

We've probably all glanced at the tabloid headlines while waiting in line at the grocery store. With amazing regularity they announce another sighting of Elvis Presley—"the king of rock and roll." Elvis died in August of 1977, but some of his fans simply cannot acknowledge that an out-of-control lifestyle led him to an early grave. As if to keep the delusion alive nearly a quarter of a century after his death, there are still competitions to see which Elvis impersonator looks most like his idol.

Ted Harrison, author of *Elvis People—The Cult of the King*, says, "The worship, adoration and the perpetuation of the memory of Elvis today closely resembles a religious cult." He cites the thousands of fans who go to Presley's Graceland mansion in Memphis every year on the anniversary of his death, as well as the talk of being loved by Elvis and having a personal relationship with him! Harrison's verdict is that the "Elvis cult" could eventually become a "full-fledged religion."

Home Daily Bible Readings

Monday, Apr. 3—Knowledge Puffs Up; Love Builds Up (1 Corinthians 8:1-6)

Tuesday, Apr. 4—Don't Cause Another to Stumble (1 Corinthians 8:7-13)

Wednesday, Apr. 5—Love Has Priority Over "Rights" (1 Corinthians 9:1-12)

Thursday, Apr. 6—Preaching the Gospel Is Reward Enough (1 Corinthians 9:13-18)

Friday, Apr. 7—Do Whatever It Takes (1 Corinthians 9:19-27)

Saturday, Apr. 8—Learn From Lessons of the Past (1 Corinthians 10:1-13)

Sunday, Apr. 9—Flee From the Worship of Idols (1 Corinthians 10:14-22)

This phenomenon shows how little human nature has changed in twenty centuries. It is tragic that spiritually needy people still create their own gods just as they did in Paul's day. Whether the god is an idol of stone or the memory of a musician who destroyed himself with alcohol and drugs, it makes no difference. The truth is as Paul states it: "There is but one God." Let us worship Him—the King of kings!

—C. R. B.

C. A Weak Christian's Conscience (vv. 7, 8)

7. Howbeit there is not in every man that knowledge: for some with conscience of the idol unto this hour eat it as a thing offered unto an idol; and their conscience being weak is defiled.

We noted in last week's lesson how the pagan environment out of which the Corinthian Christians came may have influenced their views on marriage and sex. The same was probably true with attitudes concerning idols. Some Christians saw great harm in eating meat offered to an *idol* because it had been used for pagan purposes. To them, eating the meat offered to an idol was tantamount to worshiping the idol.

Instead of scolding the *weak* Christians who were not secure in the knowledge described in verse 6, Paul encouraged the stronger Christians to be careful lest they cause the weaker ones to stumble. The strong Christian had no problem with meat sacrificed to idols, but the weak Christian, following the example of the strong, might be tempted to eat the meat even though it violated his *conscience*. As a result his conscience would become *defiled;* he would be more susceptible to engage in acts that were clearly sinful, without remorse. [See question #2, page 280.]

8. But meat commendeth us not to God: for neither, if we eat, are we the better; neither, if we eat not, are we the worse.

The act of eating *meat* was in itself neither morally good nor bad. It *commendeth us not to God;* that is, in the eyes of God eating did not gain any merit for the Christian, nor was anyone *the worse* for abstaining from eating meat.

II. Living by Love
(1 Corinthians 8:9-13)

A. Not Misleading Others (vv. 9, 10)

9. But take heed lest by any means this liberty of yours become a stumblingblock to them that are weak.

Paul acknowledged that the stronger Christians have the *liberty,* or freedom, to eat meat sacrificed to idols. Had they been in a different situation where there were no Christians with sensitive consciences, Paul's discussion might have ended

---

How to Say It

CORINTH. *Kor*-inth.
CORINTHIANS. Kor-*in*-thee-unz.
POLYTHEISM. *pahl*-uh-thee-iz-um.

---

at this point. They would have been free to eat the meat without hesitation. But freedom in Christ does not mean complete lack of restraints on a Christian's behavior. When the stronger Christian uses his freedom without carefully considering the impact his actions may have on *weak* Christians, then he is abusing his freedom. He may become a *stumblingblock* to others.

Whenever our freedom to participate in certain actions poses a threat to the spiritual well-being of another person, then our love for that person must transcend our personal freedom, or our "rights," as we are more likely to say. Paul told the Galatians, "Brethren, ye have been called unto liberty; only use not liberty for an occasion to the flesh, but by love serve one another" (Galatians 5:13). [See question #3, page 280.]

10. For if any man see thee which hast knowledge sit at meat in the idol's temple, shall not the conscience of him which is weak be emboldened to eat those things which are offered to idols?

Could it be that some Christians were actually sitting in an *idol's temple* and eating the *meat* from the sacrifice? Not necessarily. The expression may be a hyperbole, describing the effect on the weaker brother. To him, eating the meat that had been sacrificed to an idol was equivalent to participating in the ceremony at the temple.

Another suggestion has also been offered. Paul may refer to attending a banquet of a civic or social nature that was held in pagan temples. These temples provided convenient meeting places for such gatherings, and Christians might occasionally attend these kinds of banquets. (Perhaps it is just such an occasion Paul refers to in 1 Corinthians 10:27.) Upon seeing other Christians present at one of these occasions, a weaker Christian who did not know better might suppose that they were participating in a pagan ceremony. Or the weaker brother might believe that any activity performed in the temple had religious significance—even social or civic functions. In either case, the weaker brother would be emboldened to participate also, violating his *conscience* in the matter.

B. Considering Christ (vv. 11, 12)

11. And through thy knowledge shall the weak brother perish, for whom Christ died?

By thus violating his conscience, the *weak brother* might be led into further actions that were clearly sinful (a result similar to his conscience being "defiled" in verse 7). This could lead to his being lost eternally—and all because the stronger brother, perhaps not realizing the impact of his deeds, had acted by his *knowledge* rather than his love for a fellow Christian.

The same may happen today. Suppose a Christian attends an "R" rated movie that he has carefully selected according to what he considers strict standards. Another believer, knowing the former is a strong Christian, may conclude that attending any "R" rated movie is okay—with tragic results!

Paul's point is that we must always consider how our actions may influence others. This may seem a heavy burden to carry, limiting our freedom in many ways. But when we consider that *Christ died* for the weaker brother—as well as the stronger one—we really have no choice but to shoulder this burden, relying on the Lord to give us the strength to carry it graciously. [See question #4, page 280.]

12. But when ye sin so against the brethren, and wound their weak conscience, ye sin against Christ.

We do not live the Christian life in a vacuum. We do have a clear responsibility to our brothers and sisters. If we neglect this responsibility and *wound their weak conscience,* increasing the likelihood that they will fall deeper into sin, we *sin . . . against* them. But that does not conclude the matter. We also *sin against Christ.* We harm someone for whom Jesus died, and we do damage to a part of His body. A part of that body cannot be hurt without the Head's feeling the pain.

C. Willing to Adapt (v. 13)

13. Wherefore, if meat make my brother to offend, I will eat no flesh while the world standeth, lest I make my brother to offend.

Paul concluded his discussion with a statement of his own convictions and of how much he was willing to sacrifice his freedom in Christ for the sake of a weaker Christian. *Meat* in this context refers to meat sacrificed to idols. *Make my brother to offend* describes the process of causing a fellow Christian to fall into sin.

It was not Paul's intent to argue that Christians should give up all meat and become vegetarians. He is setting forth a fundamental rule governing the behavior of Christians. The standards of Christian behavior are not to be set by knowledge or law, but by love—love for Christ and love for one's Christian brothers and sisters. What a difference it would make if Christians everywhere understood this principle and applied it in their daily living! [See question #5, page 280.]

How Much Is a Person Worth?

Suppose you were asked, "What would be the perfect job?" Most people have a fantasy about a "dream job" in which the responsibilities, working conditions, co-workers, and salary all combine to approach perfection.

Many people (especially children!) might say that John Harrison of Oakland, California, has such a job. He is the official taste tester for Dreyer's Ice Cream—one of the premium brands on the U.S. West Coast. Harrison's trained taste buds are so important to him (and to the company) that they are insured for one million dollars! To make sure that he stays in top form for his job, Harrison avoids spicy foods, alcoholic beverages, tobacco, and caffeine. All of these substances either "clog the taste buds," deaden them, or distort the flavor of the ice cream.

So, what are taste buds *really* worth? One million dollars? Five million? Ten million? Another question: what is the spiritual welfare of another person worth? There is no way to put any monetary value on it, but Paul suggests that there is a way to show how much we value it: whether we are willing to limit (or even sacrifice) our freedom in order to protect a Christian brother or sister from stumbling.

How highly do we value fellow Christians? As highly as Christ valued us?   —C. R. B.

Conclusion

A. I-Strain

"Do your own thing!" How many times have we heard that expression in recent years! Someone has observed that our culture suffers from a severe case of "I-strain." On every hand we see examples of the insistence on one's "rights" to the neglect or even injury of others. It is this selfish attitude that Paul rejects in today's lesson.

As we labor to set forth the Christian ideal that the individual must be willing to subordinate his own wishes and desires for the good of others,

Visual for lessons 4 & 6

Use this visual to remind students of the prevalence of paganism in Corinth and how that would have been the occasion for temptations in every area of life.

we must recognize that we are going against the flow of our times. For every individual who gives his or her life in selfless service to others, there are millions who think only of themselves. As we examine our own lives, we are forced to admit that we have on many occasions fallen short of the ideal Paul sets forth. If we desire to change our own lives to measure up to this ideal, we need to recognize that it will not be an easy task. People are likely to misunderstand us, question our motives, and laugh at us.

B. Our Brothers' Keepers

"Am I my brother's keeper?" Cain's hypocritical answer, which he gave in an effort to cover up the murder of his brother Abel, has echoed down through the centuries. For the Christian the answer is *yes* and *no*. The answer is *yes* in the sense that we do have a responsibility first to God and then second to every part of God's creation. This especially applies to the crowning gem of God's creation—the human race, made in His own image.

Obviously we cannot extend our concern to all of creation in the way that God can, but He does expect us to act appropriately within the limits of our wisdom and strength. For example, not so very long ago many Christians took a strong stand against any use of alcoholic beverages. In our more morally relaxed times, some Christians have taken the position that such a viewpoint denies them their freedom. How would Paul react to this thinking? In view of the high cost that alcohol imposes on our society—broken homes, crime, and shattered lives—there is little doubt that he would say, "If drinking alcohol (even only a beer now and then) causes my brother to offend, then I will drink no alcohol so long as the world stands." He would take the same position against many other activities in our current society, including many of the movies and television programs we see and the literature we read.

On the other hand, we must also answer *no* to the question, "Am I my brother's keeper?" First of all, we must recognize that we cannot control all the actions of all the people around us. We can teach and we can set good examples, but each person ultimately must make his or her own decision about moral matters.

At times in the past, efforts have been made to control the behavior of people by laws. Recall how the Pharisees in Jesus' day, for example, attempted to control people's actions by laws that spelled out right and wrong behavior in great detail. In real life it didn't work. In addition, it produced a spiritual pride and arrogance on the part of the Pharisees that led them to oppose Jesus and eventually nail Him to the cross.

Paul's solution is not to ignore our brothers or attempt to legislate their behavior, but to try to live our lives in such a way that we are sensitive and loving examples for others.

C. The Weaker Brother

Many years ago when the game of Monopoly was first introduced, my brother, my cousin, and several neighborhood youngsters would spend hours on rainy days playing the game. But a problem soon arose when we played at our house. To determine moves we had to roll dice. In the eyes of my grandmother, this was sinful because dice were used in gambling. We finally solved the problem by devising a spinner that determined our moves. The irony of all this is that no one questioned the object of the game, which was to bankrupt your opponent by lucky moves or clever trading. Perhaps the game was relatively harmless, yet its subtle emphasis was on greed.

We may smile at this childhood experience, but it does point to a problem that we must face as we try to live in such a way that we do not cause others to stumble. By concentrating on minor details, we may neglect the larger, more important issues of Christian living.

In Romans 14 Paul discusses in greater detail the principle of concern for the weaker brother. There he points out that we cannot make the conscience of the weaker brother the only standard for our actions. If we do, the weaker brother may become a moral dictator, controlling everyone's behavior by his delicate conscience.

In the Romans passage Paul warns the strong not to despise the weak and the weak not to judge the strong (Romans 14:3). Interestingly enough, Paul makes no mention, either in the Romans passage or in today's lesson text, that the weak should become strong. In many matters we may not know which position the inspired apostle would label "weak" and which he would call "strong." All we know is that we disagree. No matter. Act according to your own conscience and accept the brother who disagrees without judging—whether weak or strong.

D. Prayer

Dear God, help us to be sensitive to the spiritual needs of those about us. Show us how to live in such a way that we will never be a hindrance or a stumblingblock to others. Help us to have knowledge, but above all help us to love You and Your children. In Christ's name we pray. Amen.

E. Thought to Remember

"If meat make my brother to offend, I will eat no flesh while the world standeth" (1 Corinthians 8:13).

Learning by Doing

This page contains an alternate lesson plan emphasizing learning activities.
Classes desiring such student involvement will find these suggestions helpful.

Learning Goals

After this lesson, each of your students should be able to:

1. Summarize Paul's teaching about love and knowledge as it applies to the issue of eating meat sacrificed to idols.

2. Compare the issue Paul addressed with disputable matters that concern Christians today.

3. Determine to make choices based on love for Christ and His church more than on personal freedom.

Into the Lesson

Distribute copies of the following scenario and ask your students to pretend they are members of the same church as "James." Ask them what they might say to him in response to this incident.

> James is a professional athlete who claims to be a "born-again Christian." After his arrest for drunk driving, he told reporters, "It's a free country and what I do with my life, as long as I don't hurt anyone else, is my business. I've never told anyone else to pattern his life after mine, and I don't need anyone to tell me how to live my life."

Discuss their responses briefly for now; then move on to the next exercise.

Into the Word

Introduce the issue of eating meat offered to idols as background information. (Use the material in the comments on 1 Corinthians 8:1.) Then divide your class into groups of three or four each. Distribute copies of Exercise 1 to half the groups and copies of Exercise 2 to the other half (or refer them to the student books). Ask each group to complete its exercise (correct answers are in parentheses). Allow five to ten minutes for the group activities; then bring the class together to review their conclusions.

Exercise 1

Read 1 Corinthians 8:1-3, 10-13, and complete the chart below, contrasting knowledge and love. Then discuss the questions that follow.

Verse	Knowledge	Love
1	Puffs up	(Edifies)
2, 3	(Lacks full knowledge)	Is known of God
10-13	Can destroy a weak brother	(Won't cause a weak brother to stumble)

1. What kind of knowledge was Paul talking about in verse 1?

2. What does it mean that a person who thinks he knows anything knows nothing (v. 2)?

3. How are love and knowledge related (v. 3)?

4. How could one Christian's knowledge cause another to stumble (vv. 10-13)?

5. How could wounding a weak conscience be a sin against Christ (v. 12)?

6. Should a Christian avoid doing something that is not sinful simply because someone might be offended by it? Why or why not?

Exercise 2

From 1 Corinthians 8:4-10, identify the statements below as true or false; then discuss the questions that follow:

1. Paul said that idols are not real beings. (True, v. 4.)

2. According to Paul, there really are many gods. (False, vv. 5, 6.)

3. Some consciences are defiled by eating meat offered to idols. (True, v. 7.)

4. We are better, in God's eyes, for not eating some foods. (False, v. 8.)

5. Our liberty can cause others to stumble into sin. (True, vv. 9, 10.)

1. What did Paul mean when he said an idol is "nothing in the world" (v. 4)?

2. Did Paul really believe that there are many "gods" (vv. 5, 6)?

3. How would eating meat offered to an idol defile another's weak conscience (v. 7)?

4. What does verse 8 mean, "But meat commendeth us not to God"?

5. How can a Christian's liberty become a stumblingblock to a weak brother (vv. 9, 10)?

Into Life

Ask your students to identify some current issues that parallel the problem of eating meat offered to idols. What should be our key principle to settle such issues? Are there limits to how far or how often a believer must surrender his liberty for the sake of the weaker brother? If so, what? Why?

Return to the "Into the Lesson" exercise. In light of Paul's teaching, would your students make any changes or additions to their first efforts?

Let's Talk It Over

The questions on this page are designed to encourage review of the lesson Scriptures and to promote discussion of the lesson by the class. The answers provided are only discussion starters. Let your class talk it over from there.

1. How can we overcome tendencies toward excessive pride regarding our Biblical and religious knowledge?

As 1 Corinthians 8:2 reminds us, we do not know as much as we should know. How can we be proud when we realize that through laziness, indifference, prejudice, and stubbornness we have failed to take advantage of learning opportunities? Reading 1 Corinthians 4:7 should also humble us as we recognize that it is God who has made our present level of knowledge possible. Gratitude, not arrogance, is the proper response. Finally, a reading of 1 Corinthians 4:1, 2 should remind us that we, like Paul and the apostles, are stewards of what God has given us. We should look upon our knowledge as a resource for service rather than seeing it as a reason for pride.

2. Not many people have a problem with meat sacrificed to idols today. Suggest a contemporary issue in which "strong" and "weak" Christians may take differing views. How should the "strong" and the "weak" relate to one another?

Any issue of conscience for which the Bible makes no specific command or prohibition may fall into this category. Attending movies, especially those rated "PG-13" or "R," may be an issue among believers in your church. Other issues may include playing the lottery, smoking, buying products from companies that endorse or sponsor anti-Christian activities, or skipping the midweek church services. As you continue to explore the Scripture text, relate the principles learned to the issues raised in this discussion.

3. The poet R. L. Sharpe has written:

    Each is given a bag of tools,
    A shapeless mass, a book of rules;
    And each must make, ere life is flown,
    A stumbling-block or a stepping stone.

How might keeping this in mind help us as we make decisions about what we do?

Paul's point in today's text is that we must avoid being a stumblingblock to fellow Christians. We will sacrifice enjoyment of what to us is harmless pleasure if it could pose a serious temptation to another Christian. This is the negative side of the issue. To that we must add the positive side of being a "stepping-stone" by which others can gain a richer life of discipleship. Instead of asking, "Will it hurt anyone if I engage in this or that behavior?" we would do better to ask, "What can I do that will help someone?"

4. First Corinthians 8:11 speaks of the danger of causing a weak brother, "for whom Christ died," to perish. How can we cultivate better concern for our Christian brothers and sisters to see that this does not happen? What difference would it make in our lives if we did?

We need to be aware that the eternal destiny of any fellow member in our church could depend on us. Participating in worldly forms of entertainment, carelessly speaking an unkind word, failing to be regular in worship attendance, refusing to serve, or criticizing the church's leaders may be seen or heard by others and cause harm. Some will suggest that they need to be careful another does not see them when they engage in such behavior. How much better to cultivate a lifestyle that need never to ask whether someone is watching! If we always assume some younger or weaker Christian is watching, we will behave in a more loving and Christlike manner.

5. How can we balance our "rights" with our responsibility to serve others? What are some examples of circumstances in which we must achieve such a balance?

At times we must stand up for our rights, for certain unscrupulous people will prey upon us if we do not. We have a right, for example, to expect that someone who damages our house or car will reimburse us for repairs. We have a right to receive adequate payment for work we perform. But we must beware of insisting on our rights even when other people will be hurt, or when we can be of more help to another by yielding.

We also can expect our church to provide us Biblically sound, Christ-exalting teaching and preaching. We have good reason to anticipate support from fellow members when we face a crisis, and we should graciously voice our disappointment if that does not occur. But when matters of personal opinion are at stake, we must be prepared to yield our "rights." We may insist that Christians should not watch certain television programs, subscribe to certain magazines, or patronize restaurants that serve alcohol. But we dare not make these points of conflict and division.

Spiritual Gifts

DEVOTIONAL READING: Romans 12:1-8.

BACKGROUND SCRIPTURE: 1 Corinthians 12: 1-30.

PRINTED TEXT: 1 Corinthians 12:4-20, 24b-26.

1 Corinthians 12:4-20, 24b-26

4 Now there are diversities of gifts, but the same Spirit.

5 And there are differences of administrations, but the same Lord.

6 And there are diversities of operations, but it is the same God which worketh all in all.

7 But the manifestation of the Spirit is given to every man to profit withal.

8 For to one is given by the Spirit the word of wisdom; to another the word of knowledge by the same Spirit;

9 To another faith by the same Spirit; to another the gifts of healing by the same Spirit;

10 To another the working of miracles; to another prophecy; to another discerning of spirits; to another divers kinds of tongues; to another the interpretation of tongues:

11 But all these worketh that one and the selfsame Spirit, dividing to every man severally as he will.

12 For as the body is one, and hath many members and all the members of that one body, being many, are one body: so also is Christ.

13 For by one Spirit are we all baptized into one body, whether we be Jews or Gentiles, whether we be bond or free; and have been all made to drink into one Spirit.

14 For the body is not one member, but many.

15 If the foot shall say, Because I am not the hand, I am not of the body; is it therefore not of the body?

16 And if the ear shall say, Because I am not the eye, I am not of the body; is it therefore not of the body?

17 If the whole body were an eye, where were the hearing? If the whole were hearing, where were the smelling?

18 But now hath God set the members every one of them in the body, as it hath pleased him.

19 And if they were all one member, where were the body?

20 But now are they many members, yet but one body.

· · · · · · · · · · · · ·

24b But God hath tempered the body together, having given more abundant honor to that part which lacked:

25 That there should be no schism in the body; but that the members should have the same care one for another.

26 And whether one member suffer, all the members suffer with it; or one member be honored, all the members rejoice with it.

Apr 16

GOLDEN TEXT: Now there are diversities of gifts, but the same Spirit. . . .
And there are diversities of operations, but it is the same God
which worketh all in all.—1 Corinthians 12:4, 6.

Helping a Church Confront Crisis
Unit 2: Unity in Human Relationships
(Lessons 5-9)

Lesson Aims

After completing this lesson, each student should be able to:

1. Tell how the various spiritual gifts in a church body function together for the health and unity of the body.

2. Tell what Paul says about the variety of gifts and why that variety is so important in the church.

3. Identify at least one spiritual gift he or she possesses and describe how it can be used to edify others in the body.

Lesson Outline

INTRODUCTION
  A. Nailed Together
  B. Lesson Background
 I. DIVERSITY OF GIFTS (1 Corinthians 12:4-11)
  A. Source of Gifts (vv. 4-6)
  B. Variety of Gifts (vv. 7-11)
    For the Good of Everyone
 II. ANALOGY OF THE BODY (1 Corinthians 12:12-20)
  A. One Body, Many Members (v. 12)
  B. Unity by One Spirit (v. 13)
  C. Unity in Diversity (vv. 14-20)
III. GOD'S CONCERN FOR THE BODY (1 Corinthians 12:24b-26)
  A. God Honors All Parts (v. 24b)
  B. So Should His People (vv. 25, 26)
    An Act of Unusual Concern
CONCLUSION
  A. Gifts and Unity
  B. Prayer
  C. Thought to Remember

Introduction

A. Nailed Together

One day the parts of a sailing vessel got into a terrible argument about which was the most important. "I am the most important," said the sail, "for I enable the ship to move."

"But," responded the mast, "without me you would be nothing but a piece of cloth."

Then the deck got into the argument: "Without me there would be no place for the sailors who man the ship to stand."

"Yes," replied the rudder, "but without me no one could steer the ship."

Thus the argument went back and forth. Finally, in the midst of all the debate, a tiny voice was heard: "Without me none of you would be part of a boat at all." Looking around, the various parts discovered that the tiny voice came from the nails that were absolutely necessary to hold the boat together.

Thus it is with the church. Every member of the church is important, but without the power of the Holy Spirit to hold the parts together there could be no church. That is the point Paul makes in today's lesson.

B. Lesson Background

The previous lessons in this quarter have dealt with some of the problems and controversies plaguing the church at Corinth. Today's lesson deals with another controversial matter—the place of spiritual gifts in the church. This issue was not settled once and for all in the first century. In fact, within the past three or four decades it has become a subject of debate in hundreds of congregations and most major denominations.

God has poured out many wonderful gifts upon mankind, including the "unspeakable gift" of His only Son (2 Corinthians 9:15). Today's lesson, however, deals with the special gifts that He granted to His church, which are often called "spiritual gifts" or "charismatic gifts." Several of these gifts are mentioned in the New Testament (Romans 12:6-8; 1 Corinthians 12:4-11, 28-30; Ephesians 4:7-12).

The term *charismatic* is derived from the Greek word *charisma*, meaning "gift." It is noteworthy that this word is used to describe much more than just the gifts mentioned in today's text. Eternal life is called a *charisma* in Romans 6:23. The lifestyle of being single or married is called a *charisma* in 1 Corinthians 7:7.

Spiritual gifts have afforded great blessings to the church. However, they have also been a source of problems, as illustrated by the situation in Corinth. There spiritual gifts became a source of unholy pride on the part of those who possessed them. Some were jealous of the possession of certain gifts, especially the ability to speak in other tongues (1 Corinthians 14:1-25). Thus the gifts had become a divisive force, threatening the unity of the church.

Paul begins 1 Corinthians 12 with these words: "Now concerning spiritual gifts, brethren, I would not have you ignorant." This wording has been seen before (see 7:1; 8:1). It is generally agreed that this refers to another matter raised in the letter from the Corinthians to Paul. One reason this question may have been raised was that certain activities associated with pagan worship resembled some of the spiritual gifts. It is also obvious from Paul's emphasis on *one body* throughout chapter 12 that the exercise of these gifts had become more important than the pursuit of unity in Christ.

I. Diversity of Gifts
(1 Corinthians 12:4-11)
A. Source of Gifts (vv. 4-6)

4. Now there are diversities of gifts, but the same Spirit.

In verses 1-3 of 1 Corinthians 12 Paul reminds his readers that they had come from pagan backgrounds and from the worship of "dumb idols" (v. 2). In the pagan temples and religious services, they had likely witnessed a variety of phenomena that they had believed were evidence of the pagan gods' activities. The point Paul makes is that the real test of any "gift" is whether or not it leads people to acclaim Jesus as Lord.

The members of the Corinthian church had displayed a variety of *gifts.* Since in the pagan world different gods were associated with different gifts, Paul wanted to assure the Corinthians that the *diversities* of gifts within the church all had a common source—*the same Spirit.*

5. And there are differences of administrations, but the same Lord.

While Paul speaks of *differences of administrations,* the intent is the same as "diversities of gifts" in the previous verse. The source of these is described as *the same Lord.*

6. And there are diversities of operations, but it is the same God which worketh all in all.

Another similar phrase, *diversities of operations,* is seen in this verse. All spiritual gifts come from the Godhead, whose triune nature is expressed in verses 4-6 as the Spirit, the Lord (Jesus), and *God.* Such harmony of purpose ought to be demonstrated by God's people.

B. Variety of Gifts (vv. 7-11)

7. But the manifestation of the Spirit is given to every man to profit withal.

The *manifestation of the Spirit* is the gift of God given through the Holy Spirit. Paul affirms here that some such gift *is given to every man.* Every Christian has received one or more spiritual gifts. In the verses that follow Paul specifically mentions some of these, but it does not appear that he intends to make this list exhaustive (other lists include gifts that Paul does not mention here, and he includes some here that are not mentioned elsewhere). The purpose of these gifts must not be overlooked: it is to *profit* Christians—that is, to provide for their mutual encouragement and edification. [See question #1, page 288.]

[See question #1, page 288.]

FOR THE GOOD OF EVERYONE

Can you remember when making a telephone call involved picking up the earpiece, cranking the handle on the box on the wall, and shouting into the mouthpiece so the operator could hear you? Then she would connect you with the person to whom you wished to talk.

Then came dial phones, and soon we had prefixes to the numbers, such as "Gladstone" or "Jackson." Next came all-number dialing, and an ever-increasing number of digits in the phone numbers. Now we have push-button phones and a growing number of area codes; sometimes area codes even overlap within the same area.

This might seem unnecessarily complicated, but those hundreds of millions of phone lines are essential if we are to benefit from the fax machines and computers in our homes and offices, not to mention conduct ordinary conversation. The multiplicity of numbers lets our technology work for the greater good of everyone.

The gifts that the Spirit gives are a lot like those phone numbers. The multiplicity of gifts lets the various members of a congregation work for the "profit" of everyone (1 Corinthians 12:7). Those who fail to discover and use the gift or gifts that the Spirit has given them deprive themselves and their church of numerous blessings. When the church isn't blessed by the use of our gifts, the fault is with *us*—not the Spirit!

—C. R. B.

8. For to one is given by the Spirit the word of wisdom; to another the word of knowledge by the same Spirit.

One of the difficulties we have in understanding spiritual gifts lies in the fact that Paul does not explain what each of these gifts enabled someone to do. In some cases, the best we can do is to use the names themselves and try to determine what the exercise of the gifts may have included.

One may gain certain types of *wisdom* through experience and study. The wisdom Paul lists here as a gift must be something beyond such "ordinary" wisdom. The same is true of *knowledge.* It

---

How to Say It

AGABUS. *Ag*-uh-bus.
CHARISMA (Greek). kah-*riss*-ma.
CHARISMATIC. care-iz-*mat*-ik.
CORINTH. *Kor*-inth.
CORINTHIANS. Kor-*in*-thee-unz.

would seem that both of these had something to do with God's revelation of truth to an individual. This was especially important during the early years of the church, before the written New Testament was completed.

9. To another faith by the same Spirit; to another the gifts of healing by the same Spirit.

The word *faith* carries several different meanings in the New Testament. Here it may describe an extraordinary level of faith, such as the "mountain-moving" faith described in 1 Corinthians 13:2, where faith is listed among several other gifts that clearly are miraculous.

The phrase *gifts of healing* refers to healings that are miraculous, instantaneous, and complete. (The plural *gifts* may be used because of the many kinds of sickness that were healed.) The healings produced by this gift should not be confused with the healings that came in answer to prayer. These latter healings would have differed from miraculous healings primarily in two ways. First, healings that came in answer to prayer did not usually occur instantaneously. Furthermore, all Christians could have prayed for healing, not just a few persons who had the gift of miraculous healing.

10. To another the working of miracles; to another prophecy; to another discerning of spirits; to another divers kinds of tongues; to another the interpretation of tongues.

A more literal translation of *working of miracles* is "workings of powers." This expression would include miracles other than those of healing. Some suggest that it may refer to such acts as raising people from the dead or drinking poison without any ill effects (Mark 16:18).

Literature of the Greco-Roman period contains numerous references to so-called prophecies, often known as oracles. The *prophecy* mentioned here differs from these accounts in that it came from the Holy Spirit, insuring its accuracy. The role of the prophet was not merely to predict the future (recall Agabus's warning to Paul—in Acts 21:10, 11—that if he went to Jerusalem, he would be bound and delivered to the Gentiles), but more importantly to teach spiritual truth. It is this aspect of prophecy that Paul especially commended to the church at Corinth (as in 1 Corinthians 14:1-5). [See question #2, page 288.]

Next, Paul mentions the *discerning of spirits*. It is appropriate that the mention of this gift followed that of prophecy, for it would allow its possessor to distinguish false prophets from true prophets.

On the Day of Pentecost, the apostles began to speak with "other tongues" (Acts 2:4). This was the result of a unique outpouring of the Holy Spirit, and the listeners heard the message in their own languages (Acts 2:8). The *divers kinds of tongues* here refers to languages as well.

The *interpretation of tongues* was the ability to translate instantaneously something spoken in an unfamiliar language—especially if it was spoken as an expression of the gift of tongues. Paul later called tongues a "sign" to unbelievers (1 Corinthians 14:22), and he taught that Christians should not speak in tongues in public worship unless an interpreter was present (1 Corinthians 14:27, 28). These gifts would have been quite useful in a busy commercial city such as Corinth, where people from many nations were found.

It is important to note that all of these miraculous gifts served a vital purpose in the early church. In the case of gifts such as wisdom and knowledge, the purpose was to provide divine guidance until the time when the writings of the New Testament were completed. The working of miracles and the speaking in tongues served to confirm the gospel message when it was first delivered (Mark 16:17-20).

Note that these miraculous gifts (prophecies, tongues, knowledge) are described as those that will "fail," "cease," and "vanish away" when "that which is perfect is come" (1 Corinthians 13:8-10). Some believe that the "perfect" describes the New Testament Scriptures. Once these were completed, there was no need for additional revelation or for the gifts of confirmation to continue; for the record of the confirmation could be found in the Scriptures.

11. But all these worketh that one and the selfsame Spirit, dividing to every man severally as he will.

Paul emphasizes that all gifts come from the *Spirit*. No one has any reason to boast about the gift or gifts that he has received.

II. Analogy of the Body
(1 Corinthians 12:12-20)

A. One Body, Many Members (v. 12)

12. For as the body is one, and hath many members and all the members of that one body, being many, are one body: so also is Christ.

Even though the human *body* has *many members*, it still functions as a unit. *So also is Christ*. In the verses that follow, Paul compares the diversity of gifts in the body of Christ with the various members of the human body that work together to make the body complete.

B. Unity by One Spirit (v. 13)

13. For by one Spirit are we all baptized into one body, whether we be Jews or Gentiles, whether we be bond or free; and have been all made to drink into one Spirit.

Visual for lesson 7

Today's visual illustrates our Golden Text. Discuss how unity is seen in diversity in the church today as well as in the first century.

Through being *baptized,* believers become a part of the *one body* of Christ. The *Spirit* is closely involved in this process. On the Day of Pentecost Peter proclaimed that penitent believers would receive the "gift of the Holy Ghost [Spirit]" when they were baptized (Acts 2:38).

Paul also notes that in the body of Christ, the various categories into which people are often placed lose their significance. *Jews, Gentiles, bond,* and *free* are equal before God because they *have been all made to drink into one Spirit.* This is a figurative way of saying that all have received the Holy Spirit, who, like God the Father, is no respecter of persons (Acts 10:34).

C. Unity in Diversity (vv. 14-20)

14. For the body is not one member, but many.

This verse states what is obvious to anyone who has ever given the matter even a passing thought. It sets the stage for the specific examples that Paul uses in the verses that follow.

15. If the foot shall say, Because I am not the hand, I am not of the body; is it therefore not of the body?

We do not think much about a *foot* unless it is hurt or crippled. Otherwise, our feet do not receive much attention or respect. Paul may have deliberately chosen to use the feet as an example for that very reason. Perhaps they represented some members of the Corinthian church who were snubbed because their spiritual gifts did not seem so important. But that did not provide them an excuse to try to secede from the rest of the *body.* To suggest that something like that could happen to the human body, Paul points out, is absurd. [See question #3, page 288.]

16. And if the ear shall say, Because I am not the eye, I am not of the body; is it therefore not of the body?

After considering two extremities, the feet and the hands, Paul now turns to two sensory organs, the *ear* and the *eye.* While these two organs perform two very different functions, both

are necessary if *the body* is to operate at its greatest efficiency.

17. If the whole body were an eye, where were the hearing? If the whole were hearing, where were the smelling?

No one organ or other member of the body can exist apart from the other members. Each part performs a unique function that is necessary for the well-being of the *whole body.* This fact is perfectly obvious when dealing with the human body, and is just as true of Christ's body.

18. But now hath God set the members every one of them in the body, as it hath pleased him.

While the human body's diversity in function is quite evident to nearly everyone, that same diversity in the church is often not as appreciated as it should be. Paul reminds the fragmented Corinthians that the source of that diversity is *God.*

19, 20. And if they were all one member, where were the body? But now are they many members, yet but one body.

Paul clinches his argument with a rhetorical question. What kind of a *body* would one have if every *member* were exactly like every other member? The church would be totally helpless if every member were exactly alike, coming from the same mold. The immediate application of this principle was to the variety and use of gifts within the Corinthian church, but it is equally applicable to other aspects of church life today. [See question #4, page 288.]

III. God's Concern for the Body (1 Corinthians 12:24b-26)

A. God Honors All Parts (v. 24b)

24b. But God hath tempered the body together, having given more abundant honor to that part which lacked.

Paul now draws a practical application from the statements he had previously made about the body. *Tempered* means mixed or mingled. God has desi_ _d the physical *body* so that every member performs a function that is essential to the well-being of the whole body. Some organs or members of the body that are the smallest or most obscure may actually be among the most important. Thus has God *given more abundant honor* to a *part* that seems to lack it. Every part of the human body should be respected for its contribution to the good of the body. This also holds true for the body of Christ.

B. So Should His People (vv. 25, 26)

25. That there should be no schism in the body; but that the members should have the same care one for another.

Paul insists that there not be any *schism,* or division, within the *body* of Christ. The church at Corinth seems to have been more blessed with spiritual gifts than other congregations in New Testament times, yet it was characterized by a more divisive spirit than that found in other congregations.

Paul's words indicate that this divisiveness stemmed from the Corinthians' lack of *care one for another.* Were Paul to visit many congregations today, he would, unfortunately, find this same condition. If the situation in Corinth mirrors the situation in the church where we serve, then we ought to repent in humility and act to restore the unity that God wants in His church and for which Jesus prayed (John 17:20, 21).

AN ACT OF UNUSUAL CONCERN

Too often the focus of the news media seems to be only on crime, violence, and natural disasters. So it is refreshing when good news is reported, even if it comes as the result of something bad that has happened.

Such was the case a couple of years ago. An eighty-year-old woman carrying a puppy was put off a commercial bus at a deserted Florida truck stop at 3:00 A.M. She did not know that animals were not allowed on the bus. Her plight was made more serious by the fact that her hearing and eyesight were failing and that she used a crutch.

The good news is that a security guard called the area sheriff, who enlisted the help of deputies in five neighboring counties. They gave the woman food and carried her in their patrol cars, one after the other, to her home. The last deputy helped her walk right to her front door.

The fact that this woman was elderly may have helped her obtain some extra care from the deputies, but isn't it refreshing to see the institutions of society working together to accomplish good? However, in society at large—*and* in the church—we should not have to rely on "officials" to do good. The Biblical principle is that we *all* "have the same care one for another" (1 Corinthians 12:25).

Can the world count on us who are Christians to live this way? Is this the way you and I are known for living *our* lives?   —C. R. B.

26. And whether one member suffer, all the members suffer with it; or one member be honored, all the members rejoice with it.

All of us recognize how true this is of our own bodies. If we have a severe headache, the whole body suffers; if we catch a cold, the whole body is uncomfortable. The reverse is just as true. When the members of our body are well, we feel good all over and we are also mentally and emotionally healthy. The application to the church is obvious. (See Paul's admonition in Romans 12:15 to "rejoice with them that do rejoice, and weep with them that weep.") [See question #5, page 288.]

Conclusion

A. Gifts and Unity

Today we have studied Paul's use of the human body to illustrate that unity and diversity can (and must) exist alongside one another in the body of Christ. The world of music provides other helpful examples. Certainly an orchestra includes many different instruments of various shapes and sounds. However, this diversity does not stand in the way of unity. A skilled conductor knows just how to bring harmony out of the diversity, resulting in a pleasant listening experience for an audience.

Let us resolve that our church's diversity in gifts and abilities will be united under the direction of our "Conductor"—Jesus Christ.

B. Prayer

Loving heavenly Father, we pray for forgiveness for the times we have allowed our feelings and opinions to become sources of division within the church. Teach us how to deal with the divisive forces both outside and inside the church that threaten its unity and thus weaken its efforts to reach a dying world. In the name of Him who came to save the world. Amen.

C. Thought to Remember

"That there should be no schism in the body; but that the members should have the same care one for another" (1 Corinthians 12:25).

Home Daily Bible Readings

Monday, Apr. 10—Understand the Source of Spiritual Gifts (1 Corinthians 12:1-6)

Tuesday, Apr. 11—Many Spiritual Gifts, but One Spirit (1 Corinthians 12:7-11)

Wednesday, Apr. 12—One Body, Many Members (1 Corinthians 12:12-19)

Thursday, Apr. 13—We Need One Another (1 Corinthians 12:20-31)

Friday, Apr. 14—Transformed by New Life in Christ (Romans 12:1-8)

Saturday, Apr. 15—Marks of a Faithful Christian (Romans 12:9-15)

Sunday, Apr. 16—Guidance for Living the Christian Life (Romans 12:16-21)

Learning by Doing

This page contains an alternate lesson plan emphasizing learning activities.
Classes desiring such student involvement will find these suggestions helpful.

Learning Goals

After this lesson each student will be able to:

1. Tell how the various spiritual gifts in a church body function together for the health and unity of the body.

2. Tell what Paul says about the variety of gifts and why that variety is so important in the church.

3. Identify at least one spiritual gift he or she possesses and describe how it can be used to edify others in the body.

Into the Lesson

Display three small pieces of wood: one of natural wood, one of plywood, and one of particleboard. Tell the class members to assume that all three pieces are from the same type of tree, such as a pine. Then ask them to rate the three pieces in terms of strength, from weakest to strongest. (Particleboard is weakest because it is simply made of wood particles held together by glue. The board is only as strong as the glue that binds the pieces together. Natural wood is much stronger than particleboard, but it can crack and split along the grain. Plywood is strongest because it is made of thin layers of wood glued and pressed together with the grain of each layer running in a different direction to prevent splitting. Thus, each layer reinforces the others around it, making the whole piece strong.)

Discuss your class's ratings, then explain to them that today's lesson from 1 Corinthians 12 will show how God unites individual Christians with their particular gifts to make a strong church.

Into the Word

Distribute copies of the following exercise. (If your class uses the student books, you can refer the class to them, as this activity is printed there for your convenience.) Ask each student to read 1 Corinthians 12:4-20, 24-26 and then to fill in the blanks for each statement below. (Correct answers and the verses where they are found are supplied in parentheses.)

1. There are diversities of gifts, but the same _____. There are differences of _____, but the same Lord. *(Spirit, administrations, vv. 4, 5)*

2. There are diversities of _____, but the same God. *(operations, v. 6)*

3. The _____ of the Spirit is given to every man. *(manifestation, v. 7)*

4. To one is given by the Spirit the word of _____; to another the word of _____. *(wisdom, knowledge, v. 8)*

5. To another _____ by the same Spirit; to another the gifts of _____ by the same Spirit; to another the working of _____; to another _____; to another _____ of spirits; to another _____ kinds of _____; to another the _____ of tongues. *(faith, healing, miracles, prophecy, discerning, divers, tongues, interpretation, vv. 9, 10)*

6. For by one _____ are we all _____ into one body, whether we be _____ or _____, whether we be bond or _____. *(Spirit, baptized, Jews, Gentiles, free, v. 13)*

7. If the _____ shall say, Because I am not the _____, I am not of the _____; is it therefore not of the body? *(foot, hand, body, v. 15)*

8. And if the _____ shall say, Because I am not the _____, I am not of the _____; is it therefore not of the body? *(ear, eye, body, v. 16)*

9. If the whole body were an eye, where were the _____? If the whole were hearing, where were the _____? *(hearing, smelling, v. 17)*

10. But God hath tempered the body together, having given more abundant _____ to that part which lacked. *(honor, v. 24)*

11. That there should be no _____ in the body; but that the members should have the same _____ one for another. *(schism, care, v. 25)*

12. Whether one member _____, all the members suffer with it; or one member be _____, all the members rejoice with it. *(suffer, honored, v. 26)*

Using the students' answers and the lesson commentary, discuss Paul's teaching on the variety of spiritual gifts in the church.

Into Life

There is a saying, "Our strength is our diversity." Ask the class in what way that slogan is true of the church. Have students give some examples of how diverse gifts strengthen the body of Christ.

Divide the class into pairs. Ask each student to list the spiritual gifts he or she has and to make another list of the gifts of his or her partner. Have the partners compare their lists and to discuss any gifts that appear on both lists but are not currently being used. Have them discuss ways to put those gifts to work for the church's good and to pray together for opportunities to do that.

Let's Talk It Over

The questions on this page are designed to encourage review of the lesson Scriptures and to promote discussion of the lesson by the class. The answers provided are only discussion starters. Let your class talk it over from there.

1. First Corinthians 12:7 tells us that every spiritual gift is given "to profit withal," or "for the common good" (*New International Version*). How does thinking of our gifts or talents as existing "for the common good" help you to appreciate the value of your gifts and the gifts of others?

Every believer should be excited to realize that he or she has something to contribute to the good of the church. We often hear the lament, "I don't feel like a part of the church!" But when we ponder how a certain talent we possess is important to the congregation's evangelistic outreach or worship or teaching programs, we will be assured that we are an important part. Also, thinking of our gifts as existing for the common good is a safeguard against using them selfishly. We can sing for our own pleasure or for the good of others. We can write for our own profit or for the benefit of others. We can lead as a means of bolstering our own pride or to edify others.

2. Compare the role of the "prophet" with that of the "preacher" in today's church. How are they alike? How are they different?

When we think about a prophet's ministry, certain characteristics come to mind. One of these is boldness. Paul was a prophet (Acts 13:1), and he desired to speak the word boldly or fearlessly (Ephesians 6:19, 20). Another prophetic characteristic is plainspokenness. We have seen earlier in 1 Corinthians 2:1 how Paul disclaimed using "excellency of speech or of wisdom." The preacher should possess these characteristics. But the prophet received his message by inspiration. Today's preacher must study the inspired Word of God for his message. In fact, study of the Word must be a priority if his ministry is to have real spiritual power.

3. What are some gifts or ministries that we may be inclined to regard as less important in the church? Why do we do that? How can we correct the situation?

Some may think of janitorial work as far below the tasks of evangelism and teaching. However, a soiled and cluttered church building can be a distraction for those who should be learning from sermons and Bible lessons. Other areas of service in the church that may be seen as less important are those of preparing the Communion emblems, or

secretarial work, or working in the nursery. Usually, it's the gift that is least public or the one we don't have that is seen as "unimportant." This is a worldly trait that we need to get rid of. As Christians we need to practice "preferring one another" over ourselves (Romans 12:10). If we will see ourselves as servants of Christ, then we will seek to please Him instead of comparing ourselves with others.

4. What are some church programs in which the blending of the members' various talents and gifts can be vividly demonstrated?

A choir or ensemble is a vivid illustration. While all the members have a similar gift, there are differences that provide beautiful harmony when they sing together. Vacation Bible School provides another demonstration. Certain individuals must employ their gifts of teaching children. Others are skilled at working with crafts. People with musical skills are required. And the children would count as very important those persons who plan recreational activities and prepare refreshments. We dare not forget those who organize this program and those who work at publicizing it. (Use this discussion to recognize those who help, especially from behind the scenes, in the different programs the class mentions.)

5. As fellow members of Christ's body we are to share each other's sufferings and successes. How can we do this?

Paul expressed our responsibility clearly in Romans 12:15, when he said, "Rejoice with them that do rejoice, and weep with them that weep." We should make it a priority to be present for occasions of rejoicing in the lives of fellow church members. Among these are weddings, graduations, retirement celebrations, and occasions of public recognition. It is also important to be there for our brothers and sisters in Christ in times of suffering. Our visits to hospitals, nursing homes, and funeral homes are much needed. Even when we are unable to be present on these glad or sad occasions, we can still fulfill Paul's exhortation. An appropriate card or gift or telephone call can provide a way of expressing our participation in the rejoicing. When we are unable to be present during a time of suffering, a card or flowers can serve as our message.

Christ's Resurrection and Ours

DEVOTIONAL READING: 1 Corinthians 15:12-19, 50-58.

BACKGROUND SCRIPTURE: 1 Corinthians 15.

PRINTED TEXT: 1 Corinthians 15:20-27, 35-44.

1 Corinthians 15:20-27, 35-44

20 But now is Christ risen from the dead, and become the firstfruits of them that slept.

21 For since by man came death, by man came also the resurrection of the dead.

22 For as in Adam all die, even so in Christ shall all be made alive.

23 But every man in his own order: Christ the firstfruits; afterward they that are Christ's at his coming.

24 Then cometh the end, when he shall have delivered up the kingdom to God, even the Father; when he shall have put down all rule, and all authority and power.

25 For he must reign, till he hath put all enemies under his feet.

26 The last enemy that shall be destroyed is death.

27 For he hath put all things under his feet. But when he saith, All things are put under him, it is manifest that he is excepted, which did put all things under him.

. . . .

35 But some man will say, How are the dead raised up? and with what body do they come?

36 Thou fool, that which thou sowest is not quickened, except it die:

37 And that which thou sowest, thou sowest not that body that shall be, but bare grain, it may chance of wheat, or of some other grain:

38 But God giveth it a body as it hath pleased him, and to every seed his own body.

39 All flesh is not the same flesh: but there is one kind of flesh of men, another flesh of beasts, another of fishes, and another of birds.

40 There are also celestial bodies, and bodies terrestrial: but the glory of the celestial is one, and the glory of the terrestrial is another.

41 There is one glory of the sun, and another glory of the moon, and another glory of the stars; for one star differeth from another star in glory.

42 So also is the resurrection of the dead. It is sown in corruption, it is raised in incorruption:

43 It is sown in dishonor, it is raised in glory: it is sown in weakness, it is raised in power:

44 It is sown a natural body, it is raised a spiritual body. There is a natural body, and there is a spiritual body.

Apr 23

GOLDEN TEXT: But now is Christ risen from the dead, and become the firstfruits of them that slept. . . . For as in Adam all die, even so in Christ shall all be made alive.
—1 Corinthians 15:20, 22.

Helping a Church Confront Crisis
Unit 2: Unity in Human Relationships
(Lessons 5-9)

Lesson Aims

After completing this lesson, each student should be able to:

1. Tell what Paul says about the certainty of Christ's resurrection and His role as the "firstfruits," guaranteeing believers' resurrection.

2. Contrast the Christian perspective on the future with that of the unbeliever.

3. Give thanks to God that the resurrection of Christ remains the sure foundation of Christian faith and hope.

Lesson Outline

INTRODUCTION
  A. Recycled Rags
  B. Lesson Background
I. CHRIST'S RESURRECTION (1 Corinthians 15:20-23)
  A. Its Certainty (v. 20)
  B. Adam and Christ Contrasted (vv. 21-23)
    Renewed, Not Reburied
II. CHRIST'S ULTIMATE VICTORY (1 Corinthians 15:24-27)
  A. Authority Asserted (v. 24)
  B. All Enemies Conquered (vv. 25-27)
III. OUR RESURRECTION (1 Corinthians 15:35-44)
  A. Key Questions (v. 35)
  B. Earthly Bodies (vv. 36-39)
  C. Heavenly Bodies (vv. 40, 41)
  D. Our Resurrected Bodies (vv. 42-44)
CONCLUSION
  A. Skeptics of the Resurrection
  B. What Kind of Body?
  C. Prayer
  D. Thought to Remember

Introduction

A. Recycled Rags

In the process of producing textiles, there are always scraps of material that cannot be used. These are sometimes sent to a paper mill. From other sources, old and worn-out clothes are gathered and sent to the same mill. All of these are then processed and added to wood pulp. The end product is a beautiful, high-grade bond paper on which especially important documents are printed.

If a paper maker can take useless scraps and ragged old clothes and make a valuable product from them, why should we doubt that God, the "people maker," can take our feeble, worn-out bodies and make glorious new bodies from them?

B. Lesson Background

In today's lesson Paul deals with yet another problem that was troubling the Corinthian church. Some in the church were denying the resurrection of the dead (1 Corinthians 15:12). Students of the Bible disagree as to the exact details of this false belief, but Paul leaves no doubt about its consequences if it is carried out to its logical conclusion. "If there be no resurrection of the dead, then is Christ not risen" (v. 13). This in turn meant that the Corinthians' (and all Christians') faith was in vain and that they were still in their sins.

The disheartening conclusion of Paul's argument is stated in verse 19: "If in this life only we have hope in Christ, we are of all men most miserable." Our printed text begins with the next verse, where Paul begins to examine some of the key issues surrounding the resurrection.

I. Christ's Resurrection
(1 Corinthians 15:20-23)
A. Its Certainty (v. 20)

20. But now is Christ risen from the dead, and become the firstfruits of them that slept.

Paul's intent in the previous verses (vv. 12-19) was to demonstrate how illogical was the position of those who denied the resurrection. But it was more than just illogical; it was tragic, for it left them "of all men most miserable" or "most pitiable" (*American Standard Version*).

Bible students have debated the origin of this skepticism toward the resurrection. Some believe that it may have stemmed from certain Greek philosophers who believed that the soul was immortal but that the body was not resurrected. Others see its source in an early form of the philosophy that later came to be known as Gnosticism, which insisted that the material world was evil.

In the face of this doubt, Paul thundered forth an absolute certainty: *now is Christ risen from the dead*. The resurrection of Christ marks the *firstfruits* of those who have died. This term had rich overtones for those who understood the Old Testament. In dedicating the firstfruits of a crop, a farmer was demonstrating his assurance that God would provide the entire harvest. The portion offered was a pledge, signifying that the rest of the harvest would one day be gathered. Thus

Christ's resurrection stands as the assurance that all others who have died will also be raised. Since this is true, it was appropriate for Paul to speak of them as *them that slept.* Death is not final; we shall "awaken" from it. [See question #1, page 296.]

B. Adam and Christ Contrasted (vv. 21-23)

21, 22. For since by man came death, by man came also the resurrection of the dead. For as in Adam all die, even so in Christ shall all be made alive.

Because of the sin of *Adam, death* came as a punishment, not to Adam alone but to the entire human race. As a result, man's eternal status remained hopeless until *Christ* came. His *resurrection* has given new hope to humanity. In Him *shall all be made alive.* All who have died will be raised when He returns, as the next verse states. This does not mean that all will be saved. Assuredly all will be raised, but some to eternal life and some to eternal punishment (John 5:28, 29; Acts 24:15).

23. But every man in his own order: Christ the firstfruits; afterward they that are Christ's at his coming.

The Greek word translated *order* was a military term that described an army unit properly organized to move in a strategic manner. Thus, declared Paul, the resurrection will proceed according to a plan—obviously a divine plan. Christ will be the head of the procession, for He has already risen; then *they that are Christ's at his coming* will follow. First Thessalonians 4:13-18 tells us that at Jesus' return "the dead in Christ shall rise first," then those who "are alive and remain shall be caught up . . . to meet the Lord in the air."

RENEWED, NOT REBURIED

Czar Nicholas II went into exile in 1917 as the Russian Revolution was beginning. He and his family were assassinated by a Bolshevik firing squad the following year. Their bodies were burned in a pit and then buried.

More than sixty years later the bones were discovered. After several more years went by, and following the collapse of the Communist empire, the royal remains were transferred to a morgue. Finally, on July 17, 1998, eighty years to the day after their murders, the members of the royal family were given a belated Russian state funeral and reburied in a ceremony of "repentance and atonement," as one report of the event described it.

Such an act reminds us of man's limitations concerning death. People can conduct a reburial, even adding touches of dignity and decor, but they cannot bring about a resurrection.

Because of Jesus' resurrection, however, man's limitations are overshadowed by God's power. When the dead in Christ are raised at His return, not only will our decayed physical bodies be changed into a new and glorious form, they shall be inhabited again by our spirits, never to die again. That is far better than any state funeral, no matter how belated or how richly deserved.

—C. R. B.

II. Christ's Ultimate Victory (1 Corinthians 15:24-27)

A. Authority Asserted (v. 24)

24. Then cometh the end, when he shall have delivered up the kingdom to God, even the Father; when he shall have put down all rule, and all authority and power.

The end refers to the end of this present age. While men have attempted to discern when this will occur, we really know for certain only this: Jesus will return! The book of Revelation speaks of the occasion in these words: "The kingdoms of this world are become the kingdoms of our Lord, and of his Christ: and he shall reign for ever and ever" (Revelation 11:15).

Obviously that time has not yet come. While, in a sense, Christ does rule even now, the kingdoms of this world are anything but in subjection to Him. In fact, many of the kingdoms of our day stand in defiant rejection of His authority.

When Jesus returns, He will *put down all rule, and all authority and power.* He will not wait until we have everything in order before He comes to take complete charge. He will come at the time so designated by His Father, and He will come with full and absolute authority. As Paul tells us in Philippians 2:10 and 11, every knee will then bow at the name of Jesus and every tongue will confess Him as Lord. It is urgent, therefore that we so live that we will be ready whenever that triumphant day arrives. [See question #2, page 296.]

The glorious resurrection of Christ is the theme of today's visual. You may want to display it on other occasions besides today's class session.

Visual for lesson 8

B. All Enemies Conquered (vv. 25-27)

25. For he must reign, till he hath put all enemies under his feet.

Paul told the Ephesian church that God has set Jesus "at his own right hand . . . far above all principality, and power, and might, and dominion, and every name that is named." From this lofty throne He reigns "not only in this world, but also in that which is to come." God "hath put all things under his feet, and gave him to be the head over all things to the church" (Ephesians 1:20-22).

This passage in Ephesians helps us to understand what Paul means here. Jesus will continue to *reign* as Head of the church until "the end" (verse 24), when He will have *put all enemies under his feet*—an expression that conveys the idea of total victory over an enemy and the enemy's complete subjection. This language has its roots in the Old Testament, specifically the Messianic prophecy of Psalm 110:1: "The Lord said unto my Lord, Sit thou at my right hand, until I make thine enemies thy footstool." [See question #3, page 296.]

26. The last enemy that shall be destroyed is death.

Death is the ultimate *enemy* of the human race. Every person born into this world must, unless the Lord returns first, exit through the gate of death. The Bible records the resurrection of several persons, but each of these persons eventually had to drink the cup of mortality. Medical science has made many advances in the past generation and has extended the life expectancy of human beings. All that these breakthroughs have done, however, is to postpone the inevitable.

With the coming of Christ, man's outlook on death changed dramatically. That death has already been dealt a fatal blow because of Jesus is clear from Hebrews 2:14, 15: "that through death he might destroy him that had the power of death, that is, the devil; and deliver them, who through fear of death were all their lifetime subject to bondage." Thus those who are born into the new life in Christ have already begun to experience some of the blessings that come by knowing that death is no longer able to cast a dark shadow over their lives. Jesus has given us the promise that those who believe on God and who know God have eternal life already (John 5:24; 17:3). When Jesus returns and has finally put all of His other enemies under His feet, then death itself will be *destroyed*—for eternity (Revelation 20:14). [See question #4, page 296.]

27. For he hath put all things under his feet. But when he saith, All things are put under him, it is manifest that he is excepted, which did put all things under him.

Here Paul adds a further comment on his previous statements. That *all things* are *under* Jesus' *feet* does not literally mean *all things*. The exception is God, the One *which did put all things under* Jesus. Though Christ will eventually subject all things to His authority, He Himself will still be subordinate to the Father. Verse 28 completes Paul's thought in regard to this matter. When Christ returns and has put all other things in subjection to Himself, then He in turn will "be subject" to God.

III. Our Resurrection
(1 Corinthians 15:35-44)

A. Key Questions (v. 35)

35. But some man will say, How are the dead raised up? and with what body do they come?

In the first part of today's printed text, Paul has firmly established the fact of the resurrection; but he realizes that this has not completely satisfied the skeptics. Two of their questions are stated in this verse. The first is, *How are the dead raised up?* Paul does not specifically address this question, for God has not revealed to any of us the process of how He will accomplish this. However, he does respond to the second question (*with what body do they come?*) by drawing on illustrations from nature.

B. Earthly Bodies (vv. 36-39)

36. Thou fool, that which thou sowest is not quickened, except it die.

Paul used rather strong language (*fool*) to express his criticism of someone who raised questions about the resurrection. He certainly would have been more gentle toward one whom he considered an honest seeker after truth. Apparently Paul knew his readers better than we do and addressed his reply to those who stubbornly persisted in their doubts. Perhaps he had in mind the kind of person described in Psalm 14:1: "The fool hath said in his heart, There is no God."

Paul then proceeded to discuss the nature of the resurrection. In this verse he emphasized the fact that death must precede a resurrection. That is quite obvious with the sowing of seeds. The original seed is decomposed and is absorbed into the new life that later emerges from the ground.

37. And that which thou sowest, thou sowest not that body that shall be, but bare grain, it may chance of wheat, or of some other grain.

When wheat or some other *grain* is planted, it sprouts and grows. The green plant does not at all resemble the brown grain of wheat. What is sown is not what *shall be*. It was planted as one kind of a *body* and is raised a different kind of a body.

Undoubtedly the Corinthians had witnessed this process many times and had accepted it as part of life. Paul's implied question was, "Why, then, do you have trouble accepting the resurrection of the human body in a new and different form?"

38. But God giveth it a body as it hath pleased him, and to every seed his own body.

Seeds come in all kinds of sizes and shapes, from a tiny mustard seed to a coconut. The plants they produce vary just as widely. All of these differences are planned by God in His infinite wisdom. Grain is planted as one kind of body, and it is raised a different kind of body. If God can accomplish this in the physical realm, why should He not be able to do the same in the spiritual realm?

39. All flesh is not the same flesh: but there is one kind of flesh of men, another flesh of beasts, another of fishes, and another of birds.

To reinforce his point, Paul then turned to the animal kingdom. *All flesh is not the same flesh.* This is obvious to anyone who is at all observant of nature. *Men, beasts, fishes,* and *birds* all have different types of flesh and different bodies. If God could make such a variety of physical bodies to populate His earth, why should the Corinthians have any problem believing that He could also create the spiritual body to be different from the physical body?

C. Heavenly Bodies (vv. 40, 41)

40. There are also celestial bodies, and bodies terrestrial: but the glory of the celestial is one, and the glory of the terrestrial is another.

Paul then drew an illustration from some of the inanimate objects of creation. In this verse he contrasts *celestial* (heavenly) *bodies* (sun, moon, and stars, note v. 41) with *bodies terrestrial* (meaning "of the earth"). We do not know exactly what earthly bodies Paul had in mind (some believe the great mountains, canyons, and seas), but that information is not essential to understanding the point he is making. Each of the bodies has a different *glory*, or splendor. The heavenly bodies are entirely different in their composition from the earthly bodies. God is able to take similar physical material and design it to accomplish His purposes, whether in the heavens or on the earth.

41. There is one glory of the sun, and another glory of the moon, and another glory of the stars; for one star differeth from another star in glory.

In the previous verse, Paul had highlighted the distinction between two very different categories of objects—earthly bodies and heavenly bodies. Now, in this verse, he focused on the differences between the bodies in the celestial class. Every-

---

How to Say It

BOLSHEVIK. *Bowl*-sheh-vick.
CORINTH. *Kor*-inth.
CORINTHIANS. Kor-*in*-thee-unz.
EPHESIAN. Ee-*fee*-zhun.
GNOSTICISM. *Nahss*-tih-sizz-um.
MESSIANIC. Mess-ee-*an*-ick.

---

one would readily acknowledge the difference between the *glory of the sun* and the *glory of the moon.* Even if one did not understand that the brightness of the sun is caused by a vast and continuous nuclear reaction while the moon simply reflects the light of the sun, the difference in their brightness would still be obvious. No one has to be an astronomer to understand the point Paul is making here.

D. Our Resurrected Bodies (vv. 42-44)

42. So also is the resurrection of the dead. It is sown in corruption, it is raised in incorruption.

Paul now applied the comparisons he had made to the issue at hand—*the resurrection of the dead. It* (referring to the physical body) *is sown in corruption.* Just as the seed must decay when it is planted, so the physical body, composed of mortal flesh, must also decompose when it is *sown* (planted or buried) at death.

But that is not the end of the story. Just as the decaying seed is transformed into new life as a plant springs forth, the body *is raised in incorruption.* The new body sheds its mortality and takes on immortality, no longer subject to the limitations of the flesh.

43. It is sown in dishonor, it is raised in glory: it is sown in weakness, it is raised in power.

Paul continued a series of contrasts in order to drive home his point. The body *is sown in dishonor.* No matter how great a person may be in the eyes of the world, he or she must face death. But, praise God, because of Jesus' resurrection that dishonor is replaced by *glory* and that mortal *weakness* is exchanged for eternal *power.*

44. It is sown a natural body, it is raised a spiritual body. There is a natural body, and there is a spiritual body.

Just as there are many differences between one form of animal and another, Paul says, so there is a difference between one form of human *body* (the *natural*) and the other (*spiritual*). And just as there are differences between one celestial body and another, so there are differences between these two forms of human body. But there is a body in that spiritual realm—*there is a spiritual body.*

Some of the Corinthians may have believed that the physical or *natural body* was weak, even evil, and that the ideal situation was attained when one could free himself from it and become a disembodied spirit. Paul completely rejected this notion. A Christian will be *raised a spiritual body.* We cannot begin to understand what this resurrected body will be like, but we can be absolutely sure of this: it will be different from (and far superior to) the natural body with all of its limitations and frailties. [See question #5, page 296.]

Conclusion

A. Skeptics of the Resurrection

The doctrine of the resurrection is at the very heart of the gospel. Without it there really is no gospel—no good news. Today those who believe in the resurrection are under attack from at least two directions. Leading one attack are the materialists, who believe that the only real world is the physical world. In their view, anything that cannot be seen, touched, or weighed simply does not exist. They reject the account of Jesus' resurrection and the belief in a resurrected life after this life as myths that educated people no longer believe. Unfortunately, some who claim to be Christians (even some who hold prominent positions within the church) have accepted this materialistic view of Christianity. Such a view makes observing Easter (or going to church at all, for that matter) an empty charade.

A second challenge to the Christian view of the resurrection comes from strange religious beliefs that have recently become prominent in the Western world. Some of these, such as Hinduism and Buddhism, are ancient religions imported from the East. Reports indicate that both of these religions are gaining followers because they claim to fill a spiritual need that many feel. What an indictment against Christians! Why have we not found ways to fill this void with the truth of the gospel?

Christians are also challenged by many new cults, often built around a person with unusual personal charisma. Claiming special knowledge or some unique revelation about topics such as life after death, these cults have been able to lead many astray.

Just as Paul countered the doubts toward and rejections of the resurrection with a vigorous affirmation of this doctrine, so must we today. Jesus' resurrection allows us to say, with enthusiasm, "Thanks be to God, which giveth us the victory through our Lord Jesus Christ" (1 Corinthians 15:57).

B. What Kind of Body?

When we come to believe in the resurrection, we are tempted to speculate about what kind of a body we will have in the world to come. Today's lesson affirms certain important facts about the resurrection, but it leaves many questions unanswered. What will we look like in the future life? Will we be able to recognize one another? Will there be work for us to do in the next world?

On one occasion Paul was "caught up to the third heaven." There he heard words "not lawful for a man to utter" (2 Corinthians 12:2-4), meaning, presumably, that he could not find words to describe what he witnessed during that experience. We would be wise to follow Paul's example here and avoid undue speculation about all that the resurrected life will involve. The Scripture in today's lesson indicates that the next world will be different from this world. Other passages of Scripture (for example, Revelation 21 and 22) indicate that it will be far better than anything we can imagine. This ought to provide us with the confidence that we need to face each day joyfully and triumphantly!

C. Prayer

Troubled as we are by so many things in the world about us, dear Father, we offer up thanks to You for the assurance that beyond the resurrection there awaits a glorious life for all those who accept Your Son as Lord and Savior. In His name we offer this prayer. Amen.

D. Thought to Remember

"Now is Christ risen from the dead" (1 Corinthians 15:20).

Home Daily Bible Readings

Monday, Apr. 17—The Resurrection of Christ the Lord (1 Corinthians 15:1-11)

Tuesday, Apr. 18—How Can You Deny the Resurrection? (1 Corinthians 15:12-19)

Wednesday, Apr. 19— The Resurrected Christ Destroys Death (1 Corinthians 15:20-28)

Thursday, Apr. 20—The Dead Are Raised: Believe It! (1 Corinthians 15:29-34)

Friday, Apr. 21—How Are the Dead Raised? (1 Corinthians 15:35-41)

Saturday, Apr. 22—Raised a Spiritual Body (1 Corinthians 15:42-49)

Sunday, Apr. 23—We Have Victory Through Jesus Christ! (1 Corinthians 15:50-58)

Learning by Doing

This page contains an alternate lesson plan emphasizing learning activities.
Classes desiring such student involvement will find these suggestions helpful.

Learning Goals

After this lesson each of your students should be able to:

1. Tell what Paul says about the certainty of Christ's resurrection and His role as the "first-fruits," guaranteeing believers' resurrection.

2. Contrast the Christian perspective on the future with that of the unbeliever.

3. Give thanks to God that the resurrection of Christ remains the sure foundation of Christian faith and hope.

Into the Lesson

Distribute copies of Henry Wadsworth Longfellow's "A Psalm of Life" (or refer your students to the poem in their student books).

Life is real! Life is earnest!
 And the grave is not its goal;
Dust thou art, to dust returnest
 Was not spoken of the soul.

Ask your students whether they agree or disagree with Longfellow. Have each one write his or her evaluation of the verse. Then have several volunteers share their evaluations and briefly discuss their views. Tell your students that in the first century, as today, many people rejected the possibility of life after death (see Acts 17:32). Today's lesson deals with Paul's arguments against such skepticism.

Into the Word

Divide your class into pairs and give each pair a copy of the following arguments against the possibility of our resurrection. (They are printed in the student books.) Using today's text, 1 Corinthians 15:20-27, 35-44, each pair of students should write a brief response to each argument. Verses relevant to each argument are indicated in parentheses.

1. Even if Jesus rose from the dead, there is no guarantee that we will. (vv. 20-23)

2. If Jesus were going to return, He would have done so already, so we have no hope of a future resurrection. (vv. 24-27)

3. Resurrection is impossible because there is nothing left to raise; the body is decayed, gone. (vv. 35-39)

4. Even if God did raise our bodies from the dead, we would simply grow old and die again. (vv. 40-44)

After your students finish their responses, ask several to share their work, one argument at a time. Using your lesson commentary and the questions below, discuss the meaning of each section of the text.

Verses 20-23

1. What are "firstfruits"? (See Leviticus 23:9-14.) How is Jesus, by virtue of His resurrection, the firstfruits of our resurrection?

2. What contrast does Paul make between Adam and Christ?

3. How was Jesus' resurrection different from those before His, such as that of Lazarus?

4. What order of resurrection is indicated in this section? Compare verse 23 with Daniel 12:2 and 1 Thessalonians 4:16.

Verses 24-27

1. How long must Christ reign before the end of the world?

2. What must happen before Christ can deliver up the kingdom to God? What does it mean to "put all enemies under his feet"? Who is exempted from that subjection?

3. How is death an enemy? See Hebrews 2:14, 15. How will it be destroyed?

Verses 35-39

1. How is the resurrection likened to a seed that has been planted?

2. Why must something die to come to life (be "quickened")?

3. How, from his reference to beasts, fish, and birds, does Paul demonstrate that the resurrected body is different from the natural body?

Verses 40-44

1. How is Paul's argument in verses 40, 41 parallel to the one in verse 39?

2. What argument does Paul offer to prove that resurrected people will not die again?

3. In what sense is the natural body sown in dishonor and weakness? What gives the resurrected body its glory and power?

Into Life

Return to the discussion of Longfellow's poem from the opening activity. How accurately did the poet capture Paul's teaching in today's text? Distribute paper and pencils as needed, and ask your students to write their own poems, based on 1 Corinthians 15, praising God for the promise of the resurrection. To conclude the lesson, ask for volunteers to share their poetry.

Let's Talk It Over

The questions on this page are designed to encourage review of the lesson Scriptures and to promote discussion of the lesson by the class. The answers provided are only discussion starters. Let your class talk it over from there.

1. Skeptics deny that Jesus actually rose from the dead. How would you answer if an unbeliever challenged your faith in His resurrection?

The good news of Jesus Christ's resurrection comes to us primarily through the New Testament. It is well to keep in mind that while the New Testament is one book, it is also a collection of twenty-seven books. Each of these separate books bears its own witness to the resurrection. The four Gospels are four unique works by four very distinct authors. The book of Acts is a careful work of history that frequently makes reference to the resurrection. In the letters of Paul (see Romans 4:24, 25), Peter (see 1 Peter 1:3), and other writers the resurrection is often presented as a historical reality. The multiple witnesses and the absence of any other plausible explanation for the empty tomb make the case for Jesus' resurrection compelling.

2. What excites you about the idea that Jesus will at last reign? Why? Do you feel any other emotions about it? If so, what? Why?

It is wearisome now to endure the rejection and ridicule that unbelievers direct toward Jesus and His followers. It is painful to see how they twist His teachings and scoff at His miracles. We are distressed when we hear people profaning the name of Jesus Christ with thoughtless angry curses. In view of all this, how we anticipate the time when "every tongue [shall] confess that Jesus Christ is Lord, to the glory of God the Father" (Philippians 2:11).

Perhaps there are some who fear that time. Do they need to get serious about following Christ? Perhaps they have unsaved loved ones. If so, the need to share their faith has never been more urgent!

3. Not only do we anticipate Christ's future reign, but Paul tells us that we can enjoy Christ's present reign as Head of the church. What excites you about the idea that Jesus is even now reigning? Why?

When problems arise in the church, it is easy to become discouraged. Some churches go through periods of weak leadership, and people may become disgruntled or even divisive as a result. But the human leaders are not the head of the church. Jesus still reigns, and "must reign" until the end. We can take heart that no matter what problems we face in the church, Jesus has the answer. He can lead us out of the difficulty and into fruitful service if we will continually seek His will. Even if our local church does not survive some terrible difficulty (and many churches are forced to close every year), Jesus is still Lord and can put us into a body of believers where we can continue to serve Him faithfully.

4. Many unbelievers declare, "When you're dead, you're dead!" Others hold to a vague kind of hope regarding life after death. How do we respond to them?

Those who confidently assert that there is no life after death have no evidence to back up that assertion. Those who believe in a life after death without reference to the gospel do so on the basis of mere hunches and hopes. We have solid truth to back up our claim. If someone says, "No one has come back from the grave to assure us of life after death," we can answer, "You are mistaken! Jesus Christ has come back and given us clear evidence." Paul wrote in 2 Timothy 1:10 that "Jesus Christ . . . hath abolished death, and hath brought life and immortality to light through the gospel." We Christians possess the brilliant light of truth regarding this crucial topic. We should not hesitate to declare our confidence in victory over death and the grave through Jesus Christ.

5. Even Christians have many questions about the exact nature of the life we will live in our new body. How would you answer a new Christian who says he just can't figure out what life after death will be like?

We recognize that human beings are limited in their capacity for certain kinds of knowledge. Small children are not ready to learn to drive an automobile or program a computer. When it comes to truths regarding life after the resurrection, we are all limited. God has revealed to us what we need to know and what we are capable of understanding. We know that we will dwell in the presence of God and the Lamb, Jesus Christ, and that we will serve the Lord (Revelation 21:3, 4). We are aware that all forms of sin will be banished (Revelation 21:8, 27; 22:15). Our other questions will be answered when we enter that life and are capable of a higher level of understanding.

Love's Better Way

DEVOTIONAL READING: 1 John 4:7-21.

BACKGROUND SCRIPTURE: 1 Corinthians 12:31—13:13.

PRINTED TEXT: 1 Corinthians 12:31—13:13.

1 Corinthians 12:31

31 But covet earnestly the best gifts. And yet show I unto you a more excellent way.

1 Corinthians 13:1-13

1 Though I speak with the tongues of men and of angels, and have not charity, I am become as sounding brass, or a tinkling cymbal.

2 And though I have the gift of prophecy, and understand all mysteries, and all knowledge; and though I have all faith, so that I could remove mountains, and have not charity, I am nothing.

3 And though I bestow all my goods to feed the poor, and though I give my body to be burned, and have not charity, it profiteth me nothing.

4 Charity suffereth long, and is kind; charity envieth not; charity vaunteth not itself, is not puffed up,

5 Doth not behave itself unseemly, seeketh not her own, is not easily provoked, thinketh no evil;

6 Rejoiceth not in iniquity, but rejoiceth in the truth;

7 Beareth all things, believeth all things, hopeth all things, endureth all things.

8 Charity never faileth: but whether there be prophecies, they shall fail; whether there be tongues, they shall cease; whether there be knowledge, it shall vanish away.

9 For we know in part, and we prophesy in part.

10 But when that which is perfect is come, then that which is in part shall be done away.

11 When I was a child, I spake as a child, I understood as a child, I thought as a child: but when I became a man, I put away childish things.

12 For now we see through a glass, darkly, but then face to face: now I know in part; but then shall I know even as also I am known.

13 And now abideth faith, hope, charity, these three; but the greatest of these is charity.

GOLDEN TEXT: And now abideth faith, hope, charity, these three;
but the greatest of these is charity. —1 Corinthians 13:13.

Helping a Church Confront Crisis
Unit 2: Unity in Human Relationships
(Lessons 5-9)

Lesson Aims

After this lesson each student will be able to:

1. Summarize what Paul says about love and what makes it the "more excellent way."

2. Suggest some actions love might prompt a person to take.

3. Commit himself or herself to act with genuine love toward a specific person.

Lesson Outline

INTRODUCTION
    A. Love "Seeketh Not Her Own"
    B. Lesson Background
  I. PRIORITY OF LOVE (1 Corinthians 12:31—13:3)
    A. Eloquence Without Love (12:31—13:1)
    B. Gifts Without Love (v. 2)
    C. Giving Without Love (v. 3)
      Mixed Message
 II. PRACTICE OF LOVE (1 Corinthians 13:4-7)
    A. Love Is Humble (v. 4)
    B. Love Is Unselfish (v. 5)
    C. Love Rejoices in the Truth (v. 6)
    D. Love Is Patient (v. 7)
III. PERMANENCE OF LOVE (1 Corinthians 13:8-13)
    A. Gifts Will Cease (v. 8)
    B. The Partial and the Perfect (vv. 9-12)
    C. "The Greatest of These" (v. 13)
      Symbol of Lasting Love
CONCLUSION
    A. Love Acts
    B. Prayer
    C. Thought to Remember

Introduction

A. Love "Seeketh Not Her Own"

Early in the nineteenth century a missionary worked alone among the slaves in the British West Indies. The planters sneered at him or ignored him, but the slaves came to love him. Eventually the missionary, exhausted by his hard labors, fell dangerously ill. With no one to attend him, it seemed certain that he would never recover. Then one day one of the slaves who had become a faithful Christian through the missionary's efforts appeared at the door with the simple announcement: "I am yours now. Just tell me what to do."

Inquiry disclosed that the slave converts had become worried about the missionary's health, but were not certain what they could do to help. Finally they arrived at a solution. By combining their meager savings, earned through years of extra work, they were able to purchase one of their own number from his master and present him to the missionary. In so doing each had postponed indefinitely his or her individual hope of freedom in order to comfort the one who had taught them the meaning of brotherly love.

B. Lesson Background

In the lesson two weeks ago we saw that a problem had developed within the Corinthian church regarding spiritual gifts. The church was blessed with a variety of spiritual gifts, but pride and selfishness had led some of the members to abuse these gifts so that they had become a source of division rather than the harmony that God intended.

Today's lesson text is actually a continuation of the theme Paul began in 1 Corinthians 12. At the conclusion of that chapter, Paul pointed the Corinthians to "a more excellent way"—the way of *agape* love. The chapter that follows is one of the most cherished portions of Scripture in the entire Bible. In it Paul gives us a description of what Christian love is and challenges us to live by its standards.

I. Priority of Love
(1 Corinthians 12:31—13:3)

A. Eloquence Without Love (12:31—13:1)

31. But covet earnestly the best gifts. And yet show I unto you a more excellent way.

But covet earnestly the best gifts. In the previous verses of chapter 12, Paul had discussed the use of spiritual gifts in the Corinthian church. The word *covet* does not necessarily have a negative connotation (as in the tenth Commandment); here it simply means "desire" earnestly. As Paul's statement reads, it is a command; however, the Greek construction of this statement can also be understood as a description of what the people were actually doing ("you are earnestly desiring").

The best gifts were those gifts that the Corinthians had thought most important—perhaps the gifts that Paul cited in 1 Corinthians 13:1 and 2. There Paul wanted to emphasize the supremacy of love over the gifts: love is the *more excellent way.* Love is not a spiritual gift; it is a fruit of the Spirit (Galatians 5:22) that must govern how gifts are used. If the Corinthians are to *covet,* or desire, anything, it should be to love one another. This leads to Paul's timeless description of love. [See question #1, page 304.]

1. Though I speak with the tongues of men and of angels, and have not charity, I am become as sounding brass, or a tinkling cymbal.

Since Paul uses the personal pronoun in verses 1-3, some commentators think that these verses are autobiographical, with Paul describing some of his own gifts. However, it seems more likely that he was presenting hypothetical situations and making himself the subject of them out of consideration for the feelings of the Corinthians.

Since the gift of *tongues* was particularly controversial in Corinth, it was appropriate for Paul to mention it here in order to draw attention to the importance of love. *Charity* is an old English translation of the Greek word *agape*, which is usually translated "love." The phrase *sounding brass, or a tinkling cymbal* suggests discordant notes that are little more than noise. That, says Paul, is what speaking in tongues amounts to unless it is done with a discerning love for the members of the congregation.

B. Gifts Without Love (v. 2)

2. And though I have the gift of prophecy, and understand all mysteries, and all knowledge; and though I have all faith, so that I could remove mountains, and have not charity, I am nothing.

Paul now calls attention to three of the spiritual gifts that he had mentioned in the previous chapter. While he esteemed the gift of prophecy quite highly (as 1 Corinthians 14:1 indicates), if it was practiced without love it was *nothing*. The gift of *knowledge* apparently gave one the power to understand some of the *mysteries* of God's dealings with man—an understanding that not everyone possessed.

The power to *remove mountains* may have included the ability to work miracles in the realm of nature. Jesus mentioned moving mountains on occasion (Matthew 17:20; 21:21; Mark 11:23), although He may have used this expression as a hyperbole (an extreme exaggeration for emphasis). In any case, the point of Paul's proposition is obvious. One might perform the most astounding miracle imaginable, but if it is done without love, it is *nothing*.

C. Giving Without Love (v. 3)

3. And though I bestow all my goods to feed the poor, and though I give my body to be burned, and have not charity, it profiteth me nothing.

[See question #2, page 304.] People have been known to give part of their *goods*, or possessions, to benefit others, but they did so in order to receive the plaudits of men (Matthew 6:1-4). Paul's hypothetical example goes far beyond giving just a part of one's goods; here, the donor uses *all* his goods *to feed the poor*.

Then Paul goes a step further, supposing that the person gives not merely all his possessions but himself—his *body to be burned* in an act of martyrdom. Such extreme examples of giving highlight the importance of love; as impressive as they may seem, they are totally meaningless if one does not do them out of love.

MIXED MESSAGE

A twenty-six-year-old woman in Tustin, California, provided an interesting example of the "road rage" phenomenon. This term describes an aggressive driving style that some people adopt in which they take out their frustrations on other drivers. This young woman became angry at the driver of the truck in front of her because she thought he wasn't driving fast enough. So she took a baseball bat that she had in her car and attempted to hit the side of the truck several times as she pulled alongside it.

The policeman who arrested her noted that her license plate read "PEACE 95." When he questioned her about it, she told the officer that she got the personalized plate because she thought there was too much violence in our society!

Psychologists would probably call this a case of "cognitive dissonance." It's what happens when a person's behavior doesn't match his stated beliefs—and yet the person himself sees no contradiction. This was the situation in the Corinthian church that Paul was addressing. When we pride ourselves on the gifts or talents that make us seem very spiritual, and yet do not exercise them in a spirit of love, something is seriously wrong with our Christianity.   —C. R. B.

II. Practice of Love
(1 Corinthians 13:4-7)

A. Love Is Humble (v. 4)

4. Charity suffereth long, and is kind; charity envieth not; charity vaunteth not itself, is not puffed up.

Having identified several actions that are meaningless without love, Paul turns to love's positive side. Some of these attributes were conspicuously absent from the Corinthian congregation.

A very important part of love is humility. *Charity suffereth long;* that is, love leads one to work patiently with others, even those who may be considered "difficult." The loving person is willing to labor in the shadow of others, allowing them to receive credit for what he may have done. Love is also *kind*. It is not merely passive in its longsuffering; it actively pursues what is in the best interests of another.

Charity envieth not. It is clear that some in the Corinthian church had become envious of the gifts that others had received. Envy, however, is not a mark of true love. *Charity vaunteth not itself, is not puffed up.* One who lives a life controlled by love is not proud or arrogant. Yet how subtly Satan tempts us in this respect. We want to be "number one," or to "keep up with the Joneses." Such pride blinds us to the source of our possessions and our talents. They all come from God.

B. Love Is Unselfish (v. 5)

5. Doth not behave itself unseemly, seeketh not her own, is not easily provoked, thinketh no evil.

Love *doth not behave itself unseemly.* Unseemly behavior is any conduct that brings reproach to Christ or His church. The *New International Version* translates this "rude." Many of us are shocked by the growing rudeness we see in the society around us. Often this stems from ignorance; children have not been taught simple politeness such as saying "please" and "thank you." But in other cases rudeness is the product of the selfish spirit that seems to be the trademark of our times.

Love *is not easily provoked.* Some people are like prickly cactuses. It is painful to approach them from any direction. Nearly every office and every church probably has at least one person who is irritable and hard to get along with. Whatever reasons one may have for this attitude, the underlying problem is that such a person lacks love and consideration for others.

Love *thinketh no evil.* The Greek word for *thinketh* describes the keeping of an account or record. Love "keeps no record of wrongs" (*New International Version*); it does not dwell on wrongs done, trying to devise ways of "getting even." Love forgives and forgets. [See question #3, page 304.]

C. Love Rejoices in the Truth (v. 6)

6. Rejoiceth not in iniquity, but rejoiceth in the truth.

Today we are immersed in a sea of *iniquity.* Radio, movies, television, and now various electronic media intrude into our homes with offensive words and images. We have to be alert every minute to keep our minds pure. Living by God's *truth* can help us attain that purity because it helps us determine right from wrong.

D. Love Is Patient (v. 7)

7. Beareth all things, believeth all things, hopeth all things, endureth all things.

Love *beareth all things.* The Greek word translated *beareth* comes from the word for "roof." Thus love protects others (from threatening situ-

ations or negative talk), as a roof protects what is inside a building.

Love *believeth all things.* This certainly does not mean that we are to be naive, believing everything that we are told or chasing after every strange idea that appears on the horizon. The point here is that love gives us a positive attitude toward others that is eager to believe the best, not the worst, about people. Love continues to believe that God has ways of reaching out and saving wayward souls. It gives us an optimistic, patient perspective toward life. [See question #4, page 304.]

Love also *hopeth all things* and *endureth all things.* Love looks toward the future positively. It refuses to fold in the face of difficult people or circumstances. It is thoroughly loyal—to God and to others.

III. Permanence of Love (1 Corinthians 13:8-13)

A. Gifts Will Cease (v. 8)

8. Charity never faileth: but whether there be prophecies, they shall fail; whether there be tongues, they shall cease; whether there be knowledge, it shall vanish away.

In verses 1-3 Paul declared that even the most coveted spiritual gifts and the most commendable actions, if exercised without love, are empty and meaningless. In verses 4-7 he listed the qualities of love that make it the "more excellent way." Now in the closing verses of this chapter he shows that love is superior to the spiritual gifts because love is permanent, while the gifts are temporary.

B. The Partial and the Perfect (vv. 9-12)

9. For we know in part, and we prophesy in part.

Knowledge and prophecy refer back to two of the spiritual gifts that were mentioned in 1 Corinthians 12:8 and 10. Although Paul, as an apostle,

The beautiful visual that goes with today's lesson reminds us of the importance and power of love. Display it as you begin to discuss verse 13.

Visual for lesson 9

How to Say It

AGAPE (Greek). uh-*gah*-pay.
CLAIRVAUX. Clair-*voh*.
CORINTH. *Kor*-inth.
CORINTHIANS. Kor-*in*-thee-unz.

had received by revelation a special knowledge of God's purposes in Christ (Galatians 1:11, 12), he readily recognized that his understanding was only partial. There were at least two reasons for this. First of all, God in His infinite wisdom had not chosen to reveal all of His mysteries at that time. Second, if He had, man in his human weakness would not have been able to comprehend it. In the same way, the ability to *prophesy* resulted in only partial understanding.

10. But when that which is perfect is come, then that which is in part shall be done away.

This verse has been the source of considerable discussion. Some understand *perfect* to refer to the revelation of the New Covenant embodied in the New Testament Scriptures. The special spiritual gifts were necessary in the first century and shortly thereafter to authenticate this new and final revelation of God's will to man. (See the reference to "confirming the word" in Mark 16:20.) According to this view, the gifts ceased once the New Testament was completed.

Another view is that *perfect* looks to the second coming of Christ. When He who is the perfect revelation of God returns, then special gifts will no longer be needed.

Still others believe that *perfect* means "mature," as it does in various passages (Ephesians 4:12, 13; Colossians 1:28). As such, it may refer to a mature individual or a mature church. When a person or congregation has attained "the unity of the faith, and of the knowledge of the Son of God" and "the measure of the stature of the fulness of Christ" (Ephesians 4:13), there will no longer be a need for the gifts of knowledge and prophecy. Or when the church as a whole becomes "mature," it no longer needs the foundational gifts of the apostles and prophets (Ephesians 2:20).

11. When I was a child, I spake as a child, I understood as a child, I thought as a child: but when I became a man, I put away childish things.

Paul elaborates on the point he made in the previous verse. The *child* represents the time in which Paul was writing (first century) while the *man* points to maturity at some time future to Paul. As noted under verse 10, the time represented by this analogy varies according to one's view of what the "perfect" is. Under the first

view—and probably the third—we are in that time now. But if one takes the "perfect" to be the return of Christ, then that time is, obviously, still future to us today. [See question #5, page 304.]

12. For now we see through a glass, darkly, but then face to face: now I know in part; but then shall I know even as also I am known.

The *glass* refers to a mirror, which in Paul's day was not made of glass but of polished metal. With such a mirror one's reflection would be dim and distorted. But at some future time we will *see . . . face to face.* To use a contemporary illustration, we might compare a person's photograph to the person himself. A photograph may show certain aspects of a person accurately, but it in no way adequately shows the real person. When "that which is perfect is come" (v. 10), we will have more complete knowledge about those matters that we now *know in part.*

Again, one's understanding of when this happens depends on his interpretation of what the "perfect" means. Those who believe it refers to the return of Jesus would say that at that time we will see Him face to face. Those who say that the "perfect" designates the completion of the New Testament or the attainment of maturity may take a more symbolic understanding of *face to face.* Some will combine both views, seeing the arrival of the "perfect" as beginning a process that makes the foundational gifts unnecessary before Christ returns, but not necessarily granting full knowledge *even as also I am known* until His return.

C. "The Greatest of These" (v. 13)

13. And now abideth faith, hope, charity, these three; but the greatest of these is charity.

The closing verse of this chapter brings Paul's discussion to a fitting conclusion. The spiritual gifts that had created so much controversy in the Corinthian church were not permanent. What really matters are the qualities of *faith, hope,* and *charity* (love). This triad sums up quite succinctly the crucial elements that lie at the heart of Christian living.

In one sense, faith will not be needed in the next world, for then we shall "walk by sight." But in another sense it will exist there as fulfilled faith. The same is true of hope. Hope is a wonderful source of encouragement in this life, but in Heaven we will no longer need that kind of hope. However, it will exist as hope that has been realized and rewarded.

The greatest of these is charity. Love is greater than faith and hope, because in Heaven it will be most necessary. Faith and hope are not divine attributes, but human ones. After all, God does not need faith and hope; we do. But "God is love" (1 John 4:8), and if we are to relate to Him throughout all eternity, then we must possess love above all else.

SYMBOL OF LASTING LOVE

Yvonne Saunders runs an unusual business in West Vancouver, British Columbia: she preserves wedding bouquets. She sends an airtight shipping box to the bride who wants her bouquet preserved. When the flowers arrive at Saunders' studio, they are photographed, disassembled, and dried, flower by flower, in chemicals that will preserve even the colors of the petals, leaves, and stems. Then the bouquet is reassembled, placed on a background of velvet (or a piece of the fabric from which the bride's gown was made), and sealed in a frame. The cost of this service ranges from under $100 to over $600.

The carefully preserved flowers are intended to symbolize the eternal nature of the love that the happy couple have pledged to each other. (One might observe that this could be a symbolic first lesson to the newlyweds of how much love can cost!)

Paul describes the eternal nature of love in 1 Corinthians 13, noting that it "never faileth" (v. 8). While the words of this chapter are often read as part of a wedding ceremony, they can truly be understood only by looking to the God who is this kind of love. His love is a love that lasts a lifetime and beyond.   —C. R. B.

Conclusion

A. Love Acts

Love is not just a term that theologians discuss or about which scholars write books. It is at the heart of everything that Christianity stands for. Love must be active and involved in the real, everyday world. Consider the extent and variety of circumstances in today's world where love can make a genuine difference.

For example, love transcends race and nationality. Paul wrote in Ephesians 2:14 that the sacrificial love of Christ "hath broken down the middle wall of partition" between Jews and Gentiles. Laws may sometimes help dissipate the racism that so plagues our world; but until our hearts have surrendered to the power of *agape* love, racism will never be eliminated.

We are distressed by the ethical behavior of men and women in places of prominence in our land. Codes of ethics and laws may be helpful, but without love our society will never solve this problem.

In our major cities are thousands of homeless individuals without adequate food or shelter.

Home Daily Bible Readings

Monday, Apr. 24—The Gift of Love (1 Corinthians 13:1-7)
Tuesday, Apr. 25—Love Is the Greatest Gift (1 Corinthians 13:8-13)
Wednesday, Apr. 26—Love: An Old New Commandment (1 John 2:7-17)
Thursday, Apr. 27—Show Your Love for One Another (1 John 3:11-17)
Friday, Apr. 28—Believe in Jesus and Love One Another (1 John 3:18-24)
Saturday, Apr. 29—Let Us Love as God Loves (1 John 4:7-12)
Sunday, Apr. 30—We Abide in God If We Love (1 John 4:13-21)

Unless the power of *agape* love compels us to leave our comfortable suburbs and go down into the inner city to minister to them, the problem will remain.

All of us are distressed by the growing number of broken marriages and single-parent families and the countless problems they cause. Yet without love, all of the efforts to meet these problems are like adhesive bandage strips plastered over a gnawing cancer.

Our society has surrendered its soul to materialism. Many are blessed beyond their dreams by God's gifts, and yet in the midst of their plenty they never seem to be satisfied; they always want more and better things. They pursue these items with the love and zeal that rightly should be directed toward God and His creation. Until they are willing to make God and others the objects of their love, they are doomed to drown in their own discontent.

Deep down, we usually come to realize that we all need to embrace *agape* love; but *agape* love exacts a price. We must be willing to surrender to Christ, accept His love, and then share His love with others.

B. Prayer

Loving Father, we raise our voices in a prayer for forgiveness—forgiveness for not loving You as we should, forgiveness for not accepting Your love, and forgiveness for not sharing that love with others. Melt our hearts now, and give us the strength and wisdom to become the kind of people You want us to be. In Jesus' name. Amen.

C. Thought to Remember

"The true measure of loving God is to love Him without measure."   —Bernard of Clairvaux

Learning by Doing

This page contains an alternate lesson plan emphasizing learning activities.
Classes desiring such student involvement will find these suggestions helpful.

Learning Goals

After this lesson each student will be able to:

1. Summarize what Paul says about love and what makes it the "more excellent way."

2. Suggest some actions love might prompt a person to take.

3. Commit himself or herself to act with genuine love toward a specific person.

Into the Lesson

Over the years, many writers, poets, and lyricists have tried to capture the essence of love. Ask your students to read the following statements and decide which ones accurately reflect the meaning of love and how they do so.

"Love means never having to say you're sorry."
"Love is always sweeter the second time around."
"All you need is love."
"Love can touch us one time and last for a lifetime."
"Love was when God became a man."

Discuss these ideas briefly; then tell your class that today we will see what the Holy Spirit inspired Paul to write about the nature of love.

Into the Word

For this exercise, divide your class into three sections. Each student in section 1 will write a paraphrase of 1 Corinthians 12:31—13:3, restating the verses in his or her own words. Students in section 2 will paraphrase 13:4-7, and those in section three will paraphrase 13:8-13. Encourage your students to try to express the meaning of the passage, not simply to rewrite the verses in slightly different words.

When your students complete their work, ask for volunteers to share their paraphrases with the class. Then discuss the meaning of the chapter, using the questions below.

1. What are the "best gifts" to which Paul refers?

2. Is it wrong to desire God's gifts? Why?

3. What does Paul mean by his reference to "sounding brass" and "a tinkling cymbal"?

4. What is the relationship of love to the gifts and deeds mentioned in verses 2 and 3?

5. What does Paul mean when he says, "Charity suffereth long"?

6. What do the positive characteristics of love in verse 4 have in common?

7. How are the negative characteristics of love in verse 5 the opposite of those in verse 4?

8. What does it mean to rejoice in iniquity? How does verse 6 contradict the idea that lying is a good way to spare someone's feelings?

9. Is it naive to "believe all things," as Paul says love does? What sorts of things will love bear and endure?

10. Why will love outlast the various spiritual gifts, including prophecy, tongues, and knowledge?

11. To whom does Paul refer in verse 9? What does he mean to "prophesy in part"?

12. What is the "perfect" in verse 10? Why will its coming signify the end of the partial gifts?

13. What is the point of Paul's illustration about his childhood in verse 11?

14. What is the "glass" Paul refers to in verse 12? What does this allusion say about love?

15. Why is love the "more excellent way" (12:31), even greater than faith or hope (13:13)?

Into Life

Distribute copies of the chart below, omitting the material in parentheses. (Or direct your students to this activity in the student books.) Have each class member look up the following passages; then write a brief description of what God expects a Christian to do to express love. Ask students to add to the list other loving deeds that are not mentioned in these passages.

After his list is complete, each student should then go back and evaluate it. If a student believes he is now expressing love in this way to the best of his ability, he should put a plus (+) next to the verse. If he believes he could do better, he should put a minus (−). From the deeds marked with the minus signs, each student should select at least one loving deed that he will determine to do this week and put an asterisk (*) beside it. Emphasize that he will *not* be asked to share his evaluation with the class.

VERSE	LOVING DEED	EVALUATION (+, −, *)
1 John 3:17	(Help the needy)	
1 John 5:2, 3	(Keep commands)	
James 2:1-9	(Be impartial)	
3 John 5-8	(Show hospitality)	
Romans 14	(Respect a brother's conscience)	

Discuss the meaning of the passages as well as other ways to express love. Close with prayer for your students, that they may follow through in their plans to demonstrate love this week.

Let's Talk It Over

The questions on this page are designed to encourage review of the lesson Scriptures and to promote discussion of the lesson by the class. The answers provided are only discussion starters. Let your class talk it over from there.

1. Some people speak of love as merely a feeling, something one "falls" into—and just as easily falls out of. But in speaking of love as a requirement, Paul makes it clear that we have the ability to control whether or not we demonstrate love. What can we do to be sure we are acting with love?

One helpful practice is to study and meditate on the love of Jesus. He commanded us to love one another in the same way He has loved us (John 13:34; 15:12). If we fill our hearts and minds with His words and works of love, we can do that. Since love is part of the "fruit of the Spirit" (Galatians 5:22, 23), then cultivating our spiritual life will help us to grow in love. In 1 Thessalonians 3:12 Paul prayed that the Thessalonians would grow in love for one another. While we are praying for other needs, both for ourselves and others, we should also be sure to pray for a stronger love.

2. Paul pointed out that acts of charity and sacrifice toward others do us little good if they are not done in love. Why not?

Without question, some people today donate to religious and benevolent causes out of impure motives. They are perhaps seeking to earn favor with God, or they desire to impress other human beings with their generosity.

Such people think they can earn God's favor—even salvation—by good deeds. But the Bible repeatedly tells us that we cannot be saved by good works (cf. Galatians 2:16; 2 Timothy 1:9; Titus 3:5). God desires a pure heart, not mere outward acts of kindness. Insincere acts of kindness may do some good for the person for whom they are done, but they earn nothing in God's eyes.

Love is important because God Himself is love (1 John 4:8). Love, Jesus said, will be the hallmark of a disciple (John 13:35).

3. What are some forms of selfish behavior in the church that love can overcome?

Many churches have members who feel that the congregation should cater to their own personal needs and desires. They are upset by any deviation from the style of worship they prefer. They have a time limit they do not want the preacher to exceed in his sermons. They are staunch supporters of a certain kind of curriculum for use in Bible

teaching. Through love such members must develop a flexibility in accepting changes that will benefit their brothers and sisters. Another problem seen in many congregations are those people who are much too sensitive. They can easily get their feelings hurt, or they can readily misinterpret what a fellow member has said or done to them. These members must develop the kind of love that will lift them out of their preoccupation with self. They must learn to concentrate on service rather than sensitivity.

4. Through love Christians can learn to believe the best about one another. How important do you think this quality is? Why?

It is a very human tendency to want to imagine ourselves superior to others. In order to fulfill this tendency, we focus on what we perceive as the faults or inadequacies of others. This happens in the church, as it does elsewhere.

If we are in the habit of looking for flaws in our fellow Christians, it is not surprising that dissensions and divisions develop. On the other hand, if we make it a practice to look for positive traits and expect positive actions, the church can enjoy a remarkable atmosphere of love, cooperation, and harmony. Paul's admonition in Philippians 2:3 is appropriate here: "In lowliness of mind let each esteem other better than themselves."

5. Whatever view one takes of when "that which is perfect" arrives, Paul's point of adults' "put[ting] away childish things" is applicable to us today. How does the mature Christian demonstrate love in ways a non-Christian might not? What are some goals we might set for ourselves in order to grow in love?

In 2 Corinthians 13:11 Paul wrote, "Finally, brethren, farewell. Be perfect, be of good comfort, be of one mind, live in peace; and the God of love and peace shall be with you." The mature Christian seeks the welfare of others and harmony in the church. These are acts of love.

In addition, the mature Christian more consistently focuses on Jesus. Such a focus inspires us to greater love. The more we recognize His presence in our worship and service, the deeper will be our experience of His love. This is particularly true of the Lord's Supper. We should aim to make it a genuine communion with our loving Savior.

Christian March of Triumph

DEVOTIONAL READING: 2 Corinthians 1:3-11.

BACKGROUND SCRIPTURE: 2 Corinthians 1, 2.

PRINTED TEXT: 2 Corinthians 2:4-17.

2 Corinthians 2:4-17

4 For out of much affliction and anguish of heart I wrote unto you with many tears; not that ye should be grieved, but that ye might know the love which I have more abundantly unto you.

5 But if any have caused grief, he hath not grieved me, but in part: that I may not overcharge you all.

6 Sufficient to such a man is this punishment, which was inflicted of many.

7 So that contrariwise ye ought rather to forgive him, and comfort him, lest perhaps such a one should be swallowed up with overmuch sorrow.

8 Wherefore I beseech you that ye would confirm your love toward him.

9 For to this end also did I write, that I might know the proof of you, whether ye be obedient in all things.

10 To whom ye forgive any thing, I forgive also: for if I forgave any thing, to whom I forgave it, for your sakes forgave I it in the person of Christ;

11 Lest Satan should get an advantage of us: for we are not ignorant of his devices.

12 Furthermore, when I came to Troas to preach Christ's gospel, and a door was opened unto me of the Lord,

13 I had no rest in my spirit, because I found not Titus my brother; but taking my leave of them, I went from thence into Macedonia.

14 Now thanks be unto God, which always causeth us to triumph in Christ, and maketh manifest the savor of his knowledge by us in every place.

15 For we are unto God a sweet savor of Christ, in them that are saved, and in them that perish:

16 To the one we are the savor of death unto death; and to the other the savor of life unto life. And who is sufficient for these things?

17 For we are not as many, which corrupt the word of God: but as of sincerity, but as of God, in the sight of God speak we in Christ.

GOLDEN TEXT: Thanks be unto God, which always causeth us to triumph in Christ, and maketh manifest the savor of his knowledge by us in every place.—2 Corinthians 2:14.

Lesson Aims

After this lesson students will be able to:

1. Tell the reasons for Paul's sense of triumph concerning the Corinthians.

2. Suggest some situations over which God's love and grace can triumph today.

3. Pinpoint a current situation in the church or in their personal relationships where Christian love needs to triumph.

Lesson Outline

INTRODUCTION
    A. From a Blot to a Blessing
    B. Lesson Background
  I. CHRISTIAN LOVE UNITES (2 Corinthians 2:4-11)
    A. In Sympathy (v. 4)
     "Big Boys Don't Cry"
    B. In Punishment (vv. 5, 6)
    C. In Forgiveness (vv. 7-11)
     Saving a Sinking Church
  II. CHRISTIAN LOVE REACHES OUT (2 Corinthians 2:12-17)
    A. In Evangelism (vv. 12, 13)
    B. In Triumph (vv. 14-16)
    C. In Sincerity (v. 17)
CONCLUSION
    A. Apostolic Triumphs
    B. Satan's Devices
    C. Prayer
    D. Thought to Remember

Introduction

A. From a Blot to a Blessing

A friend once showed John Ruskin, a nineteenth-century British writer, a very expensive silk handkerchief that had been ruined by an ink blot. All efforts to remove the stain from the handkerchief had failed, so the man decided to throw it away. Ruskin, however, offered to find some way to save it. A few days later he returned the handkerchief to the man. He had not removed the stain, but, using the stain as a starting point, he had used a pen and some India ink to create an intricate and attractive design. From a ruined handkerchief, Ruskin created a valuable work of art.

This somewhat resembles the situation that Paul dealt with in the Corinthian church. In 1 Corinthians 5 he urged that a man involved in a serious sin be disciplined. It is apparent in today's lesson that the man had repented, so Paul encouraged the church to welcome him back in love. In this way the Corinthians were able to help in turning an individual badly stained by sin into a spiritual "work of art."

B. Lesson Background

The remaining four lessons in this quarter will be based on texts taken from the book of 2 Corinthians. Before considering the background for today's printed text, let us examine the background of the letter itself. After Paul's successful ministry in Corinth, which lasted about a year and a half (Acts 18:11), he had traveled to Jerusalem and then returned to Antioch, thus completing his second missionary journey (Acts 18:22).

Not long afterward, Paul began his third missionary journey, which took him through Galatia and Phrygia to Ephesus (Acts 18:23; 19:1). Here he had another very successful ministry, which lasted about three years (20:31). Its success, however, brought him into conflict with the silversmiths of Ephesus, whose lucrative business had been impinged by the message of the gospel (19:23-27). While in Ephesus, Paul had written 1 Corinthians. In this letter (as we have noted in previous studies this quarter), he addressed some of the situations in the church that had threatened its unity and had undermined its witness to the pagans.

At this point, a question arises concerning Paul's visits to the Corinthians. It appears that some time after the writing of 1 Corinthians, Paul made a brief stop in Corinth to try to address personally the problems there. We know that a second visit occurred because 2 Corinthians 12:14 and 13:1, 2 mention *two* prior visits. In addition, 2 Corinthians 2:1 indicates that one of the two earlier visits was "in heaviness" or "painful" (*New International Version*). This does not seem to be a good description of Paul's first visit to Corinth, recorded in Acts 18:1-18, so it must refer to another. In 2 Corinthians 1:15-23 Paul mentions his plans for a third visit to Corinth; in fact, he was on his way when he wrote 2 Corinthians. He had left Ephesus, passed through Troas, and had gone as far as Macedonia when he met Titus, returning from Corinth, and penned the epistle (2 Corinthians 2:12, 13; 7:5-7).

Though some believe that the man mentioned in today's lesson text is someone who had attacked Paul by challenging his apostolic credentials (someone whom he had met during his second visit to Corinth), it has generally been held that he is the man mentioned in 1 Corinthians 5, who was involved in an incestuous relationship with his father's wife. Today's lesson gives us a good example of how Paul, a man with a servant's heart, dealt with sin in the body of Christ—firmly and yet with mercy and forgiveness.

I. Christian Love Unites
(2 Corinthians 2:4-11)

A. In Sympathy (v. 4)

4. For out of much affliction and anguish of heart I wrote unto you with many tears; not that ye should be grieved, but that ye might know the love which I have more abundantly unto you.

The phrase *out of much affliction and anguish of heart* describes the emotions that Paul experienced when he felt compelled to write to the Corinthian church in rather firm tones. Some believe that the words *I wrote* refer to a letter Paul had written to the Corinthians after the letter that we today call 1 Corinthians. According to this view, this "lost epistle" or "severe letter" contained very harsh language, which is the reason Paul felt so anguished about it. Others maintain that 1 Corinthians is this letter, and that the situations it describes would certainly have been disturbing enough to move an earnest man like Paul to *many tears.*

Paul took no pleasure in admonishing the Corinthians, just as a parent takes no joy in punishing a child. But his *love* for them required him to take this action. Paul wanted to assure the Corinthians of how *abundantly* he loved them. [See question #1, page 312.]

"BIG BOYS DON'T CRY"

There may be a scientific reason behind the old adage that "big boys don't cry." Ramsey Clinic in St. Paul, Minnesota, has a Dry Eye and Tear Research Center. Researchers at the Center have found that, up to approximately age twelve, boys and girls cry about the same amount; but by the time they are adults, women cry much more frequently than men. Women in the study experienced crying on an average of 5.3 times per month; men cried only 1.4 times a month. Seventy-one percent of men said that they had only watery eyes when they cried, but forty-seven percent of women reported that tears flowed when they cried. Forty-five percent of men versus six percent of women said they did not cry at all.

Of course, part of the differences may be attributed to the different ways in which women and men are conditioned by cultural factors to respond in a certain manner. But the researchers think that some of these differences have to do with biochemistry. Tears that are triggered by our emotions contain the hormone prolactin, and women have sixty percent more of it in their blood than men do.

Nevertheless, it is significant when a man such as Paul acknowledges that his love and concern for the Corinthian church had caused him anguish of heart and had brought "many tears." Perhaps Paul is telling us, by word and example, that in our modern sophistication we may not be moved to tears as often as we should be at the sin we find in the world—and sometimes even in the church.   —C. R. B.

B. In Punishment (vv. 5, 6)

5, 6. But if any have caused grief, he hath not grieved me, but in part: that I may not overcharge you all. Sufficient to such a man is this punishment, which was inflicted of many.

As noted in the Lesson Background, the *man* mentioned here is likely the man guilty of incest, whom Paul had told the Corinthians to discipline (1 Corinthians 5). Paul noted that the *grief* the man had caused was not confined to Paul but affected the entire congregation. As Christians we need to realize that when we sin, or even engage in questionable activities, our actions reflect negatively on the congregation where we serve.

Sufficient to such a man is this punishment. The incestuous man was to be delivered "unto Satan for the destruction of the flesh" (1 Corinthians 5:5). (See the comments on this verse in lesson 4.) This punishment, which had been *inflicted of many* and thus represented the entire congregation, had achieved the desired results.

C. In Forgiveness (vv. 7-11)

7, 8. So that contrariwise ye ought rather to forgive him, and comfort him, lest perhaps such a one should be swallowed up with overmuch sorrow. Wherefore I beseech you that ye would confirm your love toward him.

In Paul's opinion the man had suffered enough. Two steps were now necessary. First,

---

How to Say It

ANANIAS. An-nuh-*nigh*-us.
ANTIOCH. *An*-tee-ock.
CORINTH. *Kor*-inth.
EPHESUS. *Eff*-uh-sus.
GALATIA. Guh-*lay*-shuh.
MACEDONIA. Mass-eh-*doe*-nee-uh.
PHRYGIA. *Frij*-ee-uh.
SAPPHIRA. Suh-*fye*-ruh.
TROAS. *Tro*-az.

Home Daily Bible Readings

Monday, May 1—God Consoles Us in Our Afflictions (2 Corinthians 1:1-11)
Tuesday, May 2—Sealed by God's Spirit (2 Corinthians 1:12-22)
Wednesday, May 3—Love Prevails Over Pain and Conflict (2 Corinthians 1:23—2:4)
Thursday, May 4—Christian Forgiveness for the Offender (2 Corinthians 2:5-11)
Friday, May 5—The Gospel: the Fragrance of Life (2 Corinthians 2:12-17)
Saturday, May 6—Good News Written on Human Hearts (2 Corinthians 3:1-11)
Sunday, May 7—Freed and Transformed by the Spirit (2 Corinthians 3:12-18)

the Corinthians were to *forgive him*, perhaps in a public meeting of the congregation. The restoration process then required another step. The man needed to sense the *comfort*, or support, of the congregation, lest he *be swallowed up with overmuch sorrow*. In some situations an offender may be so overwhelmed with remorse that he needs continued help and support from other Christians. If he does not sense that they have forgiven him, he may find it difficult, if not impossible, to forgive himself.

When the offense against others has been quite painful, this is not an easy step to take. In such a situation the most effective tool that one can use is the kind of love Paul describes in 1 Corinthians 13. [See question #2, page 312.]

9. For to this end also did I write, that I might know the proof of you, whether ye be obedient in all things.

Paul had written the Corinthians primarily out of a concern that the man living in sin be disciplined, but he had another motive. He was testing whether the Corinthians had the maturity to deal with this problem effectively. No doubt Paul was pleased that they had accepted his authority, which some in the congregation had challenged. Paul's response to their criticism is found in 2 Corinthians 10:1—11:33.

10. To whom ye forgive any thing, I forgive also: for if I forgave any thing, to whom I forgave it, for your sakes forgave I it in the person of Christ.

Forgive is the key word in this verse. Since the man in question had shown repentance and had been punished by being excommunicated from the congregation, it was time for healing to begin. The congregation had already started the process, and Paul now gave his approval to their actions.

When the problem first arose, Paul had to prod the Corinthians to take action; but in extending forgiveness, they had taken the initiative. Paul commended them by expressing his agreement with their action.

Forgave I it in the person of Christ. Paul's statement is not an indication that he had some unique authority from Christ to forgive sins. By forgiving the man Paul was acting in the spirit of Christ—the spirit that he wanted the Corinthians to demonstrate. It is difficult for people to know that Christ forgives them if those who claim to follow Christ do not forgive them.

SAVING A SINKING CHURCH

Construction of Mexico City's Metropolitan Cathedral began in 1563. Builders were warned that the ground was unstable, and, proving the skeptics right, the building started to sink soon after construction was started.

During the growth of the city to its present population of more than eighteen million, aquifers beneath the city have been its water supply. So much ground water has been pumped that in the last hundred years, the ground has subsided more than twenty-five feet. As a result, the great cathedral has also been sinking. Because it sank unevenly, a point was reached a few years ago where one end was eight feet lower than the other. Engineers proposed a radical, counterintuitive scheme to solve the problem: remove the earth that supports the high end of the building in order to level it. It is working, and the church has been stabilized.

The Corinthian church was "sinking" also—not the building, but the body of Christ in Corinth. Paul's solution to at least one of their problems was bold and perhaps counterintuitive to some. Rather than gloating over the sin of their stumbling member and their success in having forced him to repent, they were to forgive him—especially once the desired end of their discipline had been realized. The sinking moral tone of the church had been stopped. Forgiving love would put the situation in Corinth back "on the level."

—C. R. B.

11. Lest Satan should get an advantage of us: for we are not ignorant of his devices.

Paul had another reason for being encouraged by the Corinthians' decision. Had the church or some of its leaders remained at odds with Paul or defiant of his advice, *Satan* would have taken *advantage* of the opportunity to create havoc among the believers. Satan has many *devices*, many weapons in his arsenal. Immorality is a weapon he often uses to ensnare Christians. But he also uses disagreements to create a spirit of division among believers, and in many situations this weapon can be just as devastating. [See question #3, page 312.]

II. Christian Love Reaches Out (2 Corinthians 2:12-17)

A. In Evangelism (vv. 12, 13)

12. Furthermore, when I came to Troas to preach Christ's gospel, and a door was opened unto me of the Lord.

Earlier Paul had expressed his intention to visit the Corinthians on his way from Ephesus to Macedonia, then to stop by Corinth again on his way to Judea (1:15, 16). However, he had changed his mind about the visit, no doubt out of a concern that the time was not right: "to spare you I came not as yet unto Corinth" (v. 23).

Instead he sent Titus to check on things in Corinth and to bring him word, intending to meet Titus in Troas (verse 13). Apparently Paul left Ephesus because of the riot recorded in Acts 19 (see Acts 20:1). He *came to Troas* (Acts 20:6) where he found that *a door was opened* for him *to preach Christ's gospel.* (Compare Paul's language with that in 1 Corinthians 16:9, where "a great door and effectual" was "opened" to Paul in Ephesus.) Paul preached enough in Troas to determine that the door was open, but, as the next verse tells us, he was not able to continue long in that city.

13. I had no rest in my spirit, because I found not Titus my brother; but taking my leave of them, I went from thence into Macedonia.

Because of the circumstances under which Paul left Ephesus, we may assume he left somewhat sooner than he had intended when he sent *Titus* to Corinth with plans to meet him in Troas. Thus Titus was not in Troas when Paul was, and Paul was not able to learn of the conditions in Corinth. This left him restless—his *spirit* could find *no rest.* So in spite of the "open door" in Troas, Paul felt compelled to go on *into Macedonia* and to continue his search for Titus. [See question #4, page 312.]

B. In Triumph (vv. 14-16)

14. Now thanks be unto God, which always causeth us to triumph in Christ, and maketh manifest the savor of his knowledge by us in every place.

Apparently somewhere in Macedonia, Paul finally met with Titus and was relieved to learn that the Corinthians had received his letter in a positive spirit and were working to address the matters about which he had written (2 Corinthians 7:4-9, 13-16). This led Paul, as he often did in his writings, to offer a tribute of praise to God.

To emphasize his gratitude, Paul used a striking metaphor. The phrase *causeth us to triumph in Christ* is translated "leads us in triumphal procession in Christ" in the *New International Version.* The picture is that of a conquering Roman general at the head of a victory parade in his honor. Behind him marched his victorious troops; then came the prisoners and the spoils of war that had been seized. Christians are likely represented by the triumphant soldiers, for they march victoriously behind the leadership of Christ (though some believe that Christians are portrayed by the prisoners, for they have given themselves as willing "captives" of Christ).

The phrase *savor of his knowledge* alludes to another practice that accompanied victory processions. Incense was offered as part of the sacrifices that were made to give thanks to the Roman gods. The victory was also celebrated with the release of perfumes along the parade route. Paul equates these fragrances with the spread of the knowledge of Christ wherever His gospel is preached.

15, 16. For we are unto God a sweet savor of Christ, in them that are saved, and in them that perish: to the one we are the savor of death unto death; and to the other the savor of life unto life. And who is sufficient for these things?

Whereas in the previous verse Paul used "savor" to describe the knowledge of Christ as it is spread through the efforts of Christians, here *sweet savor* is used of Christians themselves. Certainly this is a sweet aroma *in them that are saved.* In contrast, those who refuse to accept the message that Christians proclaim are doomed to *perish.* So it was with the aroma of incense and perfume at the Roman victory procession; it was the *savor of death* to the conquered peoples, for they would be executed at the conclusion of the celebration. Paul expressed a similar contrast in 1 Corinthians 1:18: "For the preaching of the cross is to them that perish, foolishness; but unto us which are saved, it is the power of God."

Visual for lesson 10

The "procession" in today's visual is comprised of young people from missionary families displaying the flags of the many nations where they serve.

Who is sufficient for these things? With this rhetorical question Paul raises the issue of the awesome responsibility of those who convey the gospel message. In a sense no human is fully worthy or competent to deliver this message. Yet this is the means that God has chosen to convey His saving truths—through fallible human beings. Thus we must always enter into the ministry of the Word with humility and trembling.

Later Paul gives an answer to this question, asserting that his "sufficiency is of God" (2 Corinthians 3:5). It behooves us to be imitators of Paul in this respect, looking to God for direction and strength as we carry out the ministry He has given us. As Jesus emphasized in His teaching on the vine and the branches, "Without me ye can do nothing" (John 15:5). [See question #5, page 312.]

C. In Sincerity (v. 17)

17. For we are not as many, which corrupt the word of God: but as of sincerity, but as of God, in the sight of God speak we in Christ.

Paul established himself as an authentic spokesman for God in contrast to *the many, which corrupt the word of God.* The *many* does not necessarily indicate that there were a great number of false teachers, only that the number was large in comparison with the teachers of truth. This certainly would have included false teachers in other churches as well as in Corinth. The word *corrupt* is more accurately translated "peddling" or "hawking," indicating that the false teachers were greedy and interested primarily in making a profit from their teaching.

Conclusion

A. Apostolic Triumphs

In today's lesson text Paul expresses his thanks for the triumph he had experienced in Christ. There were several blessings for which he could be thankful. First of all, he was thankful that the man who had been overtaken by sin had repented. Paul found great joy in the man's change of heart.

Second, the Corinthians' actions in disciplining the man brought joy to Paul's heart. They could have resented Paul's criticism of their slowness to act in this case. Many today react negatively to any criticism, even when it is appropriate and given sincerely and gently. The Corinthians accepted Paul's counsel and acted to correct the problem.

Third, Paul found joy in the Corinthians' willingness to forgive the man who had created the problem. All too often when conflict occurs within a congregation, people are slow to forgive

and even slower to forget. Some find it much easier to blame everyone else for their problems, and they hold grudges that cripple a church for years. But the Corinthians forgave the man and encouraged him, lest he be "swallowed up with overmuch sorrow" (2 Corinthians 2:7). Serious wounds that result from conflicts within a congregation are sometimes slow to heal. The soothing balm of love must be applied frequently and over a long period of time to effect complete healing.

Finally, Paul could rejoice that he had been given the opportunity to preach in Troas. While he could not take full advantage of the open door there, he was never happier than when he was sharing the good news with those who had never heard it. He was ready to preach in any circumstance—in jail, to angry mobs, to legalistic Jews, to scholars. No situation could curb his desire to preach.

B. Satan's Devices

Satan never seems to lack ways to attack Christians. Sometimes he is a "roaring lion" that "walketh about, seeking whom he may devour" (1 Peter 5:8). At other times he is subtle, appearing as an "angel of light" (2 Corinthians 11:14). He often attacks us through our enemies, using them to lead us into temptation. But he may also get to us through our friends or members of our own families.

Paul could say that "we are not ignorant of [Satan's] devices" (2 Corinthians 2:11); however, he did not mean by that that we can take him for granted. Just the opposite! We know he will attempt to catch us at our weakest moment—that is one of his favorite "devices"! Thus, we need all the help we can get to protect us from Satan's wiles. Since "we wrestle not against flesh and blood, but against principalities, against powers, against the rulers of the darkness of this world, against spiritual wickedness in high places," we need to "put on the whole armor of God" (Ephesians 6:11, 12). Among other items, this includes a better understanding of the Scriptures—something that this present study is designed to give.

C. Prayer

We thank You, O Father, for the inspired words of Paul and the other Biblical writers that give us practical guidance for the problems that we face as we serve in Your church. Give us the grace and wisdom to accept and apply these lessons in a manner pleasing to You. In Jesus' name. Amen.

D. Thought to Remember

Lord, teach us how to forgive—and to forget.

Learning by Doing

This page contains an alternate lesson plan emphasizing learning activities. Classes desiring such student involvement will find these suggestions helpful.

Learning Goals

After this lesson students will be able to:

1. Tell the reasons for Paul's sense of triumph concerning the Corinthians.

2. Suggest some situations over which God's love and grace can triumph today.

3. Pinpoint a current situation in the church or in their personal relationships where Christian love needs to triumph.

Into the Lesson

Prior to students' arriving, write the word "conflict" on the chalkboard. Begin the lesson by directing their attention to the board and asking them to "identify the various types of conflict there are in the world today." Write their suggested answers (racial, marital, interpersonal, religious, employer/employee, ideological, political, international) on the board.

After looking at these various types of conflict, ask the class to "describe how conflict affects people's attitudes and behavior—the way people relate to each other while in conflict." Possible responses include the following: separation of people, avoidance of people, refusal to make eye contact, lack of communication, angry criticism.

Next, ask the class to describe what often happens between people who are in conflict—i.e., how conflict is "acted out" (fighting, lawsuits, verbal and/or physical abuse). In today's study, we find that a conflict that could have separated people was not acted out but was resolved by love. God, who is love, causes us to triumph in Christ (v. 14)—by restoring not only broken relationships between people, but broken relationships with God.

Into the Word

Read 2 Corinthians 2:4-11 aloud. Write on the chalkboard "Steps to Unite Broken Relationships." Ask the class to identify the ways that the Corinthians' faith united their congregation and resolved their conflict. Write their answers on the board. From the text, possible answers include forgive the erring brother, comfort him, confirm your love. Ask: "Why should the Corinthians forgive the erring brother?" Paul gives three possible answers: 1. punishment was sufficient to bring repentance (v. 6); 2. failure to forgive would overwhelm the man with sorrow (v. 7); and 3. failure to forgive would give Satan an advantage (v. 11).

Point out that love triumphs in restoring a broken relationship with God. Have a volunteer read 2 Corinthians 2:12-17. Ask the students to work with a neighbor in answering the following questions:

1. What is meant by the "opened" door (v. 12)?

2. Describe how you believe Paul felt when he said, "I had no rest in my spirit" (v. 13).

3. What is meant by the phrase, "sweet savor" (v. 15)?

4. Why does the savor result in two different responses (v. 16)?

Allow four or five minutes to complete this activity. Then go over the questions, having the students respond with their answers.

Into Life

Place the students into at least three groups of three to five individuals. Pass out a sheet of poster board and colored markers for each group. On the poster should be the following two headings: "Satan's Schemes" and "Savior's Solutions." Ask each group to complete the table by writing under the first heading possible ways that Satan deceives, separates, and causes conflict among people. *(Possible answers include immorality, worry, false teaching, disagreements, divisiveness, worldliness, and arguments.)* Likewise, have each group identify and write possible solutions to avoid those schemes under the second heading, Savior's Solutions. *(Suggested answers: knowledge of God's Word; obedience to God; personal confrontation of sin; genuine concern for the person; active involvement in sharing the message of Christ; indwelling presence of the Holy Spirit; personal forgiveness, love, and comfort.)*

Answers will come from the text as well as from inference and personal experience. Have each group present its work to the class, and compile a master list.

Next, pass out a sheet of paper to each student. With assurances that the students will not be asked to reveal what they write, have each one write the five "Schemes" that most often give them trouble in their personal relationships and one or two specific actions he or she can take to address each of the five. These action steps may be direct applications of some of the solutions above or original ideas. Close with prayer that love will triumph in your students' relationships.

Let's Talk It Over

The questions on this page are designed to encourage review of the lesson Scriptures and to promote discussion of the lesson by the class. The answers provided are only discussion starters. Let your class talk it over from there.

1. The Corinthians had caused Paul "much affliction and anguish of heart." Still, he loved them and worked hard to help them. How do you think a leader develops the kind of love that keeps on in spite of "affliction and anguish"?

Some people are disillusioned by petty bickering, backbiting, and unrest in a congregation. Loving leaders, however, keep in mind that churches are made up of human beings, who are subject to temptation and sin. They realize that people will err occasionally, and they need loving guidance to bring them back to the right path.

A leader may have to remember what God told Samuel. When people reject the truth, they are not rejecting the human leader so much as they are rejecting God (1 Samuel 8:7). Loving leaders do not take such rejection personally, but keep on in their ministries in spite of the opposition.

2. It has been said that a church leader is to "comfort the afflicted and afflict the comfortable." How would you apply this maxim to the problem of dealing with a member's sin?

We dare not be too hasty in comforting the sinner. There is a danger in giving the impression that sin is not so serious after all. Furthermore, we may hinder the process of repentance if we are too quick to assure the offender that we still regard him as a beloved brother. If an offender is inclined to justify his behavior or blame someone else, he may need to be afflicted—sternly reminded of God's judgment on sin. But once he has come to genuine repentance, he should be comforted, assured, and encouraged.

3. What are some devices Satan employs to wreak havoc in a typical church?

[CAUTION: Teacher, if there is an issue causing more than the usual differences of opinion in your church, be very careful that this discussion does not erupt into a "blame game." Keep the discussion focused on issues, not people.]

In the context here, *failure to forgive* a repentant brother is immediately connected with Satan's schemes. This might include *feeling superior* to the errant brother, or *failing to see one's own weaknesses*. Peter identified Satan as the inspiration for the *lying and deception* practiced by Ananias and Sapphira in the Jerusalem church (Acts 5:1-3). Satan is still active in stirring up

trouble this way. Another device of the devil is *envy*. In James 3:15 and 16 "envy and selfish ambition" are connected with the "wisdom [that is] of the devil" (*New International Version*). In Ephesians 4:26 and 27 Paul indicated that holding on to *anger*—holding on to a grudge, as we sometimes put it—gives the devil a foothold that he can use in tempting and trying us.

4. Paul seems to have left an open door in Troas unentered because of his great concern for the Corinthians. When do you think it is okay to ignore an open door "of the Lord," and when would you feel compelled to enter in spite of other circumstances?

Frequently we see many opportunities open to us. In that each one bears some promise of doing God's will, each might be seen as an open door from God. But to enter one is to ignore the others—some or all of which may never again be open.

Paul had an opportunity for prolonged ministry at Troas. He also had opportunity to go on to Macedonia and then to Corinth. Because of the urgency of the situation in Corinth, and because his heart was with the Corinthians, he chose to go on. We today need to determine which open doors represent the best use of our gifts, the most prudent consideration of urgency, and the honest expression of the burden of our own hearts.

5. In what kind of efforts or ministries are you most likely to say with Paul, "Who is sufficient for these things?" Name some situations when you have most appreciated that "our sufficiency is of God."

Paul's declaration is consistent with Jesus' words in John 15:5: "Without me ye can do nothing." But also inherent in these statements is the truth expressed in Luke 1:37, "With God nothing shall be impossible." Perhaps your students have heard the expression, "Attempt something so big that, if God is not in it, it is sure to fail." Have any of them done that? Perhaps they can tell of feeling overwhelmed at first, but of giving thanks to God when He brought it to a successful conclusion.

Parenting is another area in which many people feel insufficient. New parents, or parents of children with special needs, may feel overwhelmed by the challenge at first. But later they realize that God's grace has empowered them for the task.

Trials and Triumphs of Christian Ministry

DEVOTIONAL READING: 2 Corinthians 6:1-10.

BACKGROUND SCRIPTURE: 2 Corinthians 4.

PRINTED TEXT: 2 Corinthians 4:5-18.

2 Corinthians 4:5-18

5 For we preach not ourselves, but Christ Jesus the Lord; and ourselves your servants for Jesus' sake.

6 For God, who commanded the light to shine out of darkness, hath shined in our hearts, to give the light of the knowledge of the glory of God in the face of Jesus Christ.

7 But we have this treasure in earthen vessels, that the excellency of the power may be of God, and not of us.

8 We are troubled on every side, yet not distressed; we are perplexed, but not in despair;

9 Persecuted, but not forsaken; cast down, but not destroyed;

10 Always bearing about in the body the dying of the Lord Jesus, that the life also of Jesus might be made manifest in our body.

11 For we which live are alway delivered unto death for Jesus' sake, that the life also of Jesus might be made manifest in our mortal flesh.

12 So then death worketh in us, but life in you.

13 We having the same spirit of faith, according as it is written, I believed, and therefore have I spoken; we also believe, and therefore speak;

14 Knowing that he which raised up the Lord Jesus shall raise up us also by Jesus, and shall present us with you.

15 For all things are for your sakes, that the abundant grace might through the thanksgiving of many redound to the glory of God.

16 For which cause we faint not; but though our outward man perish, yet the inward man is renewed day by day.

17 For our light affliction, which is but for a moment, worketh for us a far more exceeding and eternal weight of glory;

18 While we look not at the things which are seen, but at the things which are not seen: for the things which are seen are temporal; but the things which are not seen are eternal.

**May
14**

GOLDEN TEXT: We are troubled on every side, yet not distressed; we are perplexed, but not in despair; persecuted, but not forsaken; cast down, but not destroyed.
—2 Corinthians 4:8, 9.

Helping a Church Confront Crisis
Unit 3: Unity Expressed in Ministry
(Lessons 10-13)

Lesson Aims

After completing this lesson, students should be able to:

1. Recite the trials and the blessings Paul said accompanied his service for the Lord.

2. Explain how we, like Paul, can persevere through the trials of Christian ministry.

3. Focus on the eternal in order to bear the trials and appreciate the blessings that come with serving Christ.

Lesson Outline

Introduction

A. A Greater Honor

During the American Civil War, General William T. Sherman created a special corps to carry out his campaign against the Confederates in Georgia. He passed over the man who had expected to command this corps, giving this duty instead to General O. O. Howard, a man of strong Christian faith who had a distinguished combat record. When the war was over, the Union army prepared for a victory parade in Washington, D.C. The night before the grand parade, General Sherman called Howard to his quarters.

"General Howard," said Sherman, "I have a problem. The man that you were chosen ahead of to direct the special corps has some powerful friends in Washington, and they are demanding that he lead the corps in the parade."

"But, General Sherman," Howard protested, "I earned the right to lead that corps."

"I know that, Howard," Sherman replied. "But I also know that you are a Christian and that you know how to handle disappointment."

"Since you put it that way," Howard replied, "I'll accept your decision."

"Thank you, Howard. Report to me at nine in the morning." When General Howard reported the next morning, General Sherman brought him to the head of the parade and ordered him to ride by his side.

This is similar to the experience of Paul, who endured much suffering and many disappointments in his service for Christ. But he never complained, for he knew that he would one day be part of the heavenly parade, enjoying the "eternal weight of glory."

B. Lesson Background

Despite Paul's best efforts to help the Corinthian church and address its problems, some in the church had become critical of Paul and his ministry. He begins his response to these critics in the third chapter of 2 Corinthians. In today's lesson text (taken from chapter 4), Paul continues the defense of his ministry by affirming his complete trust in Christ and his desire to make Christ the heart of his ministry. The trials and personal conflicts he experienced had not shaken that trust. Because Paul's vision was focused on that which is eternal, he could deal with any trials with an attitude of triumph.

Every Christian at one time or another has experienced trials or setbacks while serving Christ, some of them quite severe. Paul's testimony is one from which we can draw strength and encouragement for these occasions. The Source of Paul's triumph can be ours as well!

I. Ministry's Focus
(2 Corinthians 4:5-7)

A. The Message (vv. 5, 6)

5. For we preach not ourselves, but Christ Jesus the Lord; and ourselves your servants for Jesus' sake.

In the previous verses of this chapter, Paul referred to those who were accusing him of preaching the gospel for his own personal gain and glory. He asserted that he had never engaged in behaving dishonestly, "walking in craftiness," or "handling the word of God deceitfully." *We preach not ourselves,* he declares (apparently including those who had accompanied him on his journeys); instead, we preach *Christ Jesus the Lord.* Paul had stated in his first letter: "I determined not to know any thing among you, save Jesus Christ, and him crucified" (1 Corinthians 2:2).

Paul was also clear about his and his companions' duty, speaking of them as *your servants for Jesus' sake.* The word translated "servants" is more accurately rendered "bondservants" or "slaves." Paul's emphasis is one that every follower of Christ ought to emulate. [See question #1, page 320.]

6. For God, who commanded the light to shine out of darkness, hath shined in our hearts, to give the light of the knowledge of the glory of God in the face of Jesus Christ.

Here Paul states the reason that he had become a slave of Christ. In mentioning the *light* that shone *out of darkness,* he describes the experience of all who come to know Christ as "the light of the world" (John 8:12). They are thereby delivered from spiritual "darkness" (Colossians 1:12, 13) "into his marvelous light" (1 Peter 2:9). Their lifestyle is described as walking in the light (Ephesians 5:8; 1 John 1:7).

Paul's words call to mind God's announcement at the beginning of creation: "Let there be light" (Genesis 1:3). Through Jesus God has initiated a spiritual re-creation, declaring to those in the darkness of sin, "Let there be light!" The reference to seeing *the glory of God* in *the face of Jesus Christ* recalls Paul's contrast of Moses' veiled face under the Old Covenant with Christ's unveiled face under the New Covenant (3:12-18).

B. The Messengers (v. 7)

7. But we have this treasure in earthen vessels, that the excellency of the power may be of God, and not of us.

God in His infinite wisdom has chosen to reveal His message of salvation through human beings. This message is the *treasure* of which Paul speaks. We who carry the message are the *earthen vessels,* or clay pots! In using this expression, Paul probably had in mind the practice of rulers of that day who kept their captured wealth of gold and silver in clay pots. The cheap clay vessels, contrasting sharply with the vast wealth they contained, did not attract the attention of potential robbers.

In the same way, the use of weak human vessels to convey God's message is contrasted with the *excellency of the power* of that message. That power is not in us; it is *of God.* We are merely the clay pots; the treasure is that which is in us—the power of the indwelling Spirit of God. Later Paul would note how his "thorn in the flesh" was

How to Say It

CORINTH. *Kor*-inth.
CORINTHIANS. Kor-*in*-thee-unz.
DAMASCUS. Duh-*mass*-kus.
LYSTRA. *Liss*-truh.

used of God to demonstrate the sufficiency of His grace and the power of Christ (12:7-10). [See question #2, page 320.]

WORTHLESS TREASURE

In 1857 the S.S. *Central America* sank off the coast of South Carolina during a hurricane. It was carrying passengers from the California gold fields and a cargo of gold bullion worth about twenty-one million dollars in today's value.

For 130 years the wreckage lay lost on the ocean floor. Then in 1987 a group of investors funded an expedition that found the ruined ship. In the process of recovering the cargo, the salvagers spent some thirty million dollars. To add insult to injury, a court awarded ten percent of the twenty-one million dollars to the company that originally insured the cargo. The judge commented that he wished the cargo had been worth a billion dollars so that it would have been worth the salvage effort.

Compare that vessel and its cargo with the "earthen vessels" and their contents of which Paul wrote. The vessels in each case are mere physical "stuff," but how much the contents differ! The things of this world often are not worth either the trouble or the cost that is required to obtain them.

Paul, however, was speaking of the gospel—a treasure of which Jesus also spoke, saying that a person ought to give all he has to possess it (Matthew 13:44). It is a prize that life's storms cannot harm or destroy. This treasure also has a unique power: it is able to "salvage" the one who seeks it!   —C. R. B.

II. Ministry's Trials (2 Corinthians 4:8-12)

A. Severe but Bearable (vv. 8, 9)

8, 9. We are troubled on every side, yet not distressed; we are perplexed, but not in despair; persecuted, but not forsaken; cast down, but not destroyed.

At this point (approximately A.D. 56) there was very little persecution of Christians by the Roman Empire. That would not become severe until the next decade under Emperor Nero. The Jewish leaders, however, exerted whatever pressure they could in an effort to stop the spread of Christianity. For Paul and his companions, the problems and sufferings they had endured for Christ's sake had often been intense. Later in this same letter Paul gave a more detailed and graphic description of some of his own trials (11:23-28). In spite of the severity of these circumstances, Paul was *not distressed, not in despair, not forsaken*, and *not destroyed*. Whenever the Corinthians faced persecution, they could look to Paul's example and take courage. The key to his perseverance was not his own strength but his trust in God to sustain him through each crisis. [See question #3, page 320.]

B. Serving a Purpose (vv. 10-12)

10. Always bearing about in the body the dying of the Lord Jesus, that the life also of Jesus might be made manifest in our body.

According to 2 Corinthians 11:24 and 25, five times Paul received thirty-nine lashes with a whip, three times he was beaten with rods, and once he was stoned. Not all of these incidents are mentioned in the New Testament; the record of his stoning at Lystra during his first missionary journey is found in Acts 14:19.

The phrase *bearing about in the body the dying of the Lord Jesus* does not mean that Paul believed he could suffer in the way that Jesus did on the cross. Its meaning is explained in the next verse.

11. For we which live are alway delivered unto death for Jesus' sake, that the life also of Jesus might be made manifest in our mortal flesh.

For Paul to bear in his body "the dying of the Lord Jesus" means being *delivered unto death for Jesus' sake*. Paul constantly faced hazardous, life-threatening situations for the cause of Christ. This theme is found in other writings of Paul. In Romans 8:36 he quotes Psalm 44:22: "For thy sake we are killed all the day long." In 1 Corinthians 15:31 he writes, "I die daily."

The *we* in this verse may include Paul and his companions, or it may be more extensive, including the apostles and others who had been martyred for Christ. Paul and others were willing to suffer in order that *the life of Jesus might be made manifest*. This is similar in meaning to the "clay pot" language of verse 7: God uses human frailty to demonstrate His power.

12. So then death worketh in us, but life in you.

Death was at work in Paul and others who brought the gospel in the sense that they frequently suffered potentially lethal persecution. Those who courageously faced such circumstances did so in order that their example might call attention to the message of eternal *life*. Paul was not saying that suffering and death in themselves have intrinsic value. Their value lies in the fact that the manner in which the Christian faces suffering and death provides a compelling testimony to others of the reality of his faith.

TARGET PRACTICE

William Tell was a legendary Swiss patriot. No doubt the most familiar story told about him is reputed to have taken place in the year 1307. Tell was forced to shoot an arrow into an apple placed on his son's head, because he refused to acknowledge Austrian authority over his land. Tell's aim was true, and his son was spared any injury. Tell was still imprisoned, however, because he later commented that if he had injured his son, he would have put his second arrow through the Austrian governor's heart.

Perhaps inspired by this tale, a Portland, Oregon, man tried to shoot a one-gallon fuel can off the head of his friend, Anthony Roberts. The incident took place as part of an initiation into an adventurers' group called Mountain Men Anonymous. As you might have guessed, both men were reported to have been drinking at the time. Roberts lost an eye, but suffered no brain damage. He later said, "I feel really stupid."

Roberts suffered a serious injury and came very close to being killed, and for no legitimate purpose whatsoever. Paul, however, was willing to be a target of the devil's "arrows" for the noblest purpose of all—spreading the gospel of Christ. The injuries he suffered he willingly endured for the sake of bringing others to know Christ, whose power had made such a dramatic change in his own life.   —C. R. B.

III. Ministry's Hope
(2 Corinthians 4:13-18)

A. Firmly Founded (vv. 13, 14)

13, 14. We having the same spirit of faith, according as it is written, I believed, and therefore have I spoken; we also believe, and therefore speak; knowing that he which raised up the Lord Jesus shall raise up us also by Jesus, and shall present us with you.

The word *spirit* in the phrase *spirit of faith* probably does not refer to the Holy Spirit, but to the attitude or perspective of faith, since faith is the subject of the Old Testament text that Paul cites. The quotation from this particular Psalm (116:10) is appropriate, for the writer seems to have been experiencing some of the same difficulties that Paul was facing. In verse 3 of the psalm he writes: "The sorrows of death compassed me, and the pains of hell gat hold upon

While there's nothing funny about persecution, the humorous illustration on today's visual reminds us that God is with us in these tough times as well as in good times.

Visual for lesson 11

me: I found trouble and sorrow." Paul could readily identify with this situation. No doubt he also found consolation in the later verses of the Psalm (vv. 12-19) in which the writer testifies how he found deliverance in the Lord.

Paul's hope for deliverance from his present troubles was grounded in his faith in the resurrection of Jesus. He knew that as God *raised up the Lord Jesus,* He *shall raise up us also by Jesus, and shall present us with you.* On the day Jesus returns, God will raise those who have "fallen asleep in Christ" (1 Corinthians 15:18) and present the faithful before His throne in glory and honor. Paul's faith in the resurrection and in the return of Christ sustained him through all kinds of difficulties. He encouraged his readers in Corinth to live by that same faith.

B. Renewed Daily (vv. 15, 16)

15. For all things are for your sakes, that the abundant grace might through the thanksgiving of many redound to the glory of God.

All things refers to the afflictions and humiliations that Paul had suffered. Paul never suggests that there is any virtue in suffering as such. Rather, his suffering had been *for your sakes.* Whatever pain he may have experienced in the past was for the purpose of bringing others like the Corinthians into a saving relationship with Jesus Christ.

Paul had committed his life to winning as *many* people to Christ as he could. In so doing he was making available God's *abundant grace.* God is glorified when people accept His grace, so the greater the number who accept it, the greater the number who offer their thanks *to the glory of God.*

This principle is still valid. Jesus' Great Commission to carry the gospel into all the world has never been repealed. Unfortunately, many Christians today have never understood the Great Commission or have little concern for it. With perhaps as many as four billion people in the world who have never come to God through

Jesus Christ, we have vast opportunities to labor for God's glory.

16. For which cause we faint not; but though our outward man perish, yet the inward man is renewed day by day.

We faint not. Paul used this same expression in verse 1 of this chapter. The word may refer to physical weariness, but it can also mean "to become fainthearted" or "to fall into despair." On many occasions Paul must have become physically exhausted, but he never became disheartened to the point that he wanted to quit the Lord's work.

God never intended our physical bodies to be immortal. The *outward man* cannot escape the limitations imposed by time and disease. Paul had no problem accepting these limitations, for he was able to rejoice that the *inward man is renewed day by day.* That renewal comes through daily communion with God through prayer and the study of His Word. [See question #4, page 320.]

C. Fixed on Eternity (vv. 17, 18)

17. For our light affliction, which is but for a moment, worketh for us a far more exceeding and eternal weight of glory.

Most of us would not look upon all that Paul suffered as *light affliction*! For most of us these experiences would represent crushing burdens. But Paul knew that his afflictions were *but for a moment.* Many today live just for the moment, or view life and set priorities by temporal standards. Paul, on the other hand, saw life through an eternal telescope, which allowed him to see the *eternal weight of glory* that made his present afflictions seem light in comparison. [See question #5, page 320.]

18. While we look not at the things which are seen, but at the things which are not seen: for the things which are seen are temporal; but the things which are not seen are eternal.

Many today are obsessed with the *things which are seen.* To them, if something cannot be experienced through one or more of the five senses, then it does not really exist, or at least it cannot be important. Paul turns this view on its head, asserting that just the opposite is true. What we see is only *temporal* (temporary) and is relatively insignificant in view of the unseen, but lasting, realities of eternity.

Conclusion

A. "We Faint Not"

On every hand the forces of secularism, demonstrated by a ceaseless quest for pleasure and possessions, seem to be winning. Pollsters tell us that many people still believe in God, but we know very well that such an expression of faith is at best shallow and uninformed. People in some parts of the world are facing severe persecution such as Paul suffered, while the worst that many of us may suffer for Christ's sake is a polite rebuff or a condescending sneer when we present the claims of the gospel to others. Yet even this "light affliction" may cause us to become fainthearted and discouraged.

Paul's response to the trials he faced was a ringing "we faint not." His words were not based on youthful bravado or blissful ignorance. Nor were they the response of an emotionally unstable man who did not know what he was talking about. At the time that Paul (then known as Saul) journeyed to Damascus for the purpose of persecuting Christians (about two decades prior to writing this letter to the Corinthians), he had gained a reputation among his Jewish countrymen as a scholar and a zealot for the Jewish faith.

Paul knew that once he became a disciple of Jesus, all that would change. He knew that his conversion to Christianity would cost him most of his friends and the honors that he had gained among his own people. He knew that his actions could lead to his imprisonment and even his death. Yet Paul did not hesitate in making the decision to follow Christ. Years later he looked back with this observation: "I count all things but loss for the excellency of the knowledge of Christ Jesus my Lord: for whom I have suffered the loss of all things, and do count them but dung, that I may win Christ" (Philippians 3:8).

B. This World Is Not My Home

There was a reason that Paul could endure trials and persecutions: he realized that this world is in no way the real or final home of Christians; we are just passing through. Like Abraham, we are strangers and sojourners looking for "a better country, that is, a heavenly" (Hebrews 11:16). Of necessity we must live under a worldly government, and that citizenship requires us to behave in a certain way. We ought to obey the laws of the land unless they require us to engage in an activity that violates God's laws. However, our true citizenship is in Heaven; and that citizenship also carries certain obligations. Concerning this issue, Peter wrote, "I beseech you as strangers and pilgrims, abstain from fleshly lusts, which war against the soul" (1 Peter 2:11).

Paul understood the principle of dual citizenship, and he knew where his priorities lay. His "outward man" (his physical body) might suffer and even perish; but that did not greatly concern him, for the "inward man" (his spirit) was "renewed day by day." Through the eyes of faith he could "look . . . at the things which are not seen," and this gave him the assurance that he would share in the glory that is promised to all who faithfully serve Jesus.

C. Christians Can!

Christians can handle disappointments because they are not self-centered. We often suffer disappointments because we want the wrong things for selfish purposes. But if we put Christ and others first, these lesser goals are seen for what they are—short-sighted and inadequate.

Christians can handle disappointments because they help bear one another's burdens. Every church ought to be a caring support group for its members in times of trouble. Whether these times involve illness, financial difficulties, or moral issues, the church should always be there to offer guidance and assistance.

Christians can handle disappointments because they understand that any present "light affliction" is but for a moment. They can look beyond such temporary inconveniences, knowing that God has in store for them the "eternal weight of glory!"

D. Prayer

O God, give us the eyes to see beyond the temporary trials we all must face and to catch a glimpse of the grand triumph You have in store for us. At the same time, give us the zeal to share that vision with others about us who are lost in the darkness. In Jesus' name. Amen.

E. Thought to Remember

Keep your eyes on "the things which are not seen."

Home Daily Bible Readings

Monday, May 8—God's Light Shines in Our Hearts (2 Corinthians 4:1-7)
Tuesday, May 9—God Raised Jesus and Will Raise Us (2 Corinthians 4:8-15)
Wednesday, May 10—We Walk and Live by Faith (2 Corinthians 4:16—5:10)
Thursday, May 11—Reconciled to Be Reconcilers (2 Corinthians 5:11-21)
Friday, May 12—Open Wide Your Hearts (2 Corinthians 6:1-11)
Saturday, May 13—We Are Temples of the Living God (2 Corinthians 6:14—7:1)
Sunday, May 14—Paul's Joy at the Corinthians' Repentance (2 Corinthians 7:2-16)

Learning by Doing

This page contains an alternate lesson plan emphasizing learning activities.
Classes desiring such student involvement will find these suggestions helpful.

Learning Goals

After this lesson each student will be able to:

1. Recite the trials and the blessings Paul said accompanied his service for the Lord.

2. Explain how we, like Paul, can persevere through the trials of Christian ministry.

3. Focus on the eternal in order to bear the trials and appreciate the blessings that come with serving Christ.

Into the Lesson

Write the words "Trials" and "Blessings" on the chalkboard or an overhead projector transparency. Draw a horizontal line underneath them and a vertical line between them. Open the lesson by asking the class to suggest blessings they have experienced since coming to know the Lord, and list these under the word *Blessings*. Do the same with *Trials*. Continue until you have more than just a few. Ask, "Which ones—from either column—have come to us specifically because we are Christians? Which have also come to many non-Christians? How did we Christians react differently to these blessings and trials from the way non-Christians reacted?" Lead into the Bible text by stating: "In today's lesson, the apostle Paul presents himself as one who persisted in his faith in spite of many trials. Through it all he remained joyful because God helped him—just as He can help us to triumph over the trials we face."

Into the Word

Divide the class into at least three groups of three to five students. Assign one of the following sections to each group. Have them write their answers and then report them to the class.

1. Proclaim the Message. Read 2 Corinthians 4:1-7, 13. Paul had received a ministry (v. 1) and as a result had "renounced the hidden things of dishonesty" (v. 2). Answer the following questions to better understand that ministry: 1. What specific characteristics describe this putting away of dishonesty (v. 2)? *(not walking in craftiness; not handling the word of God deceitfully; manifestation of the truth)* 2. What is the "treasure in earthen vessels" (v. 7)? *(gospel message that Jesus Christ is Lord)* 3. With whom does Paul say he has the "same spirit of faith" (v. 13)? *(the psalmist who wrote Psalm 116:10)* 4. What is the point of this comparison? *(making an audible expression of faith regardless—even when facing death.)*

2. Persist Under God's Power. Read 2 Corinthians 4:1, 7-12, 16. In this section Paul affirms his unyielding loyalty to the lordship of Christ. The phrase that is translated "faint not" in verses 1 and 16 is used four more times in the New Testament (Luke 18:1; Galatians 6:9; Ephesians 3:13; 2 Thessalonians 3:13). 1. What does *faint* mean? *(to lose heart, give up; it implies becoming discouraged or brokenhearted)* 2. Paul contrasts the eternal, incorruptible, glorious gospel with the temporal, corruptible, non-glorious human vessel that proclaims it. How does Paul identify the frailty of the earthen vessel (vv. 8, 9)? *(troubled, perplexed, persecuted, cast down)* 3. What is the point of this description of weakness? *(God manifests His power in His servant's weakness so that we never have to give up)* 4. What does Paul mean by the phrase "bearing about in the body the dying of the Lord Jesus" (v. 10)? *(servanthood involves self-sacrifice, a willingness to suffer physically, mentally, socially, etc.)*

3. Point to Eternal Glory. Read 2 Corinthians 4:13-18. Paul was able to remain loyal to the lordship of Jesus in spite of severe trials because of his continuous focus. 1. What guarantee does Paul give for our own resurrection (v. 14)? *(Christ's resurrection)* 2. To what does the "all things" refer in v. 15? *(whatever is suffered or endured for Christ)* 3. What terms in this chapter refer to the "outward man" (v. 16)? *(earthen vessel, v. 7; body, v. 10; mortal flesh, v. 11)* 4. Why does Paul's focus help him to persist? *(trials are seen in the light of the eternal perspective)*

Into Life

Paul would not give up when he faced trials or difficulties. Yet, many Christians give up on God when they face problems. Discuss why this happens and how a focus on eternity affects one's personal attitude about the difficulties of life.

Ask the class to brainstorm the following question: "What trials or difficulties do you believe most Christians struggle under today?" Write their ideas on the chalkboard. Then ask: What trials or difficulties do you personally face today? Based upon this study, how should our attitudes be adjusted when we encounter trials?

State: "Let's put on our eternal goggles and see life as only a brief moment in time, and rejoice that God gives us the power to triumph in Christ."

Let's Talk It Over

The questions on this page are designed to encourage review of the lesson Scriptures and to promote discussion of the lesson by the class. The answers provided are only discussion starters. Let your class talk it over from there.

1. The lesson writer says Paul's view of himself as the church's servant "is one that every follower of Christ ought to emulate." What do you think would happen if every Christian took such a view? What difference would it make?

Jesus once pointed out that "the Son of man came not to be ministered unto, but to minister, and to give his life a ransom for many" (Mark 10:45). The Sunday school class that sees itself as "servants for Jesus' sake" will go beyond learning Bible truths to meeting needs of others in the church. The youth group that sees itself as "servants for Jesus' sake" will go beyond fun activities to service projects and ministry activities. The individual Christian who takes such a view will stop evaluating the church's services and ministries by what he or she "gets out of it" and start looking for ways to put something into it.

2. How important do you think it is to see yourself as an "earthen vessel" containing the priceless treasure of the gospel? Why?

The entertainment industry has served us a steady diet of handsome, rugged heroes and beautiful heroines. We often go to great lengths to make ourselves similarly handsome and beautiful. It is easy to imagine that we would be more effective in Christian witness if we were more physically attractive. But often the opposite is true. Perhaps we have listened to a speaker who was born with a physical handicap or was disfigured by an accident or fire. We may have been amazed by the way God's love radiated from that person. Christians who are of average appearance can accomplish something similar. When we are concentrating on demonstrating the beauty of the gospel instead of our own beauty, we will have a better chance of success in our witnessing.

3. In spite of all the trouble Paul faced, he never felt defeated. What resources do we Christians have so that, as we face disappointments, frustrations, and trials, we can have confidence of victory?

As fallible human beings we are prone to wanting to impose our own will on God. And when that does not work, frustration is the result. By using Jesus' prayer, "Not my will, but thine," we can bring our "spiritual compass needle" back to God and His will. Also we enjoy great support in our Christian fellowship. Perhaps some in your class can tell how other Sunday school students or participants in small groups helped to encourage them when they needed it most.

4. How can we make sure that we, like Paul, are "renewed day by day" in the "inward man"?

This is one of the many places in the New Testament that indicates the importance of what we call "daily devotions." How can we handle the pressures of service, the distractions of the world, and the weaknesses of our physical body without these? The renewing of the inward man is accomplished in part through a daily reading of and meditation on the Word of God. And it is well to point out that the renewing requires something more than a hasty, cursory reading. We must give the Word a chance to permeate our thoughts and hopes and goals. This renewing is also accomplished through daily prayer. This must be a genuine communion with the heavenly Father and not a perfunctory religious exercise. In it we can constantly seek God's guidance and strength for our service and gain victory over the temptations to compromise or give up.

Perhaps your students can tell some of the methods or materials they have used for effective quiet times with the Word.

5. How can we keep the "eternal weight of glory" in focus while facing our "light affliction"?

When we face afflictions, it is hard to think of them as "light." Perhaps we need to focus more on Jesus—see Hebrews 12:2, 3. It is also good to remind ourselves that affliction is only temporary. With the passing of days and weeks many of our trials fade away. Even those that linger for months or years are nevertheless temporary and certain to give way at last to a glorious eternity.

Paul advised us in Colossians 3:1 to "seek those things which are above, where Christ sitteth on the right hand of God." Of course, there is much about our heavenly life that we do not yet understand. But it is very helpful simply to imagine ourselves in the presence of our loving and compassionate Savior. We can anticipate seeing His smile of welcome, hearing His words of forgiveness and reassurance, feeling the touch of His hand upon ours, and realizing that we will never be separated from Him.

Collection for Jerusalem Christians

DEVOTIONAL READING: 2 Corinthians 8:1-15.

BACKGROUND SCRIPTURE: 2 Corinthians 9.

PRINTED TEXT: 2 Corinthians 9:1-13.

2 Corinthians 9:1-13

1 For as touching the ministering to the saints, it is superfluous for me to write to you:

2 For I know the forwardness of your mind, for which I boast of you to them of Macedonia, that Achaia was ready a year ago; and your zeal hath provoked very many.

3 Yet have I sent the brethren, lest our boasting of you should be in vain in this behalf; that, as I said, ye may be ready:

4 Lest haply if they of Macedonia come with me, and find you unprepared, we (that we say not, ye) should be ashamed in this same confident boasting.

5 Therefore I thought it necessary to exhort the brethren, that they would go before unto you, and make up beforehand your bounty, whereof ye had notice before, that the same might be ready, as a matter of bounty, and not as of covetousness.

6 But this I say, He which soweth sparingly shall reap also sparingly; and he which soweth bountifully shall reap also bountifully.

7 Every man according as he purposeth in his heart, so let him give; not grudgingly, or of necessity: for God loveth a cheerful giver.

8 And God is able to make all grace abound toward you; that ye, always having all sufficiency in all things, may abound to every good work:

9 (As it is written, He hath dispersed abroad; he hath given to the poor: his righteousness remaineth for ever.

10 Now he that ministereth seed to the sower both minister bread for your food, and multiply your seed sown, and increase the fruits of your righteousness:)

11 Being enriched in every thing to all bountifulness, which causeth through us thanksgiving to God.

12 For the administration of this service not only supplieth the want of the saints, but is abundant also by many thanksgivings unto God;

13 While by the experiment of this ministration they glorify God for your professed subjection unto the gospel of Christ, and for your liberal distribution unto them, and unto all men.

GOLDEN TEXT: Every man according as he purposeth in his heart, so let him give; not grudgingly, or of necessity: for God loveth a cheerful giver.—2 Corinthians 9:7.

Lesson Aims

After this lesson students will be able to:

1. Summarize Paul's instructions about the Corinthians' participation in the collection for the Jerusalem Christians.

2. Summarize the principles of Christian giving found in today's text.

3. Apply the principles in today's text to their personal financial giving to the Lord's work.

Lesson Outline

INTRODUCTION
   A. Knotty Generosity
   B. Lesson Background
 I. CHALLENGED TO GIVE (2 Corinthians 9:1-5)
   A. Paul's Commendation (vv. 1, 2)
   B. The Church's Preparation (vv. 3, 4)
   C. Paul's Concern (v. 5)
     Encouragement to Give
II. PRINCIPLES OF GIVING (2 Corinthians 9:6-13)
   A. Sowing Bountifully (v. 6)
   B. Giving Cheerfully (v. 7)
   C. Trusting God's Promises (vv. 8-11)
   D. Meeting Needs (v. 12)
     An Anonymous Donor
   E. Glorifying God (v. 13)
CONCLUSION
   A. Rules for Giving
   B. Purposes for Giving
   C. Prayer
   D. Thought to Remember

Introduction

A. Knotty Generosity

John Eliot, a seventeenth-century missionary to the Indians of New England, was noted for his unbounded generosity. His yearly salary of fifty pounds was often given almost entirely to charity. On one occasion the secretary of the missionary society that supported Eliot tried to protect him from his own generosity. To keep him from giving away his entire quarterly stipend before he reached home, the secretary took Eliot's pay and tied a portion of it in each of the four corners of a handkerchief. Then he pulled the knots and tightened them as much as he could before handing the handkerchief to the missionary.

On his way home Eliot met a woman whose appearance indicated dire poverty. He stopped to speak to her, and soon his heart was so touched that he reached into his pocket to get a coin for her. For some time he pulled and pulled at the knots in his handkerchief, trying to loosen one of them. But he could not do so. Finally he rolled the handkerchief up into a ball and handed it to the astonished woman with these words: "My dear woman, I think the Lord meant for you to have it all."

Eliot had learned what many Christians need to learn: "God loveth a cheerful giver."

B. Lesson Background

Being a follower of Jesus Christ in first-century Jerusalem was not always easy. Poverty was a problem for some right from the beginning, but it seems that other believers had the resources to deal with the situation (Acts 4:32-37; 6:1). Intimidation and persecution were growing problems (Acts 4:1-18; 5:17, 18, 26-40; 6:9-12), increasing after the stoning of Stephen (Acts 7:54-60) to the point that most of the Christians fled. "At that time," says Acts 8:1, "there was a great persecution against the church which was at Jerusalem."

Persecution and poverty continued. It may be that some of the believers had property confiscated at this time (see Hebrews 10:34). In addition, a great "dearth," or famine (Acts 11:27, 28), added to their poverty. In response—or, rather, in prophetic anticipation—the church at Antioch of Syria sent a contribution to the elders of the Jerusalem church "by the hands of Barnabas and Saul" (Acts 11:29, 30).

Later, at the Jerusalem conference reported in Acts 15, the issue of poverty was apparently discussed. Luke does not mention this in Acts, but Paul says in Galatians 2:9 and 10 that the apostles and elders (he mentions "James, Cephas, and John") encouraged him to "remember the poor," something Paul was "forward [or eager] to do."

Paul began his second missionary journey "some days after" that conference (Acts 15:36-41). During this journey, Paul demonstrated his eagerness to "remember the poor" by arranging to gather contributions from the churches he visited and to have them sent to the church at Jerusalem. Apparently Paul began this effort among the Galatian churches and then urged the Corinthians to follow their example (1 Corinthians 16:1). In the eighth chapter of 2 Corinthians, Paul mentioned the need once again, citing the generosity of the churches in Macedonia in order to challenge the Corinthians in their giving (vv. 1-6). In the ninth chapter, from which today's text is taken, Paul provided further and more detailed instructions about giving.

I. Challenged to Give
(2 Corinthians 9:1-5)

A. Paul's Commendation (vv. 1, 2)

1, 2. For as touching the ministering to the saints, it is superfluous for me to write to you: for I know the forwardness of your mind, for which I boast of you to them of Macedonia, that Achaia was ready a year ago; and your zeal hath provoked very many.

In the previous chapter Paul mentioned that he was sending Titus and two other brothers to Corinth to oversee the collection for *the ministering to the saints*—that is, to help the Jerusalem Christians (vv. 18-22). Since Paul had come under attack by some in the Corinthian church, he wisely limited his involvement in this activity, lest his enemies would have an occasion to bring further charges against him.

It is unfortunate that some in the ministry have handled money in such a way as to arouse suspicions about their honesty. By sending these men, all of whom were known and respected by the churches, Paul removed the likelihood that any could challenge his integrity. We today would be wise to follow his example of "providing for honest things, not only in the sight of the Lord, but also in the sight of men" (2 Corinthians 8:21). [See question #1, page 328.]

It is superfluous for me to write to you. Paul thus complimented the Corinthians on their *forwardness* (willingness) to fulfill their ministry to the Jerusalem Christians. In fact, he had *boasted* about the generosity of the churches in *Achaia* (the province in which Corinth was located) to the churches in *Macedonia* (the province in northern Greece where cities such as Philippi and Thessalonica were located).

Your zeal hath provoked very many. To us the word *provoked* carries primarily negative connotations: one who is provoked is likely upset about something. However, in some passages (including this one) it means simply to stir up someone in a positive sense. Such a passage is Hebrews 10:24: "Let us consider one another to provoke unto love and to good works."

B. The Church's Preparation (vv. 3, 4)

3. Yet have I sent the brethren, lest our boasting of you should be in vain in this behalf; that, as I said, ye may be ready.

Titus and the two other *brethren* had been *sent* on ahead to make the necessary preparations for receiving the collection. After Paul had commended the generosity of the Corinthians, he did not want his words to *be in vain*. We do not know how this collection was organized, but in 1 Corinthians 16:2, Paul wrote, "Upon the first day of the week let every one of you lay by him in store, as God hath prospered him." Evidently the collections were taken weekly when the congregation assembled for worship.

4. Lest haply if they of Macedonia come with me, and find you unprepared, we (that we say not, ye) should be ashamed in this same confident boasting.

Paul said that some of the Christians from *Macedonia* might accompany him when he returned to Corinth. (Whether they did or not we do not know.) Should that happen, Paul said, then not only those in Corinth but also he and his companions would have been embarrassed because of Paul's *confident boasting* about the Corinthians. [See question #2, page 328.]

C. Paul's Concern (v. 5)

5. Therefore I thought it necessary to exhort the brethren, that they would go before unto you, and make up beforehand your bounty, whereof ye had notice before, that the same might be ready, as a matter of bounty, and not as of covetousness.

The Greek word translated *bounty* is the source of our word "eulogy," which literally means "to speak well of." Here it describes the item that became well spoken of because of the blessing it brought both to the giver and to the recipient.

Paul wanted the Corinthians' collection to be *ready* before he arrived so that he would not have to press the issue of giving with them. If he should have to coerce them or plead with them to give, it would appear as though he were trying to obtain the money for himself. This would look like *covetousness* on Paul's part. (In that day it was not uncommon for itinerant teachers to extort money from their students.) Paul wanted to avoid any controversy about his motives, for this would only further antagonize those in Corinth who were already critical of him.

ENCOURAGEMENT TO GIVE

How do you finance a college education? These days it is not at all uncommon for a year's tuition, room and board, and incidentals to total ten thousand dollars or more. Of course, if "incidentals" include the three "C"s—computer, car, and cash for extracurricular activities—the cost can go *much* higher!

A few years ago Mike Hayes of Rochelle, Illinois, wrote to Bob Greene, a columnist for the *Chicago Tribune*. Mike asked each of Greene's readers to send him a penny to help finance his college education.

The response was amazing: Mike received eighty-eight thousand letters, and the contributions totaled more than fourteen thousand dollars!

In addition to pennies, he received dollar bills and checks for one hundred dollars. (With this kind of entrepreneurial spirit, we'll assume Mike decided to become a business major!) However, just to make sure Mike would be the right kind of student, one donor wrote, "Here's a penny. If you use it to buy drugs I hope a bolt of lightning strikes you dead."

While Mike Hayes may be commended for his creativity, Paul is a more noble example for us. Paul encouraged the Corinthians to give, not for his own profit, but for the benefit of impoverished Christians in the Jerusalem church. Most of us don't need any encouragement to be selfish! We need encouragement to give willingly and even sacrificially for the good of others—as Jesus did. —C. R. B.

II. Principles of Giving
(2 Corinthians 9:6-13)

A. Sowing Bountifully (v. 6)

6. But this I say, He which soweth sparingly shall reap also sparingly; and he which soweth bountifully shall reap also bountifully.

Paul's words sound like a proverb; however, nothing resembling this saying can be found in the book of Proverbs. His observation is quite apparent: a farmer who plants a small plot is not as likely to enjoy as large a harvest as the farmer who plants a large plot. Likewise, if one skimps on seeds in order to save money, he is not likely to enjoy the abundant harvest of one who plants the necessary amount of seeds.

We should not understand Paul to mean that one should give much in order to get much in return. More important than the amount one gives is his motive in giving (a point that Paul will touch on shortly). Jesus commended the poor widow, who gave her two mites ("all the living that she had"), rather than the rich who gave "of their abundance" (Luke 21:1-4).

B. Giving Cheerfully (v. 7)

7. Every man according as he purposeth in his heart, so let him give; not grudgingly, or of necessity: for God loveth a cheerful giver.

When one is cajoled or pressured into giving, his gift is likely to be given *grudgingly*. No doubt Paul would have serious reservations about some of the fund-raising tactics used today by churches and Christian organizations. One who gives *as he purposeth in his heart* is more likely to give generously and certainly more cheerfully than one who has been pressured or manipulated into giving.

Giving from the heart, however, does not mean that giving should be based entirely on emotions. Good Christian stewardship requires

that we give intelligently as well as emotionally. In fact, long-lasting joy is more likely to result from intelligent giving than from giving that is the product of spur-of-the-moment emotions. [See question #3, page 328.]

C. Trusting God's Promises (vv. 8-11)

8. And God is able to make all grace abound toward you; that ye, always having all sufficiency in all things, may abound to every good work.

Some argue that if we give generously, God will reward us generously. This may seem to be true in some cases. When we are seriously committed to Christ and give generously to His church, we are likely to be better off financially, in part because we no longer need or want many of the expensive "toys" that have become status symbols in our culture. But that is not Paul's point here. God provides *all sufficiency* in order that we *may abound to every good work.* In other words, He blesses us that we may use those blessings to help others, not to better ourselves.

9. (As it is written, He hath dispersed abroad; he hath given to the poor: his righteousness remaineth for ever.

Paul reinforced his point with a quotation from Psalm 112:9. *He hath dispersed abroad.* In the context of the Psalm, this statement is describing a righteous man. One mark of such a man is his generosity. Because of his deep concern for others, as reflected in the fact that *he hath given to the poor, his righteousness remaineth for ever.* This *righteousness* refers to good deeds that often have positive consequences long after the initial gift has been given. For example, a child may give money to support

How to Say It

ABRAM. *Ay*-brum.
ACHAIA. Uh-*kay*-uh.
ANTIOCH. *An*-tee-ock.
BARNABAS. *Barn*-uh-bus.
CEPHAS. *See*-fuss.
CORINTH. *Kor*-inth.
CORINTHIANS. Kor-*in*-thee-unz.
GALATIAN. Guh-*lay*-shun.
ISAIAH. Eye-*zay*-uh.
LEVITES. *Lee*-vites.
LUZ. Luzz.
MACEDONIA. Mass-eh-*doe*-nee-uh.
MELCHIZEDEK. Mel-*kizz*-eh-dek.
PHILIPPI. Fih-*lip*-pie or *Fill*-ih-pie.
SYRIA. *Sear*-ee-uh.
THESSALONICA. *Thess*-uh-low-*nye*-kuh
(strong accent on *nye*).

Visual for
lesson 12

*Use today's visual to illustrate verse 7. Discuss
what it means to give "grudgingly, or of necessity,"
and what it means to be a "cheerful giver."*

a missionary who carries the gospel to some who
had never heard it. These converts pass their
faith on to their children, who do the same with
their children, and so forth, resulting in many
generations' becoming Christians. Only eternity
will measure the worth and the impact of the
child's gift.

**10. Now he that ministereth seed to the sower
both minister bread for your food, and multiply
your seed sown, and increase the fruits of your
righteousness.)**

This verse seems to reflect in part Isaiah 55:10.
Here the word *he* refers to God, rather than to a
righteous man. Such a man who is also generous
does not really create the wealth that he shares
with others. Both the *seed* and the *bread* come
from God. Paul is reminding us that as we have
freely received from God, so we should freely
share with others our blessings. God will *multiply* and *increase* our giving beyond anything we
can imagine.

**11. Being enriched in every thing to all boun-
tifulness, which causeth through us thanksgiving to God.**

The contributions that the Corinthians and others were sending to the saints in Jerusalem would
provide relief for some of their physical needs. But
it would also benefit the givers, providing them
the joy that comes from helping others. Furthermore, this gift would lead the recipients to render
thanksgiving to God. No doubt the Jerusalem
Christians had prayed for help in their time of
need. The fact that their prayers had been answered through the generosity of the Gentile
churches would strengthen their faith in God and
help dispel any reservations they may have had
toward Gentile Christians. [See question #4, page
328.]

D. Meeting Needs (v. 12)

**12. For the administration of this service not
only supplieth the want of the saints, but is
abundant also by many thanksgivings unto God.**

In this verse Paul reiterated two important
blessings that resulted from the Gentile churches'
generosity (and should accompany ours as well).
First, they were supplying *the want of the saints;*
that is, they supplied what the Jerusalem Christians needed or lacked. Second, their giving was
the source of *many thanksgivings unto God*—a
point that Paul elaborates on in verse 13.

AN ANONYMOUS DONOR

The severe winter of 1996-97 combined with a
very wet spring to bring disastrous flooding to
the upper Midwest of the United States. Thousands of square miles of farmland were inun-
dated by the Red River, which flows between
Minnesota and North Dakota. Ninety percent of
the twin cities of Grand Forks, North Dakota, and
East Grand Forks, Minnesota, were destroyed.
Many buildings in those cities were first flooded,
then they burned to the waterline when the fire
department could not get to them to fight the
fires that came in the flood's wake.

But spirits of the flood victims were raised
when someone gave fifteen million dollars to be
distributed, two thousand dollars to each family.
The donor requested that her identity not be revealed. The news media could not resist re-
searching such a story, however, and finally
traced the gift to Joan Kroc, the widow of Ray
Kroc, who made the McDonald's restaurant
chain a success. Mrs. Kroc said that the press's
attention should be given to the victims and not
to her. She didn't want to "take away from their
story."

Paul gets to the "heart" of the matter concerning giving when he challenges us to look at our
motives. We should seek to supply the "want of
the saints," and we should desire that God be
glorified through what we do (2 Corinthians
9:12). We ought to be more interested in doing
good *for* others to God's glory than in receiving
acclaim *from* others to our own glory.

Each of us would do well to ask himself,
"What are *my* aims in giving?"   —C. R. B.

E. Glorifying God (v. 13)

**13. While by the experiment of this ministra-
tion they glorify God for your professed subjection unto the gospel of Christ, and for your liberal distribution unto them, and unto all men.**

The Jerusalem Christians would *glorify God*,
being convinced of the Corinthians' *subjection
unto the gospel of Christ* as demonstrated by their
liberal distribution. One's faith can be measured
by how well his life measures up to the standards set by Jesus. Our Lord's life was a living
example of generosity. The Corinthians would
demonstrate that they understood this if they

gave generously. In other words, they could put some "walk in their talk" or "put their money where their mouth is" by their giving.

The phrase *unto all men* reminds us that while Christians have a special responsibility to those of the "household of faith," their benevolence must not be limited to fellow Christians (Galatians 6:10).

Conclusion

A. Rules for Giving

The Old Testament set some specific standards, both by example and by law, for giving. Abram, returning from a victory over a coalition of invading kings, gave Melchizedek, a "priest of the most high God," a tithe (a tenth) of the goods he had recovered (Genesis 14:17-20). After his dream at Luz (Bethel), Jacob promised to return to God a tenth of all that God gave him (Genesis 28:19-22).

According to the law of Moses, each Israelite was required to give a tenth of his crops, herds, and flocks to the Lord (Leviticus 27:30-32). This tithe went to support the Levites who cared for the tabernacle and helped conduct worship services (Numbers 18:24). The Levites, in turn, gave a tenth of what they received to support the priests (Numbers 18:25-32). In addition, other tithes were required under the law.

However, under the New Covenant no such specific requirements are set. Our motives for giving are to be guided, not by law, but by grace. We are not our own; we have been "bought with a price" (1 Corinthians 6:20)—the death of God's Son on the cross. Thus we are slaves, and our lives, our talents, and *all* our possessions belong to God. We are required to be good stewards of *all* that God has entrusted to us, using everything carefully and wisely for His glory. One who gives only a tithe of his income and feels generous does not understand the New Testament concept of stewardship.

B. Purposes for Giving

Christians must give, but they also must give intelligently. It is important that we know *why* we are giving. Jesus left His heavenly home, humbled Himself by taking on the form of a human being, and died on the cross for our sins. What have we done for Christ?

Not only do we give because of what Christ has given us, but we also give because there are real needs in the world. Many of us reside in comfortable suburban areas where our lives are rarely touched by many of these needs. We have been content to allow the government to address them. However, Christians can and should make a real difference in reaching the lives of those in need. Jesus set the standard for what God expects of us in Matthew 25:40: "Inasmuch as ye have done it unto one of the least of these my brethren, ye have done it unto me." [See question #5, page 328.]

We give for another important reason. How we give will determine in a large measure how the world receives the gospel we offer to them. If we are selfish toward others and stingy in our giving, we are not likely to convince many in the unbelieving world that we serve a loving and generous God. Someone who serves Christ selflessly in the squalor of an inner city slum is likely to have a far greater impact on the world than all the pronouncements we make in our solemn assemblies.

One other important reason for giving is that it will bring happiness and personal satisfaction to us. To feed a hungry person, to clothe and house an orphan, to visit one who is sick or lonely, to counsel one who is in the depths of despair— these are actions that Jesus equated with caring for Him (Matthew 25:34-40). And as He said in another context, "If ye know these things, happy are ye if ye do them" (John 13:17).

C. Prayer

O gracious Father, we thank You for the generous blessings You have poured out upon us. Help us, we pray, to use these blessings, not for our own selfish desires, but wisely for others and for Your kingdom. In Jesus' name we pray. Amen.

D. Thought to Remember

"It is more blessed to give than to receive" (Acts 20:35).

Home Daily Bible Readings

Monday, May 15—Exceeding Generosity (2 Corinthians 8:1-7)

Tuesday, May 16—Show Your Love by Your Giving (2 Corinthians 8:8-15)

Wednesday, May 17—A Generous Gift Glorifies God (2 Corinthians 8:16-24)

Thursday, May 18—God Loves and Blesses Cheerful Givers (2 Corinthians 9:1-9)

Friday, May 19—Generous Giving Brings Joy to All (2 Corinthians 9:10-15)

Saturday, May 20—A Collection for Jerusalem Christians (1 Corinthians 16:1-9)

Sunday, May 21—Paul Intends to Visit Roman Christians (Romans 15:22-29)

Learning by Doing

This page contains an alternate lesson plan emphasizing learning activities.
Classes desiring such student involvement will find these suggestions helpful.

Learning Goals

After this lesson students will be able to:

1. Summarize Paul's instructions about the Corinthians' participation in the collection for the Jerusalem Christians.

2. Summarize the principles of Christian giving found in today's text.

3. Apply the principles in today's text to their personal financial giving to the Lord's work.

Into the Lesson

Before class prepare one set of index cards for every three students (i.e., a class of fifteen will need five sets of cards). Each set will contain five cards with one of the following scrambled words written on each: DGO VHEOLT A FECLURHE VGEIR. Place each set of cards in an envelope.

At the beginning of class, move the students into groups of three (if you have one or two students left over, then make one or two groups of four). Give an envelope to each group and explain that it contains five index cards with scrambled words on them. The group's task is to unscramble the words on each card and then rearrange the cards in the proper order. The correct answer is: "God loveth a cheerful giver" (2 Corinthians 9:7). The group that completes the task first should receive a small reward (i.e., a doughnut hole, small muffin, etc.) for each person in the group.

State: "Just as these letters and words were scrambled, sometimes our thinking is scrambled too—especially on today's subject of giving. Some people think that they just can't afford to give. But the lesson today teaches us that we can't afford *not* to give."

Into the Word

Ask for a volunteer to read 2 Corinthians 9:1-13 aloud. Divide the class into two groups and assign each group one of the following sections. Allow several minutes for the students to work with someone sitting nearby; then review the questions, having the students give the answers.

Giving Explained (2 Corinthians 9:1-5)

1. Who are the "brethren" of v. 3? *(See 2 Corinthians 8:16-24 to find Titus and two others.)*

2. What was Paul's twofold purpose in sending the brethren to Corinth? *(His boasting would not be in vain, v. 3; Their bounty would be prepared prior to his coming, v. 5.)*

3. Whose honor was at stake if the Corinthians failed to fulfill their promised commitment to give? *(Paul's, v. 3, and the Corinthians', v. 4.)*

Giving Encouraged (2 Corinthians 9:6-13)

1. Read 2 Corinthians 9:6; Proverbs 11:24, 25; Luke 6:38. Describe how these verses teach that giving is a demonstration of faith. *(Giving generously beyond what you can spare is a statement of faith and trust in God's ability to supply what you need; reaping is dependent upon the sowing.)*

2. What is the meaning of the term *sufficiency* (v. 8)? *(A feeling of being independent, not needing to rely on others for help; a contentment that results from being self-sufficient.)*

3. How should the act of giving be done? *(Intentional, "as he purposeth in his heart," v. 7; cheerfully, v. 7; faithfully, v. 8.)*

4. How should the act of giving *not* be done? *(Sparingly, v. 6; grudgingly, v. 7; of necessity, v. 7.)*

After a brief discussion, ask for some volunteers to form three teams of at least two people. Each team will write and perform a brief skit to demonstrate giving in one of the three ways listed in question 4 above. Allow a couple of minutes to prepare. These skits will be easy for the students to prepare, and they will probably be quite humorous.

After the presentations, state: "Though we laughed about these improper ways to give, perhaps we need to look a little more closely at our own giving in light of today's Biblical teaching."

Into Life

Begin this section by stating, "Sometimes we need to feel the emotions that rise up within a person as a result of generous giving." Ask the class to write a thank-you note on behalf of a young widow in Jerusalem with three children who was helped by a generous gift from the Corinthian Christians. They should try to describe how this person felt. Provide both paper and pens for this exercise. After several minutes, have several volunteers read their thank-you notes.

Next, have the class evaluate their own giving to the local church, to missions, to other religious, non-profit organizations, and in response to emergency situations. After sufficient time has been given, ask the students to select one of those four and make a commitment to increase their giving. Close with a prayer of commitment.

Let's Talk It Over

The questions on this page are designed to encourage review of the lesson Scriptures and to promote discussion of the lesson by the class. The answers provided are only discussion starters. Let your class talk it over from there.

1. What principles can you suggest for churches and individual Christians to avoid any charge of wrongdoing in their handling of finances?

Paul's earlier instructions to the Corinthians spoke of giving proportionately "upon the first day of the week" (1 Corinthians 16:2). That can be the starting point for drawing up a budget that will demonstrate a sensible stewardship of God's money. Churches can also follow a budget and keep thorough records of income and expenditures to demonstrate their careful use of monies entrusted to them. They need a system of checks and balances to hold those who handle the money accountable and to protect them from false charges. Having one person alone count the money and prepare the bank deposit, for example, is an open invitation to criticism or worse.

2. How do you think Paul's concern that the Corinthians would be embarrassed if any Macedonians came to Corinth with him and found their gift not ready compares with what Jesus said about giving in secret (Matthew 6:1-4)?

Paul's words may offer a corrective to the way Jesus' words are sometimes used. Some people believe that giving should be so secret that no one has any knowledge of it at all—even whether it occurs. This concept would eliminate accountability. (One wonders whether this isn't precisely what some who hold the view want!)

Jesus said people should be able to see our good works, and that the experience should lead them to praise God (Matthew 5:16). What He condemned in Matthew 6 was doing good works *just* to be seen and, thus, to receive the praise that should go to God. Paul wanted the Corinthians' good work of giving to be seen by the Macedonians so that God would be praised. Our giving and other good works can properly serve as examples to others and as sources of praise to God.

3. Our lesson writer says, "Good Christian stewardship requires that we give intelligently as well as emotionally." How can we achieve a proper balance in this?

Human emotions are prone to going up and down. If we give only when we "feel like it," our giving will be inconsistent. On the other hand, giving must not be only a cold, calculated act—just another item in our budgets. Giving is an act of worship, and both our emotions and our intellect must be involved in that worship. It should touch our emotions to ponder what God has done for us and what Christ has given us. When we focus on our receiving forgiveness of sin and eternal life, it should stir in us the desire to give to God in return. At the same time we can intelligently acknowledge the ongoing needs of our church, our missionaries, the lost, and the poor. We must give to these, even when our emotions are quiet.

4. When we give to people in need, we generate occasions of praise and thanksgiving to God. How important do you think this is? Why?

We should fervently hope that as many people as possible will come to praise the Lord. We should pray with the psalmist, "Let the people praise thee, O God; let all the people praise thee" (Psalm 67:3). God is worthy of such praise, and human beings need to praise Him. It is healthier both spiritually and physically for people to replace lamentation and complaint with praise and thanksgiving. When the recipients of our gifts are unsaved people, we can hope for a further benefit. By coming to the point of praising God, they may be ready to learn to trust Him and obey Him. If they are truly grateful toward Him, we may gain the opportunity to show them that the best gifts that they can give in return are their own hearts.

5. There was no "welfare" or other government relief in the first century, but we today have a variety of sources of secular help for the poor. How, if at all, does the presence of this aid affect our responsibility to minister to the poor today?

The government can arrange for poor people to obtain money for food and other necessities. In time of disaster certain organizations go into action to supply housing, medical help, food, and clothing to the victims. But only the church can minister to the whole person. The church is God's instrument for feeding human souls and helping human beings overcome the ravages of sin. Even if we think only of meeting physical needs, there is plenty of work for the church to do. Not every person in need of food or medical care or other help is eligible for government aid. Many people who are eligible are unaware of it. The church can learn of these people's needs and minister in a personal and loving way.

Living in the Faith

DEVOTIONAL READING: Acts 4:32-37.

BACKGROUND SCRIPTURE: 2 Corinthians 13.

PRINTED TEXT: 2 Corinthians 13.

2 Corinthians 13

1 This is the third time I am coming to you. In the mouth of two or three witnesses shall every word be established.

2 I told you before, and foretell you, as if I were present, the second time; and being absent now I write to them which heretofore have sinned, and to all other, that, if I come again, I will not spare:

3 Since ye seek a proof of Christ speaking in me, which to you-ward is not weak, but is mighty in you.

4 For though he was crucified through weakness, yet he liveth by the power of God. For we also are weak in him, but we shall live with him by the power of God toward you.

5 Examine yourselves, whether ye be in the faith; prove your own selves. Know ye not your own selves, how that Jesus Christ is in you, except ye be reprobates?

6 But I trust that ye shall know that we are not reprobates.

7 Now I pray to God that ye do no evil; not that we should appear approved, but that ye should do that which is honest, though we be as reprobates.

8 For we can do nothing against the truth, but for the truth.

9 For we are glad, when we are weak, and ye are strong: and this also we wish, even your perfection.

10 Therefore I write these things being absent, lest being present I should use sharpness, according to the power which the Lord hath given me to edification, and not to destruction.

11 Finally, brethren, farewell. Be perfect, be of good comfort, be of one mind, live in peace; and the God of love and peace shall be with you.

12 Greet one another with a holy kiss.

13 All the saints salute you.

14 The grace of the Lord Jesus Christ, and the love of God, and the communion of the Holy Ghost, be with you all. Amen.

GOLDEN TEXT: Examine yourselves, whether ye be in the faith; prove your own selves. Know ye not your own selves, how that Jesus Christ is in you, except ye be reprobates?
—2 Corinthians 13:5.

Lesson Aims

After this lesson each student should be able to:

1. Summarize Paul's challenge to the Corinthians as he prepared for his third visit to them.

2. Tell why the discipline of examining one's self is so important for the Christian.

3. Set up a plan (perhaps involving another Christian) by which regular self-examination can take place.

Lesson Outline

INTRODUCTION
   A. Authority Under Attack
   B. Lesson Background
 I. FINAL APPEALS (2 Corinthians 13:1-10)
   A. Paul's Warnings (vv. 1-4)
   B. Paul's Concerns (vv. 5-9)
     A Spiritual Beauty Contest
   C. Paul's Purpose (v. 10)
     To Build or to Destroy?
II. FINAL COUNSEL (2 Corinthians 13:11-14)
   A. Challenges (v. 11)
   B. Greetings (vv. 12, 13)
   C. Benediction (v. 14)
CONCLUSION
   A. Good Leaders
   B. Good Followers
   C. Prayer
   D. Thought to Remember

Introduction

A. Authority Under Attack

A young lieutenant was assigned the command of a company of soldiers that had a reputation of being sullen and unruly. Not only was the lieutenant green and inexperienced, he was also short of stature, making him a ready target for the men's remarks.

The young officer was overwhelmed by this lack of respect, and finally blurted out in desperation, "Tomorrow at zero seven hundred you will assemble here in full field equipment. I will lead you on a twenty-five-mile hike." His words were met with sneers and defiance.

Just then, a tough old veteran officer stepped out from behind the barracks where he had been observing the episode. "You heard Lieutenant Jones," he shouted. "You will do exactly as he commanded. You will assemble here in the morning with full field equipment to take a twenty-five-mile hike. And Lieutenant Jones will lead you—riding my horse!"

The situation facing the young lieutenant was somewhat similar to the one that confronted Paul in dealing with some of the people in the Corinthian church. They had made derogatory comments about him and had questioned his authority as an apostle. According to today's printed text, Paul told them that he planned to return to Corinth to address the situation, using whatever "sharpness" (v. 10) was necessary to bring about the Corinthians' obedience.

B. Lesson Background

In 2 Corinthians 10–12 Paul went to some length to defend himself against his detractors in Corinth. They accused him of being a coward because he wrote strong letters but was weak in his personal appearance (10:10). They apparently accused him of preaching only for money. Paul defended himself by pointing out that he "was chargeable to no man" while he labored in Corinth and that any support he needed had been received from the Macedonian churches (11:7-9). Some of Paul's critics may have been Jews, which led Paul to present his impeccable Jewish credentials (11:22).

Paul deeply regretted that he was forced to boast about his accomplishments and his sufferings for Christ (12:1, 11). He related an experience of having been "caught up to the third heaven," as further proof of authority from God for his ministry (12:2-6). Immediately following this account, he told of how a messenger of Satan (a "thorn in the flesh") had been allowed to torment him. Paul prayed three times for its removal, but God did not grant his request. Instead He promised, "My grace is sufficient for thee" (vv. 7-10).

Although the situation in Corinth made Paul's disclosure of this information necessary, he was not at all happy about having to spend his time and energy in such an effort. He concluded the letter with a final appeal for the Corinthians to set their house in order lest he be forced to be more aggressive with them when he returned.

I. Final Appeals
(2 Corinthians 13:1-10)

A. Paul's Warnings (vv. 1-4)

1. This is the third time I am coming to you. In the mouth of two or three witnesses shall every word be established.

The phrase *the third time* raises the issue of Paul's visits to Corinth and when these occurred. The book of Acts mentions only one previous visit to Corinth (Acts 18:1). We do not know exactly where to fit a second visit into a chronology of Paul's life. (See the discussion of this matter in the Lesson Background for lesson 10.) Apparently it occurred sometime during Paul's three-year ministry in Ephesus (Acts 20:31).

Paul had already stated his plan to visit the Corinthians a third time in 12:14. By repeating his intentions, perhaps he hoped that his warnings to them would be taken seriously.

In the mouth of two or three witnesses refers to a judicial procedure under the Mosaic law (Deuteronomy 19:15). It is not clear just what Paul meant by using this quotation. Some understand him to mean that each of his visits to the Corinthians counted as a witness to his integrity and apostolic authority; thus his third visit would provide the three witnesses that the law deemed sufficient to consider a matter *established,* or adequately proven.

Others hold that this reference was Paul's way of affirming that he would institute disciplinary proceedings against his detractors when he returned to Corinth (similar to those actions taken against the man mentioned in 1 Corinthians 5). The *three witnesses* would then be three of Paul's supporters in the Corinthian church.

2. I told you before, and foretell you, as if I were present, the second time; and being absent now I write to them which heretofore have sinned, and to all other, that, if I come again, I will not spare.

Apparently on his *second* visit to Corinth Paul had confronted his critics, but his efforts to correct them had been ignored. Since we have no specific information about this confrontation, we are led to conclude that it was a somewhat mild one. This may have been the reason that Paul's opponents accused him of weakness (2 Corinthians 10:10) and ignored his efforts to correct them.

I will not spare. It will be different the next time, Paul assured the Corinthians. He wanted to make sure that they understood his resolve to settle this matter decisively. The most severe step he could take was to excommunicate those who had *sinned* (1 Corinthians 5:1-5). [See question #1, page 336.]

3. Since ye seek a proof of Christ speaking in me, which to you-ward is not weak, but is mighty in you.

Paul's critics had been asking for *proof* that Paul really spoke for *Christ.* While we do not know what specific miracles Paul performed in Corinth, he mentions that everyone there had had an opportunity to witness this manifestation of God's power: "Truly the signs of an apostle were wrought among you in all patience, in signs, and wonders, and mighty deeds" (2 Corinthians 12:12). Paul assured the Corinthians that if they wanted further proof of his authority, the severity with which he would deal with the rebels among them would show that the Christ he represented was *not weak, but . . . mighty.*

4. For though he was crucified through weakness, yet he liveth by the power of God. For we also are weak in him, but we shall live with him by the power of God toward you.

Though Christ had unlimited power, He meekly submitted to His persecutors, surrendering Himself to be *crucified.* His enemies saw this as *weakness,* but that weakness was transformed into the victory of the resurrection *by the power of God.* In similar fashion Paul had seemed *weak* in Christ to the Corinthians (10:1, 10), but he now assured them that he would *live with him by the power of God.* Most likely this is not referring to the future resurrection when Jesus returns. Paul was reiterating that his next visit to the Corinthians would demonstrate the power that some thought was lacking in his ministry.

B. Paul's Concerns (vv. 5-9)

5. Examine yourselves, whether ye be in the faith; prove your own selves. Know ye not your own selves, how that Jesus Christ is in you, except ye be reprobates?

Paul's critics had been demanding proof of his apostleship and authority. Now he turned the challenge back on them: *Examine yourselves.* The test was *whether ye be in the faith.* The Corinthians' questioning of Paul's authority and their defiant attitude had raised serious doubts

Home Daily Bible Readings

Monday, May 22—Paul Defends His Ministry (2 Corinthians 10:1-11)

Tuesday, May 23—If You Boast, Boast in the Lord (2 Corinthians 10:12-18)

Wednesday, May 24—Paul and the False Apostles (2 Corinthians 11:1-15)

Thursday, May 25—Paul's Sufferings as an Apostle (2 Corinthians 11:16-29)

Friday, May 26—Paul's Visions and Revelations (2 Corinthians 12:1-10)

Saturday, May 27—Paul's Concern for the Corinthian Christians (2 Corinthians 12:11-21)

Sunday, May 28—Live in Faith: Christ Is in You (2 Corinthians 13:1-14)

about whether they really understood the nature of the Christian faith. The issue was not just whether *Jesus Christ* was present in Paul (v. 3), but whether He lived in the Corinthians. One of the themes of Paul's ministry was, "Christ in you, the hope of glory" (Colossians 1:27). [See question #2, page 336.]

Paul did not use gentle language to describe the Corinthians' condition. If they were not in the faith and Christ was not in them, they were *reprobates!* The Greek word literally means someone who fails the test, as though he is "weighed in the balances, and . . . found wanting" (Daniel 5:27).

A SPIRITUAL BEAUTY CONTEST

We are all familiar with beauty contests such as the Miss America pageant, in which hopeful young women compete for college scholarships and a few minutes of fame.

A less well-known form of beauty pageant is the "Pride & Polish Truck Beauty Contest." As many as twenty such contests are held each year across North America. We are not talking about pickups here; these are "eighteen-wheelers," dump trucks, and other heavy-duty industrial vehicles. They are judged for their extra equipment, perfection of paint and bodywork, and "spit-and-polish" cleanliness—even of their chassis and engine compartments.

It is common for such vehicles to cost over a hundred thousand dollars, in part because of their special equipment. Contestants have been known to spend as much as forty thousand dollars on the interior of the cab, complete with a kitchen equipped with microwave oven, refrigerator, and freezer (not to mention the on-board shower)!

Our Scripture today urges us to "examine" ourselves to see that we are approved by God. In other words, we are to do our best to appear beautiful before Him, with lives that match the standards by which He shall judge us and award our eternal prize.   —C. R. B.

6. But I trust that ye shall know that we are not reprobates.

If the Corinthians really had Christ in them, they would have had no trouble understanding that while Paul was among them, he possessed all the credentials that demonstrated his apostolic authority.

7. Now I pray to God that ye do no evil; not that we should appear approved, but that ye should do that which is honest, though we be as reprobates.

Paul had already made it clear that as an apostle he had the authority to discipline the erring brothers in Corinth who were demeaning him

and challenging his apostleship. However, he preferred that they cease their *evil* ways and do what was *honest* and right. If they chose to change their behavior and end their defiant spirit, then Paul would not need to exert his apostolic authority.

Of course, if Paul did not use his authority, then some might conclude that he was bluffing and really did not have the power he claimed. Paul was willing to accept such a judgment, even if it made him and his companions look like the *reprobates* that he had claimed they were not in verse 6. Paul was more concerned with the Corinthians' spiritual well-being than with his own reputation. [See question #3, page 336.]

8, 9. For we can do nothing against the truth, but for the truth. For we are glad, when we are weak, and ye are strong: and this also we wish, even your perfection.

Paul elaborates on the point he made in verse 7. If the Corinthians have been acting according to *the truth*, then he has no need to reprimand them. When he does not exercise his authority as an apostle, he may seem *weak;* but he is willing to accept that, if it makes the Corinthians appear *strong.*

Paul's fervent desire was that the Corinthians continue to grow in the faith even to *perfection.* This word does not imply sinlessness. In New Testament times, the Greek word was used to describe the act of a physician in setting a broken bone; it may be translated "restoration."

In these verses Paul reveals his servant's heart. Even though he had the authority of an apostle of Christ, he chose not to use that power in an authoritarian way. He chose instead to defer to the best interests of the Corinthians. Christian leaders can learn much from Paul's example, whose primary concern was always his people, not his ego.

C. Paul's Purpose (v. 10)

10. Therefore I write these things being absent, lest being present I should use sharpness, according to the power which the Lord hath given me to edification, and not to destruction.

This verse concludes the section of 2 Corinthians that began with chapter 10. In these previous chapters Paul had dealt with the claims of his detractors that he wrote strong, bold letters but was weak and powerless in person. Here Paul explained his actions. He wrote forceful letters so that when he did come in person, he would not have to use *sharpness* in his dealings with the Corinthians. He assured them once again that *the Lord* had given him *power* (authority) to deal forcefully should the situation require it. However, his goal was to work for their *edification* (building them up), not their *destruction.* The choice of whether Paul would have to take harsher measures with the Corinthians was really up to them, as he had written previously: "What will ye? shall I come unto you with a rod, or in love, and in the spirit of meekness?" (1 Corinthians 4:21). [See question #4, page 336.]

To Build or to Destroy?

Attitudes of American citizens toward the Internal Revenue Service range from "it's a necessary evil" to "it's an unconstitutional means the government uses to destroy its citizens." The latter attitude owes much to the well-publicized troubles of citizens such as Thomas Treadway, a Pennsylvania businessman.

Agents from the IRS audited one of Treadway's tax returns and erroneously assessed him $247,000. In fighting the claim, Treadway lost his business and everything he owned. Finally, an appeals officer revoked the assessment, but IRS agents threatened "to do the whole thing all over again." Even a former IRS official has acknowledged that the agency "is intent on driving taxpayers to the wall."

The severity of Paul's dealings with the Corinthians was not intended to destroy them, regardless of what some in Corinth might have thought. Paul used his apostolic authority for the "edification" of the Corinthians—an example of how *all* authority ought to be used.

We who are in positions of authority over others must continually be watchful of how we exercise that authority. —C. R. B.

II. Final Counsel (2 Corinthians 13:11-14)

A. Challenges (v. 11)

11. Finally, brethren, farewell. Be perfect, be of good comfort, be of one mind, live in peace; and the God of love and peace shall be with you.

Paul closed this letter on a warm note with a series of general admonitions, as he did certain other letters (1 Corinthians 16:13, 14; 1 Thessalonians 5:16-22, 25, 26). The Greek word translated *farewell* literally means "rejoice." The command to *be perfect* reflects Paul's concern for the Corinthians' "perfection" in verse 9. As noted in the comments on that verse, this Greek word signifies a restoration of strength and wholeness. Paul was urging the Corinthians to restore their relationships with one another and with God.

The command *be of good comfort* is rendered "listen to my appeal" (*New International Version*), while the *New English Bible* reads, "take our appeal to heart." Paul was gently urging the

Visual for lesson 13

Today's visual illustrates the need to "prove your own selves," to see whether your own pattern of behavior reflects Biblical standards.

Corinthians to accept those teachings in the earlier part of the letter that might have seemed harsh. With the command *be of one mind,* Paul was not suggesting that they agree on everything, but on "the faith"—those doctrines that are central to Christianity.

Paul's final challenge was to *live in peace,* especially concerning the matters that were dividing the congregation. If the Corinthians followed Paul's admonitions, they could be assured that *the God of love and peace* would be *with* them.

B. Greetings (vv. 12, 13)

12, 13. Greet one another with a holy kiss. All the saints salute you.

The *kiss* was a typical greeting in the first century (see Luke 7:44, 45; 22:47, 48), even as it is in some cultures today. (In other Western cultures the handshake is what the kiss was then.) Among Christians it was considered *holy* because it symbolized a common commitment to Christ and would be a mark of peace and reconciliation among the members of the Corinthian church.

All the saints included not only Paul and his companions, but the members of the Macedonian churches to whom Paul had referred previously (8:1; 9:1-4; 11:9). While most of them were not personally acquainted with the saints in Corinth, their joint concern for the cause of Christ united them in spite of the miles that separated them.

C. Benediction (v. 14)

14. The grace of the Lord Jesus Christ, and the love of God, and the communion of the Holy Ghost, be with you all. Amen.

Paul includes a reference to *grace* at the conclusion of each of his letters. Here he specifies *the grace of the Lord Jesus Christ* and adds *the love of God, and the communion of the Holy Ghost* as a reminder that the Father, the Son, and the Holy Spirit will be involved in every aspect of the Corinthians' daily lives. The Corinthians should seek to be one in the same way that the members of the Godhead are one (John 17:21). [See question #5, page 336.]

Conclusion

A. Good Leaders

Observers who evaluate our society today all acknowledge that one of the biggest problems we face is the lack of adequate leadership. This complaint is heard from business, industry, education, government, and, sadly, even from the church. Leadership comes in many styles. One who is a leader in education might make a very poor military leader. In turn, a great military leader would not likely make a good leader in the field of medicine.

What attributes are required in a good leader? Some qualities are obvious: intelligence, appearance, good education, speaking ability, people skills, patience, stamina, good health, willingness to delegate responsibilities, high moral standards, commitment to an important cause, and courage. The list could go on for several paragraphs.

How would the apostle Paul measure up to some of these standards? Intelligence he certainly had, but appearance? Some traditions indicate that he was not at all attractive. He had a good education and apparently was a powerful preacher. He had the stamina to travel great distances without all the conveniences of modern travel, but he apparently had some physical disability (a "thorn in the flesh") that plagued him. Paul had inexhaustible courage and a commitment to the greatest of all causes—carrying the gospel to dying sinners.

While Paul lacked some of the qualities that we may deem important in a leader, still he provides an excellent model for leadership in our congregations. His handling of the difficult situation in the Corinthian church gives us insight into his leadership during a time of crisis. The challenge to his authority, which came from certain elements in the church, was one he could not ignore. To do so would have allowed control of the church to fall into the hands of arrogant and self-serving men.

In his counsel to the Corinthians, Paul encouraged them to solve problems on their own without his intervention. However, he left no doubt that he would act firmly to address these problems if he had to. In other situations, Paul knew how to be gentle and forgiving. Most important, he never allowed his ego to get in the way of his ministry. As we have seen in today's lesson, he was quite willing to become "weak" if it allowed the Corinthians to become strong.

How can we develop good leaders for our churches? One method Paul used was to serve as a mentor for younger, less experienced men, such as Timothy, Titus, Silas, and others who accompanied him on his missionary ventures. Older, experienced leaders in the congregation can render a great service by following Paul's example.

B. Good Followers

Good leadership is necessary if the church is to grow and prosper in our times. But good leaders are almost powerless unless they are supported by good followers. And in case anyone hasn't noticed, good followers are about as hard to come by as are good leaders.

Many of the same qualities that we look for in our leaders are also necessary traits for good followers. In addition, good followers need a sense of humility that allows them to work in the background and out of the limelight. In the New Testament we see Andrew bringing Peter to Christ and then quietly moving to the background as Peter assumed leadership among the disciples. We watch John the Baptist, who was content to take a secondary role when Jesus arrived on the scene. "He must increase," said John, "but I must decrease" (John 3:30).

Followers may have skills that qualify them as experts, and yet if they refuse to follow their leaders, chaos can result. Imagine how a choir would sound if the members refused to follow the direction of the leader. That is how the church "sounds" to the world when we fail to support our leaders and when we all fail to follow the leadership of Jesus.

C. Prayer

Thank You, Father, for giving us glimpses of the ministry of Paul to the Corinthians. May his example of dealing with their problems provide us guidance as we strive to become better leaders and followers. In our Master's name. Amen.

D. Thought to Remember

Rarely can one become a good leader until he has learned to be a good follower.

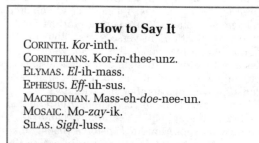

How to Say It

CORINTH. *Kor*-inth.
CORINTHIANS. Kor-*in*-thee-unz.
ELYMAS. *El*-ih-mass.
EPHESUS. *Eff*-uh-sus.
MACEDONIAN. Mass-eh-*doe*-nee-un.
MOSAIC. Mo-*zay*-ik.
SILAS. *Sigh*-luss.

Learning by Doing

This page contains an alternate lesson plan emphasizing learning activities.
Classes desiring such student involvement will find these suggestions helpful.

Learning Goals

After this lesson each student will be able to:

1. Summarize Paul's challenge to the Corinthians as he prepared for his third visit to them.

2. Tell why the discipline of examining one's self is so important for the Christian.

3. Set up a plan (perhaps involving another Christian) by which regular self-examination can take place.

Into the Lesson

Prior to the lesson prepare two graffiti statements: "A Leader likes . . ." and "A Leader dislikes. . . ." Write them on two sheets of blank newsprint or butcher paper. Tape them near the door and hang a couple of markers there so students coming to class can jot down items to complete the sentences.

After the class arrives, move the filled-in newsprint to the front of the classroom. Briefly review the items written under each statement. Ask, "What would happen to a leader who did only those responsibilities he liked to do?" *(He would not fulfill his own leadership responsibilities and would probably be fired.)* State: "Effective leaders fulfill both kinds of responsibilities. In our lesson today, the apostle Paul reveals those responsibilities he does not like to fulfill but will if the Corinthians fail to follow his leadership. Let's read our lesson text, 2 Corinthians 13, and find out what those are."

Into the Word

Ask each student to select a partner with whom to answer the following questions. (They are listed in the student book.) Each group of two should be assigned two questions from the following:

1. What is the meaning of the "two or three witnesses" in v. 1? *(See Deuteronomy 19:15. Possible views are: each of his visits represents a witness; when he arrives, he will verify all charges against some of the Corinthians with witnesses.)*

2. What do you think Paul meant by the phrase, "I will not spare" (v. 2)? *(See 1 Corinthians 5:1-5; 2 Corinthians 1:23. Possible views: public humiliation and censure; excommunication.)*

3. Why did the Corinthians seek proof that Paul really spoke for Christ? *(See 2 Corinthians 10:1; 13:2, 3, 10. Paul was accused of being bold and authoritative in his letters but meek and too lenient in person.)*

4. What does Paul mean by the term "reprobates" (v. 5)? *(Untested, unapproved, not accepted, counterfeit, disqualified.)*

5. What was Paul's primary desire for the Corinthians (vv. 7, 9)? *(Repent and do what is right, to become perfect in Christ.)*

6. What was Paul's primary desire for himself (vv. 7, 10)? *(He did not want to use his authority and inflict punishment even though he would appear to be weak.)*

7. Why did Paul give the command to "examine yourselves" in verse 5? *(The Corinthians' questioning of Paul's authority raised doubts about their own faith.)*

8. What is the predominant idea of the word "perfection" in v. 9? *(See page 332.)*

Allow time to review the questions; then ask for the students' answers. State: "Church leaders today experience similar kinds of problems."

Into Life

Ask the students to recall their experiences of being in the church and brainstorm the various types of problems or difficulties that church leadership has faced or faces today. *(Possible answers: incorrect doctrine of teachers; immorality among the leadership or church members; strife and dissension; undermining efforts for growth.)*

Churches are sometimes held back by unruly members who stymie the leaders' vision for growth. Ask, "How do you think Paul felt about the situation in Corinth?" *(See 2 Corinthians 2:4, 13.)* Leaders today find no pleasure in confronting individuals in the church. Yet, such confrontation and admonition are necessary if leaders are going to lead with integrity and be true to Scripture. "For we can do nothing against the truth, but for the truth" (2 Corinthians 13:8).

Ask, "What are some ways that followers in the church could be better at following?" *(See Hebrews 13:17—"obey leaders," "submit" to leaders; 2 Corinthians 13—do no evil; be honest; be of one mind; live in peace; be perfect or complete.)* Encourage the students to be very specific in this application to life. Write all ideas on the chalkboard. Then ask each to select one way that he or she can become a better follower. Ask each student to make a commitment to God, asking for His strength, so that the leaders "may do [their tasks] with joy, and not with grief: for that is unprofitable for you" (Hebrews 13:17).

Let's Talk It Over

The questions on this page are designed to encourage review of the lesson Scriptures and to promote discussion of the lesson by the class. The answers provided are only discussion starters. Let your class talk it over from there.

1. When, if ever, should church leaders take so firm a stand against a church member or group of church members? Why?

We are tempted to two extremes on this issue: some believe we should never take such a stand, and others are much too quick to run to judgment. We need to recognize that Paul acted with apostolic authority and that we today do not have the same authority.

Still, Paul made it clear in 1 Corinthians 5 that the church can and must take strong disciplinary action. If a member is involved in a blatant sin for which he or she refuses to repent, then the church must take action. Leaders must take the responsibility to initiate the action in such circumstances. If they must express righteous indignation, so be it. If they must gravely point out the consequences of continuing in sin or doctrinal error, then let them do it. It is painful to administer discipline, but it is essential to the church's genuine peace and harmony.

2. Self-examination can be a healthy thing, or it can become a kind of brooding, unhealthy self-consciousness. How can we develop the healthy kind and avoid that which is unhealthy?

What is our standard for self-examination? Are we measuring ourselves by what we see in Jesus Christ (Ephesians 4:13, 15), or are we laboring under some human standard of perfection? Are we concerned primarily with pleasing God, or are we occupied with impressing fellow human beings? The New Testament provides us with many tools for a healthy, spiritual self-examination. First Corinthians 13:4-7 offers a kind of checklist to test the quality of our love. Galatians 5:22, 23 enables us to take inventory of the fruit the Holy Spirit has been producing in us. Jesus' famous Beatitudes (Matthew 5:1-12) show us how we are progressing as citizens of His kingdom.

3. The lesson writer says, "Paul was more concerned with the Corinthians' spiritual well-being than with his own reputation." How important do you think such an attitude is for Christian leaders today? What difference does it make?

Someone has said, "It's amazing how much gets done when we are more concerned with getting the job done than with who gets the credit." Leaders who are out to make a name for themselves

have a divided loyalty. Their own egos compete with the Lord for first place. They are tempted to lead according to popular opinion (like politicians who always check the opinion polls).

The church needs leaders who look out first and foremost for their members' welfare. Paul's admonition to the Ephesian elders is a good lesson for all leaders (Acts 20:28-32).

4. Paul said his authority was given to him to build people up, not to tear them down. We all probably know leaders who were quicker to tear down whatever did not suit them than they were to build people up. Without mentioning the names of any contemporary leaders, contrast the two styles.

Paul had the authority of an apostle. With that authority he could pronounce blindness on Elymas (Acts 13:8-11), and it happened. By that authority he could command the Corinthians to expel the immoral brother from their fellowship (1 Corinthians 5). But Paul's leadership was tempered by love. His priority was in seeing people saved, not in making a name for himself (see Philippians 1:15-18). Leaders with that attitude are able to use even a little authority to get big results. Leaders who are more interested in the perks of a leadership position are more likely to abuse their authority. They tear people down in an effort to make themselves look better.

5. In spite of all the strong words he had to write, Paul concluded 2 Corinthians in a very gracious, winsome manner. What does that say about the way we handle difficult situations?

Paul practiced what we call "the sandwich method." He began 2 Corinthians in a gracious way, speaking of the Christians as fellow sufferers and his helpers in prayer. He concluded it with a series of gentle reminders, a word of final greeting, and a beautiful benediction. In between he dealt firmly with the church's problems. We also know how important it is to surround a criticism with some sincere words of praise. In that way we demonstrate how we appreciate the good things the offender has done. We make it clear from the outset that we still love our erring brother or sister. And we do our best to keep lines of communication open rather than to cause the offender to separate himself or herself from us.

Summer Quarter, 2000

New Life in Christ
(Ephesians, Philippians, Colossians, Philemon)

Special Features

Lessons

Unit 1: Living in Christ

Unit 2: Called by Christ

Unit 3: Christ Above All

About These Lessons

The lessons for the present quarter give us a special look at the heart of the apostle Paul as well as timeless words of wisdom to live by. Paul wrote these letters while a prisoner in Rome, yet they show no bitterness, no anger, no resentment. May Paul's example be as instructive as his words as you study these texts.

Jun 4

Jun 11

Jun 18

Jun 25

Jul 2

Jul 9

Jul 16

Jul 23

Jul 30

Aug 6

Aug 13

Aug 20

Aug 27

Quarterly Quiz

The questions on this page may be used in several ways: as a pretest at the beginning of the quarter; as a review at the end of the quarter; or as a review after each lesson. The questions are based on the Scripture text of each lesson (King James Version). **The answers are on page 340.**

Lesson 1

1. Paul told the Philippians that his "bonds in Christ" had become known in what place? (the synagogue, the palace, or the marketplace?) *Philippians 1:13*

2. Paul wrote, "To _____ is _____, and to _____ is _____." *Philippians 1:21*

Lesson 2

1. Paul tells us to let the *MIND* of Christ be in us. *Philippians 2:5*

2. We are to work out our own *SALVATION* with fear and trembling. *Philippians 2:12*

Lesson 3

1. Paul wanted to know the power of Christ's _____ and the fellowship of His _____. *Philippians 3:10*

2. Paul recognized that he had not achieved all he could be in Christ. T/F *Philippians 3:12, 13*

Lesson 4

1. What will keep our "hearts and minds through Christ Jesus"? *Philippians 4:7* *PEACE OF GOD*

2. Paul said that the Philippians had sent gifts to him "once and again" when he was in what city? *Philippians 4:16*

3. From whom had Paul received the gifts that the Philippians had sent him? *Philippians 4:18*

Lesson 5

1. Paul says that God chose us in Him before the *FOUNDATION* of the *WORLD*. *Ephesians 1:4*

2. Who is described as "the earnest of our inheritance"? *Ephesians 1:13, 14*

Lesson 6

1. "For by _____ are ye _____ through _____." *Ephesians 2:8*

2. In the past, Gentiles were called by what name? *Ephesians 2:11*

3. What or who is the foundation on which Christians are built? Who is the "chief corner stone"? *Ephesians 2:20*

Lesson 7

1. Paul described himself as the *PRISONER* of the Lord. (soldier, herald, or prisoner?) *Ephesians 4:1*

2. Paul lists seven items of whom or what there is only one. Name them. *Ephesians 4:4-6*

Lesson 8

1. We are not to be drunk with wine, but filled with the *SPIRIT*. *Ephesians 5:18*

2. With what three kinds of music did Paul encourage the believers in Ephesus to speak to one another? *Ephesians 5:19*

3. What is described as "the first commandment with promise"? *Ephesians 6:2* *Honore Thy Father & mother*

Lesson 9

1. Fill in the blanks to identify some of the parts of the Christian's "armor": the breastplate of *Righteousness*; the shield of *FAITH*; the helmet of *SALVATION*. *Ephesians 6:14, 16, 17*

2. What is the sword of the Spirit? *Ephesians 6:17*

3. Whom did Paul send to inform the Christians about his condition? *Ephesians 6:21*

Lesson 10

1. Jesus is described as both the firstborn of every creature and the firstborn from the dead. T/F *Colossians 1:15, 18*

2. Paul describes "Christ in you" as the *HOPE* of *GLORY*. *Colossians 1:27*

Lesson 11

1. In Jesus dwells "all the *Fulness* of the *Goohead* bodily." *Colossians 2:9*

2. Paul urged the Colossians not to participate in the worship of *Angels* (himself, Moses, or angels?) *Colossians 2:18*

Lesson 12

1. What does Paul describe as the "bond of perfectness"? *Colossians 3:14*

2. What should we allow to rule in our hearts? *Colossians 3:15* *PEACE OF GOD*

3. What should we allow to "dwell in [us] richly"? *Colossians 3:16*

Lesson 13

1. Which of the following words did Paul use to describe himself to Philemon? (the aged, the apostle, or the persecuted?) *Philemon 9*

2. In his letter to Philemon, whom did Paul describe as "my son"? *Philemon 10*

3. Paul said that he was willing to pay any debts that Onesimus owed to Philemon. T/F *Philemon 18, 19*

Christ Is the Center

by J. Michael Shannon

THE STUDIES FOR THIS SUMMER quarter of lessons are focused on Jesus Christ. That is most appropriate, since Jesus is the center of our faith. It is also noteworthy, because all of these lessons are drawn from the portion of the New Testament commonly called the Prison Epistles. These include Ephesians, Philippians, Colossians, and Philemon.

Observe that this study immediately follows the quarter that covered the letters of 1 and 2 Corinthians. Together these two quarters give us some interesting insights into Paul and into the conditions of the early church. They remind us that the early church was composed of real people facing real problems. These people had misunderstandings and disagreements among themselves just as we do today. However, what made this era such a golden age of growth for the church was the Christians' extraordinary, noncompromising commitment to Jesus Christ. It is a commitment that Christians today must model if we are to make an impact on our world for Jesus in the same way that the early Christians made an impact on theirs.

The thirteen lessons of this quarter are divided into three units: "Living in Christ," "Called by Christ," and "Christ Above All." Each lesson calls attention to an important element of our walk with Christ. Each challenges us to make Him the center of every area of life so that we may say with Paul, "To live is Christ" (Philippians 1:21).

Unit 1: Living in Christ

The first unit of lessons is entitled, "Living in Christ." It consists of four lessons from the book of Philippians. These lessons will discuss what it means to give Christ a position of primary importance in our lives and what it means to take on His mind, or attitude. They will also emphasize how Christ can help us persevere in our struggles and how He can give us a reason to rejoice—even in the darkest of circumstances.

Lesson 1, entitled, "Living Is Christ," comes from Philippians 1:12-26. The teacher should strive to communicate how Christians can face extraordinarily difficult circumstances with a firm and unshakable hope. For example, many people struggle with how to face the issue of death. This lesson will speak to that concern. It will encourage us to be Christ's person in every situation and to seek to glorify Him, "whether it be by life, or by death" (Philippians 1:20).

Lesson 2, "Having the Mind of Christ," is taken from Philippians 2:1-13. In this lesson the class will learn the importance of a humble, Christlike attitude. In particular, verses 5-11 of this passage describe the humility and exaltation of Jesus in one of the most stirring portions of Scripture.

Lesson 3 is entitled, "Pressing On in Christ." Through studying this text (Philippians 3:7-21), class members will learn something of what it takes to remain faithful to Christ when they feel like giving up. Using images from the athletic world, Paul will inspire Christians to run in the face of weariness. We should be motivated both by our promised reward and by the consistent example of faithful Christians such as Paul. Like them, let us "press toward the mark for the prize of the high calling of God in Christ Jesus" (Philippians 3:14).

Lesson 4, "Rejoicing in Christ," is taken from Philippians 4:4-19. It will challenge followers of Jesus to "rejoice in the Lord" even when their surroundings are less than ideal. We should keep in mind that Paul's words were not written in a vacuum. He was a prisoner of Rome when he wrote these letters. His faith challenges us to evaluate our circumstances in light of our faith in Christ, not to evaluate Christ in light of our circumstances. Regardless of our situation, Christ is unchanging and always faithful.

Unit 2: Called by Christ

The five lessons in Unit 2 are taken from the book of Ephesians. In this unit the class will deal with such subjects as the many spiritual blessings that believers receive in Christ, the unity that is possible in Christ, the spiritual gifts that Christ gives us to build His church, and the importance of reflecting Christian principles in the church and in the home. We will study Paul's admonitions to live responsibly and his encouragement to stand firm in the face of the devil's attacks. (Ephesians covers many of the same great themes as the book of Romans, but in a more concise way.)

Lesson 5, a study of Ephesians 1:1-14, is entitled, "Called to Spiritual Blessings in Christ." This lesson directs our attention to a beautiful outburst of praise in which Paul describes the wondrous "riches" that we possess in Jesus. It is filled with truths that give any believer many reasons to be thankful for God's work in his or her life.

Lesson 6, which is based on Ephesians 2:8-22, will center on unity in Christ. We will learn that unity has two dimensions: Jesus unites us to the Father, and He unites us to others who are united to the Father! While there are many causes for division, Paul will remind us of the possibility of oneness in Christ. As he deals with this vital theme, he will also touch on significant issues, such as being saved by grace for good works.

Lesson 7 (from Ephesians 4:1-16) will deal with the topic of spiritual gifts. Too often the discussion of spiritual gifts tends to center on one or two of the more controversial or spectacular gifts. This text will provide a helpful balance by emphasizing that every Christian has at least one gift that should be used to edify the church. No one's gift is insignificant.

Lesson 8, taken from selected passages in Ephesians 5 and 6, will deal with the Christian's responsibility to live a life consistent with his calling. Though this is a heavenly calling, it must be lived out on earth. Sometimes, when people emphasize being saved by grace, they almost sound as if behavior does not matter. This should not be. A genuine understanding of grace should be followed by a desire to live a life that is pleasing to God. This lesson will deal particularly with our responsibilities to honor Christ in our homes.

The text for **lesson 9** is Ephesians 6:10-24, a passage that describes "the whole armor of God." This passage could be very familiar to some members of your class. (If they grew up in the church, they may have memorized it at some point.) Borrowing imagery from the military world, Paul encourages Christians with the assurance that, even though we are under attack from the devil, God has provided the resources necessary for victory.

Unit 3: Christ Above All

The third unit of this quarter includes three lessons from the book of Colossians and one from the book of Philemon. In this unit the students will learn about the special position that Christ holds over all creation, the blessing of knowing that we are complete in Christ, the wonderful graces that will make us more effective Christians, and the ability of the gospel to break down barriers that often divide people.

The first lesson in the unit (**lesson 10**) is entitled, "The Supremacy of Christ." In this lesson, taken from Colossians 1:15-29, students will consider the uniqueness and absolute authority of Jesus. This study will provide a panoramic view of the glory of Jesus as Lord of creation and Lord of the church.

Lesson 11, "Complete Life in Christ," emphasizes the importance of finding our completeness in Christ alone. It also warns against the seduction of false philosophies. This lesson deals with issues and heresies that are no longer prevalent, although there are certain false teachings today that seek to attack the all-sufficiency of Christ as some in Colossae did.

Lesson 12 is entitled, "The Way to Righteousness." In this lesson, the students will discuss specific character qualities that should accompany the new life in Christ. The text of this lesson, Colossians 3:1-17, presents a clear contrast between the way Christians and non-Christians behave.

Lesson 13 comes from Paul's brief letter to Philemon, which is probably his most personal correspondence. Although this letter focuses on the relationship between a master (Philemon) and his slave (Onesimus), it can be applied to a variety of more contemporary settings that involve individuals of a different background, race, or economic status. The lesson will give you as the teacher an opportunity to show how the gospel speaks directly and powerfully to current social concerns.

This quarter will teach us about significant individuals such as Paul, Epaphroditus, Philemon, and Onesimus. It will teach us many great doctrines and instruct us about many great virtues. But above all, this quarter is about *Jesus Christ.* May you prepare and teach these lessons "to the praise of his glory" (Ephesians 1:12)!

Answers to Quarterly Quiz on page 338

Lesson 1—1. the palace. 2. live, Christ, die, gain. **Lesson 2**—1. mind. 2. salvation. **Lesson 3**—1. resurrection, suffering. 2. true. **Lesson 4**—1. the peace of God. 2. Thessalonica. 3. Epaphroditus. **Lesson 5**—1. foundation, world. 2. the Holy Spirit. **Lesson 6**—1. grace, saved, faith. 2. Uncircumcision. 3. the apostles and prophets, Jesus Christ. **Lesson 7**—1. prisoner. 2. one body, one Spirit, one hope, one Lord, one faith, one baptism, one God and Father. **Lesson 8**—1. Spirit. 2. psalms, hymns, and spiritual songs. 3. "Honor thy father and mother." **Lesson 9**—1. righteousness, faith, salvation. 2. the Word of God. 3. Tychicus. **Lesson 10**—1. true. 2. hope, glory. **Lesson 11**—1. fulness, Godhead. 2. angels. **Lesson 12**—1. charity (love). 2. the peace of God. 3. the word of Christ. **Lesson 13**—1. the aged. 2. Onesimus. 3. true.

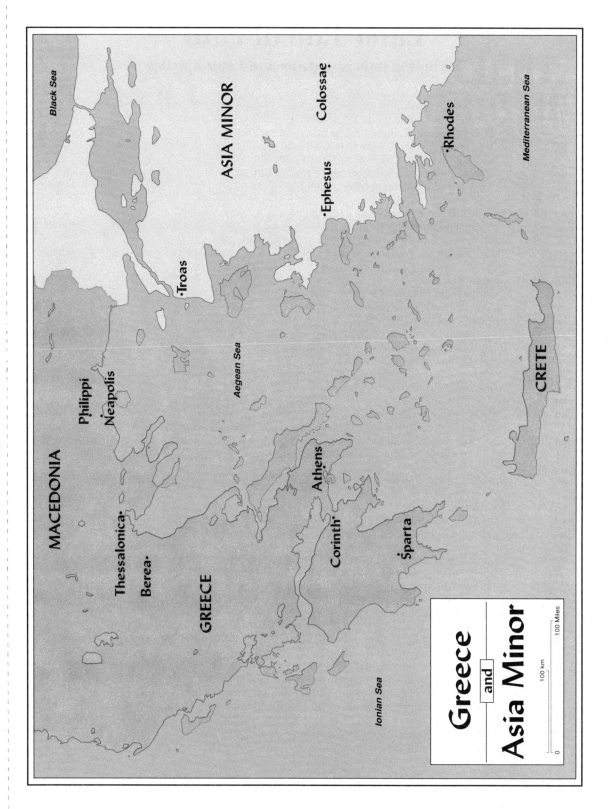

Greece and Asia Minor

MACEDONIA

Philippi
Neapolis
Thessalonica
Berea

GREECE

Athens
Corinth
Sparta

Troas

ASIA MINOR

Colossae
Ephesus

Rhodes

CRETE

Black Sea

Aegean Sea

Mediterranean Sea

Ionian Sea

100 km
100 Miles
0

Later Life of Paul

Including Imprisonments and Later Epistles

Date	Event
A.D. 58	Arrest in Jerusalem (Acts 21:17, 27-36)
	Held in Tower of Antonia (Acts 21:37; 22:24; 23:10)
	Defense Before the People (Acts 22:1-23)
	Defense Before the Sanhedrin (Acts 22:30—23:10)
	Plot Against Paul's Life Discovered (Acts 23:11-22)
	Transferred to Caesarea (Acts 23:23-33)
A.D. 58–60	Imprisoned in Caesarea (Acts 23:35; 24:27)
	Defense Before Felix (Acts 24:1-27)
	Defense Before Festus and Appeal to Caesar (Acts 25:1-12)
	Defense Before Agrippa (Acts 25:13—26:32)
A.D. 60, 61	Journey to Rome
	Shipwrecked (Acts 27:9—28:1)
	Ministry on Melita (Acts 28:2-10)
	Arrival in Rome (Acts 28:16)
A.D. 61–63	Imprisoned in Rome (Acts 28:16, 30)
	Preaching in Prison (Acts 28:17-31)
	Prison Epistles (Colossians, Philemon, Ephesians, Philippians) Written
	Hebrews Written?
A.D. 63	Released From Prison
	(Acts closes with Paul "two whole years" under house arrest in Rome [28:30]. Probably Paul was released at that time, but the evidence for what he did after that is scant. The following is one possible scenario.)
A.D. 63	Traveled to Crete (Titus 1:5)
A.D. 64	Traveled to Ephesus (1 Timothy 1:3)
	Joined by Timothy (1 Timothy 1:3)
	Trip to Colossae and Return to Ephesus (Philemon 22)
A.D. 65	Traveled to Macedonia (1 Timothy 1:3), including Philippi (Philippians 2:24)
	First Timothy Written
	Titus Written
A.D. 65, 66	Spent Winter in Nicopolis (Titus 3:12)
A.D. 66	Traveled to Corinth (2 Timothy 4:20)
A.D. 67	Traveled to Troas (2 Timothy 4:13)
	Possibly Stopped at Miletus on the Way (2 Timothy 4:20)
	Arrested (That Paul left his cloak and parchments in Troas [2 Timothy 4:13] suggests to many a hasty departure, as in an arrest.)
A.D. 67, 68	Imprisoned in Rome (2 Timothy 2:9)
	First Trial (2 Timothy 4:16, 17)
	Second Timothy Written
	Second Trial (2 Timothy 4:6)
	Executed in Rome

Put It in Writing

How Writing Can Help Students Learn and Apply Bible Truths

by Ronald G. Davis

RITTEN WORDS STAND STARK and demanding on the page. When they are personalized, they call for attention and response. That is the nature of God's written Word: "O child, I love you. I want the very best for you in life; I want the very best for you eternally! Obey me." All the words that His Spirit moved men to write are to that end. They are that stark, demanding, and personal.

Paul's letters are just such written, Spirit-inspired words—"able to make thee wise unto salvation . . . profitable for doctrine, for reproof, for correction, for instruction in righteousness" (2 Timothy 3:15, 16). Words spoken orally carry all the power and authority of the one who speaks; words in print carry that, plus the permanence that allows pondering and personalizing. God is wise. He "spake in time past unto the fathers" (Hebrews 1:1), but He also had His words and will "secured" in print. Through the written Word of God, we know the mind of God—His love and grace, His holiness and judgment.

Three Opportunities

Adult teachers will want to take advantage of this phenomenon in instructing their learners. The mind of the learner heard in speech is important; the mind of the learner seen in print adds one more dimension to the teaching-learning bond. The perceptive teacher should examine every lesson text closely to see whether there is that opportunity for learners to put pen to paper.

Three ingredients of the successful lesson offer an opportunity to have the learners write something: first, helping the learners see exactly what the text says; second, helping the learners understand what the text means; and third, helping the learners put God's truth to work in daily living. So sharpen those pencils! Get your adults to "Put It in Writing." Examples related to each of the three opportunities and to this quarter of lessons follow.

What Does It Say?

One easy way to get started is to have the class create a simple "test" based on the lesson text. Assign each member a verse of the text (or two verses, or two students to a verse) and ask that he write a true-false statement that can be answered by his assigned verse(s).

Lesson 10 of this quarter, "The Supremacy of Christ" (from Colossians 1:15-29), provides an appropriate text. Look at sample possibilities from verses 15 and 16 alone. Verse 15: "In a certain sense, Jesus is the firstborn of/over all creation" (true); "Jesus is obviously lower than God for He is 'the image of the invisible God' and 'the firstborn of every creature'" (false). Verse 16: "Jesus was an active, full participant in creation" (true); "There are elements of creation unseen to the human eye" (true); "Creation was not only *by* Jesus but *for* Jesus" (true).

The statements that students prepare can be used several ways in class. Each student can stand randomly and read his or her statement, anticipating that others will respond with "true" or "false" or with the relevant verse number. Or you could collect all the statements, shuffle them, and then give the "test" to the entire class. (The latter approach may remove some of the intimidation that certain members may have about speaking in class.)

An even simpler approach to a text (and one involving less writing) is to ask class members to characterize a text by its "key words" or "key ideas." An index card is large enough to use for this kind of activity. Tell each student to select three or four words that best characterize a particular lesson text and its ideas.

Lesson 7, "Called to Use Spiritual Gifts" (from Ephesians 4:1-16), would work well here. The fact that the text includes a number of repeated words and a dominant theme lends itself to such an activity. Ask the class to read the text and simply write down three words that characterize the text. When they have finished, you can approach the summary in several ways. One is to ask the class to send their lists around the room simultaneously—establish a "circular" pattern for the passing—and after all lists have circulated, ask the group to identify the "most common" words and the "most uncommon" words. (You may find an idea that is not clear or obvious to some members; stop and ask the one who made the suggestion to explain his or her choice.) For the text of lesson 7, some words that you might expect to be "common" include *one, unity, Christ, love, gifts,* and *maturity;* some words that might appear but are unlikely to be as prevalent are *doctrine, design, measure,* and *objectives.* The similarities and differences in such lists will provide an excellent overview of the contents and emphases of many texts.

What Does It Mean?

Once a student sees what a text says, the next step of his study must be to obtain its true and proper meaning. The revelation of Scripture is, by God's design, clear and concise. With most texts, the expectations of God are obvious (sometimes uncomfortably so). But because the historical setting of the various portions of the Bible was "far away and long ago," because the words were originally penned in languages other than English, and because both scholars and the unlettered have sometimes distorted their intent, every text must be examined with the question, "What does this mean?" This was the question that the Ethiopian eunuch asked of Philip when he could not understand the portion of Isaiah that he was reading (Acts 8:30, 31). It must also become the question of every sincere inquirer into God's Word. The one who teaches should examine every lesson text to try to anticipate how it might appear unclear and how he can help the learner adjust the lens of his mind to bring the "image" into perfect resolution.

Paraphrasing thoughts is a helpful approach to clarifying and understanding them. Many teachers use different versions, even paraphrases, to aid their preparation. However, a better approach may be to ask students to prepare their own paraphrases of part or all of a given lesson text. (A bonus to the teacher is that such paraphrases may indicate a serious misunderstanding of the text and provide occasion for correction.)

As the teacher, you may need to give examples to get your class started in the practice of paraphrasing. If you do, consider using some of the verses surrounding the printed text. The last lesson in this series, "Welcoming Others in Christ" (taken from Philemon 4-21), provides a worthy text for such an activity. Verse 22 includes Paul's final request before his closing greetings; his words might be paraphrased as follows: "Philemon, I know you've been praying for me to be free to come and visit—get a room ready!"

Once again, assign a verse (or pairs of verses that contain a single thought) to each class member. Simply say, "Put this in your own words." Some may choose to place the message in a contemporary setting; others will personalize it. Allow them that freedom. Challenge all of your students to attempt to capture the emotion—the heart—of the assigned text.

Final products of this assignment can be utilized in more than one way. All can be collected, in verse order, and then read consecutively as listeners compare their efforts with the Bible text. Or you could shuffle the paraphrases and read them randomly, asking your students to match each paraphrase with the corresponding Bible verse.

How Do I Put This Truth to Work?

Most adults "know" all sorts of truths that often have no real impact on their lives. The adult teacher's ultimate goal is that no Bible truth is left in the mind of his learners without being "translated" into godly behavior.

Many lessons in this quarter lend themselves to application through writing personal notes of encouragement and edification. Occasionally the adult learner needs to write a commitment statement for his own edification, which can then serve as a daily challenge to right thinking, speaking, and living.

For example, give your class a completion statement to finish as a challenge for the coming days. Suggest that they keep this with them or display it prominently as a regular reminder. For lesson 2 you might have them complete and carry this statement: "Lord, in lowliness of mind, this week I will esteem _____ better than myself, and I will demonstrate that by. . . ." (See Philippians 2:3.) For lesson 4, try, "Lord, I'm exhausted by my anxiety over _____; I turn this matter over to You." (See Philippians 4:6.) For lesson 6 dare the class to affirm, "Lord, I know that I have been 'created in Christ Jesus unto good works'; therefore, I will. . . ." (See Ephesians 2:10.)

However, the more significant writing that a student can do in putting truth to work is that which he does for another: to build up a sister or brother in Christ or to offer Christ's good news to one who is suffocating under the pile of the world's (and the devil's) bad news.

To every adult with a living parent, the words of lesson 8, "Called to Responsible Living" (from Ephesians 5 and 6), are timely. The simple reminder, "Honor thy father and mother" (6:2), and the earlier command to be "followers of God, as dear children" (5:1) should strike a responsive chord. What parent would not be honored to receive a loving note, a phone call, a gift, or a visit from an adult daughter or son? The adult teacher should provide the incentive (even the stationery and postage if need be) for this activity.

Finally, for every adult student and every adult teacher, there is surely that friend or acquaintance who needs the good news of Christ. The study from Paul's letter to Philemon encourages Christians to active participation in the "communication" of our faith (Philemon 6). Here is yet another way to put truth to work: by giving it the opportunity to work in someone else!

Living Is Christ

DEVOTIONAL READING: 1 Peter 1:3-9.

BACKGROUND SCRIPTURE: Philippians 1:12-30.

PRINTED TEXT: Philippians 1:12-26.

Philippians 1:12-26

12 But I would ye should understand, brethren, that the things which happened unto me have fallen out rather unto the furtherance of the gospel;

13 So that my bonds in Christ are manifest in all the palace, and in all other places;

14 And many of the brethren in the Lord, waxing confident by my bonds, are much more bold to speak the word without fear.

15 Some indeed preach Christ even of envy and strife; and some also of good will:

16 The one preach Christ of contention, not sincerely, supposing to add affliction to my bonds:

17 But the other of love, knowing that I am set for the defense of the gospel.

18 What then? notwithstanding, every way, whether in pretense, or in truth, Christ is preached; and I therein do rejoice, yea, and will rejoice.

19 For I know that this shall turn to my salvation through your prayer, and the supply of the Spirit of Jesus Christ,

20 According to my earnest expectation and my hope, that in nothing I shall be ashamed, but that with all boldness, as always, so now also Christ shall be magnified in my body, whether it be by life, or by death.

21 For to me to live is Christ, and to die is gain.

22 But if I live in the flesh, this is the fruit of my labor: yet what I shall choose I wot not.

23 For I am in a strait betwixt two, having a desire to depart, and to be with Christ; which is far better:

24 Nevertheless to abide in the flesh is more needful for you.

25 And having this confidence, I know that I shall abide and continue with you all for your furtherance and joy of faith;

26 That your rejoicing may be more abundant in Jesus Christ for me by my coming to you again.

GOLDEN TEXT: For to me to live is Christ, and to die is gain.—Philippians 1:21.

New Life in Christ
Unit 1: Living in Christ
(Lessons 1-4)

Lesson Aims

After this lesson the student will be able to:

1. Tell how Paul used his Roman imprisonment and his concern for the Philippian Christians to illustrate that Christ must come first.

2. Explain how Paul's conviction that "to live is Christ" expresses what a Christian's priorities should be.

3. Determine to face each circumstance of the coming week with the goal that "Christ shall be magnified."

Lesson Outline

INTRODUCTION
    A. Living Space
    B. Lesson Background
I. PROGRESS OF THE CAUSE (Philippians 1:12-18)
    A. The Gospel Advances (vv. 12, 13)
    B. Others Are Encouraged (v. 14)
       A Dangerous Prisoner
    C. Minor Setbacks (vv. 15-17)
    D. Yet Christ Is Preached (v. 18)
II. PERSONAL TESTIMONY (Philippians 1:19-26)
    A. I Want to Exalt Christ (vv. 19, 20)
    B. Should I Hurry to Heaven? (vv. 21-24)
       Gain and Loss
    C. I Expect to Stay (vv. 25, 26)
CONCLUSION
    A. "We'll Be in Touch"
    B. Prayer
    C. Thought to Remember

Introduction

A. Living Space

A television series called "America's Castles" described the magnificent dwellings built by immensely wealthy men for themselves, their families, and their guests. (Perhaps some space was needed also to house symbols of their pride and vanity.) The rooms in one of "America's Castles" would number in the scores, many of them with towering ceilings and with magnificent hand-carved woodwork imported from great distances. Furniture and decor were brought from all over the world at the whim of the buyer. A dining room, splendidly furnished, would seat as many as fifty guests.

Some of the owners lived for many years in the luxury of their mansions, some died shortly after moving in, and some did not even live to see their projects finished. One is reminded of Oliver Wendell Holmes's poem about a sea creature, the chambered nautilus, that develops a shell of ever-increasing proportions until at last the creature dies and leaves an empty shell. One portion of the poem says,

> Build thee more stately mansions, O my soul,
>   As the swift seasons roll!
>   Leave thy low-vaulted past!
> Let each new temple, nobler than the last,
> Shut thee from heaven with a dome more vast,
>   Till thou at length art free,
> Leaving thine outgrown shell by life's unresting
>   sea!

Proud words are those about a proud effort. But the person who lives in Christ has a "stately mansion" of God's making rather than his own. He sees freedom, not in being "shut . . . from heaven," but in living with the sure hope of going there someday. That is the assurance described for us in today's text.

B. Lesson Background

The church in the city of Philippi, located in the province of Macedonia, was the first established by Paul in what we know as Europe. This took place during his second missionary journey. Acts 16 tells of Paul's vision of a man of Macedonia who pleaded with Paul to come there (v. 9). In Philippi the apostle's efforts resulted in the conversion of Lydia and her household, Paul and Silas's imprisonment after they cast a fortune-telling demon out of a servant girl, and finally the conversion of the prison keeper and his household. Thus began what became a strong and generous congregation. The church at Philippi sent gifts to help Paul when he moved on to Thessalonica (Philippians 4:16) and later when his journeys took him to Corinth (2 Corinthians 11:9).

That spirit of generosity was still present approximately ten years later, when, while Paul was a prisoner at Rome, the Philippian church sent Epaphroditus, one of their leaders, with a substantial gift. Epaphroditus stayed for a time as a helper to Paul, but he became seriously ill while he was there. When Epaphroditus was able to travel, Paul sent him home with the letter of thanks and encouragement that we have come to call the Epistle to the Philippians (Philippians 2:25-30). Among Paul's writings, this one is especially notable for its warm and affectionate tone and for its persistent expression of rejoicing in Christ. It will provide our texts for study in the next four lessons.

The first chapter opens with Paul's typical greeting (vv. 1, 2), then expresses affectionate thanks for the Philippians' constant fellowship in the gospel. It displays confidence in their ongoing maturity in the Lord (vv. 3-8). Verses 9-11 include a prayer for continued growth in love, knowledge, and judgment; in appreciation for what is best; in lifelong sincerity and purity; and in fruitfulness springing from the righteousness that comes through Christ Jesus.

The following verses (12-26), from which our text for today is taken, testify that Paul himself possessed the same qualities that he urged his friends in Philippi to demonstrate.

I. Progress of the Cause (Philippians 1:12-18)

A. The Gospel Advances (vv. 12, 13)

12. But I would ye should understand, brethren, that the things which happened unto me have fallen out rather unto the furtherance of the gospel.

Paul's ministry had been somewhat limited since he was seized by the Jews in the temple area of Jerusalem (Acts 21:27-33). His enemies thought that this would initiate a series of events that would destroy him and his influence—in fact, they had hoped to murder him (Acts 23:12-15). However, these men succeeded only in broadening and making more permanent the apostle's accomplishments. Letters such as this one, written from Rome during Paul's incarceration, provide examples of the apostle's ongoing ministry. [See question #1, page 352.]

Acts 28:30, 31 notes a period of two years during which Paul lived in his own "hired house" in Rome and received visitors whom he taught and counseled, "no man forbidding him" (though he was always accompanied by a soldier of the palace guard, according to Acts 28:16). Most likely those persons whom he taught were in a position to teach others. And, of course, the letters known as Paul's "prison epistles" (Ephesians, Philippians, Colossians, and Philemon) continue to teach and encourage Christians everywhere.

Persecution has often served to make the church more firm in its faith and in its eagerness to spread the gospel. The persecutors fail to realize that, while they can hinder the movements of the messengers, they cannot suppress the power of the message!

13. So that my bonds in Christ are manifest in all the palace, and in all other places.

To all the *palace* guard, beginning with and spreading from the soldiers who were with Paul most directly, it was evident that his imprisonment came not from any real crime, but from his commitment to preaching the gospel. Like Daniel, Paul could not be charged with any offense except for his unusual commitment to an unpopular form of religion (Daniel 6:4, 5). In both instances God's man won respect both for himself and for the Lord whom he served.

B. Others Are Encouraged (v. 14)

14. And many of the brethren in the Lord, waxing confident by my bonds, are much more bold to speak the word without fear.

Christians in Rome knew that Paul was physically restrained by being imprisoned. Rather than being intimidated by the fact, however, *many* of them had become encouraged by Paul's example to *speak the word* plainly and to accept the consequences. No doubt some also responded to the need for faithful persons to pick up the work where Paul had been forced to lay it down.

Paul was providing evidence of the blessings one receives in the service of Christ, even under less than ideal conditions. He was also giving a powerful demonstration that the claims he had made in other letters about God's presence during difficulties (as in Romans 8:28 and 2 Corinthians 12:9, 10) were more than mere words. [See question #2, page 352.]

A DANGEROUS PRISONER

Wherever he was, the apostle Paul was engaged in evangelism. The Christians at Philippi understood this. No doubt most of them knew of his imprisonment during his first visit to their city and how he had led the local jailer and his family to Christ. Now, with Paul in prison in Rome, they were not surprised that he continued to be concerned about the souls of others—even of those who kept him confined.

When the Communists were in control of the former Soviet Union and of eastern Europe, they encountered numerous examples of this kind of evangelistic fervor. They put Christians in prison for preaching, and the Christians continued to

Visual for
lesson 1

The visual for today is a map that locates each of the cities to which Paul addressed the prison epistles. It will be useful throughout the quarter.

preach, leading fellow prisoners and even some of their captors to faith. They were as dangerous to the Communist cause inside the prison as they had been outside. In some cases they were actually released early because their evangelistic success in prison embarrassed the government!

When John Bunyan, the seventeenth-century preacher and author, was put in prison in England, the authorities offered to release him if he would agree never to preach again. He replied, "If you release me today I will preach tomorrow." Such determination ought to shame us, who have the freedom to witness of our faith but often remain silent. Sometimes we claim we have no opportunities to win anyone to Jesus. The problem is that we have many such occasions but fail to take advantage of them.

Many may have figured that an imprisoned Paul had few or no opportunities to witness for Christ. An imprisoned *and* determined Paul *made* opportunities.   —R. C. S.

C. Minor Setbacks (vv. 15-17)

15. Some indeed preach Christ even of envy and strife; and some also of good will.

Most likely there were already leaders among the Christians in Rome before Paul arrived (Acts 28:13-15). Some of them apparently were envious of his influence and his success in winning people to Christ. They were tempted to show that whatever Paul could do, they could do better.

On the other hand, many Christians in Rome knew that Paul's highest priority was the advancement of the kingdom; and their eager efforts to cooperate in that enterprise would have pleased him greatly. He could rejoice in the demonstration of such *good will*. [See question #3, page 352.]

16, 17. The one preach Christ of contention, not sincerely, supposing to add affliction to my bonds: but the other of love, knowing that I am set for the defense of the gospel.

Love is a source of encouragement to any preacher—both love for the Lord and love for His messenger. Any church is doubly blessed when the highest priority—love for the Lord—is enforced by a warm regard for the proclaimer of His truth. It is less well served when love for the preacher (or lack of it) takes precedence over love for the Lord.

The insincere proclaimers, governed at least partly by a desire to embarrass Paul while he was imprisoned, were sufficiently rebuked by the revelation of their motives. Paul refused to go any farther in judging or suggesting any kind of discipline. Since the competitors had not succeeded in embarrassing him or hindering his ministry, why should he dwell anymore on the

subject? The mention of their tainted motivation is a rare negative element in an otherwise positive and joyous letter.

D. Yet Christ Is Preached (v. 18)

18. What then? notwithstanding, every way, whether in pretense, or in truth, Christ is preached; and I therein do rejoice, yea, and will rejoice.

The negotiable element here was the motive and spirit of the proclaimer, not the message being proclaimed. The truth in *Christ* was never to be compromised: "Though we, or an angel from heaven, preach any other gospel unto you than that which we have preached unto you, let him be accursed" (Galatians 1:8). The basis of Paul's rejoicing was the spreading of the gospel and the welfare of the church. His own welfare was a minor concern.

II. Personal Testimony (Philippians 1:19-26)

At this point the apostle turned to matters more personal—his own relationship with Christ during the present times of difficulty and the strength that this relationship supplied for what lay ahead.

A. I Want to Exalt Christ (vv. 19, 20)

19. For I know that this shall turn to my salvation through your prayer, and the supply of the Spirit of Jesus Christ.

Through the *prayer* of his friends and the help (*supply*) of God's *Spirit*, Paul's present plight would lead to better things ahead, specifically to his *salvation*. In this context *salvation* could describe the apostle's release from prison or his ultimate deliverance into the glorious presence of Christ. As Paul states the matter in verse 20, he desires to be Christ's man in either circumstance. [See question #4, page 352.]

20. According to my earnest expectation and my hope, that in nothing I shall be ashamed, but that with all boldness, as always, so now also Christ shall be magnified in my body, whether it be by life, or by death.

Earnest expectation translates a Greek expression that speaks literally of "stretching out the head." As one craning his neck to see who or what is coming, Paul eagerly expected that he would remain firm in his courageous representation of Christ. He would refuse to be ashamed of the gospel that could have appeared at times to have let him down (Romans 1:16). He would also avoid being disappointed or embarrassed by any apparent failure of God's promises. He could, and would, continue to rejoice in the gospel of Christ.

Paul desired that *Christ . . . be magnified* through the *body* in which he lived. Certainly the apostle had his physical limitations (2 Corinthians 10:10; 12:7-10), and they did not disappear with the passing of time. Yet his physical body—heart, hands, feet, eyes, voice, and mind—was his only available tool with which to serve his beloved Lord. His chief desire was that every thought, word, and act reflect the lordship of Jesus. Each day he wanted to be able to say, "I am crucified with Christ: nevertheless I live; yet not I, but Christ liveth in me" (Galatians 2:20).

The possibility of an early *death* for Paul was very real. His enemies had plotted and tried in every conceivable way to destroy him. They had testified against him in every available court, and might do so again before Caesar. But as Paul had lived for Christ, he was ready also to die for Him. That *Christ shall be magnified:* this was Paul's ultimate motive. May it be ours as well.

B. Should I Hurry to Heaven? (vv. 21-24)

21. For to me to live is Christ, and to die is gain.

To live is Christ. Paul's daily being was an expression of Christ. To be without Christ would mean spiritual and eternal death.

To die is gain. Paul expressed this more fully in 2 Corinthians 5:6-8: "We are always confident, knowing that, whilst we are at home in the body, we are absent from the Lord: (for we walk by faith, not by sight:) we are confident, I say, and willing rather to be absent from the body, and to be present with the Lord." To the Christian, physical death opens the way to the eternal fulfillment of his purpose for living. Until one can say with conviction, "To live is Christ," he cannot say with confidence, "To die is gain."

GAIN AND LOSS

We have some interesting ways to avoid using the word *death*. We use expressions such as, "He went away," "God took her," or "I lost him." But *lost* is a most inaccurate word to describe the death of a Christian.

Nowadays everyone talks about the "bottom line." For a Christian the bottom line concerning death is that it is a gain and never a loss. We all can accept this in our heads, but sometimes it is hard for us to accept it in our hearts. The apostle Paul, however, was firmly convinced that he would never *lose* his life. He might *give* his life for the cause of Christ (and we can be fairly certain that he did), but he never would have wanted anyone to speak of it as a loss. For Paul death was more like the return on an investment. He had invested his life in the service of the Lord Jesus Christ, and after death he would receive the "full benefits" from that investment.

No doubt we will always speak of death as a "loss," and that is all right as long as we remember that the loss is on our side. We grieve, and we have every right to grieve. We have lost the companionship of one we love. But if that person was a Christian, he or she has gained the eternal companionship of God the Father and Christ the Savior. For a Christian it is always true that "to die is gain."
—R. C. S.

22. But if I live in the flesh, this is the fruit of my labor: yet what I shall choose I wot not.

While "to die is gain," Paul realized that, if he should go on living in his earthly body, it would provide a means of fruitful *labor* among the people around him. This presented quite a quandary: if he had to *choose* immediately between living and dying, he wouldn't know which way to cast his ballot. (*I wot not* is an old English expression meaning, "I do not know.") Both possibilities were good; which was better? Paul was in a "win-win" situation.

Thankfully there are some issues in which we do not have to choose one way or the other. Let us join with Paul in doing God's will as we are able, and pray that He will be glorified in the result. Beyond that, it was not the prerogative of even the great apostle to know the time of his death.

23, 24. For I am in a strait betwixt two, having a desire to depart, and to be with Christ; which is far better: nevertheless to abide in the flesh is more needful for you.

Paul felt himself squeezed (*in a strait* or a narrow place) between *two* alternatives, both of which were favorable. An early death, with escape from present difficulties into the everlasting presence of his beloved Lord (2 Corinthians 5:8), would be greatly to his own advantage. On the other hand, if he were true to his own admonition in Philippians 2:3 and 1 Corinthians 10:24 (to consider others' interests ahead of one's own), he would continue making himself helpfully available to his brethren for as long as possible. [See question #5, page 352.]

C. I Expect to Stay (vv. 25, 26)

25, 26. And having this confidence, I know that I shall abide and continue with you all for your furtherance and joy of faith; that your rejoicing may be more abundant in Jesus Christ for me by my coming to you again.

Paul's conclusion brought him back to the theme of *joy* that characterizes this epistle. It was the joy that would come to the Philippian Christians as they were blessed by his further ministry, especially through his *coming* to see them *again*.

It may seem that Paul was rather presumptuous in assuming that his friends would rejoice in his continued ministry, and particularly at the prospect of seeing and hearing him again. Is it presumptuous, though, for the member of a fam-

---

Home Daily Bible Readings

Monday, May 29—Paul's Prayer for the Philippians (Philippians 1:1-11)

Tuesday, May 30—Prison Bars Cannot Imprison the Gospel (Philippians 1:12-18)

Wednesday, May 31—Paul Exalts Christ in Life or Death (Philippians 1:19-26)

Thursday, June 1—Stand Firm in Suffering (Philippians 1:27-30)

Friday, June 2—We Have a Living Hope in Christ (1 Peter 1:3-12)

Saturday, June 3—A Call to Holy Living (1 Peter 1:13-25)

Sunday, June 4—Living Stones of the Living Stone (1 Peter 2:1-10)

---

ily or the partner in a long and close friendship to expect a joy-filled welcome home? Wouldn't a relationship seem hollow if it did not exhibit that kind of expectation? And the natural warmth of Christian love is not hollow!

First Timothy 1:3 speaks of a visit by Paul to Macedonia, which evidently took place after his first imprisonment in Rome. The joyous reunion with the Philippian Christians that most likely took place during this journey surely must have fulfilled Paul's expectation that the Philippians' joy in Christ would be increased by his presence. In turn his joy would be enhanced by being able to witness how the Philippians had grown in dedication to Christ. Apart from Jesus such joy, even in the midst of severe hardship, is not possible.

Conclusion

A. "We'll Be in Touch"

In many of the telephone conversations that involve family members, the final words are, "We'll be in touch." Times, methods, and circumstances are not spelled out, but there is a firm commitment to ongoing communication. It was so, too, in Paul's relationship with the Philippians. He had said that he expected to see them in Philippi, but he was not sure exactly when. He had affirmed his commitment and his confidence with regard to living in Christ for time and eternity. Of that he was very sure!

So, regardless of when Paul saw the Philippians again, he would stay in touch, expecting to hear that they had joined him in putting Christ above all else, in being steadfast in that commitment, and in suffering with and for Christ without wavering (Philippians 1:27-30). Should not we, who also have received the message Paul wrote to the Philippians, accept the same responsibility? We'll be in touch—with one another and especially with God's Word and God's Son. In Him we live!

B. Prayer

O Lord, our God, You have provided living space for us, temporarily in this world of Your creation and eternally in Jesus Christ, Your Son and our Lord. Help us to live in Him now, with all our being and all our belongings, that we may be prepared to live with Him eternally. In His name we ask. Amen.

C. Thought to Remember

"I am crucified with Christ: nevertheless I live; yet not I, but Christ liveth in me: and the life which I now live in the flesh I live by the faith of the Son of God" (Galatians 2:20).

Learning by Doing

This page contains an alternate lesson plan emphasizing learning activities.
Classes desiring such student involvement will find these suggestions helpful.

Learning Goals

After this lesson each student will be able to:

1. Tell how Paul used his Roman imprisonment and his concern for the Philippian Christians to illustrate that Christ must come first.

2. Explain how Paul's conviction that "to live is Christ" expresses what a Christian's priorities should be.

3. Determine to face each circumstance of the coming week with the goal that "Christ shall be magnified."

Into the Lesson

Prepare a handout with a list of activities (see below) down the left side. To the right of the list make two columns with a large plus sign (+) at the top of the left column and a large minus sign (–) over the right. Students are to consider each activity and determine whether it would likely serve to advance the gospel (+) or hinder it (–). List the following (and perhaps some additional) activities:

Learning the language of the people
Economic recession or depression
Serious illness or physical handicap
The arrest of a popular preacher
Publishing Christian literature
Preaching an unpopular message

Give the students a few minutes to respond; then discuss their findings. There probably will not be complete agreement on every item; discuss how some of these may be positive or negative, depending on other factors. Tell the class that Paul made a positive out of just about all of these factors—even his arrest and imprisonment in Rome, he said, had served to advance the gospel.

Into the Word

On the chalkboard or on a large poster write, "To live is Christ." Ask the class what they think that means. After a very brief discussion, tell the class we are beginning a series of lessons from the book of Philippians that remind us of the joys and responsibilities of living in Christ's church. Remind the class of Paul's adventures in establishing the Philippian church (see Acts 16:11-40 and the "Lesson Background"). Then have a volunteer read Philippians 1:12-26.

After the text is read, recall the phrase, "To live is Christ." Ask, "How does Paul's experience in Rome illustrate this principle? How do his priorities demonstrate the truth of this statement?" Here are some possible points to note in this discussion:

Verses 12-14. Paul's imprisonment had served to advance the gospel.

Verses 15-18. Paul was not jealous of the success of others or bitter about those who tried to make him look bad. The spread of the gospel was his first concern.

Verse 19. He expressed confidence that God would answer the Philippians' prayers for his "salvation."

Verses 20-23. Paul lived with hope in Christ and could die in that hope, confident of eternal life with Christ.

Verses 24-26. Paul was eager to serve the Lord, and especially to minister to the Philippians in some way, so he was confident that God's will included his release so he could do that.

To help understand Paul's statement in verse 21, use this brainstorm activity. Write two headings on the chalkboard or marker board: "Advantages of Going to Heaven" and "Advantages in Staying Here." Then ask students to brainstorm ideas for each column as you write them on the chalkboard.

Into Life

Tell the students that the phrase "To live is Christ" is the theme of this text. The phrase is both inspirational and challenging to readers today. We live in the body of Christ. Refer to the poster completed in the introductory activity, reminding students of the joy, satisfaction, and peace that come from living in Christ's body.

Note Paul's confidence that Christ would be "magnified" in his life or in his death (verse 20). Ask, "How has Christ been magnified in your life recently?" Be prepared to give a personal example to get people thinking of tangible ways they magnify the Lord. For example, any act of kindness rendered to a person in need or taking a stand for morality in a PTA meeting or some other public forum magnifies the Lord.

Note that some people occasionally magnify the Lord while others, like Paul, seem to do it automatically. Observe that it takes a mind set on Christ to have a life that continually magnifies Him. Close with prayer that each student will develop a determination to magnify the Lord in every circumstance of life.

Let's Talk It Over

The questions on this page are designed to encourage review of the lesson Scriptures and to promote discussion of the lesson by the class. The answers provided are only discussion starters. Let your class talk it over from there.

1. What are some occasions when you have seen bad things happen to God's people, but the end result was positive? How does that affect your attitude when bad things happen to you?

Bad things occur for two reasons: (1) sin is in the world—in bad people, and (2) "natural disasters" are universal, not selective. Thus, all of your students have probably been affected by some kind of calamity, disaster, or hard times. Perhaps they can tell of strengthened family bonds, of a more credible testimony of faith, or of a realignment of priorities. Just as Paul would not have chosen prison, we would not choose the bad things that happen to us. But we can choose how we will respond and whether we will allow God to work something good through the experience.

2. Do you think having one of our Christian leaders unjustly arrested and imprisoned would make us speak more or less boldly for Christ? Why?

Seeing Paul in prison had made the Philippians more bold and less fearful. Many of us, if we have not captured the true value of Christian faith, would react with fear and silence. Rather than see the greater need for someone to "fill in" for the one imprisoned, we might see only the possibility that we could share his fate. We might even rationalize our silence by saying, "Well, the time obviously isn't right to speak out!"

If we are truly wise, we would see the leader's absolute conviction of the value of his ministry, value that rises above risk. If our faith is true and deep, we will respond with Peter and John, "We cannot but speak the things which we have seen and heard" (Acts 4:20), no matter what the threat.

3. When good is done—such as preaching Christ—in what sense does motive not matter? In what sense *does* motive matter?

Though we may be tempted to criticize those who seem to be doing good things for selfish, even ulterior motives, we should thank God that good deeds are being done in His name. That was Paul's attitude and response (v. 18). Indeed, we may want to ask God's forgiveness that we were not doing the things done, if they were within the realm of our possibility. Whatever faults and flaws the individuals or organizations have, we need to look at the good things they do as a door-

way of opportunity through which we can teach the truth as the Scripture reveals it.

The blessings that accrue to the recipients of the good deeds are real even if the motives of the doer are "unreal." Those blessings should be the focus of our view.

4. How much confidence do we have that the prayers of our friends and the "supply of the Spirit" will turn our hard situation into something better? How do we gain such confidence?

One of the first things many of us do when misfortune comes our way is relate our need to those we know and love in Christ. We do know that "the effectual fervent prayer of a righteous man availeth much" (James 5:16). Any hesitation we have in asking for prayer from church leaders and fellow saints is a mark against our faith.

Likewise, we must quickly call on the Spirit of God in order to realize His abiding presence as the Comforter. John 14 and 15 need to become watchword revelation for us in all our hard times.

Of course, confidence comes about from happy experience. The more we call on Christian friends and rely on the abiding Spirit, the more we will realize and appreciate the blessings that come from such experiences.

5. When is the last time you had to choose between your own welfare and that of another? How did you choose? Why?

Life presents daily choices between serving self or serving others, even when to do either is a good thing. Paul's dilemma (vv. 23, 24) is a large example of that which comes to us in small "bits" each day: to do what makes us happier or what blesses another. Paul made the better choice.

When we have fully grasped the concept of servanthood that Christ taught and modeled throughout His life, we are well on the way to making the better choice in such dilemmas. For a husband to choose a day on the golf course or a day with his family—which is the servant choice? For the wife to spend a day shopping at the mall or a day working with her husband on a dreaded household job—which is the servant choice? For the single person to spend thirty more dollars on new CDs or to give that money to a shelter for the homeless—which is the servant choice?

Having the Mind of Christ

DEVOTIONAL READING: **2 Peter 3:8-18.**

BACKGROUND SCRIPTURE: **Philippians 2:1-18.**

PRINTED TEXT: **Philippians 2:1-13.**

Philippians 2:1-13

1 If there be therefore any consolation in Christ, if any comfort of love, if any fellowship of the Spirit, if any bowels and mercies,

2 Fulfil ye my joy, that ye be likeminded, having the same love, being of one accord, of one mind.

3 Let nothing be done through strife or vainglory; but in lowliness of mind let each esteem other better than themselves.

4 Look not every man on his own things, but every man also on the things of others.

5 Let this mind be in you, which was also in Christ Jesus:

6 Who, being in the form of God, thought it not robbery to be equal with God:

7 But made himself of no reputation, and took upon him the form of a servant, and was made in the likeness of men:

8 And being found in fashion as a man, he humbled himself, and became obedient unto death, even the death of the cross.

9 Wherefore God also hath highly exalted him, and given him a name which is above every name:

10 That at the name of Jesus every knee should bow, of things in heaven, and things in earth, and things under the earth;

11 And that every tongue should confess that Jesus Christ is Lord, to the glory of God the Father.

12 Wherefore, my beloved, as ye have always obeyed, not as in my presence only, but now much more in my absence, work out your own salvation with fear and trembling:

13 For it is God which worketh in you both to will and to do of his good pleasure.

GOLDEN TEXT: Let this mind be in you, which was also in Christ Jesus.—Philippians 2:5.

New Life in Christ
Unit 1: Living in Christ
(Lessons 1-4)

Lesson Aims

As a result of studying this lesson, students will be able to:

1. Tell how Paul used Jesus as an example to challenge the Philippian Christians to selfless service.

2. Explain why Jesus' example is critical to church life and to the church's witness to the world.

3. Identify specific situations in their church, home, or work where demonstrating the attitude of Jesus could make a positive difference.

Lesson Outline

INTRODUCTION
  A. Of Dogs and Disciples
  B. Lesson Background
 I. BE OF ONE MIND (Philippians 2:1-4)
  A. Looking to Jesus (vv. 1, 2)
  B. Not Self-Centered (v. 3)
  C. Considering Others (v. 4)
II. CHRIST SHOWS THE WAY (Philippians 2:5-8)
  A. His Example (v. 5)
  B. His Surrender (vv. 6, 7)
    The Form of a Servant
  C. His Sacrifice (v. 8)
III. GOD HONORS HIS SON (Philippians 2:9-11)
  A. The Highest Name (v. 9)
  B. The Highest Adoration (vv. 10, 11)
    A Famous Name
IV. GOD WORKS IN HIS PEOPLE (Philippians 2:
  12, 13)
CONCLUSION
  A. What's Christian About It?
  B. Prayer
  C. Thought to Remember

Introduction

A. Of Dogs and Disciples

The dog is recognized as "man's best friend"—and with good reason. A dog tends to remain ardently loyal to a considerate master. Stories have been told about brave dogs that served courageously in war or risked their lives to save those in danger. The St. Bernard is particularly famous for its ability to travel through deep snow and rescue lost or trapped travelers.

Unfortunately, such "dogged" determination is often lacking among those who claim Jesus as Master. We are too easily influenced by the apathetic attitude of our time rather than by an unwavering devotion to duty. Today's study will challenge each of us to "let this mind be in you, which was also in Christ Jesus" (Philippians 2:5). Jesus' sole purpose was to do the will of the Father who sent Him (John 6:38). Luke 9:51 says that "when the time was come that he should be received up, he steadfastly set his face to go to Jerusalem." Knowing the cross was before Him, He boldly undertook the task He had come to perform.

Have we "set our faces" to the task at hand?

B. Lesson Background

Always in view throughout the Philippian letter is the theme of rejoicing in Christ. In last week's study, we observed how chapter 1 of Philippians deals with the manner of life—regarding matters here and hereafter—that expresses our faith in Christ and thus promotes joy and peace in the body of believers. The final four verses of chapter 1 urge steadfastness in the face of difficulties such as Paul and his Philippian friends were enduring. Their faithfulness would provide a powerful testimony to unbelievers. What, though, should be said of relationships *within* the church? That is the emphasis of chapter 2.

Philippians 2 begins by urging the readers to act in such a way as to promote peace and unity in the body. It continues by calling attention to three persons—all known to the Philippians—who demonstrated the qualities recommended by Paul. The second and third were Timothy and Epaphroditus (Philippians 2:19-30). First and most important was Jesus Himself.

I. Be of One Mind
(Philippians 2:1-4)

A. Looking to Jesus (vv. 1, 2)

1, 2. If there be therefore any consolation in Christ, if any comfort of love, if any fellowship of the Spirit, if any bowels and mercies, fulfil ye my joy, that ye be likeminded, having the same love, being of one accord, of one mind.

At the first reading of verse 1, the repeated *if* might suggest that Paul doubted whether the Philippians had received *any consolation* (encouragement) from being *in Christ, any comfort* from His *love,* any meaningful *fellowship* with the Holy *Spirit,* or any *mercies* or compassion (such qualities were thought by the ancients to reside in the *bowels*). *In Christ* all of these blessings are surely to be found without limit and enjoyed beyond measure. Any uncertainty about possessing these treasures is to be traced to the saints' limited receptiveness of them.

The *if* in this sentence introduces a construction known as a "particular condition." It means that on the condition stated in the first clause, a particular response is warranted. It does not question the fact of the condition, but simply states "if this, then that"—or even, "*since* this, then that." For this reason, we may rightly understand Paul to be saying, "Since all of the virtues listed are to be expected in persons who are in Christ, let those God-given forces be put to work where they are not present in order to achieve the healing of whatever problems exist!" [See question #1, page 360.]

Paul exhorted the Philippians to *fulfil* his joy. He had already expressed his joy in the Christian maturity that was present among them (Philippians 1:3-5). The apostle's joy would be complete when they had achieved the spiritual growth that he urged in the following directives.

Be likeminded, having the same love, . . . of one accord, of one mind. Paul did not expect total uniformity in the Philippians' preferences and opinions; but he did expect their mind-set, attitude, and commitment to be centered on Christ. When their love for Him was complete, differences in other matters would be insignificant. When their dominating purpose was to glorify Him, other loyalties would fade into the background. And when they loved Him more than all else, then they would love other persons who also belonged to Him. Those who are close to Jesus will be close to one another.

B. Not Self-Centered (v. 3)

3. Let nothing be done through strife or vainglory; but in lowliness of mind let each esteem other better than themselves.

Strife (faction or contention) is that combative spirit that puts down another for the sake of one's own advancement. *Vainglory* describes the empty honor frequently associated with wealth, position, or power. Romans 12:3 offers the correct perspective: "I say . . . to every man that is among you, not to think of himself more highly than he ought to think; but to think soberly, according as God hath dealt to every man the measure of faith."

Lowliness has been described as the position of one who has stooped down to lift another up. Paul put it this way when writing to the Roman Christians: "Be kindly affectioned one to another with brotherly love; in honor preferring one another" (Romans 12:10). "It is more blessed to give than to receive" tributes, credit, and words of encouragement as well as money and material goods! [See question #2, page 360.]

Paul's command to *esteem* others as *better* than ourselves contrasts sharply with the me-centered self-esteem philosophy of our age. But if we are honest, we can easily recognize that others are better than we at something. Let us freely acknowledge the fact, especially if doing so will encourage them in their service to the Lord.

C. Considering Others (v. 4)

4. Look not every man on his own things, but every man also on the things of others.

We are to *look . . . on the things of others,* not with a covetous heart, but with a concerned one. Thoughtful consideration of the wishes and needs of others is the order of the Christian's day. That is the reason one associate minister would whistle a tune as he walked through the empty halls of the large church building on weekdays. It assured the lone secretary that the footsteps echoing in the otherwise silent corridors were friendly ones.

The same thoughtfulness persuades a friend to listen patiently to another's long story of minor adventures when his own experience could produce vastly more interesting narratives. He doesn't need to talk; he is more than happy to let the other person do so.

This is not to say that one must neglect his own daily needs and responsibilities while caring for those of others. The word *also* tells us that others are to be considered in addition to, not instead of, one's own legitimate needs.

II. Christ Shows the Way (Philippians 2:5-8)

Some Bible students believe that verses 6-11 of this chapter comprised an early Christian hymn that Paul included in his letter at this point. However, Paul was quite capable of writing in a poetic style (as illustrated by 1 Corinthians 13), and may well have written these lines himself. (They could have become part of a hymn at a later time.) Whatever their origin, this passage is a magnificent statement concerning Jesus and illustrates the principle of serving others.

A. His Example (v. 5)

5. Let this mind be in you, which was also in Christ Jesus.

A person's basic frame of *mind* (his attitude) will be reflected in all he thinks about, says, and does. The verse before us presents *Christ Jesus* as the One who should be the determining influence in the believer's mind-set. That happens in two ways. First, Christ is the example to be followed. His attitude should be reproduced in the minds of His followers. Second, Christ Himself is the power who enables the Christian to live by that example: "Christ in you, the hope of glory" (Colossians 1:27).

B. His Surrender (vv. 6, 7)

6. Who, being in the form of God, thought it not robbery to be equal with God.

Jesus was in the *form*, or very nature, *of God*, eternally. When He did what verse 7 describes ("made himself of no reputation"), He was not surrendering a glory that He had unfairly taken; He was determining not to hold on to Heaven's glory as His possession. This is the meaning of the phrase *thought it not robbery to be equal with God* (the *New International Version* reads, "did not consider equality with God something to be grasped"). Jesus surrendered His advantages willingly for the sake of rescuing lost humanity.

7. But made himself of no reputation, and took upon him the form of a servant, and was made in the likeness of men.

The eternal Word, who was with God and was God, emptied Himself of heavenly glory and, through His birth in Bethlehem, accepted the limitations and difficulties that accompany being *made in the likeness of men.* Isaiah 53 describes Him as the suffering *servant* who was "wounded for our transgressions" and "bruised for our iniquities" (v. 5). The difference between Jesus and other men was not in His physical appearance, but in His thoughts, words, and deeds. These were all governed by the fact that the Lord of Heaven came to earth, not to be served, but to serve others (Matthew 20:28). He taught and gave directions—even issued commandments—but never for His own self-promotion. [See question #3, page 360.]

THE FORM OF A SERVANT

If you are ever in the historical district of Charleston, South Carolina, a little after seven o'clock in the morning you will see a seventy-five-year-old man carrying a plastic grocery bag. If you follow him for his two-mile walk, you will see him picking up the trash with which people have littered the streets the night before. You may then find it hard to believe that this volunteer trash collector is James J. Kilpatrick—one of the most widely read columnists in America. His column is in scores of newspapers, and he is considered an authority on the English language. He is financially secure. Yet he does not think it beneath his dignity to help clean up the streets of his beloved city.

How often people will refuse to do work that needs to be done in a community, a school, or even the church! No doubt the people who dropped the trash in the streets were far less gifted

---

How to Say It

EPAPHRODITUS. Ee-*paf*-ro-*dye*-tus (strong accent on dye).
ISAIAH. Eye-*zay*-uh.
PHILIPPI. Fih-*lip*-pie or *Fil*-ih-pie.
PHILIPPIANS. Fih-*lip*-ee-unz.
ZOROASTRIANISM. Zor-o-*as*-tree-uh-niz-um.

---

than Kilpatrick. No doubt he cleans up after people who make a lot less money than he does, and who will never know the fame he enjoys.

Of course, this kind of humble service is very minor compared with what Jesus did when He "took upon him the form of a servant." Certainly our imitation of Christ will always pale beside His example. Still, we can and should learn much from that example. Jesus stooped to wash His disciples' feet. He stooped to cook their breakfast beside the sea.

Someone has wisely observed, "Only the strong can stoop." What have we done lately to "stoop" and help another in need?   —R. C. S.

C. His Sacrifice (v. 8)

8. And being found in fashion as a man, he humbled himself, and became obedient unto death, even the death of the cross.

Jesus accepted human limitations without complaint. He knew weariness, hunger and thirst, and temptation (Matthew 4:1, 2; John 4:6, 7). He was tested just as other human beings are (Hebrews 4:15). He demonstrated the servant role most memorably when He washed His disciples' feet during the observance of the Passover meal (John 13:1-5).

Jesus became the servant of men because He was first and foremost the *obedient* servant/Son of God. *The death of the cross* was the ultimate test of that obedience. Designed as the ultimate punishment of the most despised and vicious criminals, crucifixion included the extremes of suffering and shame. For Jesus the cross demonstrates the extreme to which He was willing to go in loving, serving, and saving us.

III. God Honors His Son (Philippians 2:9-11)

A. The Highest Name (v. 9)

9. Wherefore God also hath highly exalted him, and given him a name which is above every name.

In spoken words as well as by constant empowerment, God expressed His pleasure in what Jesus did on earth (Matthew 3:17; 17:5; John

12:28-30; Acts 10:38). In response to Jesus' fulfillment of God's purpose, the Father's pleasure was expressed in this manner: God "raised him from the dead, and set him at his own right hand in the heavenly places, far above all principality, and power, and might, and dominion, and every name that is named, not only in this world, but also in that which is to come: and hath put all things under his feet, and gave him to be the head over all things to the church, which is his body, the fulness of him that filleth all in all" (Ephesians 1:20-23).

What is the superior *name* given by God? At birth His Son was to be called Jesus; following Jesus' resurrection, the titles of "Lord and Christ" took on special meaning (Acts 2:33-36). Isaiah 9:6 speaks of Him as "Wonderful, Counselor, The mighty God, The everlasting Father, The Prince of Peace." The term *name*, however, may signify position or office (as in the Ephesians passage cited above). The risen Lord Himself declared, "All power is given unto me in heaven and in earth" (Matthew 28:18).

God's recognition of His servant/Son is a compelling illustration of what Jesus told His followers: "Whosoever shall exalt himself shall be abased; and he that shall humble himself shall be exalted" (Matthew 23:12). Jesus knows and shows what He is talking about!

B. The Highest Adoration (vv. 10, 11)

10. That at the name of Jesus every knee should bow, of things in heaven, and things in earth, and things under the earth.

The purpose of Jesus' exaltation is that *every knee should bow* to His *name* and every tongue confess that He is Lord (v. 11). No realm is excluded from this expression of adoration; *things in heaven, things in earth,* and *things under the earth* (likely referring to the hosts of Satan) will pay homage to Jesus' lordship.

Jesus' claim to all authority in Matthew 28:18 was followed by His command that all nations

This visual will illustrate the principle of verse 5. Discuss what it means to have "the mind of Christ."

Visual for lessons 2, 12

are to be made His disciples and directed to follow His commands (vv. 19, 20). The recognition of Jesus' authority will occur, either willingly by faith (leading to salvation) or forcefully at the judgment (resulting in condemnation). [See question #4, page 360.]

A FAMOUS NAME

A suburban homeowner got to thinking one day about all the people who served him who were not really known to him. He didn't know the name of the policeman, the fireman, the man who delivered his newspaper, or the man who picked up his trash. He decided to remedy that; so one day he stopped the garbage man and introduced himself. The garbage man did likewise and said, "My name is Albert Einstein."

The man responded, "That's a very famous name."

And the trash collector replied, "Well, it should be. I've been collecting the trash on this street for ten years!"

No name is more widely known than the name of Jesus. No name is more honored than the name of Jesus. Even many who do not believe His claims pay a certain amount of homage to His name and His character. It always surprises us to visit a country like Mexico and see people whose first name is Jesus (pronounced Hay-*soose*). But in Jesus' day the name *Jesus* was as common as John or Joe is to us today. Jesus took an ordinary name and gave it extraordinary significance.

Is this not what Jesus has done for us? He has taken our ordinary, commonplace lives and given them extraordinary meaning. He loved us when we were dead in our sins and died "the death of the cross" for us. His name deserves to be remembered, honored, and praised—by our words and by our lives. —R. C. S.

11. And that every tongue should confess that Jesus Christ is Lord, to the glory of God the Father.

Submission to Jesus will be expressed, not only by the gesture of bending the knee, but in words. To *confess* is to say the truth plainly and boldly: *Jesus Christ is Lord.* His authority deserves to be listened to with respect and obeyed implicitly. He takes no pleasure in those who call Him Lord and do not follow His direction (Luke 6:46-49).

To the glory of God the Father. God is most highly honored when individuals agree with Him in recognizing, acknowledging, and honoring His Son. From our viewpoint that means following Jesus' example and direction in loving and serving, rather than in loving to be served.

IV. God Works in His People (Philippians 2:12, 13)

Here Paul returns to the exhortation with which the chapter began. He had urged the kind of unselfish care for one another that allows the church to grow and become one body. Then he called attention to Jesus as the perfect example of an unselfish attitude. Now he challenges the Philippians to put his words into practice.

12. Wherefore, my beloved, as ye have always obeyed, not as in my presence only, but now much more in my absence, work out your own salvation with fear and trembling.

The saints at Philippi had a good "track record" on which to build their ongoing Christian experience. They and Paul loved one another genuinely (Philippians 1:3-8; 4:1, 10, 14-16). The Philippians' eager response to Paul's teaching had reflected something of Jesus' wholehearted obedience to the will of God. They were obedient not only when Paul was in their city, but, more important, they continued to be so in his *absence*. They respected God's message for them, even when its messenger was far away.

Now Paul urged his readers to continue their consistent obedience, and to *work out* their *own salvation*. Paul is not saying that salvation is based on works; the work he commands is the expression of the Philippians' commitment to Christ (Philippians 1:6). They must follow to its fulfillment the salvation course on which they had embarked. The attitude of *fear and trembling*, which acknowledges the holiness of God and the danger posed by sin, would mark their commitment. This is not a matter to be taken lightly. We are to "serve God acceptably with reverence and godly fear" (Hebrews 12:28). [See question #5, page 360.]

Home Daily Bible Readings

Monday, June 5—Imitate Christ's Humility in Your Lives (Philippians 2:1-11)
Tuesday, June 6—Rejoice in One Another's Faithfulness (Philippians 2:12-18)
Wednesday, June 7—Timothy, a Faithful Servant of Christ (Philippians 2:19-24)
Thursday, June 8—Welcome Epaphroditus in Christ (Philippians 2:25-30)
Friday, June 9—Repay Evil With a Blessing (1 Peter 3:8-12)
Saturday, June 10—Suffering for Doing Right (1 Peter 3:13-22)
Sunday, June 11—You Are Participants in God's Nature (2 Peter 1:1-11)

13. For it is God which worketh in you both to will and to do of his good pleasure.

Our salvation is God's accomplishment, not our own. He desires that none should perish, but that all should come to repentance and salvation (1 Timothy 2:4; 2 Peter 3:9); and He works continually toward that purpose. His Holy Spirit also works to accomplish that goal—through the Scriptures and *in* individuals who are committed to carrying out God's *good pleasure* in a sinful world.

"Quench not the Spirit" (1 Thessalonians 5:19); that is, don't clog the channels of His working in us. As Christians we wear Christ's name, and God will not hold that one guiltless who wears His Son's name irreverently. Let's give God His way in us!

Conclusion

A. What's Christian About It?

A Christian minister counsels a young couple in preparation for their June wedding, to be conducted in a place dedicated to Christian worship. Much that they discuss is common to most marriage counseling: finances, personal relationships, shared responsibilities, communication, to name just a few matters. What, though, will set this wedding and this marriage apart from other June bridal arrangements?

It is not simply that the wedding will take place in a house of worship and will include prayers for God's blessing. Most important, it will focus on Jesus as both the example and the divine presence that can enable this couple to fulfill the promises they will make before God and man. It is not their personal skills that will produce success, but their recognition that the strength of their marriage depends on God working in and through them. Standing and kneeling shoulder to shoulder, they must pray as Jesus prayed, "Thy will be done."

This same principle applies if we desire a Christian home, a Christian business, or anything else that bears the name Christian. Just calling something Christian does not make it so. Calling on Christ for His power and presence will make the difference.

B. Prayer

Dear God, help us to find ways to thank You for our salvation through following Jesus' words and example and through joining with others in His work and worship. In His name, amen.

C. Thought to Remember

"Follow! follow! I would follow Jesus! Everywhere He leads me I would follow on!"

—W. O. Cushing

Learning by Doing

This page contains an alternate lesson plan emphasizing learning activities.
Classes desiring such student involvement will find these suggestions helpful.

Learning Goals

After this lesson each student will be able to:

1. Tell how Paul used Jesus as an example to challenge Christians to selfless service.

2. Explain why Jesus' example is critical to church life and to the church's witness to the world.

3. Identify a specific situation in his or her church, home, or work where demonstrating the attitude of Jesus can make a positive difference.

Into the Lesson

The introduction to the theme of this lesson will focus on the attitude of submission to Christ. The attitude of believers should be of joyful submission because we wish to please our Master.

To introduce this concept, you may choose one of several ways to use dog-obedience training as an example. The "punch line" is that the dog's ultimate motivation for submission and obedience is that he wants to please his master.

You may choose to bring a dog-obedience trainer to class. He could demonstrate dog obedience with his dog. Or, if you do not wish to have an animal present, he could talk about the key concept . . . *the dog wishes to please his master.* Or you could show a segment of a video (from your public library or a pet shop) on training dogs. Look for a segment that emphasizes the dog's pleasure in pleasing his master.

Make your transition from this activity by telling the class that the dog develops a strong attachment to its master and takes genuine delight in pleasing the one he loves. Just as Jesus found delight and purpose in doing the will of His Father who sent Him (John 6:38), we also should find joy in submitting to our Master.

Into the Word

Form at least three discussion groups of three to six people each. (If you have more than three groups, have more than one group work on the same assignment.) Give the groups written instructions, and provide a poster board and marking pens for each group.

Group 1: Read Philippians 2:5-8. Then list the illustrations of Christ's submission to the Father. Be ready to explain each of these.

Group 2: Read Philippians 2:9-11, and list the honors given Christ because He submitted to the Father. Be ready to explain each of these.

Group 3: Read Philippians 2:2-5, 12, 13. Remembering that we are to have the mind of Christ in joyful surrender to God's will, list on poster board the words and phrases in these verses that suggest practical demonstrations of Christlike obedience. Be ready to clarify or explain these concepts to the class.

Encourage the groups to do their research and prepare for reports quickly. Ask each group to put its poster on the wall after completing the assigned task.

Before the groups report, use your lesson commentary to give a brief explanation of verses 1 and 2. Explain that Paul is not calling for total uniformity by using the word *likeminded*. He is simply asking that his readers' loyalty be to Christ. Their love for Him will be the source of joyful and willful submission to His will.

A spokesperson for each group should recite the group's findings. After each group reports, you should be ready to explain or clarify concepts.

To make the transition from group 2's report to group 3, put up a poster you have prepared with these words from verse 5, "Let this mind be in you, which was also in Christ Jesus." (Or use visual 2 from the visuals pack; see page 357.) Explain that Jesus was cited by Paul in this passage as an illustration of how we are to live. Group 3 will share some of Paul's principles.

To wrap up this portion of the study, summarize group reports. Remind the students that group 1 discovered that Jesus' obedience was a willful act, something He chose to do. He was not trapped nor forced into leaving Heaven or dying on the cross. Group 2 found that Jesus' submission was pleasing to God and that God exalted Jesus. Group 3 listed practical principles for submitting to and pleasing the Master.

Into Life

Ask class members to hear these questions and answer them to themselves. Question 1: "What are two things you believe you need to do to demonstrate submission to God's authority and to please your Master?" (Give them time to think about these.) Question 2: "Which of those tasks or challenges would you like to start right now?"

Conclude by having the class sing (or recite) "In My Life, Lord, Be Glorified" or "Take My Life and Let It Be." (Be sure to provide songbooks for those who do not know the words.)

Let's Talk It Over

The questions on this page are designed to encourage review of the lesson Scriptures and to promote discussion of the lesson by the class. The answers provided are only discussion starters. Let your class talk it over from there.

1. The lesson writer notes that the *if* in verse 1 does not question the fact of the presence of "any consolation in Christ . . . comfort of love . . . fellowship of the Spirit . . . [and] bowels [or heartfelt compassion] and mercies." Tell how you have experienced some of these in significant ways or at special times.

All of your students should be able to tell of the great *consolation* it is to be "in Christ," to know salvation in Him. There may be some, however, who have experienced *comfort* in times of grief, or *fellowship* when friends or family had deserted them. Perhaps they have been on the giving end of *compassion* and *mercies* when a brother or sister was in need. Both the giving and receiving of these kinds of blessings can motivate the body of Christ to "be likeminded, having the same love, being of one accord, of one mind."

2. How can we spot the "others-oriented" person? How can we be "others oriented"?

Egotists are fairly easy to spot. Usually they can just as easily be heard! We see them "making a name for themselves." We hear them "giving themselves the names."

People committed to others are willing to work anonymously. They are more likely to listen than to talk, for they are hoping to find a need to be met, not a "byline" to be added.

When we adopt Christ's attitude of esteeming others better than self, we will find ourselves in humble circumstances, as He did. We will find ourselves with the mentally and physically afflicted. We will find ourselves at people's feet and in their lives. We will find ourselves feeding and leading.

3. In Paul's "hymn to Christ," vv. 6-11, he includes this important truth to be believed: "Christ Jesus . . . equal with God . . . in the likeness of men" (vv. 5-7). How critical is the incarnation for our evangelistic message?

We must confront all the religions devised by mankind's inadequate thinking—from atheism to Zoroastrianism—with this superior truth: God saved us by making His Son one of us. The gods did not make us one of them; to the contrary, the one God made Himself human in Christ Jesus. What a far superior scheme to any that mankind has devised! We do not strive to become God.

God gives us "power to become" His sons and daughters (John 1:12).

Our evangelistic efforts take on new zeal when we emphasize what God has done for us and not what we have to do to earn salvation. We have the most beautiful, most wonderful message of all: "When we were yet without strength. . . Christ died for the ungodly" (Romans 5:6); "while we were yet sinners, Christ died for us" (v. 8).

4. Paul reveals that "at the name of Jesus every knee should bow" (v. 10). Few Christians kneel in contemporary worship. Why is that? Is kneeling necessary? Desirable?

Many of us feel awkward about kneeling in worship. Some feel that those who do kneel are trying to demonstrate superior spirituality. Yet all of those who have named Jesus as Lord and Savior will certainly concede that He is worthy of such honor and humility on our part.

Peter knelt to pray before raising Dorcas (Acts 9:40), and Paul knelt to pray with a group of Christians at Tyre (Acts 21:5). John describes the twenty-four elders and the four living creatures in Heaven as falling down to worship (Revelation 4:10; 5:8, 14). Kneeling is not required in our worship services, but there is nothing in the Bible to prohibit it. We might want to try kneeling; we just might find it comfortable and sincere worship!

5. How do we demonstrate "fear and trembling" in relationship to our own salvation? Are we concerned enough about our status with God? Too much so? What gives assurance? What creates doubt?

Some people contrast the God of the Old Testament with the God of the New, drawing contrasts between the wrath of the former and the loving grace of the latter. God is God. He is both holy and loving, so He must demonstrate wrath and judgment as well as love and redemption.

Our salvation must be considered in the light of God's full revelation. He is a God to be feared, for He "is able to destroy both soul and body in hell" (Matthew 10:28). He is a God to be loved, for He is the Son who calls us "friends" (John 15:15).

We must have such a knowledge of God that sin makes us shudder and righteousness makes us rejoice. Only then will our "fear and trembling" be in proper perspective.

Pressing On in Christ

DEVOTIONAL READING: Hebrews 10:19-25, 32-36.

BACKGROUND SCRIPTURE: Philippians 3.

PRINTED TEXT: Philippians 3:7-21.

Philippians 3:7-21

7 But what things were gain to me, those I counted loss for Christ.

8 Yea doubtless, and I count all things but loss for the excellency of the knowledge of Christ Jesus my Lord: for whom I have suffered the loss of all things, and do count them but dung, that I may win Christ,

9 And be found in him, not having mine own righteousness, which is of the law, but that which is through the faith of Christ, the righteousness which is of God by faith:

10 That I may know him, and the power of his resurrection, and the fellowship of his sufferings, being made conformable unto his death;

11 If by any means I might attain unto the resurrection of the dead.

12 Not as though I had already attained, either were already perfect: but I follow after, if that I may apprehend that for which also I am apprehended of Christ Jesus.

13 Brethren, I count not myself to have apprehended: but this one thing I do, forgetting those things which are behind, and reaching forth unto those things which are before,

14 I press toward the mark for the prize of the high calling of God in Christ Jesus.

15 Let us therefore, as many as be perfect, be thus minded: and if in any thing ye be otherwise minded, God shall reveal even this unto you.

16 Nevertheless, whereto we have already attained, let us walk by the same rule, let us mind the same thing.

17 Brethren, be followers together of me, and mark them which walk so as ye have us for an ensample.

18 (For many walk, of whom I have told you often, and now tell you even weeping, that they are the enemies of the cross of Christ:

19 Whose end is destruction, whose God is their belly, and whose glory is in their shame, who mind earthly things.)

20 For our conversation is in heaven; from whence also we look for the Saviour, the Lord Jesus Christ:

21 Who shall change our vile body, that it may be fashioned like unto his glorious body, according to the working whereby he is able even to subdue all things unto himself.

GOLDEN TEXT: I press toward the mark for the prize of the high calling of God in Christ Jesus.—Philippians 3:14.

New Life in Christ
Unit 1: Living in Christ
(Lessons 1-4)

Lesson Aims

After this lesson each student will be able to:

1. Describe the attitude, actions, and goal that, according to Paul, are part of "pressing on in Christ."

2. List some personal possessions or activities that he or she considers expendable in his or her own discipleship.

3. Evaluate his or her life to determine whether there is any part that needs to be "counted as loss" for the sake of knowing Christ better.

Lesson Outline

Introduction

A. The Peace of Progress

Traffic moved smoothly that afternoon along the interstate, and we fully expected to reach home on schedule. Then suddenly, on the highway before us, there appeared a slowing, crowding, and finally a complete stoppage of vehicles in every lane of the wide highway. Eventually our progress was also brought to a standstill. What had happened? How long would it be until

we could move again? We waited with an increasingly tense frustration.

After what seemed like a very long hour there was movement, irregular at first, and then more steady as the mass of traffic filtered, one car at a time, past the distant roadblock. Even the first slow movement, however, brought what an acquaintance of mine used to call "the peace of progress"—relief and relaxation in the assurance that we were moving toward home.

As Christians we are on the way toward the home prepared for us by the Lord who has gone before. But are we really moving in the right direction? Or have we stalled in our progress? Is it possible that some difficulty has even caused us to move away from, rather than toward, the Lord who waits to welcome us home? Today's text from Philippians 3:7-21 points us to the way of progress and peace, guaranteed to get us home safely under the direction of Jesus.

B. Lesson Background

Philippians is a Christ-centered letter! Chapter 1 presents Jesus as the focus and goal of Paul's life: "For to me to live is Christ" (1:21). Chapter 2 presents Christ as the perfect example of the self-sacrificing spirit that will build the church in peace and unity.

Chapter 3 opens with an exhortation to "rejoice in the Lord"—a theme that rings throughout the letter. Paul then warns the Philippians of certain "dogs," or false teachers, who are encouraging people to put their "confidence in the flesh" (outward conformity to Jewish law) rather than in Christ. He proceeds to list some of the items in his own background that gave him more than enough reason to have such confidence (v. 4). He does so to emphasize that such dependence on the flesh can never make a person right with God. Only by following the course that is urged in the succeeding verses, which comprise our printed text, can we be made right with God.

I. The Goal Is Christ (Philippians 3:7-11)

In verses 5 and 6 the apostle has noted that his "bragging rights" in relation to the Jewish law were far better than those of others who depended on the law for their acceptance with God. All of that, however, constituted a *program* to be carried out. For Paul that program had been replaced with a *Person* to be loved, honored, and served for time and eternity.

A. Counting Everything Loss (vv. 7, 8)

7. But what things were gain to me, those I counted loss for Christ.

Paul recognized that any part of his background or reputation that encouraged reliance on anything but *Christ* for his salvation was a handicap to him. The more desirable these items had been, the greater would be their potential to become a hindrance. They must now be moved from the "profit" side of his personal and spiritual ledger to the *loss* side for the sake of his relationship with Christ. A Christian must ask himself occasionally which of his "assets" have become liabilities because they compete with Christ for top priority in his time and attention. [See question #1, page 368.]

8. Yea doubtless, and I count all things but loss for the excellency of the knowledge of Christ Jesus my Lord: for whom I have suffered the loss of all things, and do count them but dung, that I may win Christ.

To know and serve and be with Christ is a blessing so great as to be sought at any and all costs. It begins with considering the information about Jesus found in the Gospels; it moves to an acceptance of Jesus as Savior and Lord; it then grows into the kind of intimacy described by Paul as *the excellency of the knowledge of Christ Jesus my Lord.* Thus does one become prepared for the further intimacy of an eternity with Jesus.

Note that Paul was not promising some price that he would pay; he was giving a sober account of what he had *already paid.* His position in the Jewish community; his family and friends; his home with all its comforts and security—these and other assets had been tossed aside that he might *win Christ.*

Did the apostle miss these items and mourn their loss? To the contrary, he rejoiced in his glorious exchange, regarding the losses as *dung,* or material for the garbage can. Needless to say, that kind of evaluation by Paul did not sit well with the Jewish community whose heritage he appeared to dismiss so lightly. And the world in which we live is not inclined to look favorably on our absolute preference for Jesus Christ above any and all of the benefits or "perks" it offers. The downgrading of what the world holds dear may be taken as an insult to be resented and resisted. Can we avoid the offense? Probably not if we express our preference as clearly as Paul did. [See question #2, page 368.]

B. Having His Righteousness (v. 9)

9. And be found in him, not having mine own righteousness, which is of the law, but that which is through the faith of Christ, the righteousness which is of God by faith.

Paul says it again: a person's *righteousness,* or becoming right with God, comes not through outward conformity to *the law* of Moses but through

belief in and commitment to God through His Son Jesus. The phrase *in him* describes a vital and intimate relationship with *Christ* that begins in time and continues throughout eternity.

If one could become acceptable with God through obedience to the law, then his salvation would be by means of his good behavior and thus an earned reward. But that is impossible, because no one—except for Jesus—has yet fully kept the law. Paul recognized the hopelessness of his position under the law (in spite of his own "blameless" standing before the law; see v. 6), and recognized that his salvation must come not from himself but from God through Christ. It must be received *by faith*—the belief that expresses itself through complete trust and obedience.

C. Knowing Him (vv. 10, 11)

10. That I may know him, and the power of his resurrection, and the fellowship of his sufferings, being made conformable unto his death.

To *know* Christ was Paul's constant passion and purpose. In order to attain such an intimate acquaintance, the apostle was willing to share to the greatest possible degree the experiences of his Lord and Savior. If he was to experience the *power* that raised Christ from the dead, he would need to follow Jesus through the giving of his life daily in service to God (note his statement, "I die daily," in 1 Corinthians 15:31), and also through a willingness even to die in the service of Jesus (Revelation 2:10). This was no halfhearted effort!

A UNIQUE FELLOWSHIP

Many Christians enjoy singing the hymn, "Leaning on the Everlasting Arms." Whenever we sing, "What a fellowship, what a joy divine!" we usually think of person-to-person fellowship, though this verse is actually describing the relationship we have with Jesus. And often the occasions when we are singing the hymn are happy times spent with fellow believers.

Paul, however, recognized that there is another side to fellowship. It may surprise us to hear him speak of the fellowship of Christ's sufferings. Yet when Christians suffer for Christ's sake, they share a unique partnership with Him. They come to know Christ in a way that those of us who live in more comfortable surroundings will never experience.

At the same time, the blessing of this fellowship can encourage those who suffer in more "ordinary" ways. A minister once told of visiting a member in the hospital, who spoke of her intense pain. She said to him, "You don't know what I am suffering." He agreed that indeed he did not. Then he told her, "But Christ does. He suffered intense pain on the cross, and He knows

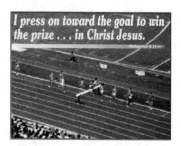

Visual for
lesson 3

Today's visual illustrates Paul's metaphor of "pressing on." Discuss the similarities between an athlete's perseverance and a Christian's.

what you are going through." The minister noted that immediately he saw a look of comfort come over the woman's face. It made a difference to her to realize that Christ knows what it is to suffer, and that when we suffer there is a unique bond between us and Him.

"What a fellowship"—the precious fellowship of suffering! —R. C. S.

11. If by any means I might attain unto the resurrection of the dead.

The Scriptures teach that a *resurrection of the dead* will be shared by both saint and sinner— the one to life eternal and the other to condemnation (John 5:28, 29; Acts 24:15). Resurrection to life with Christ is a goal worth more than whatever can be invested in striving toward it.

Attain here signifies the arrival at a chosen destination. Paul had his eye on the goal and was on his way to reaching it. This does not mean, however, that eternal life is achieved on the basis of one's personal effort. It is a gift from God to be accepted and received. Its value increases as the recipient grows in his familiarity with the Provider.

II. The Approach Is Commitment (Philippians 3:12-16)

A. Pressing On (v. 12)

12. Not as though I had already attained, either were already perfect: but I follow after, if that I may apprehend that for which also I am apprehended of Christ Jesus.

Paul described himself as *not . . . already perfect.* He was not yet a finished product of God's workmanship. That, however, did not keep him from pursuing his goal patiently to the end. *I follow after:* as a patient hunter tracks his game, so Paul resolved to stay the course with dogged persistence. [See question #3, page 368.]

Here was Paul's fervent desire: *that I may apprehend that for which also I am apprehended of*

Christ Jesus, or "take hold of that for which Christ Jesus took hold of me" (*New International Version*). The action is comparable to a drowning person's being seized by his rescuer and brought to grasp the rope he hadn't known was there. The lifesaving is accomplished by the rescuer, but it requires the cooperation of the rescued one. The Lord has laid hold on all of us through the gospel; through the same gospel we lay hold on Him and are saved.

B. Forgetting and Expecting (vv. 13, 14)

13, 14. Brethren, I count not myself to have apprehended: but this one thing I do, forgetting those things which are behind, and reaching forth unto those things which are before, I press toward the mark for the prize of the high calling of God in Christ Jesus.

What a thought to grasp all at once! Let us consider its most important elements one by one.

Brethren. Paul regarded his readers as equals with him in the family of God. He and they had shared in the opportunities and responsibilities of the gospel. We share in them, too!

Paul had not yet *apprehended* his goal: he did not claim to have laid hold of his reward. He had not yet crossed the finish line in the Christian race, but he was committed to going all out in order to reach it.

This one thing! The Greek text does not include the words *I do,* and is really more powerful without it. This is it! Nothing else matters!

Forgetting those things which are behind—this could include much of the "dung" from Paul's past: his Jewish heritage and cultural advantages; his sins and failures; his impressive array of accomplishments. None of these must be allowed to divert his attention from the opportunities before him. [See question #4, page 368.]

Reaching forth. As a runner leaning, straining, and extending himself to the limit, Paul was exerting the utmost effort to reach his goal.

I press toward the mark. Paul was not following a general compass direction of "living a good life." His eyes were fixed on a specific goal.

The verse concludes with Paul's description of his goal: *the prize of the high calling of God in Christ Jesus.* On reaching that goal Paul would receive the everlasting, never-fading "crown of righteousness" (1 Corinthians 9:25; 2 Timothy 4:8) given to those who are "faithful unto death" (Revelation 2:10). If there is anything more wonderful than being "in Christ," it will be the joy of being "with Christ!"

FACING FORWARD

During a discussion on changes and improvements in airplane design, someone suggested that airplane seats be turned around so that all the passengers are facing backward. Industry analysts claim that the public will never accept this. Why? Because people want to see where they are going, not where they have been. Everyone wants to face forward—at least physically.

In a more symbolic sense, there is always the temptation to face backward—that is, to live in the past. Sometimes this desire can be attributed to a nostalgia for supposedly better days. Sometimes it is caused by guilt over things that one did or failed to do.

In Savannah, Georgia, there is a statue in Madison Square honoring Sergeant William Jasper, who died during the siege of Savannah in 1779. The cool shaded square offers a striking contrast to the dust and heat that must have characterized the battlefield that day. But one thing is the same: Sergeant Jasper is pictured as he died—running *forward*.

Facing forward offers many advantages. One's eye is focused on future opportunities, not on past failures. One concentrates on building up character for days to come, not on reliving sins of the past. Satchel Paige, one of the greatest pitchers in the history of baseball, offered some sound advice when he said, "Don't look back. Something might be gaining on you."

Given the "prize" that awaits faithful Christians, there is no need for us to look back—ever.

—R. C. S.

C. Preserving the Gains (vv. 15, 16)

15. Let us therefore, as many as be perfect, be thus minded: and if in any thing ye be otherwise minded, God shall reveal even this unto you.

Having presented clearly his own position and perspective, the apostle recommended the same course to the *perfect* (or "mature") Christians among his readers. Any who considered themselves to be complete in their spiritual development were exhorted to be *thus minded*. However, if some differences of viewpoint still remained, Paul would leave the matter to *God*, trusting that He would *reveal* what the less mature needed to know. Such individuals required further teaching, perhaps by experience, perhaps by a more complete understanding of Christ and His Word, or perhaps by the example of mature Christians. Agreement would not be compelled, even by an apostle.

16. Nevertheless, whereto we have already attained, let us walk by the same rule, let us mind the same thing.

Even those who have not yet *attained* the level of maturity that others have should not stand around doing nothing while God is bringing

them "up to speed." Let them *walk*, or live, by the truth they have already learned. Thus they will not lose the ground they have gained, but will be in a position to advance—learning more, doing more, and growing more toward the likeness of Christ.

III. The Company Is Chosen (Philippians 3:17-21)

Neither the apostle Paul nor his friends in Philippi walked alone in the way to which they were committed. No one travels the road of life alone, but each must choose carefully his fellow travelers.

A. Follow Good Examples (v. 17)

17. Brethren, be followers together of me, and mark them which walk so as ye have us for an ensample.

Again, Paul refers to his readers as *brethren*—as equals in God's family. *Be followers together of me.* Whatever flaws might be found in Paul, he had still reached a level of commitment and maturity that merited respect and imitation. The most important aspect of his example was his steadfast imitation of Christ (1 Corinthians 11:1).

Mark them: take notice of faithful folk around you—Timothy and Epaphroditus, for examples (Philippians 2:19-30)—whose way of life is worthy of being observed, appreciated, encouraged, and followed. Then when others say, concerning some wickedness, "Everyone is doing it!" you can reply, "Not everyone, and I can point to some who are not!"

B. Shun Bad Examples (vv. 18, 19)

18, 19. (For many walk, of whom I have told you often, and now tell you even weeping, that they are the enemies of the cross of Christ: whose end is destruction, whose God is their belly, and whose glory is in their shame, who mind earthly things.)

The intensity of expression here leads one to suppose that the *enemies of the cross* included some who had claimed salvation in Christ but had forsaken the Christian way. Those who had

---

How to Say It

EPAPHRODITUS. Ee-*paf*-ro-*dye*-tus (strong accent on *dye*).
MACEDONIA. Mass-eh-*doe*-nee-uh.
PHILIPPI. Fih-*lip*-pie or *Fil*-ih-pie.
PHILIPPIANS. Fih-*lip*-ee-unz.

never known the Savior would not be likely to exert much influence on the saints in Philippi, but the falling away of those once in Christ would bring the tearful agony here expressed.

In describing the guilty ones, Paul mentions the final *end* of their wickedness—*destruction.* Paul also describes the lifestyle that leads these individuals to ruin. They give priority to physical appetites, disregarding exhortations to self-discipline. Thus their *God is their belly.* Their sense of values becomes distorted: their *glory is in their shame.* They brag about actions of which they ought to be ashamed. The Christian belongs to a better company and has a better influence to cultivate! [See question #5, page 368.]

C. Live in Hope (vv. 20, 21)

20. For our conversation is in heaven; from whence also we look for the Saviour, the Lord Jesus Christ.

In contrast with the earthbound enemies of the cross, *our* (the construction is emphatic) vital ties are elsewhere—*in heaven.* Here the word *conversation* signifies the location of one's "citizenship." That would have been very important to the Philippians, whose city was recognized as a Roman colony and whose people were citizens of Rome. They lived in the province of Macedonia, but their loyalty and their security were closely tied to a city that was some distance away.

In the same way, Christians live *in* the world and are involved *with* it; yet they are not *of* it. Their real home is far away. They must guard against becoming naturalized worldlings, giving this temporary residence top priority.

21. Who shall change our vile body, that it may be fashioned like unto his glorious body,

according to the working whereby he is able even to subdue all things unto himself.

Most of the miracles worked by our Lord during His earthly ministry dealt with the diseased, disabled, and even dead bodies of persons whom He restored to health and activity. All who saw His healings were amazed at His power. The results, however, were limited. The healed ones grew old, or became ill, and died in due time.

Immeasurably greater power will be seen when Jesus comes in glory and changes the bodies of all the saints to be like His own *glorious* spiritual *body* (1 Corinthians 15:42-53; 1 John 3:2). The physical body is called *vile,* not in the sense of being filthy or impure, but weak and lowly in contrast with the glory of Christ's body.

The miracle of conversion is seen in the spiritual change that occurs when a person is transformed from sinner to saint (Romans 6:1-11). The miracle of resurrection will be seen when the saint's physical body is transformed into one that is, like the Lord's, incorruptible and immortal (1 Corinthians 15:51-54). It is a goal worthy of our utmost attention!

Conclusion

A. "Not to Me Only"

Where, we may ask, is a race in which one participant may enjoy the "thrill of victory" without causing others to experience "the agony of defeat"? The answer is easy. The win-win outcome is most natural among those in Christ who are determined to "press toward the mark" as Paul did.

This is especially clear in Paul's final letter to Timothy. He had fought the good fight against the powers of darkness. He had finished the course. He was ready to receive the winner's crown, which the righteous Judge will bestow, "not to me only, but unto all them also that love his appearing" (2 Timothy 4:7, 8). We sense that Paul's victory would be enhanced by the presence of every one whom he had helped over the finish line. There is room in the "winners' circle" for all we can bring with us!

B. Prayer

Thank You, our Father, for Jesus—"the way, the truth, and the life." May we never lose sight of Him as the goal worthy of all our striving. When we falter or fail, lift us, please, toward a better and more successful effort for His sake. In His name, amen.

C. Thought to Remember

"So run, that ye may obtain" (1 Corinthians 9:24).

Home Daily Bible Readings

Monday, June 12—Don't Be Led Astray! (Philippians 3:1-6)

Tuesday, June 13—The Ultimate Richness: Knowing Jesus Christ (Philippians 3:7-11)

Wednesday, June 14—Press On Toward the Goal (Philippians 3:12-16)

Thursday, June 15—Our Citizenship Is in Heaven (Philippians 3:17—4:1)

Friday, June 16—Encourage One Another in Christ Jesus (Hebrews 10:19-25)

Saturday, June 17—Hold Fast Your Confidence in Christ (Hebrews 10:26-39)

Sunday, June 18—Live a Disciplined Christian Life (Hebrews 12:1-13)

Learning by Doing

This page contains an alternate lesson plan emphasizing learning activities. Classes desiring such student involvement will find these suggestions helpful.

Learning Goals

After this lesson each student will be able to:

1. Describe the attitude, actions, and goal that, according to Paul, are part of "pressing on in Christ."

2. List some personal possessions or activities that he or she considers expendable in his or her own discipleship.

3. Evaluate his or her life to determine whether there is any part that needs to be "counted as loss" for the sake of knowing Christ better.

Into the Lesson

Ask each class member to identify one or two goals he or she is working toward at the present time. Students may suggest short-range or long-range goals. The goals may involve learning new skills, perfecting some they already know, correcting disorders—any goals they may be trying to accomplish. Ask for volunteers to relate their goal(s) to the rest of the class.

Conclude this sharing time by telling the class that goal-setting is an everyday part of life. Sometimes goals are accomplished quickly. Some goals take much longer. It is important that every person determine the ultimate goal or purpose of his or her life. However, sometimes that is very difficult to do. Today's study will help you determine life's goal and how to accomplish that goal.

Into the Word

Prepare a study guide to be distributed to each class member. The study guide should have the following information: A heading should read "Determining and Accomplishing Life's Ultimate Goal." Print the Scripture reference (Philippians 3:7-21) under the heading. Print these three subheadings and references evenly spaced down the left-hand side of the page: *The Goal Is Christ* (Philippians 3:7-11), *Pressing Toward the Goal* (Philippians 3:12-16), and *Choosing Friends and Examples* (Philippians 3:17-21). At the bottom of the page, print the words, "My life's goal is. . . ."

Ask the class to work in groups of three persons. Each group should read the entire text together. Then ask the groups to go back and re-read each passage listed down the left-hand side of the page. Their first task is to summarize the primary thought of each section in one sentence and write it in the space provided.

After they have accomplished that task, ask several of the groups to read their summary sentences for the first passage. Use these discussion questions for the passage:

1. What were some of the things Paul counted as "loss" for Christ? (vv. 7, 8).

2. Paul's goal was to know Christ (v. 10). What did he mean when he said he wanted to be made "comfortable unto his death"? Then, using the lesson commentary and Romans 3:21-26, emphasize that it is impossible to become acceptable with God through the law. Righteousness comes from God through Jesus Christ.

After allowing a few groups to read summary sentences from the second passage, display the *New International Version* wording of verse 12 on a poster or a projected transparency. Explain that this translation clarifies the meaning of the verse. Using your lesson commentary, prepare a brief lecture about the colorful language and significance of verses 12-16.

Ask a couple of groups to read their summary sentences for the third passage on the work sheet. Use these questions to stimulate purposeful discussion.

1. Why do you think it is so important to identify good examples in determining our life's goal?

2. Would you consider Heaven our goal or our reward for knowing Christ (v. 20)? Why?

Into Life

The application of this lesson to life will take place in three brief activities. First, ask each class member to complete the sentence at the bottom of the worksheet, "My life's goal is. . . ."

Second, remind them that Paul had decided that his credentials were nothing but dung, or rubbish, compared with knowing Christ. Ask the students to list a few of their credentials that they would consider rubbish compared with knowing Christ. Cite examples: lots of money, parents who were Christians, position in the community, and others.

Finally, call the class's attention to the words "mark them" in verse 17. Paul asks readers to notice faithful people as examples in knowing Christ. Ask them to list one or two persons they know who would serve as good models for their lives in following Christ.

Ask the groups to pray for each other's progress in pursuing life's ultimate goal.

Let's Talk It Over

The questions on this page are designed to encourage review of the lesson Scriptures and to promote discussion of the lesson by the class. The answers provided are only discussion starters. Let your class talk it over from there.

1. What "assets" do we have that may well be "liabilities" because they compete with Christ for top priority in our lives? How can we "count them as loss for Christ"?

All too often we literally count things as an indication of a person's importance: how many cars, how many bedrooms in a house (or bathrooms!), how many windows in his or her office, how many carats of gold in the sign on the office door. Christians need to become "No-Count" people, for "a man's life consisteth not in the abundance of the things which he possesseth" (Luke 12:15).

Even in the church we are sometimes tempted to count the externals—how many services a person attends, how many ministry teams he or she is a part of, how much the person gives in offerings, and the like. These can be barometers of a person's spiritual life, but they are not replacements for true inner devotion.

2. For the Christian who minimizes the importance of the things most people value, the risk is to be resented and resisted. That threat may tempt us to compromise our value system. How can we resist that temptation?

Whenever we are deemed "different" by the majority around us, we get a little uncomfortable. People caught up in "lottery fever" may consider us elitist or just plain foolish if we reject their appeals to join in the office pool—especially if we affirm that we consider gambling to be ungodly. When co-workers gather around the "gossip fence," to stand apart may be interpreted as aloofness or self-righteousness.

No one wants to be considered an outsider. Yet that is what Christ calls us to become. We must live life "outside" the norms of general mores. Perhaps knowing we are not outsiders in Christ's body will help. Encouraging and supporting one another is important in this matter.

3. It is a universally accepted truism that "no one's perfect." How might that truth be misused to justify bad behavior? Why is it dangerous to do so?

When Paul admits imperfection (Philippians 3:12), he does not do so glibly. Sometimes we admit imperfection in such a way as to suggest we are powerless to do anything but sin. When we

glibly accept that no one's perfect, we resist the challenge to grow closer to perfection. We accept our present state and fail to grow in our faith.

The dangers of such an attitude include the tendency to take sin lightly. Our failings become "no big deal" since "no one's perfect." Besides that is the danger that failing to grow usually leads to falling away. One cannot remain stagnant in his spiritual life. Either he grows more like Christ or he moves farther away. If sin becomes insignificant, then willful sin is likely to follow. (See Hebrews 6:4-6; 10:26, 27.)

When Paul said he was not perfect, he added that he was pressing on toward perfection. So must we!

4. What kinds of things do we often have trouble forgetting and leaving behind? How can we do that?

For some of us, the sins and mistakes we made before we named Jesus as Lord are difficult to put aside: such matters as a foolish earlier marriage or a bad habit such as smoking or even the physical ravages of improper eating habits. Our concept of utter forgiveness by God is still faulty, for our understanding of His grace is inadequate.

Yet, the matters that we have trouble letting go of may be real accomplishments of our pre-Christian life. A successful career position, a desirable social position—such things can interfere with Christian growth as well. We must, like Paul, be willing to count all that as rubbish, toss it aside, and "change lanes" to the exit ramp leading to Heaven.

5. Characterize the persons "whose God is their belly." What do we see of ourselves in such a characterization?

For such a person, physical wants and drives dominate his decision-making. Eating (or satisfying another physical appetite) is his highest joy and delight. His motto for life is, "It just doesn't get any better than this," with a cold beer or warm paramour in his hand.

When we find ourselves more interested in eating (empty and excessive calories) than in reading God's Word, when we organize our daily logs more around leisure activity or rest than around opportunity to teach and counsel in the Scripture, the belly is beginning to be worshiped.

Rejoicing in Christ

DEVOTIONAL READING: 1 Thessalonians 1:2-10.

BACKGROUND SCRIPTURE: Philippians 4:4-20.

PRINTED TEXT: Philippians 4:4-19.

Philippians 4:4-19

4 Rejoice in the Lord always: and again I say, Rejoice.

5 Let your moderation be known unto all men. The Lord is at hand.

6 Be careful for nothing; but in every thing by prayer and supplication with thanksgiving let your requests be made known unto God.

7 And the peace of God, which passeth all understanding, shall keep your hearts and minds through Christ Jesus.

8 Finally, brethren, whatsoever things are true, whatsoever things are honest, whatsoever things are just, whatsoever things are pure, whatsoever things are lovely, whatsoever things are of good report; if there be any virtue, and if there be any praise, think on these things.

9 Those things, which ye have both learned, and received, and heard, and seen in me, do: and the God of peace shall be with you.

10 But I rejoiced in the Lord greatly, that now at the last your care of me hath flourished again; wherein ye were also careful, but ye lacked opportunity.

11 Not that I speak in respect of want: for I have learned, in whatsoever state I am, therewith to be content.

12 I know both how to be abased, and I know how to abound: every where and in all things I am instructed both to be full and to be hungry, both to abound and to suffer need.

13 I can do all things through Christ which strengtheneth me.

14 Notwithstanding, ye have well done, that ye did communicate with my affliction.

15 Now ye Philippians know also, that in the beginning of the gospel, when I departed from Macedonia, no church communicated with me as concerning giving and receiving, but ye only.

16 For even in Thessalonica ye sent once and again unto my necessity.

17 Not because I desire a gift: but I desire fruit that may abound to your account.

18 But I have all, and abound: I am full, having received of Epaphroditus the things which were sent from you, an odor of a sweet smell, a sacrifice acceptable, well-pleasing to God.

19 But my God shall supply all your need according to his riches in glory by Christ Jesus.

GOLDEN TEXT: Rejoice in the Lord always: and again I say, Rejoice.—Philippians 4:4.

Lesson Aims

As a result of studying this lesson, each student will be able to:

1. Describe the joy and contentment that Paul both urged and modeled for the Philippians.

2. Tell what makes Christian joy different from the surface happiness that the world promises and promotes.

3. Express appreciation to one who has helped him or her or has been an encouragement through example.

Lesson Outline

INTRODUCTION

  A. Shakespeare's Recovery Song

  B. Lesson Background

 I. CONSTANT REJOICING (Philippians 4:4-7)

  A. God's Presence (vv. 4, 5)

  B. Prayer and Peace (vv. 6, 7)

 II. CLEAR THINKING (Philippians 4:8, 9)

  A. Upbeat Thoughts (v. 8)

  B. Uplifting Example (v. 9)

III. CONTENTMENT (Philippians 4:10-13)

  A. Renewed Care (v. 10)

  B. Satisfied Regardless (vv. 11, 12)

    To Be Content

  C. Christ, the Source (v. 13)

IV. CARING CHRISTIANS (Philippians 4:14-19)

  A. The Philippians' Giving (vv. 14-16)

  B. Paul's Priorities (vv. 17, 18)

  C. God's Provision (v. 19)

CONCLUSION

  A. Courage of a "Paulyanna"

  B. Prayer

  C. Thought to Remember

Introduction

A. Shakespeare's Recovery Song

One of William Shakespeare's more familiar sonnets tells of the poet's notable recovery from a spell of the "blues." It begins on a low, low note:

When, in disgrace with fortune and men's eyes,
I all alone beweep my outcast state
And trouble deaf heaven with my bootless cries
And look upon myself and curse my fate. . . .

You may have been there, and you probably came out of it. How? Shakespeare thought of a good and generous friend:

Yet in these thoughts myself almost despising
Haply I think on thee, and then my state,
Like to the lark at break of day arising
From sullen earth, sings hymns at heaven's gate;
For thy sweet love remember'd such wealth brings
That then I scorn to change my state with kings.

The pits of a Shakespeare-like depression could be avoided entirely if, like the apostle Paul, one would spend the dark hours with Christ, the best of all friends, and so discover that the "break of day" He provides is the best of all times for pure rejoicing. That discovery is the focus of today's study.

B. Lesson Background

From beginning to end, both Paul's experience in the city of Philippi and his Philippian letter are characterized by a theme of rejoicing in the face of difficulties. Among the highlights of the apostle's ministry in Philippi is the occasion when he and Silas sang praises to God at midnight in a prison—and afterward baptized the jailer and his household as believers in Jesus (Acts 16:25-34).

Approximately ten years later we find Paul again in prison, this time at Rome, and writing to the Philippians to encourage them in their own difficulties. Each chapter in Philippians begins with an encouragement to joy and rejoicing. Paul prayed with *rejoicing* for the Philippian saints and their faithful "fellowship in the gospel" (1:3-5). He pleaded for their unity so that his *joy* might be complete (2:2). He confessed to being repetitious in exhorting them to "*rejoice* in the Lord" (3:1). He insisted that they do so always (4:4).

There were, however, occasional interruptions to the joyous mood. Some brethren were preaching the gospel with motives that were less than ideal (1:15-18). The shadow of "murmurings and disputings" lingered near (2:14). Self-seeking "enemies of the cross" persisted in their opposition (3:18, 19). And Euodias and Syntyche still needed help to overcome their differences (4:2, 3). None of these difficulties, however, must be allowed to stifle the saints' rejoicing in the Lord—always!

I. Constant Rejoicing (Philippians 4:4-7)

A. God's Presence (vv. 4, 5)

4. Rejoice in the Lord always: and again I say, Rejoice.

Rejoice is used to translate five different Greek words in the New Testament. The word found here appears in some form in approximately fifty passages, all of which are related to Christ or to the Christian's life in Christ.

Rejoice in the Lord always. Continual rejoicing requires a constant, steadfast basis. We find that constancy only in God, of whom we sing, "Thou changest not, Thy compassions, they fail not; As Thou hast been Thou forever wilt be."

That basis for rejoicing is most evident when circumstances seem to undermine any reason to rejoice. Recall Jesus' words: "Blessed are ye, when men shall revile you, and persecute you, and shall say all manner of evil against you falsely, for my sake. Rejoice, and be exceeding glad: for great is your reward in heaven" (Matthew 5:11, 12). The Christian's joy in Jesus is always "in season," whatever national, international, or personal conditions may be.

Again I say, Rejoice. Paul has said it before (3:1), and, like any effective teacher, he will say it again and again!

5. Let your moderation be known unto all men. The Lord is at hand.

Moderation translates a word that is rendered in other Bible versions as "gentleness," "forbearance," and being "considerate." It reflects the divine nature described in Psalm 103:8: "The Lord is merciful and gracious, slow to anger, and plenteous in mercy." He who constantly rejoices in the Lord will not respond angrily in word or deed to small vexations. He can answer a scowl with a smile and an insult with a favor, because he knows that the Lord is constantly present to provide patience and to dispense in His own time whatever judgment is appropriate.

B. Prayer and Peace (vv. 6, 7)

6. Be careful for nothing; but in every thing by prayer and supplication with thanksgiving let your requests be made known unto God.

"The Lord is at hand" (v. 5) to prevent the killjoy attitudes of worry, anxiety, or perplexity that haunt persons who do not acknowledge His presence. The phrase *be careful for nothing* simply means, "Don't worry" or "Do not be anxious." It echoes the themes of part of Jesus' Sermon on the Mount (Matthew 6:25-34). Many medical caregivers testify that prayer helps in the treatment of their patients; but prayer loses something of its value if it is used for anything other than communication between a child of God and the loving heavenly Father.

Our text provides a well-balanced menu for prayer. Along with general communication it includes *thanksgiving* and *requests*. A request recognizes dependence on God for all we really need—in both the material and spiritual realms. Thanksgiving brings a smile of remembrance in recalling countless blessings already received in answer to requests made (and sometimes without any requests made!). It discovers joy and covers disappointment. It is an exercise in continual rejoicing! [See question #1, page 376.]

7. And the peace of God, which passeth all understanding, shall keep your hearts and minds through Christ Jesus.

Peace suggests a wholeness and serenity of spirit very different from the pulled-apart feeling of anxiety. Anything laid before the Lord in honest prayer is on the way to a solution. Because the Lord is "able to do exceeding abundantly above all that we ask or think" (Ephesians 3:20), the resultant tranquillity indeed *passeth all understanding*. Its source, however, is clear; it comes *through Christ Jesus*. This is a peace "not as the world giveth" (John 14:27). It is Christ's answer to the trouble and fear that one encounters in the world (John 16:33).

The Greek word translated *keep* refers to the protection of a security guard standing at a door. The mind thus protected will scarcely be invaded by such intruders as bitterness, depression, or anxiety. Like the joy highlighted earlier, Heaven's peace abides within the Christian regardless of his surroundings.

II. Clear Thinking (Philippians 4:8, 9)

To be kept from invasion by negative forces, the mind needs nourishment from positive sources.

A. Upbeat Thoughts (v. 8)

8. Finally, brethren, whatsoever things are true, whatsoever things are honest, whatsoever things are just, whatsoever things are pure, whatsoever things are lovely, whatsoever things are of good report; if there be any virtue, and if there be any praise, think on these things.

Visual for lesson 4

Today's visual suggests that our rejoicing should continually "echo" throughout our lives. Post it before you begin the lesson.

Finally: Paul offers one more series of exhortations before expressing his gratitude for the Philippians' recent gift. He has written about Christians' attitudes; he turns now to the mental diet that feeds those attitudes. What are Christians to look at, listen to, think about, or discuss? Even in a wicked world filled with "junk food" for the mind, some constructive subject matter is available.

Paul names eight qualities of a good mental diet, and all of them are associated with God. The list falls naturally into four pairs: *true* and *honest, just* and *pure, lovely* and *of good report,* and having *virtue* and being worthy of *praise.* The first two describe what is upright and dependable, despising deceitfulness in all its forms. The second pair describes what is incorruptible and undefiled; it is not tainted by a sinful world. The third pair describes what is seen and known to be above reproach; it is both pleasant and admirable. The fourth pair describes what is most respectable and respected—of highest quality and known to be so.

One adjective describes all these subjects recommended for consideration: *Christlike!* "Turn your eyes [and your mind] upon Jesus." Fix and hold your attention on *these things,* and you will never lack for reasons to smile! Neither will you lack for material to occupy conversations and to form plans, imaginations, and actions that will please the God who has blessed you with a mind. [See question #2, page 376.]

B. Uplifting Example (v. 9)

9. Those things, which ye have both learned, and received, and heard, and seen in me, do: and the God of peace shall be with you.

Paul did not ask his friends to act simply on the basis of abstract principles. He provided a "visual aid" to offer guidance where needed and to show that these principles really work. And that visual aid was Paul himself!

Do! Put into practice what you have *learned.* Just as Paul's teaching would have been ineffective without the confirmation provided by his actions, so the Philippians' learning would have been empty without expression of the truth in their daily behavior. With that combination of knowing and doing firmly in place, they could be sure that *the God of peace* would shelter them with His presence. [See question #3, page 376.]

III. Contentment
(Philippians 4:10-13)
A. Renewed Care (v. 10)

10. But I rejoiced in the Lord greatly, that now at the last your care of me hath flourished again; wherein ye were also careful, but ye lacked opportunity.

Paul's own "rejoicing in the Lord always" had been encouraged by Epaphroditus's arrival from Philippi with gifts from the church. We may wonder why Paul waited until the conclusion of his letter to mention this. Perhaps he had sent a grateful acknowledgment earlier, possibly with the news of Epaphroditus's illness (Philippians 2:26).

Paul's rejoicing, however, was not so much for the gift as for the loving *care* that prompted the giving. Apparently some time had passed since the Philippians' last communication with Paul. He recognized this delay, not as a sign of their indifference, but as a reflection of circumstances. His imprisonment had placed certain restrictions on his ability to correspond with others and be contacted by them (thus one of the reasons for writing this letter). Recall that his Roman imprisonment was preceded by at least two years of imprisonment in Caesarea (Acts 24:27).

The phrase *hath flourished again* brings to mind a plant's springtime foliage that has been dormant throughout a long winter. To see such a renewal of activity is cause for rejoicing, both in flowers and in friends!

B. Satisfied Regardless (vv. 11, 12)

11. Not that I speak in respect of want: for I have learned, in whatsoever state I am, therewith to be content.

Paul wanted to make it clear that he was not expressing a need for more gifts. He had *learned* through a considerable amount of practice (read his account of his sufferings for Christ in 2 Corinthians 11:23-28) how to get along with much or with little. Thus he was indifferent to what most people consider important or necessary. He would have been keenly embarrassed to have anyone think otherwise. Paul was always concerned that others' reception of the gospel would not be affected negatively by what might be interpreted as greed on his part (1 Thessalonians 2:5, 9).

The key word in this verse is *content*. It translates a Greek word that means "self-sufficient," in the sense that Paul needed no outward props to sustain his faith. In Christ he possessed an inner strength that erased any dependence on external help. His sense of self-worth and well-being did not depend on the *state* of his outward circumstances. He could deal with companionship or solitude, popularity or rejection, comfort or pain, good health or illness. Have we *learned* to live in that same contentment? [See question #4, page 376.]

TO BE CONTENT

Many people have been caught up in the craze known as "lottery fever" and have spent huge (and unnecessary) amounts of money in trying to find a cure. However, a Kentucky newspaper reporter found some people who were not at all swept up in the enthusiasm. The reporter interviewed one lady who claimed that all that money could be more trouble than it's really worth. "Look at all the wealthy people who are still unhappy." Later the reporter talked with a man who said, "Frankly, what am I supposed to do with all those millions of dollars? I can't think of anything else I really need. I'm content."

Obviously this reporter had talked to two very astute people. It simply doesn't matter how much you have if you are discontented. And it doesn't matter how little you have if you are contented. Note that Paul said that he had *learned* to be content. It was not something that came naturally to him. More than likely it does not come naturally to any of us. But we can learn contentment, and we can do so in the same way Paul learned it—by enrollment in the school of Christian living. Here one learns not only contentment, but a host of other virtues that make one "educated" in the subjects that matter most. —R. C. S.

12. I know both how to be abased, and I know how to abound: every where and in all things I am instructed both to be full and to be hungry, both to abound and to suffer need.

To live one's life each day under conditions that seldom vary does not pose a formidable challenge to faith. However, to be able to adjust gracefully to the roller-coaster experiences of poverty and plenty, hunger and feasting, and to do so in many locations and surroundings as Paul did, requires a sense of true contentment.

This does not mean that Paul passively accepted the circumstances he faced. He prayed for relief from his "thorn in the flesh." But when he did not receive that for which he prayed, he thanked God for the grace to bear testimony to Christ's power in him (2 Corinthians 12:7-10). His contentment came from a source greater than his surroundings, as the next verse indicates.

C. Christ, the Source (v. 13)

13. I can do all things through Christ which strengtheneth me.

Paul's contentment, or self-sufficiency, was really *Christ*-sufficiency. While the word *Christ* does not appear in the Greek text of this verse, it is surely implied. Jesus supplied the strength that Paul needed to run the Christian race to its completion and receive the "crown of righteousness" (2 Timothy 4:8). At this point the strength he needed was the endurance to serve joyously in the circumstances he was now enduring. What a comfort to the apostle to know that his imprisonment could not shut out the companionship of Christ!

IV. Caring Christians (Philippians 4:14-19)

A. The Philippians' Giving (vv. 14-16)

14. Notwithstanding, ye have well done, that ye did communicate with my affliction.

Paul's comparative indifference to material things might make him seem ungrateful for his friends' generosity. That was not the case at all. The Philippians were aware of his *affliction*, living as a prisoner and probably on limited resources. Their gift made them participants in his ministry, and he sincerely appreciated such partnership.

15. Now ye Philippians know also, that in the beginning of the gospel, when I departed from

---

How to Say It

CAESAREA. Sess-uh-*ree*-uh.

CORINTH. *Kor*-inth.

CORINTHIANS. Kor-*in*-thee-unz (*th* as in *thin*).

EPAPHRODITUS. Ee-*paf*-ro-*dye*-tus (strong accent on *dye*).

EUODIAS. You-*o*-dee-us.

MACEDONIA. Mass-eh-*doe*-nee-uh.

PHILIPPI. Fih-*lip*-pie or *Fil*-ih-pie.

PHILIPPIANS. Fih-*lip*-ee-unz.

SYNTYCHE. *Sin*-tih-key.

THESSALONICA. *Thess*-uh-lo-*nye*-kuh (strong accent on *nye*; *th* as in *thin*).

Macedonia, no church communicated with me as concerning giving and receiving, but ye only.

The close bond between Paul and the *Philippians* began when the apostle first entered what we know as the European continent. Philippi was the first city in that region to receive the gospel, and it was eager to join in Paul's ministry of taking the gospel to others. Paul cites the Philippians' "fellowship in the gospel from the first day until now" (Philippians 1:5). They did not wait to receive letters of appeal from Paul or to see what other churches would do; on their own initiative they acted to participate in what Paul was doing. Theirs was the true joy of giving. It was a joy in which others could not share because they waited to be asked.

16. For even in Thessalonica ye sent once and again unto my necessity.

Here Paul recalls the Philippians' assistance during his rather stormy experience at *Thessalonica*, which was also in Macedonia (Acts 17:1-9). It appears that they also provided similar assistance to Paul at Corinth; for later he wrote to the Corinthians, "When I was present with you, and wanted, I was chargeable to no man: for that which was lacking to me the brethren which came from Macedonia supplied" (2 Corinthians 11:9).

B. Paul's Priorities (vv. 17, 18)

17. Not because I desire a gift: but I desire fruit that may abound to your account.

Paul was bold in urging liberality toward others who were in need (2 Corinthians 8, 9), but would never request, or even suggest, that any kind of *gift* be given to him. "I seek not yours, but you," he insisted (2 Corinthians 12:14).

Paul did, however, rejoice in the blessing that came to his friends from their faithful giving. Here he uses an interesting commercial term in expressing his pleasure at seeing "credits" added to the Philippians' *account*. They were laying up treasures in Heaven, which would never be lost nor depleted (Matthew 6:19-21). In that Paul openly rejoiced.

18. But I have all, and abound: I am full, having received of Epaphroditus the things which were sent from you, an odor of a sweet smell, a sacrifice acceptable, well-pleasing to God.

Paul had been "paid in *full*" and had *all* that he needed. *Epaphroditus* seems to have brought gifts of more than one kind (perhaps financial assistance and warm clothing). Here Paul referred to them in terms suited to describe Old Testament sacrifices: "a sweet savor, an offering made by fire unto the Lord" (Exodus 29:18; cf. Leviticus 1:9, 13, 17; 2:2). Sheer generosity creates its own pleasant aroma.

C. God's Provision (v. 19)

19. But my God shall supply all your need according to his riches in glory by Christ Jesus.

God had provided through Paul a dramatic demonstration of Jesus' promise concerning life's necessities: "Seek ye first the kingdom of God, and his righteousness; and all these things shall be added unto you" (Matthew 6:33). The apostle was convinced that the saints in Philippi had set these same priorities and could claim the same provision.

God's provision in Christ, however, goes far beyond material needs. It includes all the glories of living daily in Christ Jesus and the indescribable glories of His presence in eternity. Such *riches* come in their own unique and dependable "currency." They are not subject to the woes that befall worldly wealth, for they are the riches of Heaven! [See question #5, page 376.]

Conclusion

A. Courage of a "Paulyanna"

You may have heard of Pollyanna, the young minister's daughter who could find, or make, something to be glad about in whatever happened. Pollyanna's optimism was more respected in 1913, when her story was published, than it has been in more recent (and more cynical) times. Her perspective has been dubbed "vapid sentimentality" or "head-in-the-sand idealism" by those who prefer to look on the darker side of things.

The "glad" approach did not begin with Pollyanna, though, nor with Eleanor Hodgman Porter, who wrote her story. It is at least as old as the apostle Paul and the Christ-centered optimism that led him to say, "I have learned, in whatsoever state I am, therewith to be content," and to advise, "Rejoice in the Lord always."

It takes considerable courage in this present world to promote this "Paulyanna" brand of optimism. Such courage, as well as the joy that accompanies it, comes with a stubborn faith in the Son of God.

B. Prayer

Some of childhood's joys are no longer with me, Lord; so give me grace to appreciate the richer gifts of a growing faith. And when I no longer have some strengths I now enjoy, give me grace to enjoy the riper pleasures and greater expectations I then shall have in Christ my Lord. Amen.

C. Thought to Remember

Our grounds for rejoicing are as constant as the love of God.

Learning by Doing

This page contains an alternate lesson plan emphasizing learning activities.
Classes desiring such student involvement will find these suggestions helpful.

Learning Goals

As a result of studying this lesson, each student will be able to:

1. Describe the joy and contentment that Paul both urged and modeled for the Philippians.

2. Tell what makes Christian joy different from the surface happiness that the world promises and promotes.

3. Express appreciation to one who has helped him or her or has been an encouragement through example.

Into the Lesson

Before class prepare and post a banner with the words, "Rejoice in the Lord always."

Begin this study by asking the class to sing the chorus, "Rejoice in the Lord Always." (A larger class can sing the song as a round.) Tell the class the words on the banner are the words in the key verse to today's study.

Ask two class members to be the scribes at chalkboards or posters. Ask class members to call out names of other choruses and hymns that indicate Christian joy and happiness. The hymnbooks and chorus books are filled with songs of joy, such as "The Joy of the Lord," "This Is the Day," "Let There Be Praise," "He Keeps Me Singing," "Sunshine in My Soul," and "O Happy Day."

After the exercise, ask the class what this long list of songs tells them about Christianity. The answer you are looking for is that one of the products of our faith is a deep sense of joy.

Into the Word

This portion of the lesson will be done in two parts. For the first part of the Bible study, prepare handouts to be given each student and an identical large poster (or an overhead transparency) to use in this portion of the study. The heading to the posters and handouts should read "Tips for Peace and Joyful Living." Under the heading should be three columns. The smaller heading for column 1 should be "Do." The heading for column 2 should be "Do Not." Column 3's heading should read "Rewards." Ask a student to read Philippians 4:4-19. Then ask the class to scan the text looking for answers to write in the columns. As the students discover answers, write their responses on the large poster (transparency).

Do: rejoice in the Lord, v. 4; be moderate (gentle), v. 5; present your requests to God, v. 6; think on good things, v. 8; rejoice at benevolent care, v. 10; be content, v. 11; acknowledge blessings and gifts, vv. 14-17.

Do not: worry, v. 6.

Rewards: the peace of God, vv. 7, 9; I can do all things through Christ, v. 13; God shall supply all needs, v. 19.

Summarize this part of the study by observing that Paul has given us very helpful tips for joyful living. Tell the class that we will look more closely at this passage in two sections. The first section (vv. 4-9) will give us some tips for finding true joy and peace. The second section (vv. 10-19) will focus on Paul's example in learning contentment.

After re-reading vv. 4-9, use the following questions to lead a discussion:

• Why would Paul say, *"Again* I say, Rejoice" (v. 4)?

• What makes Christian joy different from and deeper than other kinds of joy?

• What kind of peace is Paul talking about?

• What is the opposite of this kind of peace (v. 7)?

• What is the key word ("do") in verse 9 and why?

Prepare a short lecture on Paul's example and tips for finding contentment (vv. 10-19), using the lesson commentary. Remember, the lecture should be brief.

Into Life

As you distribute envelopes to the students, point out that Paul says he has found joy in persons who have encouraged him. This Philippian letter expresses his gratitude for such acts. He thanks his friends for their financial help during times of trouble. Tell the class of someone who, down through the years, has been a Christian encouragement to you and brought joy to your life.

Ask each student to identify someone who has done that for him or her. Have the students write those names on their envelopes and then take the envelopes home and write letters to the ones they identified, expressing gratitude and joy for sharing in their lives.

Give the students copies of Philippians 4:4-7 and ask them to memorize this text. Make the arrangements to have a "Scripture choir" in a worship service in the near future. The Scripture recitation can become the core of a song service built around Christian joy.

Let's Talk It Over

The questions on this page are designed to encourage review of the lesson Scriptures and to promote discussion of the lesson by the class. The answers provided are only discussion starters. Let your class talk it over from there.

1. Worry and anxiety are characteristic of the modern culture. Why is that true? Why is such a mind-set so antithetical to Christian living?

Most of modern society does not have available the resource that Paul reveals in Philippians 4:6—making their needs known to God! The unbeliever has, from his perspective, real reason to be anxious for *everything*! The world is both dangerous and uncertain, in areas ranging from health to the economy. To have the weight of those dangers and uncertainties on one's own shoulders is enough to create great anxiety and worry.

For the Christian, the truth of existence is to the contrary: *God* is in control, and He is quite adequate for the task! A heart and mind filled with thanksgiving, a tongue filled with supplication—those are all the Christian needs. He knows God is adequate—and more.

2. Paul says we are to fill our minds with good and wholesome things (v. 8). How can we evaluate ourselves in this regard?

Every day believers need to run the checklist of Philippians 4:8, asking, "What is one thing I have mentally considered today that is true? honest? just? pure? lovely? well-regarded? virtuous? praiseworthy?" For any entry for which the mind is blank, Christians need to ask themselves, "Why is nothing there? What can I give attention to right now?" That kind of spiritual discipline will both cleanse and renew the mind. (See Romans 12:2.) Evil thoughts and thoughts of evil often fill our minds simply because there is room there! The mind filled with the right things has little room for the wrong.

3. What are some of the things we have *learned, received, heard,* and *seen* that we have yet to *do?*￼

Much of what we have learned of Christ from our studies of the Gospels, we have yet to apply. Few of us are as kind and compassionate, as bold and assertive, as focused and as persistent as we know He was. All that we know of His generosity and His humility we have not approached. His holiness and His servant's heart we do not imitate. Paul would have the same simple answer for us that he had for the Philippians: "Do!"

Similarly, we have failed to emulate the pattern of witnessing to the gospel that we see in the book of Acts. Rather than making difficulty into opportunity for evangelism, we are satisfied to make it into occasion for grumbling. "Do!"

Nor have we followed all that we have learned of Christian maturity in the epistles. While we should be reaching "the measure of the stature of . . . Christ" (Ephesians 4:13), many of us remain stunted spiritual dwarfs. It is time to "do!"

4. What is keeping us from reaching Paul's state of contentment?

Some people may hear this question and think of some thing or things—"If I just had this, then I would be content." Probably not! As long as a thing or things are one's priority, contentment is impossible. Only when things and circumstances are understood in the light of eternity—with all the temporal value gone—can we reach contentment. When we continue to carry a "Wants" list in our pockets or purses (or our minds), we make contentment unreachable.

Only when the mental transformation that accompanies making our bodies a living sacrifice to God (Romans 12:1, 2) is complete will we move from wanting to being—being content in Christ.

5. How well do most Christians demonstrate that they believe the truth Paul states, "God shall supply all your need according to his riches in glory by Jesus Christ"? How can we live with greater confidence in this truth?

The world constantly urges us to provide for ourselves all that money can buy—even if on credit. If we can't afford it, we can finance it. If the bank won't lend us the money, there are places that are more "creative" with their financing. All this adds up to human solutions to one's needs (or, more often, "wants").

It is difficult to be in this world but not of it. The strivings of the worldly are to become independently wealthy, providing a life of ease for themselves and the following generation. Jesus' suggestion was much simpler: ask for *daily* bread.

For the Christian to emulate a worldly lifestyle and philosophy is disastrous. When we become *independently* wealthy, where is our affirmation of God? Where is our dependence on Him? How can we witness of His adequacy when we do not demonstrate that we believe it ourselves?

Called to Spiritual Blessings in Christ

DEVOTIONAL READING: **Romans 1:8-17.**

BACKGROUND SCRIPTURE: **Ephesians 1.**

PRINTED TEXT: **Ephesians 1:1-14.**

Ephesians 1:1-14

1 Paul, an apostle of Jesus Christ by the will of God, To the saints which are at Ephesus, and to the faithful in Christ Jesus:

2 Grace be to you, and peace, from God our Father, and from the Lord Jesus Christ.

3 Blessed be the God and Father of our Lord Jesus Christ, who hath blessed us with all spiritual blessings in heavenly places in Christ:

4 According as he hath chosen us in him before the foundation of the world, that we should be holy and without blame before him in love:

5 Having predestinated us unto the adoption of children by Jesus Christ to himself, according to the good pleasure of his will,

6 To the praise of the glory of his grace, wherein he hath made us accepted in the beloved:

7 In whom we have redemption through his blood, the forgiveness of sins, according to the riches of his grace;

8 Wherein he hath abounded toward us in all wisdom and prudence;

9 Having made known unto us the mystery of his will, according to his good pleasure which he hath purposed in himself:

10 That in the dispensation of the fulness of times he might gather together in one all things in Christ, both which are in heaven, and which are on earth; even in him:

11 In whom also we have obtained an inheritance, being predestinated according to the purpose of him who worketh all things after the counsel of his own will:

12 That we should be to the praise of his glory, who first trusted in Christ.

13 In whom ye also trusted, after that ye heard the word of truth, the gospel of your salvation: in whom also, after that ye believed, ye were sealed with that Holy Spirit of promise,

14 Which is the earnest of our inheritance until the redemption of the purchased possession, unto the praise of his glory.

GOLDEN TEXT: Blessed be the God and Father of our Lord Jesus Christ, who hath blessed us with all spiritual blessings in heavenly places in Christ.—Ephesians 1:3.

New Life in Christ
Unit 2: Called by Christ
(Lessons 5-9)

Lesson Aims

After this lesson each student will be able to:

1. Summarize the "spiritual blessings" that Christians possess.

2. Tell how a knowledge of these blessings will affect their walk with Christ and witness to the world.

3. Write or say a prayer of thanksgiving for the spiritual blessings he or she has received in Christ.

Lesson Outline

INTRODUCTION
  A. Three Cheers for God!
  B. Lesson Background
I. GOD'S GRACIOUS CHOICE (Ephesians 1:1-6)
  A. Chosen for a Purpose (vv. 1-4)
  B. Added to a Family (vv. 5, 6)
II. GOD'S GRACIOUS SACRIFICE (Ephesians 1:7, 8)
  A. Providing Forgiveness (v. 7)
    The Altar of Forgiveness
  B. Providing in Abundance (v. 8)
III. GOD'S GRACIOUS MESSAGE (Ephesians 1:9, 10)
  A. Once Hidden (v. 9)
  B. Now Revealed (v. 10)
IV. GOD'S GRACIOUS PROMISE (Ephesians 1:11-14)
  A. Our Inheritance (vv. 11, 12)
  B. Our Down Payment (vv. 13, 14)
    The Notary's Seal
CONCLUSION
  A. Go Ahead—Smile!
  B. Prayer
  C. Thought to Remember

Introduction

A. Three Cheers for God!

Have you ever become so excited about something that you started talking and couldn't stop— you just talked and talked without "coming up for air"? It takes an extraordinary event to generate that degree of excitement.

The first few verses of Paul's letter to the Ephesians comprise just such an outburst. Language scholars have criticized the style, but no one can criticize the sentiment. What is it that gets Paul so excited? It is his realization of the many wonderful blessings that God has given all Christians.

If we do get as excited as Paul, it is rarely over spiritual blessings; yet these are the very topics that ought to thrill us most. The blessings and benefits we receive from God are exhilarating. That is the reason Paul begins his letter to the Ephesians by saying, in effect, "Three Cheers for God!"

B. Lesson Background

The book of Ephesians is thought by many Bible students to have been a circular letter—that is, that it was addressed to a group of churches rather than to one specific congregation. Two reasons are often cited for this conclusion. The first is the lack of personal information and references included in the letter. Paul was closely associated with the Ephesian church—he spent three years in Ephesus (Acts 20:31)—yet this letter does not contain the kind of warm, personal language that one would expect to see.

The second piece of evidence for believing that Ephesians was a circular letter is that the earliest copies of the book do not have the words "in Ephesus" in the opening verse. Why, then, did the letter come to be called the book of Ephesians? The church in Ephesus may have been the largest one or most prominent among the group of churches to which the letter was sent. Perhaps it was the church that took custody of the letter.

On the other hand, the letter is not completely without personal language. Paul mentions his prayers for the recipients (1:15-23; 3:14-19) and asks for theirs (6:18-20). He also notes that Tychicus would bring them personal information about him (6:21, 22). And, of course, we do not have the original copy of the letter, so we do not know whether the words "in Ephesus" were part of the original or not. Nor were the words necessary since the letter was probably carried directly to its destination(s) by Tychicus, one of Paul's friends (Ephesians 6:21). It did not have to be "addressed" like a modern letter sent by the post office.

The idea of a circular letter is not foreign to the New Testament. Paul told the Colossians, "When this epistle is read among you, cause that it be read also in the church of the Laodiceans; and that ye likewise read the epistle from Laodicea" (Colossians 4:16). Note, however, that both Colossians and "the epistle from Laodicea" seem to have been intended for a particular church first and for circulation second. If Ephesians was a circular letter, it was probably delivered to the Ephesians first and then circulated as much as was feasible.

Ephesus was a thriving and fairly modern city when Paul was there. (Its ruins are still being studied by archaeologists.) It was the site of a temple dedicated to the Greek goddess Artemis (also known by her Roman name Diana) and considered one of the seven wonders of the ancient world. Silversmiths established a lucrative business in making and selling silver images of Artemis. Acts 19:23-41 records how a riot resulted when Paul's success in converting people to Christianity began to affect the silversmiths' profits.

Ephesians, Philippians, Colossians, and Philemon are usually called Paul's prison epistles. What is perhaps most striking about these four letters is Paul's positive attitude in all of them. (We have already noted the theme of joy that characterizes Philippians.) It is surely an insight into the apostle's relationship with Christ that he could maintain such a vibrant faith while in prison. Paul himself may have been in bonds, but his spirit was always free—with the freedom that only Jesus can give.

I. God's Gracious Choice (Ephesians 1:1-6)

While words like *chosen, election,* and *predestination* have fueled many a theological debate, we cannot ignore them. As difficult as these issues may be to grasp, we must give attention to them and seek to examine them from a Biblical perspective.

A. Chosen for a Purpose (vv. 1-4)

1, 2. Paul, an apostle of Jesus Christ by the will of God, To the saints which are at Ephesus, and to the faithful in Christ Jesus: Grace be to you, and peace, from God our Father, and from the Lord Jesus Christ.

As with most letters in the Greco-Roman world, this one begins with the writer's identifying himself. *Paul* describes himself (as he often does in his letters) as *an apostle of Jesus Christ.* He addresses his letter *to the saints.* The world generally considers *saints* to be special people who belong to an elite class of super-spirituality. But the word *saints* simply means "holy ones" or "separated ones," which is a characteristic of all Christians.

Paul also uses his typical greeting of *grace and peace.* Since *grace* was the typical Greek greeting and *peace* was the typical Jewish greeting, the use of both terms together was particularly significant in this letter, which emphasizes the oneness of Jew and Gentile in Christ (Ephesians 2:11-22).

3. Blessed be the God and Father of our Lord Jesus Christ, who hath blessed us with all spiritual blessings in heavenly places in Christ.

The word *blessed* can have two basic connotations, both of which are present in this verse. (The Greek word here translated *blessed* literally means "to speak well of" and is the source of the English word "eulogy.") When we think of being *blessed* we often think of receiving something good, which then becomes designated as a *blessing.* Thus has God *blessed us with all spiritual blessings.* However, the word *blessed* in the phrase *blessed be . . . God* indicates speaking something good, or, in this case, praising God for the good that He has done.

Paul describes the blessings Christians have received as being *in heavenly places,* or, literally, "in the heavenlies." This is a phrase unique to Ephesians, appearing four other times in this book besides here (1:20; 2:6; 3:10; 6:12). It is instructive to note the use of the term in these passages. According to 1:20, 21, Christ is now at God's right hand *"in the heavenly places,* far above all principality, and power, and might, and dominion." Ephesians 2:6 says that Christians are privileged to "sit together *in heavenly places* in Christ Jesus." The reference in 6:12 says that Christians "wrestle . . . against spiritual wickedness *in* high [literally, *heavenly*] *places."*

These passages emphasize that the victory gained by Jesus through His resurrection is one that He shares with His followers. We are reminded that our true home is in Heaven (Philippians 3:20) and that we have a taste of that now by being "in the heavenlies" with Jesus. [See question #1, page 384.]

4. According as he hath chosen us in him before the foundation of the world, that we should be holy and without blame before him in love.

This verse takes us into controversial territory. Theologians have long debated the issues of predestination and free will. Is this verse saying that God chooses who will be saved? If so, how does this fit with Scriptures indicating that God desires that all be saved (1 Timothy 2:4) and that

The large letters on today's visual spell the word Blessings. *Ask the class what blessings Paul describes in our text; then compare the small background words to see which ones match the class's list.*

Visual for lesson 5

man has the freedom to choose whether or not to accept God's salvation (John 3:16; Revelation 22:17)? How do we reconcile the sovereignty of God with man's free will?

Some believe that *chosen* means that God has chosen (or elected) certain individuals to believe in Jesus Christ and be saved, while the rest of mankind (everyone not chosen) is condemned and lost forever. Many people, however, wonder how this position can be held in light of those Scriptures that call individuals to choose to obey God (Deuteronomy 30:19; Revelation 22:17) and that indicate that God does not want any individual to perish (Ezekiel 18:32; 2 Peter 3:9).

One way of understanding the doctrine of election is to see the choice as corporate; that is, it describes God's dealings with a group rather than with individuals. Thus, when Paul says, *"He hath chosen us in him before the foundation of the world,"* he may be talking about the church. Just as Israel had been God's chosen people under the Old Covenant, so the church has become God's chosen people under the New Covenant.

At the same time, some Scriptures indicate that election has an individual nature as well as corporate. Peter writes to Christians whom he calls "elect according to the foreknowledge of God the Father" (1 Peter 1:2). This passage tells us that election occurs according to God's foreknowledge. This means that God chooses or elects certain individuals to be saved and to enjoy the blessings of salvation on the basis of His advance knowledge of the choice they will make concerning Jesus Christ. Thus, God does not cause some to be saved and some to be lost, but rather He knows in advance who will accept His gracious offer of salvation. And those "whom he did foreknow, he also did predestinate to be conformed to the image of his Son. . . . Moreover, whom he did predestinate, them he also called" (Romans 8:29, 30).

Note also the purpose of this election: *that we should be holy and without blame before him*— or, as Paul told the Romans, "to be conformed to the image of his Son." As God's people *in Christ*, we are to be holy (or, be "saints," see v. 1) and blameless, just as Christ was while He walked on this earth. And someday, we will be just as He is in glory (1 John 3:2).

B. Added to a Family (vv. 5, 6)

5, 6. Having predestinated us unto the adoption of children by Jesus Christ to himself, according to the good pleasure of his will, to the praise of the glory of his grace, wherein he hath made us accepted in the beloved.

Part of God's eternal plan is that we who accept His *grace* become His *children*. Paul is the only New Testament writer to use the *adoption* metaphor, though the concept is consistent with other New Testament images (see, for example, John 1:12).

All of this is pleasing to God and is *to the praise of the glory of his grace* (words similar to these are also found in verses 12 and 14). The salvation of lost individuals delights God and causes people to give Him glory.

II. God's Gracious Sacrifice (Ephesians 1:7, 8)

A. Providing Forgiveness (v. 7)

7. In whom we have redemption through his blood, the forgiveness of sins, according to the riches of his grace.

Sin exacts a terrible price; thus the plan to save mankind from it was not without a staggering cost. The word *redemption* is a word that signifies the freeing of a slave by payment of a price. The picture is clear: God saw us on the auction block, as it were, and as slaves to sin. He was willing to pay the redemption price—the *blood* of His only Son—to set us free.

God's blessings are granted *according to the riches of his grace*. Too many see God as someone who enjoys dispensing His justice but is stingy with His grace. That is not at all the picture the Bible gives us. In Ephesians, Paul refers six times to the richness of what God has done for us (here; 1:18; 2:4, 7; 3:8, 16).

THE ALTAR OF FORGIVENESS

If you ever visit the renowned cathedral in downtown Mexico City, you will see a magnificent altar known as the Altar of Forgiveness. An interesting story lies behind its construction. A young artist was accused of a capital crime and sentenced to a year in prison, after which he was to be executed. While in prison he painted such a touching and inspiring picture that he was pardoned and set free. Eventually this painting became the central feature of a majestic golden altar that was placed in the cathedral in Mexico City.

Some years ago fire destroyed much of the inside of the cathedral. When officials surveyed the ruins to determine the cause of the fire, they discovered a short circuit in the electrical system. That short circuit was in, of all places, the Altar of Forgiveness!

We need not worry that the true Altar of Forgiveness will ever experience a short circuit—for that Altar is the cross of Jesus Christ. On the cross Jesus died and offered Himself as the sacrifice that made forgiveness of sins possible for us all. He is the only person who can provide this forgiveness, and His cross is the only place where it can be found. There will never be a short circuit in this altar. The "riches of God's grace" found there will never be depleted.

—R. C. S.

B. Providing in Abundance (v. 8)

8. Wherein he hath abounded toward us in all wisdom and prudence.

Among God's other blessings, we also receive both *wisdom* and *prudence* (or insight). There is only a shade of difference in the meaning of these two words. We might understand them as telling us that God has blessed us with the ability to see situations as they are and the ability to know what to do about them. [See question #2, page 384.]

III. God's Gracious Message (Ephesians 1:9, 10)

A. Once Hidden (v. 9)

9. Having made known unto us the mystery of his will, according to his good pleasure which he hath purposed in himself.

Paul says that God has *made known unto us* what was once a *mystery*. We think of a mystery as something that we need to figure out, such as the identity of the guilty party in a mystery novel. With Paul, however, the word describes something once unknown that has now been revealed by God. Since His *good pleasure* and purposes are involved, the mystery encompasses something that it was not possible for us to reason out for ourselves. God had to reveal the answer.

B. Now Revealed (v. 10)

10. That in the dispensation of the fulness of times he might gather together in one all things in Christ, both which are in heaven, and which are on earth; even in him.

What does *dispensation* mean in this context? (We must be sure not to let other definitions with which we are acquainted affect our interpretation.) The Greek word used here is the source of our English word "economy." Literally it means "house rules." These include the rules by which a family or even a family business operates. It could refer to what we today might call a strategic plan.

As part of this plan, Paul says that in the end (at *the fulness of times*) God will *gather together in one all things in Christ.* The Greek word translated *gather together in one* is a mathematical term and describes the way that numbers were totaled in New Testament times. Whenever a column of figures was added, the total was placed at the top (not at the bottom as most of us are ac-

customed to doing). Paul is saying that at the end, everything will "add up" to Christ.

This is not to be taken as a form of syrupy universalism that says everyone will go to Heaven. (This would contradict other passages in Ephesians as well as countless other Scriptures.) It simply means that all of history is pointing to the second coming of Jesus and will be consummated when He returns (1 Corinthians 15:24-28). What an encouragement to know that we will reign with Him! [See question #3, page 384.]

IV. God's Gracious Promise (Ephesians 1:11-14)

A. Our Inheritance (vv. 11, 12)

11. In whom also we have obtained an inheritance, being predestinated according to the purpose of him who worketh all things after the counsel of his own will:

Under the Old Covenant, Israel was the recipient of God's promises. Only those who belonged to the seed of Abraham could claim such a privilege. Now, however, under the New Covenant Gentiles are included—a theme to be developed later by Paul (Ephesians 2:11-22). Christians are now "Abraham's seed" (Galatians 3:29); they are "heirs of God, and joint-heirs with Christ" (Romans 8:17). That *inheritance* includes eternal life with Christ in Heaven.

Notice once more the use of *predestinated.* From the beginning of time God has had a particular "destiny" in mind for His people, those who by faith are children of Abraham. The church was not an afterthought in God's *will*, but was part of His *purpose* all along.

12. That we should be to the praise of his glory, who first trusted in Christ.

How to Say It

ABRAHAM. *Ay*-bruh-ham.
ANTIOCH. *An*-tee-ock.
ARTEMIS. *Ar*-teh-miss.
COLOSSIANS. Kuh-*losh*-unz.
EPHESIANS. Ee-*fee*-zhunz.
EPHESUS. *Ef*-uh-sus.
EZEKIEL. E-*zeek*-yul or E-*zeek*-ee-ul.
LAODICEA. Lay-*odd*-uh-*see*-uh (strong accent on *see*).
LAODICEANS. Lay-*odd*-uh-*see*-unz (strong accent on *see*).
PHILEMON. Fih-*lee*-mun or Fye-*lee*-mun.
PHILIPPIANS. Fih-*lip*-ee-unz.
PREDESTINATED. pree-*dess*-tin-ay-ted.
TYCHICUS. *Tick*-ih-cuss.

The ultimate purpose of what God has done is that those who are blessed by His work should bring *praise* to Him. But to whom is Paul referring when he speaks of those *who first trusted in Christ?* Most likely he is describing the Jews (of whom Paul was one); since in the next verse his use of *ye also* would seem to include Gentile Christians, which would characterize most of those reading Paul's letter. [See question #4, page 384.]

B. Our Down Payment (vv. 13, 14)

13, 14. In whom ye also trusted, after that ye heard the word of truth, the gospel of your salvation: in whom also, after that ye believed, ye were sealed with that Holy Spirit of promise, which is the earnest of our inheritance until the redemption of the purchased possession, unto the praise of his glory.

Gentile Christians (*ye also*) are now described as full participants in the blessings of the *gospel* of *salvation.* They are also described as *sealed.* Just as a letter was sealed by an owner in order to guarantee its authenticity, or an item was sealed to insure its safety while being transported to another location, Christians have been "marked" as God's property by the *Holy Spirit.* [See question #5, page 384.]

In addition, the Spirit is described as *the earnest of our inheritance.* The word *earnest* was taken from the business world and described what we would call a "down payment" (as when we speak of "earnest money"). The final *redemption* (that is, the time when we receive "in full" what God has promised) will take place when we get to Heaven. Until then, we have the Holy Spirit to assist us in living the Christian life as well as to give us a touch of Heaven.

Home Daily Bible Readings

Monday, June 26—God Has Blessed Us in Christ (Ephesians 1:1-6)
Tuesday, June 27—God's Grace Lavished on Us in Christ (Ephesians 1:7-14)
Wednesday, June 28—Paul's Prayer for the Ephesian Christians (Ephesians 1:15-23)
Thursday, June 29—Called to Belong to Jesus Christ (Romans 1:1-7)
Friday, June 30—The Gospel: God's Power for Salvation (Romans 1:8-17)
Saturday, July 1—Bear the Fruit of the Spirit (Galatians 5:16-26)
Sunday, July 2—Bear One Another's Burdens (Galatians 6:1-10)

THE NOTARY'S SEAL

Most everyone is familiar with the notary's seal. It takes the place of that more ancient seal in which a bit of hot wax was placed on a document and then an image was pressed into it. Today we use a metal stamp that embosses the image signifying the author directly into the paper itself. While a photocopy machine may duplicate such a document, the presence of the seal assures you that what you have is not a copy but the real document.

In one respect, our modern notary's seal may actually serve as a better illustration of our being "sealed" with the Holy Spirit than the ancient seal. Just as the notary seal is embossed into the paper itself, so the Holy Spirit comes *into* the believer to become a part of his life. Sometimes we call this the indwelling of the Spirit. In another passage, Paul wrote that a Christian is a temple of the Spirit "which is in you" (1 Corinthians 6:19).

God does not want us to have any uncertainty about our forgiveness. The presence of the Holy Spirit gives us a blessed assurance that we truly belong to Him. We can know that our forgiveness is real and that we are members of the family of God. We ought to rejoice in the seal of the Spirit—God's assurance of His presence now and of greater blessings yet to come! —R. C. S.

Conclusion

A. Go Ahead—Smile!

One dear saint (but a very reserved one) was pondering the many blessings of the Lord. She told a friend, "The Lord's been so good to me, I can hardly keep from smiling." It should be hard not to feel some measure of gratitude when we consider all that God has done for us in Christ. It's all right to get a bit emotional about His great blessings. Emotionalism may be dangerous, but emotion based on and appropriate to the facts is always healthy.

If you put your mind to it, couldn't you, like Paul in today's text, find abundant reason to break forth into praise?

B. Prayer

Lord, thank You for the songs You place in our hearts and the smiles You place on our faces. When language fails, we will still try to praise Your holy name. Words may be inadequate, but accept the sentiment of our hearts. We are grateful for Your grace, Your gifts, and Your glory. Through Christ, who is above all, amen.

C. Thought to Remember

Don't be afraid to raise a phrase of praise.

Learning by Doing

This page contains an alternate lesson plan emphasizing learning activities.
Classes desiring such student involvement will find these suggestions helpful.

Learning Goals

After this lesson each student will be able to:

1. Summarize the "spiritual blessings" that Christians possess.

2. Tell how a knowledge of these blessings will affect their walk with Christ and witness to the world.

3. Write or say a prayer of thanksgiving for the spiritual blessings he or she has received in Christ.

Into the Lesson

Distribute copies of the handout described below. (This exercise is also included in the student book.) On the handout, print the heading "CURSE OR BLESSINGS?" Under the heading print these instructions: "Paul tells us that Christ has redeemed us from the curse of the law (Galatians 3:13). One of the final promises of the Bible is *'And there shall be no more curse'* (Revelation 22:3). Remove the letters of that promise—in order—from the list of letters below. The remaining letters will reveal a wonderful message that is the key to our study today. Write the solution below." Under these instructions print the letters "B L E A N S S E D D B E T H T H E E R G O D E W H O S H H A A T H L L B E B L E S S E D U N S W I O T H A M L O L R S E P I R I T U C A U L R B L E S S S E I N G S."

Give the students a couple of minutes to solve the puzzle; then ask for the solution, which is "Blessed be the God . . . who hath blessed us with all spiritual blessings" (Ephesians 1:3). Tell the class that today's study will provide us with a wonderful list of spiritual blessings.

Into the Word

Use your lesson commentary to outline and deliver a brief lecture about the background of the book of Ephesians. Conclude with remarks about Paul's greeting in verses 1 and 2.

Ask a student to serve as scribe to write blessings on the chalkboard. Ask the other members of the class to read Ephesians 1:1-14 and look for the blessings Paul mentions. As they discover a blessing, they are to tell it to the scribe so that he or she can add it to the list. The list will include the following: spiritual blessings in heavenly places (v. 3), God chose us (v. 4), holiness (v. 4), blamelessness (v. 4), adoption (v. 5), God's grace (v. 6), acceptance by God (v. 6), redemption (v. 7),

forgiveness of sins (v. 7), the riches of God's grace (v. 7), wisdom (v. 8), prudence (v. 8), knowledge (v. 9), an inheritance (v. 11), sealed with the Holy Spirit (v. 13), and the earnest of our inheritance (v. 14). Is it any wonder that Christians celebrate when we realize the many wonderful and powerful gifts God has given us?

Next, review and clarify the following issues:

1. The issue of predestination, vv. 4, 5. During the week before class ask a class member to prepare a brief report on this issue. Let the student study the lesson commentary and other sources you can make available. Have the student report to the class at this time.

2. Ask the class to define the following terms from the text: *redemption, forgiveness, wisdom, prudence, mystery of his will,* and *the dispensation of the fulness of times.* Use the lesson commentary to complement the class's answers.

3. Explore the concept of adoption by asking, "What are the benefits of being adopted? Why is this such a precious concept to Christians?"

4. Ask the class, "What is 'earnest money,' and how does understanding that help us understand verse 14?"

Summarize the study by reminding the class that Paul's wonderful list of blessings was written from prison. But his positive attitude, optimism, and enthusiasm tell us that his spirit remained free.

Into Life

Point to the list of blessings created earlier and remind the class that these blessings are theirs! Ask this discussion question: "What blessing 'grabbed you' during this study, and how do you feel it may influence your walk with Christ or your witness?" Repeat the question and ask them to answer it to someone sitting next to them.

Then ask the students to turn the handout over and use the blank side to express gratitude or praise by writing a prayer using the word "Bless" or "Praise" for an acrostic. (This activity is also in the student book.) Display this sample on a large red heart:

You have **B**lessed me, Lord!
I will **L**ive with the joy
of b**E**ing your child,
redeemed by your **S**on and
bathing in the riche**S** of your grace.

Let's Talk It Over

*The questions on this page are designed to encourage review of the lesson
Scriptures and to promote discussion of the lesson by the class. The answers
provided are only discussion starters. Let your class talk it over from there.*

1. What are some of the blessings with which God has "blessed us with all spiritual blessings in heavenly places in Christ"?

Certainly the blessing of salvation is one, and the one Paul immediately goes on to address in this context. The fellowship of brothers and sisters in Christ is another great blessing, perhaps one that is not fully appreciated until the strength and support of those brothers and sisters is really needed because of some crisis or trauma. Various spiritual gifts and talents are also blessings from God, and ones that vary from person to person. While these may differ, they all come from God. (See 1 Corinthians 12:4-12.) Try to keep the discussion focused on "spiritual" blessings rather than material, though there is a certain spiritual blessing that comes through physical entities like a job or house, etc.

2. If God has "abounded toward us in all wisdom and prudence," why do you think we continue to do so many foolish things? What can we do to demonstrate more of His wisdom?

Even the best of us occasionally revert to our old ways. Peter, who clearly saw that God had accepted the Gentiles (Acts 10, 11), reverted to his old way of behaving in Antioch (Galatians 2:11-14). We need to be open to the counsel of other believers and admit that our behavior is not always a demonstration of godly wisdom.

One of the most important things we can do to think the way God wants us to think is to think about the things God is concerned about—particularly the salvation of the lost. That means we will make decisions on the church program according to what will best win the lost, not by our personal preferences. It means that we will use our church facilities for His glory and not for our own convenience. For example, we might like the large room where our class has met for years, but if a different class in a smaller room has become larger than ours, we will gladly trade with them.

3. God has always had a plan culminating in Christ. He worked His plan to the letter. All history is His story. Do we have a plan? How are we doing in working it out?

Many organizations, secular and sacred, have recently been caught up in writing "mission statements" and the extended, step-by-step procedures

necessary to accomplish their missions. Certainly it is appropriate and profitable for a church to clarify and verbalize its purpose for existence. But whatever our "mission statement," it must point clearly to Jesus Christ! It is still true that the one who fails to plan plans to fail. We need constant evaluation of what works and what doesn't in the communication of the pure gospel of Christ. We need a constant willingness to make the necessary changes . . . even when we don't personally like those changes!

4. How can we "be to the praise of [God's] glory"?

Your discussion should focus not only on verse 12 of the text, from which the quotation comes, but also on the similar language in verses 6 and 14, and the immediate context for each verse. Note the similarities: predestination (vv. 5 and 11), redemption (vv. 7 and 14); God's will (vv. 5 and 9). God's purpose, as it is fulfilled in the lives of His people, leads to praise. Whatever we can do to cooperate with God's purposes, then, is "to the praise of his glory." Whatever we do to fulfill the demands of Matthew 5:16, "Let your light so shine before men, that they may see your good works, and glorify your Father which is in heaven," is "to the praise of his glory."

Certainly, we are to praise Him, in every way possible, but we must not limit that to singing and praying and pronouncing praise. We must be His praise by doing His will.

5. Gentiles as well as Jews had trusted in Christ and found salvation in Him. This represented the removal of a major barrier between peoples. What barriers need to be removed in our world today? In our church?

The gospel is for all people—of every gender, race, nationality, or any other division we may like to draw. We are all sinners—and if we are saved, it is only by Christ. Any great differences we try to draw among ourselves are flimsy ones, at best. Any feelings of superiority and inferiority we have toward one another are totally misguided.

Does your church exhibit the same demographics as your community? If not, why not? Are there barriers that need to come down? Brainstorm some ways to remove the barriers and open your church to all peoples.

Called to Oneness in Christ

DEVOTIONAL READING: John 17:1-11, 20-23.

BACKGROUND SCRIPTURE: Ephesians 2.

PRINTED TEXT: Ephesians 2:8-22.

Ephesians 2:8-22

8 For by grace are ye saved through faith; and that not of yourselves: it is the gift of God:

9 Not of works, lest any man should boast.

10 For we are his workmanship, created in Christ Jesus unto good works, which God hath before ordained that we should walk in them.

11 Wherefore remember, that ye being in time past Gentiles in the flesh, who are called Uncircumcision by that which is called the Circumcision in the flesh made by hands;

12 That at that time ye were without Christ, being aliens from the commonwealth of Israel, and strangers from the covenants of promise, having no hope, and without God in the world:

13 But now, in Christ Jesus, ye who sometime were far off are made nigh by the blood of Christ.

14 For he is our peace, who hath made both one, and hath broken down the middle wall of partition between us;

15 Having abolished in his flesh the enmity, even the law of commandments contained in ordinances; for to make in himself of twain one new man, so making peace;

16 And that he might reconcile both unto God in one body by the cross, having slain the enmity thereby:

17 And came and preached peace to you which were afar off, and to them that were nigh.

18 For through him we both have access by one Spirit unto the Father.

19 Now therefore ye are no more strangers and foreigners, but fellow citizens with the saints, and of the household of God;

20 And are built upon the foundation of the apostles and prophets, Jesus Christ himself being the chief corner stone;

21 In whom all the building fitly framed together groweth unto a holy temple in the Lord:

22 In whom ye also are builded together for a habitation of God through the Spirit.

GOLDEN TEXT: Now therefore ye are no more strangers and foreigners, but fellow citizens with the saints, and of the household of God; and are built upon the foundation of the apostles and prophets, Jesus Christ himself being the chief corner stone.
—Ephesians 2:19, 20.

New Life in Christ
Unit 2: Called by Christ
(Lessons 5-9)

Lesson Aims

As a result of studying this lesson, each student will be able to:

1. Tell how the grace that provides salvation also eliminates barriers that had previously separated those who are now saved.

2. Suggest some modern walls or barriers that need to be eliminated by the gospel.

3. Tell one specific way he or she can work for unity within the body.

Lesson Outline

INTRODUCTION
  A. Before and After
  B. Lesson Background
 I. SAVED! (Ephesians 2:8-10)
  A. By Grace Through Faith (vv. 8, 9)
    In Our Nothingness
  B. For Good Works (v. 10)
II. RECONCILED! (Ephesians 2:11-18)
  A. A Great Chasm (vv. 11, 12)
  B. A Greater Bridge (vv. 13-18)
III. INCLUDED! (Ephesians 2:19-22)
  A. In God's Family (v. 19)
  B. In God's Temple (vv. 20-22)
CONCLUSION
  A. No More Barriers
  B. Prayer
  C. Thought to Remember

Introduction

A. Before and After

People who are trying to sell diet programs or muscle-building devices often show before-and-after pictures to dramatize the difference that their products allegedly have made in the lives of people who have used the products. They hope that others will be impressed enough by this difference to buy those same products.

Paul, in our text for today, provides some before-and-after pictures comparing our lives before Christ came with what He has made of them. In particular, he calls attention to what the Gentiles were like before and after Christ came. The difference is striking!

Often the advertisers of the aforementioned products have to admit that their before-and-after

pictures are not necessarily typical and that results may vary from user to user. Paul, however, could promise results without any disclaimers. Everyone who comes to Christ can experience the changes he describes. These changes make it hard to imagine that anyone could consider them and then not want his "product."

B. Lesson Background

This lesson covers a text that contains some of the most significant doctrinal themes found in this letter to the Ephesians. In certain respects our text reminds us of the themes found in Paul's letter to the Romans, though they are considered here in a much more concise manner.

Paul was commissioned by Jesus to be an apostle to the Gentiles (Acts 26:17; cf. Romans 11:13). However, Paul was a Jew, with an especially impressive Jewish heritage and upbringing (Philippians 3:4-6). This placed him in the thick of occasional controversies, such as that which led to the convening of the Jerusalem Conference (Acts 15:1, 2) and that which resulted in Paul's confronting Peter in Antioch (Galatians 2:11-14).

In today's text Paul emphasizes that Christ died for both Jew and Gentile—to bring an end to the separation between the two. He encourages us to remember that we are all sinners who have been reconciled to God by Jesus' death on the cross. If we have been thus accepted by God, then we must accept each other—something that is often easier said than done.

We may summarize the focus of today's text by saying that it highlights what we once were because of our sins and what we now are because of what Jesus did for us.

I. Saved!
(Ephesians 2:8-10)

These verses are among the most important in the Bible, and also among the most debated.

A. By Grace Through Faith (vv. 8, 9)

8. For by grace are ye saved through faith; and that not of yourselves: it is the gift of God.

In spite of the questions that this verse raises, we all must marvel at how concisely Paul explains the substance of the gospel. He draws attention to salvation, grace, and faith in one verse.

Certainly the verse offers much comfort in the assurance that *by grace are ye saved.* This frees us from trying to earn or deserve Heaven, which we can never do in the first place.

A certain amount of controversy has arisen over the words *that not of yourselves: it is the gift of God.* What is it that is not of ourselves? What exactly is the gift of God? Some believe that faith itself is the gift of God. They maintain that those who respond to God were first given the gift of faith by the Holy Spirit so that they would believe; thus it is impossible for them not to believe. This position, however, diminishes the factor of man's free will, which is emphasized in "whosoever" passages such as John 3:16 and Revelation 22:17.

There is, in addition, a linguistic problem with this position. In the Greek text of this passage the pronoun *that* (in *that not of yourselves*) is a neuter pronoun. It cannot, then, refer to *faith* because *faith* is in the feminine gender. *That* refers not to any actual word in the text but to the concept expressed, that is, to the entire process of salvation. Our salvation is a gift from God. That this understanding is the better way to view this verse becomes more clear when the next verse is considered. Our salvation is "not of works." The idea of earning one's salvation is as ancient as it is wrong, but it still persists and shows up in some of the most surprising places. Longtime believers are sometimes caught up in a process of trying to "do enough" to merit salvation rather than accept the fact that we are saved by God's grace. Good works are important, but not as the source of our salvation. Paul addresses the role of works in verse 10. [See question #1, page 392.]

9. Not of works, lest any man should boast.

One of the consequences of understanding that we are saved by grace should be a sense of genuine humility. The plan of salvation is the work of God, *lest any man should boast*. No one can ever say that he is going to Heaven on the basis of his own *works*. While we should always seek to be obedient and to live in a manner pleasing to God, that is not what gets us to Heaven.

Let us keep in mind a phrase that appeared three times in last week's text from Ephesians 1: "to the praise of his glory" (vv. 6, 12, 14). This is one of the consequences of salvation: that God is praised by those who have received it. Obviously if we could win salvation through our own merits, we would have something about which to boast. As it is, we should boast about God: "He that glorieth, let him glory in the Lord" (1 Corinthians 1:31).

How to Say It

COLOSSIANS. Kuh-*losh*-unz.
CORNELIUS. Kor-*neel*-yus.
EPHESIANS. Ee-*fee*-zhunz.
EPHESUS. *Ef*-uh-sus.
PHILIPPIANS. Fih-*lip*-ee-unz.
PYRENEES. *Peer*-uh-neez.

IN OUR NOTHINGNESS

Our houseguests had sent their two small children upstairs to get ready for bed. Soon the older sister came down to complain about her younger brother. "He won't go to bed," she said, "and he's running around up there in his nothingness."

That's a fitting description of what we have to offer when we come to God for forgiveness: our nothingness. For Him to make something out of our nothingness is a testimony to the power of His "amazing grace." We sing of that in the beloved hymn *Rock of Ages:*

> Nothing in my hand I bring,
> Simply to Thy cross I cling;
> Naked, come to Thee for dress;
> Helpless, look to Thee for grace.

Can we name one good reason that God should forgive us? Absolutely not. The only reason is that this is the kind of God He is. Forgiveness can never be based on *our* goodness—only on *His* goodness. All our accomplishments, all our possessions, and all our abilities put together amount to nothing before God. We could not trade them all for pardon for a single sin.

We cannot earn forgiveness. We cannot buy forgiveness. We cannot barter for forgiveness. We can only accept the forgiveness lovingly offered by the God of grace. That is the reason there is no room for boasting. But there is more than enough room for gratitude and praise. A God who does so much for us who deserve so little is worthy of all the gratitude, praise, and love that we can offer. —R. C. S.

B. For Good Works (v. 10)

10. For we are his workmanship, created in Christ Jesus unto good works, which God hath before ordained that we should walk in them.

While salvation is "not of works," we must never think that works are meaningless. However, they must be understood in proper relationship to our faith. In order to emphasize the significance of *good works*, Paul points out that we were *before ordained* to do them. It is God's will for us as Christians that in this life we should display good works and thus let our light shine (Matthew 5:16). Thus works do not justify us, but they do identify us. As F. F. Bruce says, Paul "repudiated good works as a ground of salvation. [Still] no one more wholeheartedly insisted on works as the fruit of salvation."

While we cannot hope to earn Heaven by our works, the awareness of what Jesus did for us should move us to live lives filled with works that honor Him. The result of salvation is not just eternal life in Heaven, but a better, more fulfilling life on earth.

Home Daily Bible Readings

Monday, July 3—Saved and Made Alive by Grace (Ephesians 2:1-10)

Tuesday, July 4—One Body in Jesus Christ (Ephesians 2:11-16)

Wednesday, July 5—God Dwells in You (Ephesians 2:17-22)

Thursday, July 6—Jesus Commits Disciples to God's Care (John 17:1-6)

Friday, July 7—Jesus Prays for the Disciples' Protection (John 17:7-13)

Saturday, July 8—Jesus Prays for the Disciples' Unity (John 17:14-21)

Sunday, July 9—May God's Love Be in Christ's Disciples (John 17:22-26)

This verse also describes Christians as God's *workmanship*. The Greek word used here carries the connotation of a "work of art." (It is the source of our word "poem.") Perhaps we could translate it as "God's masterpiece." That's quite a goal to aspire to!

II. Reconciled!
(Ephesians 2:11-18)

Next, Paul proceeds to describe Christians as enemies of God who have been reconciled to Him. Many who are not Christians are uncomfortable with any suggestion that they are God's enemies. Most would strongly disagree with such an assessment. But while they may not see themselves as in active opposition to God, they are dead in sin and, in fact, at enmity with God.

In this section of our text, Paul deals with what we might call our "double alienation": we are separated from God and from each other.

A. A Great Chasm (vv. 11, 12)

11. Wherefore remember, that ye being in time past Gentiles in the flesh, who are called Uncircumcision by that which is called the Circumcision in the flesh made by hands.

Paul reminded his Gentile readers what their condition was like before they knew Christ. They were *called Uncircumcision* as a derisive way of noting that they lacked the covenant sign of Israelite males. [See question #2, page 392.]

Circumcision was first commanded of Abraham (Genesis 17:10-14). Eventually the practice became to the Jews a symbol of their presumed superiority to the *Gentiles*. Peter, for example, was accused of going "to men uncircumcised" and eating with them following his visit to the house of Cornelius (Acts 11:1-3).

Paul, however, explained that Christ has provided a new kind of circumcision. In Colossians 2:11 Paul wrote that Christians are "circumcised with the circumcision made without hands." To the Philippians, he wrote, "We are the circumcision, which worship God in the spirit, and rejoice in Christ Jesus, and have no confidence in the flesh" (Philippians 3:3).

12. That at that time ye were without Christ, being aliens from the commonwealth of Israel, and strangers from the covenants of promise, having no hope, and without God in the world.

At that time (before they became Christians), the Gentiles were *without Christ*. They were *aliens* and *strangers*. They were not part of God's chosen people and did not share in the *covenants of promise* made with individuals such as Abraham, Moses, and David, and given to the nation of *Israel*. Gentiles were, said Paul, both hopeless and Godless. It is hard to imagine a more desperate situation. [See question #3, page 392.]

B. A Greater Bridge (vv. 13-18)

13. But now, in Christ Jesus, ye who sometime were far off are made nigh by the blood of Christ.

Verse 13 introduces a much brighter picture, thanks to the phrase *but now*. (Other significant uses of this phrase are found in Romans 6:22; 7:6; 1 Corinthians 15:20; Colossians 3:8; Hebrews 8:6; 11:16.) The Gentiles, who for so long had been *far off* have now been *made nigh* (brought near) to God *in Christ Jesus*. Those who have been "on the outside looking in" have seen the barriers come down. No separation exists between God and the Gentiles; therefore no separation exists between Jew and Gentile. How did this happen? It happened through the cross, where Jesus shed His *blood*.

Today there is considerable concern about the divisions—racial, social, economic, and others—that exist in our society. We need to keep in mind the degree of hostility that was present between Jew and Gentile in Paul's day. Read the book of Acts to see how challenging it was for the church, which began among the Jews, to deal with the understanding that God wanted to save Gentiles as well. A gathering of the leadership (recorded in Acts 15) was required to settle the issue, and even that did not put the issue to rest. No less a figure than the apostle Peter had trouble living out the new understanding of God's love for Gentiles as well as Jews. (See Galatians 2:11-14.) Yet it is one of the impressive accomplishments of the gospel of Christ that it could and did transcend such formidable barriers.

Could anything but the gospel have accomplished this? Can anything but the gospel heal the divisions present in our fragmented world?

14. For he is our peace, who hath made both one, and hath broken down the middle wall of partition between us.

What Jesus accomplished at the cross was so significant that Paul does not say merely that Jesus brought peace, but that *he is our peace.* There are two ways Paul describes the difference Jesus has made. First, He *hath made both one.* Any differences between Jew and Gentile mean nothing now. Paul told the Galatians, "There is neither Jew nor Greek [Gentile], . . . for ye are all one in Christ Jesus" (Galatians 3:28).

Second, Paul says that Christ *hath broken down the middle wall of partition between us.* The word rendered *middle wall* is translated as "dividing wall" in the *New International Version.* (This is the only time the word appears in the New Testament.) The word for *partition* is a more common and general term that can refer to any kind of wall or fence, including a "hedge" that was used to protect a vineyard (Mark 12:1). Perhaps Paul was thinking of the "wall" that existed in the Jerusalem temple, where gates leading into the inner courts displayed warning signs barring Gentiles from going any farther. Violation of this warning was punishable by death. Recall the uproar that resulted when Paul was accused of bringing Gentiles into a forbidden area of the temple (Acts 21:27-36).

Paul declares that the wall dividing Jews and Gentiles has crumbled. The next verse describes this wall and what Christ did to demolish it.

15. Having abolished in his flesh the enmity, even the law of commandments contained in ordinances; for to make in himself of twain one new man, so making peace.

Jesus has *abolished . . . the law of commandments contained in ordinances.* Some see this statement as contradictory to Jesus' declaration that He did not come "to destroy the law, or the prophets: . . . but to fulfil" (Matthew 5:17). These two verses simply offer two different perspectives on what Jesus did concerning the law. Jesus fulfilled the law by living according to its standards of righteousness and by emphasizing its underlying principles (as seen throughout the Sermon on the Mount). Through His coming the law's purpose was fulfilled in that it is a "schoolmaster to bring us unto Christ" (Galatians 3:24).

In this passage from Ephesians, Paul seems to place special emphasis on the ceremonial aspects of the law—*commandments contained in ordinances.* These are the portions of the law (including such matters as feast days, food regulations, and rituals) that drove a wedge between Jew and Gentile. Colossians 2:14 says that Jesus blotted out "the handwriting of ordinances that was against us . . . and took it out of the way, nailing it to his cross."

Under the New Covenant, the portions of the law concerning moral issues (for example, the Ten Commandments) can still provide guidance as a standard of conduct, but not a means of salvation. Only Jesus' death supplies that. His sacrifice has allowed those who have broken the law to be forgiven.

The impact of Jesus' death is described as making *one new man* of two. Some believe that this is to be taken in a corporate sense, picturing the church as God's new humanity that includes both Jews and Gentiles. Others see the phrase as descriptive of the new individual or "new creature" in Christ (2 Corinthians 5:17). This person is neither Jew nor Gentile; he is a Christian!

16. And that he might reconcile both unto God in one body by the cross, having slain the enmity thereby.

The method *God* chose to *reconcile both* Jews and Gentiles to Himself was *the cross.* Since the cross has done away with what once separated Jews and Gentiles, and has reconciled them to God, it is now possible for them to be reconciled to each other.

17. And came and preached peace to you which were afar off, and to them that were nigh.

This verse tells us that Jesus *came and preached peace* to those *afar off* (Gentiles) and to *them that were nigh* (Jews). But Jesus' earthly ministry was primarily for the sake of "the lost sheep of the house of Israel" (Matthew 15:24). When did He preach peace to Gentiles? Probably Paul is describing the impact of Jesus' ministry, particularly His death and resurrection, on all peoples, to whom His followers are told to go and preach (Mark 16:15). Thus Peter could speak to the Gentiles in the house of Cornelius of "the word which God sent unto the children of Israel, preaching peace by Jesus Christ" (Acts 10:36). He then concluded, "Whosoever believeth in him shall receive remission of sins" (Acts 10:43).

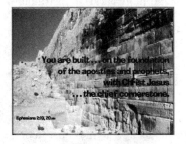

Visual for lesson 6

Today's visual illustrates our Golden Text for the day, Ephesians 2:19, 20. Display it as you begin to discuss those verses.

18. For through him we both have access by one Spirit unto the Father.

Through Jesus all peoples, Jews and Gentiles alike, have *access* to God as their *Father*. The Greek word rendered *access* is related to a word that describes the official who would usher someone into a king's presence. Now *both* Jews and Gentiles can walk in daily fellowship with the King of Heaven.

III. Included!
(Ephesians 2:19-22)

In this portion of our text, Paul uses what our high school English teacher would have called a mixed metaphor. He combines the figures of a nation, a family, and a building to illustrate that Christians (both Jews and Gentiles) belong together because they belong to God.

A. In God's Family (v. 19)

19. Now therefore ye are no more strangers and foreigners, but fellow citizens with the saints, and of the household of God.

Paul offers a before-and-after picture of what we were before Christ's coming and what we are now, thanks to Him. We were *strangers* (outsiders) and *foreigners* (a word that describes what we today would call "resident aliens"). But *now* we have been designated *fellow citizens*. We enjoy the full privileges of being citizens of the kingdom of Heaven and members of the *household* (family) *of God*. [See question #4, page 392.]

B. In God's Temple (vv. 20-22)

20. And are built upon the foundation of the apostles and prophets, Jesus Christ himself being the chief corner stone.

Paul now pictures Christians as building blocks in a great temple that God is constructing. He describes the *apostles and prophets* as the *foundation* of this building. This makes sense, since the apostles and prophets were instrumental in delivering the first inspired messages to the early church.

Then Paul designates *Jesus Christ himself* as the *chief corner stone*. Today cornerstones are largely symbolic. In the first century, however, the cornerstone was a vital part of the construction of a building. Great care was taken to be sure the cornerstone was perfectly square and level. It then stood as a standard of reference for all the measurements relating to the construction of the rest of the building.

21. In whom all the building fitly framed together groweth unto a holy temple in the Lord.

Paul then describes each Christian as what we might call a "brick" in God's *building*. He pictures this great building as in the process of constant growth. Anyone who becomes a Christian is added to the structure. Every part belongs; every part has its purpose. *Together* the parts constitute *a holy temple in the Lord*—His dwelling place (1 Corinthians 3:16). [See question #5, page 392.]

22. In whom ye also are builded together for a habitation of God through the Spirit.

Now Paul goes a step farther. Not only is this great building—this holy temple—being built by God, but He Himself dwells in it *through* the presence of His *Spirit*. Of course, Paul is not talking about a literal building. Just as God has created "one new man" including both Jews and Gentiles (v. 15), so He has constructed one new building—His church, composed of the people (both Jews and Gentiles) in whom He lives by His Spirit.

Conclusion

A. No More Barriers

When the same royal family ruled both Spain and France during the seventeenth century, someone declared, "There are no more Pyrenees." For centuries those mountains had divided the two nations, serving as both a military and a psychological barrier. When the two royal families united, it was seen as an opportunity for two nations that had been geographically and politically separated to be at least politically united. However, the mountains remained in place and so did the mistrust. The union did not last; the hopes went unfulfilled.

With Jesus the barriers that divide nations, groups, families, and individuals are meant to come down for good. When we see how much God dislikes walls of separation and the effort He put forth at the cross to tear them down, we should be motivated to do all we can to bring them down in the name of Jesus—and to refuse to allow any new walls to take their place.

B. Prayer

Thank You, gracious Father, for saving me, bringing me to Yourself, and including me in Your wonderful enterprise. I freely admit that I do not deserve such treatment. While I know I am unworthy of Your grace, I will treasure it and seek to live a life that honors You. Through Jesus, who paid the price and built the bridge between us. Amen.

C. Thought to Remember

What you were is not what you are, and what you are is not what you will be.

Learning by Doing

This page contains an alternate lesson plan emphasizing learning activities.
Classes desiring such student involvement will find these suggestions helpful.

Learning Goals

As a result of participating in this lesson, each student will be able to:

1. Tell how the grace that provides salvation also eliminates barriers that had previously separated those who are now saved.

2. Suggest some modern walls or barriers that need to be eliminated by the gospel.

3. Tell one specific way he or she can work for unity within the body.

Into the Lesson

Give every person a copy of a handout with the heading, *My Immediate Family!* Under the heading should appear these instructions: *Name each person in your immediate family. Then write something about each person named that makes him or her unique or different from other family members.* Ask the class members to take a few moments to complete the exercise and share their answers in groups of two or three persons.

Tell the class that today's Scripture identifies us as members of the "household of God." Just as members of your family are unique and different from each other, so are members of God's family. Yet, like your family, we are to enjoy a "oneness" in God's family. The questions that face us today include, "In what ways are we to be one?" And, "What can I do to promote unity in God's family?"

Into the Word

Ask the students to turn their handouts over and divide the back page into two columns. Ask them to write, "Images of the Church That Indicate Unity (Ephesians 2:19-22)" at the top of column 1. About halfway down the page they should write, "Foundations for Christian Unity (Ephesians 2:8-10)." At the very bottom of column 1 have them write, "Issues Concerning Unity in Ephesus (Ephesians 2:11-18)."

Tell the class, "Read Ephesians 2:19-22, looking for names or images that indicate unity in Christ's church. Write these under the first heading. (Answers may include *fellow citizens with the saints, the household of God, a building, a holy temple, a habitation of God.*) Prepare a visual (transparency or poster) identical to the handout and write comments on it as they are shared.

Next, have the class read verses 8-10 and look for clues to the basis for Christian unity. (Answers will focus on the means of our salvation.

Salvation is *by grace. . . through faith.* Salvation does not come *of yourselves.* Salvation is *not of works.* Instead, we are saved *unto [or "for"] good works.*) Tell the class that we will explore the wonderful truths and implications of this text later in the lesson.

Read verses 11-18. Using your lesson commentary, prepare and give a brief lecture about the issues raised in this passage. Include information about the identity and issues of the *Uncircumcision* and the *Circumcision.* While this text teaches that Gentiles are no longer separated from God, it also emphasizes the unity of Jews and Gentiles.

Into Life

Tell the class that the issue of unity in the local church is appropriate not only for the Ephesian Christians. It is important to our church as well. Ask class members to write "Implications for My Church" at the top of column 2 on the handout. Ask them, "As you read through the list of descriptions and names for the church in column 1, what principles for unity do you see implied for our church?" Again, write their comments on the large visual you have prepared.

Then ask the class to review their notes about the "Foundations for Christian Unity." Ask and discuss: "How can understanding the means of salvation help to break down the barriers or walls to unity in the church? How does understanding grace and salvation draw people together?"

Tell the class, "The issue of the relationship of Jews and Gentiles is not an issue in our church. However, there may be other walls or barriers to fellowship we may be experiencing." Ask the students to identify differences that may separate people in your congregation. The answers may focus on music, worship styles, leadership struggles, economic strata, ethnic issues, quarrels, etc.

Ask, "What have we learned today that will help to destroy these walls or barriers to fellowship in our church family?"

To make this lesson personal, ask the students to turn back to page 1 of the handout. At the bottom of the page ask them to write these words: "I am concerned about this barrier to complete fellowship and unity in our congregation," and "I will do this one thing to strengthen the fellowship in my church." Ask each student to write a response to each of those; then close with small groups praying for the concerns on their lists.

Let's Talk It Over

The questions on this page are designed to encourage review of the lesson Scriptures and to promote discussion of the lesson by the class. The answers provided are only discussion starters. Let your class talk it over from there.

1. Why do some of us have difficulty accepting the fact that salvation comes by God's grace and not by our works?

Many cannot tolerate the idea that they are not in control. Such an attitude results from pride. People who have an inflated concept of self and a distorted view of personal responsibility have difficulty conceiving of a context wherein, by their own ability and by their own drive and sense of duty, they cannot achieve success.

Submission and dependence are simply foreign to many. Only with gritted teeth and grumblings under their breath do these survive the hierarchical structure of everyday living. *Grace* and *gift* are not what these recipients want to receive. All they want is, "Congratulations! Job well done!"

2. When the Jews called Gentiles the "Uncircumcision," they were simply doing what others had done and others still do. What are the usual bases for such name-calling? Why is such a practice foolish?

Religious and ethnic differences often are the grounds for derogatory name-calling. Emphasizing differences rather than seeing what we have in common with others hardly ever accomplishes anything positive. In many times and places, such silliness has resulted in feuds and wars.

Such name-calling is sometimes a symptom of deep-seated animosity or jealousy. Christians must take care not to get caught up in such behavior. It is guaranteed never to break down walls, but only to build them.

3. Why is it that Christians sometimes act as if they do not believe that those who are "aliens" and "strangers from the covenants of promise" are without hope, when they are, in fact, "without God in the world"?

Many Christians have a hard time believing that a "good" God could let unsaved people perish in Hell. This is especially true when the unsaved seem to be decent people. But to believe otherwise is to believe that Jesus' death was unnecessary! To believe otherwise is to believe that the redemptive message of the Bible is not true. In fact, to believe otherwise is to believe that there are no "aliens" nor any "strangers"—but that everyone will eventually, somehow, be saved. Such theology is called universalism.

Another reason we might make such a mistake is that we improperly understand that salvation is by grace. We don't want to suggest we are "better" than non-Christians, so we cannot bring ourselves to believe that they are truly lost. When we appreciate that it is only by grace that we are saved, then we will know it is only by grace that others will be saved. Until they come to know Jesus, they cannot find that grace! (See John 14:6.)

4. What are the responsibilities of being a citizen of a nation? What are the responsibilities of being a citizen of "the household of God"?

Citizens have both loyalty and legal responsibilities to their nation. To pledge allegiance to the country's flag, to sing the nation's anthem, to honor the country's history and uniqueness—all are appropriate expressions of national loyalty. But legal submission is further evidence of that sense of pride and duty. To live in a country is to abide by that country's decisions on authority and rule, as conscience permits.

The citizen of God's kingdom has similar responsibilities. Declaration of that kingdom's worth should be as automatic as any secular pledges. And submission to the Lord of the kingdom should be a joyous expression of gratitude for what He has done for its citizens.

5. What are some of the human "building blocks" necessary to a church that is truly "a holy temple" in which God lives by His Spirit?

By God's design and power, He can make any stone fit. People with various talents—even undiscovered ones—He can shape and form by His Spirit. Mechanical aptitude can mend and repair and maintain. Artistic flair can decorate and inspire. Musical ear can praise and edify. Verbal skill can teach and persuade. Economic insight can support and manage. Compassionate heart can comfort and counsel. By God's design and plan, every ability can be a blessing to His church. But only by the willingness and commitment of those thus enabled can the church become the growing holy temple Paul envisions.

Every church has the right building materials, and every church has the right Builder. But the human "materials" should not choose to refuse the hand of the Builder any more than physical materials can refuse!

Called to Use Spiritual Gifts

DEVOTIONAL READING: Ephesians 3:14-21.

BACKGROUND SCRIPTURE: Ephesians 4:1-16.

PRINTED TEXT: Ephesians 4:1-16.

Ephesians 4:1-16

1 I therefore, the prisoner of the Lord, beseech you that ye walk worthy of the vocation wherewith ye are called,

2 With all lowliness and meekness, with long-suffering, forbearing one another in love;

3 Endeavoring to keep the unity of the Spirit in the bond of peace.

4 There is one body, and one Spirit, even as ye are called in one hope of your calling;

5 One Lord, one faith, one baptism,

6 One God and Father of all, who is above all, and through all, and in you all.

7 But unto every one of us is given grace according to the measure of the gift of Christ.

8 Wherefore he saith, When he ascended up on high, he led captivity captive, and gave gifts unto men.

9 (Now that he ascended, what is it but that he also descended first into the lower parts of the earth?

10 He that descended is the same also that ascended up far above all heavens, that he might fill all things.)

11 And he gave some, apostles; and some, prophets; and some, evangelists; and some, pastors and teachers;

12 For the perfecting of the saints, for the work of the ministry, for the edifying of the body of Christ:

13 Till we all come in the unity of the faith, and of the knowledge of the Son of God, unto a perfect man, unto the measure of the stature of the fulness of Christ:

14 That we henceforth be no more children, tossed to and fro, and carried about with every wind of doctrine, by the sleight of men, and cunning craftiness, whereby they lie in wait to deceive;

15 But speaking the truth in love, may grow up into him in all things, which is the head, even Christ:

16 From whom the whole body fitly joined together and compacted by that which every joint supplieth, according to the effectual working in the measure of every part, maketh increase of the body unto the edifying of itself in love.

GOLDEN TEXT: Unto every one of us is given grace according to the measure of the gift of Christ.—Ephesians 4:7.

New Life in Christ
Unit 2: Called by Christ
(Lessons 5-9)

Lesson Aims

This lesson should enable students to:

1. Summarize Paul's discussion of unity in terms of its source, expression, and result.

2. Tell how a variety of differing gifts can contribute to unity.

3. Identify a specific ministry gift that he or she has and suggest how the use of that gift can contribute to unity within the body.

Lesson Outline

INTRODUCTION
    A. Get Organized
    B. Lesson Background
  I. RECOGNIZING UNITY (Ephesians 4:1-6)
    A. Essential Attitudes (vv. 1-3)
        Unnecessary Gentleness
    B. Essential Principles (vv. 4-6)
 II. RESPECTING DIVERSITY (Ephesians 4:7-12)
    A. Source of Our Gifts (vv. 7-10)
    B. Variety of Our Gifts (v. 11)
    C. Purpose of Our Gifts (v. 12)
III. REACHING MATURITY (Ephesians 4:13-16)
    A. The Process (vv. 13, 14)
    B. The Product (vv. 15, 16)
        A Healthy Body
CONCLUSION
    A. You Are Important
    B. Prayer
    C. Thought to Remember

Introduction

A. Get Organized

In an old *Peanuts* comic strip, Lucy tries to get Linus to let her watch what she wants to see on television. Linus says, "Give me one good reason I should let you." Lucy responds, "I'll give you five." She then pulls each of her fingers one by one into a ball, makes a fist, and shakes it at Linus. In the last frame of the comic strip, Linus looks at his hand and says, "Why can't you guys get organized like that?"

Sometimes we feel like asking the church that same question. We wonder how much more powerful and effective the church could be if its members would work together and "get organized." In today's text, Paul challenges us to

"keep the unity of the Spirit in the bond of peace" for the sake of the cause of Christ.

B. Lesson Background

The first two lessons in this unit from Ephesians were taken from the doctrinal portion of the letter (chapters 1-3). Chapter 4 begins what might be considered the more practical portion of the letter, where Paul addresses concerns relevant to Christian living. (Most of Paul's letters could be outlined in this manner.)

At the same time, what Paul considers as chapter 4 begins is closely tied to the preceding material. (Note the word "therefore" in verse 1.) The doxology at the close of chapter 3 (vv. 20, 21) includes the phrase "unto him [God] be glory in the church by Christ Jesus." In chapter 4 Paul proceeds to address how the church can bring glory to God. His initial topic of concern is unity in Christ—a matter that the church must make a top priority.

I. Recognizing Unity
(Ephesians 4:1-6)

Christian unity is rarely, if ever, achieved by accident. Essential to its attainment is the cultivation of Christlike attitudes in those who claim to be His followers.

A. Essential Attitudes (vv. 1-3)

1. I therefore, the prisoner of the Lord, beseech you that ye walk worthy of the vocation wherewith ye are called.

Paul begins his discussion of unity with a sense of urgency. (Note the word *beseech*, which means to plead earnestly.) He desires his readers to *walk worthy*—to "practice what they preach," or "walk the talk." He wants that walk to reflect *the vocation wherewith ye are called*. In this case the word *vocation* does not refer to the way a person makes a living. It is a word more accurately translated as "calling." So literally Paul says, "Conduct yourselves in a manner worthy of the calling that you have accepted." All Christians are called to cultivate the attitudes that follow.

2. With all lowliness and meekness, with long-suffering, forbearing one another in love.

Here Paul begins to describe what it means to "walk worthy." His desire is that his readers be patient people: *long-suffering, forbearing one another in love.* Working together with others requires patience; and if we are going to have that kind of patience, then we must possess the related qualities of *lowliness and meekness.*

To many in the world, meekness is a sign of weakness. (Someone has suggested that if you think meekness is weakness, try being meek for a week!) True meekness is perhaps best defined as strength under control. Consider, for example, a horse brought under control for the purpose of plowing or riding. He has not lost any of his strength, but his strength has been channeled toward a useful and beneficial purpose.

Humility and meekness are absolutely necessary if Christians are to forbear (literally, "hold up") each other. People will inevitably disappoint us and will tax our patience at times. What we must never forget is how much we need people to be patient with us. [See question #1, page 400.]

UNNECESSARY GENTLENESS

One of Bud Blake's *Tiger* comic strips shows a group of children playing football. One little boy stands and watches as a girl carries the football right past him. When he is asked why he didn't tackle her, he replies, "I was afraid I would hurt her." Later, on his way home, he is complaining about what happened to him. He says, "I got thrown out for unnecessary gentleness." In certain sports a player is sometimes thrown out for unnecessary roughness, but never for unnecessary gentleness!

In the life and work of the church, we must learn to be gentle. We must follow Paul's admonition to walk "with all lowliness and meekness, with long-suffering, forbearing one another in love" (Ephesians 4:2). Roughness is always unnecessary in the church.

Love is to be the trademark that identifies followers of Jesus (John 13:35). Love demands courtesy and kindness. Love demands that we learn how to disagree without being disagreeable. Love desires to handle both the sinning believer (Galatians 6:1) and the one who requires further instruction (2 Timothy 2:24, 25) *gently*. If we exercise gentleness, we can keep the unity of the church intact. If we fail to be gentle—if we use "unnecessary roughness" with others—we risk dividing the body of Christ.

Even the soldiers who crucified Jesus would not divide the *robe* of Christ. Let us not be guilty of dividing the *body* of Christ.   —R. C. S.

3. Endeavoring to keep the unity of the Spirit in the bond of peace.

Notice that *unity* and *peace* are linked in this verse. In a sense, peace is the by-product of unity; peace, in turn, serves to keep unity alive and well. This unity is said to be *of the Spirit*. Elsewhere Paul tells us, "By one Spirit are we all baptized into one body, . . . and have been all made to drink into one Spirit" (1 Corinthians 12:13). The Spirit is also the source of the gifts (1 Corinthians 12:11) that are to be used to achieve "the unity of the faith" (Ephesians 4:13).

B. Essential Principles (vv. 4-6)

What follows is a seven-part statement of Christian unity. It seems more than coincidental that Paul lists seven items, since seven is a frequent symbol in the Scriptures for completeness.

4. There is one body, and one Spirit, even as ye are called in one hope of your calling.

The *one body*, of course, is the church. Today the various denominations that exist make it difficult for many to see the church as one body. This was not the case in Paul's day, and this is not the case in God's eyes. In spite of the divisions created by man, to Him there is still only one body.

The *one Spirit* is the Holy Spirit. Every Christian has the gift of the Holy Spirit (Acts 2:38; 5:32). Sadly, the purpose for which the Spirit has been given (to glorify Jesus, according to John 16:14) has been lost amid numerous questions and controversies concerning the Spirit's work.

The *one hope* to which we are *called* is no doubt the hope of eternal life. This hope is firmly grounded in the resurrection of Jesus, who declared, "Because I live, ye shall live also" (John 14:19). [See question #2, page 400.]

5. One Lord, one faith, one baptism.

It is obvious that the *one Lord* is Jesus Himself. What does Paul mean by *one faith*? It may refer to the fact that Christians are all "saved through faith" (Ephesians 2:8). However, it could also describe the substance of what we believe. A similar usage is found in the phrase "the faith which was once delivered unto the saints" (Jude 3).

Paul also mentions *one baptism*. Many might respond to Paul's claim by saying, "Wait a minute; there are many baptisms mentioned in the Bible: John the Baptist's baptism, baptism in the Holy Spirit, and water baptism." However, since Jesus included water baptism as part of what should be preached to all the world (Matthew 28:19, 20; Mark 16:16) and since Paul describes it as the act by which one is brought "into Christ" (Romans 6:3, 4; Galatians 3:27), it seems clear that the one baptism is water baptism.

This, however, does not end the discussion. A question might be raised concerning the mode of baptism—that is, how it is done. Some use sprinkling, others believe in pouring, and still others advocate immersion. Which is the *one baptism*? When we consider the meaning of the word *baptism* (the verb form means "to dip or plunge") and the evidence provided in the book of Acts (Acts 8:38, 39, for example, where Philip and the eunuch "went down both into the water" and "were come up out of the water"), it is clear that originally baptism was done by immersion.

6. One God and Father of all, who is above all, and through all, and in you all.

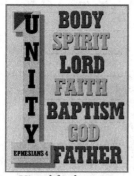

Visual for lesson 7

Today's visual is a graphic reminder that the church is called to oneness. Display it as you discuss verses 4-6 in the text.

Last in Paul's description of the basics of Christian unity (though first in prominence and authority) is *God* Himself. He is described as the *Father of all*, and His authority is affirmed in the phrase *who is above all, and through all, and in you all.*

Notice in these verses the mention of the three persons of the Godhead: one Spirit, one Lord (Jesus), and one God.

II. Respecting Diversity
(Ephesians 4:7-12)

A. Source of Our Gifts (vv. 7-10)

7. But unto every one of us is given grace according to the measure of the gift of Christ.

Paul now moves from stating the principles of unity to considering the expression of unity in church life. He reminds his readers that *every one* of them has been *given* some kind of spiritual *gift* that can be exercised in some ministry of the church. Paul describes each gift as *the gift of Christ*, but these are also gifts of the Holy Spirit, as noted in 1 Corinthians 12:7-11.

8. Wherefore he saith, When he ascended up on high, he led captivity captive, and gave gifts unto men.

Here Paul cites a passage from the Old Testament (Psalm 68:18). The text pictures a conquering hero rising up a mountain and then giving of the spoils of his victory as gifts to his people. Paul's main point is to affirm that the church has been given gifts by our Conqueror, Christ Jesus, who has *ascended* into Heaven. Each person has been given a gift, and all gifts are to be exercised for the good of the church.

What is meant by the phrase *he led captivity captive*, or "captives in his train" (*New International Version*)? Some believe that the captives are those who march in triumph behind the victorious Christ and are the recipients of His gifts. (A similar idea is expressed in 2 Corinthians 2:14.) More likely, however, the phrase here describes

Jesus' victory over His spiritual enemies. Colossians 2:15 supports this view by noting that at the cross Jesus, "having spoiled principalities and powers, made a show of them openly, triumphing over them in it." Judges 5:12 speaks of Barak leading "captivity captive" and then refers in the next verse to his having "dominion over the nobles among the people." Thus the idea of conquest over one's enemies seems to be what the phrase implies.

Of special note in considering Paul's quotation from Psalm 68:18 is that it varies from the text found there, which reads, "Thou hast *received* [not *given*] gifts for men." Perhaps Paul recognized that the gifts Christ gives to His church have been given to Him by God; however, in this verse he chooses to emphasize what Christ has given, since he has alluded to the "gift of Christ" in verse 7.

However we understand what Paul is saying, we can trust that, under the inspiration of the Holy Spirit, he is providing the correct understanding and application of the verse from Psalms.

9. (Now that he ascended, what is it but that he also descended first into the lower parts of the earth?

Since the passage Paul cited spoke of Christ's having *ascended*, then He must *also* have *descended*. To where did Christ descend? Paul says he *descended first into the lower parts of the earth*, but that phrase is also confusing. What does Paul mean?

Some believe that it refers to the earth itself and is speaking of what happened in the incarnation: Jesus left the glories of Heaven, "was made flesh, and dwelt among us" (John 1:14), and then later ascended back to Heaven. Others claim that *the lower parts of the earth* refers to the grave or to Hades, the abode of the dead. Those who hold this view often cite 1 Peter 3:18-20 for support.

10. He that descended is the same also that ascended up far above all heavens, that he might fill all things.)

When He had accomplished His Father's task ("when he had by himself purged our sins," Hebrews 1:3), Jesus *ascended up far above all heavens* to "the right hand of the throne of God" (Hebrews 12:2). He is in this position of authority and prominence *that he might fill all things*—perhaps a reference to His giving of the Spirit (Acts 2:33) and the gifts that accompany the Spirit's presence. Paul now proceeds to describe some of these gifts and their purpose.

B. Variety of Our Gifts (v. 11)

11. And he gave some, apostles; and some, prophets; and some, evangelists; and some, pastors and teachers.

This verse describes some of the people whom God has gifted in order to help the church fulfill its mission. It is not surprising that this list begins with the office of the *apostles.* They were the men commissioned by Jesus to lead in the proclamation of the gospel and the establishment of the church.

Next, Paul mentions the *prophets.* Prophets were inspired by God to utter special proclamations of divine truth. A good example is Agabus, mentioned in Acts 11:28 and 21:10-12. Both apostles and prophets make up what Paul calls the "foundation" of the church (Ephesians 2:20).

Following the prophets is the office of *evangelists.* This word comes from a Greek verb meaning "to bring good news." An evangelist proclaims the good news found in the gospel. It would seem that the main focus of the evangelist's work is to reach lost people with the gospel. (Perhaps evangelists could be considered the equivalent of today's church planters.)

Only one person in the Bible is given the title of *evangelist,* and that is Philip (Acts 21:8). Timothy is told to do the work of an evangelist (2 Timothy 4:5), so many conclude that the title properly belongs to him as well. Their conclusion is probably correct.

Paul also mentions *pastors and teachers.* Frequently in modern usage, the word *pastor* is used to refer to the preaching minister of a congregation. While the preaching minister may perform a variety of pastoral duties, such duties are usually associated in the New Testament with the office of elder (also called "overseer" or "bishop"). The word for *pastor* literally means "shepherd," and it is the elders who are exhorted to "feed the flock of God" (Acts 20:17, 28; 1 Peter 5:1, 2).

In the Greek text each of these offices has a definite article except *teachers.* Most students believe this indicates that the last two terms describe one office ("pastor-teachers" or "teaching elders"), not two. This office may well describe the "elders . . . who labor in the word and doctrine" (1 Timothy 5:17).

All of the leadership gifts mentioned in this verse are given for a special purpose, which Paul goes on to explain.

C. Purpose of Our Gifts (v. 12)

12. For the perfecting of the saints, for the work of the ministry, for the edifying of the body of Christ.

What are these gifted leaders supposed to accomplish? They are to work toward *the perfecting of the saints.* The Greek word translated *perfecting* was used in New Testament times to describe the setting of a broken bone. It is used in the New Testament itself to describe the mending of

nets (Matthew 4:21). The expression here conveys the idea of "preparing" or "equipping" the saints.

At first glance it may appear that this verse is outlining three tasks that those mentioned in verse 11 are to accomplish. However, the Greek text indicates that just one task is being assigned to the leaders of the church: to prepare the saints so that *they* can carry out their ministries and thus bless the church.

It should be noted that the term *ministry* does not refer to the work done by those in the position we often call "minister." Here it simply means "service." Christian leaders are to help those in the church to serve effectively. This, of course, does not mean that the church will ever outgrow the need for a vocational ministry. There is far too much work to do in the church for anyone in that position to work himself out of a job. It is true, however, that all Christians are in a sense ministers. And as all exercise their gifts and fulfill their ministries, they will participate in the *edifying* (building up) *of the body of Christ.* [See question #3, page 400.]

III. Reaching Maturity (Ephesians 4:13-16)

A. The Process (vv. 13, 14)

13. Till we all come in the unity of the faith, and of the knowledge of the Son of God, unto a perfect man, unto the measure of the stature of the fulness of Christ.

The church achieves *unity* in Christ and maturity (becoming *perfect*) when each Christian is willing to use his or her gift or gifts to help others grow toward *the measure of the stature of the fulness of Christ.* To be like Jesus—this is the true measure of our progress.

14. That we henceforth be no more children, tossed to and fro, and carried about with every wind of doctrine, by the sleight of men, and cunning craftiness, whereby they lie in wait to deceive.

To be childlike in humility is commended by Jesus (Matthew 18:1-4), but here the immaturity of *children* is something to be avoided. Paul wants Christians to be knowledgeable enough

---

How to Say It

AGABUS. *Ag*-uh-bus.
BARAK. *Bair*-uk.
EPHESIANS. Ee-*fee*-zhunz.
EUNUCH. *you*-nick.
HADES. *Hay*-deez.

not to be unstable. The word Paul uses for *tossed to and fro* describes a dizzying kind of spinning motion.

Christians should beware of both questionable doctrines and the men who use *sleight* (deception) and *cunning craftiness* to *deceive* others. The mature must not be taken in by spiritual con artists and their clever words. They should know the Word well enough to be able to recognize the "counterfeit" message of the dishonest teacher or preacher. [See question #4, page 400.]

B. The Product (vv. 15, 16)

15. But speaking the truth in love, may grow up into him in all things, which is the head, even Christ.

Truth without *love* can come across as harsh and vindictive. Love without truth can come across as sloppy and undisciplined sentimentality. The combination of both is necessary in order to enhance the process of growth toward the likeness of *Christ*. [See question #5, page 400.]

16. From whom the whole body fitly joined together and compacted by that which every joint supplieth, according to the effectual working in the measure of every part, maketh increase of the body unto the edifying of itself in love.

Paul uses various medical terms in this verse to describe a *body* that is healthy and fully functioning. *Every part* is important to the whole. *Love* enables the parts to work together for the *edifying* of all.

Of course, it is *from* Christ the head (v. 15) that the health of the body comes. When all parts of the body respect His headship, the body will demonstrate the unity that will lead others to believe in Jesus (John 17:21).

Home Daily Bible Readings

Monday, July 10—Gentiles Are Fellow Heirs in Christ (Ephesians 3:1-6)
Tuesday, July 11—Gentiles Receive the Gospel's Riches (Ephesians 3:7-13)
Wednesday, July 12—Paul Prays for the Ephesian Christians (Ephesians 3:14-21)
Thursday, July 13—Unity in the Body of Christ (Ephesians 4:1-10)
Friday, July 14—Grow to Maturity in Christ Jesus (Ephesians 4:11-16)
Saturday, July 15—Live in Righteousness and Holiness (Ephesians 4:17-24)
Sunday, July 16—Live a New Life in Christ (Ephesians 4:25-32)

A HEALTHY BODY

David Feldman has written a book with an interesting title: *"How Does Aspirin Find a Headache?"* Perhaps we've wondered just how medicine is able to "find" the area that it is supposed to help. Or we've gone to the doctor for treatment on one part of the body, and are surprised when he or she starts examining some other part.

These peculiarities remind us that the body is a unit, and that each part is connected to the whole. While modern medicine has become very specialized, many physicians are seeing the value of what is called holistic medicine—looking at the individual as a whole person and considering more than just one's physical problems. Some now acknowledge the need to give spiritual matters a higher priority than they once did.

This interconnectedness is the reason that the body is one of the most frequently used metaphors for the church. Each part of the church is meant to function for the spiritual health of the entire church. No part functions alone or lives in isolation from the rest.

What part of the body should you be? God has already decided that through the gifts He has given you. You need only to identify those gifts and determine that you will use them as effectively as possible—not for your own benefit, but for the good of the body.   —R. C. S.

Conclusion

A. You Are Important

Every tool in the toolbox is important. Each one has a unique role to play. A toolbox made up of all hammers or all saws is useless to the handyman. However, when it is stocked with various types of tools, it can serve the handyman well and keep him prepared for any situation he might face. No tool is unnecessary, and none is more important than another.

The same is true in the church. We should not look down on our own gift(s) or disparage the gift(s) of a brother or sister. We must all lovingly offer our gifts to be used for the common goal of building the body of Christ.

B. Prayer

Father, help me to discern the gifts You have given me. Grant me the courage to use those gifts. Help me to do my part to make my church the dynamic body of Christ that it needs to be. Through Your Son, the greatest gift of all. Amen.

C. Thought to Remember

God has given you many gifts. Your gift to Him is to use the gifts He has given you.

Learning by Doing

This page contains an alternate lesson plan emphasizing learning activities.
Classes desiring such student involvement will find these suggestions helpful.

Learning Goals

After this lesson each student will be able to:

1. Summarize Paul's discussion of unity in terms of its source, expression, and result.

2. Tell how a variety of differing gifts can contribute to unity.

3. Identify a specific ministry gift that he or she has and suggest how the use of that gift can contribute to unity within the body.

Into the Lesson

Ask class members to name their favorite books (other than the Bible). Ask them to categorize the books (historical, fiction, romance fiction, western, biography, philosophy, or some other). As they name the books and kinds of books, write on a large poster the categories named.

After the exercise, point out the diverse reading interests of the class. Then ask, "How is the church like a library of books?" *(There is a variety of interests and skills; each person is different and makes a unique contribution. Yet we are bound together into one body.)* Today, the apostle Paul will help us understand how important each of us is to the church and how the unity of believers blesses the church and each member of it.

Into the Word

As you read Ephesians 4:1-16, ask students to watch for clues to the problems Paul was concerned about at Ephesus *(unity & maturity)*. After reading the text and discovering the problems, tell the class that Paul has several tips for living together in God's family. Write these tips on a poster as you complete the following activities.

Tip #1: Qualities of a Good Family Member (vv. 2, 3). Assign each of the terms *lowliness, meekness, long-suffering, forbearing, love, unity,* and *peace* to a different person or group. Have each one define the assigned term and tell how it contributes to a healthy church.

Tip #2: Things That Bind Us Together (vv. 4-6). Ask the class to name the seven "Ones" as you write them on a visual. Ask, "In which of these areas is Christendom united? Where are the differences? What is the impact of division on the effectiveness of Christianity around the world?" Use the commentary section for help.

Tip #3: Remember That Our Various Gifts Come From God (vv. 7-10). Prepare a brief lecture on, or explanation of, these verses.

Tip #4: Appreciate the Diversity of Gifts (v. 11). Draw a sketch of books on a shelf. Ask the class to name and explain these gifts as you write their names on the spines of the books. (Explain this is not a complete list. Other teachings about gifts can be found in other New Testament passages.)

Tip #5: Reach for the Goals (vv. 12-16). Ask the class members to scan verses 12-16 and list the various goals for the church *(edification, unity, knowledge of the Son of God, maturity, doctrinal stability, etc.).* Write the class's answers on your visual poster. Then comment on Paul's imagery of a healthy body in verse 16. Point out Paul's emphasis on "each part does its work" *(New International Version).*

On the chalkboard write, "Unity in Christ's Church." Under this heading list *Source, Expression, Results.* Ask and discuss the following:

"What is the source of Christian unity?"

"How is unity expressed in the church?"

"What are the results of unity in the church?"

Into Life

Tell the class that God teaches in 1 Peter 4:10 and 11 that each Christian has a gift to contribute to the church. Discuss, "How do we discover our gifts?" Then give each student a handout with the following questions listed under the heading "How to Unwrap Your Gifts."

1. What do you WANT or LIKE to do?

2. What are you willing to TRY?

3. What spiritual abilities do OTHERS SEE in you and what are you ASKED to do?

4. What are you NEVER asked to do?

5. What kind of service can you render BEST to Christ's body?

Discuss how these questions can help, giving brief illustrations.

Tell the class that we have a "library" of gifted people in our class—and we are a part of the church. Ask groups of about four people to take a few moments to work together and list what they see are "gifts" each person in the group brings to the church. After the group discussion, ask groups to shout out some of the gifts that were in their groups.

Tell the class, "This brief exercise answered questions 3 and 4 on the handout. Now focus on question 5 and pray a silent prayer committing yourself to use your gift(s) for God to bless and strengthen His church."

Let's Talk It Over

The questions on this page are designed to encourage review of the lesson Scriptures and to promote discussion of the lesson by the class. The answers provided are only discussion starters. Let your class talk it over from there.

1. As Paul discusses unity, he begins with individual godly behavior as the basis for that unity. How does the absence of the qualities cited in verses 1 and 2 create disunity?

Sooner or later, hypocrisy always divides. It divides husbands from wives (and vice versa); it tears fathers from families. And it will divide a professed Christian from his church. That's the reason Paul's first challenge is, "Be what you claim to be!"

Losing control divides people. Arguments of anger or unreasonableness cause serious fractures. No one wants to be around a "hothead." So Paul advises, "Stay in control!"

Pride sets up barriers of superiority; it relegates some members of a group to be "the inferiors," and that becomes the first of endless divisions over differences. Paul insists, "Stay low . . . in spirit!"

Impatience throttles the spirit of unity. The short-tempered, unbearable demeanor of the ungodly doesn't leave an opportunity for unity. So Paul calls for longsuffering and forbearance in Christ's servants. "Be willing to wait and to forgive!" the Spirit dares us.

Unity depends on people who want it—people who are willing to take personal responsibility for it and to keep self secondary to the "whole."

2. Paul says that we who are called in Christ have one hope—the hope of eternal life. What value does that hope have in focusing, simplifying, and easing our lives?

Minor irritations of everyday interactions become petty when compared with eternal joy and grace. Irritating people will be left behind. Irritating aches and pains will disappear. Irritating rules, regulations, and restrictions will be replaced with freedom.

Because of that future hope, present concerns fade into irrelevance. Frightening fears are foolish when "the Lord is my shepherd." Economic pressures lose their power when one considers his riches stored up in Heaven. Fatal afflictions are but a doorway to God's presence; I have hope, hope of living forever with Him!

3. People gifted by God have God's purpose to accomplish. In what ways do we see that "gift-and-purpose" strategy at work in our church?

We see God's plan in every member who is using his or her gifts to honor the name of Christ. Those who share their homes with friends and strangers are demonstrating the gift of hospitality. Those who share their incomes in extraordinary ways for God's work are showing the gift of generosity. Those who study and lead others in the Scriptures are modeling the gift of teaching. All those and more are evidence of God's "gift-and-purpose" strategy—if the kingdom of Christ is being honored and nurtured. Use this discussion time to recognize those who use their gifts in selfless and largely unnoticed ways.

4. How are some Christians being tossed to and fro by every wind of doctrine in our culture?

In our media-saturated lifestyle, false doctrine is everywhere: at the door in our mailboxes, on the television screen of "religious" broadcasters, on-line on computer networks for private seduction, in the voices of well-meaning but mistaken family and friends and job acquaintants, and at the mall in beautifully decorated bookstores. False doctrine is much more available than is true doctrine. All too often true doctrine whispers in the corners of our lives (such as Sunday mornings between 10:00 and 12:00), while false ideas trumpet themselves in the marketplace. Every Christian needs the anchor of pure doctrine, or else he will be tossed and blown.

5. The phrase "speaking the truth in love" implies it is possible to speak the truth without love. How can truth be loveless? Can love be truthless? Why or why not?

Truth can be hard and cruel. The old expression, "Truth hurts," can obviously be true. Truth about sin can have the impact of a blow to the diaphragm; it can leave one breathless and reeling. If truth about sin is told with a vengeance, with vindictiveness as its motive, it is loveless. Rather than wanting what is right and good, that truthteller is wanting to cause harm. Loving truth places the pillow of compassion and the seat of mercy behind the one being confronted. Loving truth has the hand of encouragement and support ready in place.

Love must never be truthless. A lie is from the devil, while both love and truth are from God. They should be inseparable forever.

Called to Responsible Living

DEVOTIONAL READING: Ephesians 5:6-21.

BACKGROUND SCRIPTURE: Ephesians 5:1–6:9.

PRINTED TEXT: Ephesians 5:1-5, 18-29; 6:1-4.

Ephesians 5:1-5, 18-29

1 Be ye therefore followers of God, as dear children;

2 And walk in love, as Christ also hath loved us, and hath given himself for us an offering and a sacrifice to God for a sweet-smelling savor.

3 But fornication, and all uncleanness, or covetousness, let it not be once named among you, as becometh saints;

4 Neither filthiness, nor foolish talking, nor jesting, which are not convenient: but rather giving of thanks.

5 For this ye know, that no whoremonger, nor unclean person, nor covetous man, who is an idolater, hath any inheritance in the kingdom of Christ and of God.

. . . .

18 And be not drunk with wine, wherein is excess; but be filled with the Spirit;

19 Speaking to yourselves in psalms and hymns and spiritual songs, singing and making melody in your heart to the Lord;

20 Giving thanks always for all things unto God and the Father in the name of our Lord Jesus Christ;

21 Submitting yourselves one to another in the fear of God.

22 Wives, submit yourselves unto your own husbands, as unto the Lord.

23 For the husband is the head of the wife, even as Christ is the head of the church: and he is the saviour of the body.

24 Therefore as the church is subject unto Christ, so let the wives be to their own husbands in every thing.

25 Husbands, love your wives, even as Christ also loved the church, and gave himself for it;

26 That he might sanctify and cleanse it with the washing of water by the word,

27 That he might present it to himself a glorious church, not having spot, or wrinkle, or any such thing; but that it should be holy and without blemish.

28 So ought men to love their wives as their own bodies. He that loveth his wife loveth himself.

29 For no man ever yet hated his own flesh; but nourisheth and cherisheth it, even as the Lord the church.

Ephesians 6:1-4

1 Children, obey your parents in the Lord: for this is right.

2 Honor thy father and mother; which is the first commandment with promise;

3 That it may be well with thee, and thou mayest live long on the earth.

4 And, ye fathers, provoke not your children to wrath: but bring them up in the nurture and admonition of the Lord.

GOLDEN TEXT: Submitting yourselves one to another in the fear of God.—Ephesians 5:21.

Lesson Aims

As a result of completing this lesson, each student will be able to:

1. Relate Paul's description of proper Christian conduct in the community, the church, and the home.

2. Contrast Christ's call to responsible living with the thinking that governs much of modern society.

3. Pinpoint an area of personal, home, or church life where a more responsible commitment to Christ is needed, and devise a plan to address that need.

Lesson Outline

INTRODUCTION
    A. Wash Up
    B. Lesson Background
  I. RESPONSIBLE IN THE WORLD (Ephesians 5:1-5)
    A. Imitate the Father (v. 1)
    B. Walk in Love (v. 2)
    C. Avoid Immorality (v. 3)
    D. Avoid Impure Speech (v. 4)
    E. Remember This (v. 5)
 II. RESPONSIBLE IN THE CHURCH (Ephesians 5:18-21)
    A. Our Inner Power (v. 18)
    B. Our Corporate Worship (vv. 19, 20)
    C. A Vital Principle (v. 21)
III. RESPONSIBLE IN THE HOME (Ephesians 5:22-29; 6:1-4)
    A. Words for Wives (vv. 22-24)
    B. Words for Husbands (vv. 25-29)
    His Most Important Titles
    C. Words for Children (6:1-4)
CONCLUSION
    A. No Private Christians
    B. Prayer
    C. Thought to Remember

Introduction

A. Wash Up

A little boy was having trouble with his pronunciation. On one occasion he meant to say, "We go to church to worship." Instead it came out, "We go to church to wash up." Paul, however, may well have agreed with this young man.

We go to church both to worship God and to learn how to "wash up" our lives so that they become pleasing to God. Sunday worship and daily living are tightly bound together. Some like to try to separate these, but the Bible will not let us get away with that. Sincere Christians want to do right between Sundays as well as on them.

Worship is not for those who are perfect. No one should stay away from church because he has sinned. Going to church is probably just what such a person needs to give him what he needs to "wash up" (stop sinning) and to live in a manner pleasing to God.

B. Lesson Background

Last week's lesson brought us to the portion of Ephesians where Paul considers issues that involve practical Christian living. Beginning with 4:17, he calls followers of Jesus to "put off" the way of living associated with their pre-Christian lifestyles (v. 22) and to "put on the new man, which after God is created in righteousness and true holiness" (v. 24). Paul then gives a series of exhortations concerning a Christian's conduct (vv. 25-32).

The text for our lesson today, taken from portions of chapters 5 and 6, continues these exhortations, with a special emphasis on responsible conduct in the world, the church, and the home. In each of these areas of life, we have a duty to live by the highest standards of behavior—the standards of Christ Himself.

Despite the two thousand years that separate us from Paul's time, the need for his words is just as great today as it was then. His words speak to a society that is becoming increasingly uncivil and immoral. They speak to a society in which churches battle each other rather than the real enemy. They speak to a society that seems helpless as marriages continue to collapse at an alarming rate.

I. Responsible in the World (Ephesians 5:1-5)

A. Imitate the Father (v. 1)

1. Be ye therefore followers of God, as dear children.

Young people will always choose someone to imitate. Frequently their primary model is their parents. Since we are *children* of God, we should want to be like our Father.

The Greek word that is translated *followers* means imitators. It comes from a word that gives us our English term *mimic*. Parents consider it a great compliment when their children want to be like them. Surely it pleases our Father when we want to be like Him. [See question #1, page 408.]

B. Walk in Love (v. 2)

2. And walk in love, as Christ also hath loved us, and hath given himself for us an offering and a sacrifice to God for a sweetsmelling savor.

If we are true imitators of God, one of our first priorities will be to *walk in love.* Paul defines the standard of this love: *as Christ also hath loved us.* Our Father's love for us is illustrated by His willingness to give His Son to die for us.

The impact of Jesus' death is described using terminology taken from the Old Testament sacrificial system. The word *offering* is the term normally used for a grain, or cereal, offering. The word *sacrifice* normally indicates an offering during which an animal was slain. Both kinds of offerings would have been quite familiar to people who were acquainted with Judaism.

The presence of a *sweetsmelling savor* was frequently associated with Old Testament offerings (Exodus 29:18; Leviticus 1:9, 13, 17; 2:2). The usage of the term here indicates that God accepted Jesus' sacrifice as an atonement for the sins of the world. Paul used similar language in expressing his appreciation for a gift from the Philippians (Philippians 4:18).

C. Avoid Immorality (v. 3)

3. But fornication, and all uncleanness, or covetousness, let it not be once named among you, as becometh saints.

As Paul continues his description of behavior that is consistent with Christian commitment, he issues a warning against immorality. This was an area where those who had come to Christ out of paganism (and out of the sexual perversion associated with it) needed special guidance.

The word *fornication* translates the Greek word *porneia,* which is the source of our English word "pornography." Porneia is a general term for sexual misconduct. The word *uncleanness* is a literal translation of the Greek term and can describe any kind of immoral behavior.

We often interpret *covetousness* to mean an inordinate desire for money or possessions. The same Greek word is translated "greediness" in Ephesians 4:19, where it is again linked with "uncleanness." Carelessness in these matters is totally incompatible with the holy lifestyle that is to characterize followers of Jesus. Paul's counsel concerning each of the sins he lists is firm: *let it not be once named among you.* [See question #2, page 408.]

D. Avoid Impure Speech (v. 4)

4. Neither filthiness, nor foolish talking, nor jesting, which are not convenient: but rather giving of thanks.

Paul proceeds from the subject of immoral conduct to one's personal speech. In so doing he uses three terms that are used nowhere else in the New Testament. *Filthiness* describes any kind of shameful or obscene speech. *Foolish talking* is literally "the speech of morons." These two terms are combined with *jesting,* which could well include the double entendre and other kinds of "off-color" humor that are so prevalent in our world.

All of these forms of speech are said to be *not convenient,* meaning "inappropriate" or "unbecoming." Sadly, however, much of this kind of talk is common in our churches today. Instead of such improper speech, Paul admonishes Christians to let the trademark of their talk be the *giving of thanks.*

E. Remember This (v. 5)

5. For this ye know, that no whoremonger, nor unclean person, nor covetous man, who is an idolater, hath any inheritance in the kingdom of Christ and of God.

The persons described here are essentially those who have committed the sins mentioned in verse 3. The word *whoremonger* translates another form of the word *porneia* ("fornication"). The *covetous man* is further described as an *idolater* (Paul also links these two sins in Colossians 3:5). The connection is not hard to grasp: one who covets anything is in grave danger of allowing that item to have a more important place in his life than God does. The item, in effect, becomes that individual's idol.

One dare not treat the sins Paul has listed here as trivial, for too much is at stake. The person whose life is controlled by one of these evils has no *inheritance in the kingdom of Christ and of God.* The follower of Christ must be determined not to compromise in any way His standards of speech and behavior.

II. Responsible in the Church (Ephesians 5:18-21)

A. Our Inner Power (v. 18)

18. And be not drunk with wine, wherein is excess; but be filled with the Spirit.

This prohibition against drunkenness shows that alcohol abuse was a problem in the first century. Drunkenness not only harms the body of the person who consumes the *wine,* but it often causes behavior that harms others. Here its ill effects are described with the word *excess.* The Greek term behind this word implies waste. The staggering number of lives ruined and wasted by alcohol abuse is one of the saddest statistics of our time.

Today's visual is a delightful illustration of a child's fondness for imitating his or her parents. Discuss: "Are we as fond of imitating God?"

Visual for lesson 8

Instead of merely telling people not to drink, Paul provides a positive alternative: *be filled with the Spirit*. The Holy Spirit can bring about far better and more productive results than the artificial and temporary "high" of alcoholic "spirits." It should be noted that the verb form in the phrase *filled with the Spirit* does not indicate a one-time filling, but a constant condition ("go on being filled"). This was not something that Paul's readers had never experienced before. It was something they were already experiencing, in which Paul wanted them to continue. [See question #3, page 408.]

B. Our Corporate Worship (vv. 19, 20)

19. Speaking to yourselves in psalms and hymns and spiritual songs, singing and making melody in your heart to the Lord.

A church made up of people filled with the Spirit expresses itself in meaningful corporate worship. Christians are to speak to one another *in psalms and hymns and spiritual songs*. *Psalms* almost certainly refers to the book of Psalms in the Old Testament. No doubt the early church integrated certain Psalms into their times of worship. Some believe that the word *hymns* describes Christian compositions, examples of which may be recorded in some of Paul's letters. (See Philippians 2:6-8 and 1 Timothy 3:16.) The term *spiritual songs* may describe songs that were sung spontaneously in the worship assemblies. Whatever these words mean specifically, they indicate that there was a variety of music used in first-century worship.

Paul then mentions *singing and making melody in your heart to the Lord*. The phrase *making melody* translates a word that describes playing a stringed instrument; thus some see in the two terms used here a reference to both vocal and instrumental music. Others think that form is not at issue since this music is to be performed in the *heart*. They believe the point is one of personal sincerity and purpose in worship.

20. Giving thanks always for all things unto God and the Father in the name of our Lord Jesus Christ.

The personality of a local congregation should always be marked by an attitude of gratitude. Most definitely our thanksgiving should never be limited to one "official" Thanksgiving Day each year! [See question #4, page 408.]

C. A Vital Principle (v. 21)

21. Submitting yourselves one to another in the fear of God.

Paul now moves from the subject of worship to interpersonal relationships. The idea of *submitting* has received much attention, mostly because of its use in verse 22. At this point notice that, in the church, everyone is to submit *one to another*. Such mutual submission is based on our common *fear of God*—that is, our respect for His authority.

III. Responsible in the Home (Ephesians 5:22-29; 6:1-4)

A. Words for Wives (vv. 22-24)

22. Wives, submit yourselves unto your own husbands, as unto the Lord.

Here Paul applies the principle of submission, introduced in verse 21, to *wives*. Thus this is one expression of the submission enjoined upon all Christians. When Paul admonishes wives to *submit yourselves unto your own husbands, as unto the Lord,* he does not mean that a wife should treat her husband as if he were Jesus. Paul is saying that a wife's submission to her husband is a service that she does unto the Lord, or for the Lord's glory. A similar phrase is used in encouraging servants to obey their masters "as to the Lord" (Ephesians 6:5-7). Paul is simply applying an important spiritual principle (submission) to the God-ordained institution of marriage.

23. For the husband is the head of the wife, even as Christ is the head of the church: and he is the saviour of the body.

The authority given to the *husband* is certainly not absolute. That he is *the head of the wife* does not give him license to coerce his wife into submission. The standard against which his headship must be measured is clear: *even as Christ is the head of the church*. This indicates that marriage is truly "holy matrimony." It is meant to give both husband and wife a deeper appreciation of their relationship to Christ.

Notice the close ties between home and church: the order in the home is to reflect how Christ and the church are related. Whether a man really knows Christ and follows His example will be evident from the state of his household. Thus one qualification of the would-be elder is that he "ruleth well his own house" (1 Timothy 3:4). The next verse then asks, "For if a man know not how to rule his own house, how shall he take care of the church of God?"

24. Therefore as the church is subject unto Christ, so let the wives be to their own husbands in every thing.

Paul's teaching that *wives* must be *subject . . . to their own husbands in every thing* is not meant to demean women. (It is important to remember that Christianity brought to women a sense of dignity that the pagan world of the first century had not provided.) His teaching establishes a sense of order in the home. It does not mean that men are smarter or more valuable than women. In any football team, the quarterback may not be the smartest player; however, order in the huddle requires someone to take the role of leader. In an army the general may not be more intelligent than the private, yet the necessity of discipline and order in a military unit requires that someone be in charge. Paul is establishing a similar arrangement of authority in the Christian home, modeled on the arrangement that every Christian understands: the submission of the church to Jesus.

B. Words for Husbands (vv. 25-29)

25. Husbands, love your wives, even as Christ also loved the church, and gave himself for it.

Having established the principle of submission on the part of wives, Paul now proceeds to instruct *husbands* on how to treat their *wives.* While *submit* is the primary command to wives, *love* is to be the priority for husbands. Paul's command is followed with an extraordinary standard for husbands to follow. Husbands are to love their wives *even as Christ also loved the church.* How did He love the church? He *gave himself for it.* That is the kind of sacrificial love with which husbands are to treat their wives.

26. That he might sanctify and cleanse it with the washing of water by the word.

Paul then comments briefly on the degree with which Jesus loves the church and desires what is best for it. He says that Jesus gave Himself in order to *sanctify* (set apart or make holy) and *cleanse* His church *with the washing of water by the word.* Most likely this cleansing with water is a reference to Christian baptism (cf. Acts 22:16). *The word* is the word of God (the gospel), which Peter describes as the "incorruptible" seed that produces the new birth (1 Peter 1:23-25).

27. That he might present it to himself a glorious church, not having spot, or wrinkle, or any such thing; but that it should be holy and without blemish.

Jesus also wants His *church* (His bride) to be *a glorious church, not having spot, or wrinkle, or any such thing.* As the loving husband, Jesus took it upon Himself to do what was necessary to make His bride beautiful. He took care of all the spots, wrinkles, and blemishes caused by sin through His sacrifice on the cross.

28, 29. So ought men to love their wives as their own bodies. He that loveth his wife loveth himself. For no man ever yet hated his own flesh; but nourisheth and cherisheth it, even as the Lord the church.

Paul applies Christ's love for the *church* to the *love* of *men* for their *wives.* He says that husbands *ought to love their wives as* they do *their own bodies.*

Many men have bought into the self-centered spirit of our time and have abandoned their responsibilities at home. Believing that these duties stood in the way of their personal happiness, they have selfishly pursued interests outside the home and family. Here Paul declares that a man's love of self and of his wife are interconnected: *he that loveth his wife loveth himself.* For the husband to love his wife *as the Lord the church* is in his own best interests and brings him the greatest sense of fulfillment as a man.

Some may ask whether (or to what degree) Paul's teaching is applicable in situations where the husband or the wife is not a Christian. Guidance for proper conduct in these situations is provided in such Scriptures as 1 Corinthians 7:12-16 and 1 Peter 3:1-6. Certainly Paul's teaching should encourage us to take seriously his words about being "unequally yoked together with unbelievers" (2 Corinthians 6:14-18). Our youth need to receive special instruction in these matters to avoid substantial heartache in the future.

HIS MOST IMPORTANT TITLES

The man had already enjoyed an outstanding career of public service when he was elected a United States Congressman. After serving there, he was made head of the Central Intelligence Agency. When the United States reopened diplomatic relations with China, he was appointed Chief Liaison Officer in China. Then he was made chairman of the Republican National Committee. After that he was elected vice president of the United States. And last, but certainly not

---

How to Say It

EPHESIANS. Ee-*fee*-zhunz.
EPHESUS. *Ef*-uh-sus.
PORNEIA. por-*nye*-uh or por-*nay*-uh.

least, he was elected President of the United States. When his distinguished public life had ended, George Bush claimed that he still held his three most important titles: husband, father, and grandfather!

What an example this is for us all! It is noble to carry the title of husband. No one should ever take it lightly. It is equally noble to have the title of wife. To be a father or a mother is one of the greatest privileges one can ever enjoy. And every grandparent knows that to be a grandfather or a grandmother is such a wonderful blessing that it fully deserves the description of *grand*.

In an age and in a society that takes such wonders as these so very lightly, it is refreshing to hear a former President of the United States express his personal satisfaction in the titles of husband, father, and grandfather. Whatever our other achievements in life, the roles we fulfill in our families are of true and eternal significance.

—R. C. S.

C. Words for Children (6:1-4)

1-3. Children, obey your parents in the Lord: for this is right. Honor thy father and mother; which is the first commandment with promise; that it may be well with thee, and thou mayest live long on the earth.

Children are admonished to *obey* their *parents*. They are to do so *in the Lord,* or as part of their duty to the Lord. Similar language occurs in connection with the wife's submission to her husband (Ephesians 5:22) and with slaves' obedience of their masters (6:5-7).

Paul strengthens his words with a *promise* from the Ten Commandments (Exodus 20:12): *that it may be well with thee, and thou mayest live long on the earth.* This is not a guarantee of long life to all obedient children, but it does call attention to the fact that obedient, God-fearing children are far less likely to engage in the kind of behavior that shortens so many lives.

4. And, ye fathers, provoke not your children to wrath: but bring them up in the nurture and admonition of the Lord.

Fathers held a position of great authority in the ancient world. In some cases they possessed an almost dictatorial power over their *children.* Paul tells Christian fathers that in the exercise of their leadership they must not *provoke* their *children to wrath.* All children will get angry at times, and no parent can avoid that. Paul is encouraging fathers not to be the source of such anger by their hasty words or thoughtless actions. Remember, fathers, that our children's perception of the heavenly Father will depend in large part on the kind of fathers we are! [See question #5, page 408.]

Conclusion

A. No Private Christians

Why do we have to be concerned about the public aspects of our faith? "Isn't Christianity a private matter?" some wonder. It is true that certain areas of the Christian life are private (one's prayer life, for example), but a Christian's testimony is meant to have public consequences. This is the implication of Jesus' challenge to us: we are to be "the salt of the earth" and "the light of the world" (Matthew 5:13, 14). We are not to be hermits. We must live our lives where people can see the difference Jesus has made.

Each of us has a sphere of influence for Christ that no one else possesses. There are people we contact each day whom no one else has the opportunity to reach with the gospel. We need to accept the challenge to leave our "comfort zones" and make an impact on a world that is dying. After all, the purpose of Christianity is not just to make us comfortable. It is to make us righteous. And sometimes we have to be made uncomfortable in order to learn righteousness.

B. Prayer

Dear Father, continually remind me of the message that my life communicates to others. Help me to remember that Your forgiveness is not a license to sin again and again. Though I am forgiven, my behavior has consequences, especially at home. Help me to remember what Jesus said to the woman taken in sin: "Go, and sin no more." Forgive and empower me, in Jesus' name. Amen.

C. Thought to Remember

It's "Go, and sin no more," not, "Go, and sin on more."

Home Daily Bible Readings

Learning by Doing

This page contains an alternate lesson plan emphasizing learning activities.
Classes desiring such student involvement will find these suggestions helpful.

Learning Goals

After this lesson each student will be able to:

1. Relate Paul's description of proper Christian conduct in the community, the church, and the home.

2. Contrast Christ's call to responsible living with the thinking that governs much of modern society.

3. Pinpoint an area of personal, home, or church life where a more responsible commitment to Christ is needed, and devise a plan to address that need.

Into the Lesson

Before class, write each of the letters of the word "imitate" on a different sheet of construction paper. Begin the class time by giving the seven sheets of paper to seven class members, one to each person. Ask them to arrange themselves so they spell a word. When they have formed the word "imitate," thank them and ask them to mount the letters on a wall or bulletin board.

Then ask the class members to share with a partner the name of one person they like to imitate and why. After a moment of sharing, ask, "What are some of the qualities of character or skills that you find you like to imitate?" Write their answers on a chalkboard. Tell the class, "Sometimes it is difficult to imitate people because their lives are so much better than ours. The standards are so high. Yet Paul tells us to imitate God. What a lofty goal!"

Into the Word

Prepare a large visual poster for the class. At the top of the poster write, "Imitators of God." Below the heading make two columns headed "*Dos*" and "*Don'ts.*"

As you begin the activity, explain that the words "Followers of God" in verse 1 are better translated "Imitators of God." God gives us a very practical and easily understood list of things to do or not do as we imitate Him. Then read Ephesians 5:1-5, 18—6:4, pausing after each verse to ask, "What are we to do or not do as imitators of God?" Have a class member write the answers on the poster.

When you begin reading and listing *dos* and *don'ts* from verses 21 and following, explain this is God's will for the Christian home. Then proceed with the activity through the end of the Scripture text. Be sure to keep this activity moving. Do not let it drag.

Into Life

Ask the class to review the list of *dos* and *don'ts*, looking for teachings that are contrary to the teachings or practices of our culture. There will be many! Circle each one they mention with a colored marker, asking *why* or *how* this is different from the practice or teaching of our culture.

Then discuss the following questions:

1. Why does God ask us to do or not do the things that are listed? What are the practical outcomes of the behavior He is requesting from us? (You will need to take time to allow students to review each of the items on the list, but keep the discussion moving.)

2. Why do you think our culture reacts negatively to the teaching about wives' submitting to husbands in verse 22? Be sure to read the lesson commentary for help in applying this verse. Also ask, "Does the context of this passage imply selfish power or selfless service by the husband? Why?" Another question that could be used in this context is, "How could Paul's teaching about submission be misused or misapplied?"

3. What, according to our text, are our motivations or reasons for imitating God? (See 5:1, 2, 5.)

To make the lesson personal, give each person a letter-size sheet of paper with the heading, "My Commitment to Be an Imitator of God." Below that print, "I have been an 'Imitator of God' by obeying these teachings." (Students will write commands from the *dos* and *don'ts* list that they believe they have obeyed fairly well.)

Almost midway down the page print, "My failure to obey these commands shows that I have not always been an 'Imitator of God,' and I need to improve." (Students will write commands from the *dos* and *don'ts* list that they believe they have not obeyed well.)

Near the bottom of the page print, "My plan or steps to bring honor to God by changing the above-mentioned behavior is to do this." (Here the students will suggest specific actions they can take to improve their obedience to the Master.)

Play a tape recording of an appropriate song, such as "I Surrender All" or "More Like the Master," while the students complete the handout. Close with a prayer asking God to bless the commitments made today.

Let's Talk It Over

The questions on this page are designed to encourage review of the lesson Scriptures and to promote discussion of the lesson by the class. The answers provided are only discussion starters. Let your class talk it over from there.

1. What was it about your childhood heroes that made you want to be like them? What about God makes you want to be like Him?

Generally, heroes are chosen because they are accomplishing something out of the ordinary, and usually something that benefits others. "Good guys" rescue "damsels in distress." Generals asparkle with stars held back the evil hordes that were bent on crushing all that was right and good. Our heroes demonstrated selflessness, courage, honor, and that which is noble. That is what we so idolized.

God is the ultimate Hero. Who is so selfless as the One who gave His own Son to save us? Who else has demonstrated such a constancy of holiness? Surely there is no one else so worthy of our praise and emulation!

2. What sins do we especially need to be on guard against, that they "not be once named among [us]"? How can we do that?

Sexual sins are rampant in our age much as they were in first-century Ephesus—and the rest of the Roman world. Crude and profane talk is pandemic. Drunkenness is a national disgrace. As bad as these behaviors are in pagan non-Christians, how much more so are they in those who claim to be Christians. Paul says they simply must not be, indeed cannot be.

Strong Biblical teaching on these sins for every generation is critical. Church educational leaders cannot assume that no such instruction and guidance is needed; "head-in-the-sand" naiveté results in headlong falling into Hell.

3. Paul suggests an alternative to drunkenness: being Spirit-filled. How is true conversion the solution to such soul-killing behavior?

Sinful lifestyle does not start out as sinful lifestyle. Sin is allowed to fill in the chinks in one's personal weaknesses, only to make the chinks into cracks, the cracks into fractures, the fractures into disjointedness. Sin always fills empty spaces. The true solution is to fill in the empty spaces with something else—rather, Someone else. The devil forces himself in, and he meets little resistance. God invites Himself in, but He waits for a warm welcome. Once welcome, He will occupy just as much of a person as that person allows. And everywhere He is, sin is

not, and the devil is pushed out. The "secret" to overcoming and evicting every sin is allowing God to be the landlord.

4. Paul describes a worship service of "singing and making melody . . . to the Lord," characterized by people "giving thanks always for all things unto God"? What is the key to having such beneficial worship times?

Most worship shortcomings are brought to the assembly, not designed into the events of the worship hour. A worshipful attitude is a week-long demeanor, which needs to be heightened before arriving for "worship" and allowed to reach a "crescendo" in the fellowship of brothers and sisters. Prayer and anticipation are the keys, not simply being there and being on time. Worship needs personal—that is, individual—purpose, not only leadership purpose. Those who sincerely want to make melody in their hearts will hardly be restrained from doing so. Those who come with thankful hearts will scarcely be deterred from offering that thanks up to God.

To have a service of worship well planned and well led, with unity of theme and unity in spirit, is important. But no planning or theme can overcome the lack of personal purpose.

5. What can our church do to encourage better relationships between husbands and wives and between parents and children, relationships that more closely mirror the description Paul gives in our text?

Teaching what the Bible says about family relationships is certainly a start. In a church that takes such matters seriously and teaches Biblical standards as important and practical, members will not so easily dismiss them as archaic or unattainable. Modeling such behavior is another important help. Paul stressed that elders and deacons are to be good family men (1 Timothy 3:2, 4, 5, 12; Titus 1:6). The church that disregards these standards does so to its own peril.

Additionally, churches can sponsor marriage enrichment retreats or seminars, hold parenting classes, insist on premarital counseling for engaged couples, and give special recognition to couples who have been faithful to one another long enough to celebrate silver, golden, or diamond anniversaries.

Called to Stand Firm

DEVOTIONAL READING: John 14:15-27.

BACKGROUND SCRIPTURE: Ephesians 6:10-24.

PRINTED TEXT: Ephesians 6:10-24.

Ephesians 6:10-24

10 Finally, my brethren, be strong in the Lord, and in the power of his might.

11 Put on the whole armor of God, that ye may be able to stand against the wiles of the devil.

12 For we wrestle not against flesh and blood, but against principalities, against powers, against the rulers of the darkness of this world, against spiritual wickedness in high places.

13 Wherefore take unto you the whole armor of God, that ye may be able to withstand in the evil day, and having done all, to stand.

14 Stand therefore, having your loins girt about with truth, and having on the breastplate of righteousness;

15 And your feet shod with the preparation of the gospel of peace;

16 Above all, taking the shield of faith, wherewith ye shall be able to quench all the fiery darts of the wicked.

17 And take the helmet of salvation, and the sword of the Spirit, which is the word of God:

18 Praying always with all prayer and supplication in the Spirit, and watching thereunto with all perseverance and supplication for all saints;

19 And for me, that utterance may be given unto me, that I may open my mouth boldly, to make known the mystery of the gospel,

20 For which I am an ambassador in bonds; that therein I may speak boldly, as I ought to speak.

21 But that ye also may know my affairs, and how I do, Tychicus, a beloved brother and faithful minister in the Lord, shall make known to you all things:

22 Whom I have sent unto you for the same purpose, that ye might know our affairs, and that he might comfort your hearts.

23 Peace be to the brethren, and love with faith, from God the Father and the Lord Jesus Christ.

24 Grace be with all them that love our Lord Jesus Christ in sincerity. Amen.

GOLDEN TEXT: Finally, my brethren, be strong in the Lord, and in the power of his might.
—Ephesians 6:10.

Lesson Aims

After this lesson each student will be able to:

1. List the items included in "the whole armor of God."

2. Tell why military metaphors are appropriate for explaining the nature of the Christian life.

3. Suggest a specific way to "put on" a particular piece of the armor of God.

Lesson Outline

INTRODUCTION
  A. Is Life a Battle?
  B. Lesson Background
I. OUR CONFLICT (Ephesians 6:10-12)
  A. The Challenge (v. 10)
    We Don't Know Our Own Strength
  B. The Adversary (vv. 11, 12)
II. OUR EQUIPMENT (Ephesians 6:13-17)
  A. Its Importance (v. 13)
  B. The Belt (v. 14a)
  C. The Breastplate (v. 14b)
  D. The Shoes (v. 15)
  E. The Shield (v. 16)
  F. The Helmet (v. 17a)
  G. The Sword (v. 17b)
    Unused Armor
III. OUR CONCERNS (Ephesians 6:18-24)
  A. For All Saints (v. 18)
  B. For God's Messenger (vv. 19, 20)
  C. For Dear Friends (vv. 21-24)
CONCLUSION
  A. Sin Must Be Destroyed
  B. Prayer
  C. Thought to Remember

Introduction

A. Is Life a Battle?

Some years ago, a controversy developed within a group of churches over the use of hymns that included military terminology. The leadership convened to study the issue and made the decision to have the questionable hymns removed from church hymnals. Protests, however, immediately arose from the "rank and file" within the church.

While some likely protested because of the nostalgia associated with these hymns, others objected because they found personal strength and encouragement in these songs. Their personal experience testified that life is sometimes very much like a battle.

As we study today's text, we will see how Paul used military metaphors (particularly the parts of a soldier's armor) to emphasize the seriousness of the Christian life. For those who have experienced the battles of life, these words will offer real hope. They will reassure us that God has given us all the resources we need to wage war victoriously and to overcome our enemy.

B. Lesson Background

The passage before us today is well known to many. Young people who grew up attending church, Sunday school, and church camp may well have been asked to memorize the portion of this lesson that outlines the armor of God.

We have seen how Paul has touched on many important theological issues in his letter to the Ephesians. In the first chapter he brought us to the "heavenly places" (v. 3), where he gave us insights into God's marvelous plan for the universe. In today's text we will see how the apostle brings us "back to earth" and to the harsh realities of living a Christlike life in a hostile world. At the same time, he calls our attention to the fact that the real conflict of which we are a part is not on earth, but in "high [literally, heavenly] places" (Ephesians 6:12).

Our real enemy is not of this world; he is a spiritual being. We cannot overcome him in our own strength. Today's text will reveal the source of divine power by which we can defeat him!

I. Our Conflict (Ephesians 6:10-12)

A. The Challenge (v. 10)

10. Finally, my brethren, be strong in the Lord, and in the power of his might.

Paul reminds us that the Christian life is a conflict so intense that whatever strength we can muster of ourselves is not enough to survive. We must *be strong in the Lord, and in the power of his might.* Paul has already noted that this "mighty power" is that "which [God] wrought in Christ, when he raised him from the dead, and set him at his own right hand in the heavenly places" (1:19, 20). [See question #1, page 416.]

WE DON'T KNOW OUR OWN STRENGTH

When a person shakes our hand and squeezes too hard, or hugs us and embraces too tightly, we sometimes say, "He doesn't know his own strength!" In some cases there is more truth to that statement than meets the eye. We read of individuals coming to the aid of a loved one who is pinned under the wreckage of an automobile accident. Suddenly they find themselves able to lift something they could not ordinarily lift. The crisis gave them a "rush" of adrenaline that provided a strength far beyond their ordinary ability.

Something similar to this may be said with regard to our spiritual strength. Because that strength comes from God and not from us, it is far greater than we realize. Many people have found themselves able to endure a period of suffering that they would never have thought they could endure. Many have found victory over temptations that they had thought too strong for them. Martin Luther said it well in his great hymn, "A Mighty Fortress Is Our God": "Did we in our own strength confide, Our striving would be losing."

Regardless of the situation we face, even if we have never faced it before, God's strength will never prove inadequate. For every Christian it can truly be said, "He doesn't know his own strength"—because the Christian's strength is God's. —R. C. S.

B. The Adversary (vv. 11, 12)

11. Put on the whole armor of God, that ye may be able to stand against the wiles of the devil.

Paul was quite familiar with the *armor* used by Roman soldiers. Paul was writing this epistle as a prisoner in Rome, where, according to Acts 28:16, he "was suffered to dwell by himself with a soldier that kept him." Perhaps Paul was reflecting on this soldier's attire when writing these words in our text. (Of course, he had been in the presence of Roman soldiers on other occasions.) It is also possible that Paul's words were based on an Old Testament passage in Isaiah 59:17, where God Himself is portrayed as wearing certain pieces of armor. If so, Paul would have truly been describing the "armor of God."

The purpose of equipping ourselves with this *armor* is so that we will *be able to stand against the wiles of the devil*. The word *wiles* means methods, schemes, or strategies. Paul could say of the devil, "We are not ignorant of his devices" (2 Corinthians 2:11). Can we say the same?

The word Paul uses for *stand* is the common military term for holding one's ground. Paul reminds us that however difficult our struggle, at the end of the battle we will stand—victorious—in the strength of the Lord.

12. For we wrestle not against flesh and blood, but against principalities, against powers, against the rulers of the darkness of this world, against spiritual wickedness in high places.

Paul points out that our battle is first and foremost a *spiritual* battle. It is not against people (the unsaved are not our enemy). Our struggle is *not against flesh and blood, but against principalities, powers,* and *the rulers of the darkness of this world.* Clearly these are references to Satan and his forces; Satan is called "the prince of this world" (John 12:31; 14:30; 16:11) and "the prince of the power of the air" (Ephesians 2:2). In Acts 26:18 darkness is associated with the power of Satan. [See question #2, page 416.]

Literally translated, the phrase *in high places* is "in the heavenlies." It is the same realm where both Christ (Ephesians 1:20) and His followers (2:6) are said to dwell. Thus to be "in the heavenlies" is to be part of the spiritual battlefield, where God's forces and the forces of the devil continue to wage war.

II. Our Equipment
(Ephesians 6:13-17)
A. Its Importance (v. 13)

13. Wherefore take unto you the whole armor of God, that ye may be able to withstand in the evil day, and having done all, to stand.

When all is said and done, the forces of God will *withstand* the attacks of the opponents described in verse 12. The book of Revelation shows that Christ and His church will reign forever. However, in the here and now the church must be prepared for an intense battle. Christians are told to put on the *whole armor of God.* Every piece has its purpose, as we shall see.

The evil day does not likely refer to some great outpouring of evil over the whole world. It probably describes any period of time during which the Christian finds himself under severe attack from the enemy. (The *New English Bible* translates it, "when things are at their worst.") Obviously Satan can mount an assault at any time, yet most of us can testify to instances when his opposition seemed especially fierce. On those occasions, the

FINALLY, MY BRETHREN, BE STRONG IN THE LORD, AND IN THE POWER OF HIS MIGHT.

The humorous illustration in today's visual reminds us that we have a strength not our own as we face the wiles and the assaults of the devil.

Visual for lesson 9

armor of God will never let us down or prove to be inferior. [See question #3, page 416.]

B. The Belt (v. 14a)

14a. Stand therefore, having your loins girt about with truth.

The first piece of armor mentioned is the belt, for that is the object with which the soldier would *girt* his *loins*. The belt was a basic and practical piece of equipment. First, it helped to keep the breastplate in place. It also included a place for the soldier to keep his sword where it could be drawn at a moment's notice. Besides that, the soldier could pull his tunic up and tuck it under his belt, which would allow him to run without hindrance.

Paul states that the Christian's belt is *truth*. Our enemy Satan is the father of lies (John 8:44), so truth is, like the belt, a basic and practical piece of our equipment. The believer knows, not only that "the truth is in Jesus" (Ephesians 4:21), but that Jesus Himself is the truth (John 14:6). Such knowledge gives the Christian the ability to detect falsehood whenever it surfaces.

C. The Breastplate (v. 14b)

14b. And having on the breastplate of righteousness.

The second item mentioned is *the breastplate of righteousness*. The main purpose of the *breastplate* was to protect the vital organs, particularly the heart and lungs, where a wound would almost certainly be fatal. Some have maintained that, since breastplates would not have covered one's back, Paul's words are to be understood as exhorting Christians to face the enemy and never retreat. That is good advice; however, breastplates in the first century commonly covered the back as well as the front of the soldier.

Home Daily Bible Readings

Monday, July 24—Be Strong in the Lord (Ephesians 6:10-15)
Tuesday, July 25—Pray Always in the Spirit (Ephesians 6:16-20)
Wednesday, July 26—Grace, Peace, and Love From God (Ephesians 6:21-24)
Thursday, July 27—God's Spirit Will Strengthen You (John 14:15-27)
Friday, July 28—Abide in Christ and Bear Fruit (John 15:1-11)
Saturday July 29—Chosen by Christ (John 15:12-27)
Sunday, July 30—Your Pain Will Turn to Rejoicing (John 16:16-24)

What is meant by the word *righteousness*? Frequently in his writings Paul uses this word to describe the righteousness that we receive through Jesus (Romans 3:21, 22; 2 Corinthians 5:21; Philippians 3:9), for we can never be righteous enough on our own to deserve Heaven. At other times he uses the term to refer to the Christian's righteous lifestyle (Romans 6:19; Ephesians 5:8, 9). Righteousness in either form is a powerful and effective defense against evil.

The fact that the breastplate covered the heart is also worth noting, given the importance of the heart in Scripture. Among other things, the heart is the center of one's moral discernment. That is the reason Jesus spoke in the Beatitudes of those who are "pure in heart" (Matthew 5:8). Satan would like nothing more than to see that purity soiled and ruined.

D. The Shoes (v. 15)

15. And your feet shod with the preparation of the gospel of peace.

Since an army marches on its *feet*, its footwear is very important. Often soldiers would wear shoes with spikes in the soles to give additional stability on especially rugged terrain. Here Paul says that the Christian's footwear is *the preparation of the gospel of peace*. While we are at war with the devil, we are to communicate to the world a message of *peace*—peace between God and man and peace between individuals who were formerly hostile toward one another. This is the peace described by Paul earlier in this letter (2:14-17).

This verse brings to mind a portion of Paul's declaration of the priority of preaching: "How beautiful are the feet of them that preach the gospel of peace, and bring glad tidings of good things!" (Romans 10:15, from Isaiah 52:7).

E. The Shield (v. 16)

16. Above all, taking the shield of faith, wherewith ye shall be able to quench all the fiery darts of the wicked.

The *shield* in New Testament times protected its bearer from spears or arrows. Here the Christian is described as having to ward off *the fiery darts*, or arrows, *of the wicked*. The word *wicked* is masculine singular, no doubt referring to the devil himself. The *New International Version* translates it "the evil one." Such a reference emphasizes the intensely personal nature of the Christian's battle. We do not fight some vague impersonal "force," but a real person: Satan.

Notice that even though the battle is intense and the enemy's weapons are life-threatening, our *shield of faith* has the ability not just to deflect the arrows but to *quench*, or extinguish, *all* of them. "This is the victory that overcometh the world, even our faith" (1 John 5:4).

F. The Helmet (v. 17a)

17a. And take the helmet of salvation.

The first-century *helmet* was a head covering made of bronze and leather. (Next to the heart, the head was the most vulnerable area of the soldier.) Today we recognize how important protecting the head is—not just to soldiers, but to football players, baseball players, bike riders, skateboarders, race car drivers, and many others.

It is fitting to think of our *salvation* as something that protects our minds. The battle for our souls is also in a very real sense a battle for our minds. It is in the mind where evil takes hold, and it is the mind that God wants to transform (Romans 12:2; Ephesians 4:23).

G. The Sword (v. 17b)

17b. And the sword of the Spirit, which is the word of God.

The final item mentioned is *the sword of the Spirit, which is the word of God.* This verse reminds us how Jesus countered the devil's temptations in the wilderness by quoting Scripture. The Word of God is infinitely more powerful than the devil. Realizing this should impress upon us how vital it is to make the diligent study and memorization of Scripture a priority in our lives.

It has been noted by some that this is the only offensive weapon that Paul mentions. This suggests that our battle with Satan is not only a matter of defending ourselves. We need also to launch an offensive against evil. Jesus' picture of the gates of Hades' not prevailing against the church (Matthew 16:18) is a picture of the church attacking and breaking down the gates, not merely holding off an offensive launched from them.

UNUSED ARMOR

In the city of Graz, Austria, there is a fascinating museum called the Provincial Arsenal. This museum dates from the seventeenth century and contains one of the largest collections of medieval weapons and armor in the world—enough, in fact, to equip twenty-eight thousand

soldiers! Despite such an impressive display of swords, spears, helmets, and shields, this armor and weaponry will never be used. It is meant only to be seen and admired.

The Christian's armor is not simply for decorative purposes. We do not wear it so that people will admire our virtues. We wear it to use it in battle. Perhaps someday the armor in Graz *may* be brought out for some reenactment of an historical event. But our spiritual battle is not a mock battle; it is real spiritual warfare, and we all desperately need "the whole armor of God" if we are to triumph.

Are you wearing the belt of truth? Is your breastplate of righteousness in place? Are your feet fitted with the preparation of the gospel of peace? Do you have the shield of faith always at hand? Are you protected by the helmet of salvation? Do you know how to wield "the sword of the Spirit"? Christians are not mannequins in a museum to be viewed, admired, and later forgotten. The battle is real. War has been declared.

We must be prepared.   —R. C. S.

III. Our Concerns (Ephesians 6:18-24)

A. For All Saints (v. 18)

18. Praying always with all prayer and supplication in the Spirit, and watching thereunto with all perseverance and supplication for all saints.

Paul now moves to the subject of *prayer.* While prayer is not described using a specific piece of armor, it is without question part of our battle against "spiritual wickedness in high places" (v. 12). Paul recommends that Christians pray *always.* No circumstance that we face ever provides an inappropriate time to pray.

What does it mean to pray *in the Spirit*? Perhaps it means that when we pray, we are in communication with the Holy Spirit. Possibly it means that when we pray, the power of the Holy Spirit is applied to answering our prayer. Or, Paul may be saying that our prayer is aided in some sense by the Holy Spirit. This latter position is supported by Paul's teaching in Romans 8:26, where he notes that the Spirit "maketh intercession for us with groanings which cannot be uttered."

Notice that not only are we to pray at all times, but we are to pray *for all saints.* Such prayer acknowledges that all Christians have been targeted by the enemy and must therefore be undergirded with prayer. Just as Satan is unrelenting in his efforts toward Christians, so Christians must pray with *perseverance.* [See question #4, page 416.]

B. For God's Messenger (vv. 19, 20)

19. And for me, that utterance may be given unto me, that I may open my mouth boldly, to make known the mystery of the gospel.

Paul was not afraid or ashamed to ask for prayer on his own behalf. Here he has a specific request in mind. He wants his readers to pray for his *utterance* in his preaching and teaching. He wants to be able to express *the mystery of the gospel* with boldness. Earlier he had explained that mystery in these words: "that the Gentiles should be fellow heirs, and of the same body, and partakers of [God's] promise in Christ by the gospel" (Ephesians 3:6).

20. For which I am an ambassador in bonds; that therein I may speak boldly, as I ought to speak.

In this verse Paul uses a strange image that seems to some to be a contradiction in terms. He describes himself as *an ambassador in bonds*. An ambassador's performance of his duties would appear to require that he not be restricted in any way. He must have free access so that he may represent his nation to the officials of a foreign government. However, it is characteristic of Paul's optimistic spirit that even though he was imprisoned, he still saw himself as an *ambassador* for Christ. Paul had the knack for turning every event in his life into an evangelistic opportunity. He refused to be silenced or intimidated by his surroundings.

C. For Dear Friends (vv. 21-24)

21. But that ye also may know my affairs, and how I do, Tychicus, a beloved brother and faithful minister in the Lord, shall make known to you all things.

Paul also wanted to communicate to his friends how his ministry was progressing, so he promised that *Tychicus* would tell them *all things* that they needed to know. Tychicus is also described as fulfilling the same role (in much the same language) for the Christians in Colossae (Colossians 4:7-9). We do not know much more about Tychicus, but the other times he is mentioned indicate that Paul must have considered him a very dependable servant of the Lord (Acts 20:4; 2 Timothy 4:12; Titus 3:12). Tychicus may have been from the region around Ephesus. It is even possible that he took the dictation for this letter.

22. Whom I have sent unto you for the same purpose, that ye might know our affairs, and that he might comfort your hearts.

Part of Tychicus's *purpose* was to *comfort* those who were concerned about Paul. Paul did not want his friends to be discouraged because of what had happened to him. He wanted them to know that the work of the Lord was progressing and that the gospel was being preached even during his imprisonment (Philippians 1:12-14). [See question #5, page 416.]

23. Peace be to the brethren, and love with faith, from God the Father and the Lord Jesus Christ.

This is a fairly typical benediction, with some slight variations from the closing words in Paul's other epistles. Here he mentions the blessings of *peace, love,* and *faith.* We recall other places where the apostle makes a triad out of faith, hope, and love (the most notable in 1 Corinthians 13:13). In this letter *peace* replaces hope. That is appropriate, however, because peace, love, and faith have been important themes in this letter. The reference to *peace* may reflect Paul's burden that Jews and Gentiles understand and express their oneness in Christ (Ephesians 2:13-18).

24. Grace be with all them that love our Lord Jesus Christ in sincerity. Amen.

Thus this powerful epistle begins (1:2) and ends with the blessing of *grace.*

Conclusion

A. Sin Must Be Destroyed

The Roman orator Cato is said to have ended every speech he made in the Roman senate with the words, "Carthage must be destroyed." He saw the threat of this north African city as so ominous that he constantly reminded his audience of what he thought needed to be done. His persistent warnings were a factor in Carthage's ultimate defeat.

In the back of our minds there should always be the words, "Sin must be destroyed." When we fight against sin, it is not because we are prudish; it is not because we want to oppress people. We are against sin because it is so terribly harmful to society as a whole and to the individual in particular. The defeat of sin is the defeat of what dehumanizes us and makes us far less than what God created us to be.

Yes, sin must be destroyed. Praise God that He has given us all the resources we need to do so!

B. Prayer

Father, we will face many challenges in life. Those challenges will often fill us with fear. Relieve us, not by removing the challenges, but by helping us to be ready for them. In the name of Christ our Conqueror we pray. Amen.

C. Thought to Remember

The battle belongs to the Lord, but you must fight it.

Learning by Doing

This page contains an alternate lesson plan emphasizing learning activities.
Classes desiring such student involvement will find these suggestions helpful.

Learning Goals

After this lesson each student will be able to:

1. List the items included in "the whole armor of God."

2. Tell why military metaphors are appropriate for explaining the nature of the Christian life.

3. Suggest a specific way to "put on" a particular piece of the armor of God.

Into the Lesson

To introduce the lesson, ask class members to name songs and choruses that picture the Christian life as a battle or use military terms to describe the Christian life. Many are listed under headings like "Victory" or "Christian Warfare" in songbooks. You can stimulate thought by naming a song or two, such as "A Mighty Fortress Is Our God," "Lead On, O King Eternal," "Stand Up, Stand Up for Jesus," "The Battle Belongs to the Lord," etc. As the students suggest a song or chorus, ask, "What is some of the imagery and its significance in the lines of that song?" For example, from "A Mighty Fortress" we learn that God is our protector from evil. (You may wish to have a songbook ready for reference.)

Make the transition to Bible study by telling the class that the writers of Christian music with militaristic themes have a Scriptural model. Today's text includes imagery from the Roman soldier to teach us how to be firm in our faith.

Into the Word

Prepare and distribute a handout with today's Scripture text printed on the left side and room on the right half for the students to write notes. Print the heading "Our Conflict" over verses 10-12 of the text, "Our Equipment" over verses 13-17, and "Our Concerns" over verses 18-24. Also include on the handout the activities described in "Into Life."

Assign the following tasks to discussion groups of three to six persons each. Larger classes may need more than one group to do the same task. Give each group a piece of poster board with one of the following assignments printed at the top.

Group 1: Read Ephesians 6:10-12. Notice the words "wiles of the devil." List on this poster some of the strategies Satan uses to attack Christians in today's world.

Group 2: Read Ephesians 6:13-17. List the six pieces of armor mentioned and write the purpose or significance of each piece for contemporary Christians.

Group 3: Read Ephesians 6:18-24. Prayer is an important part of our preparation for the battle with Satan. Please list and answer the following questions: 1. Pray How? 2. Pray for Whom? 3. Pray When? 4. How does prayer fit into the battle with Satan?

Ask a reporter from each group to put its poster on the wall and report the group's conclusions. After group 1 reports, ask, "What is at stake if we are *not* prepared for the battle against Satan?" After group 2 reports, highlight the significance of the battle for our hearts and minds. (See the lesson commentary on verses 14 and 17.) After group 3 reports, mention the significance of prayer for *all* the saints. We are part of a team that fights and stands together.

Into Life

Distribute a handout on which you have written, "Evaluate Your Spiritual Armor." Below this heading list the six pieces of armor in the left column: "My Belt of Truth," "My Breastplate of Righteousness," "My Shoes of the Gospel of Peace," "My Shield of Faith," "My Helmet of Salvation," "My Sword of the Spirit." To the right of each piece of armor print the words, "Good Shape"; "Moldy and Rusty"; "Non-existent." Ask the class members to evaluate each piece of their own spiritual armor and circle the word that best describes its condition and effectiveness.

Below that activity have printed the words, "What is the focus of your battle with Satan? Where is he attacking you the hardest?" Encourage class members to answer the questions by describing their fiercest struggles with Satan. Assure them they will not have to reveal their answers to these questions to anyone else.

A third item on the page also should be printed: "What do I need to do to be better prepared for spiritual battle with Satan?" Ask each student to decide what piece of armor he or she needs to put on to deal with Satan's attacks.

Conclude by reminding the class that Paul calls us to pray for the saints. Ask class members to share with their small group what piece of armor they need in order to be better prepared for spiritual battle with Satan. Ask persons in the small groups to pray for the person to their left and the need mentioned.

Let's Talk It Over

The questions on this page are designed to encourage review of the lesson Scriptures and to promote discussion of the lesson by the class. The answers provided are only discussion starters. Let your class talk it over from there.

1. Adults move from stronger to weaker physically. Spiritually, they should be moving from weaker to stronger. What kinds of things can we do to be sure we are growing stronger?

Age should demonstrate to us the foolishness of depending on self and the absurdity of accumulating more and more stuff. Self proves more and more inadequate. Stuff reveals its inability to satisfy and its truly temporal nature.

Being stronger spiritually is ultimately based on Bible study and successful Christian living. Thus, whatever we do to increase our exposure to Bible study will help us to grow stronger. Regular Sunday school attendance, personal Bible study, and joining a small group are all excellent spiritual "muscle builders." As for "successful Christian living," getting involved in ministry, stepping out of our comfort zones to serve "the least of these," and establishing a relationship with another Christian who can serve as a mentor or an accountability partner are of inestimable value.

2. What makes an enemy fearsome? How is the devil just such an enemy?

An enemy is fearsome when he is "bigger" than we. But size is not the only fear-producing element. (Every Goliath has a weak spot!) When the enemy's nature is not fully understood and when we know him to be devious and deceitful, our fear is multiplied.

All this is true of the devil. As a spiritual creature, he is "bigger" than those of us limited by flesh and blood and time and space. We have not fully understood the limits God has placed on his powers. And we certainly know his "wiles"; he is both "a liar, and the father of it" (John 8:44).

We have a fearsome enemy. But, praise the Lord, God is bigger and more powerful, and He is our Friend!

3. Why is it that sometimes we do not feel very well equipped for battle with the devil?

Truth, righteousness, peace, and faith may wobble in our lives. Every time one or another is compromised, our battle readiness is compromised. Too often we have underestimated our enemy's strength. We think we can warm ourselves at his fire and not get burned. We take the easy way out of a tough situation and find it costs us a lie. We put ourselves in a position where we know there will be temptation, and then we are surprised that we failed the test when it came.

A lie, an evil deed, an anxiety, a doubt—each one leaves an opening for another attack from the devil. When our salvation helmets are laid aside for a "break," and when our sword skills are unpracticed, we have every reason to feel ill-prepared. What soldier would move to the front lines with all his safety equipment and weapons left in a trunk somewhere "back there"? He would feel very exposed. So do we.

4. Who are some of the saints you are praying for "with all perseverance"? For whom should you be praying?

Perhaps your church has a prayer list suggesting people for whom the saints should pray. Look the list over. How many of the requests relate to physical issues (health, needing a job, etc.), and how many relate to spiritual warfare?

All the saints occasionally have "armor flaws," and they need the prayer support of all the rest of us. The devil is after every single one. And each of us knows Christians in other congregations and in other Christian endeavors far and near. They are all included in the "all the saints" of verse 18. Paul's challenge is a large one—but not impossible. Let's get started!

(Perhaps your class could take the names of all your church members, divide them into seven groups, and then pray for one group every day.)

5. The letters of Paul were designed to let Paul's loved ones know his condition and to bring comfort and encouragement to the readers. What do we do that is similar?

Though modern travel allows us much greater opportunity to visit those across cities and across nations and continents, we can and do use a variety of media to communicate ourselves and our wishes. From letters to greeting cards to telephones to E-mail, we have marvelous potential to accomplish Paul's purposes with our Christian brethren. The marvel of the first century is that the Christians maintained any contact. The marvel of the twenty-first is that Christians do not.

We still need the edification of knowing what Christians in other places are doing. We still need the encouragement other Christians can offer. It has to start with someone. Why not us?

The Supremacy of Christ

DEVOTIONAL READING: John 3:25-36.

BACKGROUND SCRIPTURE: Colossians 1.

PRINTED TEXT: Colossians 1:15-29.

Colossians 1:15-29

15 Who is the image of the invisible God, the firstborn of every creature:

16 For by him were all things created, that are in heaven, and that are in earth, visible and invisible, whether they be thrones, or dominions, or principalities, or powers: all things were created by him, and for him:

17 And he is before all things, and by him all things consist:

18 And he is the head of the body, the church: who is the beginning, the firstborn from the dead; that in all things he might have the preeminence.

19 For it pleased the Father that in him should all fulness dwell;

20 And, having made peace through the blood of his cross, by him to reconcile all things unto himself; by him, I say, whether they be things in earth, or things in heaven.

21 And you, that were sometime alienated and enemies in your mind by wicked works, yet now hath he reconciled

22 In the body of his flesh through death, to present you holy and unblamable and unreprovable in his sight:

23 If ye continue in the faith grounded and settled, and be not moved away from the hope of the gospel, which ye have heard, and which was preached to every creature which is under heaven; whereof I Paul am made a minister;

24 Who now rejoice in my sufferings for you, and fill up that which is behind of the afflictions of Christ in my flesh for his body's sake, which is the church:

25 Whereof I am made a minister, according to the dispensation of God which is given to me for you, to fulfil the word of God;

26 Even the mystery which hath been hid from ages and from generations, but now is made manifest to his saints:

27 To whom God would make known what is the riches of the glory of this mystery among the Gentiles; which is Christ in you, the hope of glory:

28 Whom we preach, warning every man, and teaching every man in all wisdom; that we may present every man perfect in Christ Jesus:

29 Whereunto I also labor, striving according to his working, which worketh in me mightily.

Aug 6

GOLDEN TEXT: For it pleased the Father that in him should all fulness dwell; and, having made peace through the blood of his cross, by him to reconcile all things unto himself.
—Colossians 1:19, 20a.

Lesson Aims

As a result of studying this lesson, each student will be able to:

1. Summarize how Paul described the supremacy of Christ and its impact on his ministry.

2. Tell why the supremacy of Christ must continue to remain at the heart of the church's ministry and message.

3. Suggest a way to honor Christ as Lord through some specific ministry undertaken in His behalf.

Lesson Outline

INTRODUCTION
    A. "What Think Ye of Christ?"
    B. Lesson Background
 I. CHRIST, OUR CREATOR (Colossians 1:15-18)
    A. His Identity (v. 15)
    B. His Activity (v. 16)
    C. His Supremacy (vv. 17, 18)
      Liberty, Equality, Fraternity
 II. CHRIST, OUR RECONCILER (Colossians: 1:19-23a)
    A. Means of Reconciliation (vv. 19, 20)
    B. Effect of Reconciliation (vv. 21-23a)
III. CHRIST, OUR COMMANDER (Colossians 1: 23b-29)
    A. Called to Suffer (vv. 23b, 24)
      Rejoicing in Suffering
    B. Called to Speak (vv. 25-28)
    C. Called to Strive (v. 29)
CONCLUSION
    A. Filled to Overflowing
    B. Prayer
    C. Thought to Remember

Introduction

A. "What Think Ye of Christ?"

Most people who read about Jesus are attracted to Him and even admire Him. The real challenge comes when we ask someone, "Do you believe that Jesus is who He said He was?"

Today's text from Paul's letter to the Colossians highlights what makes Jesus unique. It will not allow us to get away with saying that Jesus was just a good man, a prophet, or a great teacher. Paul declares that Jesus is nothing less than "the image of the invisible God" (Colossians 1:15). People find it much more convenient to believe in a God who is indefinable, impersonal, and can be described as "way out there" because they do not believe themselves to be accountable to such a distant God. But Jesus shows us God in the flesh—"the glory as of the only begotten of the Father" (John 1:14).

Today's lesson will focus on some of the most important truths about Jesus. These are truths that we who are His followers must believe and proclaim—without compromise.

B. Lesson Background

Our study today covers the second half of the first chapter of Paul's letter to the Colossians. This letter, like Ephesians, Philippians, and Philemon, is one of Paul's "prison epistles" and, like the rest, was probably written from Rome around A.D. 63. Like Ephesians, it was sent by the hand of Tychicus (Colossians 4:7-9).

The city of Colossae was located some one hundred miles east of Ephesus, in what is modern-day Turkey. We do not know when the church there was formed, for Colossae is never mentioned in the book of Acts. Probably it was established during Paul's ministry at Ephesus. Luke tells us that Paul used the school of Tyrannus as his headquarters in Ephesus for two years, and that as a result "all they which dwelt in Asia heard the word of the Lord Jesus, both Jews and Greeks" (Acts 19:9, 10). Otherwise, all we know of the Colossian church is what we can learn from this letter and from Paul's letter to Philemon (which was carried by Onesimus, who most likely lived in Colossae).

It is important to note the similarities between Colossians and Ephesians. They cover the same basic topics and exhibit a similar structure. In some instances the wording is very similar (compare, for example, Colossians 4:7-9 and Ephesians 6:21, 22). Probably they were both written at the same time, with Tychicus delivering Ephesians first and then continuing on to Colossae to deliver Colossians.

Despite the similarities between Ephesians and Colossians, there are important differences, many of which can be attributed to the reason Paul wrote this letter. Apparently Paul had received some disturbing news from Epaphras (mentioned in Colossians 1:7 and 4:12) that certain false doctrines were being propagated in the Colossian church, including an early form of what would later be known as Gnosticism.

It is difficult to explain Gnosticism briefly, but we must make a few observations about it before our study of Colossians begins. The name *Gnosticism* comes from a Greek word meaning "knowledge." Gnostics believed that they possessed a secret knowledge of spiritual truth that the average or "unenlightened" person could not possess. That is the reason Paul, in writing to the Colossians, emphasizes that in Christ alone are "all the treasures of wisdom and knowledge" (Colossians 2:3; cf. 1:9, 10). Only in Christ (not in the Gnostics' doctrine) is God's true "mystery" revealed (1:26, 27; 2:2).

Gnostics also believed that material things, including the physical world itself, were evil, created by an evil god. There was also a good god, they believed, who was spirit only, for only the spirit was good. They believed in a spiritual world full of divine beings (one of whom was Jesus) who came forth from this good god. Apparently some of these emanations became confused with angels, resulting in the actual worship of angels among some in the Colossian church. Paul warns against this practice in Colossians 2:18.

The Gnostic teaching that all flesh was evil had a devastating impact on Christian doctrine; for if flesh is evil, then Jesus would never have come as a human being. Gnostics thus saw Jesus as a kind of phantom who only appeared to be human. We will notice, as our study in Colossians proceeds, how Paul countered this error by insisting that Jesus had a body (Colossians 1:22; 2:9).

Since Gnostics considered the body to be evil, many of them advocated treating it harshly and denying it any pleasures. This resulted in a strict set of rules governing one's conduct. Paul alludes to these rules in Colossians 2:16, 17, 20-23. Others, however, took this teaching concerning the body to the opposite extreme. They claimed that since the body was evil anyway, one's behavior did not matter. Thus they engaged in blatant immorality, against which Paul writes in Colossians 3:5.

As he does with his letter to the Ephesians, Paul begins his epistle to the Colossians with a tribute of praise to the Lord Jesus Christ. In our text the apostle presents three word pictures of Christ: He is Creator, He is Reconciler, and He is Commander.

I. Christ, Our Creator (Colossians 1:15-18)

A. His Identity (v. 15)

15. Who is the image of the invisible God, the firstborn of every creature.

Jesus is described as *the image of the invisible God.* The Greek word translated *image* is a word that gives us our English word "icon." It could describe an image on a coin or a person's reflec-

tion in a mirror. Thus does Paul counter the false teaching that Jesus was simply one of many beings who came from God. Jesus was Immanuel—"God with us." Later Paul will affirm that in Christ "dwelleth all the fulness of the Godhead bodily" (Colossians 2:9). The nature of God is perfectly represented in Jesus.

Jesus is also *the firstborn of every creature.* Although this phrase may seem to portray Jesus as a created being, such could hardly be the case, given Jesus' superiority over creation (vv. 16, 17). Paul uses *firstborn* to highlight the role of Christ, not His origin. It was common in the first century to bestow on the firstborn special rights and obligations. Paul thus sets the stage for his declaration in the next two verses that Jesus Christ is Lord over all of the created world.

B. His Activity (v. 16)

16. For by him were all things created, that are in heaven, and that are in earth, visible and invisible, whether they be thrones, or dominions, or principalities, or powers: all things were created by him, and for him.

As one with the Father, Jesus was involved in the creation of this world. (See John 1:1-3.) This verse counters the Gnostic notion of the world's creation by an evil god.

Notice also that Paul places Christ above all *thrones, dominions, principalities,* and *powers.* These include the authorities *in heaven* and *in earth.* The reference to heavenly powers may reflect Paul's concern about the worship of angels within the Colossian church.

C. His Supremacy (vv. 17, 18)

17. And he is before all things, and by him all things consist.

How to Say It

COLOSSAE. Ko-*lahss*-ee.
COLOSSIANS. Kuh-*losh*-unz.
EPAPHRAS. *Ep*-uh-frass.
EPHESIANS. Ee-*fee*-zhunz.
EPHESUS. *Ef*-uh-sus.
GNOSTICISM. *Nahss*-tih-sizz-um.
GNOSTICS. *Nahss*-tiks.
IMMANUEL. Ih-*man*-you-el.
ONESIMUS. O-*ness*-ih-muss.
PHILEMON. Fih-*lee*-mun or Fye-*lee*-mun.
PHILIPPIANS. Fih-*lip*-ee-unz.
RECONCILIATION. *rec*-un-sill-ee-*ay*-shun (strong accent on *ay*).
TYCHICUS. *Tick*-ih-cuss.
TYRANNUS. Ty-*ran*-us.

Christ is not only superior in that He existed *before* the created world, but it is through Him that the entire created world is sustained. Jesus is the "glue" of this universe. If not for Jesus, there would be chaos.

18. And he is the head of the body, the church: who is the beginning, the firstborn from the dead; that in all things he might have the preeminence.

Not only is Christ the head of the created world, but He is specifically *the head of the body, the church.* The idea of the church as a body with Jesus as the head is one of Paul's favorite images of the church. It has been wisely said that the church is not just an organization; it is an organism.

Whereas Jesus was described as "the firstborn of every creature" in verse 15 (indicating His supremacy as Creator of all things), here He is called *the firstborn from the dead.* This is obviously referring to His resurrection. Jesus raised certain individuals from the dead; however, they were brought back in their physical bodies and eventually died again. Jesus was the first to rise from the dead, never to die again. Because He is "the firstfruits of them that slept" (1 Corinthians 15:20), it is the "blessed hope" (Titus 2:13) of all followers of Jesus to be resurrected and to "put on immortality" when He returns (Romans 8:11; 1 Corinthians 15:51-53).

The resurrection is the primary reason that Jesus is given *the preeminence.* Paul says that Jesus was "declared to be the Son of God with power, . . . by the resurrection from the dead" (Romans 1:4). [See question #1, page 424.]

LIBERTY, EQUALITY, FRATERNITY

The slogan of the French Revolution in the late eighteenth century consisted of three words: *Liberty, Equality, Fraternity.* In some sense each of these three words applies to the church, yet each must be properly understood. We are certainly free in Christ. Paul's letters make that very

Today's visual recalls the supreme price paid for our reconciliation. Post it as you begin to discuss verse 19.

Visual for lesson 10

plain. But they also warn us that our liberty is not license; we cannot do as we please. The word *fraternity* fits the concept of the church as the family of God. We are brothers and sisters in Christ. But we must keep in mind that Jesus is the Elder Brother (Hebrews 2:11, 12).

The word *equality* reminds us that we are all equal before God. We are all equal in our need for a Savior. Distinctions that often separate people in society are eliminated in Christ. However, one Person in the church is above us all, and that is Jesus. He is "the head of the body, the church" (Colossians 1:18). He has the preeminence. No matter how long we have been Christians, our primary purpose as part of the body of Christ is always to lift up the Head.

Maturity is usually viewed as being able to get along independently of others, without having to resort to their help in making decisions or handling problems when they arise. But in the Christian life, maturity is shown by our increasing dependence on Jesus. We cannot exist and function apart from the Head.   —R. C. S.

II. Christ, Our Reconciler (Colossians 1:19-23a)

A. Means of Reconciliation (vv. 19, 20)

19, 20. For it pleased the Father that in him should all fulness dwell; and, having made peace through the blood of his cross, by him to reconcile all things unto himself; by him, I say, whether they be things in earth, or things in heaven.

The phrase *in him* [Jesus] *should all fulness dwell* refers to the incarnation of Christ. The Word through whom all things were created (John 1:1-3) "was made flesh, and dwelt among us, and we beheld his glory, the glory as of the only begotten of the Father" (v. 14). This is another point at which Paul refutes the Gnostics' belief that Jesus was one of many spirit beings who came from God (cf. v. 15). *All* the fullness of God is found in Jesus—and in no one else!

This verse also calls attention to the purpose for which Jesus "was made flesh": *to reconcile all things.* The means of this reconciliation was *the blood of his cross* (note the similarity to Ephesians 2:16). It is through Jesus' death and our acceptance that what happened there happened for us that we are able to be at peace with God.

Why does Paul mention both *things in earth* and *things in heaven* being reconciled? Probably he is indicating how far-reaching is the impact of Jesus' death. Just as "by him were all things created, that are in heaven, and that are in earth" (v. 16), now all things are reconciled to God by Him. That "the whole creation" is affected by the work of Christ is clear from Romans 8:19-22. Again, Paul's words are similar to his teaching in Ephesians: that God will one day "gather together in one all things in Christ" (1:10).

B. Effect of Reconciliation (vv. 21-23a)

21. And you, that were sometime alienated and enemies in your mind by wicked works, yet now hath he reconciled.

Paul now moves from considering the universal impact of the work of Christ to a more personal perspective. Our position of being *alienated* from God affects our *mind*. Man's mind is a wonderful creation; however, if unredeemed it is capable of producing increasingly *wicked works*.

22. In the body of his flesh through death, to present you holy and unblamable and unreprovable in his sight.

Notice Paul's emphasis that Jesus has reconciled us *in the body of his flesh*. As noted earlier, Gnostics rejected the idea that Jesus was really God in the flesh, for they viewed all flesh as evil. They taught that Jesus had only the appearance of humanity. Paul affirms that it was *in the body* and *through death* that Jesus accomplished the work of reconciliation.

The purpose of Christ's redeeming work is to *present* those who once were alienated as *holy, unblamable,* and *unreprovable.* The word *holy* means "set apart." Holy objects are set apart for God in service or worship. Holiness is not some attribute for the "super spiritual"; it is expected of all Christians.

The word *unblamable* is perhaps better translated as "unblemished." Such a person is not sinless, but his character is consistently Christlike. Others are drawn toward Christ, not driven away from Him, by his behavior.

Finally, we are described as *unreprovable.* This word indicates that which cannot be called to account. It describes a person whose conduct provides no basis for a charge of wrongdoing. [See question #2, page 424.]

23a. If ye continue in the faith grounded and settled, and be not moved away from the hope of the gospel, which ye have heard, and which was preached to every creature which is under heaven.

Here Paul encourages his readers to remain true to *the hope of the gospel.* The word *faith* can describe either the content of doctrinal truth or our own personal belief in those truths. We who have accepted the gospel must resolve not to be *moved away* from its truth.

Paul's description of the gospel as having been *preached to every creature which is under heaven* is a bit of hyperbole—an intentional exaggeration

to make a point. Certainly the gospel had not been preached at that point to every individual on earth. It had, however, been proclaimed in virtually all the great urban centers of the Roman world. Keep in mind also that on the Day of Pentecost people "out of every nation under heaven" (Acts 2:5) were present to hear Peter's message. [See question #3, page 424.]

III. Christ, Our Commander (Colossians 1:23b-29)

A. Called to Suffer (vv. 23b, 24)

23b, 24. Whereof I Paul am made a minister; who now rejoice in my sufferings for you, and fill up that which is behind of the afflictions of Christ in my flesh for his body's sake, which is the church.

Paul was able to *rejoice in* his *sufferings* because he saw them as coming for the benefit of the Colossians. In addition, his sufferings linked him with *the afflictions of Christ* and with *the church* as a whole. But how could Paul have expected to *fill up that which is behind of* Christ's *afflictions*? Did Paul see something insufficient in Jesus' sufferings?

It may be better to look at Paul's words, not as a statement that something was lacking in Christ's death, but that something was lacking in Paul himself. As Christ's *minister* (servant), Paul had suffered even as Jesus promised he would (Acts 9:16). Now, in prison, he was continuing to suffer in accordance with that promise; and he would do so until this part of his service to Christ was fulfilled. [See question #4, page 424.]

REJOICING IN SUFFERING

It would seem strange indeed to many in our self-centered, comfortable age to hear Paul speak

Home Daily Bible Readings

Monday, July 31—Paul Gives Thanks for the Colossians (Colossians 1:1-8)

Tuesday, Aug. 1—Paul Prays for the Colossians (Colossians 1:9-14)

Wednesday, Aug. 2—The Fullness of God Dwells in Christ (Colossians 1:15-20)

Thursday, Aug. 3—God's Mystery Revealed to the Saints (Colossians 1:21-29)

Friday, Aug. 4—Jesus Christ: God's Word and Light (John 1:1-9)

Saturday, Aug. 5—God's Word Lived Among Us (John 1:10-18)

Sunday, Aug. 6—Christ Is Superior Even to Angels (Hebrews 1:1-14)

of rejoicing in his sufferings (Colossians 1:24). Yet to Christians in other parts of the world, this does not sound strange at all. If anything, suffering is part of their routine.

For decades the Soviet Union and the Communist countries of eastern Europe persecuted Christians. Those believers' view of such suffering was surprising. They said, "Christians in the West see prosperity as a sign of God's favor. We see suffering as a sign of God's favor. It shows that God thinks that we are strong enough to endure it."

Recently the church's attention has been drawn to the intensifying persecution of believers in certain parts of the world. Their hardships reinforce the truth that the cost of following Jesus is sometimes very high—a fact that Christians who live in more comfortable surroundings can easily forget.

These sufferers, however, are our brothers and sisters. We must not forget them.   —R. C. S.

B. Called to Speak (vv. 25-28)

25. Whereof I am made a minister, according to the dispensation of God which is given to me for you, to fulfil the word of God.

Again Paul describes himself as a *minister,* or servant, of Christ, *according to the dispensation of God.* The word *dispensation* can be translated "management plan" or "strategy" (cf. Ephesians 1:10). Paul recognized that God's plan for him was that he present the *word of God* in its fullness. He explains that message and his response to it in the remaining verses of our text.

26. Even the mystery which hath been hid from ages and from generations, but now is made manifest to his saints.

The word *mystery,* as we noted in our study of Ephesians 1:9; 6:19, refers to a truth once hidden from mankind that God has revealed or *made manifest.* Paul's use of this word ran counter to the Gnostics' claim to possess secret knowledge. The *saints* are blessed with insight into the plan of God!

27. To whom God would make known what is the riches of the glory of this mystery among the Gentiles; which is Christ in you, the hope of glory.

The *mystery* involves the sharing of the riches of the gospel with the *Gentiles*—a theme that is prominent in Ephesians (Ephesians 2:11-19; 3:1-6). But it also involves something deeper and more personal. The *mystery* is more than just God's acceptance of a class of people; it is *Christ* actually dwelling *in* a person, regardless of his or her ethnic background. That personal indwelling comes through the Holy Spirit, who is described as "the earnest of our inheritance" in Ephesians 1:14. This produces *the hope of glory* within us,

allowing us to look forward to the ultimate fulfillment of God's plan in eternity.

28. Whom we preach, warning every man, and teaching every man in all wisdom; that we may present every man perfect in Christ Jesus.

Notice in this verse both a negative and a positive side to Christian work. Sometimes people need to be given words of *warning,* just as Paul warned the Colossians about the false teachings being spread among them. But we also need to engage in faithful *teaching* of the truth so that people will be able to recognize falsehood when it appears.

The purpose of these efforts is to *present* everyone *perfect in Christ Jesus.* Remember that *perfect* in this context does not mean flawless or faultless; it is better rendered as "complete," "mature," or "fully formed."

C. Called to Strive (v. 29)

29. Whereunto I also labor, striving according to his working, which worketh in me mightily.

The word Paul uses here for *labor* describes hard, demanding work—the kind that takes every ounce of one's effort. The Greek word translated *striving* is the source of our English word *agony.* But Paul does not view these rigorous labors as dependent on his own stamina. He understands that God is *working* through him and doing so *mightily.* The word translated *working* gives us our English word *energy.* No power shortage here! [See question #5, page 424.]

Conclusion

A. Filled to Overflowing

Paul has given us a marvelous picture of who Jesus is, what He has done, and what He wants to do for us. Think of it: Jesus is the One in whom all the fullness of God dwells, and we as Christians have that fullness dwelling in us!

What are we to do with this fullness? Consider what one preacher said when a lady remarked to him, "Preacher, my cup is filled to overflowing."

He responded, "Then go out there and slosh on somebody!"

We have been filled with Jesus. Is there someone we can "slosh on"?

B. Prayer

Thank You, Father, for sending Your Son Jesus to redeem us. Thank You for sending Him to reconcile us to You. Help us to give Him the preeminence that He deserves. In His name. Amen.

C. Thought to Remember

Above all, remember that Christ is above all.

Learning by Doing

This page contains an alternate lesson plan emphasizing learning activities. Classes desiring such student involvement will find these suggestions helpful.

Learning Goals

After this lesson each student will be able to:

1. Summarize how Paul described the supremacy of Christ and its impact on his ministry.

2. Tell why the supremacy of Christ must continue to remain at the heart of the church's ministry and message.

3. Suggest a way to honor Christ as Lord through some specific ministry undertaken in His behalf.

Into the Lesson

Prepare a transparency (or a handout for each student) with today's Scripture text printed on it. Ask the students to scan verses 15-22 and select words or phrases that describe Jesus. Circle these on the transparency and/or have a student write them on a poster under the heading "Jesus." Then do a similar exercise with verses 22-29, this time looking for words or phrases that describe the Christian life. Put these words on the poster under the heading "And Me."

After the exercise, tell the class this text is one of the most complete, yet concise, descriptions of Jesus in the Bible. Our faith is centered on Jesus, so we must clearly understand who He is. Some of the Christians at Colossae were confused about Jesus, and this letter was written to make Jesus' nature and authority clear to them and us.

Early in the week, ask a student to prepare a brief report on Gnosticism in the early church. Ask the student to deliver that report at this time. Summarize his or her report by saying that the beliefs of the Gnostics caused the early church great trouble, and the seeds of this destructive belief system are seen in the issues Paul addressed in Colossians. While Gnosticism is not a problem today, many people remain confused about the nature of Jesus. This text gives us tools to address the confusion in our own world even as it helped to solve ancient problems.

Into the Word

If you are a skilled lecturer, the visual list made earlier of names and qualities of Jesus and Christians provides a wonderful visual and outline for your lecture. Use the lesson commentary to clarify the significance of these descriptions.

However, to encourage active participation in studying this passage, you may want to study it in small groups. Give each group the instructions printed for that group, paper and pencils, and (if possible) a hymnbook.

Group 1: Read Colossians 1:15-18. Explain the significance of the titles and descriptive words assigned to Jesus in this text. Also, make a list of worship hymns or choruses that recall some of these qualities.

Group 2: Read Colossians 1:19-23a. Paraphrase these verses, making the major concepts in this passage as clear as possible. Also, make a list of hymns or choruses that celebrate the thoughts of this passage.

Group 3: Read Colossians 1:23b-29. Explain the significance of the words in our opening activity under the heading "And Me." Also, make a list of hymns or choruses that call these principles to mind.

Ask each group to report on its findings. Supplement the reports with information from the commentary section as needed. After group 1 reports, ask these discussion questions.

1. What are some other views of Jesus in today's world? (For example, who would the Muslim say Jesus is? the Jew? the atheist?)

2. Why is it important that Jesus' supremacy remain at the heart of the church's ministry and message?

Into Life

We will do this "So what?" time of the lesson in two activities. First, call attention to the list of words under "Jesus" on the poster made earlier. Ask each person to select one of those words or phrases and share why that description of our Lord is richer or more significant to him because of today's study. (This activity may be done in the small groups formed earlier.)

Second, observe that Paul tells us he works hard for Christ's kingdom. Ask the students to think of works they have seen other persons doing for the Lord this past year and list those on a visual. You might list these in categories such as physical labor, proclamation, spiritual encouragement, and other appropriate headings. Then draw a scale (1–10) on the chalkboard. Tell the class, "Paul was able to say he works hard for Christ. Think about where on this scale you would make a mark to measure your work for Christ." Then ask them to consider "stepping up the pace" in service and mentally circle the areas of service they would like to explore and try.

Let's Talk It Over

The questions on this page are designed to encourage review of the lesson Scriptures and to promote discussion of the lesson by the class. The answers provided are only discussion starters. Let your class talk it over from there.

1. Many today make false statements about the nature of Christ. What is there in today's text that we can use to make His claims known to those who oppose or just don't understand the real claims of the gospel?

Equality with God, participation in creation, preexistence, superiority to all things, headship of the church, incarnation, sacrificial and redemptive death, and being the basis of our hope of eternal life—all these critical doctrines of Christ are capsulized in Colossians 1. Whenever we are confronted with a contradiction or denial of any of these claims, we must turn immediately to this text and say, "Look, here is what the inspired apostle affirms about Christ. I believe him, because I believe the Spirit who enabled him."

2. Paul says that Jesus can make us "holy and unblamable and unreprovable in his sight." How does that affect our behavior?

God has taken that which was unholy, blamable, and reprovable in our lives, and—by the covering blood of Christ—made them all the opposite. In His eyes we are holy, unblamable, and unreprovable. Our friends and acquaintances might well say otherwise, but it is God's "opinion" that matters. Still, in gratitude for what God has done, we ought to make every attempt to live up to the evaluation God has made of us. We will not treat our liberty in Christ as license. We will focus on that which is holy and fill our lives with it. We will avoid that which brings blame or reproof.

3. In Paul's day the gospel had been preached in all the major urban centers of the world. Since that time, however, the gospel has been shut out from much of the world. Literally billions of people have no prospect of hearing the gospel preached in their lifetimes! What is our congregation doing to see that the gospel is once again available to all peoples? What more can we do?

Most churches have several ways of contributing to God's plan. We commission and support Christian workers in many places around the world. Probably, we are helping finance the Christian education of those who are preparing for ministry. Many are actively financing the distribution of the Scriptures. Some of us assemble or join short-term teams of Christian workers to travel to a near or far destination for benevolence

and evangelism. Try to mention by name each mission work supported by your church. Perhaps your class could adopt a missionary family and send assistance and greetings on a regular basis.

4. Paul humbly speaks of the things he does and endures for the sake of Christ's body, the church. Every Christian needs to ask himself or herself, "What am I doing, what am I enduring, for the sake of Christ's body, the church?" How would you answer the question?

Enduring may not be the right word for most of us. Our circumstances are much more blessed. We have more food, more clothing, and more house than we actually need. We need to consider those circumstances as indeed a blessing of God *for the purpose* of doing good deeds in Christ's name. The extra food and house can enable us to offer hospitality. Having extra clothing can facilitate generosity toward the destitute. God's abundance is never given to be used selfishly. Paul was willing to endure hardship in order to minister; one can be certain that when he was blessed with plenty, it did not stay long in his control!

Of course, there are Christians in the world who truly do suffer for Christ's sake. We must pray that, given that privilege for Christ, we would endure—and rejoice.

5. If Christ's power is at work in believers "mightily," then why do you think there are so many Christians who appear to be very weak?

Christ's power is certainly available to us, but we have a responsibility to access that power. Division in the church is one threat to that access. The divisions in the church at Corinth were so serious that Paul said their observance of the Lord's Supper was a judgment against them. He went on to say, "For this cause many are weak and sickly among you, and many sleep" (1 Corinthians 11:29, 30). Prayer is one important channel for the power of God to work in one's life, but even here our relationships with others may restrict the power flow. Peter warned husbands that failure to treat their wives with honor could hinder their prayers (1 Peter 3:7).

As we work for the Lord, He will work in us. But if we try to act on our own, or if we think we can serve God without maintaining good relationships with God's people, we will fail miserably!

Complete Life in Christ

DEVOTIONAL READING: **Romans 8:31-39.**

BACKGROUND SCRIPTURE: **Colossians 2:6-19.**

PRINTED TEXT: **Colossians 2:6-19.**

Colossians 2:6-19

6 As ye have therefore received Christ Jesus the Lord, so walk ye in him:

7 Rooted and built up in him, and stablished in the faith, as ye have been taught, abounding therein with thanksgiving.

8 Beware lest any man spoil you through philosophy and vain deceit, after the tradition of men, after the rudiments of the world, and not after Christ.

9 For in him dwelleth all the fulness of the Godhead bodily.

10 And ye are complete in him, which is the head of all principality and power:

11 In whom also ye are circumcised with the circumcision made without hands, in putting off the body of the sins of the flesh by the circumcision of Christ:

12 Buried with him in baptism, wherein also ye are risen with him through the faith of the operation of God, who hath raised him from the dead.

13 And you, being dead in your sins and the uncircumcision of your flesh, hath he quickened together with him, having forgiven you all trespasses;

14 Blotting out the handwriting of ordinances that was against us, which was contrary to us, and took it out of the way, nailing it to his cross;

15 And having spoiled principalities and powers, he made a show of them openly, triumphing over them in it.

16 Let no man therefore judge you in meat, or in drink, or in respect of a holyday, or of the new moon, or of the sabbath days:

17 Which are a shadow of things to come; but the body is of Christ.

18 Let no man beguile you of your reward in a voluntary humility and worshipping of angels, intruding into those things which he hath not seen, vainly puffed up by his fleshly mind,

19 And not holding the Head, from which all the body by joints and bands having nourishment ministered, and knit together, increaseth with the increase of God.

Aug
13

GOLDEN TEXT: As ye have therefore received Christ Jesus the Lord, so walk ye in him: rooted and built up in him, and stablished in the faith, as ye have been taught, abounding therein with thanksgiving.—Colossians 2:6, 7.

Lesson Aims

After this lesson each student will be able to:

1. Explain how Paul describes the Christian's completeness in Christ, and the ways in which the Colossians were being led astray from their completeness.

2. Give some modern examples of teachings and philosophies that constitute a threat to our completeness in Christ.

3. Express an exclusive faith in Jesus, rejecting all other systems of belief.

Lesson Outline

INTRODUCTION
    A. Bargains?
    B. Lesson Background
  I. THE STEADY CHRISTIAN (Colossians 2:6, 7)
    A. Walking in Christ (v. 6)
    B. Rooted in Christ (v. 7)
      No Forwarding Address
  II. THE DISCERNING CHRISTIAN (Colossians 2:8-10)
    A. Cautious of Error (v. 8)
    B. Complete in Christ (vv. 9, 10)
      The Complete Package
  III. THE FORGIVEN CHRISTIAN (Colossians 2:11-13)
    A. Dead to Sin (v. 11)
    B. Alive in Christ (vv. 12, 13)
  IV. THE LIBERATED CHRISTIAN (Colossians 2:14-19)
    A. Free From the Law (vv. 14, 15)
    B. Free From Legalism (vv. 16, 17)
    C. Free From Deception (vv. 18, 19)
CONCLUSION
    A. Follow the Signs
    B. Prayer
    C. Thought to Remember

Introduction

A. Bargains?

An auto mechanic once put up this sign in his shop: "Beware of bargains in life rafts, brain surgery, parachutes, and auto repairs." We have all, no doubt, had the experience of getting a bargain that turned out to be no bargain! Yet some people apply a "bargain mentality" to religious faith. They want what promises the most and requires the least. They don't want to do the hard work of maturing in the faith.

Christian maturity doesn't happen overnight any more than physical maturity does. Yes, there are numerous blessings to being a Christian; we have considered many of them during this quarter's study, and we will examine more in today's lesson. But these blessings are not automatic. They come as a result of our committing ourselves to the never-ending process of Christian growth.

Christianity is a bargain in the sense that we can never earn, or deserve, the blessings God gives us. It is a bargain in the sense that we will receive far more than we ever contribute. Still, we must recognize that while one can become a Christian in just a few moments, it takes a lifetime to learn the Christian life. (In a similar way, we may get married in a ceremony of only minutes, but it takes a lifetime to make a marriage.) Today's lesson will describe what it means to grow in Christ. It will both encourage us to remain faithful and warn us to beware of obstacles to our growth.

B. Lesson Background

In last week's lesson we touched on how what appears to be the seeds of a false teaching called Gnosticism had infiltrated the Colossian church. (See the Lesson Background to last week's study.) In today's text we see Paul issuing more direct warnings concerning some of these pre-Gnostic doctrines.

The heretical teachings in Colossae included elements from different sources. Some teachings appeared to be derived from pagan philosophy, but they used certain Christian terminology to heighten their appeal. Other teachings seemed to advocate a rigid adherence to the Old Testament ceremonial regulations. Much of the language that the false teachers used appeared to correspond to what Paul was teaching. It is easy to see how newer Christians especially could be led astray.

If these false teachers had one characteristic in common, it was probably their attempt to add to the gospel, thus saying, in effect, that the work and ministry of Jesus was insufficient. Such a position was something that Paul could not tolerate. Chapter 2 of Colossians begins with his expression of concern for the Colossians' spiritual welfare (and for others besides them). He notes that in Christ "are hid all the treasures of wisdom and knowledge" (v. 3), thereby countering the Gnostics' claim to a special secret knowledge of spiritual matters. He wants the Colossians to possess a "steadfastness of . . . faith in Christ" (v. 5). Paul is doing more than just exposing false information; he is acting to preserve the eternal destiny of brothers and sisters in Christ!

I. The Steady Christian
(Colossians 2:6, 7)

A. Walking in Christ (v. 6)

6. As ye have therefore received Christ Jesus the Lord, so walk ye in him.

To Paul, the logical conclusion of having *received Christ Jesus* as *Lord* is that we *walk,* or live, as He would have us to walk. Every aspect of our lives and our conduct should be influenced by our relationship with Jesus Christ.

B. Rooted in Christ (v. 7)

7. Rooted and built up in him, and stablished in the faith, as ye have been taught, abounding therein with thanksgiving.

Paul, by describing us as being *rooted,* illustrates the stability that should characterize all Christians. The verb *rooted* is in the perfect tense, which indicates a past event. By our acceptance of Jesus as Savior and Lord, we became planted in Him.

Not only are we rooted in Christ, but Paul also says that we are *built up in him.* Here the verb is present tense, which indicates an ongoing process. Growing in the Lord is just that. Consider the growth of a plant: the better rooted it is, the better chance it has to grow strong and the better it will be able to withstand storms and other threats to its existence.

The word *stablished* means made stable, or strengthened. Paul says that we are strengthened *in the faith.* In this verse, the word *faith* probably refers to the entire system of doctrinal truth that Christians believe, since faith is described as something that the Colossians have been *taught.*

Paul also describes the prevailing attitude of our life in Christ—that we should be *abounding . . . with thanksgiving.* Christians should be constantly thanking God for His blessings and for His work in their lives. [See question #1, page 432.]

No Forwarding Address

Some years ago the television program *Real People* told a story about a package that had been mailed to an inmate of a penitentiary. The package was returned to the sender marked: "ESCAPED: LEFT NO FORWARDING ADDRESS." You can be certain that an escaped prisoner left no forwarding address!

By God's grace we have escaped from sin—and we must not leave a forwarding address! As Paul stated the matter in Romans 13:14, "Make not provision for the flesh, to fulfil the lusts thereof." In today's lesson Paul emphasizes the fact that we who have found forgiveness in Jesus must now walk in Him and remain rooted in Him. Our break with sin must be complete and final. Our new allegiance to Christ must be complete and final.

It is said that Augustine, one of the outstanding theologians of early church history, once met a woman whom he had known before his conversion. She called to him, "Augustine! It is I!" He replied, "But it is not I!" He was a new person! His break with sin was such that he could not go back to the old ways.

Unfortunately, some who claim allegiance to Christ make only a tentative break with sin. They escape, but they leave a forwarding address so that the devil will know where to find them. A gospel song we often sing at Christian camps reminds us of the commitment we have made: "I have decided to follow Jesus. . . . No turning back. No turning back." —R. C. S.

II. The Discerning Christian
(Colossians 2:8-10)

A. Cautious of Error (v. 8)

8. Beware lest any man spoil you through philosophy and vain deceit, after the tradition of men, after the rudiments of the world, and not after Christ.

Is Paul condemning the study of *philosophy* in this verse? Not exactly. What he is condemning is false philosophy, or philosophy that refuses to acknowledge God. Since *philosophy* literally means "love of wisdom," and since "all the treasures of wisdom and knowledge" are in Christ (Colossians 2:3), then genuine philosophy must pay homage to Christ. Obviously the philosophy being promoted by the false teachers in Colossae included ideas contrary to Christian truth.

Paul describes some as having been taken as *spoil* by these so-called philosophies. The word refers to items or individuals taken captive during battle. Those who are thus captured are robbed of all they have been given in Christ.

This false philosophy is accompanied by *vain deceit.* The word *vain* means empty or hollow (as

The visual for today's lesson is a striking representation of the Christian's need to be "rooted" in Christ. Display it as you discuss verses 6 and 7.

Visual for lesson 11

in the third Commandment, which prohibits taking God's name "in vain"). This counterfeit teaching also follows *the tradition of men*. Paul could be referring to either Jewish or pagan traditions, either of which were to be avoided if they led their followers away from Christ. These traditions were as dangerous as those of which Jesus warned the Pharisees and scribes (Mark 7:5-13). All such teachings must give way to the authoritative word of Jesus.

Paul also labels the false teaching as being *after the rudiments of the world*. The Greek word rendered *rudiments* means elements. It was often used to describe the components of something. Here it could refer to either the fundamental principles of the false teachers' philosophy or to the beings who were part of the spirit world and whose worship was promoted by the false teachers (Colossians 2:18). In either case, Paul was exposing the error in something that was clearly *not after Christ*. [See question #2, page 432.]

B. Complete in Christ (vv. 9, 10)

9. For in him dwelleth all the fulness of the Godhead bodily.

This is a very important verse when considering the nature of Christ. It stresses Jesus' human and divine nature. Jesus was divine *(all the fulness of the Godhead)*, even though that divinity was housed in humanity *(bodily)*. This is the significance of the term *incarnation*, which literally means being in flesh. It is part of what Paul describes as "the mystery of godliness: God was manifest in the flesh" (1 Timothy 3:16). This refutes the Gnostic contention that Jesus was just one of many manifestations of God.

10. And ye are complete in him, which is the head of all principality and power.

The Greek word translated *complete* is a form of the word rendered "fulness" in verse 9. Christians have found their fulness in the One who is the fulness of God. How could any false teacher improve on this—then or now? Why seek after any other claims of authority when Jesus is *the head of all principality and power*?

THE COMPLETE PACKAGE

The June 1969 issue of *National Geographic* reported the discovery of relics from a Spanish ship that had sunk in the year 1588. A man named Robert Senuit located the wreckage of the ship off the coast of Ireland. Among the objects he found was a man's engagement ring. Although some 380 years had passed since the tragic death of the person who wore it, one could still see that engraved on the ring was an outstretched hand and a phrase written in Spanish meaning, "I have nothing more to give."

How to Say It

COLOSSAE. Ko-*lahss*-ee.
COLOSSIANS. Kuh-*losh*-unz.
EPHESIANS. Ee-*fee*-zhunz.
GNOSTICISM. *Nahss*-tih-sizz-um.
GNOSTICS. *Nahss*-tiks.
PHILIPPIANS. Fih-*lip*-ee-unz.

The Lord Jesus could have spoken those very words at Calvary. When He gave His life on the cross, He had nothing more to give. Indeed nothing more *needed* to be given. His work of atonement was complete.

The same words can also describe our response to Jesus' sacrifice at Calvary. When we give our lives to Him, we have nothing more to give. It may seem that giving our lives to Him is not really much of a gift. Sin has ruined our lives, making them distorted, dirty, and ugly. But they are the very gifts Jesus wants. He died so that ruined lives could be made new.

Is this not part of what Paul means when he writes that we are complete in Christ (Colossians 2:10)? His gift of life for us was complete. The gift of our lives to Him must also be complete. Then we can sing, "Jesus Paid It *All*" and "*All* to Jesus I Surrender."   —R. C. S.

III. The Forgiven Christian (Colossians 2:11-13)

A. Dead to Sin (v. 11)

11. In whom also ye are circumcised with the circumcision made without hands, in putting off the body of the sins of the flesh by the circumcision of Christ.

Circumcision was the covenant sign instituted by God with Abraham (Genesis 17:10-14) and performed on all Israelite males. Here Paul describes a spiritual *circumcision*. It cannot be done by human *hands*, for it involves a procedure that only *Christ* can perform. Instead of cutting away part of human flesh (as physical circumcision does), the spiritual circumcision cuts away from one's life *the sins of the flesh*. Gentiles were not required to undergo physical circumcision, but all believers in Jesus from whatever background must receive the spiritual circumcision, which Paul proceeds to explain.

B. Alive in Christ (vv. 12, 13)

12. Buried with him in baptism, wherein also ye are risen with him through the faith of the operation of God, who hath raised him from the dead.

The book of Hebrews tells of many Old Testament practices and institutions that were given a deeper and fuller meaning with the coming of Christ. Here Paul points out that circumcision's fuller meaning is found in the act of Christian *baptism*. It would be wrong to say that circumcision and baptism are exactly parallel to one another, for circumcision was performed on male Israelite infants when they were eight days old. The spiritual circumcision of baptism follows repentance from sins (Acts 2:38) and provides a washing away of sins (Acts 22:16), or a "putting off . . . of the sins of the flesh," as verse 11 says.

Paul also describes baptism as a burial. This alludes to the normal mode of baptism in the New Testament, which was by immersion in water. (The word *baptism* comes from a verb meaning to immerse.) Because baptism follows a dying to sin, the candidate for baptism is symbolically *buried* (lowered into the water) and raised up from it, symbolizing his resurrection to "newness of life" (Romans 6:3-6). Paul then links baptism with faith when he says that we *are risen with him* [Christ] *through the faith of the operation of God.* Baptism without faith is of no use and has no real meaning. Faith in Jesus expressed by the obedience of baptism receives the full blessing of God.

13. And you, being dead in your sins and the uncircumcision of your flesh, hath he quickened together with him, having forgiven you all trespasses.

This describes what happens in the process of experiencing the spiritual circumcision. We who were once uncircumcised (in a spiritual sense, indicating our separation from God and from His people) and who were *dead in* our *sins* are *quickened* (or made alive) *with* Christ. Note that we are made alive after we have died *to* sins, and we

are made alive by being brought out of the state of being dead *in* sins. We are *forgiven* of *all trespasses;* they cannot be held against us anymore. [See question #3, page 432.]

IV. The Liberated Christian (Colossians 2:14-19)

A. Free From the Law (vv. 14, 15)

14. Blotting out the handwriting of ordinances that was against us, which was contrary to us, and took it out of the way, nailing it to his cross.

What does this *handwriting of ordinances* mean? The Greek word rendered *handwriting* is taken from the business world and describes a certificate of indebtedness signed by the debtor acknowledging his obligation. Some believe that this phrase is describing a list of our sins. However, the emphasis of the verse is on *ordinances,* which most likely refers to the law of Moses and the many commandments found within it. While the Colossian church was largely made up of Gentiles, part of the false teaching there seems to have been a legalistic insistence on keeping the Mosaic law. This code *was against us* and *was contrary to us* because it was impossible for us to keep its requirements. But because Jesus kept the law perfectly and then took the penalty that was due lawbreakers, the debt has been canceled. Jesus *took it out of the way* at the *cross.*

15. And having spoiled principalities and powers, he made a show of them openly, triumphing over them in it.

Roman generals celebrated their victories on the battlefield by marching in an impressive parade. All prisoners of war were forced to march in this parade, and all the spoils of battle that the army had captured were displayed.

Here Paul uses the description of such a celebration to highlight the triumph of Jesus at the cross. At the cross Jesus *spoiled principalities and powers.* Most likely this phrase refers to those "rulers of the darkness of this world" that hold individuals captive to sin and against whom Christians still "wrestle" (Ephesians 6:12). Jesus broke the stranglehold of these powers so that their captives could be set free.

B. Free From Legalism (vv. 16, 17)

16. Let no man therefore judge you in meat, or in drink, or in respect of a holyday, or of the new moon, or of the sabbath days.

Here Paul specifically addresses the false teachers in the Colossian church who were promoting a rigid legalism. The Colossians need not concern themselves with those who *judge* them on the basis of how they handle certain religious rituals—in this case, keeping various Old Testament

---

Home Daily Bible Readings

Monday, Aug. 7—Paul Commends the Colossian Christians (Colossians 2:1-5)

Tuesday, Aug. 8—God Dwells Fully in Jesus Christ (Colossians 2:6-10)

Wednesday, Aug. 9—Dead to the Flesh, Alive in Christ (Colossians 2:11-15)

Thursday, Aug. 10—Hold Fast to Christ, Our Head (Colossians 2:16-23)

Friday, Aug. 11—Jesus: Mediator of a New Covenant (Hebrews 8:1-7)

Saturday, Aug. 12—The Blood of Christ Purifies Us (Hebrews 9:11-15)

Sunday, Aug. 13—Christ Perfects Those Who Are Sanctified (Hebrews 10:11-18)

regulations and holidays (our word *holiday* was originally *holyday*, which is used here). This is indicated from the references to the *new moon* and to the *sabbath days*, which were part of the Jewish calendar. The references to *meat* and *drink* likely called attention to the dietary regulations of the law of Moses. It is also possible that the false teachers in Colossae had developed their own dietary restrictions.

It was not wrong for Jewish Christians to observe the customs outlined in the law of Moses. Paul himself observed some of them (Acts 16:3; 18:20, 21; 21:26). The key issue in the early church was whether Christians—especially Gentile converts—should be *required* to observe them. While Paul voluntarily circumcised Timothy (Acts 16:3), in another circumstance he refused to have Titus circumcised because others (certain false teachers) were trying to force the issue (Galatians 2:3-5).

Brothers and sisters in Christ should not judge each other on the basis of whether they keep or do not keep certain customs. The false teachers in Colossae were only promoting division when they encouraged such activity. Read Paul's additional teaching on this matter in Romans 14:1-12.

17. Which are a shadow of things to come; but the body is of Christ.

Paul maintains that the Old Testament regulations and holy days were just *a shadow* of the substance (the meaning of *body*) that would come later in *Christ*. This is the reason they should not become tests of faith and fellowship. We should not grasp at shadows when we can embrace the reality and the fullness found in Jesus. [See question #4, page 432.]

C. Free From Deception (vv. 18, 19)

18. Let no man beguile you of your reward in a voluntary humility and worshipping of angels, intruding into those things which he hath not seen, vainly puffed up by his fleshly mind.

The Greek word translated *beguile* refers to the decision of a judge to disqualify someone from competition in an athletic event. Thus Paul describes the high price of being led astray by the false teachers. The word rendered *reward* is the same word translated as "prize" in Philippians 3:14. Some of the Christians in Colossae were in danger of forfeiting that prize by following after those who had lost contact with Christ the Head (v. 19).

Later Paul will encourage the Colossians to "put on . . . humbleness of mind" (Colossians 3:12). Here, however, he speaks of a *voluntary humility* (although the word he uses is the same word found in 3:12). Obviously this is a false, or pretended, humility, and seems to be tied in some way to the *worshipping of angels*. Perhaps the false teachers were claiming to be humble by worshiping angels rather than the sovereign God. We have noted that the erroneous teaching in Colossae was characterized by a belief in a series of spirit beings who were thought to have come from God.

In addition, the false teachers seemed to take great pride in informing their hearers about *those things* that they had *not seen*. In other words, they were claiming to have received special visions of some kind. These were not, however, visions from God, but simply the product of a *fleshly*, or unspiritual, *mind*. [See question #5, page 432.]

19. And not holding the Head, from which all the body by joints and bands having nourishment ministered, and knit together, increaseth with the increase of God.

Here is the real cause of the false teachers' problems: they are *not holding the Head;* that is, they have lost their connection with Christ, the Head of the church. For any part of *the body* of Christ to stay spiritually healthy, it must remain connected to the Head. Paul's description of how the body grows is similar to his words in Ephesians 4:16.

Conclusion

A. Follow the Signs

In many cities, when spring melts the heavy snows of winter and cars splash the resulting "slush" on everything nearby, road crews must come along and scrub all the street signs. They become obscured to the point that people cannot read what they say.

In a sense, that is what Paul is doing in our lesson today. He is trying to wash off the spiritual warning signs (which have been obscured by the "slush" of the false teachers) so that the Christians in Colossae can know where to go and what to do. These signs have not been posted to limit our freedom; they are there to give us the freedom to travel the right road and avoid danger. Thus we can reach our destination safely.

B. Prayer

Forgive me, Father, when I have been content with what is partial and "shadowy." Help me to be dissatisfied with stunted spiritual growth. Keep me aware of all the riches that I have in Christ, and help me to find my completeness in Him. Through Him I pray. Amen.

C. Thought to Remember

To be a complete Christian, I need to be completely Christ's.

Learning by Doing

This page contains an alternate lesson plan emphasizing learning activities.
Classes desiring such student involvement will find these suggestions helpful.

Learning Goals

As a result of participating in this lesson, each student will be able to:

1. Explain how Paul describes the Christian's completeness in Christ, and the ways in which the Colossians were being led astray from their completeness.

2. Give some modern examples of teachings and philosophies that constitute a threat to our completeness in Christ.

3. Express an exclusive faith in Jesus, rejecting all other systems of belief.

Into the Lesson

Be sure there is a supply of paper and pencils available, and begin this lesson by playing a "word association" game. This is a light, fast-moving activity that will involve all students in a non-threatening way. You will say a word, and the students will quickly write down the first word or thought that comes to mind. Use the following words: *Faith, Jesus, Baptism, Circumcision,* and *Complete.*

Review the list, asking for a few volunteers to tell what they wrote in response to each word. Keep this activity moving quickly.

Then say, "We might ask, 'What do these five words have in common?' While some words have an obvious commonality, some just don't seem to fit the list. For example, what do *circumcision* and *baptism* have in common? All five are key words in today's text. And all five words are clues to living a full and mature Christian life."

Into the Word

Do a brief lecture, reviewing the setting for this text, from the Lesson Background in the commentary. Then ask students to turn over the papers they used earlier and write these verse numbers down the left-hand side: 6, 7, 8, 11, 12, 13, 16 and 17, 18 and 19. Observe that verse 10 tells us we are complete in Christ and that today's text is filled with clues to what it means to be complete or full or mature in Christ. Have the students work individually or in small groups to search these verses, looking for marks of a Christian who is complete or mature. Next to each verse number they should write one or more answers.

6: Walking in Christ.

7: Rooted and built up in Him, stablished in the faith, and giving thanks.

8: Refusing to be robbed or taken captive by human philosophies.

11: Putting off, or dead to, sin.

12: Buried and raised with Christ in baptism.

13: Dead in one's sins, quickened together with Christ, forgiven.

16, 17: Free from traditions or legalism.

18, 19: Committed to Christ's headship, free from falsehood.

Allow eight to ten minutes for this activity. Then review the students' findings, using the lesson commentary to explain passages that seem difficult to understand. Read and review the text in the four sections listed in your commentary (vv. 6, 7; 8-10; 11-13; 14-19). After reading and discussing each section, write on a poster the words "The complete Christian is _____." Beneath that write each of the following headings (taken from the commentary) as you summarize your discussion: *steady* (vv. 6, 7); *discerning* (vv. 8-10); *forgiven* (vv. 11-13); *liberated* (vv. 14-19).

As you review these verses, be sure to include the following:

Explain Paul's warning about "philosophy" and "tradition" (v. 8). Ask, "What does this warning mean to us today? What philosophies or traditions might be 'of the world, and not after Christ'? Why is the Christian perspective superior to these teachings?"

Explain the human and divine nature of Christ (v. 9).

Review Christ's work on our behalf (vv. 14, 15).

Into Life

Display this incomplete statement: "Living as a complete or mature Christian is like living as a _____." Have persons fill in the blank with their own vocations (e.g., carpenter, salesperson, retiree, housewife). Then have them think why this statement is an appropriate analogy. Example: An investment counselor might say his life is vested in Christ and growing beyond his imagination. Or a farmer might say that completeness in Christ is like being a laborer in God's harvest. Members of the class can share their analogies in small groups, with those sitting next to them, or with the entire class.

Remind the class that we may be tested in our maturity or completeness in Christ as the Colossians were tested. Christ, however, is the only true way to know and worship God.

Let's Talk It Over

The questions on this page are designed to encourage review of the lesson Scriptures and to promote discussion of the lesson by the class. The answers provided are only discussion starters. Let your class talk it over from there.

1. In what ways can our church help to ensure that its members are "rooted" in Christ?

Biologists tell us that a root's primary function is to give the plant stability. The church must provide stability for its members by providing an atmosphere where Bible study, worship, and encouragement can flourish. Roots are also the plant's connection to its sources of nourishment. Paul mentions that rooting is based upon what one has "been taught" (v. 7). The church must provide a solid teaching program.

The Sunday school is one way the church fulfills that role. What others can your class list? You might include solid Biblical preaching, small groups, and a midweek Bible study. What *new* programs can your class suggest, or what new emphasis could be added to a current program to help members grow better "roots"?

2. What are some philosophies and examples of "vain deceit" in the contemporary world that threaten to subvert Christian faith?

One of the most dangerous false philosophies is the so-called "New Age" movement. Based on ancient Oriental teachings, New Age thought assumes that man can make himself enlightened through his own efforts and self-discipline. Such teachings fly in the face of all that God has revealed about man's weakness and finiteness and what He *needed* to do to save us.

Materialism is another major problem. People with little or nothing envy those who have more and covet what they have. Wealthier people seem equally dissatisfied. Temporal things have displaced the eternal God in the hearts of many.

3. Jesus taught us to pray, "Forgive us our debts" (Matthew 6:12). Paul says God has "forgiven you all trespasses." Why do we need to pray for forgiveness if we're already forgiven?

Paul is discussing the beginning of the Christian life. When we accept Christ, as Paul has described, then our sins are forgiven. We were dead in our sins, but now we are risen with Christ. Yet sin still besets us—even in our "post-resurrection" life. We need continually to pray, "Forgive us our debts," as we live from day to day. Those new sins are also covered by the blood of Jesus, but we dare not take them lightly. Hebrews 10:26 and 27 warn of the danger of continuing to sin willfully,

and 1 John 1:9 reaffirms the promise of forgiveness when we confess our sins to the Lord.

4. It seems that people in every era and every generation fall prey to the trap of legalism. Why is legalism so appealing? How can we avoid it in our own lives?

In the Old Testament, God's prophet Micah had to ask, "What doth the Lord require of thee, but to do justly, and to love mercy, and to walk humbly with thy God?" (Micah 6:8). Even in that prescribed system of law, God was concerned about the heart and the mind. Yet some still judge their fellow Christians according to rules not taught in the New Testament.

Legalism appeals to some because it seems to make life easier: no need to evaluate and decide, for right is right and wrong is wrong. Black-and-white thinking is easier than weighing the issues and applying a variety of ethical principles. Legalism is very attractive for the mentally lazy.

Some are, no doubt, attracted to legalism for the same reason the Pharisees were. The Pharisees used it to justify themselves and make themselves appear superior to others. Thus, legalism quickly becomes elitism.

5. From television to collectibles, angels are very popular today! How, if at all, is the modern fascination with angels similar to the Colossian heresy of worshiping angels?

Angels are real beings, and we ought to believe in them. They are God's servants, "sent forth to minister for them who shall be heirs of salvation" (Hebrews 1:14). If we want to display representations of angels, this can become an affirmation of our belief in the beings the Bible calls angels.

As it has with other Biblical realities, however, the secular world has reinvented angels. Many believe in "guardian angels" who protect us from our foolishness and from the threat of other persons and disasters. They give us our wishes, like a genie we can cork and uncork at our own convenience and need. Yet they make no demands on us. We are the masters; they are our servants.

To many, angels are mysterious and intriguing, beautiful and benevolent. They are not the striking figures of the Bible that virtually always struck fear—or, at least, awe—in the hearts of those few who saw and recognized them.

The Way to Righteousness

DEVOTIONAL READING: Mark 12:28-34.

BACKGROUND SCRIPTURE: Colossians 3:1-17.

PRINTED TEXT: Colossians 3:1-17.

Colossians 3:1-17

1 If ye then be risen with Christ, seek those things which are above, where Christ sitteth on the right hand of God.

2 Set your affection on things above, not on things on the earth.

3 For ye are dead, and your life is hid with Christ in God.

4 When Christ, who is our life, shall appear, then shall ye also appear with him in glory.

5 Mortify therefore your members which are upon the earth; fornication, uncleanness, inordinate affection, evil concupiscence, and covetousness, which is idolatry:

6 For which things' sake the wrath of God cometh on the children of disobedience:

7 In the which ye also walked sometime, when ye lived in them.

8 But now ye also put off all these; anger, wrath, malice, blasphemy, filthy communication out of your mouth.

9 Lie not one to another, seeing that ye have put off the old man with his deeds;

10 And have put on the new man, which is renewed in knowledge after the image of him that created him:

11 Where there is neither Greek nor Jew, circumcision nor uncircumcision, Barbarian, Scythian, bond nor free: but Christ is all, and in all.

12 Put on therefore, as the elect of God, holy and beloved, bowels of mercies, kindness, humbleness of mind, meekness, longsuffering;

13 Forbearing one another, and forgiving one another, if any man have a quarrel against any: even as Christ forgave you, so also do ye.

14 And above all these things put on charity, which is the bond of perfectness.

15 And let the peace of God rule in your hearts, to the which also ye are called in one body; and be ye thankful.

16 Let the word of Christ dwell in you richly in all wisdom; teaching and admonishing one another in psalms and hymns and spiritual songs, singing with grace in your hearts to the Lord.

17 And whatsoever ye do in word or deed, do all in the name of the Lord Jesus, giving thanks to God and the Father by him.

Aug 20

GOLDEN TEXT: Whatsoever ye do in word or deed, do all in the name of the Lord Jesus, giving thanks to God and the Father by him.—Colossians 3:17.

New Life in Christ
Unit 3: Christ Above All
(Lessons 10-13)

Lesson Aims

After this lesson students will be able to:

1. List several things Paul says a Christian must "put off" and things he says a Christian must "put on" to grow in the way of righteousness.

2. Tell why the process of "putting off" and "putting on" is a continual challenge for the Christian.

3. Suggest a specific way to "put on" one of the virtues Paul commends.

Lesson Outline

INTRODUCTION
    A. The Mirror
    B. Lesson Background
  I. TRUTHS TO CELEBRATE (Colossians 3:1-4)
    A. Risen With Christ (vv. 1, 2)
       The Man Who Came Back From the Dead
    B. Hidden With Christ (v. 3)
    C. Glorified With Christ (v. 4)
 II. VICES TO ELIMINATE (Colossians 3:5-11)
    A. Immoral Behavior (vv. 5-7)
    B. Hostile Attitudes (v. 8a)
    C. Improper Speech (vv. 8b, 9a)
    D. Remember Who You Are (vv. 9b-11)
III. VIRTUES TO CULTIVATE (Colossians 3:12-17)
    A. A Merciful Spirit (v. 12)
    B. A Forgiving Spirit (v. 13)
    C. A Loving Spirit (v. 14)
    D. A Peaceful Spirit (v. 15)
       Celebrate Thanksgiving Days
    E. A Grateful Spirit (vv. 16, 17)
CONCLUSION
    A. Stay Focused
    B. Prayer
    C. Thought to Remember

Introduction

A. The Mirror

In one of Hans Christian Andersen's stories, he tells of a mirror that made every good and pretty thing look bad. Many people have just such a distorted view of life. Paul once made this observation: "Unto the pure all things are pure: but unto them that are defiled and unbelieving is nothing pure; but even their mind and conscience is defiled" (Titus 1:15). Often those who use such a "mirror" find that it also makes bad things look good.

Today's study from Colossians reminds us that only when we find new life in Christ and begin to look at people and situations through the mirror of God's Word (James 1:23-25) can we enjoy a clear view of them. The best way to see the world is from Heaven's perspective!

B. Lesson Background

Our two previous studies from Colossians were taken from the portions of the letter that focus particularly on doctrinal issues. The lesson from chapter 1 dealt with the preeminence of Christ. Last week's study from chapter 2 examined some of the false teachings being spread among the Colossians. Both lessons highlighted the fullness of the Father that dwelt in Jesus (Colossians 1:19; 2:9) and the fact that Christians are "complete" through the presence of Christ in us (1:27; 2:10).

Today's study moves on to the more practical part of Colossians, challenging us who have been "risen with Christ" (3:1) to express that new life in our attitudes, words, and deeds.

I. Truths to Celebrate (Colossians 3:1-4)

A. Risen With Christ (vv. 1, 2)

1. If ye then be risen with Christ, seek those things which are above, where Christ sitteth on the right hand of God.

Paul urges Christians to *seek* after the highest possible ideals—*those things which are above*, or, the things of Heaven. The word *seek* has the sense of "keep on seeking." This emphasizes that the seeking must become a priority in our lives. To accept Christ as Savior is, in one sense, the end of our searching—we have found the one and only source of salvation! In another sense, however, it is just the beginning. The Christian life is a continual adventure of seeking to know Christ better.

The expression *risen with Christ* recalls Paul's words in the previous chapter. Colossians 2:12 says: "Buried with [Christ] in baptism, wherein also ye are *risen with him* through the faith of the operation of God, who hath raised him from the dead." Baptism marks a rebirth—a beginning of "newness of life" (Romans 6:4). The one so raised must continually walk with the Lord, seeking those things that are above.

Here Jesus is described as seated at *the right hand of God*. To be at the right hand of a sovereign or king is to be stationed at the place of highest privilege. Even today a person may refer to a close friend or associate as his right-hand man.

THE MAN WHO CAME BACK FROM THE DEAD

When a guest minister came to a certain church one Sunday to preach, the people asked him, "Would you like to meet a man who came back from the dead?" They then introduced him to an older man in the congregation. They explained that some time ago the man had become very ill and was taken to the hospital, where he was declared dead. Then someone noticed a slight movement. Quickly doctors resuscitated the man, who soon became known as "the man who came back from the dead."

Of course, these people understood that their friend was not really dead, though he was certainly near death. Only Jesus is honored as the One who really came back from the dead.

In a spiritual sense, however, all Christians have come back from the dead. We died to sin. Our old person was buried with Christ in baptism (Colossians 2:12), and a new person was raised up. We are now declared "risen with Christ" (Colossians 3:1). As He came back from physical death we have come back from spiritual death—and the same power is responsible for both events! Now that resurrection power lives in us, enabling us to live as Christ lived.

We ought to remind ourselves from time to time of the radical difference Christ has made in our lives. We are indeed people who have come back from the dead.　　　　　—R. C. S.

2. Set your affection on things above, not on things on the earth.

Perhaps we have known someone whom we would describe as having a mind that was "in the gutter." Here Paul admonishes us to have the opposite. We are to set our *affection* (our minds or our thinking) on *things above*. True, not all *things on the earth* are evil, but they are inferior to what is heavenly. [See question #1, page 440.]

B. Hidden With Christ (v. 3)

3. For ye are dead, and your life is hid with Christ in God.

What does Paul mean by telling us that we are *dead*? He means that our old sinful life is dead with Christ (Romans 6:8-11). Now our *life is hid with Christ in God*. We dwell "in heavenly places" (Ephesians 2:6) with Christ (Ephesians 1:20). *Hid* calls attention to the fact that the world does not understand our new life; it is too preoccupied with "things on earth." The word may also carry with it the idea of being protected.

C. Glorified With Christ (v. 4)

4. When Christ, who is our life, shall appear, then shall ye also appear with him in glory.

This describes what will happen at the second coming of *Christ*. This "blessed hope" (Titus 2:13) provides a strong motivation to continue thinking about heavenly things and thus to keep ourselves pure (1 John 3:3). We will be part of the great victory that Christ achieves when He returns. The life once "hid" from the world (v. 3) will be gloriously revealed, for Christ Himself *is our life*. [See question #2, page 440.]

II. Vices to Eliminate (Colossians 3:5-11)

A. Immoral Behavior (vv. 5-7)

5. Mortify therefore your members which are upon the earth; fornication, uncleanness, inordinate affection, evil concupiscence, and covetousness, which is idolatry.

While we have died to sin (Romans 6:2) so that sin is no longer controlling our lives as it once did, we still have to deal with individual temptations. To do this, says Paul, we must *mortify* our *members*. To *mortify* means to "put to death." The word *members* refers to the parts of the body and here represents the entire body and its desires. Paul is obviously not asking for a literal killing of the body; he is telling us to avoid the sins he proceeds to list, which involve the use of the body. (Read his similar exhortation in Romans 6:19.)

First, Paul condemns *fornication*. This word is a very general word for sexual immorality. The Greek word is the source of our English word *pornography*. Paul's counsel is deemed irrelevant by many in our society today, where sexual standards have been greatly relaxed. However, regardless of what society says, Christians are still obligated to live lives of purity before a holy God.

Paul then mentions *uncleanness*, which literally means impurity. It covers a much wider area of behavior than *fornication*. Then comes *inordinate affection*. Some versions translate this "lust." It is actually the Greek word *pathos*, which is the root of such words as empathy and sympathy. While the Greeks used *pathos* to describe either a good or bad feeling or desire, in the New Testament it always refers to inappropriate feelings or uncontrolled desires.

The word *concupiscence* speaks of intense desire, particularly sexual desire—though the word is not limited to the sexual context. Of itself it can be good or evil. It is the same word used of Jesus' "desire" to eat the Last Supper with His apostles (Luke 22:15). But Paul makes clear that it is the *evil* desires that must be put to death, not just intense desires of any kind. Indeed, a Christian should have an ardent desire for good causes.

The last sin Paul cites is *covetousness*. This means more than just greed for money; it is a warning against a selfish desire for anything or anyone. Note how Paul equates covetousness with *idolatry:* if we put our desires and wants above what God wants for us, then we have indeed made idols and worshiped them.

6. For which things' sake the wrath of God cometh on the children of disobedience.

While God is loving and forgiving, we dare not think that He is casual about sin. Paul reminds us that these sins provoke *the wrath of God*. The phrase *children of disobedience* refers to those who make sinning their habitual practice and are in an unsaved condition (Ephesians 2:2, 3).

7. In the which ye also walked sometime, when ye lived in them.

Paul reminds the Colossians that at one time they committed these sins. Their lives prior to being "risen with Christ" were characterized by all kinds of evil. [See question #3, page 440.]

B. Hostile Attitudes (v. 8a)

8a. But now ye also put off all these; anger, wrath, malice.

Paul continues with another list of evils that the Christian is to *put off* like soiled clothing. These sins deal more with our attitudes and our speech toward others. The first three words are all related: *anger, wrath,* and *malice.* James tells us simply, "The wrath of man worketh not the righteousness of God" (James 1:20).

C. Improper Speech (vv. 8b, 9a)

8b, 9a. Blasphemy, filthy communication out of your mouth. Lie not one to another.

Blasphemy means insulting talk. It can be directed toward God or toward other people. This is the reason the word can also be translated "slander."

Filthy communication translates a Greek word that suggests communication that is abusive or obscene. This is another word of Paul that seems especially relevant in our day. Nearly every movie and television program contains what might be described as filthy communication. The

---

How to Say It

AGAPE. uh-*gah*-pay.
BARBARIAN. Bar-*bare*-ee-un.
COLOSSIANS. Kuh-*losh*-unz.
CONCUPISCENCE. con-*kew*-pih-sense.
EPHESIANS. Ee-*fee*-zhunz.
PATHOS. *pay*-thahss.
SCYTHIAN. *Sith*-ee-un.

---

language is used either to shock or to provide a twisted form of humor, neither of which is an acceptable use of God's precious gift of speech.

Verse 9 continues the admonitions concerning our speech by reminding us that Christians are to be honest people. Anyone who claims to be a follower of the One who is the truth (John 14:6) should find lying intolerable. It is actually the speech of the devil (John 8:44). A Christian's speech, Paul will later say, should be "always with grace, seasoned with salt" (Colossians 4:6).

D. Remember Who You Are (vv. 9b-11)

9b, 10. Seeing that ye have put off the old man with his deeds; and have put on the new man, which is renewed in knowledge after the image of him that created him.

Again the language of *put off* and *put on* is used to highlight the difference that being "risen with Christ" ought to make in the resurrected person's life. The *new man,* or new person, in Christ is *renewed in knowledge*. This is probably a reference to the knowledge of God, since the knowledge mentioned here causes the individual to become more and more like God. Such a person grows into *the image of him that created him,* thus becoming what God created him to be.

11. Where there is neither Greek nor Jew, circumcision nor uncircumcision, Barbarian, Scythian, bond nor free: but Christ is all, and in all.

This verse emphasizes the unity found in Christ. Paul says that in Him those barriers that divide and frustrate people are brought down. There is *neither Greek nor Jew.* Since the time of Alexander the Great, Greek culture had been spread over the entire world. But since it was a pagan culture, it was resisted by the Jews. The love of Christ was able to penetrate such barriers of culture and nationalism.

A religious barrier divided the *circumcision* and the *uncircumcision.* The *circumcision* referred to the Jews, for whom this act was the covenant sign required of all males. To the Jews, all non-Jews were labeled *uncircumcision.* But the sign of the Old Covenant is meaningless in the New, so this barrier was also removed in Christ.

The term *Barbarian* referred to anyone who did not speak Greek. The Greek word used here imitated how foreigners sounded to Greek ears— as if they were saying, "baa, baa, baa, baa." Thus we get the term *barbarian.* Perhaps this suggests that the language barrier is removed in Christ.

A *Scythian* was part of a particularly hated group of barbarians in Paul's day. They originated from what is today southern Russia. The term probably suggests that no one is beyond the reach of God's grace in Christ.

Finally, Paul declares that in Christ there is neither *bond nor free.* Slavery was a fact of life in the Biblical world. Few probably even considered the possibility of its nonexistence. Here Paul does not speak directly to the issue of slavery; he simply affirms that in Christ the slave and the free person are one.

That the distinctions Paul mentions in this verse could be eliminated in Christ is a testimony to the power of the gospel. It also challenges us as Christians today to apply that same power to the divisions around us. [See question #4, page 440.]

III. Virtues to Cultivate (Colossians 3:12-17)

A. A Merciful Spirit (v. 12)

12. Put on therefore, as the elect of God, holy and beloved, bowels of mercies, kindness, humbleness of mind, meekness, long-suffering.

Earlier Paul described what we should "put off." Now he tells us what we must *put on.* He describes us as *elect of God,* or chosen ones. (See the discussion of the term *elect* in lesson 5, pages 379, 380.) This term, along with *holy and beloved,* calls attention to our standing as the people of God. Note that being *elect* does not do away with human responsibility. We are to take to heart all the commands that Paul proceeds to give.

Paul follows this reminder of who we are with a list of qualities that we need to cultivate. First, he says that we should put on *bowels of mercies.* Just as we often think of emotion and compassion as coming from the heart, in Paul's day these were believed to originate in the intestinal area. It is still true that people often feel strong emotion in their stomachs. (Thus we occasionally speak of a "gut feeling.")

The word for *kindness* is the common word for this virtue. In the original language it sounds very much like the name *Christ. Humbleness of mind* and *meekness* are attitudes that will produce acts of kindness toward others. Meekness has often been misunderstood as weakness. Actually it describes a kind of balance between extremes, or strength that is brought under control for a useful purpose.

Finally, Paul admonishes us to put on *long-suffering,* or patience, which we will also demonstrate if we have cultivated humility and meekness. Patience is a virtue both in handling the trials and struggles of life and in dealing with people and all of their complexities.

B. A Forgiving Spirit (v. 13)

13. Forbearing one another, and forgiving one another, if any man have a quarrel against any: even as Christ forgave you, so also do ye.

This visual illustrates the principle of verse 17. Discuss how a believer can do everything ("whatsoever ye do") in the name of Christ.

Visual for lessons 2, 12

The word *forbearing* describes a willingness to bear with others whose actions or words irritate us. It is demonstrated by what we do not do. On the other hand, *forgiving* is a more active virtue in that we determine not to hold someone's offensive act or deed against him anymore. This admonition is made stronger by the challenge to forgive in the same way *Christ forgave* us. All of us have been the recipients of an "amazing grace," and it behooves us to exhibit it toward others. This is the point of Jesus' parable of the unforgiving servant (Matthew 18:21-35). [See question #5, page 440.]

C. A Loving Spirit (v. 14)

14. And above all these things put on charity, which is the bond of perfectness.

Paul completes his list of virtues with the "crown jewel" of *charity,* or love. The word for *charity* is the Greek word *agape.* Paul calls love *the bond of perfectness,* meaning that love binds together, or is the gluing power behind, all the other virtues he has listed. This is consistent with his teaching in 1 Corinthians 13 about the priority and excellence of love.

D. A Peaceful Spirit (v. 15)

15. And let the peace of God rule in your hearts, to the which also ye are called in one body; and be ye thankful.

The word for *rule* is taken from the sports world of Paul's day. The word described the action of a judge, or umpire, in deciding the outcome of a competition. Thus Paul is saying that God's peace is to act as an arbiter governing all of our relationships in the church. He even goes so far as to say that we are *called* to peace. We are not to treat peace as optional; Paul tells the Romans, "If it be possible, as much as lieth in you, live peaceably with all men" (Romans 12:18). If Christians would give peace this kind of priority, we would go a long way toward becoming *one body.*

Then Paul adds *and be ye thankful.* Certainly the refreshing change in our lives that results from removing the vices and embracing the virtues should make us grateful people indeed.

CELEBRATE THANKSGIVING DAYS

On the island of St. Croix (*kroy*) in the Virgin Islands, two Thanksgiving days are celebrated. In addition to the one celebrated by all Americans, the residents observe a Hurricane Thanksgiving Day on October 25. It is linked to the observance of Supplication Day, which is on July 25, the beginning of hurricane season. On Supplication Day all the citizens of St. Croix are urged to pray that their tiny island will be spared the ravages of a hurricane. They have then appointed a day at the end of hurricane season, October 25, to thank God for answering their prayers.

Most of us probably have many supplication days, but far too few thanksgiving days. Over and over we receive that for which we prayed, yet we seldom thank God for His answers. Of course, we don't need something as dramatic as a hurricane to make us thankful. One little boy made a list of blessings for Thanksgiving Day and showed it to his family. One item on the list was quite puzzling: the boy said that he was thankful for his eyeglasses. Since most little boys don't want to wear glasses, the family wondered why he would list that. He explained that he was thankful for his glasses for two reasons: "They keep the boys from hitting me, and they keep the girls from kissing me."

All of us have unnoticed blessings for which we need to be thankful. And we need to remember that it is just as important to thank God for the little things as it is to thank Him for the big things. —R. C. S.

Home Daily Bible Readings

Monday, Aug. 14—Revealed With Christ in Glory (Colossians 3:1-6)

Tuesday, Aug. 15—Put on the New Self (Colossians 3:7-11)

Wednesday, Aug. 16—Live Faithfully, Joyfully, and Thankfully (Colossians 3:12-17)

Thursday, Aug. 17—Love And Honor All People (Colossians 3:18—4:1)

Friday, Aug. 18—Live and Speak in Christian Love (Colossians 4:2-6)

Saturday, Aug. 19—Paul's Faithful Supporters (Colossians 4:7-11)

Sunday, Aug. 20—Paul's Final Words to the Colossians (Colossians 4:12-18)

E. A Grateful Spirit (vv. 16, 17)

16. Let the word of Christ dwell in you richly in all wisdom; teaching and admonishing one another in psalms and hymns and spiritual songs, singing with grace in your hearts to the Lord.

What does it mean to *let the word of Christ dwell in* us? The *word of Christ* probably refers to the message of the gospel. The gospel is not just truth to be grasped intellectually; it should find a home in our minds and in our hearts, affecting all our relationships. Its presence allows us to share a rich fellowship with others in the church, who also know that indwelling.

Paul says that we are to express this fellowship by *teaching and admonishing one another* in our worship. The terms *psalms, hymns,* and *spiritual songs* were discussed in lesson 8 under the study of Ephesians 5:19 (page 404).

17. And whatsoever ye do in word or deed, do all in the name of the Lord Jesus, giving thanks to God and the Father by him.

This is an appropriate summary of Paul's exhortations in this passage. He tells us that every *deed* we *do* and every *word* we speak ought to be done *in the name of the Lord Jesus.* Every aspect of our lives should be lived in recognition of His lordship, *giving thanks to* our heavenly *Father* for His goodness.

Conclusion

A. Stay Focused

Have you ever watched a crowd of people watching a tennis match? No doubt you have noticed how their heads move back and forth in perfect unison as they follow the flight of the ball from one side of the court to the other and back again.

Many people try to live the Christian life in just that manner. They want to give their allegiance to *both* God and the world in an effort to gain "the best of both worlds." Paul tells us, "Set your affection on things above, not on things on the earth" (Colossians 3:2). What works for watching a tennis match spells disaster in the spiritual realm. Let's stay focused, for this is a "match" with eternity at stake!

B. Prayer

Father, we ask You to help us fix our minds on "those things which are above." If we do that, then we will want to get rid of all that displeases You and embrace all that pleases You. Through Christ, who is our life. Amen.

C. Thought to Remember

The way of righteousness is the way of Christ.

Learning by Doing

This page contains an alternate lesson plan emphasizing learning activities.
Classes desiring such student involvement will find these suggestions helpful.

Learning Goals

As a result of studying this lesson, each student will be able to:

1. List several things Paul says a Christian must "put off" and things he says a Christian must "put on" in order to grow in the way of righteousness.

2. Tell why the process of "putting off" and "putting on" is a continual challenge for the Christian.

3. Suggest a specific way to "put on" one of the virtues Paul commends.

Into the Lesson

On the chalkboard or on a large poster list the following events: the inauguration of a president (or other government leader), a football game, a wedding, a polar expedition, an engine overhaul. Divide the class into small groups and assign one event to each group, or have the entire class consider each item on the list. Ask, "How would you dress to attend or participate in this event?" (or, ". . . in each of these events?")

Obviously the way one dresses to attend an inauguration will be much different from the way he dresses to overhaul an engine! A polar expedition requires one to "put on" some very special clothing. Observe that today's lesson will tell us how to dress for the Christian life—what to take off and what to put on.

Into the Word

This portion of the lesson can be done in small groups or with the entire class. If using small groups, give each group two pieces of paper. The heading for one should read "Behaviors of My Old Self." The heading for the other paper should read "Qualities or Behaviors of My New Self." (If you are doing this activity as a class, put the headings on two large pieces of poster board.) Ask each group (or the class) to read Colossians 3:1-17 and then list all the old and new qualities or behaviors cited in the text. Ask the groups or individuals also to list or cite the verse that mentions the behaviors or qualities. ("Old Self" behaviors will be found in verses 5, 8, and 9. "New Self" behaviors may be found in verses 1, 2, 3, 5, 10, 11, 12, 13, 14, 15, and 16.)

After the exercise is completed, it will be necessary to explain or define some of the behaviors or qualities listed. Give one person (or each group) a dictionary. Begin by reviewing the "Old Self" qualities. Ask for definitions or examples of each. Write these definitions on the poster. If a definition is unknown or uncertain, refer it to the person with a dictionary. After completing the first list, remind the class these are behaviors that God expects His children to abandon or avoid.

To review the "New Self" behaviors and qualities, ask these questions:

1. Paul tells us to "seek . . . things above" in verses 1 and 2. Why? Does he assume that all things on earth are evil?

2. What does it mean to be "dead" (v. 3)?

3. What does it mean to "mortify . . . your members" (v. 5)?

4. What are the differences in the three types of music mentioned in verse 16? How can they be used to teach and admonish one another?

Use the commentary section to help answer questions and clarify other issues as needed.

Into Life

Tell the class, "This list appears to be a 'before and after' list." Then discuss these questions:

1. Do you think this transformation is likely to be completed at the moment of conversion? Or, do you think this transformation is a continuing process? Why?

2. What can make this transition to the "new self" difficult for believers? What can we as a church do to encourage this transformation in our members?

Read verse 17. Point out that this verse is a great summary statement of Paul's teaching and of living as a Christian.

Make the lesson personal by distributing lists of the characteristics of the old and new self. (Prepare these lists before class.) They may not be identical to the lists prepared earlier, but will be very similar. Ask class members to take a moment to look at the first list. Ask them to circle one of the behaviors of the "Old Self" that they may be having trouble letting go. Have a time for silent, personal prayer, asking God's help to abandon this dishonoring behavior.

Then ask each person to look at the second list and place a check mark by each virtue he or she would like to develop or improve to bring honor to Christ. Ask each to share one of those items with a person sitting next to him or her. Ask the students to pray for each other's goals; then close with a prayer for all your students.

Let's Talk It Over

*The questions on this page are designed to encourage review of the lesson
Scriptures and to promote discussion of the lesson by the class. The answers
provided are only discussion starters. Let your class talk it over from there.*

1. How do we set our minds on things above, and not on the things of the earth?

Earthly things pound persistently on our mind's door, demanding to be let in. Basic human needs and desires must be met, but we must not let them dominate and control our thinking.

We need to read the sources and engage in conversations that stimulate heavenly thinking. We need to eliminate or minimize the sources of earthly thought—whether from books, magazines, television, movies, or other media. We cannot remove ourselves entirely from the world or its influences, but we can be more discerning. What specific books or other sources can your students suggest that they have found helpful?

2. The second coming of Christ gets very little thought time and talk time with most of us. What can we do to give it more attention, more space in our lives?

If we are preoccupied with the demands and pleasures of everyday living, anything future can easily be ignored. Until we develop the "soon" concept of Christ's coming that the first-century Christians had, most of us will give it little thought.

We need often to pray John's prayer: "Even so, come, Lord Jesus" (Revelation 22:20). Maybe we could make a plaque with these words on it and hang it in a prominent place in our home or office. Perhaps we could borrow the Jewish farewell of "Next year in Jerusalem" and make it, "Next year in the New Jerusalem!" The second coming is the climax of our Christian hope—we ought to focus more and more on that "blessed hope"!

3. We, too, "walked sometime" in evil practices and a wrong lifestyle. How much thought do you think a Christian should give to his or her former life? How can an awareness of the past help the believer to be faithful in the present and into the future?

When some Christians talk about their past, they seem to be thinking of "the good old days"! Such recall is not what Paul has in mind here. Rather, he encourages a memory of that from which we have been delivered by the power of Christ. Keeping in mind that we, too, are saved by grace will help us to be more accepting of others still in need of His grace.

Recalling our past can also be an encouragement to faithful living. Paul reminded the Corinthians that the wicked have no part in God's kingdom. Then he said, "And such were some of you: but ye are washed, but ye are sanctified, but ye are justified in the name of the Lord Jesus, and by the Spirit of our God" (1 Corinthians 6:11).

4. What can we do about eliminating the divisions that separate people in our world?

Our divisions are the same as those in Paul's day. Cultural, ethnic, and national differences frequently divide us. Reaching across cultural lines may pull us out of our comfort zones, but we must make the effort. The cross was outside Jesus' comfort zone, too!

History and tradition can be as much a barrier today as circumcision and uncircumcision were in Paul's day. We must recognize that such issues have no merit on the eternal scale.

Supporting the work of Bible translators can be an important step to breaking down language barriers. The Scythians of our day may be incarcerated criminals, alcoholics, drug addicts, and the like. What are we doing to be sure the gospel is heard by and modeled before these groups?

Economic differences are among the hardest to overcome. It seems to be very difficult to minister to people who are much poorer or much richer than oneself. But difficulty does not excuse us from making the effort.

5. Why are forbearing and forgiving often forgotten among Christian friends? How can we cultivate an ability to practice these more faithfully?

We tend to expect better behavior from those we know best. When they offend us or neglect us, we think, "They should know better!" At the same time, we may lower the standards for ourselves. "I ought to be able to be myself around my friends. They're supposed to understand me."

Paul reminds us of the utmost reason we must be forbearing and forgiving to one another: "Even as Christ forgave you, so also do ye" (v. 13). We of all people ought to understand our need for one another's support and encouragement. We have understood the insidiousness of sin and what it has done and keeps on trying to do to us. We know how difficult it is to try to be righteous, how impossible, in and of ourselves.

Welcoming Others in Christ

DEVOTIONAL READING: James 2:1-13.

BACKGROUND SCRIPTURE: Philemon.

PRINTED TEXT: Philemon 4-21.

Philemon 4-21

4 I thank my God, making mention of thee always in my prayers,

5 Hearing of thy love and faith, which thou hast toward the Lord Jesus, and toward all saints;

6 That the communication of thy faith may become effectual by the acknowledging of every good thing which is in you in Christ Jesus.

7 For we have great joy and consolation in thy love, because the bowels of the saints are refreshed by thee, brother.

8 Wherefore, though I might be much bold in Christ to enjoin thee that which is convenient,

9 Yet for love's sake I rather beseech thee, being such a one as Paul the aged, and now also a prisoner of Jesus Christ.

10 I beseech thee for my son Onesimus, whom I have begotten in my bonds:

11 Which in time past was to thee unprofitable, but now profitable to thee and to me:

12 Whom I have sent again: thou therefore receive him, that is, mine own bowels:

13 Whom I would have retained with me, that in thy stead he might have ministered unto me in the bonds of the gospel:

14 But without thy mind would I do nothing; that thy benefit should not be as it were of necessity, but willingly.

15 For perhaps he therefore departed for a season, that thou shouldest receive him for ever;

16 Not now as a servant, but above a servant, a brother beloved, specially to me, but how much more unto thee, both in the flesh, and in the Lord?

17 If thou count me therefore a partner, receive him as myself.

18 If he hath wronged thee, or oweth thee aught, put that on mine account;

19 I Paul have written it with mine own hand, I will repay it: albeit I do not say to thee how thou owest unto me even thine own self besides.

20 Yea, brother, let me have joy of thee in the Lord: refresh my bowels in the Lord.

21 Having confidence in thy obedience I wrote unto thee, knowing that thou wilt also do more than I say.

GOLDEN TEXT: [I pray] that the communication of thy faith may become effectual by the acknowledging of every good thing which is in you in Christ Jesus.—Philemon 6.

New Life in Christ
Unit 3: Christ Above All
(Lessons 10-13)

Lesson Aims

After completing this lesson, each student should be able to:

1. Identify Philemon and Onesimus and tell what Paul hoped to accomplish on their behalf with his letter to Philemon.

2. Tell what made Paul's actions regarding Onesimus such a bold testimony to Christ's love.

3. Take steps to break down barriers and develop a friendship for Christ's sake with someone who needs a Christian's testimony.

Lesson Outline

Introduction

A. People Like Us

It is generally true that we like people who are most like ourselves. And, in contrast, we tend not to build friendships as quickly with people who are not like us. Sometimes, if we are not careful, prejudices can develop toward those who are not like us.

Today's lesson from Philemon encourages us to take a closer look at how we view people and to see them as Jesus sees them. This letter is not a theological treatise; it is a very personal letter permeated with genuine emotion. It does not deal with issues in the abstract; it deals with them in the context of a very real set of circumstances being addressed by very real people.

Obviously Philemon was one of the individuals involved in the situation behind Paul's writing of this letter, for it is addressed to him. The other was an escaped slave named Onesimus. They were asked to become models of the reconciliation made possible through Jesus. This was no easy task for either of them. In the world of the first century they were miles apart on the socio-economic scale: Philemon was an apparently well-to-do businessman; Onesimus, a humble slave. How they responded to Paul's appeal had the potential to provide an impressive testimony to the uniting power of the gospel.

There is an important lesson here for all of us. It is quite possible for us to believe that the gospel should go to everyone, even people who are not like us, but at the same time refuse to accept such people into our own fellowship. Paul appealed to Philemon to display a willingness to break down social barriers in the name of Jesus. His appeal is addressed to us, too.

However, we will see in this study that there is more than just social change at stake; the importance of forgiveness is also a pivotal issue. This, too, is difficult. According to the standards of the day, Philemon would have been under no obligation to be kind to or forgive his slave. But Paul knew of Philemon's Christian commitment and appealed to him to "go the second mile" with a person whom society would have said did not deserve such treatment. This appeal also is addressed to us.

B. Lesson Background

Some believe that Philemon is the most personal book in the Bible. Certainly there is no other book quite like it. It deals with a very sensitive set of circumstances. The problem was a runaway slave named Onesimus. He had fled from his master, Philemon (and may even have stolen something before he left). When Onesimus reached Rome, he met Paul and his companions. As a result, he became a Christian.

Now what was Paul to do? Should he tell Onesimus to go back to his master (where he might be punished), or should he tell him to stay in Rome and thus remain a fugitive? Paul chose a third course of action—one that illustrates the gospel's ability to heal the divisions that characterize a sinful world. He would send Onesimus back, but plead for Philemon to treat him as a brother rather than a slave—in other words, to allow their relationship in Christ to overrule their relationship in society.

Some Bible students wish that Paul (and the New Testament in general) had more to say about the evils of slavery. Actually it comments very little on the subject (perhaps the closest to a criticism of slavery comes in Paul's reference to "mensteelers," i.e., slave traders, in 1 Timothy 1:10). Slavery was simply a part of first-century culture. No one would have given serious consideration to abandoning it, for they could not have conceived of an alternative. But Paul put into effect the transformation of the master-slave relationship by urging Philemon to treat Onesimus as a brother in Christ rather than as a slave. It seems that Paul did not try to change society as such, but to change individuals and to encourage them to apply Christian principles to every situation. In that way, society would be changed.

Not only does Paul address Philemon in this letter, but he also mentions Apphia and Archippus (v. 2). Some Bible students believe Apphia to be Philemon's wife and Archippus his son, but there is no proof of this.

Philemon is one of the prison epistles, most likely written around the same time as Ephesians, Philippians, and Colossians. Since Paul sent Onesimus with Tychicus to Colossae (see Colossians 4:7-9), it seems likely that Philemon lived in or near that town. Onesimus probably delivered Paul's letter to Philemon. This, of course, would have added an extra touch of tenderness to Paul's appeal.

I. Paul's Old Friend (Philemon 4-7)

A. His Love and Faith (vv. 4, 5)

4. I thank my God, making mention of thee always in my prayers.

Paul begins the body of this letter in much the same fashion as he does his other letters. He expresses thanksgiving to God and reminds the recipient, Philemon, of his *prayers* for him. So much of our prayer lives is devoted to our wants. It appears that much of Paul's prayer life was devoted to others rather than to his own wants or needs.

Paul does not identify himself as an "apostle" in this letter, though that is common in his other letters (Romans 1:1; 1 Corinthians 1:1; 2 Corinthians 1:1; Galatians 1:1; Ephesians 1:1; Colossians 1:1; 1 Timothy 1:1; 2 Timothy 1:1; Titus 1:1). This attests to the personal nature of this letter. Titles are not as important when corresponding with a friend.

Paul was particularly grateful for the household of Philemon and for the church that met in his house (v. 2). This indicates that Philemon was a man of hospitality and of some means, and that he was probably a leader in that church. And if he was a leader, then his response in the matter involving Onesimus would set a compelling example for others in the church.

5. Hearing of thy love and faith, which thou hast toward the Lord Jesus, and toward all saints.

Interestingly, the name *Philemon* means loving. Philemon's Christian commitment was expressed in his *love* for *the Lord Jesus* and his love for the *saints*. (Of course, Paul was about to ask Philemon to do a very loving thing for Onesimus.)

This twofold dimension of love should call to mind Jesus' statement of the two greatest commandments: love God with all your heart, soul, mind, and strength; and love your neighbor as yourself. It is not possible to separate these two aspects of Christianity. Our relationship with God will always affect the relationships we have with others. It has often been noted that the Christian faith has both a vertical dimension (toward God) and a horizontal dimension (toward others). These two dimensions are also seen in the Ten Commandments; the first four of them emphasize our reverence for God, and the last six stress our responsibility to others.

B. His Evangelistic Success (v. 6)

6. That the communication of thy faith may become effectual by the acknowledging of every good thing which is in you in Christ Jesus.

As Philemon participates in the *communication* of his *faith* in Christ, that faith will become more *effectual* (effective) because he will understand more fully the goodness of God. It is certainly true that the more we give our faith away, the more it grows.

C. His Support (v. 7)

7. For we have great joy and consolation in thy love, because the bowels of the saints are refreshed by thee, brother.

Paul notes that Philemon's *love* has been a source of *great joy and consolation* to him and to others. The word translated *consolation* can also

Visual for lesson 13

Paul prayed that Philemon would be active in sharing his faith. Today's visual illustrates a modern believer sharing his faith.

be translated "encouragement." It literally means a calling alongside (for the purpose of rendering some kind of assistance). Paul says that *the saints* had been *refreshed by* Philemon.

As noted in last week's study (under Colossians 3:12), *the bowels* were believed to be the source of emotions in Paul's day. Paul was commending Philemon because other Christians had been encouraged and *refreshed* through his efforts.

It is obvious at this point that Paul is preparing Philemon for the favor he will ask. He is depending on Philemon's compassion to govern how he will treat his runaway slave. [See question #1, page 448.]

II. Paul's New Son
(Philemon 8-16)

A. No Longer Useless (vv. 8-11)

8. Wherefore, though I might be much bold in Christ to enjoin thee that which is convenient.

Paul now begins his appeal to Philemon. He first suggests to Philemon that there is abundant reason for him to *enjoin,* or order, Philemon to do what he desires, but he will not do so. Paul prefers to appeal to Philemon's own conscience that he will do what he ought to do simply because it is the right thing to do.

The word *convenient* is not used as we use it today. Paul does not mean that Philemon should make a choice on the basis of what is easiest for him. In the English of the *King James* translators *convenient* meant what is fitting and appropriate. (See comments on Ephesians 5:4, page 403.)

9. Yet for love's sake I rather beseech thee, being such a one as Paul the aged, and now also a prisoner of Jesus Christ.

Although Paul appeals to Philemon to grant his request *for love's sake,* he is not unwilling to tug at Philemon's emotions. His description of himself as *Paul the aged* is a bit of hyperbole. While Paul was a mature man at this point, he probably was not what we would consider *aged.* Perhaps Paul used the term in a spiritual sense, describing himself as someone older in the faith, which would have given some degree of authority to his request. Along with his reference to being *also a prisoner of Jesus Christ,* it would have appealed to Philemon's sympathy. [See question #2, page 448.]

10. I beseech thee for my son Onesimus, whom I have begotten in my bonds.

Paul finally mentions the name of the person for whom he is interceding: *Onesimus,* a slave. Philemon must have been surprised to see the words *my son* attached to the name of Onesimus. It was clear he would have to begin to see his slave in a new light!

As far as we know, Paul had no children (none is mentioned in the New Testament). But he had many "sons in the faith," including Titus (Titus 1:4), Timothy (1 Timothy 1:2), and others whom he led to Christ (1 Corinthians 4:14, 15).

Onesimus was someone Paul had *begotten in* his *bonds.* Even while in prison Paul had many opportunities to present the gospel (Philippians 1:12, 13). Onesimus had responded positively and had become a son to Paul. The issue now was whether Philemon would treat him as a brother.

Something should be said about the faith of Onesimus. He was doing something quite courageous by returning to Philemon—something that demonstrated the sincerity of his commitment to Christ. Onesimus could have remained a fugitive, but he chose to return instead. Paul said he was sending Onesimus (v. 12), but Paul was in no position to force him to return. While Paul may have urged him, we have to see this as a voluntary act on the part of Onesimus.

OPEN MY EYES

Anyone who puts on glasses for the very first time is amazed at the difference they make in his vision. A person doesn't realize what he has been missing! Only after wearing and using his glasses does he realize how blurred different objects and people have looked.

Today's study of Philemon and Onesimus challenges us to see people as God sees them and as they can be in Christ. Sometimes it is hard to see the potential in others. Their past obscures the possibilities for their future. Yet every one of us probably knows someone who, by the grace of God, has made a dramatic change in his or her life and achieved a level of spirituality we never dreamed the person could reach. (In fact, we would probably be surprised at how many people think that about us!)

In today's lesson we have two examples of being able to see others better because of the improved vision that God provides. Paul saw the potential in Onesimus. He knew that the runaway slave could become a trusted servant. He also saw the potential in Philemon. He knew that this master could become a brother to the man who was his slave.

Many today have given up on humanity, and they see no hope. (Suppose God had felt that way!) As Christians we are relieved of this pessimism when we see by faith the potential that God sees in the human race. May it be said of us, "Wherefore henceforth know we no man after the flesh" (2 Corinthians 5:16).   —R. C. S.

11. Which in time past was to thee unprofitable, but now profitable to thee and to me.

This verse includes an interesting play on words. The name Onesimus means *profitable,* but he had been to Philemon quite *unprofitable*—especially since he had run away. Paul claims that Onesimus will no longer be profitable in name only, but in reality. Paul then proceeds to explain how this is so.

B. No Longer a Slave (vv. 12-16)

12. Whom I have sent again: thou therefore receive him, that is, mine own bowels.

Paul continues to include emotion in his appeal. By describing Onesimus as *mine own bowels,* he indicates that this slave is not just another convert. He is very precious to Paul.

13. Whom I would have retained with me, that in thy stead he might have ministered unto me in the bonds of the gospel.

Paul admits that he considered keeping Onesimus with him so that *he might have ministered unto* him and helped him during his imprisonment in the proclamation of the *gospel.* If he had done so, Onesimus would have been serving Paul on Philemon's behalf. To do this, however, would have violated the law and jeopardized the friendship of Paul and Philemon. However helpful this new brother might be to Paul, the apostle chose a different course of action.

14. But without thy mind would I do nothing; that thy benefit should not be as it were of necessity, but willingly.

Paul does not mention the legal issue involved in keeping Onesimus with him but goes right to the matter of his friendship with Philemon. He does not want to take advantage of his friend by acting *without* Philemon's consent. He does not want to force Philemon to accept Onesimus, but for Philemon to act *willingly.* A gift given out of *necessity* is no gift at all, but "God loveth a cheerful giver" (2 Corinthians 9:7).

15, 16. For perhaps he therefore departed for a season, that thou shouldest receive him for ever; not now as a servant, but above a servant, a brother beloved, specially to me, but how much more unto thee, both in the flesh, and in the Lord?

Paul believed that in some way God had been at work in this situation. He suggests that there may have been a purpose behind Onesimus's running away and eventually meeting Paul. Although Onesimus had *departed for a season* (temporarily), now, in Christ, Philemon would have Onesimus *for ever*—not as a slave, but as a brother.

There is some speculation that Paul was also hinting that Philemon should free Onesimus and send him back to Paul. This, however, involves speculation and a reading between the lines.

There is no evidence that this was either Paul's intention or the eventual result of his letter to Philemon. [See question #3, page 448.]

III. Philemon's New Brother (Philemon 17-21)

A. Count Him a Friend (v. 17)

17. If thou count me therefore a partner, receive him as myself.

As if Paul had not already appealed to Philemon enough, he now says that Philemon should *receive* Onesimus as if he were Paul himself. Can you imagine the respect and honor that Philemon would have given Paul if he were his house guest? Can he show that kind of hospitality to Onesimus? Paul depends on Philemon's fellowship as a *partner* in Christ as a basis for his request.

B. Forgive His Past Offenses (vv. 18-21)

18. If he hath wronged thee, or oweth thee aught, put that on mine account.

This verse suggests that Onesimus may have taken some money or something else of value from Philemon. Paul says that all of Onesimus's debts should be placed on his *account.* Such a gesture showed that Paul was willing to do more than just request favors of Philemon; he, too, was offering to make some sacrifices on behalf of Onesimus. [See question #4, page 448.]

19. I Paul have written it with mine own hand, I will repay it: albeit I do not say to thee how thou owest unto me even thine own self besides.

Why does Paul emphasize that he has *written* this with his *own hand*? We know that Paul dictated his epistle to the Romans to an individual (Romans 16:22). In another letter he mentions writing the closing salutation with his own hand, "which is the token [trademark] in every epistle" (2 Thessalonians 3:17). Here Paul was probably trying to demonstrate the earnestness of his

---

How to Say It

APPHIA. *Af*-ee-uh or *Ap*-fee-uh.
ARCHIPPUS. Ar-*kip*-us.
COLOSSAE. Ko-*lahss*-ee.
COLOSSIANS. Kuh-*losh*-unz.
EPHESIANS. Ee-*fee*-zhunz.
EPHESUS. *Ef*-uh-sus.
ONESIMUS. O-*ness*-ih-muss.
PHILEMON. Fih-*lee*-mun or Fye-*lee*-mun.
PHILIPPIANS. Fih-*lip*-ee-unz.
TYCHICUS. *Tick*-ih-cuss.

appeal to Philemon by taking the pen in his own hand and concluding his letter.

In addition, Paul reminds Philemon that he owes his very life to Paul. This may refer to the part Paul played in leading Philemon to Christ.

20. Yea, brother, let me have joy of thee in the Lord: refresh my bowels in the Lord.

Philemon could become the source of true *joy* to Paul by doing exactly as he requested in his treatment of Onesimus. Philemon had a reputation as a man of great compassion. Paul calls upon him to manifest that compassion (note once more the reference to the *bowels*) in the midst of a very delicate situation. [See question #5, page 448.]

21. Having confidence in thy obedience I wrote unto thee, knowing that thou wilt also do more than I say.

Paul has *confidence* that Philemon will *do* as he has asked. Paul goes a step farther and expresses his conviction that Philemon will do even *more*. Again, this calls attention to Philemon's reputation as a deeply committed and compassionate servant of Christ.

According to tradition, early in the second century one of the leaders of the church in the city of Ephesus was a man named Onesimus. Is this the same man as the Onesimus in today's study? There is no way to know, but isn't it fascinating to think of this runaway slave becoming a leader in the church?

BROTHER LOVE

Gil Contreras is a Mexican preacher who works among the Otomi Indians in his native land. During his efforts to communicate the gospel to them, he discovered that they had no word for love. They could only say, "I hate you" or "I don't hate you." Contreras lived among those Indians,

---

Home Daily Bible Readings

---

ate their meager food, and slept on their rough benches. Through such acts they began to comprehend the idea of love. As a result they borrowed a word from the Spanish language, and now they call Contreras "Brother Love."

We do not know how the situation involving Philemon and Onesimus turned out. Given Philemon's reputation as a loving and compassionate Christian, we trust that the master/slave relationship became one between brothers in Christ. Think of the impact this must have had on those who became aware of what had happened!

This is the kind of love that Christians are called to demonstrate as their trademark (John 13:35). Our culture has so overworked the word *love* that merely talking about it will not suffice. We must support our talk with actions so that others will be drawn to the true love—God's love.

If others are to know that the Father loves them, they must see that love in the lives of His children.   —R. C. S.

Conclusion

A. Down With the Walls

The day that the Iron Curtain came down is one that will be remembered as one of the twentieth century's most remarkable events. The collapse of the wall that once divided the city of Berlin spoke of a new hope for freedom and for reconciliation between cultures and political systems that once seemed forever alienated from one another.

Paul's letter to Philemon tells of the apostle's efforts to tear down one of the most intimidating social walls of his day: the wall between a master and a runaway slave. The usual response to such an occurrence included severe punishment. But the presence of Christ in the parties involved meant that this was not to be handled in the usual way. Whether the century is the first or the twenty-first, any man-made barriers that separate groups or individuals can be torn down—through the love of Jesus Christ.

B. Prayer

Give me the grace, dear Lord, to treat people the way You would have me treat them. Help me to realize that You do not take note of social status. Forgive me when I have done so. Help me not to think so highly of myself that I demean other people. Help me to forgive those who have wronged me. Through Jesus, in whom there is true unity. Amen.

C. Thought to Remember

All are family who have God as Father and Christ as Elder Brother.

Learning by Doing

This page contains an alternate lesson plan emphasizing learning activities.
Classes desiring such student involvement will find these suggestions helpful.

Learning Goals

After completing this lesson, each student should be able to:

1. Identify Philemon and Onesimus and tell what Paul hoped to accomplish on their behalf with his letter to Philemon.

2. Tell what made Paul's actions regarding Onesimus such a bold testimony to Christ's love.

3. Take steps to break down barriers and develop a friendship for Christ's sake with someone who needs a Christian's testimony.

Into the Lesson

Begin this lesson with a "brainstorming" activity. Ask the class to "brainstorm," or list quickly, a few kinds or illustrations of human prejudices in today's world. Write their answers on a visual under the heading "Human Prejudice." (Their list might include religious prejudice, racial prejudice, prejudice against handicapped persons, political prejudice, economic prejudice, and others). Then make the transition to Bible study by saying, "It seems that we tend to like people who are like us and not to like people who are different from us. Today's text forces us to address and deal with our differences and the impact they have on our attitudes toward each other."

Into the Word

First, use the Lesson Background to prepare and deliver a lecture using the following outline:

A. The Problem. Tell how Onesimus ran away from Philemon and was converted by Paul. Mention Paul's dilemma about sending Onesimus back to Philemon.

B. Paul's Plea. Tell what Paul expected from Philemon and why.

Have a volunteer read Philemon 4-21 aloud. Explain the word *bowels* (which is used three times in today's text) as the equivalent to using the word *heart* today. It is a poetic concept indicating the seat of emotions. Then write the italicized headings listed below on the chalkboard. Ask the questions that follow each heading before writing the next.

A Snapshot of Philemon
1. What does this text imply or say about Philemon's stature in the community?
2. What does it imply about his faith?
3. For what does Paul thank Philemon?

A Snapshot of Onesimus
1. What was his occupation?
2. At the writing of the letter, what was his relationship with the Lord?
3. Why would Paul say Onesimus was once unprofitable but now is profitable? (Tell the class that Onesimus's name means profitable.)

Paul's Plea
1. What was Paul asking of Philemon?
2. Paul said he would like to keep Onesimus, but was sending him back to Philemon. Why? What was the ethical issue at stake?
3. What was the basis of Paul's plea with Philemon (v. 9)?
4. Why would Paul mention his age as he makes this request of Philemon?
5. What point of leverage is Paul making in verse 12? Verse 17? Verse 19?
6. What did Paul mean by his remark in verse 15?

Into Life

Point out that there were great differences between Philemon and Onesimus. One was a slave, the other a slave owner. One was well-to-do, the other was a debtor. One had social status, the other had none. Yet Paul urges Philemon to accept Onesimus as a Christian brother and forgive him.

Then remind the class of the introductory activity. Differences and prejudices often have the potential to divide believers. However, our differences can also be a blessing. Ask how the following differences can be a blessing to the church: Religious Backgrounds, Racial Differences, Economic Differences, Physical Handicaps.

Tell the class you are confident Paul would encourage acceptance and fellowship with everyone we've talked about. Ask, "What are the attitudes or values that are necessary to bring fellowship, harmony, and a sense of purpose among Christians who come from different backgrounds?" Write their answers on the chalkboard. Then ask, "What can we do to foster these attitudes or values in our church and community?"

Ask each class member to identify a Christian who comes from a different background from himself or herself. Ask the students to evaluate their acceptance of and fellowship with the individuals they identified. Ask each student to determine to become better acquainted with that person and to work together for God's glory.

Let's Talk It Over

The questions on this page are designed to encourage review of the lesson Scriptures and to promote discussion of the lesson by the class. The answers provided are only discussion starters. Let your class talk it over from there.

1. Paul has some very nice—even flattering—things to say about Philemon before asking of him a huge favor. Do you think it's okay, then, to "butter up" a person before asking a favor? Why or why not?

Manipulation of another person through insincere flattery or by any other means is never appropriate. It does not respect the person; it uses him or her for the flatterer's own purposes. A false compliment uttered in the process is not even believed by the person offering it. It is a lie. But Paul's compliments were sincere and true.

Paul often began letters with words of praise, and the praise was always genuine. His approach here was not uncommon to him, nor was it unrelated to his subject matter in this case. Paul was doing more than asking a favor. He was urging his friend to make a right moral choice. It was a choice that would be difficult, given the social climate of the day. But it was one that needed to be made, not only for Philemon's own sake, but for the many who would follow his example. Paul was justly reminding Philemon of the good walk he had been making and urging him to continue in that right way.

2. Sometimes even when we are in a position to insist on another's doing our bidding, it is better to make a request than an order. What circumstances tell us the right times to do this?

Some might say that such an approach is always to be preferred when it can be used. If a person is capable of making the right choice without coercion, he will be happier about the result than if forced to "do the right thing." To allow one the freedom to decide is to allow him an occasion for growth. To refuse him the opportunity is possibly to stunt his growth or, worse yet, to generate resentment, anger, or vindictiveness, and thus be party to spiritual regression.

Paul knew Philemon was capable of righteousness; he wanted him to have the growth experience of forgiving and loving. We need to look diligently for occasions to allow our friends in Christ to choose to do right, without threatening them, without ordering them, without shaming them.

3. Paul suggests that perhaps Onesimus's running away was within the providence and plan of God. Onesimus had found faith in meeting Paul.

Now things could be better than they ever had been before. What can we generalize about God's providence on the basis of fortuitous happenings?

It is assuredly a good thing when we see in events the possibility that God is at work. Why should we be surprised? That truth is at the heart of our whole understanding of God's scheme in history: God is at work! But to make some evidential claim for such an event is pressing what God reveals. Even the inspired apostle used *perhaps* here (v. 15), and we should likewise be careful about making dogmatic assertions of exactly what God is doing and how He is doing it. It is enough to know He is working in our behalf (Romans 8:28). We do not always have to know the details.

4. For whom could you say, "If he hath wronged thee, or oweth thee aught, put that on mine account"? Why?

It takes a special kind of love to agree to be accountable for another's debts. Certainly a husband or wife would do that for his or her spouse. Many parents would do so for their children. Essentially we do the same thing if we co-sign for another's loan. Now the Bible offers strict warnings about co-signing. If taking on another's debts simply allows that person to act irresponsibly, we are doing him no favors to assume those debts! There are times, however, when offering such help can demonstrate faith in, and love toward, another. And, of course, if we agree to be held accountable, we ought not to be surprised if we are indeed held accountable. If we are not willing, we ought not to make the offer, whether by co-signing or by verbal promise.

5. How do we plead with others to "let [us] have joy of thee in the Lord"?

Whatever opportunity we have to call for obedience to God's revealed will is an opportunity for us to experience joy. Whether as parent, spouse, teacher, deacon, ministry leader, or other, our call to those who are under our influence to obey God offers us the possibility of great joy. For what Paul could say to the Thessalonians, we can say to our charges: "Ye are our glory and joy" (1 Thessalonians 2:20). If there is anything that ought to bring us joy, it is seeing brothers and sisters obeying God, doing the right thing in love and forgiveness.